Men of God

Confluencias

SERIES EDITORS

Susie S. Porter
University of Utah

María L. O. Muñoz
Susquehanna University

Diana Montaño
Washington University in St. Louis

Men of God

Mendicant Orders in Colonial Mexico

ASUNCIÓN LAVRIN

University of Nebraska Press
LINCOLN

© 2024 by the Board of Regents of the University of Nebraska
All rights reserved

The University of Nebraska Press is part of a land-grant institution with campuses and programs on the past, present, and future homelands of the Pawnee, Ponca, Otoe-Missouria, Omaha, Dakota, Lakota, Kaw, Cheyenne, and Arapaho Peoples, as well as those of the relocated Ho-Chunk, Sac and Fox, and Iowa Peoples.

An earlier and shorter version of chapter 2 appeared as "El Umbral de la Vida Religiosa," in *De la historia económica a la historia social y cultural. Homenaje a Gisela von Wobeser*, coord. María del Pilar Martínez López-Cano (Mexico: UNAM, 2016), 235–61.

Library of Congress Cataloging-in-Publication Data
Names: Lavrin, Asunción, author.
Title: Men of God : mendicant orders in colonial Mexico / Asunción Lavrin.
Description: Lincoln: University of Nebraska Press, [2024] | Series: Confluencias | Includes bibliographical references and index.
Identifiers: LCCN 2024021574
ISBN 9781496237804 (hardcover)
ISBN 9781496240446 (paperback)
ISBN 9781496240750 (epub)
ISBN 9781496240767 (pdf)
Subjects: LCSH: Friars—Mexico—History. | Monasticism and religious orders—Mexico—History. | Masculinity—Religious aspects—Catholic Church—History. | Mexico—History—Spanish colony, 1540–1810. | BISAC: HISTORY / Latin America / Mexico | RELIGION / Christianity / Catholic
Classification: LCC BX2820 .L37 2024 | DDC 271/.06072—dc23/eng/20240905
LC record available at https://lccn.loc.gov/2024021574

Set in Minion Pro by Scribe Inc.

CONTENTS

List of Illustrations vii
Acknowledgments ix
Introduction xiii
1. Childhood: Prescriptions and Memories 1
2. The Threshold of Religious Life: The Novitiate 38
3. Lay Brothers: An Alternate Choice 76
4. Sexuality: The Treacherous Flesh 120
5. Missionaries: Preaching Their Faith 166
6. Martyrs: The Offer of Life 213
7. Death: The Test of Faith 253
Epilogue 289
Notes 293
Bibliography 343
Index 387

ILLUSTRATIONS

Figures

1. *Eighteenth-Century Mexican Elite Family* — 4
2. *Eighteenth-Century Mexican Children* — 5
3. *Idea de un príncipe político cristiano* — 20
4. *El discreto estudiante* — 23
5. Profession of Fr. Hernando de San Pablo — 41
6. *Instrucción y Doctrina de Novicios* (1685) — 50
7. *Instrucción y Doctrina de Novicios* (1733) — 51
8. *Oratorio de religiosos* — 55
9. Portrait-Drawing of Fr. Diego de Basalenque — 63
10. *Guía de religiosos* — 72
11. Recruited friars at Colegio de Propaganda Fide in Zacatecas — 84
12. Age of lay brothers in two Franciscan convents in Mexico City — 86
13. Sebastián de Aparicio — 105
14. Portrait of Fr. Antonio de los Ángeles — 114
15. The Inquisition vs. Fr. Joseph María López Aguado — 129
16. Fr. Antonio Margil de Jesús — 175
17. Map of the trip of Fr. Pedro Font — 182
18. *Deberes y obligaciones ... de los misioneros en el Norte de Nueva España* — 187
19. *Fr. Junípero Serra Preaching to All People* — 194
20. *Vida, martirio y beatificación* — 241

21. *Destierro de Ignorancias . . . Arte de ayudar a bien morir*   256
22. *Sermón . . . en las Solemnes Honras de los . . . Misioneros*   286

Table

1. Cases of solicitation before the Inquisition, Mexico, 1614–20 and 1621   125

ACKNOWLEDGMENTS

This work was researched and written after retirement from active teaching and with the leisure and intensity one can enjoy after disengaging from academic duties, but I still owe many thanks to the colleagues and institutions who supported my work. Seed money for the initial research was provided by a John Simon Guggenheim Memorial Foundation Fellowship. The foundation had faith in my proposal to study men in clerical robes as members of a society in which the pursuit of a career within the Catholic Church was a legitimate and desirable choice beneficial to society and a valid expression of manhood. The Guggenheim support meant more than the stipend provided by the foundation. It validated a new topic worth pursuing and gave me the opportunity to set up the necessary connections with research institutions and the free time to initiate the voyage of discovery.

The navigation of a topic that was new to me and with scant supporting published research was made easier by friends and institutions in Mexico and Spain. Among them, Dr. Manuel Ramos Medina and Fr. Francisco Morales, OFM, stand out. Dr. Ramos Medina, director of the Centro de Estudios de Historia de México Carso, opened the resources of that center as a most gracious host. As a historian himself, I could not ask for a more understanding and sympathetic host. I am equally indebted to Francisco Morales, OFM, who hosted my visits to the admirable collection of Franciscan history at the archives of the Franciscan province of the Holy Gospel at the convent in Cholula, Mexico. As a well-known historian of the Franciscan order, he also acted as reader and evaluator of one of my published works on the friars. Ramos Medina and Morales have been my friends for decades, and my debt of gratitude to them will never be repaid properly. The Archivo General de la Nación (AGN) in Mexico City and its extensive Inquisition records were also very important to my research. I am indebted to its former director and also fellow historian, Dra. Aurora Gómez Galvarriato Freer, who supported my research and arranged for a public lecture on its objectives and initial results, held at the archive's premises. The past and current directors of the archives of the Franciscan order of the province of San Pedro y San Pablo in the city of Celaya, Michoacán, and its former librarian, Ana Maria Marín, were very supportive of my research in the extensive holdings of the province.

Next on my list are the two readers of this manuscript, much respected and appreciated colleagues, Drs. John Chuchiak and Martin Nesvig. The time and intellectual effort they invested in improving my manuscript is the most priceless gift I have received from them. Both have a deep understanding of the history of the Catholic Church in colonial Mexico (New Spain) and all the patience in the world to indicate problems in my writing and interpretations. Their critiques were necessary, and their support of the project was essential. Nesvig and Chuchiak were very precise in their recommendations and helped strengthen and refine the contents and the general objectives of my work. As often stated by most authors, any shortcomings remain my responsibility, and most improvements are owed to my great readers. I would like to extend my appreciation to the personnel of the National Library of Mexico; the AGN; the Archive of the Franciscan province of San Pedro y San Pablo in the city of Celaya, Michoacán; the General Archives of the Indies in Seville; and the National Library of Spain in Madrid. In this age of digital reproductions, other libraries and librarians in the United States and in Europe should be gratefully—if anonymously—acknowledged for making their books accessible through the internet. Dylan J. Joy of the Benson Library at the University of Texas at Austin went out of his way to help me identify and download several of the documents in that collection. My grateful thanks to him. I must also thank Anne E. Pedrotti Gomez, chief communications officer at Our Lady of the Lake University in San Antonio, who granted permission to use a painting of Fr. Antonio Margil de Jesús in the art museum of the university.

This is the third book I publish with the University of Nebraska Press. Its editorial support throughout the years has been essential for my development as a historian, and I want to express my gratitude to its current editor in chief, Bridget Barret, and to its senior acquisitions editor, Dr. W. Clark Whitehorn, with whom I first exchanged letters about historical issues in 1998. Many thanks also go to Emily Casillas, associate acquisitions editor of the University of Nebraska Press; Brianna Blackburn, editor and project manager of Scribe Inc.; and Judy Staigmiller, the book's indexer, upon whose advice and unflagging help I have relied throughout the preparation of this manuscript. All of them have shown the patience of Job in dealing with me as an author. Thanks are also due to Dr. Ben Vinson III, past directing editor of *The Americas*, and Fr. Benedikt Mertens, general editor of *Archivum Franciscanum Historicum* (Rome), for supporting the publication of two articles based on my research on Franciscan friars and nuns.

Friends, who are also historians, must be acknowledged because they have tolerated my stories, thoughts, and sometimes vagaries about friars. For their patience I thank Ann Twinam, Rosalva Loreto and Francisco Cervantes, Manuel Ramos Medina, Rafael Castañeda, Felipe Burgueño, Virginia Sánchez-Korroll, Vicky Ruiz, Judith Raftery, and César Favila, historian and musicologist. My children, Cecilia and Andrew, and their spouses, Chris Hauge and Laura Schubert, and my grandchildren, Erik and Nora Hauge, enrich my life as mother and grandmother—for which I am very thankful. As always, the memory of my late and supportive husband, David Lavrin, remains inspirational.

INTRODUCTION

After many years of writing on women in history, including feminists and nuns, I decided to write on men, specifically on men in the mendicant orders, as a companion research project to my book on nuns in colonial Mexico. The result is this book, where I follow men of three mendicant orders, Franciscans, Dominicans, and Augustinians, through their life experience from childhood to death. The mendicant orders had their origins in Europe in the low Middle Ages, and each one created a special charisma of its own to convey its understanding of God's message. Early in the sixteenth century, these orders obtained special papal permission to preach and convert the Native inhabitants of the New World. This is how they arrived in New Spain—colonial Mexico—among the many other men who came to either make a fortune or govern the new territories. The Crown supported their activities and entrusted them to convert the Indigenous peoples to Roman Catholicism and to foster their loyalty to the Spanish monarchy. In sixteenth-century Europe, Christianity was torn into many pieces, causing an irrevocable departure from a belief in a single Church to many churches upholding variations of the same faith. In the New World, there was the promise of finding a unity of belief. The men entrusted with reviving that unity were awed by the prospect but had an enduring belief in their own ability to carry out the task. They never questioned their "right" to change the beliefs of others; it was not a concern in a period characterized by self-righteousness and imperial visions of world dominance.

The activities of the mendicant orders have been studied by many scholars since the late nineteenth century. They have given preference to their territorial expansion, their institutional development, their methods and policies of indoctrination, the personalities involved in the process, and their clashes with the secular Church. The controversial nature of religious conversion and the personal character of some of the men involved in it have fueled debates and counterdebates reflecting the evolving understanding of the facts by several generations of historians. A perusal of the titles included in this book's bibliography suggests the breadth of existing studies.

Here I attempt a different approach. I pursue a thematic study of the life experience of the members of the orders. By "life experience" I mean following the friars as a group of men from childhood to death. The rules of the mendicant orders changed very little throughout time and applied to all members without exception. They imposed a basic "homogeneity" to the friars as a group that can be pursued throughout time to establish a common thread of belief and behavior among them. I have drawn examples from the three orders mentioned previously to find meaningful similarities among them. My chronological focus is largely on the seventeenth and eighteenth centuries, given the abundance of studies on the first century after the political conquest. The availability of historical material favors the Franciscan order in some topics because, since the beginning of the colonial period, Franciscans bore the largest burden and responsibility of catechizing the Indigenous peoples, and in the eighteenth century, they were granted complete control of that task in some key areas of the northern frontiers. Franciscans engaged in catechesis and spiritual work among all members of society throughout the colonial period and remained the most "popular" mendicant order with the largest number of members across the territory of New Spain. Also, Franciscan archival resources are far more accessible and complete than those of the other two orders.

My objective is to approach my subjects as men living their lives as they understood them. Where should the life experience of mendicant friars begin? The logical answer is childhood. It was a common experience for all of them, and it is essential to understand how the process of becoming a man was shaped by current notions of manhood. As children, friars grew up within a system of ideas that predisposed their futures as adults and pointed to the choice of religious life as appropriate and even desirable. I do not cover some topics common to the history of childhood, such as school curricula or child care in the nursery at home. More relevant to the purpose of this work are the ideas of leading thinkers about what was appropriate for boys to learn to become men and to be different from women. Adult manhood began to take shape early in life and took place in the family, in the school, in the streets, and wherever boys went as they grew up. The very freedom of movement boys enjoyed was a defining factor in their social education and the achievement of their manhood. Since it is difficult to collect systematically the notions of how to educate boys from unwritten sources, I pursue the concept of an appropriate and desirable manhood as it was explained in the writings on how to educate boys, since all friars grew up shaped by those ideas.

It is important to understand that socialization is not the same as formal education. However, as a form of education, it is more powerful than school education because it affects all men regardless of their social or economic status. The chapter on childhood examines ideas about the social education of boys as defined by the intellectual and social leaders of the sixteenth through the eighteenth centuries. Many of those writers were friars or members of the secular church, a fact that explains why secular education contained many of the elements of piety and self-discipline that we also find in conventual life. Most of the friars living in New Spain in the sixteenth century came from Spain, where they had been raised following the ideas explained in this chapter. Although the ethnic composition of the orders changed slowly throughout the seventeenth century, becoming increasingly American-born, this change did not necessarily affect the orders' expectations regarding the personal character of incoming aspirants. Standard ideas about the socialization of male children remained largely unchanged and applied to all the children who would eventually qualify for admission into the orders.

At the end of childhood, between the ages of fourteen and seventeen (and sometimes earlier), a boy was expected to choose an occupation. Vocation for the religious state was natural to many who had been raised in very religious families and had been under a strong religious influence. Becoming a member of a male order was the choice of thousands of young men and one regarded favorably by society. Life as a friar offered a much-sought-after intellectual education and the shelter of a home with a new "family" whose members shared a similar lifestyle and bonded as a same-sex group sharing strong spiritual ties. Belonging to a male order also conferred social and spiritual authority to the bearer of a robe. The depth of personal faith leading to profession cannot be fathomed. Some friars had a deeper spiritual commitment than others, but once they joined a religious community, friars shared the spiritual traditions and objectives that permanently defined who they were, how they wrote and spoke, and how they were perceived and received in their society.

The recruitment of new members was essential for the survival of the mendicant orders. The orders relied on a set of selective rules for admission that guaranteed a basic homogeneity in terms of race and education. Race was a nonnegotiable factor designed to keep the orders free from racial admixtures. Social extraction was aligned with the prerequisites of race. The majority of friars came from families of similar economic standing that could afford the minimum education required to be admitted or had the means to have their child educated by a religious order seeking talent and future members. Further formal education would be completed in the convent. Judging "vocation," or affinity to become a friar, was a delicate and crucial task left to the elders of the orders. No single rule could apply to all aspirants because the friary was in need of a variety of services from its members. Intellectual abilities were balanced by the necessity of depending on an "in-house" labor force to serve the daily housekeeping needs of the premises. Thus, the friary sheltered a group of "lay," or *legos*, to carry out those tasks. They were selected from among those who lacked formal education but fulfilled the race requirement demanded for admission. However, there were exceptional lay friars with a good education and an economically comfortable familial background who chose to profess as *legos* to follow their own spiritual call.

Bonding was the base of the male religious community and the foundation of its identity as a brotherhood. It was the social cement that kept men of diverse social backgrounds together irrespective of personality traits. The process of bonding and "becoming" a friar took place during the novitiate and its sequel, the *corista* stage, a period of living in the community while studying for the final consecration to the priesthood. While being a *corista* was in itself an important period in the formation of a friar, it was the novitiate that really reshaped the secular man into a friar. This formative period has not received as much attention as it deserves. The novitiate reconfigured the sense of "self" of the young man who entered the convent. While as a child the boy had been socialized as a "man in the making," the very idea of his maleness had to be reoriented to fit into the one acceptable to the Church. This process also applied to men who professed as adults. For the latter, the renunciation to the "world" meant a shift in gears, giving up many of the prerogatives they had enjoyed as men and accepting a new set of values in their lives. Each of the mendicant orders put special emphasis on certain activities they considered to be their own spiritual signature, such as teaching, preaching, writing, taking care of the sick, rescuing abducted Christians from Muslim countries, and so forth. All members of a given order had to learn and share its special sense of mission. The chapter on the novitiate covers the training of the novices, the practice of conventual discipline, and the process of bonding as a spiritual family. As a transition from the culture of manhood in the world to a culture of manhood in the convent, the novitiate was of the greatest importance to shaping the future friar's behavior. During the novitiate the future friar was expected to learn how to place the principles of religion and the charisma of his order above all other concerns. To understand a friar as a person, one must understand the novitiate.

Not all novices achieved the status of professed religious men with the full spiritual powers ascribed to that state. There was the choice of lay brotherhood, an option that included membership in the mendicant orders to serve the ordained priests and, as it was often stated, to liberate them from the chores of daily life and allow them complete dedication to higher educational and spiritual training. The lay brother received the spiritual benefits of belonging to his order, but his appointed task was the service of the community. Historical attention has always focused on the priests, the men entitled to perform the Mass, to confess and assess the health of the soul, to prescribe penitence and absolution, and to preach in public backed by their knowledge of theology and their various degrees of learning. Lay brothers have been more often ignored despite the fact that they were essential to the functioning of the friars as the backbone of their labor force, carrying out a variety of manual tasks. To be sure, all convents counted on the additional help of servants, but lay brothers served others in the name of God and *belonged* to the religious family. While performing their household tasks, they were in touch with a broad sample of the lay population in ways not experienced by the ordained friars. Their connection with the humbler members of society strengthened the convents' ties with the majority of the common folk. They were not judges of people's behavior, did not appear threatening, and connected with laypeople through empathy and piety. As they dispensed the leftovers of conventual meals among the poor, lay brothers conveyed the goodness of small acts of charity that endeared the orders to the common folk. The lives of three exceptional lay brothers have been chosen to illustrate how their personal activities elevated them above the meager memory of other regular lay brothers. Franciscan Beato Aparicio, a late sixteenth-century muleteer who died in the odor of sanctity, and Fr. Cristóbal de Molina, a seventeenth-century Augustinian lay brother, were born in families of rather limited means. They cut a striking contrast with Fr. Antonio de los Ángeles, a wealthy merchant who, by joining the Franciscan order as a lay brother, became a model for the type of marvelous conversions that fueled piety among common folk.

Rather different from the piety exemplified by the lay brothers was the behavior of those transgressors of the vow of celibacy, known as *solicitantes*. They could not be missing from a study of friars' lives because they broke the vow of chastity and exercised their biological virility in ways forbidden by the orders. A chapter on sexuality is not only desirable but necessary in the understanding of how men of the cloth faced the restriction of what most other men understood as a masculine entitlement: physical sex. Since the patristic period, the Christian Church proposed an alternate form of masculinity that nullified the relevance of sex in men's lives. Those chosen to serve as spiritual guides to the rest of the flock were expected to be celibate, which meant renouncing matrimony and mastering their sexual desires. By adopting a vow of chastity, mendicant orders hoped to guarantee the observance of celibacy.

Throughout centuries the outstanding spiritual leaders of Christianity addressed the issue of sexual abstention by giving all members of the clergy and the regular orders advice on how to avoid being ensnared in the temptations of the flesh. Moral theology, the discipline of establishing the principles of ethical advice to Christians, regulated sexual conduct among the clergy and members of the regular orders as well as the laity. Sexual control rested on the individual, who, exercising his understanding, his memory, and his will, would battle the temptations of the flesh. The observance of clerical celibacy had a patched record throughout the Middle Ages. Sexual engagements were not unusual among the clergy and among the regulars. The Catholic Church's answer was to reaffirm the principle of celibacy at the Council of Trent (1645–63).

Women religious were interned in cloisters to guarantee and preserve their chastity. Men never prescribed that solution for themselves. Instead, spiritual advice on the preservation of celibacy and chastity intensified, reinforced by precise description and regulation of the mental processes known to rule human sexuality. For the Catholic Church, however, there was another pressing moral issue to confront and resolve: solicitation for sexual purposes during the act of confession. Solicitants breached the sacredness of one of the sacraments of the church: the sacrament of penance. That was a more serious issue than breaking the vow of celibacy, and that is why it was placed under the jurisdiction of the Inquisition. The chapter on solicitation thus addresses one of the most serious disruptions of the theological and doctrinal base of Roman Catholicism. Solicitation is best understood through the examination of individual cases, as detailed in the records of the Inquisition. Chapter 4 examines several cases in depth to understand the behavior of *solicitantes* as men with full use of their sexuality. Seduction is not a process often described in detail in historical records, and those furnished by the Inquisition are particularly rich and only rivaled by those contained in civil criminal cases. Since the Inquisition pried into people's minds, a disclosure of the inner feelings of the solicitant and his victims is often available. The inclusion of the women's voices—whenever possible—adds important nuances in these cases, and it is essential insofar as the friars' actions were not his own alone. The third set of voices inserted in this chapter is that of the prosecuting attorney and the judges of the Inquisition. They represent the moral compass of the Church and society. The opinion of the attorneys dictating the final verdict is illuminating, given the inefficiency of the regulations followed by the regular orders to cope with this thorny issue. Having these key actors engaged with one another in this chapter is a desirable form of adding resonance to their respective roles and gaining a deeper understanding of their personal behavior.

Friars remain much-discussed and controversial subjects of historical debate in their role as missionaries. Since the sixteenth century, they carried out the task of converting the Indigenous populations to a faith that was not theirs and were in no position to reject. The basic assumption of all European crowns in Europe was *cuis regio eius religio*, "the faith of the king is the faith of the people." This principle was extended to the New World as a natural and unquestioned assumption, and the missionaries were the first body of men actively enforcing this policy on the American continent. The compulsory nature of this conversion has been under discussion for centuries and has cast historians in two camps: those who see the conversion as a benevolent action and those who decry it as an act of cultural dispossession of the Natives' beliefs. I will not take sides in this discussion because there is no reconciliation in sight. However, understanding the principles ruling the faith of people in Europe helps explain the policy. Further, the conviction that the salvation of the souls of all people depended on conversion to the "correct" religion was the strongest drive in the friars' lives. Spiritually convinced of the righteousness of their cause, they never had any doubt about their conduct, and this chapter reviews their viewpoint.

The complexity of the missionary as a topic of study invites writing a book rather than a chapter. Facing the strictures of space, I chose to focus on the second wave of missionary activity in the vulnerable distant borders, where the missionaries engaged in conversion while the military carried out the task of making the secular government effective to protect the boundaries of the viceroyalty. To focus on the lives of the missionaries, I use personal letters and reports of the missionaries of the Colegios de Propaganda Fide. They do not disappoint in the detail of historical information they furnish. They engaged in what was a daring adventure in remote lands. The common denominator in their experience *as* men was their constant confrontations and forced accommodations with the military governors. Today, we would call it an encounter between the religious masculinity of the missionary and the overpowering masculinity of the military. New insights into missionary history can be seen when viewed in the light of masculine behavior: the governors trying to subject the missionaries to the will of the state and the missionaries resisting the challenge, bearing their "cross," and continuing on their chosen path as "soldiers of God." The personal burden of administration under constant pressure and the ties they created among the friars reveal the involvement of these men in nondoctrinal issues and disclose angles of their character that belong to a potential future history of the emotions of men of the cloth.

A chapter on martyrdom points to the fact that violent death for the sake of faith had an unexpected "revival" in the sixteenth and seventeenth centuries as a result of the spread of Christianity beyond the Mediterranean and Europe. Martyrdom became a "global" experience, and, ironically, injected new life into the concept of personal sacrifice. The distinctiveness of martyrdom beyond its original scenario in antiquity makes it a desirable topic, separate from that dedicated to death. The "exoticism" of the new geographical scenarios added a form of death revered by early Christians and was an unexpected spiritual bounty for the defenders of traditional Roman Catholicism. A life snuffed out by unconverted and resistant Indigenous made a terrible statement about the effectiveness of evangelization. However, that was not the way the blood of martyrdom was understood at the time. Personal sacrifice was admired and praised as a form of fertilizing the metaphorical grounds of religion. Every martyr signified the challenge of the "unconverted" Natives to the territorial expansion of an alien faith and an alien king. That challenge is minimized in the historical sources created by the ultimate victor. The deaths of the Natives were never considered a form of manliness by the men in control. That topic remains a challenge for future historiography. The eulogies of the martyred brothers and the sermons in praise of their sacrifice were in line with current beliefs on the promise of eternal blessing within a militant Church. Personal letters and reports reveal that many missionaries rejected the potential holocaust of their lives. The idealized image of a sixteenth-century missionary dying for Christ rang hollow for them, and their rejection poses a challenge to the rhetoric of praise in official histories.

The chapter on death closes this study as a logical ending to a journey that began with infancy. Death was a subject of serious theological thought. For the faithful, it meant the closure of life in this world and the beginning of eternal life for the soul. That certainty remained one of the pillars of Christianity. Preparation for death was a lifelong project, according to theologians and spiritual advisors. Only a good life could ensure a good death, and a good death was a "teachable" subject. To die well meant to have lived virtuously and also to have the aid of the Church at the critical moment of departing the physical world. This chapter moves the topic of a good death from its understanding by the general population, to the personal experiences of the friars who thought and wrote about it, and to the religious community that enacted the appropriate rituals when death struck one of its members. The death of a brother involved the entire community as witness to the last moments of someone with whom they had shared their lives. The relevance of death as a topic for meditation and spiritual didactic purposes is completed by the detailed description of the last moments of some outstanding members of the community in several chroniclers' and biographers' narratives.

The privacy of death in the friar's cell had a counterpoint in the very public funerals of notable friars. People gathered to pay homage to men of saintly reputation, to have a good cry, to reinforce their own personal hope in the afterlife, and to listen to the sermon in eulogy of the departed. Sermons were literary and intellectual efforts that the best minds of the colonial period appreciated as an aural experience of scholarship and eloquence. Often studied separately as examples of rhetorical literature, they also reveal the emotions of the friary's collective. Although there are few sermons honoring friars, they are important as summations of a life seen through the lens of faith as well as expressions of the sentiments of the religious community on their loss. Closing this book with the end of life as viewed and felt by the community of brothers is, in my view, a fitting way to finish my work. Other themes related to the life experience of friars await study, especially with the potential inclusion of other men of the cloth, such as the Carmelites and the Jesuits. As always, I hope that the guidelines I have used in this work suggest even better paths to other historians.

How can we use the life experience of men of the cloth to illuminate the construction of masculine models? No specific pattern of hegemonic masculinity has been posited for the entire colonial period, and there might be none, but there are examples of multiple masculinities contesting one another. Contrasted with the aggressiveness of male conquistadors in the sixteenth century, the friar trekking the land and refusing to use arms could be regarded as a masculine countermodel. In the shared memory of the orders' chronicles, the men of the first and even the second generation of arrivals were described *and* remembered as requiring boldness, valor, and stamina, qualifications that suggest they were regarded as examples of strong male behavior. Evangelizers were eulogized by their chroniclers as men fighting against Satan to recover the souls of the Indigenous and overcoming physical challenges while carrying out their task. It was important to masculinize the activities of men who customarily were not associated with warfare to equate them with secular men who wielded swords and participated in military campaigns. Friars were members of another form of soldiering in a special militia: God's militia. Dominican historian Agustín Dávila Padilla refers to bishops as "soldiers of humility" or "soldiers in virtue." Fr. Jerónimo de Mendieta remembers the sacrifice of martyrs in a special section of his history and presents them as active soldiers of Christ who had paid the highest Christian debt in a manly fashion. The actions of that militia of God exceeded the value of a life of conventual physical retreat employed in reading and devotional practices.

Colonial history is replete with examples of men of the cloth whose activities could and should be analyzed in terms of constructions of masculinities. The internal affairs of conventual politics, such as the one cited in the chapter on the novitiate, offer the possibility of studying the orders' rivalries and personal conflicts as expressions of masculinity. The orders also antagonized the Crown and its royal agents and fought among themselves for the management of Indigenous labor and for attracting patrons to support the construction of churches and the maintenance of the cult. On a personal level, friars sailed across oceans, walked long distances, climbed rugged mountains, crossed dangerous rivers, and explored dense jungles and dry deserts, as did settlers and men of arms. They dared to go alone into the territory of antagonistic tribes, and some paid with their lives. There were battles of a more personal nature that echoed the principles of their religion: battles with their own pride and personal free will to submit to the discipline and obedience demanded by community living. The hardest battle, according to some, was that against the temptations of the flesh. In their days, the determination to engage daily with those challenges was regarded as evidence of straightforward and effective manhood, proof of character that went beyond the donning of a robe. There was also the world of letters, where the aspiration to intellectual preeminence moved many members of the orders to excel in the erudite activities appreciated by their society. Writing, teaching, and preaching created rivalries in the exclusively masculine world of letters. We must remember that they were also expressions of the intellect open *only* to men. Finally, the mere fact of having been born men made them members of the sex destined to command. Friars took an alternative route for exercising their masculine privileges, and the nuances they experienced as they walked the path determined by their sex and their choice of lifestyle are infinitely intriguing. In a very modest way, some of them are explored in this work.

Men of God

1

Childhood

Prescriptions and Memories

> The blessed and venerable Father Fr. Francisco de Loaysa was from the town of Béjar, of the Duchy of the same name in Spain, and son of noble parents. He passed to this New Spain as a young man.
> —Fr. Hernando de Ojea, *Libro Tercero*

Childhood seemed to have little meaning in the remembered lives of mendicant friars. Its memory was no more than a ripple in the often terse language of biographies and chronicles that focused largely on men in their midlives with the gravitas of a significant number of years in the practice of religion. The grown-up man in his habit obliterated the experience of the friar as a child despite the fact that childhood and early youth were the periods of life when the process of "socializing" boys prepared them to fulfill the expectations of manhood. The child was unable to discern his future as a man, but those around him were intent on shaping a future generation as good as or better than their own to live productive lives and to serve king and God to the best of their abilities.

Current studies on the history of children and early youth focus on all children, and while they are very precise about the differences in the educational possibilities among children of different economic and racial backgrounds, they do not make specific references to those who could or would eventually become members of religious orders.[1] There are very good reasons for this. Mature men who achieved notoriety or positions of social influence rarely spoke or wrote about their childhoods. Biographies of notable men skip childhood as unnecessary or irrelevant in explaining the accomplishments of their subjects. Childhood was held as a state of emotional immaturity, a period in which a person was "in the process" of becoming a rational adult.

It was a state of life subject to emotional vagaries in need of control and the inculcation of the discipline and polish that were necessary to succeed as a full-grown person. There was no reason to linger for long on this period of life. And yet, all religious orders assumed their applicants arrived at their doors with a firmly grounded set of moral and religious values and specific traits of behavior that distinguished them from others and made them good "material" for the religious life. We find those values clearly explained by educators and men of letters who addressed the features of character they thought would make children and youth grow into respected and outstanding men. They were writing with the objective of creating not men destined for religion but respected members of their communities. In the selection of their future members, the mendicant orders looked for the same good qualities of character suggested for all boys by educators. Once a boy entered the friary, the rules of the order reshaped him to become who he ought to be as a man of the cloth.

The childhood of future friars was not different from that of other children, since the decision to join a religious order was not feasible until the age fixed by the rules of the mendicant orders, and the commitment to become a friar did not become real until the candidate entered the novitiate in late puberty or early youth. By that time, the potential future friar had already been socialized into being a man, with all the burdens and prerogatives of his biological sex, as well as having been deeply grounded in his religious beliefs. There was still a lot to do to turn him into a friar, but what lay before reception was the work of others. Here we will see what the men who undertook the task of guiding the child into manhood had to say about that process.

Social Education for the Male Sex

Social or informal education was the sum of expected, appropriate, gendered behavior a child acquired during his formative years. The early years of a male child were channeled toward social activities and intellectual training considered appropriate for a boy that would differentiate him from girls and femaleness. Boys and girls were separated at a relatively early age to learn how to behave according to their biological sex. A boy's demeanor and behavior, as well as his prerogatives as a male, were slowly inculcated in him so that they would coalesce in his early teens.[2] This "social education" guided boys into predesigned channels of behavior, and it was administered by parents, religious instructors, and their own peers between late infancy and adolescence. There was no homogeneous set of rules or practices because models of manhood responded to the economic, social, and racial or ethnic affiliations of the boys. The socialization of the son of a merchant or the son of a lawyer differed from that of the son of an artisan or a street vendor. Their formal schooling was also different and geared to fulfill different roles in their adulthood. As children, the sons of merchants or lawyers, for example, wore different clothes, spoke a more educated language, and were taught how to adopt manners fitting their family's social station. Male comportment was slowly acquired as the boy grew up by observing how other men of his social milieu behaved and by imitating what was appropriate to his status in society. By the time a male adolescent was faced with a choice of occupation, he was socially educated in his prerogatives and rights as a male and those of his own social and/or racial affiliation, and his own behavior followed those guidelines.[3]

In Western societies the process of socializing male children was also one of "gendering"—that is, the process of training them in the behavior that society considered as belonging to a man. Gendering began at the age of four or five and continued through the decisive puberty years, when, by personal or familial choice, the boy began another training period more focused on his economic future. For boys of the lower socioeconomic and racial groups, making a living superseded formal education, and they began helping their parents very early in life, well before puberty. To define childhood cultural models in viceregal Mexico means to focus on the socialization process and not on demographic data, such as infant mortality, the features of child care such as the nursing of infants or young children, or the features of formal education boys received in schools. Doubtless, the latter mattered, since formal schooling was in itself a defining feature of manliness, as it was reserved for boys and men.[4] Girls did not often receive formal education and never attended the same schools as boys. Not ever seeing a woman as a peer through the early schooling process was a factor that caused young men to believe in masculine entitlement to education and in women's intellectual inferiority.

Historical materials that could help depict the childhood of elite men are not abundant in Mexico until the eighteenth century. The *mestizaje* series is one of the best visual sources to appreciate the differences among boys of various social and racial provenances, even though they are idealized portraits

FIG. 1. Anonymous, *Eighteenth-Century Mexican Elite Family*, n.d., Dr. Robert H. Lamborn Collection, 1903–29, Philadelphia Museum of Art.

of reality.[5] With some exceptions, these paintings show families with children engaged in their daily activities, whether in the intimacy of the home or in the streets. The relationship among the subjects may be affectionate or not, and the role of the father in the picture is not necessarily dominant insofar as the mother, especially women of the lower classes, had a key role in the economy of the home. On the other hand, what the boys are doing and how they are dressed are worth noticing. Upper-class children, those closer to the Spanish prototype, are fashionably dressed and never engaged in physical "labor." They are small men resembling their fathers, suggesting the expectation of their future lives as copies of the paternal image.

In the few other examples of family and children's portraiture of the eighteenth century, we see children rehearsing the roles they would adopt in their adulthood.[6] Boys are dressed up as adults, some even wearing wigs, while others wear hats. In one case a boy is fitted with a small sword, and he rests his hand on the hilt in a typical manly pose.[7] A portrait of the

FIG. 2. Anonymous, *Eighteenth-Century Mexican Children*, n.d., Dr. Robert H. Lamborn Collection, 1903–29, Philadelphia Museum of Art.

Fagoaga-Arozqueta family shows Josefa Arozqueta and Francisco Fagoaga with their nine children, four boys and five girls. In the portrait they are physically separated, with all the girls on the left-hand side with their mother and the boys on the right-hand side with their father. The children of various ages are dressed up like their parents, looking like miniature adults, and they are kneeling before an icon of the Virgin of Aránzazu. The painting mixes piety with social elegance and urbanity, elements of which all the children partook. The division of the family into boys and girls is more than a visual strategy; it reflects the different destinies of the children.

The girls are on the side of the mother because they will become mothers. Boys belonged to the father and would follow male-appropriate occupations. Another iconic portrait of children of the upper classes shows two brothers and a sister of an elite family. Also dressed as adults, the boys are on either side of the little girl in a protective pose.[8] Their clothes suggest the path they would likely follow in their lives as adults.[9] One boy is dressed as a *letrado* (lawyer or intellectual) and the other as a priest.

Paintings and portraiture provide visual clues of how clothing defined important distinctions among children and their futures since the earliest days of their lives. However, there were other factors more relevant than clothing in developing guidelines for "maleness" in childhood. They were the rules of behavior expected from boys and taught in a practical manner in the family or in the daily intercourse among families of similar social standing. Such rules were taught directly by tutors and confessors and indirectly by the behavioral example of other male adults close to the family and worth imitating. The pedagogical rules that reinforce the social education of a boy are gathered in treatises that deal with more than formal school education and include guidelines on how to make a boy aware of his gender and learn the appropriate behavior of a man. In addition, and very important for the purposes of this study, are the biographical data of their own notable men gathered by the mendicant orders. Although meager in information, these accounts were an effort to perpetuate a general model of childhood that crystallized in a man of the cloth. The mendicant orders' spiritual and social male models are also delineated in the manuals of instruction of the Christian doctrine. I will examine both sources of information.

Intellectual Models for the Education of Boys

The Church was a privileged party in the definition of social and moral education principles applicable to all boys, regardless of class and family provenance. Men of the cloth wrote most books for children's social education. There was no practical separation between secular and religious instruction in matters of character formation. An early Christian childhood defined an upright Christian manhood. The aim of educators was to train all boys, regardless of class, as future men of honor and faith as defined by the Catholic Church. Printed sources on the social education of men in Spain between the sixteenth and the eighteenth centuries serve as guidelines for understanding the socialization of young men in New Spain. The elements of a Christian education did not change because of location, and there are publications of that nature in Mexico until the eighteenth century. Those who eventually took the vows as members of the mendicant orders in Mexico were raised by the standards of the socializing literature produced in Spain.[10] Further, a significant number of friars of the mendicant orders were born and raised in Spain, a situation that remained true through the eighteenth century. This fact validates the study of Spanish authors and sources as applicable to all—Spaniards and Mexican-born.

As Spain became a world power by the mid-sixteenth century, the Crown needed educated men to run the country, and thus, didactic and advice literature on social and personal behavior appropriate for boys developed in full in the sixteenth and seventeenth centuries. This social education should not be confused with the academic or formal learning required to advance socially. The latter consisted of learning subjects such as Latin, rhetoric and grammar, geometry, and mathematics, the disciplines that would enable the boys to pursue a career in law, religion, public administration, or politics. That type of education was available to a thin layer of upper urban society until the eighteenth century, when education for the lower classes became desirable and education for a larger number of children became a worthwhile social goal. However, the patterns of personal and social behavior that were identified as being specifically "male" and signifiers of masculinity had little to do with formal schooling in the classroom. Regardless of class, ethnicity, or race, men had, for example, an unquestioned freedom of movement that permitted them to walk in the streets of a city, roam in the countryside, or even move from one continent to another. As heads of the household, they had authority over their families and over women in general, although in theory, women gained legal self-government after age twenty-five if they remained single. Social mores, despite exceptions, dictated that, regardless of age, a woman be under the authority or protection of a man and within a home or, alternatively, a convent. Her personal movements beyond those protected sanctuaries were always under surveillance. As boys grew up, they learned they would inherit the authority of their fathers and male relatives and the personal freedom to be away from the home. They learned how to ride a horse and use arms for self-defense. Swords and daggers were openly worn as part of their public manhood. Any legal restriction in the use of arms or a horse, to some men, was an explicit public denial of their male authority. Boys also learned that as grown-up men, they would have a respected "voice" to express themselves in public. It was a right they enjoyed as soon as they gained legal majority. The voice of a family was always the voice of a man, although it could be socially muffled by class and race. A male servant would not raise his voice over that of his master, but he could raise it in the home he headed. A woman's voice had its place, largely at home, but it was greatly restrained outside it and had to find specific social niches, such as a convent, to gain authority.[11] Some masculine prerogatives were alien to friars and priests, such as the use of arms and biological fatherhood, but a young man entering a religious order to become an ordained priest knew that in exchange for what he gave up as a layman, he would retain a "voice" respected by almost all members of society. The authority of the voice of a preacher in a church or a confessor in the confessional was undeniable. All other men, from the king down, had a confessor to pass judgment on their behavior.

Formal education reinforced authority, but it had to be accompanied by "proper" social behavior, expressed as courteous social manners among one's peers. Social polish was in great demand as an asset to enter not just the orders but the complex bureaucracy operated by the state.[12] The elements of social polish were *urbanidad*, *cortesía*, *policía*, and *civilidad*, qualifications of behavior showing culture, education, and civility.[13] The lay and religious teachers hired by urban elites and noble families to educate their boys were in charge of teaching them social polish (*buena crianza*) as part of a basic Christian education. The main caveat about social educational guides is that, with notable exceptions, they focused largely on boys of the urban elite, excluding poor urban and peasant or rural boys who would become simply laborers. In New Spain they would also exclude the vast majority of Indians and "mixed-bloods." Doubtless, men of the lower economic and social classes had their own rules of socialization. We cannot assume that they lacked the social guidelines of *urbanidad* or *cortesía*, but they also learned the etiquette of social distancing and respect that they had to observe when dealing with their social "betters." A peon, a street vendor, or a muleteer would learn how to be obsequious, tune down his voice, and show he understood who his social superiors were; their children learned by example. Their public *urbanidad* consisted of assuming a polite behavior of submission and deference. For boys of the elite, the process was similar, but in reverse. They learned from family members and teachers the prerogatives they had over others and how to behave and command to elicit respect and validate their authority. Training on how to "command" was part of the social apprenticeship of the male elite, but such subtleties were not recorded in books; they were learned in daily life.

Male children of colonial elites faced different circumstances than their counterparts in Spain, although they were heavily influenced by Spanish culture. Racial variations in the New World created special behavioral expectations for boys. González and Premo have pointed out that children born to Spanish parents or to Creoles descending from Spaniards in the American continent grew up with children of different races. Their formal education followed Spanish patterns, but their social behavior reflected the fact that they were surrounded by other boys who were racially different and socially below them.[14] Different social spheres became more sharply delineated in a multiracial society. Lipsett-Rivera's study on the social issues facing mostly boys of the lower classes and mixed race in eighteenth-century Mexico underlines the significant differences between them and upper-class boys. They learned the general rules of manly behavior *suited to their state* precisely through social intercourse.[15]

Race and social class were not the only factors affecting a child. Legitimacy and illegitimacy created different childhood experiences, *especially* among elites. As Ann Twinam has shown, the childhood of elite children born out of wedlock posed personal emotional challenges to them and elicited manipulations of the social codes for bringing them up.[16] Although their parents made efforts to provide comfortable lives for children born out of wedlock, illegitimacy created special circumstances that children were unable to grasp until they grew up. Twinam notes imbalances in the education and social future of those children based on whether they were raised by their father or by their mother, with the most favorable outcome on the side of those raised or backed by the fathers. All that being said, the socialization of boys that matters in this study pertains to those who could become members of the church. Given the exclusionary terms followed by religious orders in the acceptance of their members, we are looking at the socialization of young men who came from families of the social elite in the New World, even if they were not wealthy. Economic standing did not matter as much as the biological tag of Spanish descent.

The education and behavior of the colonial male elite remained close to the models set in Spain.[17] Children born in the New World were not aware in their early childhood years that they were criollos. Assumption of the "otherness" of *criollismo* was probably not acquired until the late teenage years. A "Mexican" identity developed slowly throughout the seventeenth century, but even then, it was not part of early childhood education.[18] However, some men were conscious of the difference in their social standing by the late sixteenth century. When Fr. Agustín Dávila Padilla wrote the prologue to his history of the Dominican order in 1596, he declared that having been born in New Spain put him at some disadvantage as a scholar and writer. Dávila Padilla excused his book's possible faults as being due to his own birth in the New World among "barbarous Indians" and his resulting lack of urbanity and polish (*urbanidad y policía*) possessed by those born in Spain.[19] This preamble revealed much about him as a Spaniard born in the Americas (*español americano*) in the sixteenth century. It seems that he was apprehensive about the reception American-born authors could expect in the mother country. However, Dávila Padilla could have been simply using an expected literary *diminutio*, or under the cover of irony, he could have been "mocking" peninsular authors, since he knew how well educated and knowledgeable he was. In either case his comments suggest that for American-born authors, Spain remained the intellectual and cultural source of their own ideas and target of their work, even though when Dávila Padilla published his book, there was already a vibrant cultural life in the viceroyalty.[20] Qualifying his own aptitude for writing as in need of peninsular approval, Dávila Padilla was acknowledging that his education as a writer, as a young man, and later as a member of a religious order was part of a complex cultural world whose foundations he sought and found in the motherland.[21]

How to Shape a Boy: Didactic Literature

Education was regulated to suit the biological stages of life as perceived in most educational treatises.[22] Formal education could begin between ages seven and ten. For Augustinian Fr. Pedro Salguero, "infancy" was when children were babies in the nursery and cared for by mothers and women.[23] "Childhood" began when a child was able to walk and acquired the ability to speak and lasted through age fifteen. Childhood was naturally extroverted and lacking in self-regulation; it demanded much discipline and correction. Between the ages of fifteen and twenty-one or twenty-two was *mocedad*, a period of transition to full manhood. It was during this stage that men underwent key physiological changes and experienced the onset of the "sensual vices." The luxuriance of that age inclined to lust. Nature pressed life forward, and the "vegetative" part of the body was in haste to achieve its natural purpose. The moral education of men during *mocedad* should curb such inclinations and "drown Venus in the waters of the flood." Some religious orders accepted postulants as probationary pupils when they were between twelve and fifteen to take advantage of the last years of childhood and before the physical transformations of the body began to take place, giving them the opportunity to "drown Venus." Conversely, secular youths learned manly behavior precisely in those years of *mocedad*, before full manhood and its responsibilities arrived.[24] A smooth transition from childhood into early youth was not experienced by all men. Some were simply propelled into adulthood by the economic circumstances of their lives. Learning a trade as an apprentice, working in the fields with the men of their family, or accompanying a street vendor father in his daily perambulations were "educational" circumstances determined by class and race. Maturity and responsibility arrived earlier for nonelite boys.[25]

There was an abundance of didactic literature in early modern Spain aimed at those boys who could have the benefit of education. A distinction must be drawn between the literature addressed to instruct in letters and sciences and that destined to shape the social behavior of boys.[26] Most socialization treatises belonged to the latter category and addressed the formative years of childhood and early youth, when the boy was still pliable and sensitive to the guidelines adopted by parents and teachers. Legislation and social custom expected parents to assume physical care and early moral guidance.[27] The observance or evasion of those responsibilities created different moral choices for men and women, as amply discussed by Ann Twinam.[28] Parents, especially fathers, received advice to make them aware of their moral responsibility in training future good men by raising up good boys.[29] Fathers were told to be aware that children would perpetuate their "memory," family prestige, and honor, and thus they should endeavor to make that memory as polished and flawless as possible. Projecting themselves into the future through their own children was a call to men's personal pride.[30] Fostering a devotional life was expected to be another parental duty, and it was in this area that women assumed a leading role, as they were in charge of teaching their children the basic notions of religion, the basic prayers, and regular attendance to church services.

A full religious education was a required part of a child's upbringing regardless of sex, and it was beyond what mothers could teach, since it was believed to open the gates to salvation, a matter of the highest importance for all believers. Full religious instruction belonged to ministers of the Church, not the parents. To begin constructing their moral foundation, all children had to learn the basics of Christian (Catholic) doctrine to take their first Communion after age seven using the *Doctrinas Cristianas*. *Doctrinas* prepared the child in the basics of the faith and made ethical behavior compulsory to all—race, social, or economic status notwithstanding.[31] That fundamental indoctrination in Roman Catholicism would affect the child's behavior for the rest of his life. *Doctrinas*, also called *cartillas*, were the first books printed in Mexico City for the instruction of Indigenous children.[32] Sent from Spain to its territories overseas, they were among the most ubiquitous books in the book trade.[33]

One of the best *doctrina* examples is the anonymous *Libro de Doctrina Cristiana*, printed in Toledo in 1564.[34] This book went beyond teaching the basis of religion; it was a comprehensive treaty on moral doctrine that taught young men proper social behavior and guided them to follow a formal education. The *doctrina* addressed all aspects of personal comportment, including sleep hours, appropriate behavior in the streets and in the privacy of the home, table manners and politeness toward the family's guests, appropriate forms of play and leisure, and how to establish and respect friendships. Some *doctrinas* remarked on the "wisdom" of following the father's occupation. The breadth of the themes discussed by the *doctrinas* indicates how "education" went beyond the teaching of religion and embraced a preparation for life. The *Doctrinas Cristianas* first published in Mexico were more limited in content, as they aimed at educating Indians in the principles of religion.[35] Thus, we assume that the first generations of young white boys raised in New Spain used fuller *doctrinas* printed in Spain and not the books to teach non-Christians about Christianity. In the sixteenth century, there were also books called *catones* for the education of children. They were still in print in early nineteenth-century Spain and Mexico. The *catón* contained more than the basic tenets of catechism by including advice on proper social behavior as a signifier of moral virtues.[36]

The task of writing didactic works, whether *doctrinas cristianas*, *catones*, or manuals of social behavior, was in the hands of men who never received any specific training as "educators." They were either members of the Church or seculars with experience in the courts of princes and nobles and men of a vast culture, with a reputation for possessing respectable moral qualities and experience in dealing with the children of the elite families. Their works went through many printings and helped build a general cultural understanding of models of male behavior since childhood. For example, Franciscan Fr. Diego Murillo stressed that good manners and virtuous social behavior (*buenas costumbres*) were as desirable as a deep religious belief and faithful observance of the Christian faith. If acquired early, he posited, *buenas costumbres* would help avert the natural inclination of youth to vices and bad habits.[37] The common ground of all male education was instruction in piety, respect for family lineage, and the volatile but much-quoted sense of honor, which applied to him and his family.[38] All children should learn moral doctrine because it was a *bien común*, or "common good," for society.[39]

Etiquette, as an expression of codified urbanity governing public behavior, was very important for a well-educated man. Social polish was not universal. It was displayed largely in the royal court, in the homes of the rich and noble, and among the aspiring urban bourgeoisie that would serve in administrative offices. Urbanity, as courtesy and deference to others, was displayed wherever and whenever educated men met in open spaces to guarantee courteous, polite behavior. Some rules of urbanity were also enforced at home because their observance was deemed useful to maintaining the patriarchal authority of the father and harmony among the family members. The lack of civility and urbanity could bring embarrassment and social ostracism to those who violated the rules of courtesy.[40] The abundance of advice literature and the variety of printed venues used as guides for the education of nobles indicate that the education in social courtesies and social know-how was a subject of great interest in Spain. However, some contemporaneous scholars cast doubt on the effectiveness of scholarly instruction among the nobility, since many nobles lacked interest in formal education.[41] This was not the case among the young men aspiring to enter the mendicant orders. They knew that scholarly knowledge and social urbanity had a place in the ambits of the church. The rules of the mendicant orders included sections addressing the behavior expected from its members that were the equivalent of the rules or urbanity for the layman. Conventual urbanity was intended to keep civility and manners as well as respect for the hierarchical order within the convent. Any aspirant to church membership was well advised to learn social manners.

Other Texts and Models

The distinction between *doctrinas* and books on social manners was sharp enough to make them two distinctive genres. *Doctrinas* taught mostly moral values and Christian behavior in society, while the books that I will review here addressed the proper manly behavior expected from the nobility and upper classes. Works on the education of princes and the high nobility flourished in Spain in the sixteenth and seventeenth centuries. The didactic literature may have been officially written for princes and the nobility, but the authors also had in mind a burgeoning urban population and men in various occupations and social levels. While addressing the education of a prince, the treatises written for royal education contained intellectual and behavioral precepts that, assimilated by less-exalted male subjects, became useful guides to behavior for the male children of the social elite.[42] Despite changes in the political and social makeup of the Hispanic cultural world, the definition of upright or "proper" manhood changed little through several centuries because social education was infused with ethical models that were resilient to any challenge.

Among the many authors who flourished in the sixteenth and seventeenth centuries, one stands out: Juan Huarte de San Juan (1530–92). He published a widely read analysis of people's natural abilities to guide parents and teachers on how best to use a child's potential and provide the most effective education to all according to their wit (*ingenio*).[43] This work achieved meteoric popularity and readership despite having been placed in the Spanish *Index* of forbidden books in 1583 and 1584.[44] Huarte de San Juan posited that it was in the state's interest to channel every man in the right direction according to his "natural," or inborn, capabilities rather than trying to defeat nature. Educators and statesmen should learn how to detect personal abilities and instruct children accordingly. He was a firm believer in the theories of humors: how different parts of the body influenced one another and how people were born with abilities that were unlikely to change. Although lacking in scientific base, those theories were held in great respect at the time. His didactic conclusions applied to all male children, and, as such, were probably more influential than some treatises addressed only to certain social male elites.

Huarte de San Juan agreed with most contemporaries that formal education should begin early in life and follow a methodic development suitable to the mental capabilities of children. He showed little interest in urbane behavior, but his understanding of why, when, and how children should be educated had definite social implications. Children could learn Latin best when they were young because at that stage, memory was strong. Adolescence, the second stage in life, would be the time to introduce the art of reasoning and train the brain to think rationally. In subsequent stages of their adult lives, men were to be guided to the more complex sciences, each according to his abilities, until they reached the apex of their intellectual aptitude between the ages of thirty and fifty. Ethical qualities such as prudence and understanding could not be taught; they were "inherent" to each person. Since he posited that some men were not meant for any education, his work supported the process of selection of men for civil service and religious life and relegated most boys to remain uneducated and in the lower levels of social expectations and opportunities. His ideas went against early sixteenth-century humanistic teachings that all people were capable of understanding goodness in the same fashion that all could achieve salvation. Despite his official banishment, Huarte de San Juan was widely discussed among those in charge of training the clergy.[45]

Huarte de San Juan's ideas were not the only guide for social or informal male education. Other sources conveyed different models of manly behavior. Two sixteenth-century non-Spanish works were very influential in Spain and its colonial cultural centers: Erasmus of Rotterdam's *Education of a Christian Prince* and Castiglione's *The Courtier*, although Erasmus stood above Castiglione.[46] Machiavelli's *The Prince* was not popular in the peninsula, and he was more a model to negate than one to follow. Erasmus, on the other hand, was widely read in the early sixteenth century until his humanist bent put him on the wrong side of the conservative wing of Spanish Roman Catholicism. His writings were placed in the Inquisition's *Index* by the mid-sixteenth century. Although proscribed, he was read behind closed doors. His works on education, especially the *Familiar Colloquies*, were copied or rephrased by Spanish authors.[47] Rather than dwell on the well-known educational theories of Erasmus, a topic well developed by many other authors, it is more appropriate in my opinion to review Spanish authors who encountered no state or clerical proscription. Throughout the sixteenth century, the assumption among intellectuals was that Spain had no need for foreign educational models, a sentiment that strengthened with time. Spain was the strongest monarchy of Western Europe, and its writers could provide kings and princes with texts on courtly manners and moral instruction.

Spain had its own "Erasmus" in the figure of Franciscan Fr. Antonio de Guevara (ca. 1481–1545), who was the bishop of Mondoñedo and Guadix and author of the *Libro Áureo* and the *Reloj de Príncipes*.[48] The latter was a revised and expanded version of the former. The *Libro Áureo* (1518), possibly his best-known work, contained a good dosage of social and educational guidance for all laymen. It was written for Charles I of Spain and pretended to be based on the life of Roman emperor Marcus Aurelius. Guevara shared with Erasmus the honor of authoring a book addressed to the education of a prince. *Libro Áureo* circulated in clandestine editions, including one in 1528 that prompted Guevara to rework it and publish the revised version as *Reloj de Príncipes*. In his prologue, Guevara posited that the highest ideal for a man (he also included women in the text of his book) was to live a virtuous life. Virtue was the combination of uprightness and good behavior. It was the base of *fama*, or "good reputation," and it was the most important signifier of a good life. Men living virtuous and well-regulated lives ensured the well-being of society. To achieve that objective, Guevara prescribed rules on how to work and to rest; how to speak properly, to eat well, and to sleep adequately; and how to engage and deal with others in a polite, urbane fashion. These rules helped all men, not only princes, establish order in their lives, and they should be taught and learned as the basis of general education.[49] Guevara placed the responsibility of determining the quality of a boys' education squarely on their fathers, who, by assuming their paternal duty faithfully, discharged their greatest moral obligation and ensured that their property and the family's name were safely preserved. Fathers, however, were not expected to assume the technical aspects of education. For this purpose, they should choose a good teacher, or *ayo*, whose character they should verify.[50] Guevara also did not hesitate in recommending that parents punish their children, since for lack of discipline, many became insufferable adults.[51]

A contemporary of Guevara, Luis Vives (1493–1540) was a prolific writer in Latin and the best-known Spanish humanist of his time. Given the fact that the circulation of Erasmus's work was restricted in Spain, Vives had a deep influence on the social education of men in the Spanish world. He wrote his *Diálogos* (1538) as an exercise to teach children Latin. Thus, he fulfilled two objectives: teaching Latin *and* social manners.[52] *Diálogos* was reprinted hundreds of times in several languages in Europe. In Spain, it reached around thirty-five editions between the sixteenth and the seventeenth centuries.[53] *Diálogos* recorded a conversation between two boys as they rose in the morning and went around the city throughout the day. It was divided into several chapters focusing on home, school, food, books and teachers, clothing, games and gaming, customs in other countries, the need to study, the nature of governing men, the vanity and emptiness of courtesan life, and unsocial behavior. In Vives's world, a male child attended school to become "human" and different from "beasts," but they learned how to behave in society by moving freely in their environment, observing others, and noting what was proper and good and what was wrong or bad. This social learning complemented the teacher's instruction in formal studies and assumed that the young learned not just from books but from their betters in a social context. The behavior of the adults mirrored the moral mettle of the individual, and the young learned how to behave by observing wise older men in their world. He did not address the issue of bad moral examples among the adults.

The social learning Vives endorsed was accessible only to men and brimming with values applicable only to them, despite the fact that they visited a kitchen during their perambulations. What the male child learned from his exposure to the world was composure and good habits such as personal cleanliness, the choice of appropriate clothing, and the observance of restraint in eating and drinking. He also learned how to walk properly, to control his gestures, to maintain a pleasant face, and to speak correctly and politely. Vives adhered to the humanist moral tenet that all men, regardless of class, have something to give to society and should learn how to behave in it. There was a certain modicum of social critique addressed to the newly rich who wanted to imitate the nobility. Vives was interested in raising not a courtier but a regular man who cultivated his intelligence by learning how to make the "right" choices, which inevitably were more traditional than innovative.

Respect for God and the Catholic religion were underlying assumptions in his work, but the moral values and ethical behavior derived from religious principles were more relevant than formal piety. One of the most important lessons for children and young men was to respect the authority of the elders not because they were old but because they were wise. Rebellion, whether political or personal, was not encouraged. Vives helped spread respect for authority, control of the body, and upright social behavior as the guiding principles of social and personal education for the next two centuries. In Mexico City, Francisco Cervantes de Salazar (1514–75) glossed and published Vives's works in 1554, thus becoming the conveyor of European culture to a very young society. It was one of the first books published in the capital of the viceroyalty. Written originally in Latin to help young students of the language, Cervantes de Salazar also wrote a description of the city in three dialogues carried by two young students.[54] Current analyses of his work today focus on its "Mexican" character, but its value as a manual for social education is just as important.

Another author worth noticing was Cristóbal de Villalón (1510?–88?). He was a tutor of the sons of the Count of Lemos for two years (1532–34), but he is better remembered for being an excellent grammarian and the presumed author of *El Crótalon*, possibly written around 1553–54, under the pen name of Cristophoro Gnophoso. Although his work was not written specifically on "education," he had very strong ideas on what a proper man should be.[55] *El Crótalon* is fashioned as a dialogue between a rooster, Crótalon, and Micilas, a poor cobbler. It is a critique of bad children, bad women, false religious behavior, and vain philosophers and courtiers. As a social critic, he addressed the nature of manhood and the objective of a boy's education, but his broader target was Spanish society and the international politics of his time. In his view, the only acceptable evidence of personal strength was the control of one's passions. Like other moralists of the early modern period, Villalón sustained that the senses were the gates to the corruption of the integrity of men's moral capabilities. Men who indulged in their bodies' sensual weaknesses "feminized" themselves and shamed their manhood.[56] He condemned the pursuit of venereal pleasure, sharing with Catholic theologians the notion that the rejection of sexuality was an expression of moral strength.[57] He was an admirer of the regular clergy, and his focus on "proper" manly sexuality had many similarities with the instruction imparted to novitiates in the mendicant orders. Villalón targeted corrupt men in the secular clergy who partook in many of the vices of laymen and admired the regular orders, contrasting their "nobility" to the vices of the clergy. In fact, Villalón asserted that the monastic life was the best possible life. Certainly not all monks were perfect, but many had achieved a high degree of sanctity.[58] His opinion was shared by many on the peninsula, and it traveled with them to New Spain and the New World.

The interest in didactic works expanded throughout the sixteenth century, resulting in a body of works that cemented the principles of social and academic education. Among the best known are the works of Juan Lorenzo Palmireno (1514–79), a humanist and Latin scholar from Aragón and author of *El estudioso de la aldea* (1568) and *El estudioso cortesano* (1573). The first was written for the education in social manners of rural and poor young men who lacked the savoir faire they needed to get along in urban society, while the second addressed the needs of courtly men. Palmireno's methodology was based on quotes and sayings that conveyed popular wisdom on all topics of daily social behavior.[59] Like other educators, he extended the meaning of education beyond the formal curriculum to the realm of appropriate behavior based on a code of etiquette and common sense. Works such as Palmireno's approached male socialization from a nonestablishment angle, whereby wisdom is not always on the lips of savants and may also be found in the common man. His works appealed to the emergent urban bourgeois seeking advice to enhance their social standing.

In general, texts addressing the education of princes did not seek to apply to men other than the young prince and courtiers in the highest social ranks who may have wished to mirror the ideal of a prince. They shared a solid core of advice of an ethical nature and proposed that a rounded education would make rulers examples of prudence, personal valor, piety, a sense of justice based on moral philosophy, and elegance and restrained behavior.[60] In other words, the prince should be a mirror of perfection to his subjects.[61] He should inspire other men to become *hombres de bien*, even though his special mission was to govern and protect his people.[62] Spain had its share of publications on the education of princes through the end of the seventeenth century. A brief overview of this genre should include Francisco de Monzón (?–1575), who published *Espejo del Principe Cristiano* in 1544 and was among the earliest authors of such treatises in the sixteenth century.[63] Another author

FIG. 3. Diego de Saavedra Fajardo, *Idea de un príncipe político cristiano. Representada en cien empresas* (Amberes: Casa de Ieronymo y Juan Baptista Verdussen, 1655).

who merits citation is the Jesuit Pedro de Ribadeneira (1527–1611). He joined the ranks of royal advisors with his *Tratado del Príncipe Cristiano* (1595), written to counter Machiavelli's *The Prince* and for the benefit of Phillip II and Phillip III of Spain.[64] Ribadeneira's *Tratado* is an excellent example of the incursion of men of the cloth in the field of education and politics. He considered the art of ruling the highest and most difficult task facing a man. A virtuous prince would put himself above all men and become a model of manliness. Juan de Torres, SJ (1547–99), wrote a treatise on the *buena crianza* of princes addressed to the Marquis of Velada, who was in charge of the education of Phillip III. It focused on the moral values of the ruler as a public person.[65] Like other authors, he mixed religious indoctrination with advice on teaching liberal arts and science and considered his teachings useful for young men of all social levels. Andrés Mendo, SJ (1608–84), writing during the reign of Phillip IV, authored *Príncipe Perfecto y Ministros Ajustados. Documentos Políticos y Morales en Emblemas* (1626).[66] Using the explanation of emblems or moral examples, Mendo reiterated the by then well-established notions of the desirability of social and formal education to harness the impulses of nature. Straightening a young tree and channeling the young river were the tasks of a good teacher. Achieving "composure" and control over one's expressions and body enabled men to interact responsibly with one another in society. Freedom was useless if the individual became a slave of his vices.[67] These concepts reiterated the message of educators of the sixteenth century, which, by then, had become "orthodox" pedagogy.[68]

Arguably the most important writer of educational treatises for princes was Diego de Saavedra Fajardo (1594–1648), knight of Santiago and member of the Council of the Indies. He wrote *Idea de un Príncipe Christiano Representada en Cien Empresas* (1640) for the ill-fated Baltasar Carlos, son of Phillip IV, who died in childhood. It was one of the most complete expressions of political pedagogy of its time.[69] Saavedra Fajardo, like Ribadeneira, targeted Machiavelli's *The Prince*, pointing out what he considered fallacies and duplicity in the understanding of the role of a prince and countering them with his own Counter-Reformation principles of ethical and Christian leadership. To make his points and to teach the prince the mistakes as well as the successes of his forefathers, Saavedra Fajardo relied on examples of Spanish history rather than ancient history. While primarily addressed to a future ruler and focused on the principles of government, this work also deals with childhood and puberty, with the understanding that moral character is formed in those early years. He reiterated the parental duty to foster a child's future by providing education, either by the father or by carefully chosen teachers. The plastic nature of childhood made children vulnerable to bad influences, and he objected to the intrusion of women in the education of men, fearing they would foster "emotions" or "affections" that would weaken the young man. His distrust of women disregarded the very strong role played by a number of queens serving as regents to the throne in the seventeenth century and the sterling precedent of Isabella of Castile.[70] In his understanding, a rounded education for a boy should include Latin as a base, the subjects of the trivium and quadrivium, the moderation of sentiments and physical appetites, and respect for the concepts of justice and the arts of war.[71] As a seventeenth-century man, Saavedra Fajardo regarded the physical senses differently from his sixteenth-century predecessor, Cristóbal de Villalón. Rather than venues for moral corruption, the eyes and the ears were venues for learning.[72] He also incorporated current ideas on early physical exercise to strengthen boys' bodies as well as helping them develop a masculine identity. Fencing, learning how to use several types of arms, horse riding, and hunting were appropriate training not just for the prince but for all men of the better social classes.[73] Saavedra Fajardo believed so intensely in the need to train young men in the martial arts that he suggested that all orphan male children be made useful to Spain by training them as soldiers ready to serve their king, imitating the Turkish custom of raising men totally loyal to their ruler.[74] The association of arms with childhood was by no means regarded as negative. Handling arms was part of learning what was desirable for a man destined for a public role. The hand on the sword should be ready to act for self-defense and the defense of the monarchy.[75] This admiration for soldiering and arms sometimes overcame Saavedra Fajardo's advice for political and diplomatic caution, which was understandable in a Spain stressed by European wars and engaged in constant military struggle.

The principles of self-control and civil social behavior were still viable and vibrant in the eighteenth century. The *Reglas de la buena crianza civil y christiana*, published in Barcelona in 1781, reiterated earlier guidelines for raising children properly.[76] The anonymous author addressed the virtue of *cortesanía*, the art of regulating the behavior of men in social life. *Cortesanía*

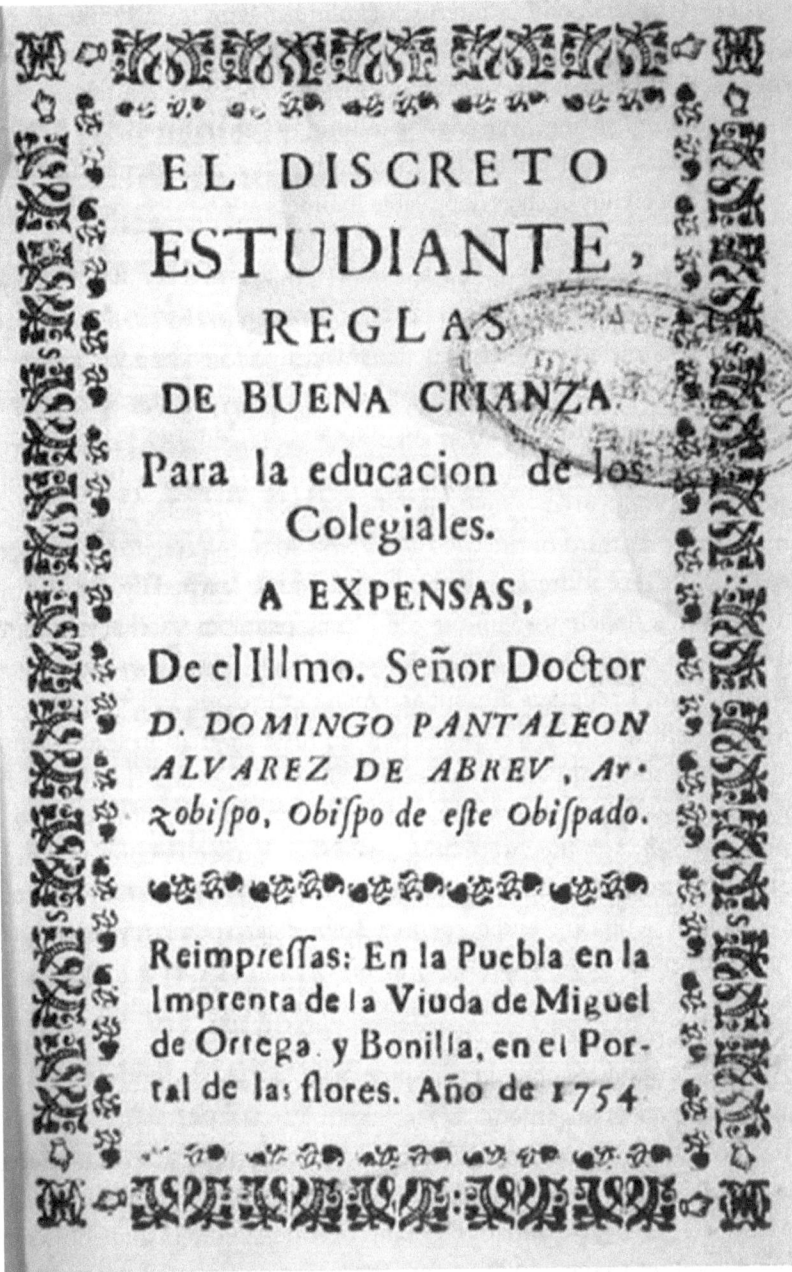

FIG. 4. Anonymous, *El discreto estudiante. Reglas de la buena crianza* (Puebla: Imprenta de la Viuda de Miguel de Ortega y Bonilla, 1754).

consisted of the harmonious mixture of good behavior toward others, civility, and courtesy, which should be learned early in life and practiced as a form of self-discipline. It reiterated the message that a body under control (when standing, sitting, walking, or talking to others) spoke of intellectual and moral values. The anonymous author also paid attention to other expressions of civility such as good table manners and respect for elders and those in higher social positions. Not surprisingly, this work was prologued and recommended by an anonymous man of the cloth who added his own recommendations on how to respect God through prayers. He also urged readers to acknowledge God's presence inwardly as well as outwardly.

Spiritual life, initiated early in life, remained a key element of education in the eighteenth century, as corroborated by Antonio Vila y Camps, clergyman and theologian, who published a book on the education of a gentleman in Madrid in 1776.[77] His concern about the religious education of men took one-third of the work—the first 86 of the treatise's 285 pages. The rest of the text addressed the "social arts" to be learned by young boys, such as riding, dancing, swimming, hunting, pistol and archery training, and fencing. Obviously, the cultivation of physical exercise was more for a secular than for a religious life, but as a man of the cloth, Vila y Camps was writing for all men, and it was not beyond his imagination that a future man of the cloth could and should learn such skills in his childhood. He was defining activities that were desirable in the building of manhood in general, even though they were not part of the regimen of conventual life. For that reason, he also included advice on training in utilitarian arts such as agriculture, sculpting, and carpentry. To be clear, such knowledge was a form of "diversion" to make the gentleman a better-educated person, but in a slanted fashion, he was endorsing the desirability of trades and the "mechanical arts." Religious orders were grateful to some of their members who designed and helped build churches and convents as well as those who took care of vegetable gardens.

In contrast with the traditional nature of academic education and more in tune with the spirit of enlightenment of the period, Francisco Gabriel Malo de Medina (1732–93) expanded the radius of education to include boys who belonged neither to the nobility nor to the legion of educated state officials. As a priest and founder of elementary schools in the Castilian heartland, he addressed the practical education of peasants (*labradores*), shepherds, artisans, and laborers, since he was interested in promoting better living conditions for the Spanish peasantry and the laboring classes.[78] His interest was beyond reading, writing, and proper enunciation. He would have peasant children and those born in families of laborers learn to master the tasks specific to their occupations. This book unambiguously addressed the needs of most boys who would take up their fathers' occupations and would be apprenticed as artisans. Malo de Medina provides a window into the world of men who worked with their hands and for whom he envisioned a better practice of their métier through an improved practical education. There is no emphasis on etiquette in this work; formal education consisted of learning the catechism and the rules of elementary reading and math as well as a smattering of geography and history.

New Spain had its own seventeenth- and eighteenth-century mentors for moral and social education among the urban elite. None other than Carlos Sigüenza y Góngora, the well-known seventeenth-century Mexican savant, published a *Theatro de virtudes políticas que constituyen un príncipe* in 1680. This work dwelled on the moral virtues of Aztec rulers as positive indexes of their culture. His intention was to build a countermodel to European nobles based on autochthonous royalty. Its pedagogical message for young men was implicit rather than explicit, and its influence on the upbringing of Mexican children is questionable.[79] On the other hand, eighteenth-century philosopher Juan Benito Díaz de Gamarra, author of *Máximas de educación en la piedad Cristiana*, was more relevant as an educator. In 1772 he was the rector of the Colegio de San Francisco de Sales in the city of Zamora.[80] The purpose of the college was to impart good education to all "well-born" youth and "to form men useful to the republic, and also to the Church." As rector of the school, Díaz de Gamarra wrote guidelines for the students who, in his words, were at the age when they were most inclined to listen to either vice or virtue. Being surrounded by social dangers, young men could err if they lacked educational and moral guidance. Gamarra, using his voice as that of a "father," intended to guide the youth under his care by recommending the observance of the basic rules of piety, respect for authority and the school's daily discipline, and the cultivation of their intellect. It is telling that his first recommendations were for the observance of piety and devotion through a daily regimen of prayers, attendance to mass, practice of regular confession and communion, spiritual talks, and the reading of "spiritual" books. Respect for authority prescribed the unquestioned obedience of teachers and men of the cloth. The control of the body, cited as an educational principle since the sixteenth century, was an important element in his agenda. Self-restraint was a virtue to be practiced by the students in their usual daily intercourse with their school companions and outside the college. Calling other students names or engaging in rough play belonged to street boys lacking in manners and education.

Díaz de Gamarra's school followed a daily routine reminiscent of a male convent in the ordering of its inner activities and the regulation of the students' behavior. The boys had to observe correct table manners and uniformity in clothing—always wear black—as well as regular attendance to religious services. Loyalty to the king was promoted by praying for his welfare and promising not to defraud him of his taxes, to respect his ministers, and to abhor the "monstrous" concepts of regicide and tyrannicide. Díaz de Gamarra was only twenty-eight years old when he wrote the rules for the school, but he was already a traditionalist in terms of educating and socializing young men. By advising respect for king and Church, he politicized education but not more so than our own contemporary practices that demand recitations of vows of allegiance to the nation or singing the national anthem in schools. Elite education traditionally fostered a "civic" identification with king and Church as the pillars of a social life. This ensured that the men of the better social strata upheld the status quo and respected the laws of the land.

The educational treatises surveyed here addressed the body as well as the intellect. Physical exercise, such as walking and playing ball games, was seen as appropriate for developing a manly, firm, and robust body, regardless of class.[81] Elite men were also advised to learn sword fighting, shooting, and not surprisingly, dancing. As a venue for socializing with women, dancing was worth learning among men of the upper classes. Rowdiness and drinking were not "commendable," but they were indulgences men could engage in at their own discretion. The authors of these works hoped to control the coarser aspects of the body implicit in all human beings. Above all, more than a mere facade, they upheld social manners as a means of expression of intellectual maturity and self-control.

The educational treatises reflected widely held notions about important phases in the social and moral education of men being tied to their physical growth. A child belonged to the feminine circle of mothers and nurses during his first five years of life. Once beyond that age he passed to the masculine circle of *ayos* and teachers, and his life acquired a tougher and less compromising tone. The social and moral pressure exercised on male children passed their early childhood was considerable. The burden of acting like "little men" was placed on their shoulders as soon as academic pressure began to bear down on their lives. Teachers and parents had no inhibitions about corporal punishment to rebuke "bad" behavior and reinforce conformity and obedience. At the same time, when children were judged apt for taking the "first communion," those in charge of their spiritual and moral education began to inculcate in them notions of sin and guilt as well as a disdain for the female sex. The "sin" of Eve was a foundational concept of religious education that no boy or girl could escape from. Among men who chose to don a clerical robe as adults, the disparagement of women's bodies, their intellectual abilities, and moral character was not uncommon, being the result of social and educational notions on how to shape a "proper" man.

Educational treatises help us understand the basic social and moral notions supporting the concept of manhood. However, at some point, some of the behavior taught as properly "masculine" for a secular man had to be proscribed for a man in a habit. That moment came during the novitiate, as it will be seen later. We cannot venture to state that the majority of books on the education of children circulating in Spain were widely read or used in New Spain, but information on well-known secular libraries of the sixteenth century shows that the books of instruction for formal education were the core of private libraries and would be found even in conventual ones.[82] The *catones* and the *cartillas* designed to help boys learn their first letters were the fundamental texts for instructing boys of all social classes in male social behavior, but other complementary notions of appropriate masculinity circulated in Mexico by oral tradition through private tutors, educated men, and clerical advisors. Their transmission and assimilation depended not on readership only but on usage and on imitation as key components of male behavior, as the educators themselves postulated. For those who lacked formal education and were to live in the lower ranks of society, education meant to follow the example of their male forebearers and the moral advice imparted by the ubiquitous members of the Church.

Childhood Mirrored in Mendicant Order Chronicles

To move beyond the prescriptive literature on masculine behavior, it would be desirable to find memories of childhood or autobiographical information concerning the earlier years of members of the regular orders. Sadly, friars rarely engaged in autobiographical reminiscences of their childhoods. Chronicles and biographical data focus on their adult years, and information on childhood is like a cobweb, where delicate but tenuous lines of information are found in the midst of a prevailing emptiness. A lot is left to the imagination of the reader. The information in those biographies consists of brief statements on the child's moral character and *buenas costumbres* resulting from the virtues of a good Christian education imparted by pious parents who instilled in them the love and the fear of God.[83] The emphasis on piety is similar to that found in prescriptive sources, and its objective is to underline how the virtues and spirituality of the adult friars had their roots in a home that practiced traditional religious values. Most chroniclers and biographers were older men, far removed from their own childhoods. They were likely to regard that period of life as temporary and largely inconsequential in the account of a man's experience, albeit with some exceptional features promising a full flowering of virtues in adulthood. The writers, intentionally or not, tended to create a cardboard image of a *niño santo* who intuitively or willfully understood his destiny as a man of the cloth around the age of seven and succeeded in fulfilling it in their *mocedad*, when, as teenagers, they were ready to enter religious life. Those who professed late in life, having taken a different course in their youth or even their adulthood, were assumed to have returned to a call ignored for years, but one strong enough to correct the course of the rest of their lives. A delayed adoption of conventual life carried a heavy moral message: there was always time to correct youthful confusion. The ways of the world could not rival the benefits of a religious life.

There is no distinction between peninsular and Mexican-born authors in conveying these images of childhood. Chroniclers writing in the late sixteenth- or early seventeenth-century Mexico were mostly peninsular-born because that was the demographic reality of the regular orders. Their texts do not depart significantly from the correct models established by the historical biographies and the hagiographical literature of the peninsula at the time. Their vision of religious childhood was narrow given their limited interest in it.[84] When writing on the childhood of exemplary friars, most were satisfied with stating that they were born to honest and pious parents and that at some point in their childhood or early youth, they had received the call of God and had answered it. Only a few had followed the occupation of their fathers, had served as soldiers, or had sought a future in trade before making a significant turn to join the orders. Those born in Spain and landing in the New World as young children traveled with their parents or relatives or were sent to join relatives in the viceroyalty. The influence that Mexican society had on their lives as children is barely documented in most cases.[85] Exceptional information is found in the case of Fr. Alonso de Molina, author of the Nahuatl and Mexican dictionary, *Arte de la lengua mexicana y castellana*. He arrived in New Spain shortly after the conquest (ca. 1523) with a brother and a widowed mother. He soon learned Nahuatl by playing with Native children and then became a teacher of the language to the first evangelizers, who asked "Alonsito's" mother to lend them the boy to learn that language from him. Later he became a friar himself and the author of a grammar in Spanish and Nahuatl.[86] The majority of peninsular friars throughout the colonial period arrived as adults carrying the spiritual and intellectual baggage of their social and religious upbringing. With notable exceptions, their attempt to understand their charges would focus on learning their language in order to indoctrinate them.[87]

As American-born youths (criollos) began to join the ranks of the mendicant orders in the late sixteenth century, their birth and upbringing in an increasingly complex society began to be "relevant" in terms of their admission to the orders. By 1570, the Dominicans of the province of Chiapas and Guatemala were defining criollo as a person who was born or brought up until age ten in New Spain. It was believed that those first ten years of life were key in character molding, and some Spanish-born friars began advancing the theory that bringing up children in the new land did not favor the formation of a strong character. Such prejudiced opinion was based on observed practices of child upbringing, such as the use of Indigenous nannies among the upper classes and the indulgence of children among the newly enriched members of the elite.[88] The environmental influence was also a point of discussion when a medical doctor, Juan de Cárdenas, wrote a book in 1591 to explain to Europeans all the marvels of the New World. Cárdenas was born in Spain but traveled as a young man to Mexico, where despite an uneven lifestyle, he succeeded in getting a degree in medicine after having studied with some notable teachers. Among other topics, Cárdenas discussed the character of those born and raised in the Americas.[89] Broaching the thorny discussion on the differences between Spanish- and Mexican-born people, he was an ardent defendant of the latter, who, in his opinion, had a sharper wit (*ingenio*) than their Spanish-born counterpoints.[90] He contended that any humble Indian had such polished, courtesan, and dainty delicacy in his speech, as if he had been raised in a court in the company of well-spoken and discreet people. He perceived similar qualities in women. In contrast, people coming from Spain were rough in their speech and behavior. In terms of intellectual understanding, the American-born accomplished anything they decided to do, as he had witnessed dealing with them in school. Without going into further detail about his Galenic-inspired interpretation of character and ability, Cárdenas's emphasis on wit, a quality underscored by Saavedra Fajardo, and on polished manners and behavior as features of a proper education support the notion that educational treatises had some impact on the opinion of lettered men. Having a natural wit was a significant boost to the Spanish American's self-esteem, but we cannot assume that Cárdenas's opinions were influential in the process of selecting novices for the orders in New Spain. The orders adhered to well-established rules of member selection crafted in Spain and Europe and shared the educational ideas synthesized above. The prejudice against criollos would remain a feature of the Spanish-controlled clerical hierarchy for a long time thereafter, and it was largely based on the features of their upbringing as children.

Ironically, looking into the biographies of notable friars born in New Spain, there is little evidence that their childhood education was different from that of *peninsulares*, although there is very little stated in such reminiscences. The already mentioned Fr. Agustín Dávila Padilla, the undisputed star of early Dominican historiography, was born in Mexico to Spanish parents. His older brother also became a distinguished Dominican. Agustín was a prodigy in terms of his ability to learn fast and well. His formal education began at age nine. By twelve he had mastered Latin, grammar, and rhetoric. He was also reputed to be knowledgeable in history, including that of the Indigenous peoples. He showed similar ability in the liberal arts. By thirteen, he had earned a bachelor in arts; by sixteen, a master's degree. At eighteen (1585), he professed in the Dominican order. He could be a perfect model for Cárdenas's image of the wit of children born in New Spain. His biographer, Fr. Alonso Franco, underlined the personal social qualifications that made him agreeable to all, which coincide with those expected of well-educated young men. His conversation was straightforward, affable, graceful, and witty—obviously a persuasive and useful tool in his social circles. He behaved like a prince in his generosity, his fidelity to his friends, and his *cortesanía* (urbanity) to all. Franco regarded such qualities as an outward expression of his *discreción*. *Discreción* was a complex amalgam of such personal qualities as speaking and acting appropriately, having good judgment in one's own behavior, and being reserved and prudent. Add to that his devotion to the Virgin Mary and his frequency at the sacraments, the love his teachers felt for this modest and brilliant young man explains itself.[91] He was a living model of a perfect child who inevitably matured into an exemplary well-educated man and friar. Since he was Mexican-born and raised, his accomplishments suggest that his rearing reflected well current Spanish-originated patterns of male socialization and ideas on how to rear perfect male children.

Not all biographers were interested in their subjects' childhoods. Franciscan Agustín de Vetancurt, author of a *menologio*, or biographical register, of the Franciscan friars in the province of the Holy Gospel, was an example. He was largely satisfied with stating that his chosen subjects were of old Christian families and were raised well by their parents. Fr. Juan González de la Puente, the chronicler for the Augustinian province of Michoacán, published the lives of nine distinguished men of his order, seeking to enhance its prestige. Like other chroniclers he did not provide dates systematically and dispatched their childhood information with a formulaic reference to their parents and early virtues as children. The slim gleanings from his stylistic brevity corroborate early life and family connections as strong influences on the destinies of future friars. Among his biographees we find Fr. Juan Montalvo and his uncle Pedro Guerrero, archbishop of Granada. Fr. Juan was raised by the archbishop, who paid for his education, and unsurprisingly, he became a friar and eventually landed in New Spain, answering the call for Spanish-born members to strengthen the presence of the order in the new "pastures." Another future friar with well-connected parents was Fray Antonio de los Reyes, who lived in the house of the Dukes of Arcos, as did other children who acted as pages or were in the retinue of the rich. He left his life as a courtier to study in Salamanca and eventually became a

Dominican in the convent of San Esteban, leaving for New Spain in 1555.[92] He was among many others who traveled to Mexico with a royal official or relatives and helped strengthen the number of friars in the new land.

Other examples were closer to fitting the pattern of model childhood. Fr. Juan Martínez had a good social and religious education. Brought to New Spain by his parents, he caught the eye of the Dominicans for his physical good looks, measured movements, circumspect speech, and attentive behavior in the religious services. In other words, he performed the model youth behavior prescribed in socialization treatises and was admitted to the order. An abundance of model social qualifications also marked Fr. Pedro de la Cueva, a young *oaxaqueño* who also entered the Dominican order.[93] According to the chronicler, he shone in courtesy, respect, urbanity, discretion, and seriousness in his conversation as well as in composure and modesty in his countenance. Such "qualities" guaranteed his admission to the order.

Writing for the Dominican order in the province of Oaxaca, Fr. Francisco de Burgoa sought to preserve its history by outlining the lives of twenty-six of its members.[94] As young boys, Burgoa's biographees share typical similarities: their parents, relatives, or patrons had provided them with a good formal education in the hope that such training would enable them to find a secure position in life by becoming friars. One of his biographees, Fr. Martín de Zárate, was a relative of the first bishop of Oaxaca. He applied to enter a Dominican convent at age eleven. By then, he was already well trained in Latin. In addition, he had very favorable character traits. He had a *lindo ingenio* (quick wit) and was a virtuous, "modest and grave" child. After trying him as a *donado*, or "adjunct," owing to his age, the Dominicans saw such good potential in him that they sent him to study in Spain, where he could receive the best education for a life in the order. After gaining experience in oratory by preaching in Toledo, Córdoba, and Extremadura, Fr. Martín returned to his local *patria* (motherland) to share the fruits of his education and serve his order in the provinces of Oaxaca and Mexico.[95]

The life of Fr. Diego de Basalenque (1577–1651), historian of the Augustinian order in New Spain, was lovingly written by his brother in religion Fr. Pedro Salguero.[96] The future friar migrated to the viceroyalty with his parents at age nine at the invitation of a maternal uncle. This relative paid for his studies in Puebla and later in Mexico City. There, he was instructed by a gentleman who took only twelve boys of the best families to teach them the basic subjects of the educational curriculum and the principles of devotional life in the critical years of late childhood. This type of private instruction by educated men was not uncommon in the urban centers of New Spain. The intelligent, small *gachupincito*, as Basalenque is described by Salguero, was then placed under the wings of the Jesuits, from whom he learned the coveted grammar and rhetoric before he was fifteen, early in his *mocedad*. At that age he entered the Augustinian order as a novice.

Fr. Cristóbal de Molina, a lay brother in the Augustinian order in Puebla, moved from Spain with his family to the viceroyalty when he was a very young child. The biographer praised his parents for teaching him the fear of God and good behavior. His father encouraged him to become an apprentice embroiderer (*bordador*). This occupation would have earned Cristóbal a reasonable living, but he never gained the title of master in that art because, as he said, he decided to profess in 1612 as a lay brother to avoid the sexual attentions of his master's wife.[97] Since he lacked the formal education required to become an ordained priest, his only option was a secure life in a convent as a lay brother. He gained notoriety as a pious and accomplished spiritual man, becoming the subject of one of the few biographies devoted to a lay brother to be published in New Spain.

Another interesting example of a man of his time was Fr. Felipe de Jesús.[98] Born in Mexico City around 1571–72, he became a religious martyr in Japan and was beatified in 1627. The scant information on his youth indicates that his father was a merchant importing Asian textiles. Two of his brothers professed in the Augustinian order, suggesting that piety ran in the family. One biographer skipped the "menudencias de la niñez primera" (inconsequential details of his childhood) for lack of verifiable information.[99] Educated by the Jesuits, Felipe attempted a novitiate in the Franciscan order but gave it up, and one of his biographers suggests that he lacked a serious aim in life and possibly engaged in what the hagiography calls restlessness and entertainment. However, another biographer argued vigorously that whatever *travesuras* (pranks) and *veleidades* (fickleness) he might have shown in his youth, they were not scandalous or vile.[100] It was taken for granted that young men could engage in revel and carousal if they were not too disturbing. He may have been an apprentice silversmith in Mexico City, but that detail remains uncorroborated. More trustworthy is the information that he became an assistant to his merchant father, who eventually gave him money to follow a trading career buying merchandise in the Philippines. His destiny changed while in Manila. He became a Franciscan novice in May 1594, and in 1596 he reembarked to return to Mexico to receive his consecration as a priest. Unfortunately, he and several other Franciscans were captured in Japan, and not long thereafter they were martyred. His engagement in trade on behalf of his father marks a desire to leave his early youth behind to assume the responsibilities of a young adult. His attempt at religious life suggests a desire to redirect his life after his experience as a merchant. It was not unusual for some young men who took the path to the convent to face years of indecision while weighing their options. In contrast, others made early decisions that stood firm. Fr. Domingo de la Anunciación, a Dominican cited by historian Dávila Padilla, was brought up by a pious widowed mother and began seeking the habit at age thirteen while still in Spain. Yet the family wished a different career for him. In 1528 his brother took him to New Spain, where, after a brief, successful career, he became a gambler. Facing his brother's mismanaged life, Domingo returned to his original pursuit of the habit. The order needed men like him. Dávila Padilla comments that in the early years of the Dominican order in Mexico, novices abounded but professions were few. In 1530 out of twenty-nine aspiring novices, only two professed. Fr. Domingo was one of them. In those early years of the viceroyalty, young men bided their time to make a final decision on their careers as presumptive novices, opting out of taking the vows if they found other opportunities to make a living in administration or commerce.[101]

Not all who came to New Spain and joined the orders were examples of proper behavior, but the errant sheep could return the fold and become exemplary models to serve the moralizing purpose of the chroniclers and demonstrate the possibility of changing a youth gone wrong. Among them were a few who, after arriving in New Spain, lost their moral compasses but repented and entered a convent as mature adults. Their example of repentance and renunciation to the world could not be overlooked by those in charge of writing the history of their orders. Such was Augustinian Fr. Francisco de Acosta, born near Seville, who, like many other *mancebos galanes* (graceful gentlemen), went to New Spain and then traveled to Zacatecas in search of a new and better life. However, he apparently got embroiled in sexual adventures that obliged him to escape the area and eventually enter the Augustinian order as a repentant adult.[102] Dominican Dávila Padilla also paints us a portrait of how a young man could deviate from the straight path to find redemption in religion in his biography of Fr. Cristóbal de Lugo. He was born in Sevilla, no date provided, and was a protégée of none other than Inquisitor Francisco Tello de Sandoval, who in 1543 was sent to Mexico by Charles V to study the situation of the Indians in the viceroyalty and to enact the New Laws. Lugo, of a humble family, was put under the care of Tello de Sandoval to be educated and secure a career under the wing of a powerful man, a frequent enough situation in Spain in the sixteenth century. During his early youth, Cristóbal did well in his studies, and as soon as he entered pubescence (*hombrecito*), he was taken to Toledo when Sandoval became inquisitor general. There he diverted from the "straight" path and began a life of dissipation and gambling in taverns in the company of "ruffians" and women—not untypical behavior among young men trying the freedom of early manhood. Dávila Padilla called that period his "lost mocedad." Tello de Sandoval kept his faith in Cristóbal, possibly trusting that the passions of youth would dissipate. In order to bring him back to the fold, Tello ordained him in the lower grades of the clergy. This move apparently worked, and he was eventually ordained as a priest. In 1544, when Tello was appointed to review the activities of the Mexican *audiencia*, he took Cristóbal with him. Apparently, this new mission changed his life again. In 1548, after Tello returned to Spain, Cristóbal de Lugo remained in Mexico and professed in the Dominican order as Fr. Cristóbal de la Cruz. The information on the "reckless" years of a young layman called attention to the course correction that took place when the rowdiness of early manhood was replaced by a quieter life in the orders. The mendicant orders appear as an appropriate choice for those who felt a call for a more spiritual life as they matured. Lugo's life was such a didactic example that it became the subject of one of Miguel de Cervantes's hagiographic comedies.[103] The good seeds sown in childhood eventually conquered the negative influences of a negative social environment.

The biographical accounts of late seventeenth- and eighteenth-century members of the orders are equally meager in terms of information on childhood. The formative years of two of the most prominent Franciscans, Fr Antonio Margil de Jesús and Fr. Junípero Serra, are described by their devoted biographers with much moral eulogy and hagiographical froth. Both were *peninsulares* brought to New Spain to invigorate the missionary activities of their order. Margil was a founder of the Colegio de Propaganda Fide in

Zacatecas, and Serra revived the missions in the Sierra Gorda and founded those in California. Of Fr. Antonio's childhood, his two biographers state that he received religious indoctrination and support from a strong mother, whom the friar remembered later on as "saintly," thus corroborating the influence of some women on the spiritual formation of the child. Margil was attached to the Church and its liturgy since age seven and trained to become an acolyte. It was then that he received his first instruction in Latin at a local school. He was precociously inclined to prayer and spent hours in the church.[104] Biographer Vilaplana, intent on creating the image of Margil as a child inclined to virtue and religiosity, considered him extraordinary because he did not "suffer the infirmities of childhood." He belonged to that special number of men who were already "adults" in their early years, rejecting the superficialities of that age and adopting the maturity of older men. Margil "learned how to mingle the flowers of childhood with the fruits of a disillusioned [*desengañada*] old age," states the biographer.[105] For his part, another biographer, Fr. Isidro Félix de Espinosa, commended young Margil's horror of sin, his fear of God, and his early devotion to Christ and religious activities.[106]

In these hagiographical visions of childhood, there was no space for games and the carefree behavior of normal children. They stayed close to home, were obedient and dedicated to their studies, and were full participants in the liturgy of the church under the direction of a spiritual director. Fr. Manuel Bravo, who commented as a referee on Espinosa's biography of Margil, added his own opinion of his socially desirable qualities. As a young man, Margil, he wrote, possessed those virtues praised by didactic literature: modesty, gravity, and civility (*cortesanía*). Modesty was his golden rule to deal with all men. Gravity and civility served him to be "agreeable and urbane," treating everyone according to their status regardless of their personal shortcomings. The latter comment was assumed to be a eulogy of social urbanity. Despite being a man of the cloth, Margil was praised for not engaging in the moral condemnation of others unless he learned about their failings in the confessional.[107]

Fr. Junípero Serra (1713–84) was born into a humble family on the island of Majorca, part of the Balearic Islands. He learned Latin in a Franciscan school adjacent to the village, and his parents took him to the city of Palma, capital of the islands, to study to qualify for admission to the order. He was a sickly and small child but succeeded in entering the order in 1730 at age sixteen and professed one year later. Family strategies were at play when parents took their promising male children to be educated in a convent to ease their way into the stable careers of jurisprudence or religious life. However, not all families regarded conventual life as a promising career. The parents of Dominican Fr. Diego de Alcázar gave him the good education expected in members of the rising elite in sixteenth-century Mexico City. They wished their son to follow the "arms" rather than the "letters" and become a *caballero* like others in his family. They were disappointed when the young man, escaping his family's grip, took refuge in the convent of Santo Domingo after participating in some local fiestas in 1566 and eventually professed as a friar.[108]

The unblemished portraits of children presented in religious texts were not necessarily true to reality. The childhood remembered by the Church was a construct built with some facts and embellished by the set of norms prescribed by educators and churchmen who wrote on the boyhood of model men. By pretending that all postulants followed the perfect rules of behavior set up for that stage in life, chroniclers and biographers set up a strong base for an alternate form of masculine behavior that would bloom in adulthood. They were creating models of childhood not necessarily reflective of the true experience of children in general—and possibly not even that of most members of the orders. Closer to reality were the data on the care of their parents, relatives, and protectors, who ensured they received a good religious and intellectual education.[109] In real life, boys could not really be protagonists of their own lives until they reached physical manhood.

The narrative brevity of the childhood of real friars simply enunciates and reformulates the principles set by those who wrote on the social education of children. The family, the state, and the church had a common interest in setting up norms that would guide little boys to become upright men in the hope of building a stable society. Socially accepted behavioral models found in historical and literary narratives introduced to readers men praised as fulfilling the prescribed behavior of perfect childhood. Another set of norms laid before those who chose to profess. To obtain full membership in any of the mendicant orders, the young novice required further social, academic, and spiritual training. Just as secular men would have to readjust their lives to the heavier demands of adulthood, religious life would retrain the novice to enter into a different type of adult manhood. They are described and analyzed in the next chapter.

2

The Threshold of Religious Life
The Novitiate

> All religions have a novitiate, and all crafts, apprenticeship. Therefore, it is important that before they become ecclesiastics, men exercise themselves in the virtuous and exemplary life they will have to live until they die to obtain salvation.
> —Antonio Arbiol, *Vocación eclesiástica*

The transition from *mocedad* to adulthood was more than a physical change for some men. It was the time to decide whether he would enter a convent and follow a life in the service of God. The intellectual and spiritual process behind that decision remains rarely explained by those who made it, even though it was the most crucial moment in a man's life. Unlike nuns, friars rarely kept intimate writings that could have disclosed their personal reasons for choosing conventual life. The act of profession was a brief statement recorded in conventual books with the name of the professant and the date of the act; nothing else was required. We may assume that at a young age, a novice might have been emotionally motivated but lacking the right words to explain his decision. Those who professed well past their youth had a more meditated experience, but they often resort to generalities to explain it. Their scarce testimonials talk about being disgusted with the vanities of the world and wanting to seek refuge and the love of God in the friary. Regardless of age and motivation, those entering a mendicant order with the intent of becoming a man of the cloth had to undergo a period of training known as the novitiate. It was meant to initiate them into the arduous physical and spiritual training that would mark them forever as dedicated to a different but acceptable expression of manhood. The novitiate was essential to learning the discipline followed by the community on a daily basis as well as the order's spiritual profile.

In chapter 1, we have seen the young aspirant to religious life arriving at his decision in the years of his *mocedad*. For some of them, that decision was a "natural" sequel to their education. In some families the boys were "expected" to join the ranks of the Church as a mark of the family's piety. In families of limited means, becoming a friar was a viable and desirable way of channeling the boy into a respected role in society. Friaries did not expect "dowries" because in their act of marrying into the Church, men followed the secular practice of grooms, who simply offered themselves in body and spirit to the bride—the order, in this case. Initiation into conventual life could be as early as fourteen, the minimum age established by the Council of Trent (1540–63).[1] In New Spain, Trent's rule was observed faithfully, as verified by Elsa Malvido's studies of the long-term admission to the recollect Franciscans of the friary of San Cosme in Mexico. Her figures corroborate that those novices came largely from the capital (63 percent) and that they entered San Cosme between fifteen and eighteen years of age, while among those traveling from the provinces to the capital to profess, the ages fluctuated between fourteen and nineteen years.[2] Age was not as important as the piety and sincerity shown by the candidate.

All novices were an investment in the order's future, whether spiritual or material. Mendicant orders needed priests, preachers, and writers because they aspired to be bastions of religious and philosophical knowledge as well as active venues for sustaining and propagating the faith among the general secular population. They also needed humbler men who would attend to the daily needs of the community. The decision to admit an aspirant was made by the friary's elders, working as a rotating committee of admission that evaluated the candidates. These gatekeepers took into consideration the needs of the community and the ability of the candidates to satisfy them. On the one hand, to guarantee the continuity of their intellectual status, the orders had to cultivate the education of the most gifted of their novices. On the other hand, those whose task was to serve their brothers in religion were to be educated too, but only to the extent required by their future services. The novices considered in this chapter are those destined to become priests. Those destined to serve as lay brothers will be seen in chapter 3.

As the symbolic threshold of religious life, the novitiate was designed to reeducate the candidate by removing many of the features of his previous secular life to build a new person through a daily physical and spiritual regimen that would make of him a *mendicant* in thought and behavior. Once the novice made his final vows, he was a rightful member of the community, a *corista* with rights to belong to the *coro*, or "community," of priests of the convent. The first few years after profession were also known as the *jovenado*, or "youthful years." The *corista* spent one or two years studying theology and liturgy until he was ready for the final ordination that gave him the right to perform the Mass and become a full-fledged pastor of souls.

It would have been desirable to rely on direct personal accounts of how the novice experienced his transformation into a friar. A few nuns left written memories of their experience as novices.[3] Men, on the other hand, at least in New Spain, did not indulge in such autobiographical exercises. Lacking such personal testimonies, we have to resort to institutional sources and the information they can provide in order to understand the significance of the transition into conventual life. Since the key actor in this process was the candidate for admission and eventual profession, we focus on him first.

When they knocked at the friary's door, candidates to become ordained priests brought with them reading and writing skills and at least some basic Latin acquired through their early education. The depth and breadth of that education were assessed on a personal basis so that the novice could pursue mastery of several subjects as part of his training in the convent. Physical health and spiritual aptitude for religious life were also of the uppermost importance. The latter was not measurable by any prescribed rule; it was a matter of judgment left to the small group of friars who oversaw the selection of candidates and the teacher of novices who would be in charge of training him in conventual observance for at least one year. During that period of time, the teacher had to decipher the complexities of each aspirant's personality and assess the quality of his spiritual potential known as vocation. Fr. Antonio Arbiol, a rigorous commentator on religious life and observance, devoted a book of over five hundred printed pages to examine vocations and provide guidance to those examining the aspirants as well as to the novices themselves.[4] Conventual life was a commitment for life, and it deserved that kind of intensive study and advice.

Historically, all mendicant orders began to develop some guidelines for admission shortly after their foundation in the late Middle Ages. In 1603 Pope Clement VIII intervened to establish general rules on the process of reception for all orders, thus completing a task that had begun at the Council

FIG. 5. Profession of Fr. Hernando de San Pablo, April 26, 1565, in *Book of Professions from the Convent of Saint Augustine, Mexico City*, Genaro García Collection, Benson Latin American Collection, LLILAS Benson Latin American Studies and Collections, University of Texas at Austin.

of Trent. The rules gave guidance in the selection of the aspirants, but the friars could also consult their own institutional memory and the combined wisdom of their acknowledged spiritual leaders.[5] In chapter 1, I have reviewed some of the general "impressions" that endeared an aspirant to the community. It's worthwhile to quote the testimony of a chronicler on this point. In a full description of a very young candidate, Dominican Fr. Francisco de Burgoa tells how Fr. Jerónimo de Abrego was admitted to the novitiate at the Dominican convent of Oaxaca. Born in the Gran Canarias, Abrego traveled to Mexico with his parents, who settled in Puebla. Jerónimo was at the convent's door before he was fifteen. He had letters recommending his good character, but the friars were just as impressed by his modesty and the logic of his persuasive request for admission. The prior and several elder priests understood "at first sight" the potential of this "chosen vessel" to become a Dominican preacher. On his second visit to the convent, Jerónimo put so much "force in his arguments" that the friars agreed to receive him even though he was a few months short of his fifteenth birthday.[6]

Social Selection of the Novice

While the task of assessing a candidate's vocation was subtle and personal, the social qualifications of the aspirant relied on stronger bases. There were rules with juridical weight behind them and a complex system of enunciations and redefinitions that gave predictability to the process of judging a candidate. Terms of exclusion defined who could *not* be a candidate. By the early sixteenth century, documents called *informaciones* certified key personal facts demanded from all candidates. To become a member of the orders, one had to be "old Christian"—that is, without any direct descent from converted Jews and a practicing Christian for several generations.[7] This requirement was known as *limpieza de sangre*, or "purity of blood." In peninsular Spain an unblemished religious affiliation also required proof of not having any practitioners of the Muslim faith in the family. Other key elements in the aspirant's candidacy were legitimacy of birth, personal reputation as an honorable person, lack of criminal records, good health, and being single. All were facts that required corroboration in a notarial affidavit.[8] In New Spain, the weight of purity of blood had become overwhelming by the end of the sixteenth century. The key factor for purity was the absence not of Muslim or Jewish ancestry—although that was included in the text—but of Indigenous or African blood. The uncontrolled mixing of Spaniards with the Natives and the imported Africans injected diversity into the racial profile of the population but created individuals judged undesirable for religious profession. The exclusion of racial admixtures was enshrined in the rules of all mendicant orders, and it closed the doors of the convents to the majority of the male population, reserving membership in the Church solely for the proven descendants of Europeans.

Well before the condition of *limpieza* began to be discussed in the midsixteenth century, the orders had decided not to admit Indians to their ranks.[9] The doors were even more firmly closed to any admixtures of Africans. The Dominican order in New Spain defended this position with Fr. Domingo Betanzos, its first vicar general, as its strongest advocate. Its 1642 general chapter reiterated the exclusion of any aspirant with Indian or African ancestry.[10] The reasoning was that while some Indians showed aptitude, most of them were too new in the faith and had some weaknesses of character that would dilute the purity of the observance. Some early members of the Franciscan order were inclined to ordain Indians and mestizos and began to instruct them to meet the requirements for acceptance as novices. They were defeated by a series of sometimes contradicting arguments by individual members of the order against such broad terms of admission. Indians, it was argued, not only were "new" Christians but had too much natural "humility" to assume leadership. They lacked discipline for religious life, were prone to weaknesses of the flesh, and had a limited capacity for the abstruse theological points of Christianity. Indians, by these reasonings, would remain "new" Christians forever.[11] Considering the Indigenous as neophytes and as "children" never reaching adulthood in the faith, the evangelization process was on a path to becoming a perpetual process: missionary activity would never cease as long as there were Indigenous people under indefinite care as wards of the Church.

Pro-forma limpieza took an interesting twist when it began to apply to mestizos.[12] Mestizos were rebuffed on account of having "suckled" the Indian weaknesses through their mother's milk. Negotiation became possible when the ability to speak Native languages and forge good social connections gave a few mestizos access to the order in the Franciscan province of the Holy Gospel. Francisco Morales, OFM, confirmed cases of aspirants of Indian descent in their grandparent's generation who were admitted to the province of the Holy Gospel. The vagueness of ancestry information committed to paper gave a few postulants the desired passport for profession, while the order gained someone who could deal with Native speakers. However, Morales admits that despite exceptions, the rejection of aspirants owing to social blemishes increased in the eighteenth century.[13] He recorded six rejections in the seventeenth century on account of "blemished lineage." In the eighteenth century, there were thirty-three. These were low numbers relative to the total number of admissions, but they meant that the order remained committed to carrying out its policy of exclusion.

The growth of the American-born of Spanish descent (criollos) and the decline of immigrants from Spain favored the admission of criollos in the mendicant orders in the seventeenth century, since their need for more members could not be met solely by migration from Spain. The Dominican order found itself declining in terms of the total number of admissions by the end of the sixteenth century and was forced to admit Mexican-born to halt the trend.[14] A recent study of the Dominican order between 1570 and 1661 by Maria Fernanda Mora Reyes amplifies our knowledge of the order's standing in terms of ethnicity and admissions. She verifies the decline of Spanish-born Dominicans in the province of Santiago, a fact already noted by 1601. In 1624 Fr. Agustín de Alderete reported that for every peninsular professing, six criollos took the habit. This imbalance created political issues that affected the admission of novices. In 1627 the Dominican order's visitor instructed the province of Santiago to restrict the access of criollo novices in order to guarantee Spaniards equal access to the conventual government. This order was rejected by the Dominican convents in Oaxaca and Puebla, and in 1628 a royal order voided the enforcement of such restriction.[15] There would not be any official ethnic discrimination against those of Spanish descent to favor those moving from Spain to its viceroyalty.

In an attempt to maintain a balance between ethnicities, the Augustinian provincial chapter of 1619 tried to close the door of the novitiate to criollos until the numbers of Spanish-born friars equaled those born in New Spain. This was an obviously impossible goal to reach. When Fr. Diego Basalenque finished his chronicle in 1646, the Augustinian order was experiencing some internal struggles resulting from the enforcement of that measure.[16] The imbalance in the elective offices created by the majority of criollo members among the Augustinians and Dominicans was offset by the adoption of an alternating system for the election (*alternativa*) of key posts in each convent, whereby a Spaniard was elected after a criollo finished his term. The Dominicans of Michoacán, with a majority of criollo members, accepted the *alternativa* in 1630.[17] The Franciscan province of the Holy Gospel, the leading Franciscan branch in the viceroyalty, was overwhelmingly criollo by the end of the seventeenth century. Spanish-born represented only 8.6 percent of a total of 703 friars. Criollos represented 79.5 percent. There was nothing that Spanish-born friars could do to change that reality except adopt the *alternativa*. A small number of Franciscan friars were classified as *hijos de provincia* (sons of the province) and not by their ethnicity. A novice professing in the province of Oaxaca, for example, would be an *hijo* of that province.[18] This added some complexity to the issue of adscriptions but did not alter the election process or the fact that criollos became the backbone of the mendicant orders by the end of the seventeenth century.[19]

The Franciscan Colegios de Propaganda Fide, introduced in New Spain in the late seventeenth century, adopted *limpieza*.[20] Its records in New Spain show no admission of anyone with Indian ancestry to any degree. David Rex Galindo's study of the college in Querétaro confirms the steadfastness of the policy of exclusion.[21] In fact, reforms to the order approved in 1791 advised the father guardian to be very careful about the racial affiliation of the candidates. He should seek the advice of individuals who could distinguish among the various "infected" pedigrees in New Spain, thus separating the "precious from the lowly."[22] Those wanting to join the mendicant orders as lay brothers went through the same process of racial qualification.[23]

Another stipulation that had a long-lasting impact on the acceptance of novices was that of legitimacy of birth. This requirement was not difficult to fulfill in Spain, where the rate of illegitimacy was low. The rate of children born out of wedlock was considerably higher in New Spain than in Spain or Europe.[24] This fact incentivized the orders to enforce the legitimacy qualification faithfully, with occasional exceptions when the well-educated novices had been registered as "hijos de Iglesia" (sons of the Church) or were of unknown parentage that could be determined as having been white.[25]

Quantitative studies of novice admissions are only possible when archival data supply long-term numbers. The Franciscan order offers the largest number of records on this topic. Several recent studies have succeeded in providing partial but important views of this process. Fr. Francisco Morales's study of the reception of novices in the province of the Holy Gospel in the seventeenth century stands out in terms of information. Between 1600 and 1699, 2,281 aspirants entered the novitiate in Mexico City's main convent of San Cosme, also in the capital, and in the convent in Puebla.[26] He found that 1,573 novices, or 73 percent of admissions, were criollos. The comparison between the first decade of the century, when criollos represented only 28 percent, and the last decade, when they represented 75 percent of the total number, corroborates the dramatic takeover of criollos. Only 260 missionaries arrived from Spain after midcentury. To carry out its doctrinal and missionary activities, the province needed all the criollo applicants it could get. Elsa Malvido's study of the Franciscan order novices between 1649 and 1749 does not include the novices from Puebla. In terms of *peninsulares* and criollos, her numbers confirm Morales's conclusions and the steep decline of Spanish novices in that period. There were 937 novices admitted in the hundred-year period. Criollos made up 85 percent of the total.[27]

The complete records of admission at the Querétaro Colegio de Propaganda Fide, a branch of the Franciscan order, afford some conclusive data on the number and percentage of admissions of criollos and *peninsulares* in this institution since it began to register professions in 1680. Two different studies indicate that there was a numerical majority of Mexican-born novices. David Rex Galindo corroborates that more criollos than *peninsulares* were admitted to the novitiate and eventually professed, despite the also significant number of novices who failed to do so.[28] For the 1691–1820 period, René González Marmolejo, focusing on the application of novices (but not the professants), also registered fewer Spanish-born applicants than criollos.[29] Another source of information is the records of the Franciscan friary of San Cosme in Mexico City. The observant Franciscan province of San Diego originated in 1599, but it did not have its own convent until 1669. It was a more rigorous version of the order, and its original residential site was in a small chapel (*hermita*) in the borough of San Cosme. In 1594 the friars moved to their own home in the city, and the San Cosme site received its official recognition as a discalced convent in 1669.[30] A long-term study of the applicants to the novitiate of this province by Daniel Salvador Vázquez Conde corroborates trends in terms of criollos and *peninsulares*, adding the numbers of those who failed to profess. Between 1613 and 1764, the convent received 655 applications, but 111 dropped out, died, or were expelled.[31] There were 469 criollo novices (71.6 percent) and 152 *peninsulares* (23.2 percent).

Of this group, 25 aspirants lacked ethnicity assignation, and 9 came from other European countries and Peru. The Puebla novitiate of the Franciscan province of San Diego admitted only lay brothers, and between 1700 and 1793, only 33 applied, a very small number for such a long period of time. There was little attraction in the status of "lay brother." Willful departures—or dropouts—in all convents were due to chronic sickness or, most likely, lack of vocation and little disposition to endure the discipline of conventual life. Doubtless, some were simply expelled for bad conduct, but records are difficult to locate and have not been studied. The few studies on the historical profile of admissions, failures, or expulsions of novices in any given convent suggest not only that those novices lacked voice but that they have failed to attract historical interest.

Raising the Novice: Reception and Training

Before applying for admission, the aspirant had to interview with the guardian or head, the master of novices, and the advisory council of the convent. Their task was to test his vocation. During this introductory meeting, the novice, dressed in his secular clothes, acquainted himself with the community for three days prior to any further administrative process.[32] If he succeeded in meeting all the requirements and entered the novitiate, the aspirant was welcomed by a small number of brothers. He removed his secular clothes, which were kept until his profession as a precautionary step in case he did not reach the latter.[33] Given the number of failures for the Franciscans of the San Diego province (Dieguinos) quoted above, this was a prudent measure. The guardian commended him to divine grace, and he was taken to his cell, where he removed the rest of his clothes and received his habit.[34]

The ceremony of the reception of the habit was profoundly symbolic. By removing his secular clothes, the postulant renounced his ties to the world and entered the one in which he expected to live the rest of his life if he overcame the challenges awaiting him in his training. The habit was more than a garment. It symbolized the friar's commitment to the canons of the faith and the rules of his order as well as his ritual death to the world. He wore it even to sleep. To remove the habit was a breach of his promise to himself and to the community and carried an automatic dismissal from the order or a shameful punishment. Franciscans gave their novices a set of two habits, a short hood, and two sets of underwear. The novice hood was shorter than the ones worn by the professed brothers, and it was not attached to the habit, meaning they were not, as yet, permanent members of the community. The Dominicans did not bless the habit until the sacred profession.[35] In the mendicant orders, the habits of the lay brothers were different from those destined to become priests; their tunic was shorter and lacked the hood.[36]

From day one in the novitiate, there was a master plan to be fulfilled: to reshape the mind of the novice as a secular man and to transform him into a religious man. It was a bold objective. It proposed to discard some of the rights and prerogatives of the candidate that had been assumed to be "natural" to men since childhood. Such were his prerogatives to speak his mind and express his will with his own voice, his right to exercise his sexuality for creating a biological family, and his right to become the head of a family, manage its well-being and finances, and exercise his authority over his wife and children. He also renounced his right to conduct himself as a free man to pursue wealth and power. This was a long list of renunciations of fundamental assumptions validated by law and custom. The three vows that bound the aspirant to the order—obedience, chastity, and poverty—trumped pride and self-will, muted the novice's voice before a superior in the order, denied his sexual desire and potential fatherhood, and forbade his desire for material possessions. In theory it was a lot to give up. Fr. Leandro de Murcia, a seventeenth-century Spanish Franciscan, thought that the vows were worth the sacrifice because they sealed the commitment to live in a "state whereby men walk to Christian perfection."[37]

The vow of poverty was difficult to reconcile with the fact that religious orders were institutions that, in order to survive, depended on economic resources such as financial royal assistance, pious deeds, and real property commercialized to render an income. It was understood that the vow of poverty was "personal," not institutional. Murcia explains how the three vows intertwined in an elegant theological unity when applied to mendicants. Men had three types of wealth (*bienes*): temporal wealth or world possessions, the wealth of their own bodies, and the wealth of their souls. World possessions were renounced through the vow of poverty. The wealth of the body was offered through the vow of chastity, which forbade the "delights" of the flesh. The wealth of the soul was offered to God through the vow of obedience. Thus, the vows were a vital shield protecting each individual from all the difficulties of the world at large. As Murcia puts it, the vows were their first and last resort when the waters of spiritual calm and perfection were muddled by the continuous assaults of the secular world. Such a thorough disavowal of the world and the privileges of secular manhood required several years of training. The novitiate, as the threshold to that new life, imparted the aspirant that knowledge, but it was only the beginning of a long-term existence ruled by such demanding renunciations.

The process of remaking the secular man into a religious man within the convent was often called *crianza*. The term means "to nurture" in addition to taking physical care of a person. Both meanings were implied in its use among the mendicant orders. The master of novices, the person in charge of initiating and carrying out the *crianza de novicios*, understood the difficulties posed by the novitiate. This challenging process demanded a personal relationship between teacher and novice so the teacher could better assess the novice's personal character and needs. In his Augustinian chronicle, Fr. Juan González de la Puente stated how the novice-teacher relationship had been essential in the shaping of one notable Augustinian, Fr. Diego de Villarubia. His teacher had been Fr. Gregorio de Santa María, "a living model of sanctity and virtue" himself. Santa María's personal qualities had enabled him to craft such an outstanding pupil: "The teacher's virtues had been pressed on him [Villarubia] as soft wax."[38] Chronicles did not discuss failure; only success. To achieve success the relationship had to be mutual. The novice had to be pliable and eager to receive the learning of the master. When de la Puente used the word *craft*, he was calling attention to the care and wisdom demanded from the master of novices and his ability to coax the potential virtues of the applicant and persuade him to embrace all rules and regulations. The man who emerged from the novitiate had to be different from the one who entered it. Books on instructions and guidance for the teacher helped in the performance of his duties, but since the instruction was meant to be carried out on a personal basis and with skill and care, the results depended on the master's personal character and abilities.

It was always assumed that the teacher had to learn and polish his métier. The manuals to teach the novice assumed the education of the educator as well. Acquiring the ability to coach a novice demanded time and a vocation for the role, but as far as we know, there was no "official" training for it. Teaching novices was demanding, and in addition to patience, the teacher

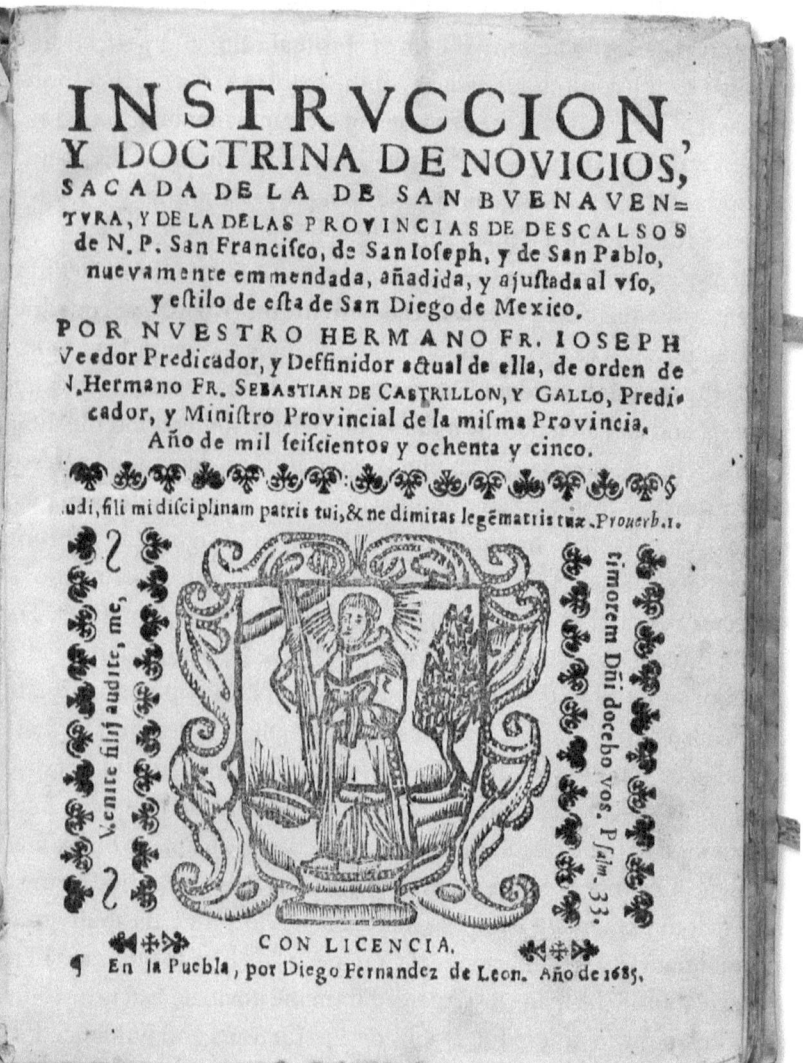

INSTRVCCION,
Y DOCTRINA DE NOVICIOS,
SACADA DE LA DE SAN BVENAVEN=
TVRA, Y DE LA DE LAS PROVINCIAS DE DESCALSOS
de N. P. San Francisco, de San Ioseph, y de San Pablo,
nuevamente emmendada, añadida, y ajuftada al vfo,
y eftilo de efta de San Diego de Mexico.
POR NVESTRO HERMANO FR. IOSEPH
Veedor Predicador, y Deffinidor actual de ella, de orden de
N. Hermano FR. SEBASTIAN DE CASTRILLON, Y GALLO, Predi-
cador, y Miniftro Provincial de la mifma Provincia.
Año de mil feifcientos y ochenta y cinco.

.udi, fili mi difciplinam patris tui, & ne dimitas legem matris tuæ. *Prouerb.* 1.

Venite filij audite, me,

timorem Dñi docebo vos. *Pfalm.* 33.

CON LICENCIA.
En la Puebla, por Diego Fernandez de Leon. Año de 1685.

FIG. 6. Joseph Veedor, *Instrucción y Doctrina de Novicios*
(Puebla: Diego Fernández de León, 1685).

INSTRUCCION,

Y DOCTRINA DE NOVICIOS,

CON LA QUAL SE HAN DE CRIAR LOS nuevos Religiosos en esta Santa Provincia de San Joseph, de los Descalzos de la Regular Observancia de los Menores.

Añadiòse al fin la forma de dàr el habito, y profession à los Novicios.

Venerabilis servus Dei S. Petrus de Alcantara Hisp...
...S. Francisci discalceatorum fundator Provincia S. Jose...
...a plures alias dimanarunt, ac P. spiritualis B. M. Teresia...

En Madrid: En la Oficina de Antonio Marín.
Año de M.DCCXXXIII.

FIG. 7. *Instrucción y Doctrina de Novicios* (Madrid, 1733).

had to assess the novice's vocation for conventual life and detect any potential weakness in his will to conform to it. His evaluation of the novice's character and religious disposition carried the most weight in the community's decision to accept or dismiss the aspirant. The relationship between novice and teacher was complex, involving a delicate balance between affection and discipline. The teacher replaced the parents of the younger aspirants who had left the family home with all its cuddling and care, only to find themselves in a new community of totally alien men. Only a few were his own age, largely the other novices. The older members of the community were distant and detached and must have inspired respect and fear. For them, the novices—young or old—were the new "children" in the family whose care was not their responsibility.

Training

The novice's closest personal contact was with his teacher. The intensity of the learning period demanded that the teacher of novices be a man with years of experience in conventual life and of an even temperament. The rules of the Dominican order stated that the teacher had to be at least thirty-five years old with ten years of experience in conventual life. Additionally, he should have desirable personal traits, such as inclination to prayer, modesty, affability, zealousness in the observance of the rule, and a placid personality not given to anger. He should be more loved than feared.[39] In New Spain, the Franciscan order published instructions for the teaching of novices three times between 1685 and 1775.[40] The discalced Franciscan province of San Diego published its own in 1738.[41] I have not found any book of instructions published by the Dominican or the Augustinian orders. According to Augustinian chronicler Juan de Grijalva, Fr. Diego de Vertavillo, a provincial of the order, had written a book for the instruction of novices that he saw in manuscript form.[42] One must assume that Augustinians and Dominicans used manuals imported from Spain. If the teacher of novices proved to be personally well equipped for his task and successful in handling the newcomers, he could serve in his post for a long time. Dominican Fr. Alonso Pérez (1523?–91) was master of novices in the convent of Mexico City for the best part of thirty-eight years.[43]

A Franciscan *cartilla*—a book for the teaching of novices—recommended that teachers treat the novices with love and charity, suffering their imperfections but never forgetting the importance of their authority. They were told to behave "like a tender mother, and the novices, in that respect, were like little children on whom . . . he could press (through divine grace) the doctrine . . . and being, as they are, like mothers, . . . treat them with the love and charity that carnal mothers have with their own, teaching them the ABCs of religion, suffering calmly their roughness and ignorance; not becoming angry if they don't succeed in doing fast what they are taught, even if they are easy things. . . . At the beginning [the easy things] are difficult to them."[44] This appropriation of the imagery of motherhood speaks of the flexibility in conceptualizing male and female roles in a milieu that lacked the presence of women. Although the language was metaphorical, the wording speaks of pedagogy understood as maternal and feminine, especially because novices were compared to little children, who were always under the care of their mothers. The teachers of novices occupied a middle ground between the discipline of a father and the affectivity of a mother. However, it was well understood that the son had to surrender his own will to that of the father. Obedience to the superiors in the community was fundamental as the first and foremost of the three vows ruling the lives of all friars. Franciscan Fr. Alonso de la Rea praised Fr. Juan de Espinosa precisely because he knew how to mix the severity of a prelate with the love of a father. While his students were busy with their lessons, Fr. Juan visited their cells to find out if they needed something. For example, if he found some old torn underwear, he would mend it or make a new garment. His preoccupation with the well-being of his novices was deemed proof of his paternal love.[45] Fr. Alonso de la Rea also praised Fr. Juan Gallina for his solicitude with the novices. His behavior was compared—on account of his name—with that of a hen with her chicks.

Teachers and Students

Two Dominican chroniclers remembered one master of novices who had a great influence on the training of the novices of the friary in Mexico City, having served for nearly thirty-eight years. He was Fr. Alonso Pérez, respectfully remembered by Fr. Hernando de Ojea and Fr. Alonso Franco, both of whom became chroniclers of the order. Fr. Alonso was the son of peasants (*labradores*) near Salamanca who had migrated to Mexico. He had been, in fact, an "old" novice himself. When he professed in 1554, he was around thirty years of age. Ojea, his pupil, described him as an excellent friar, prior, teacher, and administrator. Fr. Alonso had shown an exemplary ability in the handling of the novices, "all boys and youngsters, sons of different parents, of different habits and inclinations, and little experience. His task consisted in moderating them, making them forget [bad habits and inclinations], and adopting the discipline of the friary and the concepts of life in religion."[46]

For his part, chronicler Franco noted the intensity of Fr. Alonso's religious observance, his ascetic life, and his piety and extolled his character as a teacher. Fr Alonso demanded study and virtue. He was an excellent guide in the learning of the rites and ceremonials of the order and did not spare punishment when it was called for. Franco approved of that practice when it was administered with the novice's understanding that it was for the correction of his fault. Franco opined that punishment, coming from a virtuous master, was an expression of a paternal desire to see wrongs corrected, and it was a prudent policy, because Fr. Alonso was a model of observance himself. When he needed to "correct" a novice, Fr. Alonso waited for the appropriate moment, sometimes days after an incident, to calmly explain the fault to the student and, once the student understood it, lead him into correcting it. Franco's eulogy of Fr. Alonso's didactic directives was based on the belief that the role of teacher of novices was among the most important in religion. As a writer, historian Franco used gardening metaphors to convey his message. When they entered "the vineyards of the Lord," novices came as "new plants from all the world's un-ploughed lands." Novices required a "careful and prudent gardener who raised them well, removing old scrub and giving them a new personhood."[47] Ojea's and Franco's understandings of the role of the master of novices are reminiscent of the teachings of sixteenth-century bishop, teacher, and writer Fr. Antonio de Guevara, who in his work *Oratorio de religiosos* paid much attention to the selection of novices and their teacher. In Guevara's words, "The master [teacher] must be like a father in raising them, as a mother in cuddling them, as a brother in supporting them, as a teacher in teaching them, as a leader in guiding them, and as a tutor [*ayo*] in sheltering them."[48]

The Messages of the Texts

Learning the essence of conventual life was one of the most important objectives of the first year of training. A novice who could not learn his order's rules would never be a good friar. Texts for the instruction of novices began

FIG. 8. Antonio de Guevara, *Oratorio de religiosos* (Valladolid: Juan de Villaquirán, 1542).

circulating early in the seventeenth century under titles such as *cartillas*, *doctrinas*, or *compendios* and offered a variety of advice and thoughts on the nature of educating a friar. In 1627 Fr. Valeriano de Espinosa, a member of the order of Saint Bernard, wrote a *Guía de religiosos* dedicated to *anyone* considering joining *any* mendicant order.[49] A fifth of the total text—126 pages—explained the transition from secular to religious life and extolled the strength of character of those who followed the call of religion. The novitiate was, in his words, a form of death leading to a new life, free of all the vanities of the world. However, this death was only figurative and led to the engagement in a double battle: one against the world and one against the self. Both demanded an iron will. Those who called the professed friars "poor in spirit" did not understand that there was much personal valor in their decision. Subjecting one's will and passions to someone else's will was a form of "violence" against oneself because obedience to others was not a natural instinct in men.[50] Religious life was for men of courage, not for soft, weak, or careless men. In his words, "Virtue is not for the tender or lazy; its rigors demand steel and suffering," and, "There is no glorious victory if the battle is not difficult."[51] This was a message supporting the manly nature of religious life, an appeal for recognition of the virility of character lying under the robe. Military metaphors used in some texts placed the friar as an equal to the soldier in resolve and courage, an interesting evaluation during a period in which Spain was involved in numerous military challenges in continental Europe. Military metaphors, however, were tempered with advice that reminded the novice of his expected humility and obedience. Espinosa compared the novices to lambs adapting themselves to the convent's discipline. Some of the battles to be endured were battles against the rebellious self, and victory would mean accepting the meaning of the vow of obedience. The soldier had to learn how to be a lamb as well.

The military metaphors reappeared in the eighteenth century. The anonymous author of a guide for Franciscan novices published in Madrid in 1733 compared religious life to that of a soldier engaged in a constant battle. In his words, the self-control demanded from a friar was a more heroic deed than capturing a city by arms. The novice, with the help of God and his virile will (*ánimo varonil*), could and would win the battle against himself and any temptations from outside. *Ánimo varonil* was a frequently used concept in the treatises of religious observance and the biographies of notable friars. These expressions supported an alternative—and special—form of masculinity as being the essence of religious manhood. However, and in contrast, Joseph Veedor, a Franciscan writing from Puebla in 1685, stressed the manly valor of submission. Valor was required to renounce one's own will, an act that he considered the greatest triumph in anybody's life. He also eulogized perseverance, the virtue required to reach the finish line—profession. Beginning a task without perseverance to finish it, he wrote, was like leaving the field half plowed.[52] Dominican Fr. Francisco Romero, writing in the first quarter of the eighteenth century, saw novices as tender plants that could grow into strong trees only through time and perseverance and advised the novice to examine his conscience and motivations before knocking at the convent's door.[53] The coexistence of such antagonistic traits as defining a friar's life was an indication of the difficulties writers found in encapsulating its essence. The encouragement to exhibit the virtues and strengths of a man was paired with the treatment of novices as "children" learning their métier. Ultimately, the fiercest battle was that between the novice's natural will and the obedience he owed his superiors. Pride was cured by humility. Arrogance, Espinosa reminded his readers, had caused the fall of the angels exiled from heaven.[54] Facing the multiplicity and subtlety of the messages conveyed by the authors of didactic treatises for the novitiate, the task of the teacher of novices was not an easy one. It could only be overcome by patience and dedication in the teacher and docility and acceptance in the novice. Their relationship became filial in nature.

In 1738 Fr. Joseph de Herize ordered the publication of a new book of guidance for the discalced Franciscan of San Diego in Mexico City, he highlighted the filial relationship between novice and teacher. He advised the novice to open his heart to his teacher or, with license, to any other old and knowledgeable friar.[55] Since the teacher of novices was also their confessor, he was expected to encourage the novice not to keep any secrets from him and to rely on his elders' advice. Thus, Herize was forging ties of dependence between the young novice and his superiors. At the same time, he added an interesting subtle dimension: the teacher should "spy" on his pupils' behavior to learn their inclinations and correct them by calling attention, admonishing, reprehending, and if necessary, physically punishing the novice, publicly or privately.

For spiritual instruction, Herize recommended that the teacher should instruct the novices to read the works of Fr. Pedro de Alcántara and Fr. Luis de Granada, two of the most notable mystics of the sixteenth century. They also should read and learn well the *Rules and Constitutions* of the Franciscan order, the breviary, and the ceremonials of the divine offices, which he included in his book. He advised the teacher to occupy the novices in all the domestic chores of the convent, such as cleaning the kitchen and tending the convent's vegetable garden. These assignments would strengthen their ability to remain humble and learn the value of all those who performed the lowest tasks in the convent. In sum, the master of novices should be the source of complete instruction, spiritual and material, and his responsibility (theoretically) was eulogized and admired. As expected, failures remained discreetly unacknowledged in official records.

The Practice of Conventual Discipline

The guides for teaching the novices suggested that they lived in a disciplined world totally lacking in self-expression and personal will, dedicated instead to introspection and meditation to find their calling while seeking God's grace. But beyond learning about the depth of his own commitment, there were rules regulating the novice's daily life that had to be learned and obeyed. Breaking conventual discipline put the novice at risk of being evicted from the convent. Augustinian Fr. Diego de Basalenque summoned his experience as a teacher of novices with the advice that the best way to raise novices was to have them follow the daily routine of the community and engage them in continuous study and attention to the liturgy.[56] He rightly pointed out that the greatest difficulty for the novice was learning the complicated and rigid formulation of prayers and offerings of the liturgy of the Mass and the religious feasts. This task took a significant part of the novice's learning time. To facilitate the training, novices were physically separated from the rest of the community and placed directly under the rule of the master of novices. They were forbidden from establishing personal friendships among themselves or having any contact with the professed members of the community. The need to adapt to the discipline and total personal control of the novitiate, and the isolation necessary to find his own spiritual truth, pulled the novice in two different directions, probably causing significant emotional stress, for which we lack any testimony. There was also the issue of how to learn the discipline of his own body.

The education of the novice began with a reeducation of his body. He had to learn composure, meaning that his personal appearance and physical bearing had to be appropriate for his "state" and express his renunciation of the world. Young men outside the convent were advised to watch their demeanor; so was the future friar.[57] He should walk straight in posture and with measured steps. His demeanor should express modesty by fixing his eyes on the ground, like a woman.[58] This was a form not of feminization but of self-control. If not looking at the ground, he should walk with the eyes fixed ahead, hands under the scapulary, and an expression of serenity on his face. He should not show any curiosity in the surroundings. Everything in him should express the gravity of a man dedicated to God. Within the convent he should walk close to the walls. If two novices walked together, one should walk ahead of the other and they should not talk to each other. They should remove their hood before a religious icon or before a conventual superior as a sign of respect. If the novice was called by a prelate, he should kneel before him and kiss his hand, asking for his blessing, before engaging in conversation. If he met a prelate in the staircase, he would cede the way. He would not engage in any conversation with other friars; if his help was requested for any task and he was free to do so, he should always comply. Such behavioral mandates taught the novice to accept his low status within the conventual hierarchy. They were not too different from those required of a child or minor.[59]

Within the convent, the refectory was the theater where social etiquette and behavior were displayed and observed by the entire community. The refectory ritual reflected the degree of personal discipline each member of the community had to observe and was similar to the etiquette prescribed in books for the education of secular youths. The principles of urbanity were regarded as universal. For the novice, eating in the refectory was the only instance, except during the religious services, that he could spend time with the rest of the community. Before going to the refectory, the novices gathered in the chapel called De Profundis and prayed for the souls of the dead brothers. Guided by their teacher, they joined the community, sat down, and waited for the prior or prelate to give the blessing of the bread. Then they should place their napkin half on the table and half hanging so they could clean themselves if necessary. The napkin should not be used to blow their noses or clean their teeth. The novice would sit straight, never putting his elbows on the table, and should avoid coughing on the food. While he ate, he should not put his fingers on the food or fill his mouth excessively. He would chew diligently to help digestion. The bread was cut in equal portions for all; any leftovers were reserved for a soup that was distributed among the city poor. When he needed water, bread, salt, or vinegar, he should tap the table lightly or tap his drinking mug twice. For any other need, he would request his companion at the table to express it to avoid calling attention to himself. At the end of the meal, he had to wait until the prelate stood up and gave thanks for the food, signaling that the meal was over. No food was eaten between meals.

Novices were in charge of lifting the dirty dishes from the table and washing them in the kitchen. This task was alternated among them. Author Francisco Romero pointed out that it was important to accept all food with humility. Novices should never raise complaints about the quality of the food they were served. For the hungry, there was no bad bread, and if the food was humble, that was God's will. Those entering the orders, he stated, were not intent on becoming sybarites. Excess food was bad for the mind and obstructed prayer. Saints were not gluttons.[60] In the Dominican order, some novices would rehearse preaching during the refectory period to have the prior and the professed members of the community judge if they could meet the demands of a future preacher.[61] Franciscan novices were expected to learn their precepts—the prescriptive heart of their order—by heart, and they could test their knowledge of the rules by reciting them at mealtimes. Serving as the reader during the meal was also an assignment for the Franciscan novice.[62]

The refectory was also the space where acts of penitence took place. Among the Franciscans penitence was administered three times a week. Penitence rituals followed a prescribed formula of punishments and expressions of repentance. The novice knelt, raised his hands, confessed his faults or sins, and asked for the clemency of the prelate. Prescribed forms of penitence could include eating while sitting on the floor (*comer en tierra*) until he received a dispensation or pardon from the prelate. The teacher of novices could prescribe other forms of penitence, such as kissing the habit or the feet of the rest of the community or lying on the threshold of the door so that all the community would step on him.[63]

The church choir (*coro*) was the place to learn all the essentials of the liturgy.[64] Prayer was the soul of conventual life. It was spiritual food rather than duty. If the refectory mixed the physical need to eat together with the urbanity demanded in such social act, behavior at the *coro* had to express respect and submission to God as a preamble to the spiritual nourishment received from prayer and the adoration of God's majesty. Wherever and whenever the bells called for prayers, the novice should stop whatever he was doing, meet his teacher and his companions in the novitiate, and go with them "with all composure" to the choir. Novices should be the first to arrive and the last to leave. They entered and left the choir with their heads bare and knelt and kissed the ground as a sign of reverence. Modesty in bearing, interiority (*recogimiento*), the proper pronunciation of prayers and hymns, and a good knowledge of the correct order of the liturgy were learned during the novitiate. Ceremonial was not the essence of religion, stated the Franciscan *cartilla*, but it was a thing of beauty, like ashes keeping the fire within.[65] Novices were also called to maintain the sacristy and help the priest at Mass as acolytes, having all the necessary essentials ready for him.

The conventual regimen the novice learned covered other aspects of daily life, such as caring for his habit, washing his underwear, and cleaning his cell.[66] There was no prescription for the frequency of baths, but in a biography of a Puebla Augustinian lay brother, we know that the order appreciated personal cleanliness without exaggeration in terms of baths.[67] Novices also helped the lay brothers who were in charge of housekeeping tasks. They could be asked to help wash the dishes in the kitchen, clean the conventual latrines, or ring the conventual bells.[68] At the end of the day, on retiring to his cell, the rules prescribed how to rest. The last prayers of the day prepared him to be free of sin in case of unexpected death. Beyond the prayers the novice was advised how to sleep. He should sleep in his habit and on his right side, with his hands crossed over his chest. He should never sleep on his stomach to prevent snoring and bad thoughts, implying those of a sexual nature. At night and in his cell, the novice could experience thoughts of lust. The teachers were aware of the possibility of masturbation, sexual dreams, or lingering thoughts on the temptations of the flesh.[69]

Despite its importance as the initiation in conventual life, chroniclers rarely address the experience of the novitiate. Dominican Fr. Alonso Franco left a formulaic note on the novitiate of Fr. Jordán de Santa Catarina: "Since he received the habit and during the novitiate year, one could see samples of the sanctity in which he shone later. He was very penitent and notable in his abstinence; many days he only ate bread and water, and in the long hours of prayer and discipline he planned well his religious lessons and was marvelously good in all virtues."⁷⁰ There is more information on Augustinian Fr. Diego de Basalenque (1577–1651), who spent his novitiate in the convent of Mexico City. He was born in Salamanca and was educated by the Jesuits before he joined the Augustinian order in 1593, at age sixteen. He became a linguist and chronicler of his order's province of Michoacán. The description of his own novitiate is very unusual in the literature and is worth quoting:

> Throughout the entire year of his novitiate, he was not allowed in the church to help with the mass because he was very small in body, tender and delicate, and he looked like a small devout friar. On the other hand, in the novitiate his work was doubled when he helped Fr. Gerónimo de Santa María at mass, and because he [Santa María] usually took too long, he was told to say mass upstairs . . . and he also helped two older friars; thus, he spent all morning kneeling in that saintly exercise. Despite his being delicate he bore all the rigor of the community, the *coro* during the day, and matins at midnight, and all the rigors and asperities of religion, the fasting and mortifications, all faithfully followed in the convent in Mexico . . . and on his own, and out of curiosity, he cleaned and ordered the choir song books and he made a Table to register *invitatorios*, *introitos* and *comunicandas*, and it is still in use today for our government . . . and he made such a perfect a novice that he looked like a much older religious. When the time came for his profession after the one year of probation, he was admitted by all the religious, at age sixteen, without a single dissenting vote.⁷¹

This biographical summary is more detailed than the standard synoptic attention to this stage in the progress of a friar's life. The intention of the biographer was to remark on the strength of the candidate as a potential friar: a small, delicate boy who earned approval through discipline and work.

Intellectual and Devotional Training

Some novices arrived at the convent with a good base of Latin and the arts and good reading habits; others did not. Those expected to become priests would have to continue their education on a more focused religious culture after they took their vows. The novitiate only took one year, and learning how to live in the convent and accept conventual discipline was probably the most important subject during that period. After profession, the newly

FIG. 9. Fr. Pedro Salguero, *Portrait-Drawing of Fr. Diego de Basalenque*, in *La vida del muy Reverendo Padre y Venerable Maestro Fray Diego Basalenque*, 1660, MS 2561, Biblioteca Digital Hispánica, Biblioteca Nacional de España, Madrid, Spain.

minted friar, now a *corista*, passed to a stage known as *jovenado*. He was still not considered a fully formed priest and had to undergo intensive intellectual training before he could ascend the steps of the altar to perform his first Mass. Promising choristers were groomed to read the arts and theology while polishing their Latin, Roman, and Christian authors and studying the Bible. Augustinian Fr. Diego de Villarubia was such a promising novice, and his order encouraged him to proceed with the study of theology. After his profession he was sent to the province of Michoacán to teach arts and theology to other *coristas*. He also taught in Mexico's premier teaching college of San Pablo and later in Cuyseo, Michoacán, and Guadalajara.[72]

Since not all convents were suited to train novices, the orders selected several convents in their respective provinces to provide further study in theology, Indigenous languages, and Latin. They were known as *casas de estudio*. Augustinian Fr. Alonso de la Veracruz (1507–84) established studies in the classic arts and in Native languages in the convent of Tiripetío, where he also served as master of novices. The training school was moved to Atotonilco in 1546. He eventually founded the College of San Pablo in the city of Mexico in 1575. The order had higher studies programs in several other smaller convents.[73] The Franciscan College of San Buenaventura in the capital received friars from other Franciscan provinces for higher training.[74] Between 1530 and 1535, the Dominican order established courses in grammar and theology in its main convent in the capital, and by 1541 it had twelve novices learning the arts. The order also imparted higher-education courses at the College of Porta Coeli in Mexico City and the College of San Luis in the bishopric of Puebla.[75] The training furnished by the colleges was essential in the creation and maintenance of a body of *coristas* who provided intellectual leadership within the orders. Their program of studies was not reduced to theology or philosophy. As centers for the study of Indigenous languages, they supported mendicants' efforts to retain their Indigenous doctrines. By 1667 the Franciscans had convents designed to teach languages specific to some regions. The mendicants were under attack from the diocesan for being unprepared to care for the spiritual needs of the Indigenous, since fewer and fewer friars spoke their languages. It's difficult to evaluate the veracity of this accusation, especially when the orders had well-laid-out schemes to teach Native languages in their convents. The Franciscan convent of Toluca was designated to teach Matlatzinga and Otomí, and those in Huichapan and Huamantla taught Otomí. The convents of Tlaxcala, Xochimilco, and Texcoco would teach Nahuatl in addition to arts and theology. The convents of Mexico, Puebla, and Santiago Tlatelolco had theology chairs, and the order had two colleges destined to train the members: the already mentioned San Buenaventura in Mexico and Purísima Concepción in Celaya, where students were trained in Latin, moral and mystic theology, plainsong, and one Indigenous language.[76] Masters and lecturers in those academic disciplines had to pass a rigorous exam administered by two previous masters and were required to give a sample of their erudition in a public lecture.[77]

The instruction of novices took place in a separate section, although the teacher could also impart some lessons in his own cell. One of the most significant acquisitions for a novice was "space of his own" in the friary. The cell was his only *private* space where he would study, pray, and reflect. Mendicant orders were not contemplative; they were very much part of the secular world inasmuch as their purpose was to spread the word of God. Yet the meaning of the cell as a place of spiritual and intellectual refuge ran deeply in their religious tradition. Herize remarked on the value of the cell to the future friar: "Since you have come to this sainted religion . . . you must learn that to accomplish your sainted purpose, the cell is the place for your own peace, rest, and most convenient relief, and that is why our religion has granted it to you. In it you find peace and calm difficult to find outside it. . . . Therefore, you must be fond of it, and love it as a thing from which you will derive so much good."[78]

The cell was the anchor for spiritual interiority (*recogimiento*).[79] Even after the Council of Trent, when personal meditation became second to the practice of guided prayers, spiritual *recogimiento* remained an important part of conventual praxis.[80] The cell protected the friar's individuality as a person against the very strong requirements of communal life. Dominican Francisco Romero defined the cell as the place where the friar would be free from the three distractions that he should most urgently elude: listening, talking, and seeing. Citing Bernard de Clairvaux, he said that, for the novice, the cell was the path to heaven.[81] It could also be the place where very devout novices could practice bodily discipline, an exercise that demanded privacy.[82] On the other hand, Valeriano de Espinosa, although acknowledging the value of the cell as a place of refuge and *recogimiento*, also cited Clairvaux's thoughts on the dangers of solitude. Those lacking strength of character could also find the path to hell in the solitude of their cells.[83] His concern was echoed by Herize, who advised against entering the cell with perturbing thoughts because solitude could strengthen them, and the cell could become "arid and sterile ground, full of thistles and throngs."[84]

The life of the novice, like that of the professed friar, was organized around the sequence of prayers. All daily activities in the friary were marked by prayer at specific hours, a ritual that had roots in the origins of Christianity. Typically, the day in the three orders began at midnight with matins and the Oficio Parvo of Our Lady.[85] This was a strong tradition among Dominicans. At 5 a.m. friars and novices rose for the first prayer, Prima, and half an hour of more prayer to organize their day. Manual labor in the convent followed until the novice returned to his cell at Terce, 9 a.m. for Mass and meditation. Before refectory he attended De Profundis, with all the other novices, to pray for the souls of the dead. After refectory he returned to his cell until 2 p.m., when he visited the cell of the teacher to review or receive instruction for one hour. At 3 p.m. he followed the prayer of Vespers. Then he would be at his teacher's disposal for instruction or return to his cell until 6 p.m., time for Compline, the last prayer of the day. It was followed by an hour of communal meditation until the community gathered for the last meal of the day. After that, the novices would gather for another round of prayers and a last visit to the teacher, who could, for example, instruct a novice in one of his topics of study. At 9 p.m., a last prayer to the Eucharist was followed by the night's rest.[86] The rigidity of this scheme deteriorated in some convents. In 1772 at least one of the convents of Franciscans of the province of San Diego was not carrying out matins at midnight.[87]

The teachers of novices did not assume that their pupils were perfectly educated in Christian doctrine when they arrived. One of their first tasks was to assess the novice's knowledge of the sacraments, the articles of faith, and other basic principles of Catholicism. They also worked on refining the spiritual tools of the novice, such as the practice of mental and vocal prayer and meditation on sacred topics, on the objectives of religious life as a friar, and on the practice of a lifestyle in imitation of Christ. Vocal and mental prayer were highly recommended by the Council of Trent. For the Franciscan order, prayer was "precept," an essential obligation, but all mendicant orders agreed on regarding prayer as a compulsory bonding element for the community. Another bonding activity was gathering in the *coro* to pray and sing during the divine services, a practice that nourished the spiritual confraternity of the friary. Since part of the services were sung, the novice had to study the special form of liturgical singing. Typically, and through the end of the eighteenth century, it was *canto llano* (plainsong) with only one melodic line, sung a cappella, without music accompaniment.[88] Perfecting the prayers of the liturgy and its voice elements was essential to mastering the demanding ceremonial required by all liturgical obligations. Dominican Joseph de San Joan, author of a ceremonial treatise, quoted Saint Bonaventure: "Strengthen your body as a man, restrain it, oblige it to serve the spirit, and in the Coro, you will be reverent, and will sing with happiness and devotion before the angels, who are there present with you."[89] Learning the ceremonial liturgy was not a mechanical exercise; each one of the steps had a symbolic and spiritual meaning. Details prescribed by the ceremonial included the vestments to be worn, the appropriate body movements and gestures such as kneeling and bowing, the use of fingers and heads for benediction, and the correct handling of the host, the wine, and the incensory during Mass. By helping during some steps of the Mass as aides or acolytes to the priest, novices learned the ceremonial intricacies and their spiritual meaning.[90] Schooling was intense to encourage profession at the end of the year of instruction.

Profession, the consecration of the novice as an official member of the community of priests, was an intimate ceremony, in contrast with the theatrical nature of nuns' professions. The entire community was present, and the postulant, accompanied by his teacher, asked for the mercy of God and that of his prelate. The latter would explain the meaning of the vows, and after the novice repeated them, the prelate administered the profession. The novice would receive a new scapular blessed by the prelate, and the cantor in the choir sang the *Veni Creator* hymn while the novice lay on the floor in front of the altar. After he was registered in the book of professions, the novice moved to the category of *corista* in the *jovenado* as a life member of his order, although not yet an ordained priest. The intimacy of a friar's profession did not usually call for any particular celebration in the world outside or inside the cloister, but there is an interesting instance in the world of letters marking the profession of a friar that deserves mention. Carmelite friar Fr. Juan de la Anunciación (1691–1764) was a writer and a priest who resided in several convents of his order in the Bajío region. Among his poems there is a unique theater piece called a *loa* (praise), written to celebrate the ordination of a Franciscan known as Fr. Luis.[91] This *loa* has four "persons" of emblematic nature: Entendimiento (intellect) as the "leading male actor" and Voluntad and Memoria as the abstract female persons. There was also Música to introduce the piece and explain its purpose and the meaning of ordination. Memoria understands that Fr. Luis has become a priest but cannot believe that he is also "married," since priests cannot "marry." Entendimiento explains the meaning of ordination as a "marriage." If the Church is to receive a human who will become "one" with her (*church* is feminine in Spanish), he must be "elevated" through the holy orders to become her equal, since marriage was best when it was between equals. Ordination was a grace given to dignify the groom and make him worthy of the Church. It granted the friar the rights of a husband to govern the wealth of the benefits of his spouse, the Church. In return the Church demanded the purity of his body. This brief theatrical piece, written by a friar, spelled out the theological doctrine about the meaning of ordination, not often understood by seculars. It suggests that on special occasions, male religious communities engaged in celebratory gatherings on their premises.

At this point we must consider that despite the age prescriptions, not all novices were young men. Some novices were mature individuals who, after having lived as soldiers, university lecturers, courtiers, merchants, or entrepreneurs, decided to "abandon" the world for a life of prayer and meditation to better ensure the salvation of their souls. To their contemporaries, these older men were living witnesses to the fact that the call of God could be heard at any time in life. The most idiosyncratic "old" novice in New Spain was Brother Aparicio, who was admitted to the Franciscan convent of Puebla in 1574 as a lay brother at the presumed age of seventy-two. His full story is detailed in chapter 3. There are several less-well-known cases in the three orders. Their example was treasured by chroniclers pursuing hagiographic material. As their experience showed, when mature men gave up their secular lives, they sought to satisfy an intense spiritual angst or did so for the benefit of a safe and protected old age. Franciscan Fr. Salvador Hernández, born in the Canary Islands, was a pilot and soldier before he professed in the province of San Pedro y San Pablo, in Michoacán, when he was over forty years of age. As the chronicler La Rea states, he conquered the "defects of time" with his many talents, displayed through his consistent dedication to learning everything he needed to be a preacher among the Indians. He studied arts and theology after profession and enough Tarascan, Otomí, and Nahuatl to preach. He also learned *canto llano* and polyphonic singing as well as the organ to teach his parishioners and introduce the tradition of *cantores* and chapel music in the province.[92] Dominican Fr. Juan de Paz was a soldier before he traveled to New Spain, but once there he "left the arms of this world" and exchanged them for "those of God." He professed as a lay brother in 1563.[93] Besides collecting alms, he entered the homes of sick people to lay hands on them and earned a reputation as a healer. The chronicler did not question this special ability, because "divine good will" entered into this situation and faith could not be challenged. Fr. Antonio de Barboza, Portuguese-born, arrived in New Spain around 1540 and lived in Campeche as a carpenter but left for the capital city seeking to sign up as a soldier to travel to the troubled kingdom of Peru. Instead, he changed his mind and entered the Dominican order, where he chose to profess as a lay brother and exercise his abilities as a carpenter and architect, living an "exemplary" life.[94] Older men abandoned a life that was possibly unsatisfactory, and the examples picked by the chroniclers served to expand the image of their order as one that welcomed men who could bring good will among the population, whether by their personal virtues or by engagement in useful trades.

Most of the personal lives of the novices will remain unknown. They were under total control of their superiors, and any serious misbehavior led to their dismissal. Occasionally, a rare incident reveals the personal problems faced by some novices. One example is a suicide attempt. It was recorded by chronicler Fr. Juan de Ojea in his history of the Dominican order. His reasons for recording it were didactic, as an example that other novices and even seasoned friars should remember. They should understand that the devil could entice them and lead them to commit disastrous acts that would endanger their souls and their careers. The novice's name is not recorded, but he is described as noble, well brought up, devout, humble, and obedient. Unfortunately, the devil began to appear to him, trying to dissuade him from taking the habit. Despite his teacher's advice, the young man left the convent in his secular clothes and spent two days visiting other convents and churches praying to God to relieve him of his burden. That help did not seem to come. As the chronicler puts it, ill-persuaded by the devil, he then attempted suicide on the outskirts of the city by ingesting poison and cutting his throat with a razor. He did not succeed in taking his life because, as the story went, he was surrounded by some "angels," or Dominican saints, who advised him to return to the city and the Dominican convent, where he was taken care of before he was dismissed and sent home. Obviously, neither the cut nor the poison was life-threatening if the novice could walk on his own. Although he asked to be readmitted again, the friars wisely decided against it. A suicidal novice would have been a terrible example for his brothers in the novitiate. Ojea advised other novices never to give credit to any visions or revelations, since they could be a demonic temptation.[95]

The citation of this case in the chronicle was relevant in his time because in the sixteenth and seventeenth centuries, visions and apparitions were part and parcel of religious beliefs across all sectors of the population. An ordained man of the cloth should not be easily tempted to believe in them. Only the Church hierarchy could determine when a vision or a revelation was within the range of acceptable canon. Further, and more important, suicide was not an acceptable solution to life's problems in the Catholic Church. Those dying by their own hand were not buried in consecrated ground because they had disrespected God, who was the only giver of life and death. The suicide attempt points to the difficulties of the novitiate experience for some young men. Solitude and self-doubt must have affected the minds of many who did not profess or were expelled.

The Novitiate: A New Symbolic Family

The renunciation of parents, siblings, and other relatives was the first sacrifice offered to God by the novice. The transition from the biological to the spiritual family is a feature of the novitiate that merits more attention than it has received. Becoming a friar meant that a man must abandon ties to his biological family to become a member of a new artificial "family" for the rest of his life. This family was one formed voluntarily by a group of individuals of the same sex held together by fictive ties of a sacramental nature. Their bond was permanent despite their lack of blood ties. The sacramental ties were the vows of profession, irreversible in canon law and as deeply meaningful as those that bound members of a biological family to one another. Behind the renunciation of the blood family stood a very strong belief that they belonged to a privileged group of people. The sentiment of being "chosen" and better situated to obtain God's favor is clearly expressed by Franciscan Fr. Juan Sanz López in his treatise on the education of male novices.[96]

Explaining the meaning of charity, he wrote that "the religious, because of their state can achieve that perfection (the evangelical perfection of charity) more easily than the secular."[97] That was the ultimate compensation for the loss of the blood family.

In 1623, when Fr. Valeriano de Espinosa published his *Guía de religiosos* with instructions for the novices of his order, he explained how the call of God to abandon one's own family and social ties to the community of birth (*patria*) was proof of his love. The loss of worldly attachments was compensated with the gain of personal freedom to pursue spiritual perfection and the rewards of God's love. Parents who lamented the loss of a son (or daughter) should think, suggested Espinosa, about how their child gained a "greater father" who was more noble, more illustrious, richer, and saintlier than any earthly parent. In religion, he argued, one found many fathers and many brothers.[98] Most of the friars traveling from Spain to join communities in the New World cut ties with their biological families forever. Their religious family would be their permanent source of emotional and spiritual support in the new land.

A complex system of beliefs centering on a divine family filled in the vacuum left by the absence of a biological family. The worship of Mary was special among the male orders. The Franciscans and many prominent members of the secular clergy were fully committed to promoting the cause of her Immaculate Conception (the Virgin Mary not sharing the sin or procreation derived from the stain of Adam and Eve). While this belief would not become canon until the twentieth century, the Spanish Crown was a strong advocate and supporter of this proposal. Mary was a perfect mother, virtuous and modest wife, eventually queen of heaven, and protector of humankind. She was the unchallenged venue to channel the worship of a perfect woman among the male orders. There was no inhibition in the continuous veneration of her many apparitions and the important dates of her birth, the annunciation of her pregnancy, her maternal suffering at her son's crucifixion, her compassion for humankind, and her ascension to heaven. Thousands of sermons were addressed to her, and she reigned supreme in the visual arts.[99] As a faultless woman, Mary was central in helping friars channel their affectivity to one who was irreproachable and perfectly suitable to replace the loss of their own biological mothers when they joined an order.

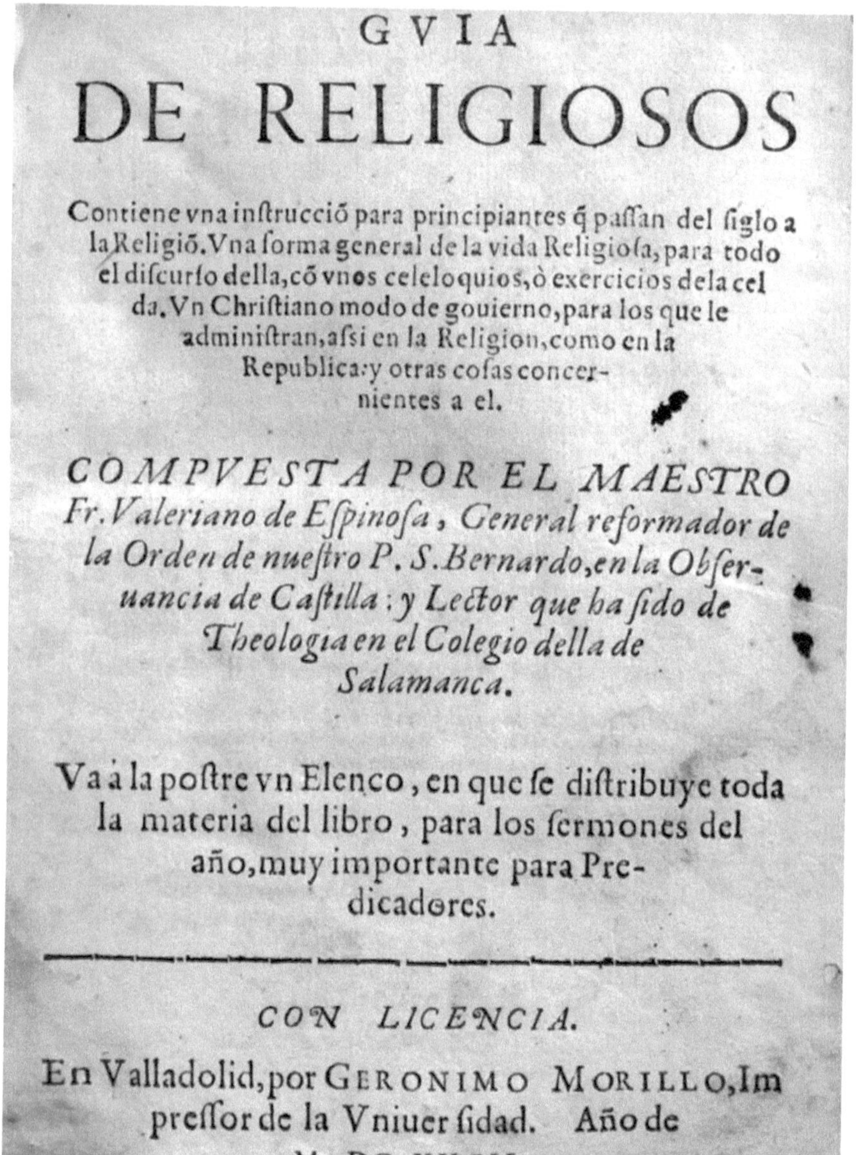

GVIA
DE RELIGIOSOS

Contiene vna instrucciõ para principiantes q̃ passan del siglo a la Religiõ. Vna forma general de la vida Religiosa, para todo el discurso della, cõ vnos celeloquios, ò exercicios de la celda. Vn Christiano modo de gouierno, para los que le administran, assi en la Religion, como en la Republica: y otras cosas concernientes a el.

COMPVESTA POR EL MAESTRO Fr. Valeriano de Espinosa, General reformador de la Orden de nuestro P. S. Bernardo, en la Observancia de Castilla: y Lector que ha sido de Theologia en el Colegio della de Salamanca.

Va à la postre vn Elenco, en que se distribuye toda la materia del libro, para los sermones del año, muy importante para Predicadores.

CON LICENCIA.

En Valladolid, por GERONIMO MORILLO, Impressor de la Vniuersidad. Año de
M. DC. XXIII.

FIG. 10. Valeriano de Espinosa, *Guía de religiosos* (Valladolid: Gerónimo Murillo, 1623).

The religious family within the friary experienced some of the natural cycles of the biological family, with the deaths of the old and their replacement by a younger generation. This family experienced symbolic births and marriages. The profession of a novice was, in a metaphorical way, the "birth" of the new member into a life in Christ. That birth was also a "marriage" to Christ. In their dialogues with the divine, friars would address Christ as their bridegroom.[100] To our modern eyes, the friars' use of the term *groom*, or *esposo*, for Christ is less familiar and feels perhaps contrived. Since the Middle Ages, however, several theologians adopted the representation of Christ as the groom of those men dedicated to his worship. This concept did not seem to raise any eyebrows as theologians manipulated such a slippery concept without any objection from the Church. Christ as the groom of male religious is not a concept that appears frequently in the mendicants' chronicles or biographies, but it is found in some of them. Addressing male novices, Franciscan Pedro Navarrete stated that "all his consideration must be fixed on his devout and celestial groom Jesus-Christ who should be the owner of his soul, living in it, ruling and governing it."[101]

The fictive ties of brotherhood within the family of friars sealed bonds of fraternity. Fr. Christobal de Agüero, vicar of the Dominican convent of Teozapotlan, writing one of the required official approvals for the publication of Fr. Francisco de Burgoa's history of the Dominican province of San Hipólito Mártir of Oaxaca, thanked God for having endowed the mother convent with such "a son of his own, and a very own brother of ours."[102] The histories of the orders created an ancestral genealogy and a shared memory that gave the religious family internal cohesiveness as well as luster and fame in the secular community. The deceased *santos varones* of a given community represented their lineage. Their deeds and virtues became property of the community and a source of pride and honor (*honra*) for all members.

The foundation of a convent was understood as an extension of the family, whereby the original community witnessed the birth of new sons to the mother convent and the addition of new brothers to the family. As mendicant orders expanded geographically, creating new provinces (large geographical units containing several friaries), the main convent was always addressed as the "mother" of the new offspring. Fr. Alonso de la Rea addressed the early years of the Franciscan province of Michoacán as "niña y novicia," implying its youth and its recent foundation as a form of novitiate in religion.[103] He took the metaphor of motherhood as far as he could when he described the foundation of the province as the first birthing (*parto*) of the province of the Holy Gospel: "And thus, we can venerate as a mother she who is the mother of this entire kingdom, and we enjoy being her first born." He also stated that the Michoacán province came "from the womb" of the Holy Gospel as a girl swaddled in the diapers of poverty, thus stretching the somatic and feminine metaphors applicable to the province as materfamilias.[104] Male writers seemed to be fond of using such metaphors of birthing. Fr. Baltasar de Medina prefaced his chronicle of the Franciscan province of San Diego by writing, "It [the chronicle] now sees the light, this history, the desired Bejamin of my studies, the son of my right hand, heir of my love. . . . Had not the pregnant one been so mysterious, the birth could seem to have been late." He continues explaining how his Franciscan province had been a beautiful Sara, sterile until her ninetieth birthday, when God appointed him, Fr. Baltasar, to help memorialize the San Diego province's birth with his writing. He described himself "as a man sustained by the powerful voice that helps in the birthing . . . applying shoulder and arm to break the tissues that hid such a son." In other words, he had acted as a midwife.[105]

Was the novitiate an experience remembered by most friars? On personal grounds this is a question that will remain unanswered for lack of testimonial evidence. Whether forgotten or remembered, this stage in the process of becoming a member of any religious order was more than pedagogically appropriate and necessary; it was essential in the spiritual shaping of the future friar. As a period of transition, the novitiate's first objective was to erase the imprint of the biological family and the attractions of secular life. The next and most important objective was to construct a different understanding of manhood, sustained by rigorous social and religious training. To achieve this end, the novice had to be willing and pliable, accepting the training administered by seasoned men whose objective was to sustain and validate the order's charisma. Dominican Fr. Francisco Romero, in his *Avisos para el Noviciado*, reminded the reader that religious men were in a "state of perfection" not because they were perfect but because they were obliged to desire perfection.[106] This argument worked for its time and explains a historical narrative that chose to present men of the cloth as always virtuous while ignoring the imperfections registered in other historical sources. The real-life behavior of the members of the mendicant orders was oftentimes far removed from the pedagogic rigors spelled in the training treatises, but the rules of the orders learned in the novitiate remained a permanent guide to a desired perfection. The transgressions recorded by history largely began after profession and ordination.[107] Without studying the objectives of the novitiate and the means to achieve them, it would be difficult to understand the internal coherence that kept the mendicant orders together. The novitiate traced a route for future behavior by training the aspirant in the charisma of the order and the discipline of conventual life, but it did not guarantee success. The personal traits of the friars would not be totally erased in the novitiate, but this transitional learning stage gave the orders an opportunity to understand the personal character of each one of its members and repurpose their abilities to serve their communal interests.

3

Lay Brothers

An Alternate Choice

In 1556, after a long trip on foot, Franciscan Fr. Pedro de Espinareda and Fr. Diego de la Cadena arrived at the then remote area of Zacatecas with the intention of founding a convent and beginning what was expected to be the crucial and difficult evangelization of the northern region of New Spain.[1] The city of Zacatecas was founded in 1546 as an urban center close to one of the richest silver mines of the viceroyalty. It was bound to become the capital of the province of New Biscay (Nueva Vizcaya) and the spearhead of missionary activity in the late sixteenth and seventeenth centuries.[2] The Franciscans followed soon after the foundation of the city in pursuit of further missionary tasks. Fr. Pedro and Fr. Diego had been preceded by several other friars who had not settled down despite having spent several years catechizing the Indigenous in the area. Along with them came one lay brother, Fr. Jacinto de San Francisco, and one *donado* simply named Lucas.[3] Fr. Jacinto and Lucas were two humble men in charge of teaching the children and the adults to pray. Chronicler Joseph Arlegui wrote a lengthy biography of Fr. Jacinto, who spent many years among the Natives and became something of a legend.[4] Lucas perished as a martyr with Fr. Juan de Tapia, another missionary. The presence of Fr. Jacinto and Lucas in the chronicle calls our attention to the participation of lay brothers and even *donados* in the task of evangelization. In New Spain, given the unusual circumstances posed by the task of conversion, some lay brothers performed leading spiritual and social roles that were not usually expected from them. Throughout time, their memory has faded in comparison to that of more-touted and better-known members of the mendicant orders partly because chroniclers, with a few notable exceptions, focused on the ordained friars, and partly because by definition, lay brothers were in charge of "humble" activities of daily life that were not regarded as "memorable." Lay brothers and *donados* embodied the social and intellectual differences that existed within the members of the regular orders. Rescuing the memory of these men at the lower echelons of the conventual hierarchy is an exercise in learning about alternative options of membership and pastoral duties among members of the orders and the church in general.

The community of men living within the walls of a mendicant convent was not a homogeneous social body despite the application of stringent racial selection in their admission. Among those chosen to become members were men whose various social and economic backgrounds, education, and intellectual abilities made of the friary a small world populated by many different characters whose sole binding ties were the rules of the order. Mendicant communities accepted two distinct categories of service to God represented by the *frailes clérigos*, or "ordained priests," and the *hermanos legos*, or "lay brothers."[5] After ending the novitiate and taking the vows of profession, the novices destined to become ordained priests pursued several years of further studies as *coristas* until they achieved the degree of intellectual preparation and spiritual maturity that allowed them to perform the Mass and provide the holy sacraments of the Church. Below them in rank were the lay brothers, who performed the manual labor in the convent and were exempted from theological studies. The distinction between lay brothers and priests had its roots in eleventh-century European monastic orders, especially the Cistercian order. These two categories were eventually approved by Pope Nicholas III (1277–80), who determined that those brothers dedicated to study should be exempt from corporal labor.[6] The menial tasks were assigned to the lay brothers.

Lay brothers carried out the most onerous but essential tasks of housekeeping: cooking, cleaning, purchasing the commodities necessary to feed the convent, and collecting alms. The nature of their service as essential company to their ordained brothers took them beyond urban areas to the moving boundaries of conversion borders and to dangerous outposts of missionary activities. Astute prelates sometimes identified skilled lay brothers who could be trusted with important tasks, such as the administration of the convent's properties or the building of churches. Some of them helped catechize the Indigenous population. Dominican chronicler Dávila Padilla explained and extolled the merits of the lay brothers as follows:

> He is a kind of person who turning his back to the world converts to God dedicating himself to corporal work, thus freeing the religious in the choir to praise God in the canonical hours and study to preach the holy Gospel. In this task they [lay brothers] deserve great merit before God, and many have achieved it. In David's camp there was equal pay for those who cared for the goods and baggage of the army and for those who fought the enemy. There is no greater proof of fidelity to our sacred Order . . . than assisting others in temporal affairs. Lay brothers keep the army's supplies, but if God's love is the same for all those who preach, their merit and prize [lay brothers'] will be the same. . . . It is true that preaching is by nature more excellent than the active life, but the fire of charity reaches the humble exercise of the lay brother in ways that surpass that of the preacher. . . . Lay brothers are in a secure and unquestioned state; by the path of simple obedience many have reached the heights of perfection.[7]

Dávila Padilla's characterization of the lay brother was a loving recognition of his merits. He also noted how the admission requirements for Dominican lay brothers were more demanding than for those who applied to become priests. Two-thirds of the total votes of the members of any given convent were required for the admission of a novice intending to become a lay brother, while the reception of a novice for the priesthood required only 51 percent of the votes of the community.[8] By establishing tougher standards for lay brothers, the Dominican order hoped to make certain that those admitted would be up to the challenges of their assignment.

There was an implicit and comforting security in religion for lay brothers. By accepting obedience and physical labor as his main duty, a lay brother was assured that he could reach the summit of spiritual benefits regardless of his social origins.[9] In fact, the histories of the orders recorded the experience of some exceptional lay brothers who, although unusual, merited special recognition as exemplary and inspirational. In Spain, Fr. José de San Benito (1654–1723), a lay brother of the order of San Benito in the convent of Montserrat in Barcelona, rose to the highest title of his order, the generalship, and became well known as a source of spiritual advice. His letters to different persons and the personal account of his life were printed with great pride.[10] Such an exceptional case did not change the fact that the majority of lay brothers never overcame the limitations imposed on them by the rules, and only a small number of them performed services that could qualify as heroic or historically memorable. However, the activities of that minority are key to understanding an alternate expression of masculine behavior and how they connected with the community in forms that the ordained priests did not.

The choice to become a lay brother was personal, and it was not necessarily determined by lack of education. Some men who could have chosen to become ordained priests chose instead to be lay brothers out of the desire to live in "true" poverty and simplicity. The paramount example of such choice is Fr. Pedro de Gante, one of the most notable Franciscan friars of the sixteenth century and a key figure in the process of conversion. As a man of letters and with the highest connections in the Spanish court, his choice of becoming a lay brother was regarded as an example of humility that could only be understood as a sign of true religiosity. In sharp contrast is the example of Fr. Francisco López (d. 1605), who professed as an Augustinian in the order's province of Michoacán. As an older man without "letters," Francisco applied to be accepted as a lay brother because he thought there was no better option in life open to him. The Augustinian prior who accepted him, however, saw enough potential in him to insist that he learned enough Latin to become an ordained friar. When he became one, Fr. Francisco acted as teacher of novices, doorkeeper, cook, and nurse, mixing the duties of lay brothers with some of those that belonged to the ordained friars.[11]

In contrast with the intensive training demanded for ordination, lay brothers went through a "fast lane" of apprenticeship in their novitiate. After a drilling in the basic principles of the faith and a few key prayers for the religious services, they were "ready" to serve. Early historians of the orders paid uneven attention to lay brothers. Typically, they remembered the notable, the learned, the martyrs, and the eminent preachers. Writing at the end of the seventeenth century, the chronicler of the Franciscan province of the Holy Gospel, Fr. Agustín de Vetancurt, lamented that the memory of lay brothers suffered from the same negligence affecting the history of most ordained brothers. One heard about their names but learned little about their personal virtues.[12] There was one notable exception to this situation, albeit not in New Spain. He was Franciscan Fr. Manuel Barbado de la Torre y Angulo, who published a history of the lay brothers of his order in 1745.[13] As he stated, all

Franciscans would benefit from the memory of these men. Since the order's inception, he wrote, the lay brothers served and revered the Franciscan clergy with steadfastness and humility. It was time to pay them back.[14] He included information on lay brothers martyred in Japan, North Africa, Eastern Europe, and Muslim Seville, but none in the New World.[15] Barbados's neglect was regrettable and invites us to make amends for the often neglected presence of lay brothers in official histories of the orders. It's worth remembering that one of the most revered saintly men in seventeenth-century New Spain was Fr. Sebastián Aparicio (1502–1600), who served most of his late life as a lay brother in the Franciscan convent in Puebla.

Lay Brothers in Profile

Even the Franciscan Minors, who could claim to observe conventual poverty and strict rules, did not dispense with lay brothers, who were legitimate members of the Church.[16] However, the number of those who felt a "call" to serve in this status was always smaller than those who became fully ordained members. The prestige of the latter was a contributing factor, since the lifestyle of lay brothers was not for everyone. Lay brothers had to excel in *mansedumbre*, the quiet acceptance of life's demands, and humility, a virtue that tempered any surge of pride. They were coached to serve and obey. These "virtues" put them in a lower position in terms of the social hierarchy and prepared them to deal quietly with the many petty problems of daily life in the convent. The amount of physical labor expected from them is not clearly detailed in the rules, but housekeeping was a demanding task. Cooking and baking were daily duties, with additional demands from the infirmary on their agenda. The relatively small number of lay brothers reported in most convents—as indicated by the numbers given below—suggests that they were probably an "overworked" sector of the conventual population even though we know that large convents had servants.[17] Information on the number of lay brothers in individual convents is scarce, owing to the dispersal of religious collections and, even today, the relative difficulty of access. In his study of the Augustinian convents up to the mid-seventeenth century, Antonio Rubial provides the total number of friars for the order, classifying them as "ordained" and "not ordained." It is unsafe to assume that the "not ordained" were lay brothers, because the figure could also include those waiting to be ordained. The only safe numbers are those for the friary of Valladolid in the years 1605–11, when the friary had a total of fifty-one members. Fifteen were ordained, five were lay brothers, and thirty-one were choristers studying to be ordained.[18] The small number of lay brothers, barely 10 percent of the total, looks inadequate to provide the labor needed in the community.

The best source of information for the lay brothers' population in the orders is that furnished by Francisco Morales, OFM, who has published a very complete and useful profile of the lay brothers of the Franciscan order in the sixteenth and seventeenth centuries. He examined 575 aspirants to the habit in the two convents receiving novices in the province of the Holy Gospel.[19] Between 1600 and 1620, only 18 men chose to be lay brothers out of a total of 489 professions. The situation did not improve much between 1640 and 1660, when 40 out of 463 men who professed chose to be lay brothers. In total, only 51 out of 801 professants were lay brothers between 1680 and 1700. Lay brotherhood was not attracting enough postulants. Morales indicates that about one-third of them came from Spain looking for some profitable occupation in the government, commerce, or farming. Failing to meet their objectives, they chose service in a convent. Lay brothers born in Mexico were younger than the Spaniards, and unlike the latter, they chose their status as a career within the Church. Morales also indicates that some relaxation of the rules of *limpieza de sangre* was possible for the candidates to lay brotherhood. This is understandable, given the low number of aspirants. He cites a Black *donado* in the main Franciscan convent who served as sacristan and organ player and who was allowed to profess as a lay brother by the demand of the community.[20] In her review of the sixteenth-century Dominican lay brothers, María Teresa Pita Moreda argues that the Dominican lay brothers were "older," indicative of men who had been active in some occupation in Spain and had passed to Mexico with some skills. Being handicapped by their age, they saw the role of lay brother as a solution to their future. Her findings are corroborated by Mora Reyes, but lacking other studies, we do not know if that remained the situation for the eighteenth century.[21]

Up to the late sixteenth century, the order of Santo Domingo had an "assigned" fixed number of friars for its convents. This rule was superseded to allow the order to expand its general population. In the mid-sixteenth century, the order had only one lay brother for each one of its convents in its key province of Santiago in central Mexico.[22] Mora Reyes's findings for the province between 1578 and 1646 show that the number of friars did not change significantly between 1604 and 1646. In 1646 Dominicans, with 436 members, had barely superseded the high number of 400 members recorded in 1598. This suggests that there was not a great demand for membership, and this situation applies to lay brothers. They represented 19 percent of the total number of members in the Dominican friaries of Mexico City, while in Puebla, they represented 23 percent of the total. In the rural convents, the number of lay brothers was small, making up roughly 1 percent of the conventual population. Rural communities possibly lacked the resources to feed the lay brothers or, more likely, had a limited need for their services.[23]

Another statistical view of the lay brother's population is furnished by David Rex Galindo in his study of the Franciscan Colegio de Propaganda Fide de la Santa Cruz in Querétaro in the eighteenth century. This convent was dedicated to training friars to preach the faith among the Catholic population as well as those yet to be converted or recently converted. The college began ordaining priests in 1683. Propaganda Fide attracted candidates because of its prestige as a training center for the priesthood and its missionary activity in the north and northwestern areas of the viceroyalty. The highest number of professions took place in the first four decades of the eighteenth century. Numbers began to decline slightly after the 1760s, when the Propaganda Fide friaries changed their policy of admission by bringing fully ordained priests from Spain while relying on Mexican-born candidates for recruiting lay brothers. A similar policy was followed by the College of San Fernando in Mexico City. Recruiting lay brothers in the land was easier than attracting migrants from Spain to serve in a low-status position in the friaries. An exception to that situation was the Queretaran Colegio de Propaganda Fide, a prestigious center for recruiting and training Franciscans. Between 1750 and 1799, the college had 87 lay brothers and 117 *coristas* preparing to become priests.[24] Rex Galindo noted that the ratio in the recruitment and professions of lay brothers and *coristas* were comparable, with only a small difference between the two categories: 3 *coristas* for 2 lay brothers. This means that in this institution, the number of professed lay brothers remained relatively high, an exceptional situation for its time.

The Colegio de Propaganda Fide in Zacatecas, an active missionary center for northern Mexico, was founded in 1707 and began to record its admissions by triennials in 1711. It sent ordained friars as missionaries to Texas, and in 1748 it assumed the responsibility of missionizing in the coastal area known as "Seno Mexicano," today's Huasteca in the province of Nuevo León. By 1752 the college had a total of fifteen missions with forty-three ordained friars. The institution was relatively successful in recruiting members for missionary activities between 1711 and 1774. Success meant attracting two or three men a year who would hopefully profess as ordained or lay brothers. Notes taken by one of its members allow a long-term view of its membership between 1711 and 1774. As shown in figure 11, there was a moderate peak of recruitment for ordained brothers in the 1730s and 1760s and a large peak in the triennial 1763–65. The number of lay brothers had high peaks in the years immediately after its foundation in 1711—which is logical—and in the triennial 1751–53, when the first-generation friars had begun to die. Recruitment figures show a steady decline in lay brothers' numbers, suggesting a lack of interest in this choice of religious life. The harsh demands of conversion and catechization in the far north attracted dedicated ordained evangelizers, but it did not have the same appeal to lay brothers. A 1758 report on the state of the seven Texas missions administered by the college states that eleven ordained friars and four lay brothers administered them. Two of the lay brothers oversaw the transportation of all the victuals (*avíos*) from Zacatecas to the missions, literally acting as *arrieros*.[25]

The Colegio de Propaganda Fide of San Fernando in Mexico City sent missionaries to California and the eastern areas of the Sierra Madre Oriental. In 1771 San Fernando had forty-three friars, seven *coristas* in training, and nineteen lay brothers. Seven of the lay brothers were reported as being very old and not "useful" for service. Three novices training for lay brotherhood and two *donados* completed the roster, giving a total of seventy-four friars.[26] The college had sent fifty-two priests to Baja and Upper California, areas of intensive missionary activity, and the order felt that the forty-three friars living in the main convent in Mexico City were inadequate to fulfill its pastoral commitment to the city. One year later, the number of friars residing in San Fernando had declined by one, with forty-two ordained friars, but the number of lay brothers had increased by three, to twenty-two, with two *donados*.[27] Since *donados* were part of the workforce, the convent had gained in terms of the availability of help with the daily tasks of the convent.[28] Its twenty-two lay brothers made up 54 percent of its total population, corroborating Rex Galindo's data on the large number of lay brothers in the order in those decades. Furnishing ordained brothers to the missions

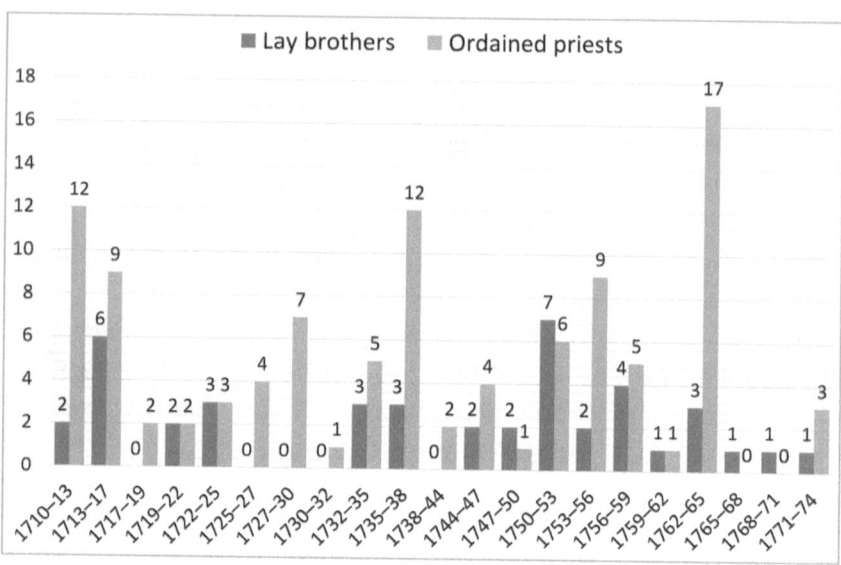

FIG. 11. Recruited friars at Colegio de Propaganda Fide in Zacatecas, in Rafael Cervantes Aguilar, *Fray Simón del Hierro (1700–1765)* (Mexico: UNAM, 1985), 325–41.

in California meant a drain in their number and created a disproportionate number of lay brothers. In contrast, the convent of San Francisco in Mexico had a more even situation in regard to the number of lay and ordained brothers. Undated data from the 1770s indicate that at some point in that decade, it had 159 religious in total. Its thirty-two lay brothers, three of whom served as *limosneros* for the convent of Corpus Christi, represented 20 percent of the total population.

The Franciscans of the province of Xalisco, in contrast with those of the capital and the Colegio de Propaganda Fide in Mexico City, were in decline. According to José Refugio de la Torre Curiel, between 1740 and 1784, the net number of novices *assumed* to be for the ordained state in the twelve Franciscan friaries of the province of Jalisco declined from twelve to eight. The number of *coristas* declined from forty in 1740 to nineteen in 1776 and remained the same in 1784. In 1740 there were twenty-seven lay brothers serving in the twelve friaries. By 1776 there were fifteen and in 1784, only eight.[29] These numbers mark a dramatic decline in vocations and represent a fall from 12.7 percent of the total conventual population in 1740 to barely 5 percent in 1784. Although the numbers are not broken down by individual friaries, it follows that the order had failed to attract lay brothers and was probably relying on hired servants for the upkeep and services in its convents. The Franciscans were hardly performing their missionary activity in that province. The regular clergy was serving the spiritual needs of the faithful while the orders were becoming less significant in that task.

Age is a factor that merits attention when numbers are available. Lay brothers were an effective labor population when their members were at the peak of their life cycles. Older brothers were unlikely to meet the labor demands as effectively. A late eighteenth-century sampler of the lay brother's population and their ages in the Colegio de Propaganda Fide and the convent of San Francisco in Mexico City show that in both convents, lay brothers were men between thirty and sixty years of age. This presupposes they were at the peak of their physical abilities.[30] Age sixty was the threshold for "old age" in those years, and "retirement" from active work was often determined by health. Between one-quarter and one-third of the total of lay brothers were "older" men. The number of aging brothers must have alerted the prelates to the need for recruitment and new admissions.

Random information from other Franciscan friaries confirms the low numbers of lay brothers. In 1743 the Franciscans of Zacatecas (not to be confused with the Colegio de Propaganda Fide in the same city) reported 163 friars and 22 lay brothers, who represented 13.4 percent of the total number of friars in the convent.[31] At the end of the eighteenth century, the Franciscan convent of Mérida on the Yucatán Peninsula had 104 priests, 6 lay brothers, and 3 choristers in what was an extremely low percentage of lay brothers and conventual "help." There may have been servants to help the lay brothers in the service, but this assumption cannot be corroborated. In general, the low percentage of lay brothers in the convents cited here indicates that lay brotherhood did not attract many candidates, possibly because the working conditions were demanding and the expectations of meekness and humility were not appealing to potential candidates.

One last demographic information of interest is that of health. Very little qualitative information is culled from official reports on this topic. Declining health relegated those brothers over the age of sixty to menial work in the convent, and when they were unable to do any work, they were classified as sick (*enfermos*).[32] The orders took care of their old and ailing. It was one of the bonuses of belonging to a religious community. All friars had a place to spend

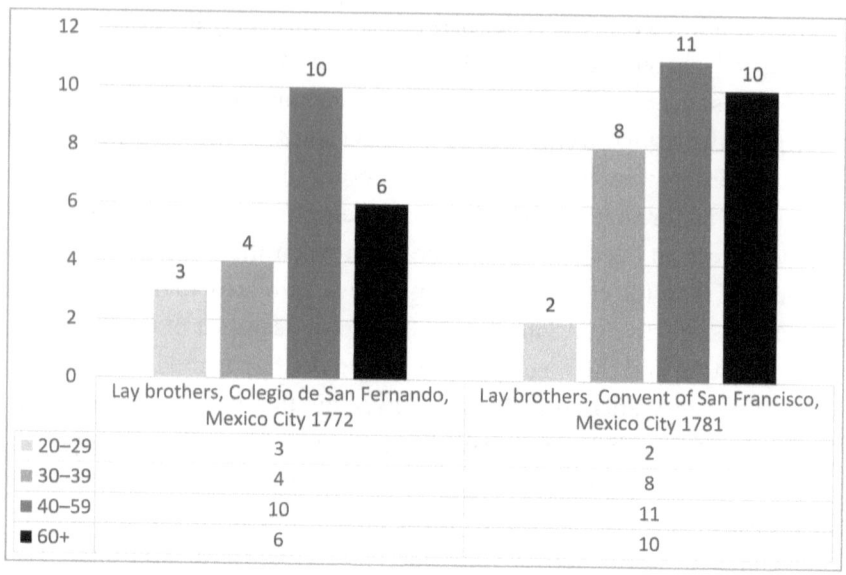

FIG. 12. Age of lay brothers in two Franciscan convents in Mexico City. Three brothers in San Francisco served as chaplains for Corpus Christi, and the age for one of them was not recorded. Created by author from Fondo Franciscano, vols. 123 and 134, Biblioteca Nacional de México, Mexico City.

their last years in comfort and with due care. For lay brothers, the prospect of personal security in the friary was a definite incentive to profess. In 1751, the College of Nuestra Sra. de Guadalupe of Propaganda Fide in Zacatecas reported an almost even number of lay brothers and ordained priests: eighteen lay brothers and twenty-two ordained priests. Of the eighteen lay brothers, five were classified as "useless" because of age and sickness. Of the twenty-two ordained priests, five were sick.[33] Turning to Puebla, in 1778 the Franciscans reported forty-three ordained friars, three of whom were sick in the infirmary, and three years later, in 1781 there were five "habitually" sick. Among the lay brothers, twenty were sick, but only one was "habitually sick."[34] These numbers do not support any hard conclusion on the issue of health, but it is obvious that the "habitually" sick were men with long-term disabilities who could render no effective "service" to the convent, while the "sick" could be restored to health. One could expect a number of sick brothers at any time of the year, making the labor of the healthy ones harder.

The difficulty in obtaining specific information on lay brothers indicates that although they were valuable members of the convent, their status limited their historical footprint. Their services were not of an intellectual nature, and this reduced their visibility. They became historical data when some of them were recognized, often postmortem, as having shone in simple piety, having been instrumental in bolstering the relations of their orders with the populace at large, or having been notable participants in the task of evangelization.

Status within the Orders

Although conventual life was expected to make every professing brother comfortable within his status, the rules of the orders made clear that there were key distinctions between the ordained and the lay friars. The constitution of the Franciscan order of San Diego clearly stated that no lay brother could ever become a chorister. This stricture made the distinction among the friars irrevocable and permanently divided the cloister population into two categories, one of which had prerogatives not enjoyed by the other.[35] In 1719 Augustinian Fr. Francisco de Avilés, a lay brother, felt compelled to make a case for the publication of the rules of his order in Spanish. He argued that lay brothers and nuns, who were not expected to understand Latin, should not lack the spiritual guidance the rules could give them. Conscious of class distinctions, he felt obliged to address the friars dedicated to higher learning in the order, asking them not to take offense or feel demeaned by his decision. They should be guided, he argued, by fraternal love and understand that his work was an attempt to come closer to those "of inferior intelligence."[36] Avilés described his publication as a path leading to higher spirituality rather than a challenge to the well-established distinctions among members of the order. In 1787 the Dominican order took a similar action and reissued its rules and constitution for the specific use of lay brothers. The author, Francisco Sáenz, was a lay brother and explained his decision as one motivated by the merits of the large number of lay brothers who had flourished in the order in several parts of the world, including Mexico.[37] He recalled the example of lay brother Fr. Diego Marini, who had been appointed as the sole companion of the sixteenth-century provincial Fr. Domingo Betanzos. He also cited the exceptional case of lay brother Bernardo Acuña de Alburquerque, who was raised to the status of clergy by his order and became a well-known theologian, prior of his convent, and later bishop of Oaxaca.[38] His listing of notables resembled that organized by Fr. Manuel Barbado for the Franciscans.[39] These publications suggest that not all lay brothers felt compelled to accept meekly the limitations of their status, but their efforts to make a case for its virtues would not shake the solid foundations of tradition that supported the separation of lay from the ordained brothers.

Beyond the explanation of the physical labor demanded from their status, the Augustinian rules for lay brothers laid out the basic instruction in Christian doctrine and prayers appropriate for their status to ensure they addressed God in the correct manner.[40] The Avilés rules minimized the spiritual goals of the lay brothers. They stressed the performance of the daily duties and prevented any spontaneity or personal deviation. Lay brothers were obliged to attend the first Mass of the day and were exempted from other Masses except for Compline (*completas*) at the end of the day. Thus, they were free to perform their house duties. They substituted other prayer commitments with simpler prayers such as the *Creed*, the *Ave Maria*, and the *Our Father*. While the ordained brothers attended three Masses in remembrance of members of the friars' biological families and for dead members of the order, lay brothers substituted their physical attendance with five hundred Our Fathers. Thus, the spiritual message of the Mass was made lighter for the lay brother, and his commitment to some forms of liturgy was reduced to the level of a numerical count of prayers. As for their garments, the lay brother's habit was different enough to distinguish him visually from the ordained brothers. For example, the Dominican lay brother would wear a black instead of a white scapulary.

The description of the tasks assigned to lay brothers in Avilés's edition is the clearest guide to the nature of their responsibilities. Some of them were similar to those performed by women in any secular household. The official in charge of directing all housekeeping tasks was the *refitolero*, a "general purveyor" or "overseer" of the convent. He was responsible for the cleanliness of the premises, the preparation of all meals to meet the daily schedule, and the governance of the brothers and servants working in the kitchen. During meals he kept the dinner table well provided with bread, water, and hand towels. Lay brothers also maintained the sacristy in perfect order and cleanliness and ready for the regular and special Masses. *Campaneros* kept time for prayers with the ringing of bells, a task that demanded punctuality and was essential for maintaining the rhythm of community duties and prayers. Doormen (*porteros*) in all convents were always lay brothers. As those responsible for the physical communication between the secular and religious worlds, they had a special set of responsibilities. Their cells were physically close to the door so that they would be ready and prompt in the performance of their duties. In addition to regulating the opening and closing hours of the convent, there was a prescribed etiquette to their task. They would receive all people with modesty and courtesy, especially brothers in religion because they deserved a loving and friendly reception. Nobles were received with due urbanity and courtesy. Prelates and bishops required reverence and genuflections. The poor should receive some alms, and lacking them, they should be treated with love for their spiritual consolation.[41] Addressing the general labor-oriented duties of the lay brothers, the rules explained that the physical labor assigned to them benefited the well-being of their souls as well as those of the ordained brothers The latter's task was saving the souls of all others—including the lay brothers'—and that explained why they were exempt from manual work in the convent.

Among the lay brothers' household duties was tending the infirmary, although under the supervision of clergy friars or an experienced lay brother. In 1781 the convent of San Francisco in Mexico City reported seven lay brothers employed in the infirmary.[42] San Francisco's infirmary in Puebla employed eight lay brothers.[43] The spiritual meaning of work at the infirmary was clear to all. Nursing the sick was an act of charity and, to some, a path to sanctity.[44] As nurses, lay brothers accompanied the doctors to their visitations, took mental notes of the medications prescribed, and administered them, which implicitly meant keeping an eye on the medical supplies of the convent.[45] Lay brothers called all community members to attend the rites of the extreme unction when death approached. They had experience in detecting it. After death, they prepared the body of the deceased for viewing and entombment. Well remembered for his role in the infirmary was Franciscan Francisco Tabares, born in Zacatecas probably in the early seventeenth century to a Portuguese doctor who had the reputation of being the best in the Indies. Trained by his father, he was also a surgeon and a barber, which meant that he could draw blood and use a scalpel. Fr. Francisco professed in Guadalajara, where he was head nurse, physician, and pharmacist in addition to working in the kitchen and collecting alms.[46] He also visited the sick in town and provided medications. He died in 1642 of typhus (*tabardillo*) contracted after one of his mercy visits.

Cooking was one of the expected and most important assignments of a lay brother. This was one of the humblest and yet most intensive forms of labor in the convent. It was supposed to be carried out in good spirits with patience and charity. To add to his hagiographical profiles, Dominican chronicler Franco cited one kitchen brother who became a model of austerity in his diet, refusing to eat meat even though he cooked it daily.[47] In large friaries, kitchen labor must have been intensive. San Francisco of Mexico City listed two cooks in 1781.[48] This number looks inadequate to serve a community of over 150 men, but they must have had helpers who were unlisted because they were servants or other members of the community who performed this labor as duty or as an act of charity. Novices would help in the kitchen and perform other menial tasks such as tidying up the premises after every meal. Some chroniclers remembered some ordained friars who chose to share in kitchen work as an act of humility and brotherly behavior. Franciscan Jerónimo de Mendieta cited an older ordained brother who helped in the kitchen as well as in the administration of the supplies and distribution of labor in his friary. His commitment to such tasks resulted from his devotion to San José, a model husband, father, and head of the household.[49] While it is impossible to fathom how often such examples were available in the daily routine of any convent, the likelihood of them being "common" is minimal. Ordained brothers had other responsibilities, such as their liturgical duties, their studies, and their pastoral work, and most likely kept their distance from the activities of lay brothers.

Other lay brothers' occupations were respected for having a long historical tradition rooted in monastic Europe and were readily adopted by New World friars. Such was keeping a vegetable garden, a traditional lay brothers' occupation in European friaries. The vegetable garden (*huerta*) provided herbs, vegetables, and fruits for the largely vegetarian meals that were the main fare of many rural and poorer convents, although the diet of *all* convents included vegetables and salads (known as *hierbas*). The climate in most of New Spain favored the adoption of *huertas*. The Augustinian rules allowed the sale of vegetables and fruit if there was an excess crop. The continuous demand for lay brothers' physical labor in these various occupations most likely required the assistance of servants who were hired to alleviate their work. That was the case of all large urban convents, where a good number of servants helped with daily duties. Even in rural convents, one finds helpers in the kitchen and the *huertas*. This fact does not diminish the important role of lay brothers as household workers.

Outside the conventual premises lay brothers carried out the duties of *limosnero*, or "alms collector," a task that in the eyes of the church demanded true humility and had important practical economic benefits for the convent. The term *alms* must be regarded with due latitude, since it really did not mean to go door to door begging for monetary help. The alms collectors went around town and into the rural areas, visiting farms and mines, sometimes with a couple of beasts of burden fitted to bring back goods given as alms. Since they were in the public eye, the Franciscan rule insisted that their behavior be exemplary. They should never leave the convent before attending the first Mass and should return home on time for the evening meal. They should not chat while performing their duty, especially with women, a rule that was probably often breached, since being a *limosnero* demanded a certain degree of sociability. *Limosneros* were well-known members of the community. Everybody saw them walking the streets of large and small towns or combing the fields of rural locations to receive pious donations in cash and goods for the convent. Some urban and rural convents list dedicated *limosneros* in their books. San Francisco in Mexico City had twelve official lay brother *limosneros* in 1781. Two additional *limosneros* collected for the Indian convent of Corpus Christi. One "limosnero de San Antonio" was possibly dedicated to collecting alms for the cult of that saint, and he was not a lay brother—maybe due to his specialized assignment.[50] The Franciscan Puebla convent reported seven official *limosneros* in 1778. Two of them had specific targets: one collected eggs and the other collected bread for daily consumption. In the 1780s the Mexico City Franciscan college of Tlatelolco for Indigenous men reported two *limosneros*, one of whom was of African descent.[51]

In rural communities, alms collection was essential for maintaining the convent's financial standing and its survival. The 1771 report of the Franciscan convent of Topoyanco, in the province of Tlaxcala and within the territory of the province of the Holy Gospel, sheds light on the collection system.[52] The convent served an Indian community located in an isolated site between a stream and the mountains. It had fifteen friars in 1771, three of whom were priests. There were three choristers in training to become priests, seven lay brothers, and two *donados*. Three of the lay brothers and one *donado* were identified as *limosneros*. The fact that the number of working friars was larger than the ordained and future priests suggests that this small rural convent strongly depended on the efforts of its lay brothers. Collecting alms did not indicate a state of penury; it was a standard practice necessary to feed the members of the friary. If the collection exceeded their needs, the products were sold in the nearby market.

Alms collection was a well-organized operation. *Limosneros* methodically visited all the towns of the province all year round. One of them collected alms in the city of Tlaxcala and its vicinity and reported a collection of five pesos weekly, "more or less"—a good sum of money for one week's work. Alms in cash would be destined to pay for the liturgical needs of the convent, such as wine and candles. A second *limosnero* performed similar duties in the towns close to Cholula such as San Martin, Huejotzingo, and San Miguel de La Ciénega. He collected around eleven pesos weekly. A third *limosnero* collected eggs in Tlaxcala and nearby towns, getting 120 eggs, "more or less," a week. Their agenda was carefully delineated in what appears to be a well-planned and executed strategy to collect livestock and farm products when they became available throughout the year, either for conventual consumption or for sale. In August two *limosneros* collected "seeds," possibly various edible grains. One of them went to Apam, Texcoco, on the shores of Lake Texcoco, Huamantla, on the eastern part of the Tlaxcala, while the other went to Atlixco, Huejotzingo, La Ciénega, and Balzequillo, all towns in the geographical radius of the city of Puebla. Between them they gathered around fifteen fanegas of wheat, twelve to fourteen of barley, fifty of corn, and three or four of fava beans. They also collected the same amount of *alverjón* (*Lathyrus sativus*), a form of leguminous pea, and potatoes; one fanega of lentils; and three or four of chile, all with an estimated value of 230 pesos.[53] In March the said *limosneros* collected sugar, honey, and fruit in Aplan and Córdoba. In May they collected around two hundred head of sheep and goats in San Juan de los Llanos, Tlaxcala, and Tepeaca. In August two of them collected the aforementioned grains and wheat, corn, beans, lentils, and chili in the towns of Aplan, Huamantla, Atlixco, Huejotzingo, La Ciénega, and Balzequillo. At Advent and Lent, they collected fish and wax for altar candles in Aumantla, Huejotzingo, La Ciénega, and Tepeaca.

They also collected cash for sung and regular Masses, blessings, and other pious ends. In 1771, the value of the total collections in goods was around 930 pesos, not an insignificant amount of money. Cash, produce, and animals were handed to the syndic, or administrator. The total value of their collection—in goods and cash—for 1771 amounted to 1,918 pesos and 3 reales. This was a substantial depletion of resources from the rural population but a bounty for the convent. Lacking the conventual accounts, it remains unclear if the syndic sold some of the products after allocating part of them to the friary or dedicated them to the consumption of the community. The latter is unlikely, since it was a relatively small friary. In either case the lay brothers' labor as *limosneros* was essential to the convent's sustainability.

The assumption that all *limosneros* were lay brothers is countered by information from the Colegio de Propaganda Fide in Zacatecas. In June 1742 an ordained father, Fr. Simón del Hierro, began a long trek (*caminata*) as a *limosnero de campo* that ended one year later in August 1743. He roamed the provinces of Zacatecas, San Luis Potosí, Coahuila, and Nuevo León, visiting ranches and haciendas to collect cattle. The landowners contributed the number of cattle heads they could afford. In his final account, it appears that he collected at least four hundred head, although it could be more; he did not know the exact round number. This large number of cattle explains the importance of the *limosnero* in that region. Fr. Simón was accompanied by a few *arrieros* (muleteers), and they walked the cattle back to Zacatecas, losing twenty on the way. The college had a ranch near the convent where it kept the animals, which were used for conventual consumption. The friars were well provided for.[54]

Lay brothers are also cited as shining in entrepreneurial tasks within the orders. Since neither Dominicans nor Augustinians adhered to official poverty rules, they owned rural properties requiring the services of a general administrator (*procurador*). Some lay brothers were good "fits" for such occupations.[55] An able friar could administer the properties of his order and save it the fees that would otherwise be paid to an administrator. Fr. Diego de Basalenque noted that some of the sixteenth-century brothers with a basic education to meet the requirements to be ordained preferred to employ themselves in tasks away from the altar. He cited Fr. Jerónimo de la Magdalena (d. 1614), who during his novitiate learned enough Latin and grammar to become an ordained friar but preferred to work in the convents' properties, where he excelled in their administration.[56] The orders did not intentionally train their members to administer their properties, but they took advantage of those who had such abilities. Two Dominican lay brothers illustrate this situation. Fr. Juan Núñez de San Pablo professed in Mexico in 1548 at age thirty-five leaving behind a successful life as a wealthy merchant. The order did not waste his talent and quickly engaged him in the task of *procurador* (attorney) in charge of the financial affairs of the main convent in the capital, and later those of the entire province. In his late years, he took care of the convent's vegetable garden.[57] Fr. Alberto de Garnica, the nephew of Phillip II's solicitor in the Royal Chancery of Valladolid, had experience as a soldier in Italy when, being "touched by God," he abandoned the world to live as a humble Dominican lay brother, first in Spain and later in Mexico, where he arrived in 1570 and died in 1598. He was recorded as being illiterate despite his social extraction. After he took the habit in Spain, he began to show his potential. He acted as the administrator of his convent in Spain and learned how to read and write to become the convent's representative in the chancery of the city. Dominican historian Franco argues that he was versed in mathematics, geometry, architecture, and the liberal arts. One wonders how he acquired that education, but convents had teachers who could have taught him as well as good libraries to complement the teacher's job. He rejected the opportunity to become an ordained priest. Instead, he remained a lay brother and single-handedly administered the convent's properties in New Spain, among which was the sugar mill in Coahuixtla de las Amilpas in the Marquesado del Valle's lands. The chronicler does not get into details as to how he managed to do that—from his viewpoint it was inconsequential—but he claimed that the heavy duties of his administrative work were his "purgatory" in life.[58] This comment deterred the potential criticism of those who might think that involvement in such activities distracted the friar from his spiritual duties, and the comment may have been the result of the chronicler's own design.[59] Garnica's career spoke of alternative forms of authority and empowerment for lay brothers as property administrators, breaking the stereotype of unlettered men useful only for kitchen work or for running errands.[60]

Lay Brothers in the Chronicles

The composite picture of the lay brothers we find in religious chronicles is the most useful guide for learning what made them different from the ordained brothers and why they deserve to be remembered in the eyes of their contemporaries. General chroniclers differed considerably in the weight they gave to the memory of lay brothers in their work. Their inclusion was a personal choice and not necessarily a trend in the historiography of the period. Peeling off the obvious pieties, we discover useful facts that help formulate the general features of the lay brothers as significant members of the mendicant orders. We also learn how the chroniclers constructed models of masculine piety.

While not the first historian of his order, Franciscan Fr. Jerónimo de Mendieta remains a good starting point to review the chroniclers' representations of lay brothers.[61] He set up a narrative style that became a prototype for other historians in the seventeenth century. As Mendieta saw it, these men, like their ordained brothers, arrived in New Spain to pursue their own personal spiritual inspiration to help plant Christianity in the land. He had at close hand one of the best-known examples of dedicated lay brotherhood in the history of the Franciscan order in New Spain, Fr. Pedro de Gante, admired as a "man of God" and a lay brother by choice. Gante, a Flemish subject of good social standing, volunteered to travel to the New World as soon as he learned of the ongoing process of conversion. What made him an appealing figure to his contemporaries and religious brothers was his renunciation of any distinction within the order and his dedication to the education of the Indigenous children. Sixteenth-century spiritual writers agreed on the desirability of shunning the vanity of the world for the rewards of the cell and subscribed to the idea that the education of the young in Christian doctrine was essential to ensure personal salvation and preserve social order. Gante personified the genteel and learned religious model proposed by men like Fr. Antonio de Guevara: men dedicated to the noble task of educating the next generation. He also represented the sum of humility and spirituality applied to a task that the mendicant orders and their members considered a destiny designed by God.

Gante also knew how to spread the faith in practical terms. Mendieta praised his "ingenuity for all the arts and offices useful for human and Christian good breeding."[62] Through teaching he transformed himself from courtier into lay brother with a hands-on approach. Teaching the Christian doctrine was not enough for him; he taught Indian children European music and crafts such as masonry, carpentry, tailoring, iron smithy, and cobbling. Those were crafts in demand by the building of cities and the introduction of European fashions. To be sure, the Indigenous people had been master city planners and had excelled in a large and diverse number of arts and crafts *prior* to the arrival of the Spaniards, but Gante, like other men of his generation, believed that they had to learn what was required to meet the demands of a culturally European labor market. An expanding militant church was in need of labor in addition to believers. Building pyramids became irrelevant after the conquest. Christianity needed churches and chapels for the diffusion of the faith, and the Indigenous labor was there to build them.

Gante also knew he had to preach in the Native languages and wrote a *Christian Doctrine* (*Doctrina Cristiana*) in Nahuatl. The initial years of evangelization forced the friars to engage in new strategies to meet the enormous challenge ahead. Those who learned the Native languages gained authority, and so Gante and others set out to "conquer" the Indigenous tongues. A friar with the ability to speak the "tongue" was a powerful tool in gaining new souls for the faith, regardless of his rank in the friary. Deciphering Nahuatl grammar and usage enabled Gante and other friars to engage in direct social contact with the Indigenous, a form of acculturation that other first-generation Spaniards did not have because they never learned the languages of the land they ruled. Being the mediators between the secular state and the Indigenous, friars like Gante had a winning card in social and political strategy. To the Natives, the fact that these men spoke their own tongue was, at least, a sign of empathy. It was also a tool of cultural penetration in the Indigenous communities. He was relentless in the destruction of "idols" and Indigenous temples, a task of imposed violence he shared with other evangelizers of his own and succeeding generations. To a contemporary brother in religion like Mendieta, Gante was performing his Christian duty. He made a personal and enduring commitment to his order and to New Spain by rejecting offers to become an ordained priest and return to Flanders to receive higher appointments. He became a lay brother without rival, mixing a unique combination of *linaje* (pedigree) and humbleness and thus becoming a model for others to understand and imitate.

In contrast to Gante's refined personal background, Mendieta recalls two other lay brothers who came with the original twelve, Fr. Andrés de Córdoba and Fr. Juan de Palos. They were men without distinguished ancestry or academic education. To eulogize them Mendieta resorted to the well-known trope of the divine election of the humblest to spread the word of God. By choosing to downplay lineage, Mendieta struck a deep spiritual chord. There was nothing more precious for sixteenth-century Spaniards than bloodlines. Reminding his readers that the lack of nobility was appealing to God, Mendieta reaffirmed the spirit of the reformed discalced Franciscans, whose emphasis on poverty, purity, and strictness was sweeping the order in the peninsula.[63] Despite being a "simple" lay brother, Fr. Juan de Palos was declared "wise," as he learned Nahuatl and preached in it, even though preaching was certainly not a lay brother's task. He died an unimaginable death. He perished of hunger in Florida with his companion Fr. Juan Suárez, the result of an ill-planned settlement attempt led by Pánfilo de Narvaez. This sad ending gave Mendieta the opportunity to extol the spiritual fraternity encouraged by the mendicants. In a poetical flight, he envisioned both, ordained and lay friar, together in glory as they had been in the pilgrimage of their lives.[64]

Another of Mendieta's lay brothers was Lucas de Almodóvar, a nurse and possibly the first lay brother to gain a reputation for this métier in New Spain. Almodóvar brought to the New World a special "gift" for healing, an almost miraculous ability understood as the silent and unfathomable message of God's charity. As a healer he represented an alternative to the incantations of Indigenous shamans. Others would follow his path, nursing their sick brothers. After Almodóvar's death a cross was said to have appeared in the air, regarded as a sign that his soul had been received by God. For Mendieta, this humble lay brother, who used charity and restored the health of others, was obviously a memorable example because an orthodox Christian healer supported the validity of the new religion, which could induce cures comparable to those of the Indigenous healers.[65] A more typical lay brother was Fr. Fernando de Leiva, who, having professed in Burgos and learned how lay brothers were helping in the conversion of the Indians, crossed the seas and resided for the rest of his life in the convent of Tlaxcala, keeping the convent clean, helping in the convent's vegetable garden, and giving food away to the Indians. Exercising the expected charity of the convent's porter, he had a pot of vegetable stew always ready for the poor. Although he never learned Nahuatl, he became popular among Indians and Spaniards as a devout, humble, and as Mendieta put it, "very simple" man. Simplicity became a running thread, a leitmotif in the development of a behavioral model for writers and readers of conventual chronicles.[66] Mendieta closed his account of sainted lay brothers (*santos varones*) with Diego de Guadalcanal, who reminded him of San Diego de Alcalá.[67] Of Spanish birth, Diego was another simple man who professed in Mexico City. He was chosen as memorable because of his devoutness and charity, his dedication to being a good Christian, and his stoic resignation when, on account of a strange disease on one of his hands, physicians had to cut off his fingers one by one. Mendieta's choice of exemplary lay brothers proposed to show how, in their different ways, these men had chosen to be "useful" to their order while shedding their personal ambitions, key points that other historians adopted to preserve other lay brothers' memory.

Dominican chroniclers Agustín Dávila Padilla, Fr. Hernando Ojea, and Fr. Alonso Franco also included lay brothers in their respective narratives. Dávila Padilla's list of lay brothers was lean. He mentioned only six lay brothers and one *donado* among the illustrious men of the order. He wrote with respect of their labor and character, reiterating the contemporaneous, idealized images of men of the cloth. He described them as penitent, devout, obedient, willing to work, and observant of the rules of their order. In his opinion lay brothers deserved the confidence they enjoyed in the order as administrators and alms collectors in the mining towns.[68] His brief biography of *donado* Miguel Ortiz gave him the opportunity to pontificate on the merits of serving a religious order in that particular status. Exceptionally, a *donado* earned a long narrative in conventual chronicles, which did not often include them because they were not frequently accepted for services. Ortiz was unusual in that he seemed to have had extraordinary intellectual abilities. Having gained the goodwill of the bishop of Guatemala, Francisco Marroquín, he was relieved from his state as a *donado* and ordained in 1545. After that, he learned Nahuatl and gained a reputation as a preacher. Lay brotherhood offered, in exceptional cases, an avenue for social mobility, although the fluidity of sixteenth-century society was a key element for such possibility.

Hernando de Ojea picked up the Dominican history where Dávila Padilla left off and chose exemplary lay brothers who lived mostly in the sixteenth century and were all Spaniards by birth. Three of them came from good families, and one had been a rich merchant in Mexico City before he chose to profess. Some of these lay brothers owned and studied devotional books, but they were not men of letters, a fact that did not compromise their moral virtue and spiritual worthiness in the eyes of the writer.[69] For example, Fr. Pedro Martínez meditated methodically on the meaning of the words of his favorite prayers, one by one, trying to get to the bottom of their message. This devotional methodology was similar to the practices promoted by Fr. Luis de León and Fr. Luis de Granada in sixteenth-century Spain.[70] Fr. Juan de Sena, Pedro de Solórzano, Juan de Paz, and Diego de Medellín openly rejected the possibility of becoming ordained friars. Pedro de Solórzano was a page of Viceroy Luis de Velazco, but when "God touched him" in 1552, he took the habit. By refusing to become anything but a lay brother, he incurred his family's displeasure and became an outcast.[71] Ojea suggested that Solórzano's virtues echoed some of the Ten Commandments, the most important rules of behavior to keep the law of God. The Ten Commandments gained great influence in the indoctrination of the faith as part of the Catholic Reformation, and Ojea's remarks seem to bear that influence.[72]

Ojea's analysis of what was understood as a "saintly" lay brother reflected the religious climate of the times. His lay brothers were truthful, did not hurt anyone in word or deed, fulfilled their promises, and did not engage in usury. These men did everything in their power to ensure for themselves the glory promised by their beliefs, regardless of difficulties and hardship. Obedience was their touchstone, and they took pleasure in accepting it as mendicants and exercising their will to make their bodies "obedient" to their spirit.[73]

By the mid-seventeenth century, chronicler Fr. Alonso Franco had his agenda set before him. He picked up some information from Ojea but made his own list of the virtuous friars who had died between 1526 and 1645. He included thirty lay brothers and 144 ordained friars, a greater proportion than other authors. He wrote in some detail on twelve of them, extolling their exemplary behavior, their spirituality, and their devotional practices. Juan de Sena and Diego de Medellín are two examples. Juan de Sena earned a reputation as a spiritual man whose advice was appreciated by some notable religious men. Francisco de Loza, a priest friend and advisor of the renowned hermit Gregorio López, considered that Sena had given him the best advice on some of his own spiritual difficulties.[74] As chroniclers, Franco and Ojea complemented each other in portraying Fr. Diego de Medellín—born in Extremadura of a good family and who took the habit of lay brother in Mexico City—as an example of social "conversion," another trope of the period to signify a challenger to established norms. Ojea stressed Medellín's robust physique and his ability to read and write, play the cittern, sing, and dance. Such "mundane" and physical attributes could have been obstacles to being a true lay brother. Franco suggested that the devil could have "tricked" him into professing as an ordained brother, but being a lay brother was the "right" state for him. The chronicler praised his renunciation of wine, his perseverance in fasting and the discipline of his body. Medellín remained humble, worked in the building of the convent, took care of the convent's music books in his old age, and never asked for a license to go outside the cloister's premises, employing his time in his devotional practices with humility and determination.[75] Here, in Ojea's eyes, was a living example of Christian manly behavior under a lay brother's habit.

Franciscan Alonso de la Rea, in his history of the Franciscan province of San Pedro y San Pablo of Michoacán, published in the mid-seventeenth century, stressed the lay brothers' self-discipline and observance of the rules of their order. They all showed *mansedumbre* (docility) and humility, the modest concealment of any ability that might draw attention to themselves. They also had total control over moral weaknesses such as pride and concupiscence. These virtues were earned through much personal struggle and a manly determination to achieve them. One of his chosen examples was Fr. Alonso Ortiz, who came from Extremadura, Spain, and joined the Franciscan order at age forty.[76] According to La Rea, he had "misspent" his youth, but following the rhetoric of moral conversion, he renounced the vanities and emptiness of the world and requested the Franciscan habit in the convent of Tzintzuntzan in the province of Michoacán. He intended to "purge" his behavior professing as a lay brother. Acknowledging the nobility of his endeavor and his personal success in curbing his bad traits, his brothers in the convent wished to admit him to full membership as an ordained friar. Alonso decided to leave the judgment to God. He prayed to be sick if he was to remain as a lay brother. As he woke up sick with fever on the following day, he accepted God's will and declined the promotion. The transformation of his character was appealing, and La Rea added some anecdotes to ratify Alonso's presumed anointment with God's grace. Alonso was said to have performed one miracle: the resuscitation of a dead girl. He was also seen levitating during his prayer sessions. Everything in this short biography accommodated the canons of seventeenth-century hagiography. Religious writers were captivated by the process of "becoming" a virtuous man and choosing to remain at a lower level of social clerical rank.

Franciscan Fr. Agustín de Vetancurt crowned the line of historians of his order at the end of the seventeenth century. He included thirty-nine biographical sketches of lay brothers in his work *Menologio*, a biographical collection of exemplary Franciscans.[77] This large corpus included men of various social backgrounds who had become lay brothers for many personal reasons and became models of spirituality by adopting behavior learned from their predecessors. They were characterized as humble, devout, and accepting. Wearing *cilicios* and imposing harsh discipline on their bodies, they became the equals of the most dedicated ordained members of the order. Some of them experienced *arrobos*, or "mystical elevations," like other saintly men. More importantly for historical purposes, Vetancurt corroborated the variety of services they rendered and how they made contact with the lay population. Several of Vetancurt's lay brothers were identified as "limosneros de trigo," "limosneros de campo," and "limosneros del pescado." In their travels throughout the countryside gathering goods as alms, they met informally with many devout believers and gained their respect as emblems of meek spirituality. Among the *limosneros* of note was Pedro Vázquez de Vega, who had been a public scribe in Mexico City and had given up his practice to become a lay brother collecting wheat. While performing this duty, he distributed beads and small objects to the faithful, encouraging their faith.[78] Vetancurt also cites Diego de Santa María, a Black *donado* who grew up in the convent of Puebla and collected wheat as a *limosnero*. Brother Diego could repeat by memory the sermons he heard in the church, and he "preached" to those he encountered on his path.[79] He had several miracles assigned to him. In the early days of the viceroyalty, nursing the sick was a much-needed service. In addition to extolling the virtues of Lucas de Almodóvar, cited previously, he included Juan Juárez, who professed in Puebla in 1634 and served in his convent's infirmary, visiting other hospitals in the city to dispense his care and knowledge.[80] These bits of information line up with the information on brother nurses in the eighteenth-century conventual population seen above.

Interest in recalling the memory of the lay brothers declined with time, but when chronicler Fr. Domingo Arricivita undertook the task of writing the history of the Colegio de Propaganda Fide in Querétaro, he remembered two exemplary men: Gonzalo Juan de Pereyra and Bartolomé de Jesús y Torres. Arricivita identified Pereyra as a native of the Canary Islands and a companion of Fr. Melchor López and Fr. Antonio Margil in their Guatemala mission. Once there, the friars gave Pereyra the habit of the Third Franciscan order to add respectability to his role as their aide and servant. Pereyra shared all the missionizing activities of López and Margil. When Margil was appointed head of the college in Querétaro in 1697, he made his way to the friary on foot. So did Pereyra. His loyalty and perseverance earned him an appointment to accompany Fr. Francisco Estévez on a trip to Spain and Rome in pursuit of the college's interests. The trip lasted five years, and when Pereyra returned to Querétaro, he was in his fifties and sick. Arricivita showered Pereyra with praise as observant, humble, and devout and as one who shared all the virtues and met the lofty standards of the few select men he chose for his chronicle. He made clear that Pereyra understood the limitations of his status in the convent, as he followed his spiritual director with the reverence and "obsequiousness of a servant, and obeyed and served him with the greatest respect."[81] The moral lesson to be derived from the behavior of this lay brother was that professing in a religious order leveled all social classes. After death, "no one is third or first." Charity embraced all brothers and washed their sins away, and they all appeared equal before God. Arricivita also added Bartolomé de Jesús y Torres to his list of special men. He was a rural *limosnero* for Propaganda Fide and gave pious talks to the almsgivers, advising them on how to pray, confess, and engage in devout practices such as meditating on the passion of Christ. To foster the passion, he carried small crosses that he set up before inviting others to engage in the prayers known as the *Via Sacra*, a special devotional practice of the Santa Cruz college. Devotional books helped him pray with his audience or request the intercession of the saints for the solution of their problems.[82]

This brief survey of several mendicants' chronicles indicates how lay brothers established close contact with common folk such as tradesmen, muleteers, farmers, and miners, a point underscored and praised in Manuel Barbados's eulogy and history of lay brothers. As they mingled with the humble, lay brothers earned their confidence, trust, and belief. When they engaged in their own unofficial form of "preaching" and catechizing in plain words, they became unpretentious teachers as well as models of living piety. Reaching to the common folk made pastoral sense. In their own unique way, lay brothers rendered an important spiritual service to the church and to their own orders.

As was the case with respected friars, when lay brothers died, the faithful crowded the churches for the funeral services and tore their habits to keep as relics. People also sought objects the brother had owned and used, such as their water mugs and sandals. After the Dominican lay brother Fr. Miguel de Zamora died, people collected pieces of his old clothes and socks and his drinking and eating utensils "as if they were precious stones."[83] Baltasar de Medina tells the story of the funeral of Fr. Marcos Sánchez Calderón, a lay brother who died in 1625 in the convent of discalced Franciscans of Oaxaca. He was very popular because of the largesse of his charitable gifts to the poor and was respected for his "miraculous cures." After his death, he was reputed to have saved men who invoked his name in dangerous situations and was supposed to have helped a couple of secular priests achieve the promotions they sought. The demonstrations of popular piety after his death took unbelievable turns, despite plans for an early internment. After the city council members arrived for his funeral services, the crowd invaded the temple and ripped off the brother's habit. The spectacle was contagious. A member of the Cathedral Council stole the mat the deceased used to sleep on, only to be assaulted at the door by anxious relic seekers who wanted a piece of it. He lost most of the mat. Further, a pious man came to kiss the corpse's feet and bit off one of the toes, which he kept as a precious relic.[84]

Chroniclers knew how to use a variety of anecdotes to appeal to the readers' sensibilities and embed their order's memory in the popular imagination and historical folklore. They chose "miracles" or prodigious events that involved the community in deeply meaningful ways, such as when Fr. Cristóbal de Molina conjured away the locusts that had invaded Puebla and kept them away from the convent's vegetable garden.[85] Given the popular appeal of stories of saintly men and their miracles during and after death, it is not surprising that some special lay friars earned a full-length biographical essay for the memory of future generations. This was an honor often reserved for the most exalted members of the church.

Hagiographical Narrative: Three Sainted Lay Brothers

Antonio Rubial has argued that the hagiographical literature that flourished in New Spain helped redefine the purpose of the Church in a period when the evangelization of most of the Indigenous of central Mexico had been officially accomplished. Further, hagiography proved that New Spain had reached the same level of spirituality as the Old World.[86] The decline in the writing of sweeping histories of the mendicant orders in the eighteenth century ended the production of minibiographies of notable figures embedded in these narratives. However, some important biographies of sainted men written in the seventeenth and eighteenth centuries preserved and favored the memory of lay brothers. The biographies of Franciscans Fr. Sebastián de Aparicio, Fr. Antonio de los Ángeles Bustamante, and Augustinian Fr. Cristóbal de Molina stand as examples of a literary and historical effort to foster the memory of a body of "elected" laymen.

Chronologically, the earliest biography of a lay brother was that of Sebastián de Aparicio (1514–1600), also known as "Beato Aparicio." Expectations regarding his potential sainthood appeared shortly after his death, and the search for corroborations of his virtues, miracles, and saintliness intensified over the course of the seventeenth century. He was the emblematic lay brother figure, simple and eccentric in his behavior but with what was then regarded as having the touch of God in his personal expression of piety. Francisco Morales points out that "simplicity" and "ignorance" were personal qualities popularized in that century.[87] God hid his message in the humble man or woman whose behavior may not have been socially correct. Aparicio fit well into this post-Tridentine trend. He was a hagiographic phenomenon in terms of his meteoric popularity and was the subject of ten biographies, five of them written in the seventeenth century to support the cause for his beatification, or sainthood. Even though the fervor around his figure began to wane in the eighteenth century, he achieved the much-sought beatification in 1789.[88]

Born in Galicia in 1502 in a large and poor family, he left home as a teenager to make a living by serving in wealthy homes or working in rural properties. The lure of the New World caught him, and he emigrated to New Spain in 1531, joining the ranks of poor Spaniards seeking a better life. Before he left, he experienced an odd personal incident with a young woman who was eloping with her suitor to escape a family-imposed marriage. Returning her to her family,

FIG. 13. *Sebastián de Aparicio*, in *Compendio della Vita del Beato Sebastiano D'Apparizio. Laico Professo . . . del P. S. Francisco della Prov. Del Santo Evangelio nel Messico* (Rome, 1789). Image from Biblioteca Digital Hispánica, Biblioteca Nacional de España, Madrid, Spain.

he later claimed that he had rejected the woman's dishonest propositions, thus establishing one of his important virtues, that of his virginity, which others claimed he preserved for the rest of his life. In the eighteenth century, he was represented as either surrounded by lilies or emerging from these flowers to signify the sexual purity that distanced him from most other men.[89]

Virginity aside, after arriving in the viceroyalty, he held various occupations related to his training as a farmer and gained a reputation as a handler of oxen. With the organization of an oxcart muleteer business, he took advantage of the introduction of the wheel for commercial purposes in New Spain, establishing a successful service to deliver merchandise to the booming mining town of Zacatecas. He also learned another personal skill: how to ingratiate himself with the volatile and feared Chichimecs, providing them with beef and corn to gain their goodwill and avoid their attacks. In itself, this was a miracle in times when the unconverted tribal men of the near north became a constant threat to the expansion of trade and population in the mining areas. This "simple" man traveled worry-free and thrived in his business until 1552, when he sold it and returned to his peasant origins by buying land between Azcapotzalco and Tlalnepantla, close to Mexico City. He was by all accounts a good manager who treated his workers well and lived frugally. In times when landowners, overseers, and encomenderos squeezed most of their workers and sought life luxuries, Aparicio's charity earned him a good reputation, albeit not that of a saint.

After he became a successful landowner, the thought of getting married entered his mind. He was getting on in years, and according to the mores of the times, his properties and wealth should be invested in a family. He married twice when he was in his sixties, in both cases to very young and poor women, whom he endowed generously, but a potential family was not part of his plan. Apparently, he was not interested in sex or heirs. The stories of both his marriages suggest a desire to test himself by maintaining his virginity in the married state. This was not inconceivable in the sixteenth century. Preserving one's virginity against the assaults of the flesh was an agenda shared by the pious of both sexes. However, if this was the case (and we have no way of knowing with certainty), his intention had no purchase with the family of the first bride. He was accused of nonconsummation by her parents. It was a cause for the annulment of marriage. The Church clearly stated that marriage was for the satisfaction of sexual needs and procreation.

Since Aparicio's first bride had not brought any dowry of her own, the family probably felt that the old man could still play foul and hurt their interests and those of their daughter if the marriage were dissolved and they could make no claim to his wealth. The death of the young woman put an end to the situation. Aparicio denied any ill intentions, compensated the parents of the first wife, and at sixty-three, married again to another young bride. He received the same disapproval of her family for nonconsummation. Secular masculinity relied on the exercise of sex within marriage, and a willful nonconsummation by the man cast doubts about his virility and the desirability of the woman. While we may ponder on Aparicio's decision to marry pubescent girls at such a late age and speculate on his physical virility, social expectations were that men would either use their sexual capabilities within marriage or give them up in the religious state. The death of his second wife was a turning point in Aparicio's life. Having rejected sex and lost two wives, he decided to follow the path of religious life. His biographers could comfortably return to the eulogy of his chastity, now exercised in the appropriate state.

Aparicio's application at the Franciscan convent in Mexico City faced difficulties owing to his lack of letters and doubts about his abilities to follow religious life at such a late age. He was accepted as *donado* and sent to serve the convent of Poor Clares, to which he willed a large share of his fortune. After serving the nuns for some time, he was eventually accepted as a lay brother by the Franciscan order in 1573. Beginning in 1577 he served in the convent of Puebla for the rest of his life. The order employed him in various occupations demanding strength and dedication, and he proved able to cope with them. He traveled for months collecting alms for his convent. For these long trips, he was allowed to ride a horse, use shoes, and drink wine, amenities other devoted friars renounced. He was scrupulously honest with the money and goods he collected. He refused to use a cell in the convent and slept under his carts, close to his animals. He wore a ragged habit, and when he returned from his long trips, he entered the convent and joined the religious services unwashed and unkempt.

It is easy to understand how the appearance of this old man, oddly dressed and begging for alms for Saint Francis, would touch the piety of common people. However, his personal appearance and his poor knowledge of the prayers, rituals, and ceremonial observance raised the eyebrows of some of his brothers in religion. At one point he was sent back to the novitiate to relearn rules and prayers. According to one of his biographers, the religious who sent him back to the novitiate became ill immediately after giving his order, a sure sign of God's displeasure with this ecclesiastical chastisement. Ultimately, Aparicio was allowed to go free and live as a simpleminded man attached to the Franciscan order, who came close to God through his own lack of pretensions. His closeness to animals evoked Saint Francis's own reputation for a similar ability, albeit exercised under different circumstances. His popularity may be ascribed to the fact that he never used or abused the authority his habit conferred on him. The humble men and women among whom he was popular appreciated his spartan life, his lack of pride, and his willingness to listen to their personal problems and do something for them.

Aparicio died in February 1600, and Fr. Juan de Torquemada published his first biography in 1602.[90] Each succeeding biography amplified the number of his prodigious hagiographical events, especially those related to medical cures. They satisfied the miracle-saturated popular imagination of people in New Spain.[91] Over time, Aparicio's biographies reflected current seventeenth-century views of what was considered "sanctity" among the public and Franciscans themselves. The order was already negotiating the saintliness of martyred Felipe de Jesús and happily undertook the cause of another potential saint. Historian Fr. Agustín de Vetancurt, writing at the end of the seventeenth century, dedicated the longest of the lay brothers' biographical sketches in his *Menologio* to Aparicio.[92] Having lived in the first century of Spanish settlement, Aparicio's life "proved" the validity of Spain's imposition over the Indigenous population. This was the line of argumentation followed by one of his biographers who criticized historians who remained interested only in the "antiquities" of Indigenous history. This barb was aimed at the likes of Motolinía, Sahagún, and Fr. Diego Durán, who described and eulogized the lives and beliefs of pre-Columbian peoples but not those of their living Christian contemporaries. This critique explains the cultivation and popularity of sacred biographies in seventeenth-century New Spain. A common sentiment at the period was that the religious orders needed men committed to writing their own history, not to praising societies that had not known Christianity.

Aparicio's popularity cooled down in the eighteenth century. As Pierre Ragon points out, the patience of people with the slow beatification process in Rome began running thin. Nonetheless, the course of beatification continued to appeal to people in his birthplace, Galicia, and Spanish regional pride sustained it. Pope Clemente XIII (1758–69) declared Aparicio's virtues "heroic" on May 2, 1768, putting him closer to beatification. Immediately thereafter, the Franciscan commissary general in New Spain supported a new biography that appeared in 1769.[93] After the secularization of the Indigenous doctrines in the mid-eighteenth century, the mendicants were barely keeping their catechizing prestige alive. A Franciscan *beato* would revitalize people's faith and support. On writing the required approval for the biography, Fr. Ignacio de la Rocha, then choirmaster (*chantre*) of the Metropolitan Church of Mexico City, expressed the "religious awe" he had experienced upon learning of the unique and extraordinary ways adopted by God to speak through a man who, by all accounts, could hardly pray properly. So inspired was he that he added the adjective *prodigious* to the title of the work. Even in the midst of a presumably "enlightened" culture, works seeking to foster piety and admiration for a simple lay brother found a warm welcome in the hearts and minds of religious authorities.[94] All these efforts yielded fruit in 1789, when Aparicio's beatification finally took place. It would be unwise to discard the element of popular religiosity still thriving in the eighteenth century.

Cristóbal de Molina

Possibly inspired by the popularity of Brother Aparicio, the Augustinian friar Nicolás Ponce de León decided to write the biography of Fr. Cristóbal de Molina (1592–1638), a lay brother of his order, which appeared in print in 1686.[95] Molina was born near Toledo, Spain, of "old Christians" and some hidalgo lineage, possibly of little means since he was apprenticed as an embroiderer as a boy. Hoping for a change in fortune, his parents traveled to New Spain when he was very young and settled in Puebla. He was twenty when he entered the convent of San Agustín in that city on May 15, 1612, professing one year later on May 16. His biographer, Fr. Nicolás Ponce de León, does not explain why Cristóbal chose to become a friar or take the status of lay brother, but it is implied that he lacked the desired degree of education to become an ordained priest. Ponce de León based his narrative on a set of notes on Fr. Cristóbal written by another friar, Fr. Estevan García, and the testimony of several members of his community, thus adding the desirable element of verifiability to his story. In fact, it appears that Fr. Estevan was a self-appointed "biographer" and recorder of Molina's "deeds" and behavior during the latter's lifetime. Augustinians seemed to have been hoping for another Aparicio in their ranks.

Ponce de León presented Fr. Cristóbal as a man close to the common people, following the example set by Aparicio's biographers. In the kitchen, where Fr. Cristóbal worked without respite, he catechized the Black men, presumably slaves, and other kitchen helpers, praying with them and teaching them the Christian doctrine amid "the fire of the hearth, pots and pans, dishes and bowls." Ponce de León stated, "That kitchen was the site of Catholic teaching and pulpit of evangelical truths."[96] Fr. Cristóbal performed miracles appropriate to his work: he made a small chicken increase in size in the pot destined to feed his sick prior, and he could touch fire and hot pots without getting burned.[97] As a very devout man, he rose at 4 a.m. for prayers before reporting to work. In addition to cooking, he was in charge of cleaning the convent, cutting wood, and shopping for the necessary victuals. Returning to the convent burdened with his purchases, he became a familiar sight in Puebla's streets, where he used to distribute some small crucifixes to the faithful while engaged in his daily errands. This activity brought him the ire of his brothers in the convent because such unblessed crosses could attract the attention of the Inquisition. His liberality with alms, leftovers, and other conventual food brought him the verbal reprimand of his own prelate for taking away resources from the community.[98] The biographer also commented on his difficulty in meeting the various daily demands of different members of the community and the humility with which he met all sorts of criticism. It is obvious that not all was harmony or fair treatment to lay brothers in male communities.

The goal of Ponce de León's biography was to extol Fr. Cristóbal's virtues, among which the observance of the rules was the foundational stone. Testing the vow of obedience, the most important for every friar, he worked for twenty-four years in the convent's bustling kitchen, which was the direct opposite of the silence of the cells where his more exalted brothers spent their time. Second to his obedience was his poverty, displayed in his habit. Cristóbal wore an old, secondhand habit and coarse underwear, a common practice among other discipline-practicing friars. However, the biographer commented, he was respectful of his habit; it was neither torn nor ill-kempt in spite of the fact that he was surrounded by cooking appliances, charcoal, and other sources of dirt. A soiled habit indicated laziness, not poverty; negligence desecrated it. In this respect he was the antithesis of Sebastián de Aparicio, and the biographer reminded the readers that Cristóbal's care of his habit reflected Augustinians' high standard of behavior. In contrast, the Franciscans showed greater tolerance toward Aparicio's unkempt figure. Biographers paid attention to such details, as they mattered in men whose character would be judged not by the heights of their intellect but by the piety expressed in the performance of the ubiquitous and humble demands of daily life.

To promote the devotional practices that the church wished to see in the general population, the biographer presented Fr. Cristóbal as displaying deep reverence for the life and passion of Christ, the Virgin Mary, and the saints of his order.[99] His penitential practices, his devotional stamina, his disregard for food, and his constant concern about his physical chastity all suggested that Molina was a living example of the perfect lay friar in his contemporaries' eyes. To his adherence to conventual discipline, his biographer added the gift of prophecy and the ability to know the arcane corners of people's minds. Ponce de León claimed he wished to exclude miracles from his narrative, arguing that while miracles and prodigies captivate the imagination of the common people, Augustinians relied more on the exercise of virtues with humility.[100] However, he contradicted his own statements by citing a string of homely miracles performed by Fr. Cristóbal. It was difficult for a seventeenth-century writer to disavow miracles, the inevitable and indispensable ornaments of hagiography. They were essential to create the proper atmosphere to elevate a candidate to the altars.

To prove that though a humble lay brother, Fr. Cristóbal was not totally devoid of intellectual abilities, Ponce de León gathered a collection of small pieces of paper with brief devotional messages written by Fr. Cristóbal in matter-of-fact language that could be understood by all. He cited some of them in the biography. They are, by no means, treatises of spirituality but a collection of statements conveying a very simple understanding of the faith. One says, "Our body is like a rental house where the soul resides; we pay for the rent with the work, affronts and persecutions we bear for the love of God." Another message reads, "The soul is a walled garden [*huerta*] where we must plant *cilicios*, discipline, fasting, mortifications, prayer and other virtues. We must strive to prevent the devil from chipping it—or give him the opportunity to do so—and live well, and exercise the virtues."[101] These pearls of simple wisdom seemed to have either confused or impressed some of his brothers in religion. To strengthen their message, Ponce de León expounded on their meaning with quotations and glosses from Saint Augustine and the New and Old Testaments. If they impressed his brothers in religion, it was because they did not expect writings from their cook. However, they would accept that God hid such wisdom from learned men and revealed it to the humble.

Biographer Ponce de León wrote *three* chapters of his book to explain one letter Fr. Cristóbal sent to two cousins who were nuns in a convent he does not bother to name.[102] The letter and the advice to the nuns speak of the relationship of cloistered women to a man other than their own confessors. Fr. Cristóbal was acting as a spiritual advisor, a role he was not supposed to have. However, his local reputation as a humble sainted man gave him enough authority to advise his relatives without infringing on the authority of a confessor or spiritual director. He probably never intended to pontificate beyond the boundaries of his state. Ponce de León's efforts to infuse this short pious letter with the depth and wisdom of well-known sources of Christian spirituality are a testimony to his desire to elevate the intellectual stature of this lay brother. He did not succeed. Molina never advanced to even the first levels of consideration for beatitude. His biography did not garner enough attention from those prelates and men who could put their money and efforts into such an objective.

Antonio de los Ángeles

Aparicio and Molina represented the seventeenth-century quest for examples of the humble but sainted man. A slightly different version of dedication to a life of quiet and devout practice of religion as a lay brother was the example of Fr. Antonio de los Ángeles Bustamante. His biography appeared in 1731, and it was written by Fr. Isidro Félix de Espinosa, one of the best-known writers and missionaries of the period.[103] Espinosa was a preacher in his own right, a chronicler of the Franciscan order, and a biographer of the notable men in his order, including the renowned Fr. Antonio Margil de Jesús.[104] Bustamante had been dead for twenty years when Espinosa published his biography in 1731. Espinosa had access to Bustamante's personal writings, his conventual records, and the testimonies of personal witnesses. Those sources were strong enough to sustain the biographer's intention to extol Fr. Antonio's spiritual virtues and the exaltation of the order that promoted his piety. To this day, his biography remains the only testimony of Fr. Antonio's life. It failed to gather any recognition for its subject or support for any aspiration to beatitude.

Straddling the seventeenth and early eighteenth centuries (1659–1711), Fr. Antonio was spiritually a seventeenth-century man and fit the trope of how God could transform a powerful man into one of his humble servants. Fr. Antonio was born in Burgos of hidalgo lineage, with a grandfather connected to the Holy Office. His father was a scrivener, and as a young man, he must have had a good education, although the biographer provides no information on the topic. An émigré from Spain to New Spain, Antonio had a successful career as an administrator to a rich merchant in Seville and had access to the perquisites of wealth and a good social position. He eventually moved to Querétaro, where, in addition to his mercantile operations, he acquired a sheep-raising property. Despite his social and financial success, he did not seem to have lived a typical life for a young man. According to Fr. Isidro, who remarked on his good looks and impressive figure on horseback, Antonio had no interest in women or marriage.

According to his biographer, a slow process of introspection and devotional conversion led him to the religious life. The sudden death of a friend, the powerful Juan de Urrutia y Retes, Marquis of Villar del Águila, prompted this conversion.[105] The narrative conveys the transformation of a man with power, wealth, and youth into a lay brother burning with the desire to please God and earn his grace through a full commitment to poverty and humility. His profession in 1690 at age thirty-one at the College of Santa Cruz gave a booster to the college. Founded in 1683, Santa Cruz was still in the process of rooting in the community and attracting future professions. Fr. Antonio became a lay brother by choice and refused to be admitted as a novice preparing for ordination, which was the desire of the college brothers. To test his vocation, he was sent to beg alms in the city where he was well known for his social prominence, displays of wealth, and youthful manhood. Ultimately, the religious community decided to accept him and employ him as a gatekeeper. It was in this task that he exercised his vocation for the rest of his life. His experience in business made him useful

FIG. 14. *Portrait of Fr. Antonio de los Ángeles*, in Fr. Isidro Félix Espinosa, *El Cherubin Custodio de el Árbol de la Vida, la Santa Cruz de Querétaro. Vida del V*^{e}. *Siervo de Dios, Fray Antonio de los Ángeles Bustamante* (Mexico: Joseph Bernardo de Hogal, 1731).

in reviewing the convent's accounts with its administrator. He also served as a conventual scrivener and performed other secretarial services such as letter writing. His patience was amply tested by the many demands of his brothers, the aggravation of one prelate's continuous requests for errands, and the duties of his assignment as gatekeeper. His biographer extolled his obedience and humility.[106]

This biography had not only an able writer in Fr. Isidro Félix Espinosa but also a venerable witness, Fr. Antonio Margil de Jesús.[107] The friendship between Margil and Fr. Antonio was well documented by Espinosa.[108] The bonding of Margil and Fr. Antonio developed as they engaged in some charitable works and devotional acts that strike modern readers as odd examples of baroque spiritual life. When Margil became the college's prelate in 1697, he and Fr. Antonio began to practice the Via Crucis together, continuing it for four years through 1701. The Via Crucis was a devotional practice introduced by the Franciscans of the Colegio de Propaganda Fide and consisted of meditation on the sufferings of Christ on his way to the cross and penitential practices in imitation of his suffering. This exercise was complemented by sessions in which Fr. Antonio read a passage from Sor María de Ágreda's writings, after which he listened to Fr. Margil's confession, gave him the advice that God guided him to give, and ended with Fr. Antonio stepping on Fr. Margil's mouth while he prayed three creeds. Then they changed places, and Fr. Margil acted as confessor and chastiser.[109] Margil left the college in 1701 to perform other duties required by his order in Guatemala and Central America. When he returned to the Querétaro convent in 1708 after his missionary absence, the two men made a spiritual pact together. Fr. Antonio renewed his commitment to God, and they declared themselves the slaves of God (Margil) and the Virgin (Fr. Antonio), becoming one body and one heart in Christ. To this effect Fr. Antonio drew a heart at the bottom of his written commitment. The heart contained the names of the two friars together. While modern readers may read a somewhat homoerotic meaning into this pact and drawing, the biographer saw it through a lens of eighteenth-century piety, calling this "a most virtuous union" whereby both men joined in meritorious exercises sharing the most secret "happening of their loving hearts; having at their disposal the key to each other's hearts."[110] The usage of the language of love among members of the masculine communities was not unusual. The bottom line is that these two men carved a spiritual brotherhood whereby Margil, the priest, and Fr. Antonio, the lay brother, disregarded differences of rank, a point the biographer wished to underline.[111]

In most other ways, Bustamante's life reads like other conventional biographies. Espinosa cast Fr. Antonio as a devotee of Saint Anthony of Padua and as a "cherub" in custody of the "mystical paradise," the College of Santa Cruz.[112] Espinosa wrote about his fortitude, his sexual chastity (albeit suggesting he had some battles to preserve it), his constant fasting, the rigor of his penitential acts, his poverty, his obedience, and similar commendable character traits. Fr. Antonio's portrait, engraved in the biography, represents an investment in the book, since illustrations were costly. It was also a persuasive means of visually conveying key features of Antonio's character. Standing in the middle of a windowless room, the friar is portrayed as bearing a chaste demeanor, looking down and holding his arms close to his body in a pose that resembles that of a saint. A rosary suggests his devotion to Mary while the keys of the convent indicate his role as porter. On the floor there is a kitchen pot, a basket of bread, and a cross. Both the basket and the kitchen pot refer to his charity toward the poor. On one occasion, he is said to have "miraculously" stretched the number of bread loaves in his basket to feed a large number of beggars. The cross lying against the wall, ready to be picked up, is a reference to the exercise of the Via Sacra. It is also an emblem of his commitment to Christ. This is one of the few portraits of a lay brother in the history of the printed book in colonial Mexico.[113]

The quality and nature of his writings, quoted by his biographer, show that Fr. Antonio could express himself well and fluidly on the vicissitudes and rewards of his spiritual life. These writings were messages sent to people with whom he was in touch and statements that he had presumably written for his own edification and may have landed in the hands of his confessors. Fr. Ángel García Duque, his confessor for twelve years, was close to Fr. Antonio, and it is possible that his writings were intended for the confessor's reading to elicit his spiritual advice. That was standard practice in the seventeenth and eighteenth centuries, but we know more about such writings among nuns than among friars. Fr. Ángel also collected several letters sent to Fr. Antonio by his spiritual brother Fr. Antonio de Jesús Margil. The writings expressed devotional and spiritual traits of the seventeenth century, such as the need for suffering. For example, addressing his spiritual struggles, he wrote, "A tribulation is the antechamber of a benefit. The latter is never true if it is not preceded by the purge of tribulation. The biggest and most fruitful benefice for our souls is suffering."[114] Another reflection on the same topic read, "Beget, Lord, in my soul, the rich treasures of gold and silver of charity; the bronze of fortitude; and the lead of guarding your honor, even though I may become insufferable to the bad ones and the demons. Wipe and dry out the humidity of the appetites; break the darkness of sins and transform them into the water of tears and penitence. Light up the love of your divine love in my soul."[115] A testimony to his devotion to the suffering of Christ as a lesson to be lived by his followers reads, "Let's carry the cross that the Lord has given us from his own hand. If one day is like hay, thank the Lord; if another day is like lead, thank the Lord. . . . Blessed be the dead who have died in the Lord."

The extent of Fr. Antonio's devotional corpus remains unknown. Unfortunately, no efforts were made to collect, let alone print this scattered collection of beatitudes, and there is no trace of their fate. The samples quoted by his biographer show a man channeling his faith through intimate writings that he had no aspirations to circulate beyond those to whom they were dedicated. His faith is anchored on Jesus and Mary, before whom he stood as a suppliant. Fr. Antonio lacked the education required for writing on theological matters. However, being a lay brother meant he was free to write on his own personal spiritual experience and faith. The excerpts quoted in his biography are rare evidence of the spirituality of an educated man who was also a member of the lower ranks of the church. There are very few extant examples of affective and intimate male spirituality in Mexican convents. Most of the writings penned by men are sermons, biographies, devotional tracts, and theological treatises. Men did not seem to have followed the nuns' practices of writing spiritual diaries expressing their inner struggles and their often visionary personal worlds.

This reconstruction of a general profile of lay brothers as men who rarely took center stage in the history of mendicant orders proposes to balance the view of men of the cloth in New Spain, which is often heavily tilted toward the "illustrious." Even the shortest biographical notes of lay brothers reveal efforts by the more educated clerical elite to prop up their figures as spiritual and morally edifying men and afford readers a view of the mendicant orders as an aggregate of men of various social categories that mirrored their own contemporary society. Biographers and chroniclers, as creators of a tradition, made sure that their chosen examples of lay brotherhood did not depart from spiritual and social orthodoxy. The majority of those chosen as exemplars were of peninsular birth, but this fact was not overstated by their biographers, who had the conviction that their subjects, having successfully acclimatized to Mexican society, were able to meet the devotional expectations of the people of New Spain. It is worthwhile to note that these peninsular men—who were the racial elite of their society—broke expectations when they embraced the role of social subordinates or manual laborers in their own communities as well as outside the convent.[116] The effect that their example may have had on the Indigenous, mestizos, and Blacks; the poor; the servants; and even the slaves they dealt with is neither quantifiable nor amenable to corroboration. Nonetheless, the sight of a member of the racial and social elite performing humble roles was what first impressed the Indigenous population about the early sixteenth-century missionary friars, and it remained a potential factor of loyalty to them that the chroniclers kept alive in their works. When chroniclers praised the role of lay brothers, they summarized the internal view of the orders about the men who voluntarily chose to remain in the lower echelon of the clerical hierarchy. In the hands of their biographers, lay brothers emerged as shining examples of what could be accomplished by the humble of society if they followed the teachings of the Church and their assigned role in life. They defined a down-to-earth religiosity that most uneducated people could understand and share by emulation.

Most lay brothers lived in relative tranquility. There was no need to challenge any institutional order because they were within the institution that offered them a decent living, spiritual support, and the opportunity to serve as role models for secular society. They were not expected to preach (even though some did, officially and unofficially), confess, or write on theological matters, but they earned respect by being members of the Church. Writing on the men who were their orders' own in-house labor force, chroniclers and religious authors extolled them because they remained exemplary in their dedication to their faith and in their willful acceptance of the obscurity of their lives. Lay brothers represented an alternative form of religious masculinity that served as a model for men of the lower social orders as well as a corrective example for those above them within the ambits of the Church itself. Historians of the orders helped memorialize this difference as an alternative and much-appreciated form of male spirituality It reminded readers and preachers of the equality of all souls before God.

4

Sexuality

The Treacherous Flesh

Chastity, understood as the abstention from exercising one's physical virility, was one of the three solemn vows a friar made at his formal profession. The renunciation of sexual activity did not mean the renunciation of manhood, but it did pose a behavioral challenge strong enough to become a test of the friar's character and his allegiance to the Church. To be sure, the other two vows, poverty and obedience, were considered as challenging as chastity and required the same dedicated exercise of the personal will. However, practicing chastity meant fighting the natural process of sexual maturation. The Catholic Church expected friars to exercise such control as part of a set of "heroic" virtues that defined the manhood of its members.

As distilled from the mendicants' chronicles and biographies, religious manhood meant a sustained capability to resist any temptation that would endanger the fidelity of men of the cloth to the vow of chastity. This vow denied the manly role of paterfamilias and also ran against the biblical mandate to multiply, found in the book of Genesis.[1] Since its earliest times, the Christian church had rejected eunuchs, welcoming only sexually capable men who were willing to accept restrictions on their physical virility. It was clearly understood by ecclesiastic and civil authorities that men of the cloth had the capacity to feel sexual desires, but they expected that the solemnity of the vow of celibacy, aided by personal will, fraternal advice, moral guidance, and the grace of God, could subdue sexual desire. To be a man of God meant to sacrifice sex for higher spiritual gains.[2]

The concept of celibacy began to develop in apostolic times, when patristic literature interpreted Jesus's advice to his married disciples to leave their wives and families to follow him as a call for celibacy. Scholars point to the fact that the early Christian Church admitted many married men as bishops and to other ecclesiastic ranks, but once they achieved those high positions, they were expected to abstain from sexual relations with their wives and stop begetting children. Many pushed back against celibacy before it eventually became a nonnegotiable obligation for both men and women joining the religious orders and the episcopal secular church.[3] After several centuries of circuitous development and struggle over its observance and enforcement, clerical celibacy was officially adopted by the Catholic Church at the Council of Trent (1545–63).[4] However, the adoption of an official position did not resolve the problem of how the spirit could completely control the flesh. Cases of secular and regular priests engaged in sexual relationships with secular women showed that the issue remained a constant discipline problem for the Church. With the transfer of Catholicism to Spanish America, it became an endemic problem in the New World too.

Sexual transgressions by members of the Church were aired at the ecclesiastical *audiencia* and the Inquisition. Regular orders had the right to deal with their own internal discipline, but the *audiencia* (also known as the *provisorato*) heard clerical criminal and civil cases such as, for example, priests involved in concubinage. The *provisorato* had no control over the Inquisition, which depended directly on the king and the Supreme Council of the Inquisition in Madrid, also known as La Suprema.[5] The Inquisition also addressed the cases of solicitation, which were a different form of sexual transgression, as explained below. This chapter focuses on cases of solicitation.

Before proceeding it is important to understand that sexual continence did not equate to virginity. Although some of the early fathers of the Church, such as Ambrose, favored virginity as the ideal religious state for Christian men and women, the early Church was more concerned with sexual abstention and celibacy for its clergy than with virginity itself.[6] Virginity was a preferred condition for women religious, but the Church also accepted many widows, and in regard to men, too many of them entered the church in their late twenties and thirties to expect a total lack of sexual experience. Virginity in men was regarded as a felicitous condition, a "special gift," resulting from a personal decision to preserve the body in its pristine state. Chroniclers and biographers of the Church had a special regard for virginity, which they considered one of the highest accomplishments of any man of the cloth, but they also acknowledged it was not for all.[7] The example of Augustine of Hippo, who spent his youth engaged in sensual pleasures and then renounced them, spoke of Christianity's flexibility to admit repentant souls and the importance of sexual continence *after* dedicating one's life to God. The writings of outstanding theologians and historians throughout time aimed at creating a model of masculinity compatible with the much-desired celibacy while not equating it with virginity. Thus historically, the Catholic Church's concept of religious manhood demanded the ability to control the body against the claims of the flesh, but it was not fixed on virginity.[8] However, although sexual control differentiated a cleric from a secular man, it took the Christian church centuries of dedicated effort to impose celibacy on its male membership.

Solicitation: Achilles Heel of Sacramental Integrity

Solicitation was not merely a transgression of the vow of celibacy; it was sexual behavior that offended one of the key sacraments of the Church, and as such, it was a greater offense than disrespecting celibacy. Besides settling the issue of clerical celibacy, the Council of Trent also reaffirmed the absolute value of the seven sacraments of the church.[9] As defined in the Catholic Church, the sacraments are rituals created by Jesus to ensure divine grace and share in God's own life. Such gifts from God must be treasured. The sacrament at risk by the act of solicitation was that of *penance*, which is a sacrament of healing, cleansing, and reconciliation with God after the confession of sins. Roman Catholic Christians had to confess their sins at least once a year, as determined by the Council of Trent. After confessing his or her sins, the penitent must express contrition and undergo a process of healing through a personal act of penitence. The feeling of remorse and shame created by sin is expiated through the suffering of the penitential act. Absolution administered by a minister of God would return the person to a state of grace and reinstate their ability to receive the body of Christ through Communion. The confessor, as a priest, is the only person authorized to listen to the confession, to judge the nature of the sins, to mete out the appropriate punishment, and to administer absolution. Thus confession, penitence, and absolution are intimately tied together in a dynamic process. A fault in the performance of even one of them invalidates the reconciliation with God.

Solicitation was defined as any action committed by a confessor to induce the penitent to commit libidinous acts (*ad turpia*) while engaged in the act of confessing the penitent's sins.[10] It was not a direct confrontation to the vow of celibacy, although it undermined it and could lead to a real transgression by the exercise of sex or the engagement in sexually charged activities. The libidinous thoughts and acts had to take place *during the act of confession*. The acts could be verbal communication, tactile advances, gestural suggestions, or *all of them together*. Also included in the definition of solicitation were lascivious conversations alien to the confession and aimed at exciting pleasure. The exchange of letters of amorous content or arrangements for trysts with the confessant were considered evidence of morally wrong activities defying the essence of the vow of chastity. These precise definitions of the physical circumstances of solicitation were legal but important technicalities that excluded many other forms of sexual misconduct from the definition of solicitation. For the theologians of the Church, the sexualization of the confessional process created an aberrant situation of deceit by the confessor and one of suffering, humiliation, and sorrow for the penitent, who, by not being able to receive absolution, forfeited the benefits of the sacrament of penance. When a confessor acted as a secular man and injected his speech and actions throughout the confession with meanings conducive to a sexual response from the penitent, he incurred solicitation and desecrated the sacrament. That was a "crime" that forced the investigation of the transgressor by the Tribunal of the Inquisition.[11]

In 1559 Pope Pius IV enacted the bull *Cum sicut nuper* defining solicitation and placing it under the jurisdiction of the Inquisition. The bull addressed acts leading to concupiscence during the act of confession and was a response to Protestant leaders' attack on the practice of confession. Under fire, it was imperative for the Catholic Church to address the problem of the corruption of a sacrament by the shady behavior of its priests.[12] The mendicant orders were brought under inquisitorial jurisdiction in 1592, when they were told that their hierarchy could not unilaterally judge the transgressions of their members against the sacraments. Friars were placed under inquisitorial jurisdiction when they acted as confessors. Papal attention to the circumstances of solicitation increased in the seventeenth century. In August 1622 Pope Gregory XV ruled against solicitants in the bull *Universi Dominici gregis*, which encouraged the faithful to denounce solicitants to the Inquisition and defined how to carry out the investigation. It also reiterated the definition of the act of solicitation as any request of a sexual nature not only at the moment and place of confession but immediately before and after it.[13] This additional precision expanded the power of the Inquisition and covered the cases in which the confessor knowingly avoided any insinuations during the act of confession but accosted his penitent before or after administering the sacrament. The process of describing all the nuances of solicitation did not end until 1741, when Benedict XIV issued the bull *Sacramentum poenitentiae*, which included any activity intended to elicit sexual thoughts or pleasure. More importantly, it forbade confessors to absolve their accomplices, a practice followed by many guilty confessors to exculpate the penitent and avoid any accusations.[14]

In 1571 Pedro Moya de Contreras arrived in Mexico as inquisitor general, and the tribunal was officially installed on November 4 of that year. Five years later, in 1576, the Mexican Inquisition received its first instruction on how to deal with solicitation cases.[15] Through the end of the sixteenth century and the first decade of the seventeenth century, the Inquisition received many denunciations, but they remained unresolved. The Holy Office was far more interested in prosecuting challenges to the orthodoxy of belief—such as blasphemy, undercover Judaism, bigamy, witchcraft, and any kind of superstitions—than the transgressions of the ministers of the faith.[16] By 1620, however, it became obvious that solicitation had become a serious problem. In that year the Holy Office had eighty-five incidents recorded in one "summary" of all cases since 1612, most of which had not been resolved.[17] In the following year, 1621, the inquisitors listed eighty-one cases of solicitants, only four of which were in the preceding 1620 list. New numbers proved a significant backlog of unattended denunciations. Such a large number of cases had not been registered before, and they could well indicate a moment of crisis in clerical moral behavior in the early seventeenth century. The regular orders were the leading culprits in this aberrant situation.[18]

Most of the cases listed for these years appear to be nonratified denunciations not leading to further investigation. One possible explanation is that the denouncers, led by their own conscience and prodded by their current confessors, were recalling solicitations that had taken place many years before. Such cases were unlikely to be prosecuted because outdated cases did not seem to have much merit for the inquisitors. However, such an impressive backlog suggests that the Inquisition either was not paying much attention to the conditions leading to denunciations, was lacking in resources to expedite them, or both. The orders were deeply embarrassed. One recorded request for relief from the weight of solicitation cases came

Table 1. Cases of solicitation before the Inquisition, Mexico, 1614–20 and 1621

	1614–20	1621
Franciscans	24	20
Dominicans	7	22
Augustinians	4	7
Other regular orders	36	22
Secular clergy	14	10
Total	85	81
Total for the three mendicant orders	35	49

Source: Created by the author based on AGN, Inquisition, vol. 334, exp. 2; and vol. 337, exp. 2. Some cases of unclear affiliations have been eliminated from this tally.

from Oaxaca, and it was signed by one Fr. Mateo de Porras (affiliation not stated) who begged mercy (*misericordia*) for the *solicitantes* of that region because of their large number.[19] Porras sent the paperwork for sixteen current and extant cases with a trusted brother in religion, pleading for a solution that would avert a scandal in town. The response was not as expected. Paying no attention to the request to preserve the honor (*honra*) of the friars, the official Inquisition's answer was that no mitigation should be used in dealing with the solicitants. The *one case* under examination at the time should continue, following the official proceedings.

A peak in the incidence of cases in the first two decades of the seventeenth century helps identify the contours of the crisis and the identity of the participants. The Franciscan order stood out as having the largest number of cases in the Inquisition's records, and that remained to be the case through the ensuing years. Although the order followed a meticulous process in the admission of novices, its inclination to admit men from all economic and social categories and its numerically large membership may explain the greater incidence of sexual slippage, but there is no conclusive explanation for this situation.[20] In his study of eighteenth-century solicitation cases, Jorge René González Marmolejo showed that Franciscans continued to lead in numbers, a situation that mirrored that of Spain.[21]

After this outburst of cases in the first decades of the seventeenth century, the number of denunciations and cases reviewed declined. For example, in a volume recording 331 extant inquisitorial denunciations investigated, mostly in 1650, only 5 cases dealt with solicitation.[22] A list of solicitation cases recorded between 1660 and 1727 shows cases dating back to 1660 that have never been addressed. Most cases were either "archived" or officially still waiting for some action from the local authorities or the Inquisition's own attorneys. Denunciations of the Inquisition were made by the "victims" of solicitation, their representatives, or the solicitants themselves, probably gnawed by their own conscience. If the victim or her witnesses did not appear before the Holy Office or its commissaries, there was no case. In rural areas "victims" had to wait for the visit of a commissioner, a person appointed by the Inquisition to initiate the process of accusation. Some suppliants waited for months or years to file a complaint because there was no official Inquisition agent available. If the aggrieved person lived far from the appointed visiting location, she could forfeit the inconvenience and cost of travel by simply not making any denunciation or not carrying out any follow-up. In 1727 some denounced solicitants were registered as already "dead."[23]

The number of solicitation cases, recorded or tried, declined significantly in the eighteenth century. A review of the cases in the Inquisition docket in the twenty-six volumes covering the 1770s and 1780s shows that of 577 expedients, or cases, only 39 addressed solicitations.[24] That was less than 1 percent. There were years with no solicitation recorded at all. It would be speculative and erroneous to conclude that solicitation was no longer a problem for the regular orders or the secular priesthood. Many cases were never recorded or tried, and while the Inquisition kept an eye on solicitants and filed and reviewed a significant number of cases, the prosecution of solicitants was not its priority.

Inquisitorial Procedure in Solicitation Cases

Solicitants were identified through denunciations that came from all over New Spain. Officials of the Inquisition, called commissaries, were deployed to key urban sites to receive denunciations and carry out the initial steps of the investigation at the local level. Once a file was assembled with all the required information, it was forwarded to the Inquisition's headquarters in Mexico City. The inquisitors assessed these denunciations in terms of credibility and the probability of proving the case. If there were sufficient grounds to make a case, one of the institution's attorneys (*fiscales*) called the plaintiffs and their witnesses to appear before its court, tell the story, and corroborate the facts and arguments in the denunciation. If the attorney was satisfied that there was a case, he then issued the *clamorosa*, or "request for the arrest, imprisonment, and questioning of the accused," who from that moment onward was called *reo* (accused prisoner).[25] The accused friar was given a legal assessor and was asked to remember and confess all the facts in his memory and tell the truth. He had three different opportunities to recall all the details of his connection with his confessants and tell the story from his viewpoint. Having gathered and studied the information in the friar's deposition and compared it to the facts in the denunciation, the attorney pressed formal charges if he saw evidence of a transgression. At this point the accused had the opportunity to accept the charges and confess or deny them and pursue his defense, either personally or assisted by an appointed lawyer. After a final review of the plaintiff's charges, the witness's depositions, and the solicitant's defense, the inquisitors passed a final judgment and its prescribed punishment.[26] There was no local appeal in Mexico. Only La Suprema, the Supreme Council of the Inquisition located in Madrid, had the right to modify the decisions of the local Inquisition tribunals, and that happened very infrequently. Processing cases at the Inquisition was slow, and any weakness in the procedure, such as the lack of witnesses, bode poorly for the case and explains the large number of cases that remained unresolved and were eventually shelved and forgotten.[27]

As a result of the complexities of the process, solicitation cases are often fragmented and incomplete. Historians have to work with denunciations without further inquiries, or with inquiries without resolution, or with the final review of a case without all the necessary preceding parts.[28] Even though sometimes incomplete, all records can be useful in assessing the human passions and social issues involved in such litigation. The morals of the clergy mattered to the Church and to the mendicant orders. The Holy Office and the regular orders took these cases seriously. Men of the cloth shaped the minds of the believers, and they were expected to observe and respect the ethical principles of the faith in their own lives. When they failed, at the most elementary level, to control their sexual urges, they tarnished the message they were assumed to convey. Mendicants, when they acted as priests, had absolute control of the sacramental process. Their authority was unquestioned, and as such, they became the real protagonists of this sad chapter in their orders' history.[29]

The Solicitants: A Human Profile

Solicitants were not the representatives of the clergy in general. The latter largely went about their pastoral duties without indulging the physical calls of their sexual virility. Even though they represented a numerical minority, however, solicitants created a serious personal and institutional discipline problem for the orders. At the root of the problem was the loneliness of men bound to sexual abstinence while men in society were free to exercise their manly physical roles. As moral and religious guides, confessors were in charge of regulating the sexuality of the rest of society and applying what was regarded as "medicine" for the souls of all sinners to restore them to the grace of God.[30] Friar confessors, also known as penitentiaries, were constantly listening to confessions concerning the sexual behavior of members of their flock, thus learning in depth about the broad catalog of human weaknesses that was meant for their ears only. This was a sacred mission but also a heavy burden for these men, and the Church itself had ruled that not everyone could assume it. The right to listen to confessions was reserved for mature men with a proven degree of knowledge in the penitential process and the tenets of moral theology who should be able to discern the good and the bad in human behavior and exercise their judgment appropriately and justly. Their own personal temperament and emotional and spiritual stability had to be exemplary to carry out such duties.[31] The secrets they learned from their penitents weighed heavily on their judgment, but learning about the secrets of those in their charge was never accepted as an attenuating circumstance for explaining their own misbehavior.

Solicitation began in the secrecy of the confessional, but solicitants came to be known fairly quickly in their respective communities, even though the scope of their activities was circumscribed to a relatively small number of parishioners. In colonial towns and cities, personal news circulated by word of mouth with considerable speed. Those involved either talked to family members, friends, and neighbors or unrelated individuals or gathered information by merely observing everybody else's behavior and passed the information around. Rumors eventually connected some confessors to "unusual" behavior in the confessional, and the presumed secrecy of their actions became common knowledge (*de voz pública*).[32] Once a solicitant was identified, he had two choices: self-denounce or wait until he was compelled to appear before the inquisitors and face charges. He could also bank on not

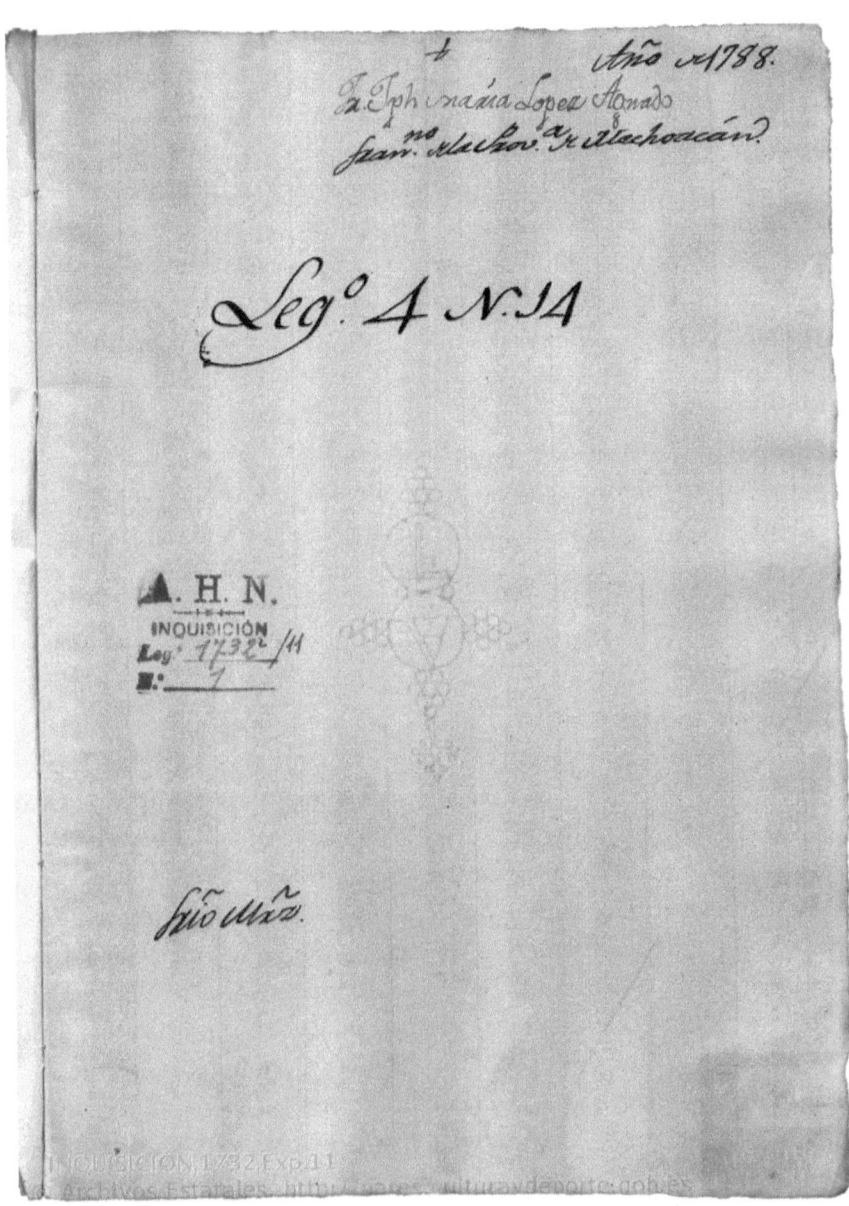

FIG. 15. *The Inquisition vs. Fr. Joseph María López Aguado, for Solicitation 1788.* Archivo Histórico Nacional, Spain.

being denounced at all. Self-denunciation was not an unusual choice. It was exercised mostly by older confessors troubled by doubts (*escrúpulos*) about their behavior who were hoping to reconcile themselves with the Church and God before they died. Alternatively, a confessor who suspected that an outside denunciation of his behavior was impending and knew his conduct was less than exemplary could preempt the process by self-denouncing. The act of volunteering the information before the inquisitors was regarded as the initiation of the process of contrition and penance for the accused and cast a positive light on the solicitant. The hope for a merciful judgment was in the minds of all self-accusers.

Even with the help of an appointed official lawyer, the solicitant had no better legal defense before the Holy Office than his own words, and it was crucial for him to use them appropriately and wisely. When moved enough by his own guilt, the friar made a first statement acknowledging his fault, thus initiating his own legal case but requesting forgiveness after penitence. Such was the 1713 case of Fr. Antonio de Luna, a Franciscan who was also the vicar, or overseer, of the nuns of Santa Clara in Mexico City.[33] He was fifty-two years old and made a deposition recalling incidents taking place thirteen years before, when he was in the prime of his manhood. He confessed to having carnal relations with a mestiza from the town of Otumba who washed his clothes. Implicit was his obvious attraction to her and her willingness to have sex with him, since no force was used. He had also sinned with a white woman who also was willing to engage in a relationship with him. Ironically, he declared that he had helped this second woman denounce another of her solicitants. The knowledge that she had been solicited by others could have opened a path to his own successful attempt with her. To be completely thorough, he also confessed to a third instance of kisses and petting with an obviously accommodating *mulata* in Atlixco. He definitely had a taste for a broad ethnic sampler of the female population. Fr. Antonio assumed that his "falls" had been a natural result of his being a sexually capable man. He repeated the phrase: it followed suit (*se siguió el efecto*) to indicate that his maleness had overcome him. This truncated process does not allow further analysis of the inquisitors' reaction to this case. Fr. Antonio may not have had to face an inquisitorial process. His acknowledged sexual activities were beyond the concern of the tribunal because they had not taken place *in the confessional*.

The solicitants who decided to "fight" their case before the inquisitors were quite often, although not always, guilty. A friar's motivation to rebut a case must have been his desire to remove any personal stain from his name and evade whatever punishment his own order may have imposed on him. It is not difficult to detect the arguments of a guilty solicitant. They would lie outright, pretend they could not remember, or shift the burden of guilt to their victim. They would resort to their own knowledge of moral theology to find arguments that would temper the guilt in their case. Knowing the terms of the papal bulls, they would argue that solicitation did not take place during the prescribed moments in the act of confession.[34] If admitting guilt, these solicitants typically represented themselves as being weak and vulnerable and having fallen to the temptations of their own flesh when their physical virility overpowered them. These were valid escape hatches provided by a religion that offered charitable forgiveness to the sincere repentant.[35] In 1758 Fr. Buenaventura Pérez was accused by three women: a young secular woman, a novice living in the convent of San Juan de la Penitencia in Mexico City, and a secular girl living in the convent of Santa Clara, also in Mexico City. As the process developed, a professed nun corroborated the testimony of the three women because she had also been a target of Fr. Buenaventura's attention. The weight of the accusations was heavy. In his role as confessor and within the space of the confessional, Fr. Buenaventura had requested that the women show him their breasts during their meetings as a form of "penitence" for their presumed sins and as a testimony of their willingness to obey him as their spiritual father. He told them that in following his request, they would be imitating Christ, who bared his breast to the bitterness of his suffering. One of the two secular women and one nun obeyed him, but the novice resisted and confided her situation to two other confessors. This led to the inquisitorial inquest. At that point, the friar decided to self-accuse and offer his own version of his behavior. He was forty-three years old and had been a teacher of male novices in the convent of San Diego in Puebla, and therefore he was acquainted with the tenets of moral theology. He did not deny the accusations. Rather, in exculpating himself, he insisted that he had not "solicited" the women. He was training them in spiritual perfection and testing their compliance with the vow of obedience. His duplicity was patent. He had instructed the novice not to talk about his demands to any other confessor, arguing that confessors had different methods for carrying out spiritual direction. His self-defense was totally disingenuous as a scurrilous attempt to escape a proven situation of solicitation.[36]

The assumption that accepting personal guilt and explaining shortcomings could elicit sympathy from the inquisitors also motivated the eventual confession of Fr. Francisco Testal, a forty-four-year-old Franciscan and custodian of the main convent of his order in the city of Guadalajara. In 1778 he was accused of solicitation by several women. When he learned that the Inquisition was investigating his behavior, he had the uncommon audacity to tell the women involved not to appeal to the Inquisition because "les había de ir mal a ambos" (it would bode badly for both of them). This was an open threat on his part to make them drop their case, and one that other guilty confessors used to instill fear in their accusers. Testal further explained to one of the women that his behavior had been "contingent" (to his duties) and tried to dissuade her from further action. However, this attempt to stop the inquisitorial investigation was ineffective because several other women were involved, and their confessors knew about his conduct. The Inquisition instructed confessors to encourage women to denounce solicitants, and they did. On one hand, confessors were entitled to withhold absolution from a victim of solicitation by another confessor if she did not denounce the solicitant. On the other hand, they could denounce the solicitor in their own name, hiding the name of the victims to avoid embarrassing them.[37]

In Testal's case, once the witnesses came forward, they corroborated the stories of the solicited women. As it happened, witnesses stated that Testal had a reputation for lascivious comments in the confessional. Public knowledge of his trait was another form of evidence accepted by the Inquisition. When Testal self-denounced, even the Inquisition's attorney considered his behavior prompted not by true repentance but by the irrefutable strength of the denunciations, and he ordered the friar's incarceration in the Inquisition's jail. When, during his trial, he was first asked if there were other instances of solicitation he could remember, he stated he could not remember well other personal negligence (*descuidos*). Eventually, and while waiting for further depositions, he "refreshed" his memory and added information voluntarily. In his own account, Testal freely admitted to and discussed two sexual engagements with women in March 1778. One of them was with a married woman. The woman's own testimony corroborated that she had gone voluntarily to his cell hoping for "help," since he had previously given her money for shoes. Once there, they had consensual sex. A woman from the town of Cocula, who had met him in the premises of the church, declared that after feigning a confession in the confessional, they went to his cell, where they engaged in sex. She was not one of his spiritual daughters and was repaid with some stockings. Several Spanish men who were also called to serve as witnesses disclosed that Testal was in the habit of giving small gifts to his "targeted" women, although he did not have sex with all of them.

Despite his attempt to manipulate the information, in October 1783 Testal was perpetually deprived of the right to confess men and women and was banned from the courts of Madrid and Mexico and any location within twenty leagues of Cocula for three years. He fought back. Shortly after his conviction and sentence, which he took with recorded outward signs of repentance and humility, Testal appealed to the bishop of New Galicia, arguing that the banishment from the confessional tarnished his own public "honor" and that of his order. He begged to have his confessional rights restored, claiming there was a scarcity of confessors in the area.[38] By August 1784 Testal had decided to appeal to the Supreme Council of the Holy Office in Madrid. His prelate had him serve in the infirmary to "dissimulate" his public absence from the confessional while his appeal ran its course. To remove him from the public eye, the Franciscan order sent him to Michoacán with the acquiescence of its bishop, and once there he was restored the right to confess by a decision of his own Franciscan prelate, who interpreted the ban as lasting for only three years. By sending a convicted solicitant away to another jurisdiction, the Franciscan order helped him manipulate the terms of his sentence and protected its own public image. The Franciscan order requested a clarification of Testal's residence and status, since he could be a potential candidate for office in the convent. In 1786 the Holy Office in Mexico City clarified that his ban from the confessional had been *in perpetuity*. In January 1787 Testal begged the Inquisition for mercy. He felt "hurt in his heart" by its decision. An inquisitorial conviction did not end the personal career or ambitions of a determined friar, especially if he expressed his deepest regrets. In Testal's case, the hope for a restoration of the right to confess and become an active member of his order and convent was based on precedent. Fr. Joaquín Perdomo, a Franciscan of the discalced San Diego branch, was successful in obtaining the restitution of his rights to perform the Mass and confess men because of the scarcity of friars in the area of Zacatecas. He was granted his request six years after his conviction for solicitation in 1763.[39] In 1804, the Franciscans of the Colegio de Propaganda Fide in Pachuca requested the rehabilitation of Fr. Antonio de Alva, who had been perpetually prohibited from confessing men and women after having been convicted for solicitation in 1790. In 1803 the Inquisition had restored his permission to confess men, but it had declined his petition to confess women.[40] His order requested his rehabilitation for all confessions on the grounds of being unable to meet the demand for confessions due to the shortage of confessors. We have no information on the outcome of Testal's request, but in theory, he could have been restored the full privilege of confession.

Ultimate Seducers: The Dynamics of Solicitation
Unlike some of the late sixteenth and early seventeenth-century records, which are either scant in information or truncated, some complete eighteenth-century records unveil the reality of sexually aggressive friars. These records also allow us to calibrate the dynamics of solicitation, as they reveal how the solicitors operated and how willing and unwilling women reacted to their advances. Some of the most stunning cases of solicitation took place in the outer geographical limits of urban Mexico, in areas still considered missionary grounds with a limited history of established Catholicism and few appointed inquisitorial officials. Among such cases was that of Fr. Francisco Conlon, one of the Spanish-born missionaries in the Colegio de Propaganda Fide in Querétaro and one of the worst sexual offenders in the records of the eighteenth-century Inquisition.[41] First denounced as a solicitant in 1777, his case was investigated through the 1790s, when he finally gave a full account of his life and activities to the Holy Office.[42] Originally from the Franciscan convent in Burgos, he served in frontier missions as well as in local missions in the province of Michoacán. He also held the post of commissary of missions in Coahuila. After ten years of service with the college, he asked to return to Spain but changed his mind and affiliated with the Franciscans of Guadalajara in 1779, serving as guardian of the convent in Ahualulco. He returned to the Querétaro college in 1782, serving in their regional missions among the Catholic population. In 1788 he quit again. He then stayed with the Franciscans of Michoacán at Valladolid and lived for a year and a half in Pátzcuaro. In May 1790 he was elected guardian of the convent of Valladolid. In other words, he held positions of administrative

and spiritual responsibility for a long time in several Franciscan convents. Whether his brothers in religion were acquainted with his improper sexual life remains unclear, but it seems highly unlikely that the community never heard about his exploits.

Conlon's active participation in the Propaganda Fide college's urban missions gained him access to and authority over women. As a confessor he could choose his targets. In his confession before the Inquisition, he admitted to having contact with forty-two women, although the Inquisition's prosecutor deposed only twenty-one witnesses. With few exceptions, all his targets were women of Spanish descent of middle social rank in the area of Michoacán, as they and their families received the treatment of dons and doñas. Only six women belonged to other ethnic affiliations and none was Indian. Most of them were also reputed to be *doncellas*, presumed virgins in good standing among the Spanish population, and their ages ranged from thirteen to their midthirties. They came from Querétaro and several small towns visited by Conlon, such as Jacoma and Sayula. The familiarity between the friar and the women cited in his legal case resulted from the women's repeated visits to the confessional, where they engaged in long conversations totally unrelated to the confession. During these exchanges Conlon utilized several techniques to seduce what appears to have been his sometimes eager accomplices. Conlon's prodigious memory supplied details about what happened in the confessionals when, as a solicitant, he met a potential target. His confession maps his personal indulgence in his own sexual desires and the means he used to accomplish his objective when he met an obliging partner. Some of the women involved with the friar seemed to have been naive about sexual knowledge but eager to engage in an opaque relationship with him to learn more about sex.[43] Others went further and were willing to engage in a sexual relationship with the friar. Among the complicit and naive but eager to learn about the facts of life was Maria Antonia de Fuente, twenty-three years old at the time of her deposition. She must have met Conlon during one of the college's "missions" to strengthen the faith among the Catholic population. After their acquaintance their "relationship" must have been rather short. While at the confessional, Conlon explained to her how women became pregnant, how they gave birth, and how they could satisfy themselves when their husbands were away. He also told her how to verify if she was still a virgin. She consulted him about some menstrual problems, a matter certainly unrelated to her spiritual needs, and he prescribed a medication. Maria Antonia flirted with him, claiming to be jealous of other women and asking him to return to her town so that they could see each other again. Although he tried to arrange for a tryst with her, he claimed he had not succeeded. Since "missions" lasted only a few days, this type of relationship had to be rather fleeting but could have been satisfying if the friar was simply pursuing the erotic nature of a fast encounter.

He was sexually more successful with others. Maria Jacinta Petra, a resident of Querétaro, still a self-declared *doncella* at age forty-seven, approached the friar seeking some financial help. She subsequently received him in her house on several occasions, had intermittent sexual relations with him, and lodged him in her house on the couple of occasions he visited Querétaro and did not want to stay at the college. María Antonia Cobián, a twenty-year-old *soltera* and therefore not reputed to be a virgin, visited him in his cell at night to have sex with him. She later told him that she had experienced physical sexual pleasure just talking to him in the confessional and was jealous of another woman who claimed that the friar favored her. Margarita Ojeda y Parra and her sister Rosalía, also of Querétaro, arranged trysts and sex with the friar. Their brother had a respectable social position, being an official scrivener in the city. Margarita's first encounter with Conlon was in 1773, and ten years later, she welcomed him back when he returned to the city. She remained loyal to him and refused to give any testimony to the inquisitors. These were not the only sisters who became the objects of Conlon's attention. Anna Josefa and Juana Josefa Carranco enticed him, and both engaged in heavy petting with the friar, who described these activities as impure touching, "tocamientos impuros." Ignacia Sánchez Cosío, the twenty-year-old sister of a priest, also willingly engaged in heavy petting, and he paid her back with a rosary, chocolate, cigarettes, and other small "favors." Jacinta Rivera, one of the few mestiza women in his coterie, seems to have actually sought him out, asking him to "visit" her, as he did other women in Querétaro. By all indications, Conlon operated freely among the city's respectable families, and women were receptive to whatever personal charms he must have had.

Fr. Francisco's modus operandi was to engage the confessant in conversation in the confessional several times until he could ascertain if she would be willing to engage in a relationship. He repeatedly assured the Holy Office that he did not confess them and, therefore, had not breached the sacrament of penance. The women knelt and pretended to confess for half an hour, and he made the presumed final gestures of blessing and absolution for the potential witnesses. Once he was hopeful of a positive response, he asked the women to request a confession at home, pretending they were ill. When he arrived, accompanied by the usual brother in religion, his companion would stay in a room with the relatives of the "sick" woman while he carried out his ministrations behind closed doors. He would stay in the room with his accomplice for about half an hour, enough time to have sex. He later described the farce as "prostituting themselves in the act" while his religious companion was duped by believing that he had actually confessed the woman. Several of his sexual partners did not bother to pretend to be sick. They made their private arrangements with female procuresses who supplied a "safe" room for the encounter. Did he force himself on any woman? María Ignacia Gutiérrez must have been between thirteen and fifteen years old when she began confessing with him during a Propaganda Fide mission in the town of Zamora. In both his and her words, he attempted to rape her in the sacristan's house, and only her firm refusal saved her from that fate. In a strange twist to her story, Conlon advised a criollo hacienda owner, Don Manuel Mariscal, to marry María Ignacia. The marriage took place, and in 1787 Conlon stayed in the couple's hacienda. During that stay Conlon accosted María Ignacia and another woman staying in the house, seeking embraces and physical petting.

 Conlon did not respect married women if they were willing to engage in sexual activities with him. When he served in Sinaloa, he had sexual relations with several Spanish *mayordomas*, or "housekeepers," of the missions of Cumuripa, Opodepe, and Río Grande. While serving as guardian at the convent in Ahualulco (near San Luis Potosí) in 1781, he had relations with two married women, Manuela Peralta and Ignacia Valdés. He claimed he had problems with another Franciscan brother who was also involved with the same women, and he decided to leave the convent to avoid further confrontations. One Josefa Pérez had sex with him before and after her marriage and after she became a widow. He also recalled calling a widow of easy virtue to the college one night when he felt desperately assailed by sexual urgings. He stated that his night visitor was also engaged in a similar relation with another friar. He also confessed to relations with the cook and her aide in the convent of Pátzcuaro in 1788. Josefa Macías, who lived with her aunt, a Franciscan *beata*, followed him during his mission stint and had several sexual encounters with him in Tangancicuaro and La Piedad in the mid-1780s.

Conlon had competition as a master seducer in Fr. Francisco Castellanos, a Mexican-born Franciscan. He was presumed to be a respectable member of the community. He was a commissary of the Third Order and a chaplain of the Indian nuns of Corpus Christi in Mexico City.[44] Castellanos confessed to nineteen cases of solicitation, which involved rape as well as consensual sex. Like Conlon, most of his partners were of Spanish descent and in their twenties. Castellanos enticed many of the women to a small room adjacent to the sacristy of the church of the Third Order, to which he had easy access. When he was successful, the women willingly accompanied him to his room or asked him to visit them in their homes. Castellanos was an aggressive seducer who did not hesitate to use force to make his advances. He confessed to having raped at least two women and attempted to force himself on several others who succeeded in escaping. After forcibly seducing one woman in her own house, they continued to see each other for months. Despite his crude and direct style, women flocked to him to confess their "temptations against chastity." There might have been an "underground" word of mouth about him that made him dangerously attractive. As the women confessed, he learned about their lives and deeds and uncovered clues about what sexual strategies he could follow to achieve full carnal relations. Given the voyeuristic details of the inquisitorial depositions, we learn that he questioned one of his regular spiritual daughters during "confession" about her orgasms. This particular woman learned from a friend that Fr. Francisco had asked her the same questions. However, with other confessants he acted properly during confessions, asking them to visit him in his private room for sexual purposes after the process ended. Among other acts, he confessed to administering physical discipline to a woman in his cell, enjoying the view of her rear and engaging in other activities of "excessive lust." He was sure to state that he did not administer Communion or absolve her, thus pretending to evade the definition of solicitation. In at least one instance, he suffered the physical attack of a despondent and jealous lover, who, brandishing a razor blade, tore his cape and his habit. Because of the obvious public nature of this man's philandering, he was eventually convicted by the Holy Office.

Solicitation was also a problem in the sparsely populated far north and small towns in the outlying areas of Jalisco and Michoacán. Although the recorded cases are fewer because the venues for denouncing solicitations were very limited, all the human factors defining solicitations come together in one thoroughly documented case against Franciscan Manuel Cadaval, a native of Galicia and member of the Colegio de Propaganda Fide of Our Lady of Guadalupe in Zacatecas. His presence at the Inquisition of Mexico City was prompted by a long history of irregular behavior at the presidio of Las Nutrias, later incorporated into the presidio of Santa Cruz Terrenate, where he carried out many solicitations spiced with testimonies of sodomy and alcohol addiction.[45] Given the physical distance, this case took seven years from inception to conviction. The inquisitorial probe unveiled a man with an irregular history as a friar with an obdurate will to deny the truth. He attempted twice to profess as a Carmelite in Puebla (1751 and 1757) but was expelled as a novice in 1758 under suspicion of sodomy with a lay brother. He moved north and was admitted and given profession in the Colegio de Propaganda Fide of Our Lady of Guadalupe in Zacatecas in 1764. He served in the Tarahumara missions for two years until 1771, when, owing to mutual dissatisfaction, he left the college and was admitted to the Franciscan convent of Zacatecas. After mission service in Mezquital, Sombrerete, and Chihuahua, he was appointed chaplain of the presidio of Las Nutrias and retained that position when the presidio changed location and name. The presidio was a small community, and the gossip about the confessors' proclivities and sexual activities, some of which had been carried out during confession, spread easily. The presidio population was obliged to suffer the behavior of the only man available for their spiritual needs.[46]

Cadaval's inquisitorial process began in 1785 at the insistence of a twenty-two-year-old illiterate married woman, a member of the Santa Cruz de Terrenate presidio in today's Arizona. The final sentence was issued in 1792. The witnesses involved were interrogated at least three times in a long process filled with convoluted details provided by many presidio witnesses, such as soldiers, officers, day laborers, and their female relatives. There were rumors that Cadaval had attempted to rape some Indian women in Arizpe, Sonora. There was also a boy who was willing to accuse the friar of sodomy. Cadaval proved to be a stubborn witness who denied or tried to whitewash all the cases brought against him. He had lived with several women in the presidio, including the one who became his first accuser. He had officiated at her marriage and had sexual relations with her shortly after the wedding. Another witness was the husband of a woman who had an illicit friendship with the friar. Yet another husband, Jacinto Montano, officially accused Cadaval of soliciting his wife and claimed that his first denunciation had not been taken seriously by the bishop of Sonora. During the Inquisition's investigation, Juan de Santiesteban, another Franciscan ministering in the mission of Cocospera (Sonora), was willing to inform that Cadaval had obtained his post in the presidio through the influence of officers of the secular government despite the fact that the Franciscan order had the lowest opinion of his ministry. The presidio military officers had received many complaints about him and wished to see this "lost lamb" removed from their premises, but they had been unable to do so, and he remained in his post due to his personal connections.

By 1789 his repeated trespasses, which included revealing the secrets of confession, prompted the inquisitorial wheels to begin turning. A brother in religion asked the governor of the Custody of San Carlos, in Sonora, to recommend that he be readmitted at the Propaganda Fide in Querétaro to save him from his own misdeeds. He was rejected by the Franciscans of Zacatecas, and when Colonel Manuel Echegaray supported all statements against the friar, Cadaval left the presidio and took refuge in a hacienda near the mining town of Indé (Durango) while seeking the protection of the bishop of Sonora. At that point the provincial of the Franciscan order intervened, and the bishop let Cadaval go. The Franciscan provincial of Zacatecas sent him to the Inquisition in Mexico City, where he arrived in March 1790 to be jailed at the Inquisition's premises. The review of his case involved twenty witnesses. His fabrications to cover his behavior did not prevent his eventual conviction. Ironically, the Holy Office sent him to the Colegio de Propaganda Fide in Querétaro to serve his sentence. The order could not rid itself of its own rotten apple.

Seduction by Women?

The seduction of a friar by a cunning woman was theoretically acknowledged by the moral theologians who had to consider the potential innocence of a man of the cloth suffering a vindictive accusation. However, was an "innocent" seduction possible? Some theologians argued that in sexual matters, "seduction" could not be "innocent," since physiologically, a man needed arousal to be "forced" into a sexual act. No case has been found, so far, to prove the *unwilling* physical surrender of a friar to a woman. On the other hand, the stories of successful seducers such as Francisco Conlon, Francisco Castellanos, and Manuel Cadaval corroborate that there were women who welcomed consensual relationships with men of the cloth. Concubinage with secular priests was hardly a novelty in the viceroyalty or in Spain, and it is not surprising to find friars in similar situations given the availability of willing women.[47] Women who engaged in sexual encounters with mendicants often began the relationship by having conversations about their sexual feelings or exchanging suggestive letters with their confessors.[48] They did not hesitate to be with the friar in either his quarters or their own homes and were not sexually innocent. As already seen, the most successful seducers found many women willing to return to the confessional to prolong a relationship on slippery personal and spiritual grounds and did not show much regret for their conduct in their depositions.[49]

In 1757 Ana María Olmedo, a married woman, denounced Franciscan Joseph Ganacia for solicitation. However, under questioning, she freely acknowledged that she feigned being sick to have a confessor come to her home. Were they acquainted before? Was she attracted to him or vice versa? Gaps in the information leave us wondering about the dynamics of this relationship. The friar and the woman spent well over half an hour alone behind closed doors and prolonged the stay for another hour after he asked for a candle for the room. She later claimed that he climbed into her bed "and asked for kisses and embraces," and she was unsure if those were "dishonest actions." He disputed her version. It was all "in jest," and there was no sex. They had simply spent a good time talking.[50] Why did she denounce him to the inquisitors if she acknowledged she was not sick and obviously was intent on seducing him? The complexities of her motivation leave much room for speculation, but she obviously felt some religious concern and remorse. Fr. Joseph had knowingly entered her room and spent time with her and was aware of her deceit. If the judges of the Holy Office had any concerns about his conduct, they followed the legal path to dismiss this case as not belonging to their purview, since there had been no confession involved.[51] This decision could have applied to yet another case in which a "worried" Dominican friar from the convent of Santa Cruz in Zacatecas penned a letter to the Holy Office to find out if he was liable to be regarded as a solicitant.[52] He had been called to the home of a woman to confess her because "she was sick." The first time he had good grounds to doubt that she was sick at all, he wrote, and did not go. On a second call from the woman, there was no request for confession, although he assumed there was. He "reprehended" her for using a pretext to give in to her passions. Nonetheless, he writes, "as the subject was so competent, and I in danger," a dishonest act followed up. His main concern was not over the fact that he had engaged in sex but whether others could have assumed that he went into the room to confess the woman. He stated that when he went in, he did not state publicly, in front of the servants, that he intended a confession. Thus he assumed that the sexual engagement did not make him liable for solicitation. Breaking his vow of celibacy was not as disturbing as breaking an inquisitorial edict about a sacrament, and he wished to be reassured about his status. No answer from the Inquisition is recorded, and probably there was none. As long as the sacrament of penance was not involved, the Holy Office had no control or jurisdiction over the sexual behavior of a friar, let alone over women who were willing to entice and have sexual encounters with members of the Church.

Women were attracted to some friars for personal and economic reasons. Despite constant indoctrination on the subject of carnal sins, some women were ready to believe and to argue that to have carnal communication with a man of the cloth was not a mortal sin. Two women were denounced to the Inquisition in 1650 for making such statements.[53] Previously, in 1612, Franciscan Fr. Alonso Cortés was denounced for stating that a woman did not sin if she had carnal knowledge with a clergyman.[54] Women who became involved with a friar for whom they had developed a physical attraction, if not desire, were not victims of solicitation. They were open to it and embraced the experience, feeling flattered to be the object of attention of a man with social and religious authority. He could provide her with not just some income but personal sexual satisfaction. For their part, solicitants were able to assess the circumstances of a potential seduction and followed what may be understood as a "courting" protocol with receptive women. They approached women, telling them that if they were willing to "be their friends" or "serve them," they would provide for them. This was tempting enough for an improvident woman such as Juana Ramos, a thirty-year-old *castiza* widow living in Querétaro, who engaged in a long relationship with Franciscan Fr. Juan Gutiérrez. She was married when they began their relationship, and they saw each other while her husband was away. Sometimes she visited him at night in the convent, leaving her baby with a compliant friend. How she accessed his cell is left unsaid. Surprisingly, she had another relationship with another friar of the same convent, a fact that was discovered during the investigation. Her relationship with Fr. Juan was deemed "public and notorious," and the Franciscan order had not done anything to stop it.[55] Another woman, Juana Gertrudis Leite, a resident in Quautla Amilpas, received visits from Fr. Manuel Popado, a Franciscan from the convent of Churubusco of the province of San Diego de Alcalá. He was her confessor and, presumably, also a friend. She had confessed to having inappropriate thoughts about a person like him, and he suspected she would welcome his advances. He advised her to fire a young male servant on the grounds that her niece's reputation could be tarnished by his presence in the house. This left the home without any potential witnesses or male protection. She was aware of his intentions, as she later confessed, and eventually during one of his visits when she was alone in the house, she "condescended" to his desire, led by what she described as "her own fragility."[56] This was a case of mutual seduction. Popado self-accused of this relationship, but there is no outcome, since the case is incomplete.

Beyond proving their unbridled sexuality, some friars' precise recollections before the Inquisition revealed the latent sexuality of many single, married, and widowed women. The line of demarcation between seduced and seducer was thin. The confessional gave those women inclined to enter a relationship with a confessor a special and somewhat secluded space to engage in conversations with a man willing to prove his sexual prowess and who could arrange trysts to satisfy their mutual desires. Seducing and being seduced by a man of the cloth must have been a risky but acceptable experience for single women with limited marital prospects in small towns or who were in dire economic straits. Maintaining a public reputation as *doncella* did not deny the existence of lust or the desire for a man's attention; it simply meant not to be discovered while engaging in covert relationships.[57] María Dolores Mota, a nineteen-year-old self-declared and improvident *doncella*, followed the lure of Fr. Ginés de la Cerda to his cell, where on several occasions they committed *torpezas*, a euphemism for "sexual acts," for which he used to give her one peso or four reales once in a while.[58] She remained a public *doncella* for the townspeople. Her case leads to the consideration of poor women who may have entered into a relationship not simply for the sake of being desired but for economic reasons. María Josefa Malaviar, a very poor single woman of twenty-one, was hoping that Fr. Juan Antonio Pico would give her a letter of recommendation so that she could become a servant to a nun in the convent of Regina Coeli. Before he gave her the letter, he twice touched her all over and incited her to give him pleasure.[59] Fr. Agustín Sánchez told a poor and orphaned thirty-one-year-old woman that he was willing to pay her rent and help her if she was willing to become his lover. He further stated he did not want "dry love" (*amores secos*), but her refusal to be deflowered led him to change his terms. He was willing to settle down to visits at her home with "petting" privileges. She still refused, and there was never any economic "help" forthcoming.[60]

The Solicited Speak Out

Whether accomplices or real victims of the sexual misconduct of confessors, women had the opportunity to speak out and gain a voice in a process that had involved them in such an intimate and personal way and in situations that were heavily weighed against them. Those targeted by solicitants were a microuniverse of womanhood: married, single, widowed, and even professed nuns.[61] They were urban and rural residents, and of all ages, although younger single women had a numerical edge over older married women. Civil status was not a determinant in the eyes of the solicitants, but social class and race were. There are fewer Indian, Black, or racially mixed women in the official records. Women of affluent means never appear in these cases, largely because they were well protected by their families and were rarely disrespected by men. Most solicitants knew their boundaries and focused on those women who could yield to their power and social authority: the young and poor, those without male protection, orphans, widows without strong family ties, or women living together in female-headed households. Some bold solicitants took risks and approached women in their own homes under the noses of their relatives and even husbands. This was possible because friars visited many homes in socially acceptable "courtesy" visits.[62] Franciscan Fr. Francisco Alva repeatedly visited a woman whom he was trying to seduce in her own home. He was not confessing her during his "courtship," but he pretended to be her confessor precisely to avoid any suspicion from her husband and have the freedom to see her personally in her house. Eventually, she declined his proposal.[63]

For a woman to be taken seriously in the denunciation of a solicitant, she had to be held in good moral standing. The sexual desires of women of good reputation were a private issue; their social reputation was something else. The majority of the women who reported cases of solicitation had to be deemed to be "decent" or respectable. As part of the pretrial inquiries, inquisitors requested reports on the character of the women denouncing solicitants in order to establish their credibility. While some women were amenable to seduction, others found sexual advances in the confession undesirable and reprehensible. They could be illiterate (even those of better families), but they were well indoctrinated in their Christian catechism. Instruction in the key principles of the faith was probably the only form of education some of them had received. They became targets precisely because they were fulfilling their expected spiritual duties of confession and reconciliation. In rural areas many women confessed only once a year, as prescribed by the Church, and usually around Lent. However, in smaller towns, women attended church as an important part of their "public" activities and confessed frequently, creating opportunities for potential solicitants.

Women who rejected solicitations reported to have been surprised and shocked or outright angry when they found libidinous words instead of spiritual consolation.[64] Those who were perturbed or even scared by the words of the confessor tried to evade any verbal confrontation with the solicitant and remained confused about the behavior of a man they were educated to respect. A few women seemed to have been naive enough to mistake the solicitant's request for another encounter elsewhere as part of the process of penitence, or so they declared. It is possible that some of these women were intentionally evasive when facing the naked gaze of the inquisitors. However, we must remember that some of the targeted women were socially unsophisticated and did not know how to challenge the word of a man, especially a man of authority as their confessor. This is how we can explain the case of fourteen-year-old Maria Manuela Calvillo, a resident of a ranch near Guadalajara, who went to confession at the Franciscan convent of the town of Temaztlan with her mother and two other women. After having confessed her, the confessor asked her to stand by his cell and wait for him until he finished other confessions. Once he returned, he took her into his cell and, after a few minutes, kissed her and suggested she stay overnight to sleep with him. She refused, and nothing else happened. This took place around 1792, and the case was posted before the commissary of Guadalajara *by order of another confessor* in 1798.[65] This lapse of time was not extraordinary in rural areas, given the scarcity of clergy and the difficulties of contacting the right ecclesiastical authorities. The girl and her family moved residence, possibly to avoid any scandal for an issue that was no longer relevant to them. Her case had very little chance of getting the attention of the Holy Office because she had not been solicited during confession.[66]

Some women were determined to denounce the advances of solicitants. They knew no moral theology but understood that the confessor's conduct was wrong. Among them was Juana de la Cruz, an Indian who, during the Lent season of 1622, was solicited by a young Franciscan after she had begun her confession. She quickly shamed him by reminding him that his profession was to confess and pardon sins rather than inciting them, and she questioned him about holding the holy sacrament in his hands during Mass when he behaved so shamefully in the confessional. This unexpected reply startled the friar, who immediately absolved her and let her go. However, Juana felt that her confession had been imperfect, and after describing her case to a Jesuit priest, she gave him permission to denounce her case, as he did.[67]

The Lent season was a propitious time for solicitants to approach women. In 1650, a woman described as *mulata ladina*—that is, astute and understanding the predominant Spanish culture—by the name of Ana María appeared before the commissar of the Holy Office in Cuautla Amilpas to inform him of an incident taking place one year before, during the Lent season. She prefaced her declaration by telling him that cases of solicitation were "public and notorious" in the church of Santo Domingo of the town of Calvario de Santiago (Guanajuato). She accused Fr. Raymundo Vallejo, a resident of the convent, of bluntly asking her, before starting confession, if she wished to have a "friendship" with him because he liked her very much. Ana Maria quickly answered, "No, because I behold you in the place of God while you are occupying that seat." The irate woman stood up and left. She found another confessor and finished her confession. On returning home she told her mother what had transpired but told no one else. This humble woman used the indoctrination she had received as a means of self-defense. Ana

Maria's statement was an attempt to exonerate herself from any possible suspicions due to her ethnicity, since *mulatas* were thought of as inclined to lust.[68] Other rebukes illustrate how women deflected unwanted solicitations. María Ramos was a young woman living in the house of the administrator of the properties of a Guanajuato mine. Sometime in late 1649, after confessing with Augustinian Fr. Joseph Galarza, he asked her if she wished "to serve him." Maria cut him off by telling him she was a *doncella* and had gone to the church only to confess. Agustina de Hinojosa, a mestiza resident of the *doctrina* of Tepaczingo, had a similar experience with Fr. Francisco Muñoz, who asked her if she wished to communicate with him and have him as a friend after asking if she had any illicit friendship with any man. She stood up to leave, but the friar begged her to continue her confession. Dissatisfied with her experience, she contacted another confessor.[69] These women gave simple but effective answers to cut the friars short and avoid solicitation. With a few sentences, they recorded their determination to maintain clean consciences and save their reputations. When they rejected and denounced solicitors, they were following the church's own instructions.

The victims of solicitation were targets because of their age and lack of experience with how to face the authority of a man of the cloth.[70] Indians were not under the purveyance of the Inquisition. Despite this important technical exclusion, Indian women appear frequently in solicitation cases from the late sixteenth century through the first quarter of the seventeenth century, especially in areas such as Yucatán, where the majority of the population was Indigenous and suspected of not knowing how to confess well and given to perjury. The personal opinions of confessors about solicitation are very hard to detect. In a rare instance of personal frankness, in 1622 Dominican Fr. Juan Bautista de Orozco advised Fr. Alonso Onrrubia that in Spain, some theologians were of the opinion that in cases of solicitation, the Inquisition should take into consideration the *calidad* (ethnic and social status) of the witnesses, citing one "Báñez" as his authority. He was possibly referring to Domingo Báñez, a distinguished theologian of the period.[71] Fr. Juan Bautista advised Fr. Alonso that if a confessor solicited an Indian woman, there was no need for another friar to denounce the transgressor to the Holy Office. He should absolve the woman and advise his brother in religion in a fraternal manner. Otherwise, the entire order, rather than the delinquent individual, would bear the "infamy" of the accusation.[72] This advice was apparently recorded in a letter originating in Mexico and circulating among some Dominicans in Guatemala. This message was contrary to the directives of the Inquisition. Although no resolution is available, the disturbing opinion held by some confessors on the validity of Indian witnesses' words casts doubts on the availability of justice to Indigenous women involved in cases of solicitation.[73] It also reveals the complicity of some friars in keeping solicitation cases under the radar of the Inquisition's attention to save the reputation of their order. The problem seems to have been more acute in areas with a large Indian population, such as Yucatán and Chiapas, where the suspicion about the veracity of women's accusations remained an issue well into the seventeenth century.[74] Some cases of solicitation of Indian women are reported into the nineteenth century, but they were in numerical decline from the mid-seventeenth century onward, suggesting that other ethnicities became more attractive to potential solicitants.[75]

Despite their lack of social leverage, some Indian women resisted as much and as well as they could and, most importantly, rose to the occasion by denouncing the aggressor. In 1581, in the distant area of Colima, ten Indian women accused Fr. Francisco Villalba, who supervised several Franciscan *doctrinas*, of attempting to force himself on them, having succeeded in at least one case.[76] They claimed that Villalba used the obligation to confess during Lent to insinuate sexual advances on them, even pushing some of them on the floor if they resisted his tactile exploration of their bodies. The women resisted and, for the most part, escaped from this physical abuse, but one of them stated she had been raped. She declared she had been called to the convent after having rebuffed the friar's first approach and was afraid of refusing the call. When she entered his cell, the friar pushed her to the floor and raped her. Another woman also confessed to having had sex with the same friar—whether she was willing is not clear—but the rest of this group of witnesses were scandalized by his words and physical contact in the confessional. In their own declarations, the women said they left frightened (*espantadas*) by the man after having refused his requests. These were not false allegations. The Franciscan order had been informed of this friar's behavior, and being unable to control him, it hoped that the Inquisition could resolve his case. Facing the inquisitor's attorney, Villalba confessed to the veracity of the accusations, which were supported by the testimony of male Indian representatives of the community. Villalba begged for a merciful punishment. The attorney verbally lashed him and gave him the strongest punishment he could mete out by divesting him of his right to confess and expelling him from his *doctrina*. The Franciscan order accepted the black sheep back into its fold, exercising its "Christian piety and charity," concepts that weakened the severity of all punishments and condemnations. In 1585, five years after he faced the Inquisition, Villalba was allowed to return to the Franciscan province of Michoacán and perform the Mass, although the rest of his punishment remained in place.[77] In Yucatán, John Chuchiak has corroborated that there was a significant lack of moral behavior among the friars but has also hinted at the possibility that some accusations resulted from an orchestrated effort against friars some communities disliked for a variety of other reasons.[78]

Far from Yucatán and in the distant northern borders of the viceroyalty, one could also find brazen examples of calculated sexual abuse. The case of Fr. Joseph Trujillo stands out. He was a Franciscan performing pastoral duties in the mining area of Parral. His victim was a Spanish-speaking Apache Native serving in the home of Captain Alonso Muñoz-Rivera, a resident landowner in the valley of San Bartolomé, near Parral (Chihuahua). She was either a recent convert or someone taken as a slave as the result of raids into Apache territory. In 1658 she denounced an incident that had taken place eight years before, a situation not unusual among rural women. Despite her lack of education, Ines, who had no surname, reported that on Tuesday of the Lent week of 1650, she had made her confession with Fr. Joseph, and after he absolved her, he took the hand in which she held a rosary and asked her if she could see him. Suspecting something wrong, she refused and then went to pray at the church. While she was there, the friar opened the door of the sacristy and invited her into the convent.[79] She demurred and answered that she had to return to her masters. Sometime later (no precise information is given) the friar was visiting the home of Captain Muñoz-Rivera as a guest. Ines was serving in the house, and her mistress ordered her to confess with the friar. She had no choice and went to confess in another room. Once there, and after closing the door, Fr. Joseph told her he had been waiting for her for a long time and proceeded to force her into sex, as she described, "against a wall behind the door, against which a cross was leaning." She would not have forgotten such a detail, and the excruciating experience had not been erased from her memory after six years. After raping her the friar asked if she wanted to confess, to which she answered in the negative while he laughed and forced himself on her again. She never saw him after the incident, but she knew he was missionizing among the Indians of San Francisco de Los Conchos (Chihuahua) because he had sent an Indian to ask her how she was doing. There is no follow-up to this case. Fr. Joseph's premeditation was obvious. He probably asked the mistress of the house to send the servant to confess as a form of revenge for her previous snub. I do not suspect any complicity in the mistress, who was probably a pious and naive woman. For Ines justice never came, but at least she left a record of her humiliation.

Black women, free or enslaved, were also vulnerable, but there are much fewer cases involving them than any other racial group, possibly for lack of social standing. In a case dating from 1598, Catalina Congo, a slave of Bernardo de Bustos in the port city of San Juan de Ulúa, denounced having been raped by Dominican Fr. Diego de Vargas. In her words, she was forced down to the floor in the middle of confession, and the friar had carnal access to her. It was Lent and she had gone for a general confession accompanied by the young son of the family. The friar asked the boy to stay outside the church. The boy later confirmed the identity of the friar, since there were only two friars in charge.[80] There are conflicting nuances in the short account of the incident. Another slave, Catalina Quiteria, who testified on behalf of Catalina Congo, stated that Catalina had confessed the rape while crying, while Lucía López, the slave's white mistress, stated that she had heard the two slaves speaking in their language and laughing. Lucía had shown interest in the story and asked the slave whether the rape had taken place after confession, a sign that she knew the circumstances that defined the act of solicitation. Whether the slave cried or laughed is irrelevant, for one cannot blame the victim in these cases, and witnesses often had conflicting narratives. The veracity of a slave's words was always under suspicion. The victim remembered the place and the violence well enough. She also recalled the fact that the friar had told her not to tell anybody and had offered to help her if she needed something. She was unlikely to invent such details. Having taken depositions from a white woman, a small white child, and the slave and her friend, no action was taken against the rapist.[81] Some Black women had physical appeal to some confessors, but hardly anybody spoke for them if they were abused. In an unusual instance early in the mid-seventeenth century, Alonso de la Portilla, a single man living in Oaxtepec in the jurisdiction of the lands of Hernán Cortés's marquisate, appeared before the Inquisition to denounce a case of solicitation of a Black woman. He felt compelled to seek some justice for Pascuala, a free Black woman who lived in a sugar mill. As he informed the Inquisition, a Franciscan friar on his way from Acapulco to the capital, having confessed all the people in the hacienda, took the liberty of offering a piece of clothing to the slave in exchange for sexual favors.[82] There is no indication that this denunciation prompted any judicial follow-up. Cases of free *mulatas* also indicate that friars were attracted to them, sometimes to the point of attempting rape. The explicit denunciation of such an attempt by Ana de la Cruz from a small town in Michoacán leaves no doubt as to the intentions of Fr. Juan de Santa María. She succeeded in freeing herself from him as he attempted to force her into a sexual act around 1619. It took six years for a layman to denounce the case in her name, a gesture that points to his human empathy and uprightness. Such individual attempts to right a wrong were often futile. The lack of resolution of this case suggests that it was never taken to trial.[83]

Special Women: Nuns

Although a fraction of the total female population, nuns were a privileged group within the church and society. They did not escape the attention of some solicitants, adding further insight into the solicitation phenomenon. Since I have written extensively on solicitation among nuns elsewhere, I will bring them here only to underline similarities and differences among their cases and those of secular women.[84] Nuns were a group of select women set apart from the majority of secular women, and nunneries were solid and respected institutions in colonial society. With the exception of the lay nuns who professed to do manual work within the convent, black-veiled nuns had a higher degree of education than most women. They were quite capable of running their convents efficiently and, on many occasions, stood up to the civil and ecclesiastic authorities. Some of them had exceptional abilities as writers and musicians. In the popular imagination as well as in their hagiographical representations, nuns were the image of purity, and convents were refuges of virgins seeking the love of God and shelter from worldly affairs. Some of these assumptions were constructions in popular belief, and not everybody shared them, but popular piety kindled and continued to rekindle them.

Respect and piety notwithstanding, the fact is that nuns were not beyond the reach of solicitants, and some of them were not beyond experiencing the pulses of sexuality. Solicitants could and would break some social and religious barriers in their pursuit of female contact. The process of soliciting a nun was not that much different from that involving a secular woman. If anything, it was easier to access a nun than a secular woman. Nuns confessed and took communion more often than most women outside the convent, and their attachment to a particular confessor was, in many instances, stronger. The need for continuity and support in their spiritual guidance led some nuns to put a great deal of trust in their confessors. Thus, the confessor's presence in the confessional was "usual" in the sense that it was expected. Under cover of such a licit situation, confessors could inject erotic actions into their relationships with their spiritual daughters, misusing their authority but sometimes finding a positive response.

Confessors engaging in such relationships must have been aware of the complicated sacramental consequences of their behavior. The sacrament of penance has already been discussed. In addition, the confessor was soliciting a "married" woman, a spiritual bride of God. That was tantamount to breaking two commandments: not to commit adultery and not to covet your neighbor's wife. That is how strict inquisitors understood the solicitation of nuns. They followed biblical and evangelical teachings closely by reasserting that anyone who looked at a woman with lustful intents had already committed adultery in his heart.[85] Further, the solicitant incurred incest because he was soliciting his spiritual daughter. One incensed inquisitor also added "rape," since the solicitant was ravishing the nun's innocence.[86] Those were formidable charges carrying heavy spiritual and legal burdens, but apparently, they were not enough to deter some solicitants. For their part, nuns were advised that if they developed an attachment to a man, they were being disloyal to their divine husband and were spiritually breaking their vow of chastity. As theologian Andrés de Borda explained, nuns were obliged to confess any break in their chastity vote, especially if it was committed with another person bound by the same vow, such as the confessor, and the activity involved tactile experiences and the spilling of semen. He added that confessors making frequent visits to a convent were under suspicion of seeking "unsaintly" objectives.[87] The Inquisition was alerted to potential cases of confessional abuse and relationships between confessors and nuns by other nuns under pressure from their own confessors. The convent was a small "village," and abnormalities in confessor-confessant relations were not difficult to detect. Once an investigation was initiated, nuns were treated like any other witness. However, when the commissaries came to the convent, they used strict *sigilo*, or "discreetness." The "honor" and reputation of consecrated women should not be endangered by the gossip of a bad apple.

Confessions within the confines of a conventual space deterred the most aggressive tactics used with secular women, even when some spiritual daughters were willing to cooperate in physical and verbal liberties. When soliciting nuns, confessors engaged in persuasive verbal entreaties sometimes accompanied by physical touching. Any embarrassment caused to the nun could be explained as part of her penitential act.[88] This kind of contorted logic did not earn the sympathy of the inquisitors. More common were entreaties aimed at having the nun become a "devotee" of her confessor. A devotee was a dedicated spiritual daughter who would confess exclusively with a certain friar and perhaps carry out a platonic amorous relationship. Questioning a witness in one such case, the Holy Office insinuated that the confessor had solicited the nun so that she would love him (*enamorandola para que lo quisiese*). This case took place in the convent of Santa Clara in Puebla, and the solicitant, Fr. Joseph de Armenta, was around twenty years old when the presumed amorous requests took place. Such extreme youth was unusual for a confessor of nuns. When the Inquisition finally completed its investigations in 1690, he was twenty-nine years old. Since the inquest yielded no results and the Holy Office could not prove that the confessor's requests had taken place in the confessional, the "legal presumption" was in favor of Fr. Joseph, and the case was "suspended."[89]

The exchange of letters between nuns and men of the cloth could serve as evidence of relationships. Letters were supposed to be read or reviewed by the abbess or Mother Superior, but it is clear that many letters received no such supervision. Corresponding with a spiritual daughter was not a forbidden practice as long as it focused on spiritual topics. Such was the correspondence carried out between Sor Maria Ignacia del Niño Jesús, of the convent of Santa Clara in Querétaro, and her confessor, Fr. Manuel Sancho de Valls.[90] There are seventy-six known letters from this nun to her confessor. Unquestionably, Sor Maria Ignacia had an emotional attachment to her confessor that could have been questionable to a strict inquisitor, but this relationship went under the radar because the content of her letters was heavily spiritual. That was not the case of Sor María de San Nicolás Obispo Herrera of the convent of Santa Clara in Querétaro. A 1758 investigation prompted her personal testimony about her relationship with Fr. Antonio Álvarez, a member of the Franciscan friary in that city. The friar was already interned in the friary's "jail," and she was asked to produce the letters he had sent her. She argued that their correspondence had been entirely innocuous and focused on advice given to her in her role as a nurse for the convent. Having admitted that some of his letters had been burned, those that were inserted in the inquest do not denote anything but simple familiarity expressed by the use of terms such as "Chatita amadísima" (Dearest little one) and his response to her complaints of his lack of attention to her. He denied her reproaches, calling himself "tu amorosísimo padre" (your loving father) and signing as "tu hijo" (your son).[91] The exchange of food and tobacco was also acknowledged as well as some advice on health issues. These letters suggested a bonding beyond a routine confessional relationship, but not one of a sexual nature. The records do not furnish any further information about Fr. Antonio's potential engagement in similar relationships with other nuns. His case was a cause for concern for his order and the Inquisition, who feared the existence of circles of devotees among friars and nuns.

Letters were also an element in another case of shared intimacy and erotic relationship between two Augustinian friars and two nuns of the convent of Nuestra Sra. de la Soledad or Santa Mónica in the city of Oaxaca in the late 1770s.[92] However, we learn that all epistolary communication among them had been burned prior to the inquest to eliminate damning evidence. The inquisitorial investigation targeted Fr. Francisco Guardia, subprior of the Augustinian friary in Oaxaca, and it began in 1776 due to "noisy and scandalous" behavior involving him; the friary's guardian, Fr. Gregorio Bouza; and three nuns, María Catarina de Jesús Nazareno (age thirty-three), María Mónica de Santa Catalina (age twenty-three), and María Manuela de la Luz (age twenty). The latter was only laterally involved as a witness and a minor participant in the conversations because of her youth. She appeared to be a novice because sometimes she was accompanied by the "teacher." The depositions of the nuns were carried out without a public notary to avoid publicity; instead, a theologian of the archbishopric, Dr. Ramón Pérez, asked all the questions and took all the notes. The case involved the repeated visits of the two friars to the convent. Fr. Francisco

Guardia was a confessor to María Mónica de Santa Catalina. Bouza had no spiritual relationship with María Catarina de Jesús Nazareno, and his visits to her in the convent were entirely personal. Both friars engaged in conversations with the nuns in the confessionals and in the conventual parlor for nearly one year in 1775. One key feature of this story is that, lacking the men's deposition, it is entirely in the voice of the women involved, with the exception of the testimonies of several confessors related to them.

The two friars involved were the two top men of the Augustinian order (prior and subprior) in Oaxaca. Bouza was older than Guardia and had been in the friary for ten years. There is no information on how or why they acted together. Bouza had known María Catarina de Jesús Nazareno for some time and had unsuccessfully attempted to become her confessor. Guardia and Bouza engaged in flirtatious courtship with the nuns, with Bouza focusing on Sor María Catarina and Guardia entertaining a relationship with María Mónica while maintaining interest in Sor María Catarina or, at least, using her to cause jealousy in María Mónica. Both men were dominant. For example, Bouza once arrived at the parlor while María Catarina was consulting her confessor, and he accused her loudly of "adultery" and told her he would kill her if he had a dagger, scandalizing the priest and the convent's chaplain, who was also present. María Mónica eventually broke up with Guardia because she was jealous of his attentions to María Catarina. She claimed that this break resulted from the advice of her spiritual advisor, Fr Aniceto del Carmen, and because Guardia was having personal "troubles" with her brother outside the convent. However, María Catarina said that their relationship was already on the rocks and that she had interceded with Guardia to return to María Mónica. The latter was piqued by those terms and dismissed the confessor.

These two nuns knew a lot about each other's relations with these men, since they shared the parlor visits of their "suitors" and read each other's letters. There were, however, undertones of internal rivalry and jealousy despite their shared complicity because of Guardia's interest in María Catarina. Both nuns did not seem very concerned or were unclear about the spiritual implications of their behavior. They acted willingly and free of any pressure. María Catarina had a regular confessor of her own, and although she claimed she never confessed with Bouza, she came to the parlor every time he called on her. She also came to see Guardia. The behavior of the friars, judging by the nuns' depositions, followed a path we have seen corroborated in other instances. They were impulsive and acted as if they were dominant secular males accustomed to dealing with women and imposing their will on them. Commissioner Ramón Pérez read Guardia's correspondence and destroyed it because he judged it offensive. He added that Guardia was also reputed to be living (*amancebado*) with a woman. A model friar he was not. Another priest, involved in the case as a witness, considered the relationships between the nuns and the friars indecorous (*torpe*) and dangerous. The outcome of this case was not surprising. Bishop Joseph Gregorio Alonso de Ortigosa referred the case to four theologians to examine whether they believed that solicitation had taken place. The theologians agreed that the friars should be referred to the Inquisition because their behavior had been dishonest and illicit before, during, and after the confessions, as suggested by the bulls dealing with such situations. On January 24, 1777, the bishop revoked Guardia's license to confess to avoid scandal, and he was sent to Mexico City by his order. Bouza was forbidden from confessing nuns, but he retained the right to confess secular men and women. It appears that Guardia was dead by 1787.[93]

The Holy Office's Viewpoint
The voices of the inquisitors were a key element in the discussion and final adjudication of solicitation cases. They were the ultimate judges and the standard-bearers of the principles of personal and social morality. Even though in their personal lives some inquisitors left much to be desired, their statements carried the weight of the law, and more importantly, they served as compass points to determine the direction of other judiciary decisions.[94] The legal punishment meted out to solicitants aimed at correcting behavior and facilitating personal reform, although the sentences seem light in view of the evidence. Sexual offenses were hard to litigate, and the lack of "correction" for the culprit and "restitution" for the victim were usual in those days. To correct the loss of confidence in a confessor incurring solicitation, the mendicant orders withdrew them from the confessionals. Expulsion or defrocking were out of the question, or extremely rare, because the Church used the sacrament of penance and reconciliation for its own members. The trespasser could repent, receive his punishment, and be restored to the Church in good grace. For the unwilling victim, there was no compensation or any official avenue to restore her personal confidence regarding the behavior

of confessors in general. The women accosted by a solicitant continued their expected religious practices, and after the review of their cases by the Inquisition, we never hear from them again.

In judging the nature of any solicitation, members of the Inquisition guided themselves by the pronouncements of moral theologians, some of whom went into the many fine details of the physical expressions of lust. For example, a Franciscan authority explained how any member of his or any other order would incur mortal sin in the act of solicitation. The physical touching during any act of solicitation had to be of such intensive nature as to produce pollution from the shameful parts of the body.[95] Such information provided guidance throughout the judicial process carried out by the Inquisition. The attorney's task was to identify and assess what was available and admissible as evidence. If he felt that the case under consideration did not merit his attention or needed further clarification and paperwork, he would ask for further details or simply stall the case for lack of compelling evidence. Archived or stalled cases had little chance of being addressed again unless a solicitant proved to be a recidivist. In 1798 such archived cases were cataloged as *causas despreciadas*—literally, "spurned" or "discarded"—for lacking a strong foundation and having little chance of being successfully prosecuted.[96] Attorneys followed closely the guidelines of canonical law, moral theology, and the papal decisions on these delicate affairs. All inquiries were to be carried out with the utmost discretion (*sigilo*) throughout the investigation, and all witnesses were sworn to silence.

One important caveat must precede this survey of the inquisitors' viewpoints: not all inquisitorial investigations of solicitation cases have a final conviction and execution of punishment. In fact, only a minority of all recorded cases have a resolution with a sentence handed down by the judges. In such instances, the voices of the inquisitors are unavailable. Inquisitors were conscious of how their conduct inspired fear and respect, and they weighed their decisions carefully. I will review several solicitation cases that preserve the statements supporting the final verdict. They serve as guides for the inquisitors' interpretations of the law as well as their personal convictions on the ethical nuances of solicitation.

The Inquisition operated on the assumption that the solicitant was guilty and that he had to prove his innocence. He received legal assistance, but that fact did not change the premises of his position as the object of an indictment. The attorneys and the judges stood for the principles of the Church's laws on moral affairs. The judges went beyond posturing, even though their written statements are often verbally grandiloquent. The callousness of some solicitants seemed to anger some attorneys and judges, and the guilt of the solicitant was painted in the darkest colors in some verdicts. From the attorney's viewpoint, the solicitant's guilt rested on the fact that rather than guiding his penitent to sincere repentance on the road to perfection, he accosted her and incited her to commit lascivious acts, forgetting his spiritual obligations and his expected fear of God. The solicitant had abused his authority, depriving the penitent of the opportunity to reconcile with God and perverting the doctrines of the Church. Thus, he had caused grave injury to her conscience while demonstrating utter contempt for the holiness and purity of the sacrament of penance.[97] The attorneys would remind friars that they were obliged to live a clean life, not one that was "carnal, dirty and dishonest." By making a habit of their turpitude, solicitants had given a bad example, causing social disruption and scandal. Women left the confessional dirtier than when they entered, claimed an attorney in the case against Fr. Joseph de Oliva, who had assiduously questioned his confessants about their knowledge of sexual mechanics and sexual experiences. If the women claimed ignorance of some facts, Fr. Joseph instructed them. When he refused to confess his transgressions, the attorney judged him a vicious and scandalous man.[98] Other terms used to shame solicitants were "lascivious" and "corrupt," and their activities were compared to those of "filthy heretics" and similar examples of malice.[99]

The lack of sympathy for solicitants shown by the Inquisition judges reflected the principles of moral theologians such as Diego de San Cristoval (Estella), who believed that the only sin Christ never incurred, or forgave in others, was the sin of the flesh.[100] Those who accosted women in the confessional committed two sins: sacrilege and lust.[101] In the eyes of the Holy Office, the act of solicitation called for punishment, regardless of whether the recipient of the solicitation consented or refused to cooperate with the confessor. When an accused solicitant tried to hide his "crimes," acting with "refined malice" in the opinion of the inquisitors, he was tagged with *diminutio confitente*, which meant the willful silencing of the true extent of his activities. Fr. Francisco Castellanos was a solicitant who incurred excommunication for having absolved his accomplices and having also misled the Inquisition in his depositions. In a show of anger, the attorney in his case recommended that the accused be given the test of torture until he confessed the whole truth. Such a recommendation was rarely executed against men of the cloth, and it is unlikely that Fr. Francisco suffered it.[102]

In 1711, attorney Francisco Antonio de Palacio del Hoyo handed down a formal indictment against Fr. Juan de Alcántara of the Dominican convent of Oaxaca, who was denounced by the nuns and secular women of the Dominican convent of Santa Catarina de Siena in that city.[103] His transgressions were revealed by a young woman living as a secular in the convent and implicated several nuns as well as another friar, who was eventually excluded from the proceedings. The preliminary investigation of the case against Fr. Juan began in 1705, six years before the actual judicial process began. Most cases moved at glacial speed. Fr. Juan was accused by Margarita Valverde de Padilla, sister of a nun and a girl of known honesty who declared that he had solicited her five times in the confessional. She also stated that two other nuns in the convent, Sor Isabel de Santiago and Sor Sebastiana de San Agustín, had also been solicited. Speaking for herself, Margarita said that the solicitation had taken place at the confessional and during confession. Three Indian servants were called to testify. They declared having "overheard" wooing phrases and words from the friar. They had acted as spies for Margarita, the accuser, and warned her when other nuns entered the area of the confessional while she was there with the friar. One of the implicated nuns had questioned the length of time spent by Margarita in the confessional, to which the confessor had answered that he "was ordering her conscience." Once Margarita decided to put an end to the friar's advances, she asked another confessor to denounce Fr. Juan. After reviewing the statements of all the women and corroborating that the solicitation had indeed taken place, the attorney decided to order Fr. Juan to the Inquisition's secret jails, which was the usual procedure in such cases in New Spain. At that point, the records described the accused as young and of "disordered conduct" in the doctrine in his charge.[104] After the evidence proved the friar guilty, Palacio del Hoyo did not mince words in his sentencing.[105] His statement reflected the passion of a powerful man carrying out his legal and moral duties to their ultimate consequences. Fr. Juan, wrote the attorney, had forgotten his moral obligation to his state as a friar and to his order and had acted against the teachings of the Church.

He had abused the sacrament of penance and the place in which it was administered, behaving as a corrupt man (*vicioso*) who in his words and deeds shamed the Christian people. Fr. Juan had also misused the confessional, a place that should be the fountain of spiritual health, making it a filthy cistern of sins.[106] The confessor had been dishonest with Margarita and lied to her, promising he would take her out of the convent to marry him. He had used two other secular women as spies to cover for him and Margarita and enticed her to come to the confessional. The friar was also accused of cultivating *devociones*, or "special friendships," with other religious women and talking to them at inappropriate times.[107] On proceeding with an indictment, the attorney used some procedural flexibility by citing "dishonest intentions," since there had been no physical contact between Margarita and the confessor. The girl was on the other side of a wall and inside the convent. Recalling theologian Martin de San Joseph's insistence on proving pollution and "liberties" with the bodies as the basis for punishable solicitation, the attorney found some ameliorating features in this case.[108] Nonetheless, the friar was jailed and sentenced because his actions carried an open message of disrespect to his religion. He also had a bad reputation in the administration of spiritual direction of the Indian women in his charge. Obviously, the attorney wished to make an example of a younger friar who should not have been appointed as confessor, as he noted in a comment in the procedural statement. Oaxaca, a somewhat distant bishopric, could use a reminder of what canon law stated and meant.

Another inquisitor, Dr. Tomas Cuber y Linián, used words similar to those of Palacio del Hoyo when he argued a solicitation case against Franciscan Gregorio de Iriarte in 1758.[109] Iriarte had not cooperated with the attorney, and Cuber y Linián could not forgive the accused for his lack of remorse and his will to "forget" his many trespasses during his deposition. Without an admission of his sins, and showing no contrition leading to repentance and penance, there could be no possibility of reconciliation with God. For a man of the cloth, that was the ultimate disrespect to his own religion. The attorney considered Fr. Gregorio's life a ruinous race in lasciviousness lacking any degree of repentance and hopelessly far from amendment. He compared the priest to an infernal wolf who changed the spiritual medicine of confession and penitence into poison, thus destroying the good faith of those who resorted to him to reconcile themselves with Jesus Christ. The friar had betrayed not only his order and the Church but the hope placed on him by his own biological family, which had raised him as an observant Catholic. His behavior stained his family's honor and trust. This statement reveals how deeply embedded was the concept of "honor" in the personal and social imagination of the period. The attorney added the charge of heresy to Iriarte's behavior. This was bordering on the unusual, and it looks like he was consciously trying to shame the friar to the greatest possible degree. Since the sixteenth century, some jurists attempted to conflate solicitation with heresy insofar as the betrayal of the sacrament denied its validity as a Christian precept, and denying a sacrament was a heretical act. When attorneys in New Spain used this argument, they softened it by inserting the clause "suspicious of incurring heresy," since *full heresy* was unlikely. In Iriarte's case the attorney also called him a perjurer who had celebrated Mass with his own sacrilegious hands. Ultimately, the impassioned words of the attorney softened Iriarte's obstinacy. He was totally cornered. He accepted a number of the charges, recalling what he could of his many trespasses, but begged the tribunal to release him of those charges he did not admit to. This trial began in 1757 and ended one year later, which was "fast" for such cases. His sentence was confirmed in the presence of twelve confessors, eight of the regular orders and four secular priests, following the Inquisition's established procedure. He was denied the right to perform Mass and was obliged to stay in his convent. He had to abjure *de levi*, a punishment used against those who had denied the validity of any of the Church's teachings, although not in a heretical manner.[110] In 1762, three and a half years after his sentence, Iriarte requested that the inquisitors allow him to return to his parents' home in Guadalajara because he was suffering from a persistent stomach ailment. That was an unheard-of request, suggesting that his presumptuousness knew no boundaries. The Inquisition denied the request, stating that as a charitable order, the Franciscans would not deny him the medical treatment he deserved and that leaving the cloisters would hardly contribute to his "spiritual remedy." Case closed.

   A strongly worded indictment expressed an attorney's desire to make his decision an edifying example for other members of the church, not the general public. Since the entire inquisitorial process was carried out in secrecy, the faithful were assumed not to know the terms of the indictment, the accused's confession, or the final verdict. People could infer that something had gone astray when a friar suddenly disappeared from the local scene. The *sigilo* in the process did not always protect solicitants from being recognized as being under indictment. Clerical sexual transgressions were common knowledge, having been discussed among the targeted women and members of their families. The Inquisition could not stop these leaks. The final verdict in any trial was issued in the presence of members of his own and other mendicant orders, the secular priesthood, and other ecclesiastical authorities. The presence of witnesses was sought to cause personal embarrassment to the culprit and was meant to be a lesson to his brothers in religion. The punishment meted out to solicitants followed a pattern that hardly deviated throughout time. The worst offenders were exiled in perpetuity from the court of Madrid, exiled for ten years from Mexico City, and deprived of voice and vote in their community for five years. During this time, the culprits would be confined to their convents, or any convent designated by the attorneys, and be the last in all community gatherings. During the first months of their sentence, the convicted had to carry out penitential tasks to "purify" his soul and reconcile with God.

The Inquisition was inclined to restore the right to perform the Mass to convicted confessors after they finished serving their penitential term, which could take several months.[111] However, the restoration of the right to confess took a longer period of time. Franciscan Fr. Antonio de Alva, originally a missionary in Zacatecas, was deprived of his rights to confess men and women in perpetuity due to proven solicitation and a sexual relationship. In 1803, twelve years after his conviction, the Colegio de Propaganda Fide in Pachuca, where he was serving his punishment, requested that he be allowed to confess men. One year later the college requested that he be permitted to confess women as well. The college argued that it had few priests to serve as confessors in its missionary activities and that Alva was already fifty-three years old and had served his punishment with humility and religiosity. The Inquisition allowed him to confess men again, but no information is available on whether he was allowed to confess women. This and other similar cases show that the inquisitors took their time to be "merciful" even under pressure from the orders.[112]

Was sex all that mattered in solicitation cases? The nature of the exchange between the confessor and the penitent inclines us to see solicitation as a purely sexual issue, but the grievances raised by the Church and the

Inquisition in regard to solicitation went beyond the issue of sexual misconduct. An important angle of solicitation charges was the confessor's betrayal of trust. He had misused the power granted to him by the Church to be the conduit of God's wisdom and justice. His disrespect for the sacrality of the place devoted to the act of penitence was a key component of the charges. The physical space of the confessional was invested with a spiritual power that was released when penitent and confessor faced each other in the act of confession. The inquisitorial procedure requested the description of the exact location of the confessional where the transgression had taken place. Any confession taking place elsewhere without permission was irregular insofar as the space lacked its spiritual dedication. In the sixteenth and seventeenth centuries, many rural areas lacked a dedicated physical confessional place, and the penitents simply knelt before the confessor. This was also the case in many distant presidios in the eighteenth century. Under such circumstances, the place of confession was temporary and was held sacred only for the duration of the confession.

When confessant and confessor gave testimony to the Holy Office, the legal procedure obliged the participants to break the secrecy of confession. The fear inspired by an inquisitorial solicitation process was that of revealed intimacy and exposed shame for both parties. The act of confession created an exceptional and volatile intimacy with the close physical proximity of the two persons involved. Confessor and penitent were bound by a temporary but totally open exchange of thoughts, memories, and emotions based on mutual trust. The faithful penitent always assumed and expected rectitude from the confessor. Some women were shocked by the breach of such spiritual boundaries and felt their dignity stained and their beliefs betrayed. A confession was tainted when the spiritual and moral restraints that allowed both participants to trust each other were broken. Finding evidence of women's sexual interests is an unexpected result of the inquisitorial records. However, while this is of great interest to historians, the Inquisition did not show any interest in learning about the erotic fantasies of the women who found the friars attractive. The Inquisition regarded all women as "victims" because it assumed that women were weak and easily misled by a skilled deceiver. They were also assumed to be sexually innocent unless information proved that not to be the case. Only a *proven* falsehood in a woman's accusation would weigh against her. To prevent such occurrences, the inquisitor's agents investigated the reputation of the female plaintiffs to ensure that they were respectable and that their allegation could be taken seriously. However, the Inquisition's role was not to judge a woman's sins. That judgment was in the hands of her confessor. The inquisitors' target was the man in the robe. He was the one responsible for misguiding a soul and for desecrating a sacrament.

Ecclesiastical authorities saw solicitation as a heterosexual problem. They were disturbed by licentious behavior between men and women. Most of the regulations issued by moral theologians and applicable to the examination of solicitation cases imagined a female confessant.[113] Sodomy was examined but without the weight given to transgressions with women.[114] When solicitation involved men, the inquisitors classified the act as "sodomy" even though the activities were often reduced to kisses and the palpation of the penitent's penis, and no sexual act had taken place.[115] In 1603 the Mexican inquisitors consulted La Suprema in Spain, begging for advice on the cases of friars accosted by their own brothers in religion and on cases of solicitation involving male parishioners. The inquisitors ordered that the male victims stop confessing with the accused friar as part of the solution to the problem.[116]

As solicitants, friars behaved as secular men exercising their male authority and power over the female sex. Their actions spoke of their intent to erode their targets' will in order to indulge their own desires. Some were awkward in their approach and gave up if they met resistance. Others enjoyed resistance and pursued their intentions in the hope of finding a point of weakness and acquiescence. Resorting to force, which some did, reduced them to the level of rapists.[117] The moment the confessor slipped into the role of a sexualized, secular man, he was no longer a member in good standing of the Church. He lost his mantle of sacred authority and demeaned himself to the status of the men who were often despised in respectable social circles for their inability to control their sexuality.[118] The slippage was regrettable, since it "humanized" friars in a way that was contrary to the ideal manhood that the Church put in so much effort to cultivate. Solicitation was, numerically speaking, a minor problem faced by the Church, given the total number of friars living in the viceroyalty throughout the entire colonial period. It was not a practice in which many friars indulged. However, examining how it expressed itself helps us grasp the fact that friars were, physically, men with sexual urges. Their vows were not enough to shield all of them from the temptations of the world and the flesh. Solicitants help us understand the struggle of those friars who succeeded in repressing their desires and the tight control they had to exert over themselves to live up to the challenge of an alternate form of masculinity without sex.

5

Missionaries

Preaching Their Faith

> A los que van a las Indias, es, a padecer trabajos.
> Lo que yo les ofrezco son espinas, no conveniencias.
> Si a esto se resuelven, vamos, y si no, libertad
> tienen para volverse a sus Provincias.
> —Isidro Félix Espinosa, *Chronica Apostólica y Seraphica*

> I beg that I be sent a complete outfit, for I have been and am appallingly short of clothing... an under-habit which I brought from Sierra Gorda serves me as a tunic, and the habit I brought from there I have now had in continuous use for five years.
> —Fray Fermín Francisco de Lasuén, letter to Fray Francisco Pangua, April 23, 1774

The characterization of missionary activity as an arduous task demanding extreme personal sacrifice came from the pen of Fr. Antonio Llinás (1635–93), founder of the Colegio de Propaganda Fide in Querétaro.[1] His words were recalled with pride by Fr. Isidro Félix Espinosa, chronicler of the Franciscan order, who had spent many years as a missionary himself. As the founding father of the new centers for missionary training centers, Llinás was writing in a period when the first conversion efforts in New Spain were already more than one hundred years in the past. For him and other members of the Colegios de Propaganda Fide, missionary work needed rekindling of its former flame. There were many "gentiles"—yet-to-be-converted Natives—who remained beyond the geographical boundaries of Catholicism as well as many lukewarm Catholics in urban and rural areas of northern and western New

Spain whose faith was in need of rejuvenation. Lasuén's dedication to the first objective was closer to the "classic" task of a sixteenth-century missionary. He worked with the California Natives in what was the last frontier of the viceroyalty and the last experience of missionary activity for the Franciscans. His 1774 call for a new habit from remote California was an indication of the not-often-stated personal sacrifices missionaries experienced in their daily tasks. When Fr. Antonio Llinás promised toil and sweat to his brothers, he was addressing missionary tasks still unaccomplished in challenging territories. He was writing on missionary activity among Indians *and* urban populations, a nuance introduced by his order in the seventeenth century.

In this chapter I review the missionary tasks carried out among the Indigenous populations by the Franciscans beyond the sixteenth century, a period that has been extensively studied by many historians. The Franciscan order took the lead in missionary activity in central New Spain and the Yucatán Peninsula since the sixteenth century and had the legal privilege of missionizing the northern territories and borderlands of the viceroyalty. Members of the order left abundant historical tracts of their personal activities as well as their plans for and thoughts on their work. The Augustinians remained limited to areas closer to the geographical core, while the Dominicans became dominant in the southern areas. By the mid-seventeenth century, the Franciscans were the only mendicant order fully committed and engaged in royal-backed missionary activity in the ever-expanding northern borders.[2] There, the key task of the missionary was to attract the unbaptized "gentiles," settle them in the enclave of the mission, and indoctrinate them in the faith until he felt confident that they understood and *practiced* Roman Catholicism. At that point the Christianized Native was granted the privilege of the sacraments, the first being baptism. From then on, the newly arrived at the faith were bound—no choice allowed—to live under the spiritual and often physical command of the missionary.

There was no ironclad uniformity in the process of missionizing. Since the early seventeenth century, the missionaries who moved into the vast north faced a variety of Indigenous communities, as complex as the geography of the land. They had various degrees of "success." Nomadic or seminomadic tribes resisted the invasion of settlers and soldiers either by mounting full-frontal attacks in the plains or by retreating to the mountains, where it was difficult to make them obey a system they did not want to adopt. Making them "come down" from the mountains was one of the most common tasks undertaken by seventeenth-century missionaries working with communities in the western and eastern cordilleras. The challenge was harder than expected, and there was disillusion among some of the missionaries. However, there was no return, even in the face of resistance and disasters such as the Pueblo Revolt of 1680. The missionary had a contract for life.

Seventeenth-Century Missionaries: A Bird's-Eye View

Since their arrival in what was to become New Spain, missionary friars were—knowingly—agents of the Crown, buttressing royal efforts to "open up" territories. Friars often referred to themselves as soldiers engaged in a spiritual battle. The metaphor reflected the real experience of meeting adversarial tribal groups who forcefully resisted the advancing members of the Spanish community in their territories. By the late sixteenth century, the assumption that the tribal groups in the near and far north were willing to convert peacefully had dissipated. Instead, they became "the enemy," prizes of war bound to be killed or bartered and enslaved for labor. The seventeenth century was one of Indigenous revolts and the loss of missionary lives even in places that appeared to have been "converted." The friars who carried out that task lived and trained in urban convents; a significant number came from Spain with no experience in meeting and dealing with Natives or the challenges posed by the land.[3] The small church with its bell tower depicted in contemporaneous maps marked the presence of a friar priest trained in a European religious culture who hoped to survive and maybe thrive against all odds in a hostile environment. The understanding and eventual practice of Christianity by the Natives was questionable the farther they were from the core of the viceroyalty in central New Spain.

The Franciscans shared missionary activity with the Jesuits, who were in Sinaloa by 1591 and in Durango by 1596, reaching the distant Yaqui River by 1617.[4] The seventeenth century tested the abilities of all missionaries, regardless of affiliation, to tame the land and its people through preaching a faith that admitted no accommodation with any other. Franciscans carved a wide radius of activities in the central land mass and pushed ahead to the most distant areas in the central, north, and Gulf areas. They were already settled in New Mexico by the early seventeenth century, although their hold on that area was strongly challenged in 1680, when the entire Spanish community had to flee key urban centers in what was "New" Mexico. However, they returned several years later and recovered the land until the end of Spanish domination. At the time of New Mexico's final resettlement, no one had any idea that the next challenging missionary enterprise would be land not yet well known to the west and discovered largely by expeditions to its coast in the ensuing century.

Missionary activity was largely a land-bound enterprise in the seventeenth century, when some long-distance-traveling missionaries scouted the northern territories and returned full of exaggerated "stories" about the possibilities of conversions among the peoples they had encountered. The spiritual conquest was an unfinished task but promising in their eyes. The future was a time of unbound opportunities. Since the sixteenth century, many friars believed that preaching was a miraculous medium that would open the minds and the hearts of the Indigenous and incite them to convert without reservations. They were men of great faith, but they did not exercise the best of judgments about the willingness of the people they encountered to adopt a new religion. Among the creators of the missionary illusion that the northern areas were *tierra de promisión*, a "promised land" of riches and opportunities, were Fr. Estevan de Perea, Fr. Alonso de Benavides, and Fr. Jerónimo de Zárate. Perea arrived in New Mexico in 1610 and established a mission south of Santa Fe, which eventually supported the creation of a Franciscan custody in 1616 to promote the conversion. The first two decades of Spanish presence in New Mexico were turbulent, and the relations between the civilian governors and the missionaries were unstable. Fr. Alonso de Benavides, as custodian since 1626, appealed to Phillip IV in a report that while not hiding problems, such as the distance and the roughness of the trip, promised marvels and miracles dictated by the Lord, such as the "great discovery of wealth, spiritual and material" of the region, including its "prosperous mines," and an imaginary population of 300,000 souls, 86,000 of whom were already baptized.[5] Such was Benavides's unbound enthusiasm about the mineral wealth of the land that he actually passed samples around to lure people to come. The rumors of the apparition of a lady in blue who encouraged the Indigenous to become Christians also cast important nuances in the spread of the faith, although in view of the Indigenous rebellions, one may doubt its effectiveness.[6] Benavides succeeded in having twenty-nine more missionaries sent to New Mexico. They arrived in 1629 led by Franciscan

Fr. Estevan Perea, who died in his office in 1638 after more than a quarter of a century of service to his cause.[7]

Seeking royal support, Benavides wrote a second report to his own Commissary General Fr. Francisco de Apodaca in 1633. The first had painted a rosy picture of a peaceful missionary activity. The second was more realistic, reporting unfriendliness among the Hopi and identifying a group of Apaches who wished peace and were willing to accept baptism in Santa Fe, the town that would become the center of the new conversion field. Benavides's text reflected his brand of missionary activity. He furnished useful ethnographic information, always necessary to calibrate the character of the people, and he was full of pious hope that God was on the Christians' side and would help them overcome the influence of the Native healers, whom he correctly identified as a challenging source of power and spiritual strength for the Indigenous peoples. The friars' activities had to counter their abilities. Friars should become "miracle makers" themselves. This was an initial tactic to break ground and recruit followers, but not necessarily a method advised by traditional missionaries.

The other important illusion maker of that century was Fr. Jerónimo de Zárate, who in 1676 made a plea to the Crown to send yet another expedition to unlock the promise of the distant land.[8] Fr. Jerónimo shared the historical concern of his period. He assessed the accomplishments and failures of previous explorers and military conquerors of the far north (Francisco Vázquez de Coronado, Antonio de Espejo, Sebastián Vizcaino, and Juan de Oñate), trying to debunk the skepticism and even disbelief of those who were of the opinion that the "New" Mexico and other northern lands were a waste of human and economic resources. Zárate reaffirmed the vision of Native people already accepting Spanish settlers and reiterated the availability of the resources they needed to remain there: wheat, corn, and vegetables and mines yielding silver, copper, lead, and magnetic stone.[9] He even insinuated the existence of gold, adding comments on the Natives' abilities to work the metal, to dispel royal concerns about feasibility and profits.[10] Fr. Jerónimo suggested that New Mexico could be settled without any cost to the Crown. The entire enterprise could be accomplished by an arrangement between the Franciscans and private parties.

Zárate did not omit some of the problems affecting potential settlements and settlers. The most important was the internecine wars among the

Indigenous groups that made them either unreliable allies or fierce enemies. They were the source of the "dangers and tribulations" facing past and contemporaneous settlers and missionaries.[11] Yet he still believed that the apostolic charisma of his brothers in religion would conquer all obstacles. He even invoked someone's prophesy to explain his faith in an eventual settlement of New Mexico. God, in his secret wisdom, had revealed to another Franciscan brother, Fr. Diego de Mercado, how a future generation would reap the wealth of New Mexico. Those men who had so far entered the region were not the "chosen" ones because they had been greedy, but divine assistance would be available to others. Fr. Juan de Escalona, guardian of the convent of Guauquecholan, had a similar revelation: the Franciscans were the chosen order to enter the land, although they would suffer spiritually and materially before achieving their reward. Martyrdom was also part of the future, but that should not stall the process of conversion of the souls in the land. In 1680, only four years after Zárate submitted his report, a large Native revolt began in New Mexico, obliging the Spanish settlers to retreat to the San Antonio mission on the Rio Grande. Divine assistance was not forthcoming. The friars experienced the naked reality of disaffection and potential revolt, but their faith compelled them to believe in a wondrous future when evil forces would be defeated.

Not all friars upheld the optimism of the founders of the New Mexican missionary enterprise. Some were more restrained in their expectations of easily opening up new territories for conversion and development. One of them was Fr. Antonio Arias y Saavedra, born in Tepic in 1627. He served as a missionary in Acaponeta, a small town in the Sierra Madre Occidental in today's Nayarit, where unconverted "gentiles," apostates, and runaways found a safe harbor. His perspective was condensed in his report to the Franciscan general commissary in March 1673. Arias still believed that his order would bring "the transformation of a stony and thorny soil, through diligent cultivation, into good soil that will render unto God a bounty of fruit as conversions."[12] His metaphor alluded to more than the geography of the new land; it spoke to the character of the potential neophytes.

A contemporary of Fr. Antonio was Fr. José Caballero Carranco, an émigré from Andalucía who arrived in New Spain in 1665. He participated in an unsuccessful expedition to Lower California in 1668 and wrote a report on Sonora and Sinaloa in 1669, seven years before Zárate's New Mexico report. Carranco Caballero dealt with the Coras, a group that had evaded the Spanish authorities and Franciscan enticement for decades by retreating to the mountains.[13] Some of the people in the mountains had escaped from Jesuit missions and remained isolated to avoid working for the Spaniards once they "converted." As a missionary, Caballero Carranco had very low esteem for the Natives. He thought that the best way to entice the non-Christian Indians was to feed them and give them gifts because their natural abilities were similar to those of "animals" and they were incapable of learning beyond a certain point or understanding the apostolic message.[14] Not all missionaries were saintly, patient, and loving, as chroniclers would have us believe. In the hands of men such as Carranco Caballero, missionary activity was bound to fail in achieving a true, noncoerced conversion. Martin Nesvig has found similar feelings of disdain or outright contempt for Indigenous peoples among the missionaries engaged in the conversion of the Puerépechas of Michoacán.[15]

The missions in the eastern Sierra Madre—specifically those of the Sierra Gorda—also had rough moments for the Indigenous and the missionaries.[16] Closer to the capital of New Spain, the Sierra Gorda attracted the attention of the three missionary orders. There, they confronted many tribes, known as *mecos*, who, like their Nayarit counterparts, proved to be difficult to missionize. It also did not help that those settlers, and eventually the military men sent to the area, openly exploited the labor of local Jonaces and Pames. The rather intricate story of the missionary efforts in this area began in the late sixteenth century and met mixed reception and rewards in the seventeenth century. It was marked by the martyrdom of Franciscans Juan Calero and Bernardo Cossin and continued with the attack and destruction of Augustinian convents in the late sixteenth century. The existence of several mines and good pasturage attracted settlers, whose presence created a tense situation among landowners, Indigenous, the three orders, and eventually, the military. The persistent efforts of missionaries who learned several languages to improve the effectiveness of their presence resulted in the establishment of "core" convents in the area despite the loss of Indigenous populations to epidemics.

Regardless of the meager spiritual rewards, the Franciscan missionaries of the provinces of San Pedro and San Pablo Michoacán disputed this eastern missionary area with the Augustinians in the first decades of the seventeenth century.[17] The establishment of the Dominicans in the area in the 1680s added complexity to the story. In 1689 the Dominicans founded a college in San Juan del Río to train their missionaries. The project was backed by viceregal support. At the end of the century, the Dominicans had several missions with a small number of affiliated families. Unfortunately, Viceroys Count of Moctezuma (1696–1701) and the Duke of Alburquerque (1702–11) adopted a confrontational policy toward the Indians, favoring military incursions to suppress any sedition from the *mecos* who had gained a reputation for being resilient to the invasion of Spanish culture and religion. The military policy created a conflictive situation that destroyed the Indigenous people's confidence in the missionaries. Missions were terminated, and the "mission" Indians were allocated among the landowners. Dominicans Felipe Galindo and Luis Guzmán sought to find a peaceful accommodation that would allow them to continue their missionary work. Guzmán favored a policy that would remove any Indigenous insurgency. Nonetheless, he was unable to stop the decline of the missions, some of which were allocated to the Franciscans of San Fernando in 1740. Fr. Junípero Serra first trained in one of those ex-Dominican missions.

In addition to the recovery of the New Mexico missions in the last years of the century, missionary activity extended into Texas and the northern Gulf Coast. Both areas were targeted by an ambitious effort to reach the Mississippi River, where the French had already established a pied-à-terre. The French failed to settle in the area, but their incursion into East Texas was a teaching lesson to the missionaries. The Indigenous of the area were fragmented and unreceptive, and the few isolated mission sites did not prosper. Missionaries were not soldiers and were incapable of protecting themselves. Evangelization by lone friars or small parties reached the limit of its capability in East Texas, and they had to retreat to safer areas in West Texas.[18]

While missionary activity changed little in its spiritual content, it was unquestionably favored by a good number of well-trained men in the period between the late seventeenth and the late eighteenth centuries. They were trained in the Franciscan Colegios de Propaganda Fide, the institutions that assumed the leadership of the last missionary effort in the north of the viceroyalty.[19] The man who best represents the foundational spirit and the transition from seventeenth- to eighteenth-century missionary activity is Fr. Antonio de Jesús Margil (1657–1726). He was born in Valencia in 1657 and traveled to New Spain as a newly minted friar, arriving in 1683.[20] His first missionary assignment beyond Querétaro took him to Yucatán, from where he left for Guatemala, via Chiapas, on foot. There he preached for two years beginning in 1685 in urban sites and among the Talamanca Indians in present-day Honduras, Nicaragua, and Costa Rica. In 1691 he learned Chol to preach in the province of Verapaz, reputed to be among the most difficult evangelical fields in the isthmus. He failed to entice the Lacandon Indians to Christianity in 1693 and continued his activities in Guatemala until he was recalled by the Querétaro college in 1697 as its elected guardian. He returned to Guatemala in 1701 to consecrate a new Colegio de Propaganda Fide and carry out more missions among the Indigenous. Elected guardian of the Querétaro college in 1703, he returned on foot to the distant city to assume office and to found a new college in Zacatecas in 1707.

Margil created a niche for himself in the new wave of missionary activity among the laity. He revitalized missionary work among lukewarm Catholics by building up a new style of "urban mission" to revive the faith, a task he began in Querétaro and took with him to Mexico City. The objective of the missions was to cleanse the spirit of the people and reconcile them to the pristine observance of the faith. The urban missions were carefully planned and highly choreographed events. He wrote the guidelines that missionaries should follow since their arrival in town and during several days of incredibly busy liturgical activities.[21] Those activities received the blessing of the local priests or bishops, a show of respect from the secular church. Reconciliation of the faithful involved confession, repentance, and a resolution to live a life close to the commands of the faith. Practically the entire town came to confession, which was carried out by a team of Franciscan brothers working during mostly the late afternoon and evening hours. In addition to confession, the mission required penitential processions and public sermons addressing the hundreds of people present as well as public communions. For the processions the *misioneros* walked barefoot with ropes around their necks, thorn crowns on their heads, and ash covering their faces while uttering praises to the Lord, Mary, and saints, called *saetas*—literally, verbal "darts" or "arrows" discharging an emotional personal message. He advised that *all* people, from the social elite to the humblest, adults *and* children, be present. These highly emotional religious "performances" drove participants to tears and acts of contrition. His prescription included the necessary adjustments for large cities, such as Mexico City. The attention to detail, physical and

FIG. 16. Nicolas Enríquez, *Fr. Antonio Margil de Jesús*, oil painting, Collection of Our Lady of the Lake University, McNay Art Museum, San Antonio, Texas.

liturgical, reveals Margil's total immersion in a spirituality that combined the personal with the public, the ludic with the serious matters of the soul.

Marfil tried preaching in the Nayarit region, but his mission there ended as one of his few "defeats." He also spent time in Nueva Vizcaya and in Texas, where he lived in extreme penury and failed to entice the Indigenous population to conversion.[22] Margil acted as guardian of the convent of Zacatecas until 1722, when he became sick and had to return to Querétaro. Despite health issues, he spent his last years engaged in his popular urban missions. He died in Mexico City in 1726.[23] Leaving behind no written record of his inspiring and influential oratory, Margil's magnetic personality is difficult to judge in literary or theological terms. Doubtless, his appeal was sui generis but well suited for a period in which religious belief was expressed verbally and communally. He became a legendary figure in his own time by reviving the sixteenth-century missionary practice of making long, personal treks that earned him the appellation Atlante Peregrino, and he continued the tradition of emotional oratory that developed in the seventeenth century.

Complex Personalities and Issues

The eighteenth century saw the expansion of missionary activity into unknown territories. From the missionized and converted areas of the northwest, the Franciscans made a daring leap into Upper California and renewed missionary activity along New Spain's Gulf Coast (Seno Mexicano). However, missionizing was substantially changed in the eighteenth century. Royal oversight was stronger and inescapable, and the friars would see their activities supervised and constrained by military leaders who succeeded in relegating the friars to a supportive role in the opening of new territories.

The Bourbon dynasty developed a different understanding of Church-state relations. Royal policy in the second half of the eighteenth century dictated the rapid absorption of the newly converted Natives into the secular polity as subjects of the Crown. Viceregal authorities relied on commanders and governors to accomplish a rapid change of mission into pueblo with Indigenous self-government. Missionary activities in the eastern Sierras and the northeastern coast of the Mexican Gulf (Huasteca) became a showcase of how new royal policies changed the dynamics between secular settlement and Indigenous conversion. In 1746, José de Escandón was appointed to carry out a "pacification" and colonization mission in the coastal areas, later named after his birthplace, Nuevo Santander. This military man embodied in his person and actions the Bourbon's secularizing policy of founding Spanish towns, uprooting Natives for presumed civilizing benefits, and ending Indigenous revolts conspiring against the authority of the king.[24] As governor—and later as Count of Sierra Gorda—Escandón was an Indian fighter, having "pacified" the Pames in Celaya and the "rebel" workers in the mines of Guanajuato, Irapuato, and San Miguel el Grande in the 1720s and 1730s. He succeeded in suffocating Indigenous "disobedience" in the coastal provinces of Huasteca, effectively incorporating those territories into the Crown. The Franciscans of the Colegio de Propaganda Fide of San Fernando derided his activities, but they had no influence on royal policies. With the blessings of Viceroy Count of Revillagigedo (1746–55), Escandón pretended to favor the establishment of missions, but in reality, he held tight control over their location and abused the prerogatives of his role as *poblador* (settler) to squeeze labor from the mission Indians.[25]

Escandón's role was a shocking eye-opener to the Franciscans, who were officially in charge of the evangelization of New Santander. The region was shared by Colegios de Propaganda Fide Nuestra Señora de Guadalupe (in Zacatecas) and La Santa Cruz (in Querétaro). The Guadalupanos had the right to missionize the southern part of the coast, and the Queretanos the northern part. Fr. Simón del Hierro, of the Zacatecas convent, accompanied Escandón in his exploration and organizational scheme for a while but, being in total disagreement with him, resigned from his position. In 1766, Fr. José Joaquín García del Santísimo Rosario, from the Zacatecan college, wrote a stinging critique of Escandón sixteen years after the "colonization" of Nueva Vizcaya had begun.[26] According to the friar, Escandón had exaggerated or lied about the suitability of his recommended sites for the foundation of towns, and when the location was acceptable, he had given preference to the secular settlers over the missions and the Indians. He had also denied military protection to some potential mission settlements, provoking an Indian revolt, the loss of Indian lives, and the murder of missionary Fr. Francisco Javier de Silva, who was killed by the Apaches. He claimed that Escandón had acted for his own benefit, and as a result, many settlers remained landless and poor. The tension between the missionaries and the military governor resulted in the abandonment of the missions by the missionaries. They rejected sharing power with a military man.

The quickly expanding northern frontier became even larger with the incorporation of the Californias, especially continental California. A royal inspector general, José de Gálvez (1765–71), visited New Spain to fine-tune the execution of a general reform in the administration of the viceroyalty, and one of the most important results of that visit was the creation of a new administrative unit in 1776, the Provincias Internas, as part of an aggressive policy to fully populate and fortify the northern frontier.[27] Relatively little was known about the territory, and a vast array of activities were deployed to secure and explore it. Among those activities were reconnoitering the territories, drawing reliable maps, establishing the viability of new routes for trade, studying the potential of mineral wealth as well as that of agriculture and ranching, and deciding where to place presidios and soldiers to defend the territory. However, no task was more important than subduing the Indigenous peoples of the north and northwest. Wars against them had begun in the mid-sixteenth century, and by the mid-eighteenth century, they were still beyond total control. Indian raids continued to endanger travelers, miners, and settlers. They were an internal "enemy" far more effective in curtailing dominion over the land than any European intrusion. Royal officers of the mid- to late eighteenth century never regarded the northern frontier lands as experimental religious sites. They were the lands of the king to be administered following royal, not religious, policies. Visitor and Inspector General José de Gálvez was appointed to oversee the administrative reforms in New Spain between 1764 and 1772. He supported the role of the missionaries as *instrumental* in the process of acclimatizing the Indigenous to Spanish culture, but missionaries would not dictate policy over the settlement of the land or the role of the Indigenous communities. The commandant of the Internal Provinces, Teodoro de Croix (1730–92), shared and enforced the new royal policy. He approved plans to carry out the conversion and assimilation of the Indians during his tenure (1777–83), but his relationship with the missionaries, while polite, was tense.[28] The problems missionaries faced in California were mostly created by the military commanders, not the Indigenous peoples. In contrast, in the province of Sonora, where Christianization had a longer history, the key problem remained the tepid reception of the new religion among the *indios de paz*, or "nonaggressive Indians," and the unrelenting attacks of unfriendly tribal Indians that the military was largely unable to control.[29]

Designing the Operation of the Missions

The extensive missionary network that developed under the leadership of the Colegios de Propaganda Fide was designed and sustained by elaborate guidelines produced in the mother colleges. The College of Santa Cruz in Querétaro managed the missions in several areas of the viceroyalty, specifically those of the provinces of Sonora. San Fernando in Mexico City designed the plan for the Californias. Fr. Rafael Verger (1722–90), of the Colegio de Propaganda Fide of San Fernando in the capital, designed the California mission plan approved by Viceroy Antonio Maria Bucareli Viceroy (1771–79).[30] The document, dated November 15, 1772, provided guidelines, not fixed policies, because the circumstances in the field required flexibility.[31]

Verger, who had been a missionary at the Sierra Gorda, cautioned against the establishment of any mission before the missionaries had attracted and won the will of the Indians of any region. The Indians, he wrote, should be aware that they were entering into a contract with the king, who was represented by the soldiers and the missionaries. Verger never explained how the Indians would reach that understanding—one of those intellectual lapses of people accustomed to prevailing. He acknowledged that military protection was essential, and missions were to be built in places appropriate for their survival. Once their basic buildings were in place, the next task was to plant crops to attract the Indians, given the fact that food and clothing were the most important magnets to the mission. "Faith enters through the mouth," he wrote.

While Verger discussed the teaching of prayers and instruction on Christian doctrine, the administration of the sacraments, and the observance of holy days, his main focus was on the administration of the missions' properties and the income derived from royal support. He had in mind that royal bureaucrats wanted to remove control of the *sínodos*—royal gratuities sustaining the missions—from the friars' hands as part of the regalist policies of the Bourbon kings. Verger argued that *sínodos*, as well as the income derived from the mission's agricultural products, should be under missionary control because unlike secular administrators, Franciscans had no intention of profiting from the missions and were personally invested in their economic success. That had also been the opinion and wishes of Visitor General José de Gálvez, who personally authorized the missionary friars in

Lower California to administer their properties. Despite his endorsement, in just a few years, money (and thus, income; *temporalidades*) became a bone of contention between secular and religious authorities in the field. Commanders and governors of the territories recommended the transfer of the administration of the missions' "temporalities" to the secular authorities, but the missionaries kept a firm hold on them. The controversy over financial administration had not even begun when Verger penned his guidelines, but he saw the writing on the wall. He inveighed against the potential interference of captains and governors and argued that any transfer of authority over the missions' income would reduce the missionaries to mere preachers. Missionaries might as well pack up their belongings and withdraw from the missions.

Verger saw many similarities between the ongoing process of evangelization and the sixteenth-century experience, but he underlined some key differences. The first evangelization, he wrote, was carried out *after* a military conquest. In the eighteenth century, military activity and missionary work happened at the same time. The missionaries preferred to attract the Natives with softer methods of persuasion and used the military *only* for their personal protection. His argument was far from being entirely true, but it was the ideological position adopted by Propaganda Fide. He was addressing an issue that would become critical in the ensuing years: who held the commanding authority in a missionary establishment. Verger stated that friars had no desire to dominate soldiers or, for that matter, dictate policy to civil governors, but he argued that the friars should maintain the standards of moral and social behavior in the missions. This responsibility entailed the disciplining of Christianized Indians who veered away from the law of God. It was a prerogative also defended by the two most notable missionaries of the period, Fr. Junípero Serra and Fr. Fermín Francisco de Lasuén.[32] The military criticized the use of physical punishment, but their disapproval was not born out of charity to the Indians. They claimed that the personal and social control of the Indians belonged to the Crown and themselves as royal representatives.

Verger was not in favor of quickly establishing missions, and he attempted to curtail plans espoused by Viceroy Bucareli and Fr. Junípero Serra for a fast-moving missionary expansion. Such plans, in his opinion, were driven by unrestrained and unrealistic religious zeal. Verger opined that there was insufficient preparation and mature thought behind the foundations already in place as well as those planned for the future.[33] As he saw it, the Indians were unwilling to accept the faith; they pretended to be friendly, and the missionaries, including Serra, were too willing to believe them. He also lamented the miserly royal allocation of funds to the missions. He wanted more soldiers to defend the missionaries and a more reliable supply of goods. He also felt that the viceroy's and Gálvez's demands to expand the number of California missions disregarded the college's capability to provide the number of missionaries necessary to carry out such a grandiose plan. The large number requested for the project would disrupt his college's ability to continue its spiritual duties in the capital city. Verger was troubled by the painful choice between missionizing among the remote Indigenous or attending to the needs of urban Catholics. Guardians were elected every three years, and Verger was replaced by others who, like him, were anguished by the burden they had to bear, but they continued to accommodate the wishes of the Crown. Matters of policy were also debated among colleges and by the missionaries in the field, but as long as the financial support for the missions was controlled by the administrative bureaucracy, the Crown had the upper hand and the last word in the design of missionary policies.

Beyond Administration: Reflections on Missionizing

Administering a mission implied more than managing its resources. Beyond issues of administration, several missionaries wrote on how to carry out missionary activities. Fr. Pedro Font and Fr. Francisco Barbastro, both members of the Colegio de la Santa Cruz in Querétaro, left writings on the topic that merit review. Both had substantial field experience. In the 1770s they were assigned to the missions in the Pimería Alta in today's Sonora while the missionaries of San Fernando carried out their duties in California.[34] Although parallel in time, the Querétaro undertakings were different from those of San Fernando. The Pimería Alta missions had been in the hands of the Jesuits until their expulsion in 1767. Under Franciscan care the missions experienced administrative and sustainability problems resulting from the remoteness and vulnerability of their location. Font and Barbastro faced and endured those circumstances, and their writings proposed changes to correct the missions' functional weaknesses.

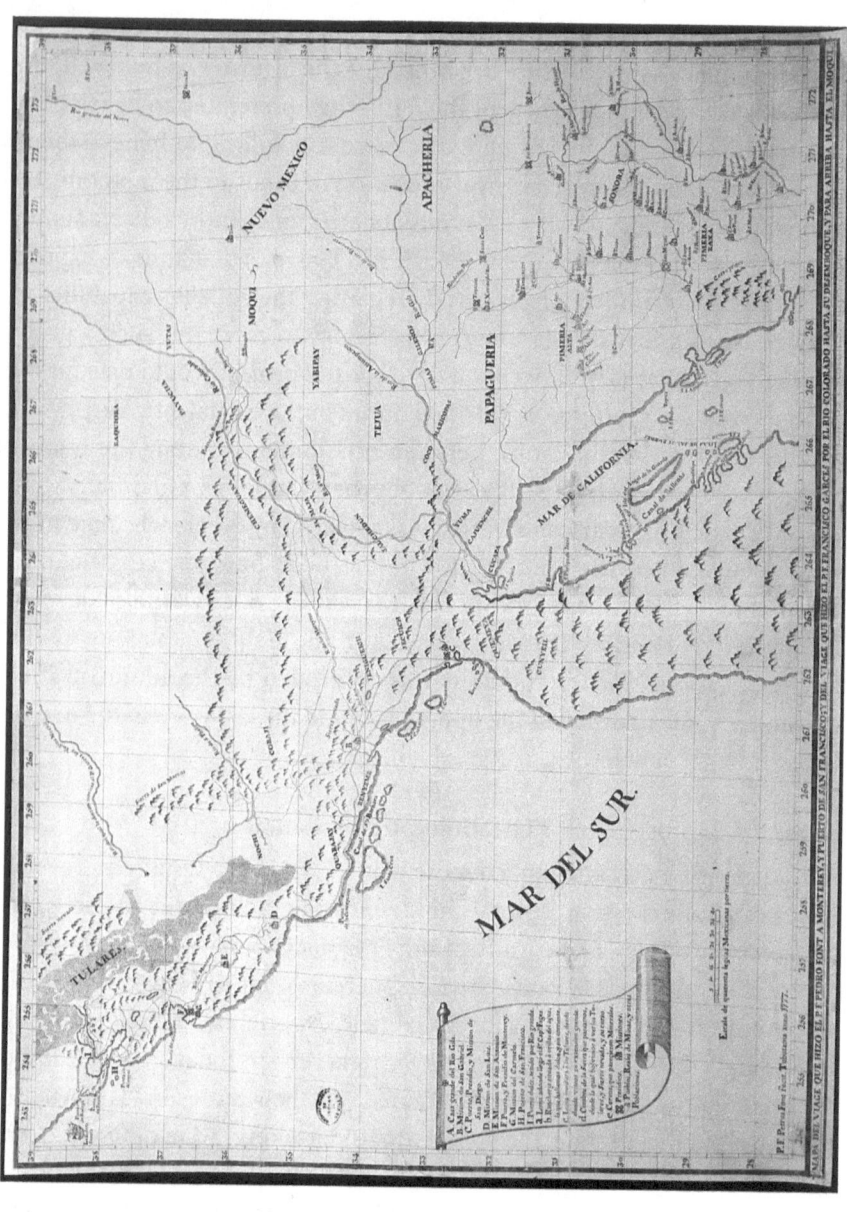

FIG. 17. Map of the trip of Fr. Pedro Font to Monterrey and the port of San Francisco, 1777. Drawn by Fr. Pedro Font. Portal de Archivos Españoles (PARES) AGI/MP-Mexico, 537.

Fr. Pedro Font (1737–81) was born in Catalonia. Little is known about him prior to his arrival at age twenty-four in New Spain to reside at the Colegio de la Santa Cruz in Querétaro. He was a sensitive and educated man, versed in music, mathematics, geography, and cartography. For ten years he sang in the college's choirs and took care of the music books. He requested and obtained an assignment to the missions of San José de Pimas in what was known as Pimería Baja in 1773.[35] After hardly two years in this mission, his cartographic and geographical knowledge earned him an appointment as chaplain and scientist in the second expedition of Juan Bautista de Anza to California in 1775.[36] He helped charter the new territory and used his expertise in managing the sextant to determine latitudes as they traveled. After his return from California, Font spent a few months in Ures and Imuris (Pimería Alta) before being assigned to the *visita* town of Santa María Magdalena in November 1776. Shortly after arriving, on November 6, he experienced an Indian attack by Seris, Piatos, and Apaches. The mission was destroyed by fire, and the people—including Font—barely survived thanks to the help sent by the nearby town of San Ignacio. After this dramatic experience, he lived in Tubutama, where he finished his diary of the California journey in 1777. He served in the missions of Pitic (Pitiquito) and Caborca, all in Sonora, and died in Pitic on September 8, 1781, after serving for eighteen years as a missionary.

In Pitic he wrote two reports. The official document, in the form of a daily travelogue, was terse and followed the procedural style expected from this type of work.[37] For his own use, he wrote a longer, more intimate, and personal report that has been dubbed *Diario Íntimo* by a Mexican historian.[38] When he returned to Sonora from California, he found out that the Colegio de la Santa Cruz had decided to abandon the Pimería Baja missions and had released them to the Franciscans of the province of Jalisco. Santa Cruz would focus on Pimería Alta, the potential gateway to the planned missions of the Gila and Colorado Rivers in today's Arizona, and Font was assigned to the town Santa María Magdalena.[39] Font regretted the abandonment of Pimería Baja missions as a matter of missionary policy and wrote three letters to Guardian Fr. Diego Ximenez explaining in detail some of the problems he saw in the management of the missions.

In his judgment, Pimería Alta was a set of poorly developed and badly defended missions, unready to sustain the planned missions on the Gila-Colorado junction. Security was a key issue for him, and he was vexed by the lack of attention paid by the college to the dangers of the missionary locations. "If the Piatos don't kill us, it may be that the Apaches will do so," he wrote, adding, "We are unable to leave the mission to go anywhere unless there is a large escort, and that cannot always be obtained. Even then, one is risking one's life."[40] To support his claims, he furnished information on the number of people killed by the Indians and the cattle stolen from the missions. A second letter dated November 30, 1776, was written at mission San José de Imuris, where he took refuge after his own mission of Santa María Magdalena was attacked and partly destroyed one week earlier. After a detailed account of the attack, he confessed that he was still suffering from "fright," the same emotion experienced by other missionaries under similar circumstances.[41] When the mission of Saric was attacked and destroyed, there was no help from the presidio of Terrenate; its personnel claimed they had to wait for "superior orders."[42] In his opinion, the college was blind to the "decadence of this land and missions, which move toward complete extinction."[43] He still thought that his chosen destiny, "the ministry and the conversion of souls," had been right for him, but he saw little hope of mending the condition of the missions and expected no miracles. Plainly stated, he wanted to "save the life God has been pleased to give [him]."[44] He was ready to leave. He requested permission from the president to "leave this country," meaning the Pimería Alta. It was denied. The college had to find replacements for any missionary wanting to leave before granting it. His third letter, dated January 20, 1777, was written at Tubutama, northwest of Imuris. The location indicates that Font had been moved again. Besides repeating his grief and fears, he reported a series of Indian attacks and thefts of horses in other missions and presidios (Altar, Cocospera, Cucuroe Tumacacori, and Tubutama). They were carried out in December 1776, and the Terrenate presidio, again, remained unable to defend the mission. Although not stated in plain words, his report denounced the incompetency of the military protection.

Font joined other missionaries in his critique of the rights granted to governors and commandants. From his viewpoint, they had stolen authority from the missionaries and perverted the "right order" that should prevail in a mission. He turned his pen against his own college, accusing it of being responsible for the decadence of the missions and maintaining a conspiracy of silence on the fact that the friars lacked authority to steer their own missions and were advised to comply with the military's or the governor's orders.[45] He also disagreed with the college's acceptance of "the Texas model," whereby missions constructed irrigation works, cultivated the land, and kept herds of cattle and horses for the community using an Indian labor force. Under this system, Font believed, the Indians did not learn how to love the land they cultivated as their own. The Texas model had failed, neither attracting people to the land nor coaxing more Indians to the missions.[46] It should not be used, he declared, in a land such as Sonora, so threatened by "enemies." He proposed a "Sonora method," a typical late eighteenth-century model of small communities of cultivators attached to their land: "Although they [the Indians] work for the mission, since they work for themselves, they learn to love the bit of earth they cultivate and have it as their own, as well as the small amount of goods they acquire by their labor." He posited that making the Indians work for the mission community while depriving them of their own lots was "unjust and not beneficial for reducing them." He concluded, "Anyone, even a poor Indian, valued something more when he considers it his own and can do with it what he would. Property held in common without the right to dispose it according to one's own desires, does not provide any incentives."[47]

Font was not alone in thinking along those lines. When Teodoro de Croix ordered the foundation of missions among the Yumas on the Colorado River in March 1780, he stipulated that once the Indians had a better understanding of how to manage private plots, they should receive them in ownership.[48] This was a recognition of the Indigenous right to have a measure of authority over their own lives. However, Font continued to believe that the Indians should remain subordinate to the final authority of the missionary.[49] He was not a proponent of democratic society.

Font's letters were a cry for help but not surrender. After his complaints and recommendations, he included a personal message as a missionary: the college should change its policies and try to "put an end to this prolonged death that [the missionaries] suffer from the hostilities of enemies." The anguish behind his words could not be stronger, but while he had many ideas for missionary reform, he did not contemplate an end to the system of which he was a part. Font died without seeing his proposals accepted. He was angry and emotional, but was he right about the doom of the missions and their potential rescue? The economic ties of the missions with their regional trade and agriculture followed the Jesuit model. On one hand, Cynthia Radding indicates that in the 1780s, the missions' assets declined markedly, and the "collective economy of the missions" was reduced to a minimum.[50] The loss of mission lands and their reduced output put the agrarian foundation of the mission in peril. The Franciscans had received those missions after they had passed their prime, and a change in their situation was unlikely. On the other hand, José Refugio de la Torre Curiel noted that Pimería Alta experienced a "brief" economic renaissance in the late eighteenth century that helped them survive into the nineteenth century.[51] The modest affluence of some of the missions was due to the trade of surplus production that allowed them to stay afloat. In the long run, it seems that Pedro Font's suggestions for amplifying the Indians' agricultural base made sense.[52]

Another set of suggestions on the foundation of missions and presidios came from Fr. Francisco Garcés, a missionary who is better known for his solo travels in the then uncharted territories of California, Arizona, and New Mexico and his ethnographic report on the Indians of the Colorado and Gila Rivers. Writing in 1777, he turned his attention to the security of the mission-presidio compounds.[53] For him, the population of the presidios was a critical element in the mission-presidio unit. He recommended that soldiers sent to presidios should be married because families provided proper models of social behavior. Settlers arriving at the presidio should have tools for cultivating the land, and there should be trained craftsmen among them. Presidios should be centers of Spanish material and social culture, while missionaries indoctrinated the Natives with full viceregal support and a suitable stipend. He understood that communication was essential to sustain those enclaves of political and religious expansion, and the routes to the northern mission-presidios should be kept safe with adequate military presence. Missions could be supplied by sea by using either the Port of San Diego or the Gulf of California. While he admitted that his recommendations might be hard to fulfill, he argued that someone could "dream up" how to change the status quo, and he was doing the "dreaming up" in the hope that his proposals could be carried out. If postponed, he warned, they would never be achieved. As for the Pimería Alta, rather than hoping for a miracle to preserve the missions, the authorities should cover the expenses required to revitalize run-down and depopulated towns. Without people, arms, and security, "the power of the enemy would finish off the Pimería Alta within twenty-four hours."

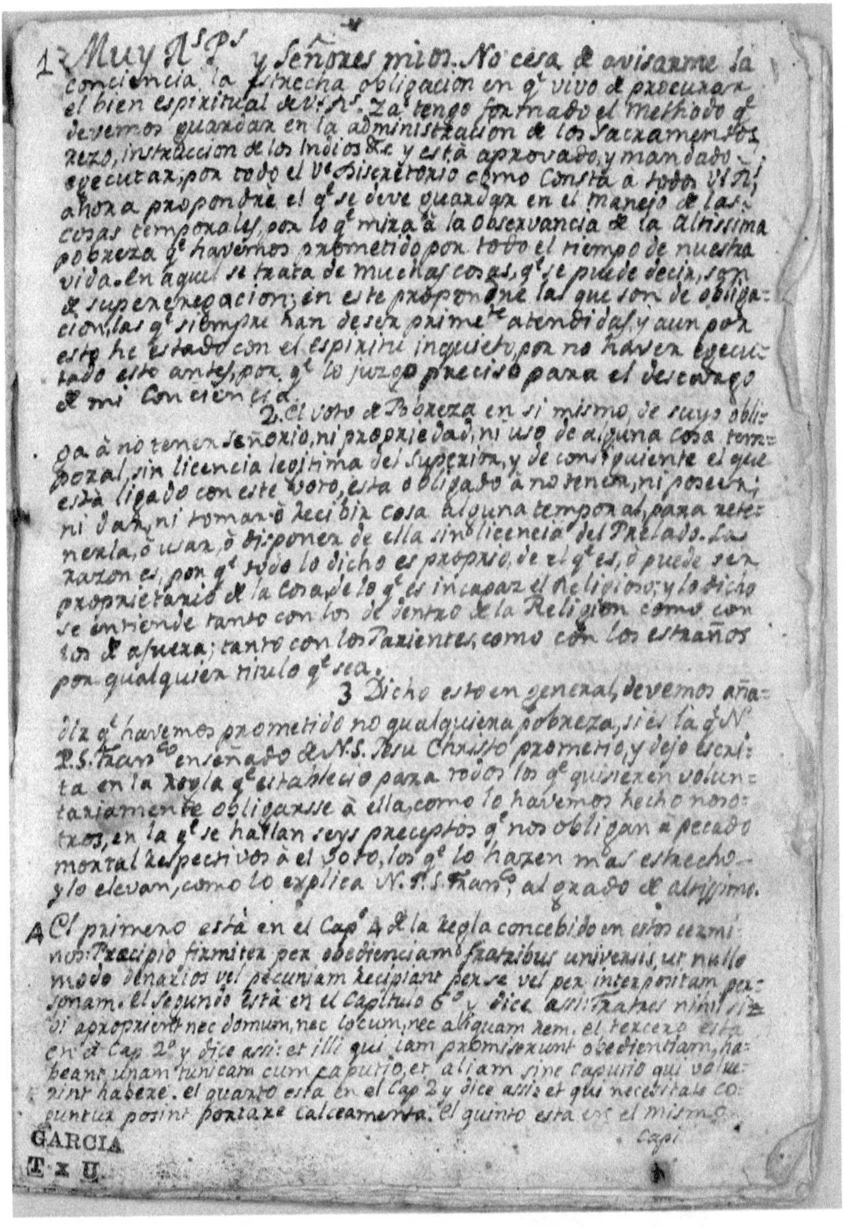
1 Muy R.s P.s y Señores mios. No cesa de avisarme la conciencia la estrecha obligacion en q.e vivo de procurar el bien espiritual de V.s R.s Ya tengo formado el methodo q.e devemos guardar en la administracion de los sacramentos, rezo, instruccion de los Indios &.c y está aprovado, y mandado executar, por todo el V.e Discretorio como consta á todos V.s R.s; ahora propondré el q.e se deve guardar en el manejo de las cosas temporales, por lo q.e mira á la observancia de la altissima pobreza q.e havemos prometido por todo el tiempo de nuestra vida. En aquel se trata de muchas cosas, q.e se puede decir, son de supererogacion; en este propondré las que son de obligacion, las q.e siempre han de ser prime.te atendidas, y aun por esto he estado con el espiritu inquieto, por no haver executado esto antes, por q.e lo juzgo preciso para el descargo de mi conciencia.

2. El voto de Pobreza en si mismo, de suyo obliga á no tener señorio, ni propriedad, ni uso de alguna cosa temporal, sin licencia legitima del Superior, y de consiguiente el que está ligado con este voto, está obligado á no tener, ni poseer, ni dar, ni tomar, ó recibir cosa alguna temporal, para retenerla, ó usar, ó disponer de ella sin licencia del Prelado. La razon es, por q.e todo lo dicho es proprio de el q.e es, ó puede ser proprietario de la cosa, de lo q.e es incapaz el Religioso; y lo dicho se entiende tanto con los de dentro de la Religion como con los de afuera; tanto con los Parientes, como con los estraños por qualquier titulo q.e sea.

3 Dicho esto en general, devemos añadir q.e havemos prometido no qualquiera pobreza, si es la q.e N. P. S. Fran.co enseñado de N. S. Jesu Christo prometio, y dejo escrita en la regla q.e establecio para todos los q.e quisieren voluntariamente obligarse á ella, como lo havemos hecho nosotros, en la q.e se hallan seys preceptos q.e nos obligan á pecado mortal respectivos á el voto, los q.e lo hazen mas estrecho, y lo elevan, como lo explica N. P. S. Fran.co al grado de altissimo.

A El primero está en el Cap.o 4 de la regla concebido en estos terminos: Praecipio firmiter per obedientiam fratribus universis, ut nullo modo denarios vel pecuniam recipiant per se vel per interpositam personam. El segundo está en el Capitulo 6.o y dice assi: Fratres nihil sibi appropient nec domum, nec locum, nec aliquam rem. El tercero está en el Cap. 2.o y dice assi: et illi qui iam promiserunt obedientiam, habeant unam tunicam cum caputio, et aliam sine caputio qui voluerint habere. El quarto esta en el Cap 2 y dice assi: et qui necessitate coguntur possint portare calceamenta. El quinto esta en el mismo

Capi

FIG. 18. Fr. Francisco Antonio Barbastro, *Deberes y obligaciones . . . de los misioneros en el Norte de Nueva España*, 1780. Benson Latin American Collection, LLILAS Benson Latin American Studies and Collections, University of Texas at Austin.

Another set of ideas came from Fr. Antonio Barbastro (1735–1800), who presided over the Custody of San Carlos from 1784 to its demise in 1791.[54] His knowledge of the Pimería Alta was better founded than Font's because he spent the better part of thirty years in the Sonora missions of Ures, Tubutama, Santa Teresa, Banámichi, and Aconchí. He had a well-defined and stern vision of the appropriate behavior for a Franciscan missionary and wrote a set of rules on how to handle the monies and properties of the missions while preserving the vow of poverty.[55] Barbastro lived in Aconchí for the longest period of his service. This experience informed a lengthy report on the state of the missions of Pimería Alta dated December 1, 1793. In this informative analysis, he took into consideration history, geography, the nature of the Indian and the Spanish populations, and the policies of the civil and religious authorities. He also injected into it his dreams for a different missionary reality.

In this carefully written report, Barbastro argued that the Sonora missions were badly in need of attention. The "spiritual fruit" represented by the number of converts remained meager, although not for lack of effort. He considered his own work as a missionary satisfactory. He had worked diligently to repair the churches, build adobe houses for the Christianized mission Indians, and provide the missions with secure walls for better defense. Nonetheless, the Seris Indians had martyred missionaries Fr. Gil de Bernabé and Fr. Felipe Guillén, and the Yumas had killed four friars in the newly founded missions of La Concepción and San Pedro y San Pablo.[56] Such deaths did not bode well for the future. Beyond his dislike for Apaches and Seris on account of their constant attacks on the mission, he openly stated he did not like some of his own charges, the Opatas of Banámichi and Aconchí. The Opatas gave no material support to their mission, did not take care of their own church, and were indolent and incapable of self-rule. To explain his opinion, it is important to know that building churches was an important symbolic statement of power for the missionaries, especially given the lack of architectural tradition among the Pimería Indians. The stunning church of San Xavier del Bac, in today's Arizona, was under construction when Barbastro was writing this report. For him missionary work meant having the cross in one hand and the masonry trowel in the other.[57] Barbastro expected the Indians to accept that notion and willingly engage in the construction and maintenance of the church as the house of God. When they did not, he complained bitterly about their lack of support.

Barbastro did not criticize the administrative supervision of the Querétaro college, but he was a staunch opponent of the new regulations of the Provincias Internas that established the election of Indian officials in each mission and granted them self-government, reducing the missionaries to spiritual activities only. The adoption of the system, he wrote, had resulted in the Natives' neglect of work for the mission and the disrespect of their religious obligations. Font went beyond criticizing the organization of the Provincias Internas. He analyzed the ecological characteristics of the area and how they affected the population and the establishment of missions.[58] He also drew a comparison between Pimas, Opatas, and Yaquis and how their different character and inclinations affected missionary activity. He was partial to the Pimas, who, he claimed, respected their ministers, loved agriculture, managed their towns well, and were peaceful. In contrast, Opatas and Yaquis were wandering and "useless" people without respect for the missionaries.[59] Having worked for eight years with the small community in Tubutama (Pimas) and despite Apache attacks and the death by martyrdom of his own companion Fr. Felipe Guillén, Barbastro claimed he had managed to build a church and keep his flock well provided. Contrariwise, in the large mission of Aconchí, Opatas refused to do anything for the church and showed their ill will by filing complaints against him. In his own defense, Barbastro argued he was the same man in Aconchí as he was in Tubutama, but his flock was different, and he did not disguise his dislike of the Opatas.[60]

In view of the local lack of cooperation with their missionary, Barbastro proposed the adoption of a policy to attract more *gente de razón* to overcome the depopulation of the area. He regarded himself as a "civilizing" agent and proposed a population scheme that would include new and more Hispanicized settlers. Physical protection of the towns was also imperative to create a feeling of security. To resolve the impasse in the development of the region, he proposed two models: one for the Spanish population and one for the Indian population. He wanted Spanish commitment to the region. Traders who came to sell merchandise and enrich themselves should be obliged to stay. Like other men of his generation, Barbastro assumed that with permanent settlements of culturally Spanish people, trade and social reform would take place, and positive spiritual fruits for the Indians would follow. He also stuck to the notion that a better future demanded the traditional method of empowering missionaries to control the administration of the missionary outposts.[61] He was also amenable to an accommodation with the secular church. Even though he opposed secularization, he suggested that since the government wanted to secularize the missions, it should create a seminary to train the secular priesthood in the mission of Oposura, directed by the two well-qualified secular priests who resided in that town.[62] The seminary would receive the best students of all Indian and mining towns.[63] By including the Indians, Barbastro crossed a line that others had not dared to approach: the formal instruction of the Indians. Those who opposed the education of the Natives, he wrote, wanted to exploit them. Indians did not lack talent; they lacked teachers. In fact, his experience told him that they were easier to teach and had more talent than the rest of the people of that province. To counter doubters and critics of his ideas, he offered his experience with his own flock. In 1788, knowing that his mission Indians paid little attention to his preaching, he proposed the foundation of a school for children under twelve years of age to give them a "better" life and the opportunity to serve their own people. The community was interested in that proposal, and in April 1788, he opened a school where, in addition to reading and writing, the children engaged in performing short plays for the holidays, a tradition that ran back to the sixteenth century. He also accepted girls in the school.[64] It is possible that this experience moved Barbastro to admit and recommend the ordination of Indians, an idea first rejected in the sixteenth century and still resisted by the ecclesiastic authorities in his own time.[65] Barbastro died in 1800 after twenty-seven years of service in Sonora. His administrative abilities as head of the missions were acknowledged in 1790 by Enrique de Grimarest, the intendant of the region, but his dreams of education and perhaps the ordination of Indians remained unfulfilled.[66]

Ironically, Barbastro's "enemy," the late bishop of Sonora, Fr. Antonio de los Reyes, had also been a proponent of Indian education.[67] The Queretaran friar's dislike of Fr. Antonio de los Reyes was personal rather than ideological and based on the fact that Reyes was a strong believer in the secularization of doctrines. Despite their unfortunate squabbles, Bishop Reyes's ideas on missionizing among the Indigenous had some points in common with those of Font and Barbastro regarding education. His proposal to Viceroy Bucareli and to the Crown included the education of the Indians in "the mechanics of soil cultivation, harvesting and making better use of the fruits, and building comfortable dwellings and houses." He concluded, "And finally, the missionaries will appoint the best trained and most intelligent natives to the political and civil government of the new settlements, teaching the local magistrates understand their obligation, love and veneration they owe to our beloved sovereign, and in his name punish the wicked justly, and act as protectors of the others."[68] Reyes also reported that the Indians preferred to cultivate their own land rather than the communal ones, an idea he shared with Fr. Pedro Font.

The intellectual content of the proposals reviewed above was the last-ditch effort, so to speak, to save a system of "entitled" evangelization that had deep roots in the past. In their own ways, these men's suggestions were intended to reform an institution that was in unstoppable decline. The Indigenous population attached to their missions was small and already mixed with other ethnic groups. Although some missions were "prosperous" by selling crafts and the surplus of their agricultural production, most of them had hardly enough income to sustain themselves. Above all, there was hardly any attempt to reform and invigorate the system.[69]

The future of the missions was in California. Some of the ideas proposed by men such as Barbastro and Font were transferred to California by members of the College of San Fernando. In California there were no Apache raids, the land was bountiful, and the Crown provided support in cash and physical protection. The founding missionaries were among the most committed members of the College of San Fernando. By the end of the century, while the Sonora missions were simply "on hold," the California missions were a success in terms of numbers and sustainability. The stories of the personal challenges faced by the California missionaries are worth examining because they are unique in the history of missionary activities as the last breath of that "peculiar" institution.

California Missionaries: Managing Remote Missions

California missions were the most remote northern enclave of missionary activity to be directed from New Spain. In its time, the experiment posed the greatest challenge to the concept of missionizing, the responsibility of the head missionary, and the relations between missionaries and the military and secular governors. The burden of carrying out that complex task fell to the two presidents of the missions: Junípero Serra and Fermín Francisco Lasuén. Both acted as missionaries in California from 1769 through 1804, when missionary activity was as much an issue of administration as conversion. For the men in charge of changing the beliefs of the Indigenous population, the materiality of daily administration became so central as to occupy most of their days and become the predominant theme in their correspondence.

As the most successful missionary of the eighteenth century, Fr. Junípero Serra had to share the burden of administrative obligations with the spiritual targets of missionary activity. He did not write any religious tracts. Neither did he pen any formal proposal for the reform of missionary activities, as did Font and Barbastro. Serra's correspondence reflects his concept of missioning as a practical endeavor to solve the concrete administrative problems he faced.[70] Serra had his initial missionary experience from 1750 to 1758 in the eastern mountains of Sierra Gorda. Then he acted as a missionary to regular members of the church in central Mexico, including Puebla. During his time of service at Sierra Gorda, the Crown began the secularization of the Indian doctrines under the regular orders.[71] As a result, the management of Indigenous flocks by the missionaries was severely restricted, and on paper, only indoctrination and activities connected to liturgy and observance remained as avenues for the exercise of the missionary's ministry.

This mixed-service background was Serra's only preparation for the assignment he received in 1768. That year he assumed the administration of a project in a territory no one knew well, with an equally unknown population whose potential reaction to religious conversion was still an enigma.[72] In his mind, he was embarking on a "new pilgrimage to a deserted land populated by a great number of gentile infidels."[73] How could the land be deserted but populated at the same time? For missionaries of all times, a land was "deserted" if it remained ignorant of the message of their own religion. As his experience proved, the difficulties of his mission were due not so much to the Natives but to the military commanders with whom he had to work.

Serra's spiritual duties as a missionary were to say daily Mass and preach (in Spanish), administer marriages and baptisms, and confirm the fully indoctrinated neophytes. It is known that Serra and Fr. Juan Crespí followed a traditional method of indoctrination: they focused on the children, from whom they learned the social character of the people, and taught them Spanish and the catechism, which the children then conveyed to their parents.[74]

Otherwise, missionaries had to rely on "translators," men who would convey the doctrine in any language discernible to the potential adult converts. Serra doesn't discuss those issues in his personal letters. His main spiritual pursuit and personal obsession was to found missions. Each mission building was a material testimony to the success of the missionary and his spiritual pursuit. In a letter written to José de Gálvez on July 2, 1770, he described in detail the celebration of Mass and a procession on the day of Corpus Christi, June 16, to mark the site of the future mission in Monterey.[75] For him, that day marked an unforgettable spiritual triumph.

Serra maintained an extensive correspondence with Viceroy Bucareli, who was keenly interested in his progress. In 1775 he wrote Bucareli ten letters reporting on the status of the five missions under his care. He included the number of baptisms, deaths, marriages, and families; the number of buildings in each mission and their style of construction; the liturgical holdings of the church sacristies; and even the number of cooking utensils and farm tools. He added the number of mules, pigs, cattle, and horses as well as how much wheat and corn were planted. He thanked the receipt of cloth to dress the Indians and combat nudity. This abundance of details indicates Serra's meticulous attention to the demanding task of housekeeping as well as his strong managerial ability.[76] Providing facts on the missions' material progress was his idea of proving that the royal monies and support were well spent.

The administrative duties of all missionaries were minutely described in guidelines written in 1787 for the Texan mission of La Purísima Concepción. They help appreciate the deep involvement in daily housekeeping demands experienced by Serra and all other missionaries.[77] The guidelines had eighty points and a supplement addressing the rituals to be followed throughout the liturgical calendar. The instruction in the basics of the faith was the most important task for all missionaries, but there were many others demanding their attention. Such were planning and supervising of the planting and harvesting of the crops, the care of pack animals and livestock, and the management and overseeing of the mission's workforce. Missionaries had to allocate the rations of tobacco, corn, and other food supplies and clothing to the mission's population. Sickness and well-being were under their purview, as were the tasks of retrieving Indian fugitives and protecting the Indians from the Spaniards who came into the mission. All these responsibilities

FIG. 19. *Fr. Junípero Serra Preaching to All People*, reproduction of an illustration originally published in Fr. Francisco Palou, *Relación histórica de la vida y apostólicas tareas del venerable padre Fray Junípero Serra* (Mexico: Zúñiga y Ontiveros, 1787).

were reported periodically to the guardian and the advisory board at San Fernando. The personal problems Serra and other missionaries faced were discussed with the guardian of his college in Mexico City as often as the flow of the maritime mail permitted. Since letters took weeks to travel between the city of Mexico and California, decisions about how to conduct daily affairs were largely in the hands of the missionary.

Serra's responsibilities as president of the California missions were heavy, and his dedication to their administration was total and time consuming. In 1774 he voiced his concern about how much time he spent writing on such issues and tending to the material needs of the missions.[78] The daily burden of administering the friary cut into his liturgical responsibilities and his own spiritual life. Serra was constantly aware of the need to make the missions more than self-sustaining because in times of need, they had to help one another as well as the presidios nearby. A poor mission like San Diego, unable to raise enough food for its people (including the Indians), received periodical help from its sister institutions. Provisions arriving from New Spain were stored in the presidios, and a quartermaster kept track of what belonged to the mission, but feeding the Indians was the mission's responsibility.

In 1774 Serra's leadership was under review in Mexico. As noted earlier, some college members had strong reservations about the success of the missions and Serra's ambitious plans. The college deemed Serra's plan prone to eventual failure.[79] The key concerns were finding personnel for the missions and the difficulties posed by the transportation of goods. President Pangua and the discretory were not satisfied with Serra's total engagement in the provisioning of merchandise, the pricing of goods, and such material issues involving money. Pangua's predecessor, Fr. Rafael Verger, apparently thought that there was too much money spent on the missions and that a "religious should not be dedicated to all that." However, in a strong response to their concerns, Serra rhetorically asked who, except for him, would tend to all the details. He argued that a spiritual mission demanded a practical head for the material aspects of a religious institute. The Lord's daily bread was earned by hard work.[80] He was fully aware of and concerned by the difficulties in receiving supplies and planning for the future owing to the irregularity of the delivery ships. He suggested the adoption of a regular, trustworthy supplier and the creation of a standard list of essential goods and cash that could be shared by the missions according to their needs.[81] These suggestions made sense, but those responsible for the task of drafting adequate policies for the California missions resided in Mexico City, and they remained skeptical of the ultimate fate of Serra's project. Serra was on the defense most of the time. In a letter to Pangua dated April 13, 1776, he explained the equity with which he treated the provisions for the missions and the needs of the missionaries.[82] He was the missions' president, but in the observance of obedience and accountability to his superiors, he remained a plain friar, as he was taught during his novitiate.

Another problem that comes to light in this correspondence is the appointment of missionaries. Doubtless, Serra's experience must have been similar to that of other presidents in missionary sites in mainland Mexico. Not all missionaries had pliable and obsequious personalities. Their work was voluntary, but they retained a voice of their own to express their thoughts to their prelates. When some of them were unhappy, they lacked no words to make their feelings clear. In Serra's case, he was willing to cajole and beg for his brothers' consent and support. For example, he had endless problems with mission San Diego. After the martyrdom of Fr. Luis Jayme in November 1775, his missionary companion, Fr. Vicente Fuster, requested to be removed from the mission on the grounds of lacking empathy for the people who had killed his brother in religion. Serra agreed, but mostly because he considered Fuster unpolished and not the best choice for the mission. When Serra tapped Fr. Vicente de Santa María for the post, he refused to go to San Diego, assuming it was a personal insult to ask him to go there. It was a poor and bottom-ranked mission. Serra wished to appoint Fr. Fermín Lasuén, but he feared that Lasuén would abandon the missionary enterprise altogether and join Commandant Fernando de Rivera as his personal chaplain. Lasuén had openly expressed his lack of desire to serve in San Diego, and Serra asked him to do it as a personal sacrifice. Sacrificing self for duty was a part of any friar's training, and Serra appealed to Lasuén's commitment to his order. Serra was willing to go himself if no one accepted because he feared a relaxation of the missionary spirit. Ultimately, Lasuén accepted the appointment, possibly following the principle of obedience to his vows.[83]

The Missionary and the Military Commander

The burden of dealing with military men was never contemplated in any manual for the conversion of the gentiles.[84] The presence of a military enclave close to the missions for protective purposes could create issues of clashing personalities and contestations of authority. Serra's life as a missionary was punctuated by recurrent struggles with the military commandants in California, Fernando de Rivera y Moncada, Pedro Fages, and Felipe de Neve. These military men were trained in dominant masculine behavior that was intolerant of contradictions. They imposed harsh terms of service on their troops, and few other men dared to challenge or question their authority, except the viceroy or the king. The missions created a unique situation where a man of the cloth, empowered by his prelates to exercise spiritual authority over the new converts, had to engage in disputes with a governor in charge of tactical operations and whose personal reputation depended on expanding his territory and maintaining it under strict control. Serra was accustomed to rendering accounts and being judged by his own prelates. However, there was no guidance or approved "code" of behavior to apply to the relationship he would have to forge with the military commander to establish the boundaries of their respective authority.

In California in the late eighteenth century, commanders were intent on making the men of the cloth understand that they had the upper hand in the management of the territory under their command, which included the missions. They outwardly and superficially respected the missionaries, especially the president of the missions, but differences of opinion on various issues were a test for both sides. Sometimes the friars prevailed; sometimes the military did. As time passed, the military had more "wins," and the religious became more accepting of a situation that gave them no voice in policymaking. To avoid misunderstandings, Serra corresponded frequently with the three commanders under whom he served to discuss the three key points of their relationship: the foundation of missions, the missionaries' rights over the Indians, and the services that missionary and commander owed each other in terms of safeguarding the missions and ensuring their viability. Serra's tone was always respectful, but he fought indefatigably to preserve what he considered the missionaries' rights and the respect he expected as a man of the cloth. He thought that his task was as important as the military's and that their mutual dependency did not mean any personal submission to the men in uniform.

Dealing with the commanders consumed a lot of Serra's energy and time. He was also answerable to his own guardian in San Fernando and to Viceroy

Antonio María de Bucareli during his term. He communicated often with Bucareli, with whom he maintained an amiable relationship and from whom he earned critical political and material support in the early years of the California missions. On the other hand, the early 1780s were years of bitter provocation and confrontation with Teodoro de Croix, Felipe de Neve, and Pedro Fages, who during their respective terms of command were intent on antagonizing Serra and diminishing his authority.[85]

Pedro Fages (1734–94) was the first uniformed governor Serra had to contend with. Fages assumed the head post of commandant at the presidio of Monterey in 1770. He replaced Gaspar de Portolá, commander in chief of the expedition that had scouted the coast between San Diego and Monterey Bay. Fages was a career military man with experience in Europe and active service against the Seris in Sonora.[86] In 1770 he was acting as governor of Upper California, sharing power with Felipe Barri in Lower California. As head of the presidio in Monterrey in 1770, the official capital of California and center of all military activities, Fages built a reputation as a strict disciplinarian and was disliked by his own soldiers. Since the early 1770s, Fages and Serra argued, among other things, over the allocation of soldiers to protect the missionaries, the appropriation of mules for service in the all-important transportation of supplies, the salary and daily ratio of servants from the mission in the presidios, and the food allocation for Indian workers. Fages was totally unconcerned about the problems he created by appropriating mission pack animals, denying Indian workers their due salaries, and failing to address complaints about the abusive sexual behavior of his soldiers.[87] Serra's relationship with Fages soured when Fages obstructed the foundation of Mission San Buenaventura due to lacking security personnel to defend that post.[88] Fages was probably correct in this; he did not want martyrs. To resolve this confrontation with the military commander, Serra traveled to Mexico City in 1773 to present his missionary plan to the newly arrived Viceroy Bucareli, in whom he found a friendly reception and support. Serra personally recommended that Viceroy Bucareli replace Pedro Fages on the grounds that the military man did not understand the situation in California.[89]

Fages's dismissal did not resolve Serra's personal encounters with successive governors. In mid-1774 Bucareli appointed Fernando de Rivera y Moncada to replace Fages as military commander and governor of California. Serra was hopeful that the new commander would be more agreeable to the missionaries. He was wrong. After a very brief period of cordial relations, Rivera showed that he had gone to California to enforce the royal policy on the administration of the frontier, not Serra's vision. Rivera began questioning Serra's decisions and judgments the moment he arrived. They barely tolerated each other. Both men were already at odds by the summer of 1775, exchanging arguments and counterarguments about provisions, the cost of feeding the mission's population, the share of provisions between missions and presidios, and the allocation of pack animals and cattle.[90] Fr. Pedro Font, who was in California in 1776, wrote down in his diary that Rivera cared more for his soldiers than for the friars and personally disliked those who got along well with the missionaries, such as Lieutenant Antonio Francisco Ortega.[91] Rivera wanted to soft-pedal some of Serra's plans for the foundation of more missions, although he eventually agreed to the foundation of San Juan Capistrano between the missions of San Diego and San Gabriel.[92] Rivera and his followers had the upper hand in determining the safety of the mission's location, a point not easily arguable or winnable by the missionaries. Serra continued to pursue his objectives regardless of tensions with the governors, but the royal policy trend to strengthen the military presence in California would undermine his plans.

In 1779, Governor Felipe de Neve wrote a *reglamento* for the government of the province of California. It was approved by the Crown in October 1780. The document, naturally, placed the commanding power clearly in the hands of the military governor, streamlined the operations of the presidios, and helped the governor exercise his authority more efficiently.[93] The *reglamento* called the missions *reducciones*, a term that irked Serra and the missionaries. As a throwback to the sixteenth century, it implied the coercive process of bringing the Indians to the missions. This was not the situation in California and definitely not Serra's understanding of the nature of the missions under his command. He was just as incensed with the attempt to classify the missions as *doctrinas*, a term applicable to religious units under the authority of a bishop. There was no bishop in California. In 1782, he was still railing about what he considered misinterpretations of the role of the missions. In a letter to Teodoro de Croix, he commented that he was pleased that Croix referred to the establishments as *misiones*, not *doctrinas*, reminding his addressee of the difference between the terms.[94]

The third governor of California, Felipe de Neve (1721–84), was also a career officer who had seen service in Querétaro and had served as governor of Lower California by appointment of Viceroy Bucareli in October 1774. He stayed in Loreto between 1775 and 1776 before he was sent to Monterrey. He served there through 1782.[95] As the author of the *reglamento* for the government of California, he continuously harassed Serra, attempting to force him to do exactly as the document stipulated. Neve's vision of California was that of a territory in need of non-Indian settlers living in pueblos defended by the presidios and men like him. He was not interested in the Indigenous population or in missions. Serra continually challenged him and tried to assert his views and make Commander Neve aware of his personal authority as a man of the cloth in charge of the souls and welfare of the neophytes. Both men felt they were "soldiering" for their own highest authority. Serra was "soldiering" for God, and Neve was soldiering for the king. Missionaries were fighting their last battle of authority, and Serra could see how they would lose it unless they held their ground.

Neve's audacity knew no bounds. He challenged Serra's right to administer confirmations to those qualifying Christians under his spiritual guidance.[96] Confirmation is a sacrament that completes the process of belonging to the church, while admission begins with baptism. Serra had the right to administer confirmations. The Franciscans had received papal approval for confirmation in 1774, but Neve engaged in a long and tedious dispute over "personally" seeing the papal papers before he would allow Serra to proceed with the confirmation process. This was a clear invasion of territories, and Serra would not relent or provide the papers, which he did not have materially in the mission.[97] Although the right to confirmation was restored to Serra, the whole incident reinforced tensions kindled by Neve's authoritarian character. In another dispute Neve refused to listen to the arguments against founding a secular pueblo close to the Santa Clara mission. Neve also wanted missions to be known as *doctrinas*.[98] As Serra put it in one of his reports, he had long altercations with Neve, but no reasoning was ever to any avail with him.[99] Serra also had confrontations with Teodoro de Croix, the commandant general of the Internal Provinces who was also invested in the policy of secularizing the frontiers.[100] In 1782 Serra and Croix were involved in a tense exchange over the latter's demand that Serra could not move any missionaries from their missions without *his* permission. Serra tersely reminded Croix that his uncle, Viceroy Carlos Francisco de Croix (1766–71), had entrusted the missions to his college with all faculties to govern themselves in matters of conversions.

In his numerous letters and reports, Serra defined the key pursuits as a missionary. He envisioned a chain of missions that would become steps in a ladder "ascending" north in pursuit of the conversion of the Indigenous population. He never relented. In 1778 he wrote to Teodoro de Croix, "Missions, Sir, missions, Sir, is what this land needs."[101] Serra understood missions and missionaries as the main vectors for "civilizing" the land. Missions would be self-sufficient and also help the presidios with labor and the produce raised by the missions. His main goal was to reaffirm the authority of the missionary over catechization and the Indigenous who were proselytized. Unfortunately for him and the rest of the missionaries, the Crown had taken a different direction on this matter and reclaimed the Indians as "subjects" in their civil status, thus weakening the principles of missionary activity. The Indigenous were, in fact, to be granted the faculty of self-government in their own "republic," as in the sixteenth century, under the assumption that they would reach maturity as Spanish subjects when they became fully Christianized and acquainted with Spanish municipal (*cabildo*) legislation. A term of ten years of indoctrination was deemed necessary for the Indians to reach full maturity in self-rule. However, the missionaries and even some secular bureaucrats doubted that the Indigenous under their supervision would attain a full degree of Spanish "civic" education in such a short time. Serra died in 1784 having accepted the diminished role of the missionaries but also having successfully helped build a chain of nine missions. They represented the newest version of the oldest institution created by Spain to deal with the Native population. His successor, Fr. Fermín Francisco de Lasuén, had an easier time dealing with the military authorities because he accepted the "new order." He complied with the regulations and tried to endear himself to the governors while discreetly pushing for the numerical expansion of the missions. He presided over the foundation of ten missions, the last one in September 1804, the year of his death, to make a total of nineteen. Having topped the number of missions founded by his mentor, he completed Serra's work. While the missionaries remained under surveillance from the military and the governors, by the end of the century, both sides had learned how to observe rules of etiquette and avoid confrontational roles of dominant masculinity.

The practice of missionizing changed a lot in the eighteenth century. How different were the late eighteenth-century missionaries from early eighteenth-century missionaries like the iconic Fr. Antonio de Jesús Margil? The answer can be only schematic and suggestive, but it is a topic that bears further analysis to assess the personal character of missionaries and the nature of missionary activity throughout time. Margil was the archetypal missionary, following traditional patterns of missionary activity but also introducing meaningful innovations. He helped extend the Colegios de Propaganda Fide with the foundation of the college in Zacatecas and by serving in *misiones vivas* among the Indigenous in Texas, Guatemala, and Central America. Unlike later missionaries, he amplified the concept of "mission" by not reducing his role to one dedicated to the Indigenous alone. He revived and redefined "urban missions" as part of Propaganda Fide's double-pronged plan for spiritual work among believers and nonbelievers. He became a living legend by practicing physical and spiritual athleticism in his long walks through the rough landscapes of the farthest reaches of New Spain.[102] Unlike late eighteenth-century missionaries, he did not have to face any restrictions or challenges from the royal administrators, as Serra and his men did. Viceregal authorities never interfered with his peregrinations or his urban missions. Religious sentiment and personal piety were strong in 1726, the year of Margil's death.[103] It was still possible to have a solemn Mass and several sermons at his funeral honoring his memory. There were no sermons to honor Serra's death in the remote land of California where he died, and his funeral was small and attended by mostly humble people. His name was not immediately promoted for any elevation to the altars, although his devoted friend Fr. Francisco Palou wrote a biography full of reverence. Margil had at least five biographers, a testimony to the reverence in which he was held. Between Margil's and Serra's time, missionary service reached a vibrant and radiant sunset that hid the fact that missions and missionaries were playing a secondary role in the geopolitical designs of the Spanish Crown. The outcome was the demotion of the men of the cloth to a secondary civic role in the early nineteenth century. After independence from Spain, the men who had helped expand New Spain's frontiers in the preceding three centuries and had assumed the task of incorporating Indigenous populations into the social and political body of the state lost their appeal to republican governments. There would be other ways to make citizens of all those who lived in the new nation.

Issues of Self and Emotions

Self-definition (or self-fashioning) as a form of understanding one's position in society is not obvious in the texts written by religious men and is a topic that remains to be explored by historians. There was more to a missionary than his duties as preacher and shepherd of new converts to the Catholic faith. Whether trekking through unknown territories seeking new converts or trying to strengthen established missions in the borderlands of the viceroyalty, missionaries became acquainted with many Indigenous tribes and their lifestyles and could not help measuring themselves against the Indian, the subject of their spiritual attention but also an alien they had to learn how to understand in order to carry out their mission. There was no "training" for learning empathy and sorting out the obstacles posed by cultural differences between the Indigenous and the missionaries. Unfortunately, everything they read or heard about the Natives before they began their journey north was negative and threatening, and their own self-definition as saviors of the Indigenous was crucial to themselves and to historians wishing to understand them.

The basic element of the missionaries' self-definition was that they were different from the Indians by divine appointment. In 1777 Fr. Francisco Garcés (1738–81) wrote a self-affirming description of his role:

> Thank be to God, I see reviving in our time the old Spanish passion for discovering and taking possession of new lands in order to gather precious pearls, the souls of men! . . . I see the great steps that are being taken for having us press further into the interior, and I firmly believe that God will favor our enterprise by bringing to us the most savage nations if we please Him by adding at once to His church so many thousands of souls as today are disposed to join it, and are awaiting us with open arms, as can be seen in my record.[104]

In the last quarter of the eighteenth century, Garcés still held the sixteenth-century utopian belief in the redemption of the "savages" by the kind word of God, with himself and others carrying the apostolic task of conversion. Pursuing that objective, he went out of his way to create friendships with all the nations in present-day Arizona and Utah in his daring explorations.[105] He learned to communicate with the Pimas and Yumas, visited their *rancherías*, partook in meals with all who came across his path, called them his friends, and acknowledged his debt to them as guides and providers of food and shelter. He was guided by his own curiosity and his understanding that learning from the Natives would help his own mission. By teaching them his own faith, he hoped that someday, they would share it. He had a lot of sympathy for their needs as people but remained emotionally detached from them. Fr. Pedro Font criticized Garcés for mixing with and trusting the Indians, not understanding that by doing so, Garcés was learning how to survive during his lone explorations.

During his travels in the Southwest, Garcés had plenty of time to observe the tribes of the region and gather materials for what became a study of their main social and cultural features.[106] His notes included a language-based classification of the tribes, and he made a detailed account of the relationships among them. It was an erudite compilation that revealed a serious ethnographic curiosity on his part, although some of his conclusions were questionable. He surmised that neither Spanish settlements nor the missions would be successful unless the Natives of the lower Colorado River were brought under Spanish control. As he put it, whatever time and effort was spent in mastering the Colorado River region would keep the missions on the coast viable. A presidio should be established in the Río de la Asunción (Gila River) to pose an obstacle to Hopi and Tewa incursions and to shelter other Indians from them. This presidio would ensure continuous contact, by either land or sea, between San Diego and northwest New Spain as well as open trade routes between Monterrey and New Mexico. In time, Garcés thought, the Hopis would lose their grip on the region and the Spaniards would be able to annex it safely. Although his conclusions were the fruit of his personal approach to the Natives and his contact with them, his report reveals him to be more than a selfless good friend of the Indians. Garcés was an observer and a "researcher" in the modern meaning of the word. He accumulated a considerable geopolitical understanding of the area and was a long-term planner and an apt player in the politics required for missionary success precisely because he learned from the Indians. To a modest extent, he revived the ethnographic interest that was so intensive and productive among some sixteenth-century missionaries.

Conversely, there was Fr. Pedro Font, whose ideas as an established missionary in the Pimería Alta were reviewed earlier and who shared with his brothers in religion the firm conviction that they were carrying the banner of God and were protected by divine forces. This self-assurance led him to self-define as "other," as different from the Indians, a sentiment he confided to his "intimate" diary when he traveled with Juan Bautista de Anza's second expedition to secure a final route to reach California overland. During that journey he had the opportunity to observe many Indian tribes in the Gila River area and southern California. He was temporarily detached from Anza's second expedition and stayed among the Yumas and Jalcheduches (Alchedoma) as a companion to Fr. Francisco Garcés. After the expedition's arrival in Monterrey on March 11, 1776, Font celebrated Mass. Junípero Serra and other friars from the mission of San Carlos del Carmelo were present, and Font took the trouble to transcribe the thrust of his sermon in his diary. He chose a passage from Matthew: "The kingdom of God is like a net; it captures all the fish in the sea."[107] God, he believed and wrote, had favored the expeditionary force, and all who had participated in it should feel chosen and protected by God during their long treks through dangerous lands. He also thanked the Virgin of Guadalupe, Saint Michael, and Saint Francis. It was a good sermon for the occasion, but during the expedition, Font had been bothered by his own mixed feelings about the Indians. He sought to "confess" them in his diary to reconcile his feelings with his beliefs.

Font's most open reckoning with himself was written on December 7, 1775. It was one of the longest entries in his diary. He wrote a series of questions and answers addressing the issue that had goaded him throughout his trip: Had God created such men to condemn them? What sins had those Indians or their ancestors committed to be born in such distant lands, warring among themselves all the time, living like beasts, with so many physical needs, in nudity, and with such ignorance of everything?[108] In a most unusual disclosure of sentiments, Font wrote how he was repelled by the Yumas he encountered on his way to California. He could not stand any intimacy with them. His opinion of the Yumas was that they were "muy asquerosos y sin vergüenza alguna" (very dirty and lacking modesty) because they went nude and never made any attempt to cover their genitals. As he understood it, "modesty" was a natural sentiment among humankind.[109] By going naked without embarrassment, he believed that the Natives lacked a *natural* instinct that civilized people had. On the other hand, he praised the cleanliness and lack of body odor of the Indians *attached to the mission* of San Luis Obispo. He also blamed the Indian women for the sexual irregularities condemned by the missionaries. The women, he wrote, seemed to be fond of the Spaniards, and this was "the reason why the soldiers were so disorderly with them." The allocation of the guilt of lasciviousness to the men was hard to accept by some men of the period. On the other hand, another missionary, Fr. Luis Jayme, had a different version of such relationships. He noted that Indian women were victims, not admirers, of the soldiers.[110] Some missionaries were more perceptive than others.

Going through a tortuous process of reconciliation between what he was taught to believe about the humanity of all peoples and God's mysterious designs and what he saw and did not like about the Indians, Font reached his own conclusions. Resorting to Old and New Testament quotes, he argued that God did not create men to be subjected to the devil. Those who belonged to God's church would be redeemed, and God would save others by some occult means of his own. That would include those who did not know God's law through no fault of their own. No man should dare to doubt God's intentions because God's mercy extended to even those of such limited understanding that they could be described as the "donkeys" of the human race. God would save them too, he concluded, although he could not know how many, or when, or how. Thus, Font unburdened his conscience on that day. From then on, he could refer to the antagonizing Indians as ungrateful, perfidious, cumbersome, and untrustworthy. God would find a way of saving them. It's difficult to reconcile these impressions with his later activities as a missionary in Pimería Alta. Obviously, Font found his duties as a missionary more bearable among Indians who had officially adopted Christianity. The lifestyle of those Natives living in the outer frontiers of northern Sonora and California took him to the border of doubting God's designs, but he pulled back when he understood the spiritual danger of his thoughts and never went beyond the edge.[111]

The contrast between "wild," "untamed" Indians and the Indians living in missions as *mansos* or *dóciles* was echoed in the correspondence of other missionaries. Fr. Gaspar José de Solís, guardian of the Colegio de Nuestra Señora de Guadalupe of Zacatecas who traveled in northern Mexico and Texas between 1767 and 1768 for an inspection of the Texas missions, also voiced sentiments that resonated with Font's judgment and conclusions.[112] Solís experienced the fear of all those who used the Zacatecas road, where the territory between missions was controlled by Apaches and Comanches.

He described the hostile Indians who preferred not to live in the missions as "barbarians, given to idleness, lazy, indolent. They are very gluttonous and ravenous and eat meat almost raw, roasted and dripping blood. . . . They are idle and given over to all kinds of vices, especially the vices of lasciviousness, robbery, systematic thieving and dancing. . . . They are cruel, inhuman and ferocious. . . . They are very dirty, foul smelling and pestiferous, and they emit such a bad odor from their body that it makes one sick." Solís changed his tune when describing the Indians of the flourishing mission of San José de San Miguel de Aguayo.[113] The neophytes there were under full missionary control and were acculturated enough to follow the work ethic the missionaries used as a yardstick of success. Solís saw them as industrious carpenters, weavers, and field-workers who grew crops of cereals, legumes, and fruits. So abundant were the yields that this mission supplied several others as well as presidios. "The Indians take care of all of this without the necessity of having white people to look after them and administer it," he said. "They are industrious workers and very skillful in everything. . . . They do not employ anyone for anything who does not belong to the mission. . . . All the Indian men and women are well trained in civilized customs and Christianity."[114] Writing in total candor, Solís, like Font, ignored the abilities the Indigenous had prior to meeting Spaniards.

Preaching to the "untamed" involved physical danger. To hide their fears, missionaries had to represent the hostile Indian as a "barbarian." There was little change for over 250 years.[115] While the reports of missionaries have been praised for offering some of the best ethnographic materials on the Natives of Sonora, Nayarit, Nueva Vizcaya, California, Arizona, New Mexico, Texas, and so on, they are perforce ethnocentric in their judgment, always seeing the Indigenous from the "outside" and belittling their ability to successfully live in hostile environments. The majority of the missionaries shared this pattern of perception. Positive nuances emerged only when the Indigenous were willing to accept the ways of the white men.[116]

There were some more generous and gentler views of the Indigenous. In the diary of his journey to California, Fr. Juan Crespí precedes his notes with a statement that extols the magnificence of the land and the good nature of the people encountered. These expressions were addressed to the expected readership. They resemble the enthusiastic exaggerations of Zárate in 1630. This missionary's own state of hope for acceptance and conversion explains his perception of the friendly Indigenous.[117] Fr. Junípero Serra showed sympathy and curiosity about the first Indigenous he encountered on his way to San Diego. On June 23, 1767, he wrote, "Their good looks and good presence, affability and happiness have made us fall in love with them."[118] In his role as a full-fledged missionary, and despite his expressed first impressions of fondness, he still acted as a severe father when he thought the situation called for it, and he also had misgivings about the character of some Indians. He regarded the Indians around San Diego as "áspera y escabrosa indiada" (rough and rugged Indians), a sentiment easy to understand given the negative reception they gave the missionaries and their continued opposition to their presence.[119] Alternatively, Serra was uncomfortable with the perception of the Indians expressed by the proponents of the foundation of a settlement—the San José pueblo—in a location too close to the Santa Clara mission. He resented that the prospective settlers were described as *gente de razón*, as "if the Indians were not" also people of rational understanding.[120] Mixed feelings about their prospective wards were to be expected. Missionaries were a group of well-educated men who had traveled from European cities to the frontiers of a new continent populated with people whose countenance and customs were so different from their own. Their efforts to understand the Indigenous were well intentioned, but too often they fell short of being satisfactory or adequate.

Bonding and Brotherhood

The intellectual and physical obstacles of missionary activity prompt questions about the esprit de corps and ties of brotherhood among those missionaries engaged in conversion in poorly known or remote areas. They had to observe a strong personal discipline to maintain their faith and endure the rigors of long treks. Once established in any of those regions, there were many challenges to their personal safety and their ability to build a sustainable relationship with the local population. They remained dependent on their "mother" convent for moral and spiritual support and on viceregal authorities for supplies and military protection. During their travels and long stays in distant missions, did they miss the sense of community fostered by life in a convent where they were members of a family of their own? The training they received in the novitiate was not simply in religion but in bonding as brothers of their order. Living in distant missions with only sporadic connections with their brothers in religion must have placed a heavy emotional burden on the missionaries.

Loneliness and lack of companionship were features of missionary life in the outer regions of their network. To attenuate the lack of personal contact with his brothers in religion, all missions were required to have two friars. A lone missionary would be unable to cope with all his religious and social obligations. He could become sick and require help to cope with his illness *and* his spiritual and catechizing duties. The need for companionship became only too relevant and necessary in the far north and in California. When the Franciscans of the Colegio of San Fernando took over the Jesuit missions of Baja California in 1767, some missions had only one minister.[121] This was not a desirable situation, and it was one rejected by Fr. Junípero Serra for Upper California, where sometimes he had several missionaries as "supernumeraries" waiting for an assignment. The official *reglamento* of 1781 for the governance of the outer regions of the viceroyalty prescribed one missionary for each mission. This rule was strongly criticized and resisted, not always successfully. There was the unstated acknowledgment that missionary friars needed the physical company of someone who shared their faith, their lifestyle, and their memory of the distant land where they were born.

Missionaries did not see one another often, and it was natural that when they did, they recorded their mutual affection and even joy. Serra was aware of the disruption that missionary service could cause in his men's lives. Before the first sixteen brothers of San Fernando began their trek from Baja California to Alta California, Fr. Juan Crespí wrote how Serra insisted that they stay for three days at Mission Loreto to celebrate Easter together. As each group left in staggered departures, Crespí wrote about "the tenderness of the farewell." He continued, "We had lived not just together but on crowded quarters and now each one was destined to live for so long in cultural and emotional solitude and with little hope of seeing each other in this mortal life."[122] Serra and Crespí had a special brotherhood bond built since childhood and relied on that bond to sustain their future trials.[123] Before he died, Serra requested to be buried next to Crespí in the modest church of their mission. Crespí had similar feelings toward other brothers in religion. Of Fr. Juan Sancho, he wrote, "[Sancho is] my father, companion, and friend to whom I owe many favors." He demonstrated his friendships with other friars with "heart-felt *abrazos*" when they occasionally met. He acknowledged favors that deserved to be paid with love (*cariño*) and graciousness.[124] Before Serra departed from Mission Guadalupe in Lower California, Fr. Juan Ignacio Gastore of Mission Santa Rosa de Mulegue came to bid him goodbye.[125] He had been Serra's companion in the Sierra Gorda missions. The two men spent three days talking and consoling each other because they expected that their farewell would mark the last time they saw each other in this life or, as Serra wrote, "hasta el mañana de después de la muerte" (until the tomorrow after death). When Serra arrived at Mission Santa Gertrudis, he was received by Fr. Dionisio de Basterra. Upon embracing, both men shed tears and stood speechless. Fr. Junípero explained that Fr. Dionisio had fallen into a sort of spiritual depression, called *tristeza*, owing to his solitude among so many Indians without a soldier or even a servant to accompany him. He had, in fact, sent many letters to Fr Junípero seeking some spiritual comfort. Serra understood his own helplessness in relieving the other friar's despondency. His several intercessions with the secular church and military authorities requesting a soldier or a companion for Fr. Dionisio had gone unheeded. Fr. Dionisio had to remain at his post, missing the warmth of conventual life and the camaraderie of his brothers. These two men had been brothers in the order and shared their decision to missionize in a remote land. They knew the emotional need for each other's company. Once he moved north, Serra arrived at Mission San Francisco de Borja, where he met Fr. Fermín Lasuén, to whom, he wrote, he owed special love (*cariño*). Their relationship had some emotional vicissitudes, but in the end, Lasuén released his conflictive feelings about Serra and accepted his missionary role in San Diego, where he trained to become Serra's successor.[126] For his part, Fr. Fermín Lasuén openly talked about loneliness in a letter to Guardian Fr. Francisco Pangua on July 8, 1782. Arguing against the possibility of having only one missionary per mission, he stated, "Loneliness in this work is for me a savage and cruel enemy which has afflicted me greatly. I fled from it, thanks to God, in face of evident risk of dying at its hands; and now as I see it raise its ugly head, even from afar. I tremble at the inconceivable danger in returning to the battle."[127]

The need to have companionship was, at times, trumped by the incompatibility of character among missionaries. In the remote California outlets, bonding had its trials. Personality issues considerably disturbed Lasuén's administration. After over two hundred Indians left Mission San Francisco in the summer of 1796, he learned that their departure might have been caused by the strong disagreement among the three friars at the mission on the conduct of Fr. Antonio Dantí, whose harsh treatment of the Indians raised concerns about the Natives' welfare and their possible flight from the mission.[128] Lasuén's feelings inclined him to protect his missionaries from outside criticism, and in this case, he officially denied the harshness of the treatment, giving Dantí a pass. Even Lasuén's sympathetic biographer concluded that in this decision, he was far from objective and that his conduct may be explained by his concern for protecting the community.[129]

However, no feeling of brotherhood could persuade a missionary to stay when he felt uncomfortable or spiritually and physically unsuited to his task. Some missionaries hated their assignment after they experienced several months or years of service in remote areas. As president of the missions, Lasuén had to resolve his men's requests to retire from service in California. All missionaries leaving Spain to serve in New Spain signed a ten-year service contract. When the time expired, they had the right to either stay in the mission, return to their Mexican friaries, or move back to Spain. In California this right met some obstacles. To retire, a missionary had to receive viceregal approval, a key feature of bureaucratic control over the missionaries. Lasuén had to listen to the insistent demands of some missionaries who could not bear the land, the Indians, or their service. In mid-July 1801 he reported to Fr. José Gasol, guardian at San Fernando, that two retiring missionaries were very vocal in their dislike of the Indians. Lasuén asked Gasol to warn and advise missionaries bound to California that they were to *work with Indians*, not others, to prevent any misunderstanding about the terms of their service.[130] In the spirit of brotherhood, his policy was to give the disenchanted friars permission to leave under a fictitious claim of "sickness" to hide the real cause.[131] He wrote, "When someone comes to me with a suggestion like that, I persuade them not to go; but if they have already made up their minds, I accept their motives."[132]

The experience of missionizing is complex in its historicity. Since, in theory, all friars in New Spain were missionaries, the evolution of the meaning of the word over three hundred years is remarkable in its flexibility to cover a variety of historical situations and complexities in its execution. The explorer missionary, with roots in the sixteenth century, continued to serve in that role through the end of the colonial period. In fact, exploration by land and sea was one of the most important consequences of the missionary endeavor. There was more than exploration in missionizing, however. The amplification of the meaning of the term *mission* to include preaching among the Catholic populations was a remarkable seventeenth-century innovation of the Franciscans of Propaganda Fide. Under their auspices missions took an urban twist, embracing all peoples, not just the Indigenous, extending the meaning of the word in an imitation of practices then current in Spain. The multiplicity of meanings of *mission* was sometimes challenging to the missionaries themselves and will remain a topic of study and discussion for years to come.

6

Martyrs

The Offer of Life

He, who loves God the most, offers what he loves the most (which is his life) for His love and service. For this reason, it is well to conclude that martyrdom is the greatest gift of love to God, and it is a most perfect act, and the greatest service we can render God.

Thus wrote Fr. Jerónimo de Mendieta near the end of the sixteenth century in a eulogy of the robed men who had already died in pursuit of the conversion of the Indigenous to Christianity. Martyrdom in Spanish America revived the early Christian and medieval experience of believers dying for their faith. When Fr. Jerónimo Mendieta began writing the history of the Franciscan order around 1574, he dedicated a special section to the martyrs. Addressing the "Christian reader," he defined the meaning of *martyr* in the context of the New World. In his words, the life of any Christian who followed the gospel was in itself a "cross and martyrdom," especially for those who "suffer willingly for Christ; those who keep His commandments; those who go naked and discalced for Christ; those who go hungry or eating lowly food simply to sustain nature rather than to satisfy hunger." However, "those with whom we deal in the final part of this book, were martyrs in the aforementioned ways, but added to their exemplary and apostolic lives that which exceeds everything else, which is to have offered their lives, and received death witnessing and extolling the name of our Savior Jesus Christ and His holy faith. They deserve more fully so, the title of martyrs."[1]

Mendieta's manuscript was not published until much later, but it was read in its time by his fellow Franciscan Fr. Juan de Torquemada, who "borrowed" a great deal of information from Mendieta and who was much luckier than him in seeing his own work published. Torquemada contributed his own thoughts to the explanation of martyrdom and explained the circumstances that met its definition. The qualifying conditions were threefold. First, the martyr was to receive torture (*tormento*), which meant that his body must have suffered a violent attack resulting in death. The second condition was that such death must have been caused for the love of Christ or in the defense of any moral virtue based on Christ's words. The third was that martyrdom must be voluntary; it must not be sought. It had to "happen." Otherwise, it could be tainted by the concept of "suicide," which was not acceptable to Christianity.[2]

Subsequent chroniclers followed those guidelines. Their narratives recalled the early Christian tradition of martyrdom, but the actors were contemporaneous to their times. Antonio Rubial has proposed that the ancient "Roman" tradition of martyrdom changed in the sixteenth century with the addition of new scenarios for martyrdom in North Africa, the Far East, and the American continent.[3] More recently, Alejandro Cañeque has reviewed martyrdom in a global context to reiterate the renewal of this type of religious phenomenon in the sixteenth century and beyond.[4] Martyrs in New Spain shared the "Roman" tradition and were immersed in the sixteenth- and seventeenth-century global wave of martyrdom. Their direct historical antecedents were in Spain, where early Christian martyrs died when the peninsula was part of the Roman Empire. Two members of the Roman militia, Emeterio and Celedonio, refused to worship pagan gods and were martyred in the city of Calahorra at the end of the fourth century.[5] Another historical element shaping the concept of martyrdom in Spain and its empire in the sixteenth century was the expansion of Islam over North Africa and the invasion of the Iberian Peninsula. Beginning in the eighth century AD, local Christian resistance resulted in martyrdom and several saints-martyrs for the church. One of them was Saint Eurosia (Orosia), who was martyred at Jaca in the Pyrenees in 714. She was followed by Valentine and Engratia, martyred at Sepúlveda (Castile) in 715. However, the center of martyrdom under Islam was the city of Córdoba in the ninth century. Between 835 and 864, forty-seven Christian men and women, some of them nuns, were martyred. All were later elevated to sainthood.[6]

While Spain had a memory of martyrdom of its own, in Mendieta's time and further into the seventeenth century, the European scenarios remained important as intellectual and spiritual inspiration. Protestants and Catholics killed one another, arguing theirs was the only true Christianity according to the New Testament and the deeds of the early Christians. Religious violence in sixteenth-century Europe made martyrs of "common" men and women.[7] Martyrdom was heavily tinted with state politics and was no longer the same process its apologists claimed it to be.[8] In his pithy survey of European martyrdom, Brad Gregory distinguished between the early and late sixteenth-century Catholic martyrs. Spain was more involved in the second phase than in the first as a result of its engagement in the religious wars in the Protestant northern provinces of the Netherlands and a diplomatic confrontation with England.[9] Military engagements, loss of life, and religious violence in Central Europe created an atmosphere of hatred toward Protestants and kindled missionary and pro-martyrdom feelings in Spain and its overseas empire.[10]

Martyrdom gained further relevance as a result of Spain's expansion on the American continent and East Asia, where the attempt at religious conversion resulted in the loss of life of Christian preachers at the hands of Indigenous peoples. Martyrdom in Mexico had no resemblance to that of Europe or Asia. It is not my purpose here to make a comparative analysis between European, Asian, and American martyrdom, but it's important to underline that the perpetrators of martyrdom in New Spain were very different from their European and Asian counterparts. In New Spain, they were members of nomadic or seminomadic tribes lacking strong political organizations, writing systems, and metal tools or arms and were in constant warfare with one another. A greater contrast in cultures could not be imagined. Cultural, technical, and political disparities notwithstanding, the tribes beyond the central areas created enormous difficulties for conquerors and settlers as well as for the missionaries who arrived to preach a new religion. The missionaries were not killed by powerful lords who imprisoned them and ordered their public execution, as in Japan, nor were they martyred by believers in a different interpretation of Christian practice, as was happening in sixteenth-century Europe.[11] It was a unique experience taking place in small, sometimes makeshift churches in remote missions; on the cart roads traversing the vast landscape of the northern territories; in remote areas of the mountain clusters of the viceroyalty; in the humid forests of the southern Yucatán Peninsula, and in the land designated as the *audiencia* of Guatemala. Those places were the domain of the Indigenous, for whom the newcomers were intruders depriving them of their habitat and their personal freedom and, just as importantly, obliging them to accept a new set of beliefs as a nonnegotiable term of subjection. Despite the difference in actors and scenarios, the Christian tradition of martyrdom was inspirational for the missionaries in New Spain during the two and half centuries of their engagement with the Native peoples.

Missionary Expansion, Indigenous Disaffection

The purpose of evangelization was not martyrdom. Martyrs were intent not on dying but on living. They were preachers seeking out Natives in order to indoctrinate them in basic Christianity and "save" their souls. The spiritual guidelines of their discourse were as straightforward as they were narrow. They were engaged in a battle against Satan, and as warriors they were engaged in the appropriately manly occupation of warfare against a resistance that was fueled by the forces of evil.[12] The opportunity to revive the pristine spirit of early Christianity among people who never heard of it was understood as a privilege by those determined friars who felt the call of God and crossed the oceans to participate in a unique enterprise. The chroniclers who wrote about them were also friars who shared the feelings of those who had died as martyrs. As brothers in religion, they understood the martyrs' sacrifice as a privilege resulting from a war against false gods. In his *Monarquía Indiana*, Fr. Juan de Torquemada, a man straddling the sixteenth and seventeenth centuries, cited the saintly law of God as the justification for a spiritual war of blood and fire against the malice and false doctrine taught by the demons to blinded peoples. His brothers in the Franciscan militia were soldiers of Christ helped by divine grace. A righteous God would help the missionary regardless of any danger he may encounter in the fulfillment of his duty.[13] Should the missionary fail to defeat the antagonistic forces and die, his blood would nourish the soil of the faith and encourage the growth of a new crop of souls for religion.[14] Such powerful metaphors fueled the spiritual energy of those who moved forward into scarcely known regions, apparently not afraid to lose their lives for such a lofty cause. It was a peculiar frame of mind shared by hundreds of European men who ventured all around the globe to convince others they should change their religious beliefs. When they perished in the course of their enterprise, they became martyrs of their cause.

In New Spain the missionary frontier began moving in all geographical directions after the conquest of Tenochtitlán. The three mendicant orders vied for territories to engage in the task of conversion in what were frequently "brotherly" skirmishes to gain a foothold in specific areas. However, by the second half of the century, it was obvious that their efforts were not spent in the same fashion and that their first impetus had slowed due to the lack of "soldiers" needed to meet the challenge of the spiritual war. The Crown had to attend to interests beyond conversion, such as the need to establish a strong bureaucracy and a viable government, support the expansion of the secular church, favor the European settlers who were reliable subjects of the king, and extract the mineral wealth of the region.[15] Most importantly, the variety of peoples in the new land and the plurality of their beliefs made the task of conversion harder than initially expected. As experience proved, under the outward acceptance of Christianity lay deep layers of unbelief in the new religion and undercover practices that were difficult to uproot. The term *conversiones vivas* (live conversions) came to mean preaching to unassimilated Indigenous in areas where open resistance could mean death for the evangelizer. By the early seventeenth century, the Augustinians opted out of live conversions, and the Dominicans cut back their efforts to defensible outposts, leaving the Franciscans as the order most consistently engaged in the search for unassimilated and quite often openly hostile peoples. The Crown acknowledged the risks involved in live conversions and provided some military protection to the Franciscans engaged in missionary work in the open frontiers, where they were liable to attack by seminomadic Natives still beyond the effective control of the monarchy. Such protection was never sufficiently thorough or strong to guarantee the lives of settlers or missionaries.

The most important missionary frontier causing the largest number of deaths was the one fanning out and north from the central basin of Mexico City and reaching as far as today's New Mexico, where three friars and a lay brother were involved in the first exploration of the land in 1581. Once these pioneers reached that remote frontier, they had a "feeling" that their work of persuasion was going well because they did not meet open resistance. Fr. Juan de Santa María, one of the members of that early party, insisted on returning to Mexico to notify the authorities of the results of the incursion. He was killed on his way, thus becoming the first martyr of the far north. His two companions eventually suffered the same fate.[16] On the western and eastern Sierra Madres, the missionaries found a diversity of ethnic groups the Spaniards called Chichimecs regardless of ethnic and tribal differences. They were peoples not conquered by the Aztecs, who had carved their own territorial spaces and defended them against all "invaders," whether Indigenous or Spanish. Consequently, the penetration of the northern territories by settlers, soldiers, and missionaries and some of their Indigenous allies was punctuated by concomitant rebellions resulting in a continuous state of war that affected the mobility and effectiveness of the missionaries and caused the martyrdom of those who tried to preach the new religion under such adverse circumstances. The regions south of the capital did not offer armed resistance to the friars or, for that matter, the new political masters. They were complex agriculturalist societies, the heirs of well-established pre-Columbian cultures with well-defined urban centers and political leadership that accepted negotiation as a practical solution to their circumstances. However, south of present-day San Cristóbal de las Casas, a new ecological and human frontier made the religious and political advance difficult and economically undesirable. The situation in the missionary scenario was also difficult in the Yucatán Peninsula. In the early 1620s, three Franciscan missionaries lost their lives trying to make inroads in the jungles of the interior of the peninsula, where the hostility of many tribes was strong and "conversions" were fragile.[17]

Widespread uprisings in New Spain began as early as 1541 with the so-called Mixtón War in the province of Jalisco (1541–42). The alliance of several tribal groups to repel the first Spanish incursion of the western territories was an eye-opener for civil and religious authorities alike. It presaged many decades of hostilities, large and small, that made the missionary task a complicated one, mixing persuasion with violence. The discovery of the silver mines of Zacatecas in 1548 and Guanajuato in 1552 opened the gates of central north New Spain to a throng of settlers, adventurers, and the bureaucracy representing the interests of the king. It also increased the raids of various groups of Chichimecs such as Xiximes, Acaxes, Zacatecos, Guachichiles, and Pames, among others, whose territorial claims were at stake. These tribal Indigenous were unlikely to accept Spanish control without a fight. It did not help that the advancing groups consisting of soldiers and bureaucrats seeking wealth and land stopped short of nothing in their cruel treatment of the population when a hostile confrontation with the tribal peoples ended with the latter's defeat or surrender. Mendieta (and Torquemada) cited an exchange between Natives in western Zacatecas, who presumably wanted to have a missionary with them, and a missionary who begged them to leave their retreat and relocate closer to the Spanish posts to safeguard the lives of the missionary. The Natives responded that they did not want to leave the mountains because the Spaniards would mistreat them and enslave them.[18] That dialogue defined the encounters of many Native groups and the missionaries throughout the colonial period as ones in which the preachers were handicapped by the actions of the civilians.

Indian slavery was one of the unfortunate outcomes of frontier warfare, and it was one of the key reasons for the antipathy shown by the Chichimecs for the men of the cloth who followed the militia and the soldiers.[19] Warfare and the ensuing Indigenous slavery in the sixteenth century prompted a strong debate among the orders on the appropriate strategies for conversion. This debate continued throughout the entire colonial period, but it was particularly acute in the second half of the sixteenth century.[20] By the end of that century, only the Dominicans remained adamant in their philosophical opposition to war against the Indigenous. Franciscans and Augustinians contemporized and believed that warfare was a necessary evil to ensure the viability of new settlements and the propagation of the faith. Frontier expansion and the ensuing warfare against Indigenous tribes had another consequence: martyrdom, mostly for members of the Franciscan order. Feeling protected by the cross, friars never carried weapons, but the symbol of Christ's death did not always afford safety to them.

By several accounts there were nineteen main Indigenous rebellion movements in the seventeenth century and eleven in the eighteenth century up to 1769.[21] After the Mixtón War (1540–42) the potential for rebellion and death increased with every mile of territory gained.[22] Between 1601 and 1603, the Acaxes rebelled in the Sierra de Topia, inspired by a leader who called himself "bishop" and imitated the episcopal functions of the Catholic hierarchy. Susan Deeds regards this first rebellion as a first-generation "pattern" that was copied throughout the century by other rebels in the northern provinces.[23] Rebellions cascaded throughout the seventeenth century with little relief in between. In 1616, the Tepehuán Indians orchestrated a massive rebellion in Nueva Vizcaya (Sonora, Sinaloa, and New Mexico). Ten missionaries lost their lives: eight Jesuits, one Franciscan, and one Dominican. More than two hundred settlers also lost theirs.[24] The attack was aimed at the Spanish presence, and the missionaries were casualties because they were Spaniards. However, in this particular rebellion, the intent to desecrate, humiliate, and reject Christianity was very clear, regardless of the cost to the rebels. The Tepehuán revolt was under control by early 1619 after the loss of thousands of Indigenous lives. Remnant splinter groups retreated into the mountains, where they remained ready for further action.[25]

In the aftermath of the 1619 rebellion, the Franciscans order, consisting largely of Spanish-born missionaries, aimed at the northern frontiers, leaving the western sierras to the Jesuits. Franciscans built up missions in Atotonilco (Guanajuato) and San Francisco de los Conchos (Chihuahua) and were able to proceed to New Mexico, where they established a toehold in the 1610s. Under the care of dedicated custodians, the missions in New Mexico seemed to be thriving by midcentury. They had established a string of missions among the Pueblo Indians in the farthest frontier of the viceroyalty, but they also collected more martyrs in the process. Two friars were killed by the Jemez and Taos by 1640.[26] In that distant frontier, Spanish civil and religious authorities did not get along, and this internal weakness helped sustain the spiritual leadership of local shamans who kept their ancient religion alive. The general Indigenous population resented the heavy labor taxation imposed by settlers and by the missionaries themselves. The Tarahumaras of the western Sierra Madre rebelled in Chihuahua in 1644 and in 1648. Other uprisings took place in 1653 and 1672. A carefully planned New Mexico revolt exploded in 1680. Twenty-one Franciscan missionaries were killed, expanding the ranks of martyrdom exponentially. The loss of human life and political control of the area were serious blows for the Crown and for the Franciscans. Among the several causes cited by historians for this revolt were famine produced by droughts, forced labor in the missions, disrespect for Indigenous culture, half-baked religious acculturation, and the lack of appeal of Christianity.[27] While a full review of these revolts is not possible here, the end result was a rejection of Roman Catholicism after decades of catechization. It took the Spaniards ten years to return to New Mexico. In 1693 they claimed a secure settlement, but another smaller revolt took place in 1696. It cost the lives of four more Franciscans. At that point, forty-nine of them had died as martyrs, making the seventeenth century the high point of martyrdom.

In the eighteenth century, the missionary and military activity in the northern areas continued to expand the frontiers to strengthen the political presence of the Spanish Crown against mostly French incursions on the Gulf Coast in the present-day states of Texas, Louisiana, and Mississippi. The perceived threat of Russian occupation on the western coast of North America expanded the Franciscan missionary field to Upper California.[28] The continental Southwest and Baja California were opened to missionary activity by the Jesuits in the seventeenth century. After their expulsion in 1757, the Franciscans took over their missions in Upper California, and the Dominican order was entrusted with the lower peninsula. This expansion of the northern frontier meant more encounters with seminomadic tribes that, theoretically, bolstered the chances of martyrdom. The Apaches, in particular, proved to be the nemesis of settlers and missionaries, but other groups such as the Seris of Sonora remained aggressive in the defense of their territory. In the northeastern part of New Spain, Franciscans reached present-day East Texas by the 1690s, but their physical presence there remained small.[29] That region was a key destination for geopolitical reasons: the French were attempting to claim the territory called Louisiana today. The Franciscan experience in the area was not very auspicious. Missionaries extended their missions inland but had to retreat for lack of material and military support in an area so far removed from provision centers.[30] After several years of fruitless missionizing in East Texas, the missions retreated to the western part of the state.

The number of martyrs in the eighteenth century was reduced dramatically despite the fact that the frontier remained a contested space. The creation of a line of presidios on the frontier enhanced the military presence, although it was not a deterrent to Indigenous raids.[31] The fate of the mission of San Sabá was symbolic of the failure of missionary activity without appropriate safeguards. Established in 1757 by the margins of the San Sabá River, which drains into the Colorado River (Texas), the mission was the brainchild of the rich miner and entrepreneur Pedro Romero de Terreros, Count of Regla. His nephew, Fr. Alonso Giraldo de Terreros, was one of the three Franciscans in charge of this missionary post when it was attacked in March 1758.[32] Fr. Alonso came from the Colegio de Propaganda Fide of San Fernando in Mexico City, and the mission of San Sabá was part of a series of projected establishments that had the Rio Grande as its central axis and stretched east in present-day Texas. Unfortunately, the area was populated by Apaches, who were under the double threat of the Comanches and the

Spanish military and missionary presence. The Comanches understood the Spanish advance as offering protection to their enemies, and on March 16, 1758, a large number of them attacked the mission and killed Fr. Alonso Giraldo and Fr. Joseph Santiesteban. The death of Terreros was by gunshot, after which he was scalped. Santiesteban was shot close to the altar. Fr. Miguel de Molina managed to escape, although wounded, reaching the presidio about five miles distant three days later. The mission was burned down by the attackers, who left the site several days later after failing to draw the presidio soldiers into battle.[33] The presidio commander gave a long explanation for his absence at the time of the attack. He claimed that the lack of an adequate number of soldiers prevented a proper defense.

The death of the socially well-connected Fr. Alonso Giraldo and the destruction of the mission ended further attempts to missionize that area. What one gleans from the official account of the attack is that the martyred missionaries were attempting to appease the Apaches in a calculated strategy of pretending to help them deliver their grievances to the presidio. The plan failed. Terreros was shot in the back in a rare instance of the use of firearms in the act of martyrdom. Presidios offered limited protection to missionaries, who did not always count on military assistance. Since the late seventeenth century, civil authorities had insisted that missionaries travel with a military escort, but not all missionaries took the offer. In the eighteenth century escorts were more frequent, but under special circumstances some missionaries traveled alone.

Although the number of martyrs declined in the eighteenth century, the circumstances of their deaths are well known. Death came by arrows or by the blunt strike of wooden *macanas*. Only exceptionally is information on the circumstances of martyrdom missing, as it was in the case of Fr. Francisco Javier Silva, a member of the Colegio de Propaganda Fide in Zacatecas, founded in 1704. He was serving in the coastal Nuevo León missions founded by the college and exposed to constant raids by the Apaches by the mid-eighteenth century when he died. No report on how he met his death is available.[34] More typical was the death of Fr. Luis Jayme, who was killed by arrows on November 4, 1775, at the mission of San Diego, which had been founded six years earlier in 1769. He was presumably addressing the attackers, invoking the love of God, when a shower of arrows pierced his body in a lethal answer to his missionary speech. The presidio was too far from the mission, and the soldiers remained unaware of the attack until dawn on the following day. Francisco Tomás Hermenegildo Garcés, Juan Díaz, Juan Antonio Barreneche, and Joseph Matías Moreno were killed on July 18 and 19, 1781, at the junction of the Gila and the Colorado Rivers in today's Arizona during a revolt that effectively stopped further missionary activity in the area. There was no military protection in that particular spot. They were the last martyrs of that century.

It is against this background of hostility, warfare, Indian enslavement, surrender, and defiance from the Indigenous peoples that the martyrs loom large in the histories of the two orders with the most intensive engagement in evangelization, the Jesuits and the Franciscans.[35] Once the circumstances of their demise are discussed, it is essential to move beyond the details of their deaths to understand what martyrdom, as the legacy of personal sacrifice from early Christian times, meant for those who envisioned and suffered it as a personal experience.

Essential Martyrdom

The eulogies of martyrs in the chronicles of the mendicant orders offer glimpses into the mindsets of the actors and guide us in understanding the meaning of martyrdom in New Spain. Direct testimonies from martyrs prior to their deaths are hard to come by, since most of the friars had no time to write anything but letters and reports to their superiors. In a few cases, some friars had time to assess the circumstances preceding a revolt and left reports to their superiors. Such reports are the closest form of evidence of a "personal" feeling about impending death, though they refer mostly to "conditions" of defense and unpreparedness.

Most missionaries did not expect to be martyrs, but they were cognizant of the possibility. Early in the seventeenth century, when missionaries were arriving regularly at the shores of New Spain and the Americas, a non-Spanish witness, Thomas Gage, reported an incident that speaks volumes about the zeal that some of those men carried with them when they departed from Spain to save souls in the New World. Having left Spain in the annual fleet in 1625, Gage's vessel anchored for water and some rest in the eastern Caribbean island of Guadalupe. Some traveling missionaries disembarked, and after contact with the Indigenous, some of them were carried away by the prospect of converting the islanders. In the ensuing discussion on board, some were of the opinion that it was a temerity to disembark and stay on the island, exposing their lives to people of unknown character and disposition. Gage records that a group of exalted would-be missionaries made their position clear: the possibility of perishing by the hand of savages was among the reasons they had left the motherland. If death should come in the fulfillment of their duties, they welcomed it.[36]

Some of those who became martyrs must have shared this attitude. A rare glimpse into the mindset of a young peninsular friar about potential martyrdom is provided in a letter written by Fr. Joseph Matías Moreno, an eighteenth-century recruit of the Colegio de Propaganda Fide in Querétaro who was killed in the Colorado River by the Yumas in 1781. A letter to his sister was rescued from his body by the Franciscan chronicler Juan Domingo Arricivita. The letter speaks of his burning desire to attain the palm of martyrdom. He confides to her that the reasons for having left Spain and his family behind were "the zeal [*celo*] of the faith, the desire of the conversion of the souls and the desire [*ansias*] of martyrdom." Those elements had moved him to put off all personal considerations for safety. As he put it, "Work, hunger, thirst, unbearable heat and roads are all true, but what are they compared to the cost of souls for Christ? If some of us do not undertake His spiritual conquest, many souls will ineluctably fall in the snares of Satan. I owe Him many benefices."[37] This young man truly believed that he was in debt to Christ and that he should repay that debt by working to save souls, regardless of discomfort or obstacles. Moreno's view reflected the personal and institutional expectations of those who made their vows a lived experience.

When chroniclers wrote about the martyrs, they infused their writing with their own personal thoughts and sympathetic sentiments for their brothers. They shared the "burning zeal" to indoctrinate the Natives and their willingness to suffer pain, sickness, calamities, and poverty. Eighteenth-century Franciscan chronicler Fr. Juan Domingo Arricivita was speaking as a missionary when he wrote, "It was not leisure, rest, security or comfort in life the missionaries pursued when among those barbarous nations, but the travails, dangers, and all that belonged to Jesus Christ and his greater glory, the exaltation of the Faith through the Gospel and the salvation of the souls."[38]

Imbued with this personal drive, the missionaries assumed practices and took risks that led some of them to their deaths. Martyrdom cases from the sixteenth through the eighteenth century share similar features, especially those in the sixteenth and seventeenth centuries, when vast expanses of the land remained open and unknown. The progress of martyrdom history had its beginnings in New Galicia with the death of Franciscan lay brothers Juan Calero early in 1541 and Fr. Antonio de Cuellar in August of the same year, both of the recently founded convent of Ezatlán, Jalisco. The Mixtón War had delayed advance into New Spain's western area, where Calero and Cuellar worked on the conversion of the Caxanes prior to their revolt. Calero died after he met with the rebels, who had abandoned the area to avoid the Spaniards and their missionaries, and tried to persuade them to return to Ezatlán. Three of his companions, newly converted to Catholicism, were also killed. To the Indians, they were social and religious "apostates" and they met the same fate as the friars. Cuellar was returning to his convent after accompanying another friar to his own when he was assaulted and killed not far from Ameca (Jalisco), a town he had helped found.[39]

Traveling in the open expanse of the northern frontiers was a daily affair for friars. The landscape had the magnetic pull of an inner spiritual call. Walking by themselves, they could have imagined being like the early missionaries in the Mediterranean and the Middle East. Protective company was not always available, but the lure of "the beyond" pushed the missionaries hundreds of leagues into the unknown. That attitude of spiritual adventure sustained four half-forgotten Franciscan friars who accompanied Captain Juan de Tolosa in September 1546 in his first entry into what was later known as Zacatecas, the site of the richest mines encountered so far.[40] One adventurous Fr. Jacinto de San Francisco visited the land later called New Mexico in 1559, accompanied by two other nameless and now forgotten friars, in pursuit of the indoctrination of the Natives of that area. This first trip was fruitless, but Fr. Jacinto believed he could return to attempt the conversion.[41] A similar strong belief in his own capacity to convert the Indigenous in totally unknown areas led a nephew of Viceroy Antonio de Mendoza, Fr. Gerónimo de Mendoza, to enter the surrounding sierras. Chronicler Arlegui calls him "another Paul," signifying the apostolic role those men had assumed and the respect they commanded in their own times. The Natives were totally stunned by his presence, and the friar probably believed he had achieved a conversion as he visited several settlements. The fact that he was not killed was in itself proof of divine protection. He settled down and began to preach in the Zacatecan language. The chronicler offers no further information on his fate.[42]

Welcoming towns and peoples did not necessarily mean a true and lasting conversion. For the Indigenous, the robed men were novelties. Once they learned about them, the Natives could decide to reject them and their message. When that happened, they became "treacherous" rebels in the eyes of the evangelizers. They could spring from the rugged sierras at any time and assault travelers. When they harmed the friars, retaliation by Spanish authorities reinforced the antagonistic feelings among the Indigenous communities. When the communities decided to accept Spanish suzerainty and the presence of a preacher-evangelizer, they had their own political or economic reasons for doing so, but they were unlikely to be truly Christianized, a process that required more than lip service to the words of a preacher.

Friars who asked to be sent north of Zacatecas, a territory known as Nueva Vizcaya, knew that the area was dangerous. The risk triggered their desire to serve their order and fulfill their missionary commitment. Friars were great trekkers. To earn the trust of their potential converts, they followed the apostolic example of the first Christian preachers traveling on foot, rather than on mule or horse, and were often alone or accompanied by a small retinue.[43] They never took food with them and lived on berries and nuts or whatever "divine providence" provided. They were defenseless and open to attack as they embarked on what today appear as reckless entries in territories populated by Indians who had no interest in the Christian religion and were ready to reject any attempts to change their ways.

Fr. Pedro de Espinareda, who arrived in Zacatecas in 1556 to help the already cited Fr. Gerónimo de Mendoza establish a missionary outpost, coordinated the foundation of missions in the roughest parts of the mountains, and by 1565 he had managed to found the required five "convents" to become a Franciscan province. The convents were flimsy constructions, not the solid stone buildings of later years. His apparent success hid the fact that the conversions were more assumed than real and the friars lived in penury, lacking any Indigenous assistance to subsist. As the first official custodian of the Franciscan convent of Zacatecas in 1566, Espinareda was the head of an enormous missionary territory that was "90 leagues from north to south and 140 from west to east."[44] He requested help from the Franciscan province of the Holy Gospel in Mexico City to begin missionary work, and he sent the newly arrived friars to the roughest mountain areas to catechize and found convents. Sending them to such places with such scarcity of resources he was sending them to their deaths.[45] In 1555, after two of his missionaries were killed, Fr. Pedro thanked God for the grace of such "benefice" and quickly "decided to send two new workers" to the new enterprise in Sinaloa, knowing that it was populated by "numberless barbarians." He was not deterred by the death of his men, who, he envisioned, had gone directly to heaven. Espinareda and his friars still retained what Mendieta described as "the desire to obtain abundant fruit from the thorns and thistles of infidelity."[46] The first martyr in the Sinaloa project was French-born Bernardo Cossin, who lasted hardly one year in his task before he was killed by arrows. After his death Espinareda sent two more friars. They managed to survive for thirteen years in their post before they were killed. Two other friars sent to the Valle de Topia in the western Sierra Madre (today's Durango) were also martyred.[47] Giudicelli and Ragon count seven martyrs in the environs of Zacatecas and Sinaloa before 1570.[48]

The circumstances of their deaths showed many similarities. Personal commitment and the vow of obedience to their superiors bound some of the first evangelizers and later martyrs to proceed into unknown territory. A review of Mendieta's account of the lives and deaths of sixteenth-century Franciscan martyrs shows that the friars, traveling without much personal protection, ventured into small settlements (*rancherías*) by themselves or accompanied by a lay brother and perhaps a couple of Christianized Indians who acted as "translators." Lacking any company and not speaking the language, they trusted in God's protection, as must have been the case with Bernardo Cossin. Sometimes they walked into dangerous areas where previous contact with abusive Spaniards had made the Natives apprehensive of any foreigner. The large number of Indigenous languages was an obstacle to any meaningful verbal communication in the initial phases, whether in the sixteenth century or in more remote areas later on in time. As the chronicles state, the friars "introduced themselves" by speaking ill of the Native gods and threatening their followers with the punishment of their own Christian God. Fr. Jerónimo de Mendieta and Fr. Joseph Arlegui use the words *reprendiéndoles* (reprimanding) and *afeandoles* (censuring) when describing the friars' approach to discussing the Natives' conduct and their gods. That was a negative approach as a first attempt at communication. In at least one case, the friar slept in the house of their gods, a possible desecration. Other friars in the seventeenth century also ventured inside such temples to break the "idols." Those tactics were unlikely to win over any followers. Those Natives who were ill disposed to any intruder would react negatively to the friar's gesturing and "preaching," since they probably looked quizzical, aggressive, or simply insufferable to them. We will never know. Bernardo Cossin is said to have died as a result of a confrontation with a group of "mountain" Chichimecs who ran out of patience with his exhortations and interrupted him with a shower of arrows, killing him instantly.[49]

When the preachers were accompanied by Christianized Indigenous, it is not always clear that they communicated effectively with the unconverted, since they were repeating whatever they knew as new Christians. The reception of the Christian message has been scrutinized and questioned by linguists and cultural historians with plausible arguments.[50] The problem with early martyrs as communicators was that their knowledge of the many Indigenous languages of the outlying tribes was questionable. Even when Indigenous people were told in their own language the principles of the alien religion, they most likely associated them with what they knew, not what they were intended to mean. Feedback from their recently converted companions was probably unreliable. Conversely, no words were necessary when a stranger arrived at any Native settlements and smashed their gods. The message conveyed by such actions was clearly aggressive and negative, and the response was, not surprisingly, violent. On one occasion, two friars whose names have been lost to history so astonished a group of the Sierra de Topia Natives with their preaching that they stood speechless until the friars finished delivering their message. Then the friars destroyed their gods. The Topias were probably impressed and confused by the initial friars' "performance," since they did not understand a word, but they seemed to have recovered their composure and killed the friars in response to the smashing of their gods.[51]

Emotions: Fear or Defiance?

Writing on martyrdom gave chroniclers an opportunity to cast death in a special light.[52] Death by martyrdom was unique because it revived the holy memory of early Christians and of Christians defending their faith against unwilling and often dangerous enemies throughout time. Martyrs were the object of reverence and inspiration to all missionaries in the dangerous frontiers of Christendom.[53] Chroniclers recast the drama of the innocent martyred hero as a victim of the evil murderers. Details, in some instances, were provided by witnesses who escaped an attack and reported the circumstances of martyrdom to ecclesiastical authorities who passed their testimonial to the chroniclers who, in turn, added pathos to the event using their writing abilities.

The information furnished by the chroniclers indicates that the martyred friars tried to engage their audience with "gestures" that would convey the message of a new god and faith. Most of the missionaries eulogized by Arlegui, for example, died preaching to their last breath. He evoked the sound of voices that would not stop, comparable to the last song of a swan.[54] Typically, the missionary fell to his knees holding a crucifix or simply yielded to the attackers without resistance as a last sacrificial gesture. Prior to departing on a missionizing tour, the friars would confess each other, pray, and share words of hope and consolation. In other instances, if an attack was expected, the missionaries prepared themselves for their demise.[55] Fr. Francisco Lorenzo and his companions came very close to death—which they escaped—as the attacking Natives inexplicably desisted from its apparent agenda, but hey had prepared for death the night before:

> That night they made the best preparations possible to receive their death for Jesus Christ. Fr. Miguel confessed to his Guardian, and the Guardian lay on the floor, with many tears begging mercy from God for all his transgressions, and having set up a crucifix on the ground, they knelt before it; they prayed at times and they consoled and encouraged each other with the hope that all would be right because they had not undertaken that journey or peregrination in search of gold, silver or any temporal goods, but only to find the lost souls that had been redeemed by the passion and blood of the son of God.[56]

Some chroniclers spared no details of the deaths of friars to ensure the empathy of their readers, casting the Indians in the worst of lights. For example, Bernardo de Lizana, in his history of Yucatán, tersely states how the Mayas of Taiza tore Fr. Diego Delgado to pieces and removed the hearts and cut off the heads of Fr. Juan Enríquez and several soldiers. Enríquez was tied to a pole while the soldiers were killed, and he continued to preach aloud until his turn came.[57]

The hagiography sometimes presents the martyr as either predestined to die or willing to die. There is probably no hyperbole on the issue of willingness to die, suspicious as it may look to our contemporary eyes. When the missionary preached the gospel, he engaged in a war against the enemy, and all wars implied the personal risk of death. Brad Gregory makes a strong case for accepting the reasons given by the European martyrs to risk their lives. As he posits, the spirituality of the late fourteenth century (*devotio moderna*), which lasted for several centuries, was based on the imitation of Christ coupled with meditation on his passion and death. Friars fully accepted the possibility of meeting a similar fate.[58] Some martyrs, according to the chroniclers, had premonitions of their own deaths. Narrating the martyrdom of Fr. Sebastián Montaño, Dominican chronicler Fr. Alonso Franco implied that since his years as a novice, he had presaged his demise at the hands of people bearing arrows, like the saint whose name he bore. Montaño arrived in Mexico City at age twelve in 1603, accompanying his father, who was a member of the retinue of Viceroy Marquis of Montesclaros (1603–7). After becoming a Dominican in 1615, Montaño asked to be sent to the convent of Zacatecas, where he arrived in 1616. It was a dangerous place to be, and all missionaries posted there were aware of the risks. Once settled, he asked to be sent to the hinterland (*tierra adentro*) to collect alms for the convent. Despite his youth and lack of acquaintance with the land, he was given the assignment, a fact that was interpreted as God's will, but it also suggests that the ecclesiastical authorities were banking on the vigor and idealism of some of the younger members of the order to carry out demanding and dangerous tasks. Following what was possibly the routine of the times under the circumstances, Fr. Sebastián made a general confession, bid his brothers farewell, and set out to travel into "mission" land, a true challenge to his youthful manhood. His first stop was in a Jesuit convent in the mission of Zape, Durango. Hospitality was extended to any brother in religion in those remote areas. There he begged confession from Juan del Valle, whom he convinced to do likewise, since he felt that both would soon die. In letters written to his superior in Zacatecas, which were retrieved from his body, Montaño wrote about his possible death and set the accounts of the alms he had so far gathered to ensure they would be carried out. This detail speaks of the inner resolve of these men, a character trait that idealistic missionaries obviously possessed. He and his Jesuit companion, who agreed to join him, were walking into a large rebellion staged by the Tepehuán Indians in 1616.[59] Neither of them returned alive to their convents.

Another chronicler who used the pathos of traveling under dangerous conditions was Fr. Joseph Arlegui. As a former missionary, Arlegui was able to describe the emotional and personal distress of missionaries under attack. When a minister left town, he wrote, he knew he was risking his life.[60] The bishop of Durango, Ignacio de la Barrera, had ordered the friars not to leave town alone and to have at least four guards when they traveled.[61] Arlegui states that the friars paid no attention to this order and, with manifest risk to their lives, traveled alone whenever they were asked to administer the sacraments. Arlegui had himself been under attack on a visit to Parral on March 28, 1726. He was traveling in the company of thirty armed men and was not in danger, but for several days he suffered the trauma that he knew others had experienced.[62] He considered the Indians of Nueva Vizcaya (Durango, Chihuahua, and part of Coahuila) more bellicose than those of Nuevo León (today's Nuevo León and part of Tamaulipas), whom he considered "noxious." Between 1685 and 1700, two missions in Nueva Vizcaya and one in Nuevo León had to be abandoned owing to the constant threat to the missionaries' lives and lack of defensive strength. Apaches and some of the mission Indians had made a mutual defense pact, and there was little hope of rebuilding the missions under such perilous circumstances.[63]

As he proceeded to tell the stories of the martyred men, Arlegui claimed that the Indians had become acquainted with the Franciscan presence and that some tribes tolerated them. The Indigenous knew that the friars traveled in pairs or alone and without weapons. These facts earned some of them a "pardon" during some attacks and a safe passage to their destination. Having learned this, some members of other mendicant orders, and even laymen, put on Franciscan habits when they went north in the hope that if they were attacked, they would escape with their lives.[64] Even if they were released, friars feared such occasions. When they were attacked, mused Arlegui, what was the use of pardoning the friars when they killed everybody else? He was not convinced that the Indians harbored any special feelings about his order. If attacked and "pardoned" while the rest of their party was killed, friars would find themselves twenty or more leagues from the nearest town and surrounded by the corpses of their traveling companions.[65] It was an appalling experience.

The respect shown to some Franciscans during such attacks could cause some strange incidents, such as when one unnamed provincial vicar carrying out the obligatory visit to his province was attacked three leagues from the city of Durango. The vicar and his accompanying friars were spared, but their secular companions were killed. After this, the attackers approached the friars with gestures of friendship and asked them to place their hands over their heads. Having been "blessed," they took the clothes of the dead corpses and left the friars alone in the midst of "that bloody spectacle." The provincial's secretary was so affected by the circumstances that he lost his mind and died shortly thereafter. Fr. Marcos de Mezquia suffered a similar fate. Having escaped an attack, he also lost his mind. He had been a scholar and a preacher, but after the attack, he could hardly remember his name. This psychological depression was called *susto* (fright), and it also affected Fr. Joseph de Rentería, of the convent of San Juan del Río, southeast of Querétaro, who was returning from confessing some sick people when he was attacked.[66] On one occasion a friar's survival was disputed by two different parties, one in favor and one against. They decided to leave it to chance, and the friar was spared by a mere strike of luck. He was described as full of "anguish and tribulation" while he prepared himself to die.[67] Arlegui summed up the effects of Indian attacks on the missionaries by stating, "When they leave those rough areas, they are speechless, pale, and almost naked; stunned by such horrifying experience." Most of the missionaries were peninsular Spaniards who had no experience of the nature of missionizing in Mexico. They had been ordained in Spain and were unacquainted with the harsh conditions of missionizing in northern New Spain. Some of these peninsular missionaries were "continually fearing and waiting the sad ending others have experienced."[68] Fear was admissible as human nature, and it did not devalue the spiritual strength that all admired in missionaries who could become martyrs. The potential martyr's character was measured by his determination—the fruit of his will—to remain faithful to his choice and his willingness to die.

As an eighteenth-century historian, Arlegui's candid acknowledgment of fear among martyrs was an admission that ran counter to the stand taken by sixteenth- and seventeenth-century chronicles, who wrote of martyrs fearlessly facing death. Friars who escaped with their lives, said Arlegui, were simply lucky, and their experiences traumatized them for the rest of their days. Thus, he wrote, "I have noted that those who fall in their hands [the Indians'] never recover well of their fright. The memory of the Indian's naked bodies, of their screams, as well as the sight of the harm they do, pulling the entrails and the heart of the corpses, leave them [the survivors] pale and withered."[69] Even when their lives were spared, the friars could be subjected to taunting, beatings, and threats by the attackers before they were allowed to go. The uncertainty about attacks and their own doubts about the loyalty of Christian converts kept the friars in suspense about their own fate and that of the Church they wanted to build.[70]

Before Arlegui wrote with such frankness about fear, some missionaries had openly expressed their unpreparedness to accept death as their reward. The 1680 and 1696 revolts in New Mexico triggered the martyrdom of a large number of friars.[71] Letters from the missionaries living in New Mexico prior to 1696 shed light on their reactions to personal threats. The missionaries were informed by spies and friendly Indians of the impending revolt and received no comfort from Governor Francisco de Vargas, who would offer military protection only to a few strategic missions. In March 1696 the custodian of the province, Fr. Francisco de Vargas, asked the friars to assess their own personal situations and their willingness to face the risks of a potential revolt. He was conscious, as he put it, that some of them could be divinely inspired "with the spirit and fervor to accept death while preaching the gospel of [their] holy faith and law, offering for God [their] Lord to suffer and sacrifice [their] lives." In doing so, he continued, the friars would "be assured the eternal good fortune and crown of [their] holy religion."[72] He offered martyrdom as an acceptable choice. However, were all the missionaries willing to accept the challenge? The correspondence between the custodian and his missionaries reveals the latter's unwillingness to risk death. They rejected martyrdom as an unwise choice. The memory of the twenty-one missionary's lives lost in the 1680 revolt was still fresh, and some friars did not want to replicate that example in their own flesh. In response to his custodian's letter, Fr. Diego de Chavarría stated that "no fruit whatsoever will be gained from the sacrilege that they [the Indians] can commit." He felt obliged to save his life so that he could return to the pueblo after the revolt.[73] Fr. Alonso Jiménez de Cisneros, of Mission San Buenaventura de Cochiti, stated on April 21 that he would remain if his prelate ordered him to do so. However, he continued, "If my inconstant frailty in regard to what is stated above leads me to believe that if the peril is too great and I am unable to endure the rabble, I will withdraw to the safest place to protect myself, which will be my salvation, sparing me from death at the hands of these traitors."[74] Fr. José García Marín thought that, being in bad health, he needed protection and that if such protection was not provided, it was not licit for him to minister baptisms or provide extreme unction.[75] In other words, he would stop his ministry.

Among those who perished in the Pueblo Revolt, some had shown reluctance to stay in their churches without military protection. Such was the case of Fr. Francisco de Jesús María Casañas, who had been a missionary in Texas before he was sent to New Mexico. In a letter dated March 19, 1696, he stated that he had "come to seek [not] death but rather the lives of these miserable ones" and reiterated his feelings in another letter dated April 18, stating that he did not expect any miracles to solve the situation because there was "little benefit gained in this evil land of apostates against the word of God."[76] His words revealed his conviction that his own ministry had born little fruit. He was killed during the revolt and died for a cause he did not believe in. Another of the martyred friars, Fr. José Arbizu, refused to return to his mission at San Cristóbal de Tanos on April 2. He reasoned, "By my death no benefit is gained at all," and on April 18 he refused again because the rebels were apostates with "wicked and depraved customs." He continued, "Yes, the priests perished by their sacrilegious hands, and now, not only is that their intention, but also that our death be by a prolonged knife in our side, and they, because of our fear, perform iniquities. . . . And so, I state that should I die, it will be in defense of that which is sacred because I am not provided with guards for its defense."[77] Arbizu was referring to the defense he owed to the sacred vessels used for worship.

Finally, another martyr, Fr. Antonio Carbonel, wrote a long letter to his prelate on March 31, lamenting the lack of protection and respect they endured, the lack of punishment for the rebels, and the rampant idolatry and lack of Christian observance he had witnessed in his flock. As he put it, he had left his province of the Holy Gospel (based in Mexico City) in the belief that he was "to go to a conquered and pacified land, which is not what it has been nor will it be until it may serve God our Lord to free it from danger." He continued, "And had they told me then that I was coming to die among infidels, I would have meditated the undertaking and would have followed the dictates of the Lord; I now consider that I was deceived." That was a strong charge against his superiors and a sad conclusion about the worth of his ministry. He had found only "thorns and brambles" in New Mexico, and he felt burdened in his conscience because he was neither gathering spiritual fruit nor serving his king. His candid expression of disappointment and the direct rebuke to his prelates was a more realistic picture of the missionaries' feelings than the one offered by most chroniclers, who wrote to create reverence for the martyrs.[78] While there was no open fear expressed in some of these letters, the misgivings about their safety and the true worth of their pastoral care suggest that for the missionaries in New Mexico, death by martyrdom had not been their choice to serve God. Unlike the missionaries of the first generation who went out as conquerors for the faith, these men had a different perception of their mission. They had imagined that their task was to convert what they thought were willing and socially pliable peoples. Facing insubordination and danger, they were not prepared to accept martyrdom blindly. They preferred to live.

Praising Martyrdom: Sermons and Chronicles

On one hand, martyrdom was something that "could happen." It was a potential danger that was known and well understood by missionaries traveling to and preaching in unsafe and vulnerable geographical areas. On the other hand, killing a missionary was a risky act. If apprehended by the Spanish authorities, those responsible would pay with their own lives. The loss of a missionary's life caused sorrow among his brothers in religion, anger among royal authorities, and fear among the settlers of sparsely populated areas. Such deaths, considered impious by all believers, also reiterated the danger lurking on the roads and at the distant settlements where many families attempted to find economic opportunities. Royal officials debated and executed retaliatory policies, but reprisals depended on the availability of cash to pay for militias to engage in military activities against insubordinate and threatening tribal groups. Some viceroys were more sensitive than others to the reports of impending revolts. The death of missionaries had to be massive—as in 1680 New Mexico, when twenty-one of thirty-three friars died—to put into action all the economic and administrative resources available to the higher authorities. The bottom line is that those most sensitive to the martyrs' deaths were the orders who lost their men. The search for bodies or bones and the funeral services in their honor were spiritual obligations rendered to those who had paid the highest prize for the goal of saving souls. Beyond performing religious services for the martyrs, the orders and the Church had the duty to express their sorrow through the spoken and the written word. The latter were the chronicles and the biographies of the deceased members. The former took the form of sermons that were delivered at the martyrs' interments or during their memorial services one year after their deaths. Preaching was a privileged means of communication and indoctrination, and sermons expressed the sentiments of the order's community as well as those of the population in general. Preaching to the converted may sound like an oxymoron, but it did have a real intellectual and spiritual value in reinforcing the Roman Catholic perspective of these events and providing nurturing support to the faithful. The spoken word reached a large number of people and was more effective than the written texts in conveying the meaning of the personal sacrifice that martyrdom required. Sermons were the indispensable means of communication between the Church and its flock in a period when few knew how to read and aurality was the venue for instruction and information. Above all, a sermon was the first and most immediate expression of the orders' reactions to their loss.

Martyrdom inspired a significant number of martyrological religious works prior to 1700, but in this period, the memorial service and sermon writers favored the missions in the Far East, where friars killed while "on duty" were among the most motivated men in their respected orders, since not all mendicants were willing to travel to the Far East.[79] Few memorial sermons for the martyrs of New Spain have survived in printed form, and the two selected here were delivered to honor the deaths of two martyrs one century apart. On March 1, 1681, the bishop of Oaxaca, Dr. Isidro Sariñana y Cuenca, ascended the pulpit of the cathedral in Mexico City to preach in honor of the twenty-one Franciscans who had perished in New Mexico on August 10, 1680. The viceroy and the entire body of the royal bureaucracy were present.[80] In his sermon Sariñana leaned on Psalm 111, "In the Lord I put my trust" (KJV), and recalled individually all the martyred friars, characterizing them as men who showed confidence in God. The missionaries had demonstrated this by exposing their breasts to the arrows of an enemy who had premeditated its treacherous attack. Sariñana presented the friars and the Indians who had killed them as two opposite actors in a morality play: the friars were purveyors of a social and spiritual good; the Natives were the impersonation of mendacity and betrayal. Deceit and treachery allowed them to hide their intentions while pretending to be loyal. Rejecting the benefits of Christianity, they had frittered away one hundred years of progress in the process of becoming "civilized." Not knowing New Mexico or the Pueblo culture at all, Sariñana spoke of Indians wandering naked in the woods and friars teaching them the art of cultivating the soil. He was confusing Pueblo Natives with tribal Chichimecs and revealing his ignorance of the land and its people, but that was irrelevant, since most people in the capital city likely shared the misconception. Sariñana's position was consonant with the Christian reaction against rebellious Indigenous since the sixteenth century. Lamenting the death of friars at the hands of insubordinate Indians, the bishop was bound to offer a Christian interpretation of their deaths under such violent circumstances. Seeking a justification for the murder of the friars as part of God's plan, Sariñana had to navigate difficult theological waters, but he had a solid base for his arguments in Christian tradition. The martyrs' suffering was, in part, caused by the will of God, who loves the suffering of the wound and rejects the sin of the aggressor. Thus, martyrdom was really a test of the love of God, who was cognizant of the suffering of the martyrs but who loved them through their ordeal. Dealing with Franciscans, an order he seemed to admire, he cited Saint Francis's determination to choose a life dedicated to God and the imitation of Christ, disregarding danger: "The imitation of Christ is most brilliant when, without being intimidated by the risk incurred, one returns with his Cross to the very place of danger."[81] To this, he added the biblical example of David returning to the dangers posed by Saul and replicated by Christ returning to Jerusalem against the wishes of his disciples. Like the biblical David and Christ, the Franciscan friars never hesitated to return to the danger and expose themselves to death. Francis's sons could never imitate Christ better, stated the bishop, than when "without endeavoring to avoid any risks they obediently bare their breasts to all danger." Thus, obedience and valor were the two outstanding qualities of the martyr.[82] The bishop thanked the king, a political move since the viceroy was present, for having appropriated money to ensure the safety of those missionaries and settlers in El Paso del Río del Norte and for planning the eventual recovery of New Mexico. As for the martyrs, they would be restored to the path of glory when their brothers restored Christianity in that remote land.

Sariñana's sermon served well his purpose and the historical moment: it was short, clear, and supportive of the Franciscan order and royal policy.

He idealized the Franciscan missionaries' lack of fear, a sentiment contrary to the emotions reflected in the testimonies of New Mexico's missionaries in 1696, but the bishop was subscribing to the notion that martyrdom was a masculine exercise in valor and it was theoretically impossible that any friar would show any trepidation on facing it.

Nearly one hundred years later, four men of the Colegio de Propaganda Fide in Querétaro died as martyrs at the missions of the Yumas, at the junction of the Gila and the Colorado Rivers. Theirs were the last deaths by martyrdom in the colonial period. A fellow Franciscan, Fr. Diego Miguel Bringas de Manzaneda, preached the funeral oration to celebrate the lives of the four missionaries.[83] His sermon merits close attention because it explains the theological bases for considering the friars "martyrs." Fr. Diego's understanding of martyrdom closed a circle of historical and spiritual interpretation that had begun two hundred years before. Fr Diego chose the theme derived from Saint Paul's Epistle to the Philippians—namely, that Christ will be magnified in the body, whether it be by life or by death. To die for Christ was a gain for those who had lived in Christ.[84] He injected a strong dose of emotional appeal into his message, taking his audience to the site of the martyrdom and describing it vividly.[85] However, he did not present the martyrs as heroes of a military nature, for they were, in his view, men of charity sacrificing their lives to save those of others. He also stated that he would not try to make "martyrs" of their Franciscan brothers because the ascription of martyrdom pertained to the Church. Having made that statement, he proceeded to make a case for them to be considered martyrs "in the eyes of God," thus bypassing the letter of canonical law. In God's eyes, he said, the friars had the merits of true martyrs for their faith, their charity, and their obedience. Desire and willingness have the same merits as deeds, he stated. It was not their deaths but their willingness to accept their fates that made them martyrs.

Preaching at their place of missionary training—the Colegio de la Santa Cruz in Querétaro—and to an audience of missionaries, Bringas eulogized them as men who had learned to adapt themselves perfectly to divine will and lived in a constant state of sacrifice of their personal needs to carry out their apostolic work. The missionaries had experienced the penuries of traveling hundreds of leagues, learning the rough language of the *bárbaros*, and suffering their scorn while trying to explain to them the intricacies of the basic Christian faith. The martyrs never departed from the path to reach their objective, and they had lived and died truly apostolic lives, showing the same strength in sacrifice and the same disposition to receive death as those who had died for their faith in Europe and Japan. By using the memory of the martyrs across the globe in the sixteenth and seventeenth centuries, Bringas de Manzaneda was reminding his audience that the cause and meaning of their deaths were still relevant and not something of the past. It was a reality for the peoples of New Spain in their own time. In his eulogy, however, he remained anchored in the vision of the past. His incursion into the history of martyrdom used the language of his predecessors, defining the Indigenous as barbarians and the friars as messengers of civilization and spiritual enlightenment.

Although Bringas eulogized all the friars for their dedication and faith, he chose Fr. Antonio Hermenegildo Garcés as the most exemplary of the martyred men. His death had cut short a brilliant career as an explorer and missionary of unusual virtues.[86] As an explorer Garcés had made repeated visits—largely alone and without requesting permission from anyone—to the vast area between Central California and Arizona and had traveled along the Colorado River as far as the Hopi settlements in today's northwestern Arizona. His reports included extensive ethnographic information on the many Indian tribes, most of whom he had befriended.[87] The friar had recorded nearly one thousand leagues of travel, and his official reports advised further exploration and settlement expeditions. Bringas de Manzaneda revealed himself as a man of the Enlightenment in his admiration of Garcés's desire for knowledge and many accomplishments. He underscored how Garcés's information on the Natives went beyond the ethnographic and geographical understanding of the territory. It had geopolitical aspirations and consequences. Garcés, he claimed, had in mind the establishment of Spanish control over the region he had traveled and had provided the tools for that accomplishment with his written work. If such a feat were accomplished, stated Bringas, the Spanish expansion in northern New Spain would be comparable to that of the Roman Empire and would likewise put as many different peoples under the suzerainty of one monarch.[88] Bringas de Manzaneda praised Garcés's desire to establish peace, obedience, union, and trade so that missionaries could safely travel in that vast territory to evangelize the Natives. In pursuit of that objective, Garcés "had listened to the call of the rivers" in his travels and had sacrificed himself for the benefit of his brothers. Bringas concluded that Garcés had been a venue of God's will.[89] He had been the obedient vessel of God's will, carrying out the task for which he professed and meeting a death that was justified by the commitment to his vows. This eulogy could have been written in the sixteenth century. At the end of the colonial period, the deeds and objectives of some of the most dedicated missionary friars replicated the behavior of those who had initiated the process of religious conversion two hundred years before, and they received the same praise.

Telling the Story of Martyrdom: The Chronicles
Oral funeral eulogies did not have the permanency of the written word, and most of them were never printed. Conversely, martyrs' deaths were memorialized in a more permanent manner in the orders' chronicles. The minibiographies of hundreds of friars formed a substantial part of the history of the orders, and those of the martyrs are the best tools to help us understand the significance of their deaths to their brothers in religion. A martyr's death created a strong bond of empathy among all friars, who saw themselves as members of a brotherhood of faith and potentially facing similar risks against a common enemy.

Having the largest number of martyrs in their ranks, Franciscan chronicles are the primary sources of information about the history and spiritual perception of martyrdom. The chronicler became the cultural interpreter of the feelings of his community. The Dominican and the Augustinian orders, lacking enough examples of martyrdom in New Spain, used some feedback from the Far East to underline the sacrifices of their brothers. For example, with no martyrs of his order in New Spain, Augustinian Fr. José Sicardo wrote a comprehensive work that included the Augustinian, Jesuit, Dominican, and Franciscan martyrs in Asia, where his own order experienced martyrdom.[90] His intention was to globalize the experience as a Christian and not as an Augustinian.

Dominican chroniclers of New Spain, Fr. Juan González de la Puente and Alonso Franco, also included the stories of those martyred in Japan and the Philippines as part of the collective memory of the order.[91] Franco had to aggrandize the presence of martyrs in his order, since up to the time of his writing, 1646, there was only one Dominican martyr in New Spain, Fr. Sebastián

FIG. 20. Fr. Baltasar de Medina, *Vida, martirio y beatificación del invicto protomártir de el Japón San Felipe de Jesús, patrón de Mexico* [...] (México: Herederos de la Viuda de Juan G. Infanzón, 1751).

Montaño. With great candor, Franco states that before he died as a martyr, no one would have imagined Montaño's name would be cited among the notable men of the order. Montaño, as stated before, was killed during the 1616 Tepehuán revolt. There was no certainty regarding how or when he perished, but his death was certified when his body was found and recovered. Franco injected an element of pathos into the story by describing how the halo of martyrdom was already attached to his name among the townspeople of Guanacevi, Durango. His body was kept as a relic after the 1623 approval of the Augustinian bishop of the province, Fr. Gonzalo de Hermosillo.[92]

Such an obscure location did not suit the sentiments of the Dominican hierarchy. Eager to have the body of a martyr in the capital city, the Dominican order commissioned and carried out a "sacred theft" of his bones from the Guanacevi church and deposited them in their main church in the capital to initiate the promotion of his cause as a martyr. The proceedings of the "cause" were stalled by bureaucracy, lost traction, and ended in oblivion. However, immediately after the news of his death reached the peninsula, he became a literary "hero" in Spain, where he was lionized in works by the greatest literary figures of the time, Lope de Vega and Calderón de la Barca. Less than two years after his death, Fr. Sebastián's name was mentioned and honored in the Dominican General Chapter celebrated in Lisbon. He was also mentioned in a sermon preached by the bishop of Córdoba, Fr. Domingo Pimentel, on the occasion of the memorial service for Phillip III.[93] However, literary fame and the occasional mention in a sermon during a solemn event were insufficient to earn him official recognition as a martyr, let alone to be elevated to the altars.

As Sebastián Montaño's case suggests, the successful promotion of a martyr had much to do with the means of recording his death and fostering his memory by his own order and among the Church hierarchy in Rome. An exceptional and successful case in terms of advocacy was that of Felipe de Jesús, who initially had the same little chance of becoming a well-known martyr as did Fr. Sebastián Montaño but became an object of increasing popular reverence in the viceroyalty and found a propitious climate of acceptance in Spain and Rome. Felipe de Jesús was Mexican by birth and a novice in the Franciscan order when he was martyred in Nagasaki, Japan, in February 1597. Thirty years later, in 1627, he and his companions were beatified. It was Rome's answer to the persecution that its members were undergoing on the islands and a sign that the Catholic Church was determined to pursue the agenda of conversion in the Far East. In New Spain the beatification was a source of great pride. The distinction of having a saintly man born in its territory came barely over one hundred years after the initial Christianization of the land. In the eyes of the clerical hierarchy, the spiritual fruit had ripened. The beatified Felipe de Jesús was fast in gaining popularity among the devout. Throughout the seventeenth and part of the eighteenth century, paintings and printed images, biographies, and sermons aimed at gaining Rome's approval for the next step: the elevation of the martyred young man to sainthood. Despite intensive efforts, public devotion began to wane with no plausible explanation. The slowness of the process had something to do with it, but despite the cooling down of the fervor, his cause for elevation to sainthood remained active in Rome throughout the colonial period. Finally, his cause was successful in 1862, when he was canonized as a saint on June 8.[94]

Felipe de Jesús was not the only native of Mexico to die as a martyr in Japan. There was another Mexican who had little chance to compete with Felipe de Jesús's sudden popularity. He was Augustinian Fr. Bartolomé Gutierrez, who was born in Mexico City in 1580 and professed in 1597.[95] In 1606 he joined a contingent of Augustinians on their way to the Philippines, and in 1612 he traveled to Japan. Banned from the land along with other regulars, he dressed up as Japanese to elude the authorities. For fifteen years he survived in Nagasaki, taking great risks in exercising his ministry. He ran out of luck in 1629, when he was apprehended by local Lord Takanawa, who became famous for persecuting Christians. After languishing for two years in prison, Fr. Bartolomé died at the stake with other mostly Japanese converts. His name and his case remained in obscurity for lack of promotion. A similar fate awaited those dying within the frontiers of the viceroyalty. The martyrs of New Spain were at a distinctive disadvantage. Their memory was revered among their brothers in religion, but popularity was reserved for "exotic" deaths in remote lands. It seems that death caused by an "enemy"—roaming Chichimecs—who was only too "familiar" and close blunted the emotional response required to create a sustained and lasting devotion to martyrs at home. In Italy, where the decision for sainthood was made, the Chichimecs were no rivals to the Japanese as symbols of evil. They did not transcend the bar of emotional response required to make them "saint-makers" when they killed a Christian friar.

Martyrs' deaths resonated among early Franciscan historians. For them, they were brothers dying heroically as extended universal symbols of aggrieved Christianity. Their deaths made the frontier a moving line fed by faith and not by economic or political reasons. The chronicles and official histories of the orders would not fail to promote their memory. The tradition was initiated by Fr. Jerónimo de Mendieta. He included twenty first-generation martyrs in his *Historia Eclesiástica Indiana* and added to the list a converted Indian boy who was killed by his own people for his perceived treachery against the old religion. Mendieta was proud to cite Fr. Juan Calero, who was the first Franciscan martyr and the first lay brother to die for the cause. Mendieta's homage to the martyrs went beyond writing. He drew a now classic illustration of martyrdom that has become an obligatory visual reference to the interaction between the Natives and the preachers of the new religion.[96] While there are different ways of "reading" this image, I will adhere to the most straightforward: It shows a Franciscan and eight armed Indians, and it tells the story of martyrdom in a compressed fashion. It reads from left to right and from top to bottom. At the top a preaching Franciscan gestures upward while the Natives point their arrows at him. In the second tier, the friar is in the center, with one Indian on each side. After approaching him frontally, they seem to have encircled him. The friar's hands signify an engagement in verbal communication. He is still preaching. In the third tier, the friar has fallen to his knees and points to the sky above, now holding a crucifix. The Natives continue to point their arrows at him. The last tier shows the friar lying on the ground, apparently dead. One of the Indians holds a *macana* over him while the other wields an arrow pointed at the dead body. Both are seemingly ready to continue battering the body, suggesting the violent frenzy that follows the downing of an animal or an enemy. This visual representation of martyrdom remains the most shocking but powerful expression of the emotional impact that martyrdom had on the friars who were liable to suffer it. Mendieta could have had the death of Fr. Juan Calero in mind when he drew the illustration. He expected that, beyond "seeing is believing," the illustration would alert the potential reading public to the sacrifice the friars were making while performing their task.

Mendieta followed with a text rich in the details of the deaths of the twenty friars. The list included lay brothers as well as ordained priests, following the principle that all souls were equal before God. He wrote of martyrdom as a sacrifice of tame sheep (*mansas ovejas*) and angels of peace (*ángeles de paz*) dying at the hands of treacherous Indians. His martyrs were quintessential in their lack of fear before death. For example, Fr. Francisco Lorenzo "did not fear any occasion that may have led to losing his life" and was extremely lucky to have the opportunity to preach in the Nayarit area with his lay brother companion Fr. Miguel de Estibaliz. His premonition of dying as a martyr came true when he revisited one of the towns and a group of "infidel" Indians attacked him at night. Mendieta describes the friar as lighting some candles and kneeling before the altar before falling under the strikes of Indian *macanas*.[97] His text has a strong emotional engagement with the martyrs, some of whom he knew personally as brothers in religion.

Martyrdom was also a close experience for three classic Franciscan chroniclers of the eighteenth century: Fr. Isidro Félix Espinosa, Fr. Joseph Arlegui, and Fr. Juan Domingo Arricivita. Espinosa and Arricivita were the official historians of the Colegios de Propaganda Fide of Franciscan missionaries, and Arlegui penned the general history of the Franciscan province of Zacatecas. Espinosa and Arricivita had a special personal interest in recording martyrdom in their respective works. They had been missionaries before becoming historians. Writing in the 1740s, Fr. Isidro Félix de Espinosa had experienced the rigors of being a missionary in Texas. His analysis of martyrdom is a mixture of hagiography and theology that reflects the vision of men of his generation. Born in 1679, one year before the Pueblo Revolt, and being a member of an institution dedicated to missionizing, his interest in martyrdom was predictable.[98] The long passages he dedicated to the death of Fr. Pedro Rebullida, who the college in Querétaro had sent to missionize in Guatemala, were inspired by the New Testament and the tradition of early Christian martyrs. Rebullida and his companion Fr. Juan Antonio de Zamora were caught in the midst of an Indian rebellion in the province of Talamancas (today's Costa Rica) in 1709. They perished along with the soldiers who accompanied them for protection during their missionary trip. Rebullida and Zamora were attacked with lances and beheaded, and their heads were taken by the Indians to be cooked and used as drinking cups, a usual war practice. Chronicler Espinosa chose to underline the theological meaning of beheading. He was persuaded that Rebullida had not died as a result of his lance wounds; rather, he had perished due to the beheading. Why? His explanation offers a fascinating insight into the conceptualization of "martyrdom" by a missionary himself. The act of beheading was a traditional way of sacrificing lambs, he wrote, and also a privileged way of dying for the lambs of God. Beheading contained a "doctrinal mystery."[99] The knife that cut the throat, according to Saint Paul, was a symbol of faith and the word of God, which penetrates the soul even deeper than a knife can penetrate the flesh. There's no resistance to God's faith, as there is no possible resistance to a knife cutting the throat. Espinosa asserted that God kept the friar alive long enough to let his soul leave his body with his last breath and fly to the celestial regions. The faith that had inspired the sacrifice of martyrdom in earlier times was still motivating that of an eighteenth-century man of the cloth.

Fr. Joseph de Arlegui, writing his chronicle of the Franciscan province of Zacatecas in the mid-1730s, had less personal experience of active missionary activity than Espinosa but knew well its circumstances and perils, having acted as guardian of his convent and provincial of the convents of the area. As he saw it, on one hand, the Franciscan custody of Zacatecas had been born through the suffering and pain inflicted by the deaths of its members, but those who died as martyrs had fought like valiant soldiers strengthened by the shield of the faith. On the other hand, he did not hesitate to describe the fear the Indian attacks inspired in the friars and the population at large. Accepting that martyrs experienced fear, Arlegui made them more human, despite his own tendency—and that of other chroniclers—to elevate them beyond the weaknesses of normal human beings. However, in the end he pinned martyrdom to a divine selection. Divine providence had determined that some Franciscans wore the red mark of martyrdom. There had been no escape from such a destiny.[100]

Juan Domingo Arricivita (1720–94) took up the history of the Colegios de Propaganda Fide where Espinosa had left off and had it ready for the press in 1791. It was the last of the chronicles written in the eighteenth century. As expected, he would focus on the missionary efforts of the Pimería Alta and the Yuma (Arizona) martyrs. He focused on the death of each martyr and used five different adjectives to characterize the event: *violent, pious, desired, happy,* and *glorious.* He began with Fr. Felipe Guillén, a native of Valencia, Spain, who, having had missionary experience in Texas, was stationed at the mission of Tubutama (Pimería Alta) in 1769, where he worked without any assistance. On April 27, 1778, while returning from his ministry in a small town, he was attacked and killed by a group of Indians who had just assaulted the mission of Ati. His death was characterized as "violent," and he was eulogized as an "intrepid athlete in the battlefield."[101] All martyrs' deaths were violent, and Arricivita could have intended to contrast Guillén's death with the "serenity of the happiness" that missionaries were expected to achieve through the service and love of God. About Fr. Juan Díaz, one of the four friars who also died in Yuma, Arricivita wrote that his death had been "pious." Díaz had a long history as a missionary. He had been the head of Mission San Pedro y San Pablo del Bicuñer, one of two destroyed in 1781 by the Yuma Indians. Fr. Juan had been previously in charge of Caborca, a Pimería Alta mission with two adjunct towns (*visitas*). Drawing the profile of this martyr, Arricivita called the reader's attention to the fact that Díaz was well aware of the unrest of the Indians in the Colorado site and the threat against his life. He was denied any further help by a military officer, and rather than abandoning the mission, he chose to return because "the adversities and suffering" he was experiencing "would not prevent him from following his destiny." This qualified his death as one resulting from his duty as a missionary and affording pride and honor to his order.[102] The death of Fr. Joseph Matías Moreno was characterized as "desired." This young missionary had expressed a strong desire for martyrdom to his sister, and "he achieved it thanks to the *bárbaros* in the Colorado," wrote Arricivita. He portrayed Fr. Joseph as full of fire and light. *Light* referred to his theological education; *fire* to the fervor in his heart.[103] Arricivita's rhetorical twist envisioned the Indigenous not only as evil but also as the means to achieve the high honor of a martyr's death. God had his mysterious ways, and to Arricivita it was obvious that evil had not triumphed, since the young missionary had certainly earned the eternal life he had always desired. The youngest member of the Yuma martyrs, Fr. Juan Antonio Barreneche, was Fr. Antonio Garcés's companion. Arricivita portrayed his death as "happy" and focused on Barreneche's virtues as a young, introverted, and pious missionary, a perfect match for the adventurous and learned Garcés.[104] Arricivita reserved "glorious" for Garcés's death based on the merits he had earned during his long and dedicated life as a missionary. Garcés was one of the most-talked-about missionaries of his time. His solo trips into the unknown lands of the northern frontiers of New Spain and his confident friendship with all the peoples he met in this vast territory gave him a knowledge of both land and people that was unrivaled by any other missionary. Arricivita eulogized Garcés for his humility, determination, lack of fear, and spiritual and physical strength. He had edified the Indians with his purity and evangelical poverty. Arricivita pointed to Garcés's confidence that his fate was in God's hands, and following God's will, he employed his life preaching, expecting to see God in his glory and be free from all the calamities of this life.[105] For the chronicler, Garcés's death was the crowning event of his life. The five adjectives Arricivita used to characterize these men's deaths—*violent, pious, desired, happy,* and *glorious*—defined the nature of martyrdom. The five Franciscans who died in Yuma exemplified the spiritual heights friars could reach through martyrdom. The official eulogy martyrdom received from historians of the Franciscan order was its strongest endorsement. As a special distinction granted by God, death by martyrdom had a great emotional and spiritual appeal associated exclusively with missionaries and their activities.

Martyrdom: A Privileged Experience

Secular people who died at the hands of Indigenous rebels were "victims," not martyrs. Martyrdom was the privilege of men of the cloth. Missionary activity, like soldiering, was essentially the choice of men deployed to carry out a task that offered the distinct possibility of death. Missionaries had the same spirit of defiance before danger as soldiers and were expected to have the same disregard for their own safety. Albeit spiritual, the process of conversion was sometimes compared to a military operation carried out as a service to God and king.

Biographers and chroniclers endeavored to put martyrdom within a religious framework, but they explicitly used military connotations in their own writings. In the perception of sixteenth-century religious authorities, there was an open war against paganism, and the "enemy" were the "gentiles" who would not accept the new religion. The switch from the appellative *gentiles*, first used in the sixteenth century, to *barbarians* resulted from meeting steady resistance from the Native inhabitants. That resistance produced anger and the ensuing use of derogatory adjectives for the perceived enemy. Once engaged in spiritual battle, friars appear protected by the "shield of the faith." Convents became castles and occasionally served to defend lay Christians.[106] Friars "hoisted" the crucifix when preaching to the enemy—the hostile Indians—in the expectation that they would "surrender" their hearts to their words. The ministers of God used the "sword of the divine word" that flowed from their mouths. The Indians' gods had to be "exterminated." Fleeing Indians left the friars in the "field of victory." The "defeat" of the enemy meant the destruction of their attachment to paganism, an emblematic victory for the souls of the defeated, since the conquered would gain their presumed salvation after the indoctrination that followed.[107] When an encounter with Indigenous resistance resulted in deaths for the soldiers of Christ, they became martyrs. The hagiographic halo was put on the heads of martyrs since Mendieta's times. Readers and writers expected miraculous events associated with their deaths. The bodies of the martyrs were typically left in open fields or among the ruins of a ravaged mission. Dismembered or heavily damaged, some of those bodies were said to have remained "fresh" and sweet smelling for days until they were rescued. Corruption was not part of the tradition of holy bodies.[108] After internment, their bones, in good Christian tradition, retained the qualities of the living person and were treated with care and dignity. Stories of miracles circulated about some of them. The murderers of Fr. Juan de Tapia (1557) confessed having seen shining shadows following them. The bones of Fr. Juan del Río, who was martyred in the 1580s, were rediscovered one hundred years later, and they were reported as being red and sweet smelling. Other remnants that escaped destruction from wild animals were recorded as remaining flexible when they were recovered. That was the case of Fr. Pablo de Acevedo's body, which was found intact but shrunken to the size of a child. Commenting on this case, Arlegui stated that God wished to equate the innocence of this martyr to the innocence of a child and had thus reduced the size of his remnants.[109] The Native who killed Fr. Esteban Benítez close to the doctrine of San Juan del Río could not move away from the victim's body, and having been found there with the stone he had used to murder the friar, he was captured and eventually hanged for his crime. The bodies of three friars knifed by apostates in their cells appeared together as if they had been confessing one another. Prodigies such as this punctuate Arlegui's narratives.[110] The blood of the martyrs had purchased their own salvation and merit for their order—but certainly not the full conversion of the Natives. However, the land was firmly in Spanish hands, the imperial objective of expanding the frontiers seemed to have been accomplished, and the mendicant martyrs were counted among those who had contributed to that end.

In Western minds Christian martyrdom was death with honor and the reward of salvation in the immolation. It was also violence. Martyrdom was violence exercised in two directions. The one who received it, the missionary, had a system of beliefs that made his death intelligible and meaningful in its consummation. It was hard for brothers in religion and chroniclers to understand the motivations of those who inflicted the violence on them, and they dubbed it demonic. And indeed, it could not have been otherwise in their eyes. As to the motivations of the Indigenous, they did not leave written statements or attempt to explain themselves beyond their actions. For the Indian side, the death of the preachers was due punishment to those who had the audacity of trespassing on their natural world and challenging their own beliefs. The missionary represented many things that were objectionable to them, and he was an easy target. It was easier to attack one individual than a group of armed men or presidios. After the Apaches killed the friars of Mission San Sabá, they stayed around for three days but never attacked the fort.

Abuses inflicted on the Indians by secular men were avenged on the friars. Arlegui states that Fr. Martín Altamirano earned the hatred of the Indians of a place called "La Silla" because the "the land was depopulated of Indians and the towns were crowding with Christians."[111] The system of *reducciones*, which obliged Indians to live close to missions or towns, away from their original habitat, drained the Native population and exposed it to the abuses of soldiers and settlers. The death of Fr. Luis Jayme at Mission San Diego in 1772 was quite possibly the result of the repeated rapes and abuses of the soldiers of the presidio against the Indian women. Fr. Jayme called attention to this insidious situation, but the military commander Pedro Fages had no interest in restraining his men. When the Indians attacked Fr. Luis, the friar told them, "Children, love God," to which they replied, "No love God anymore."[112] The Native men saw duplicity in the missionary's message and focused on the messenger. Even though he was not the perpetrator, his teachings were regarded as lies.

Occasionally there was hesitation among the attackers, but too much hesitation could be understood as cowardice. Fr. Pedro Gutiérrez, who had learned the languages of some of the tribes of Nueva Vizcaya, was in a town called Santa Catalina when it was assaulted by the Tepehuán in 1606. The townspeople took refuge in one house. Fr. Pedro came out and, speaking in their language, asked them to kill him if they were after Christian blood. His speech impressed some of the attackers, who remained indecisive for some time, until one among them called the others "cowards" and sent the first arrow against the friar. Doubtless, the Tepehuán warriors had their own male pride and could not bear to be called "cowards." The hesitation of the group speaks of the respect that some friars had managed to earn among some of the Indigenous groups. Respect as an inhibitor of behavior may have worked for others but did not work for Fr. Pedro on that occasion.[113] During the rebellions in New Mexico in 1680 and in 1696, the rebels not only killed the missionaries but destroyed all objects in the church: altars, vessels, images—anything representing Christianity. There was an obvious desire for total erasure and, above all, a will to demonstrate that they were no longer under the authority of the bearers of a new religion. Obedience and respect were discarded. The Indigenous viewpoint is never acknowledged in chronicles or biographies; they are ignored or reviled. Today we see their attacks and desire for destruction as strong expressions of their frustration. Violence was a form of speech.

Martyrdom carried a political meaning for the Crown and the orders. At the most basic level, the violence of repeated attacks and the loss of life of the missionary spoke of unaccomplished "pacification." Military efforts had to be redoubled to avert loss of life and property and to establish mastery—even a shaky one—over the terrain. On the ground, the vastness of the territory was the strongest handicap in the effort to control and command it and thus eliminate the loss of life of men of the cloth as well as civilians. The Crown never put enough resources on the northern frontier to make it a "secure" space. The July 1781 Yuma massacre effectively stopped the communication by land between northern New Spain and California. The California missions communicated by sea with the mainland and Mexico City. They were well protected by military forces that, in fact, carried out the operation of subduing the land and maintaining the peace. The Indigenous Californians never sustained constant harassment against the newcomers. Although some California missionaries lived under the threat of a potential rebellion, it never took place, and there were no martyrs in California.

Martyrdom did not deter the activities of the missionaries. Attacks occurred in some specific areas inhabited by unassimilated and seminomadic Natives and on those occasions when they perceived the possibility of success against a poorly defended traveling missionary or a missionary site.

Even though the number of martyred missionaries was high, the impact of their deaths on the orders, and most specifically on the Franciscan order, was minimized by the fact that they did not occur with any "regularity" and that those who died were quickly "replaced" by other missionaries. The deaths of missionaries were "events," not daily happenings. The psychological impact did cause personal trauma among them, but it was partially remedied with the assumption of better traveling precautions. They were regarded not as heroes but as men doing their duty.

Martyrdom carried a multiplicity of more subtle messages that were understood by the people in general, by the orders, and by the missionaries in particular. Spiritually, the martyr's death was in the flesh only. He had died for Christ and in imitation of Christ. Therefore, he lived in the spirit of Christ. Beyond those obvious foundational beliefs lay personal character features subsumed in the written and oral historical testimonies. The martyr was not an example of victimhood. He took risks voluntarily. His manhood was defiant of danger but at the same time willing to submit when the outcome of the challenge was negative. That submission was unlike that of a defeated warrior. In the world of the martyr, the humility with which he accepted his destiny was comparable to that of Christ accepting his own. Christ's meekness was not a show of weakness. His sacrifice inspired those who would suffer the same fate. Thus, the martyr's abstention from the use of force was understood as a special and tougher form of strength. The martyr's masculinity was not diminished by his refusal to defend himself. It was enhanced by it, because suffering pain and death were manly expressions of power. In the spiritual war in which they were engaged, he did not need the layman's or the soldier's sword. His words and his message were understood as his "arms." The ultimate manly feature of the martyrs was their symbolic posture against the forces of "the enemy": Satan and his militant followers. Martyrs were standing up to the tyranny of the devil personified in the nonbelievers. The "sacrifice" of his body through death was not a personal failure; it was the result of God's will and a prize for the defense of his faith, his personal toughness, his silence in suffering, and his endurance. Thus, martyrs came to represent a sophisticated and different form of masculine courage.

7

Death

The Test of Faith

We should not call death what is only a transit to a better life.

Thus reflected chronicler Fr. Isidro de Espinosa when writing the biography of lay brother Fr. Antonio de los Ángeles Bustamante, a member of the Colegio de Propaganda Fide in Querétaro. There was no more commendable task for any chronicler than to write on the lives and deaths of worthy and exemplary men who had spent their days in the service of God. The dead were more than "history"; they were inspirational examples for those still living. Chroniclers and biographers believed that the act of dying was a teachable event that would deliver to the living the lesson of how to die "properly," since theological treatises on the meaning of death were beyond the reach and understanding of most common folk. Death was also a topic of meditation and ministry for religious oratory. Preachers could tap into the emotional and spiritual message implied in death and make it accessible to a much larger audience than the chroniclers.

All religions must offer an answer to two mysteries: the mystery of life and the mystery of death. Christianity conflated both, asserting that death leads to a new birth in spirit, offering the example of the son of God living a mortal life, suffering death to redeem the souls of humanity, and resurrecting to live eternal *life* in heaven. In Roman Catholicism the symbol of Christ on the cross is emblematic of two notions: the inevitability of death and the hope of resurrection. Never an end, death is a transit through which the spirit supersedes the body's materiality to reach a final and eternal life as spirit. This transfiguration requires intensive meditation for its full comprehension. None other than Erasmus of Rotterdam, a man of the highest intellectual caliber, wrote a treatise on the subject, and for the next two and half centuries between the mid-sixteenth and the late eighteenth centuries, Protestant and

Catholic theologians wrote numerous treatises on the nature of death, on how to die properly, and on how to help others during that transit.[1]

Mendicant chroniclers recalled in detail the deaths of their distinguished brothers, assuming that in doing so, they were honoring their order and offering their members and their readers good models for reflection and imitation. Fr. Diego de Basalenque, a chronicler of the order of San Agustín, explained that in describing the death of Fr. Diego de Villarubia, one of his model friars, his intention was to prove that a good death was a mirror of a good life and that by watching a good death, friars learned how to die well themselves.[2] Not all friars' deaths were recorded or received enough attention to become more than a notation in the conventual books, with perhaps additional information on the number of Masses to be said for the salvation of his soul. Only those considered notable or exemplary received the privilege of having their last moments recorded or remembered in detail for posterity.

Facing a brother's death, the attention of the community focused more on performing the rites that would ease his transit than on taking historical notes, but a chronicler could recall the death from an actual witness or from communal memory and preserve the moment in writing. Although I have examined in detail the deaths of martyrs and their meaning, it is still intellectually necessary to analyze the deaths of less-exalted members of the religious communities. Dying as a martyr was believed to be a privilege granted by God to the few. Happening under unusual circumstances, martyrdom was not representative of the deaths of the vast majority of friars. The more typical death in the friary—after living a long life and resulting from sickness—was more appropriate to learn the spiritual lessons death could convey.

The venues to record and celebrate a friar's death and his memory were his order's chronicle, his biography, and his funeral sermon. It is not usual to find these three sources available for most members of any mendicant order. Few friars qualified, in their contemporaries' eyes, to receive such attention. Biographies and sermons are few in number and focus on the most notable men of the orders. Chronicles include biographies of various lengths but only exceptionally provide enough material to move beyond the description of death into the theological meaning of the act of dying.[3]

Death and the Art of Dying

Writing on death was an exercise that assumed that the writer understood that his narrative also conveyed an understanding of the rewards of the afterlife.[4] Chronicler Dávila Padilla explained this approach as follows: "In this life [divine] grace shows it value, but not with the sparkle of clarity it has in glory. Here it is charity commenced; there it is charity accomplished. In this life there is joy but with the risk of losing it; in the next life it is secure. In this world it means waiting; in heaven it is possessing. The good religious gives up everything in this life for God; God repays him by giving Himself through death."[5]

As a friar, Dávila Padilla knew that an afterlife in the contemplation of God had to be "earned" through a life dedicated to following the ethical and spiritual guidelines set by his order and the Church. However, regardless of how one lived one's life or how deep one's faith was, facing death still demanded enormous inner strength from all believers, including friars. Those writers who addressed the topic of death from a moral theology angle proposed a continuous intellectual and spiritual preparation for death throughout life. Laymen and members of the Church would resort to a special type of advice literature that relied on meditations on what lies beyond death, known as *novísimos*, and included final judgment, hell, and glory.[6] This mental exercise was assumed to benefit believers by encouraging them to distance themselves from sin during life. Other titles advised the readers on how to engage in meditations, prayers, and the practice of frequent confession and Communion to maintain a straight line of spiritual health throughout their lives and be ready for death when it occurred.[7]

Friars, living a life dedicated to God and following specific rules of behavior, were expected to have a deeper and more meaningful spiritual life and be stronger and less given to doubts and fears about death than the majority of people. Those assumptions notwithstanding, they were not exempt from the same apprehensions as the laity. Thus, their acquaintance with the literature addressing the end of life was of fundamental importance, especially for those invested with the rights to administer the sacraments of the church.[8] Helping the dying was a duty of the utmost seriousness, although the ultimate destiny of the soul was not in the priest's hands but hinged on the life experience of the dying. However, the mediation from a qualified member of the Church could help guide the soul toward salvation.

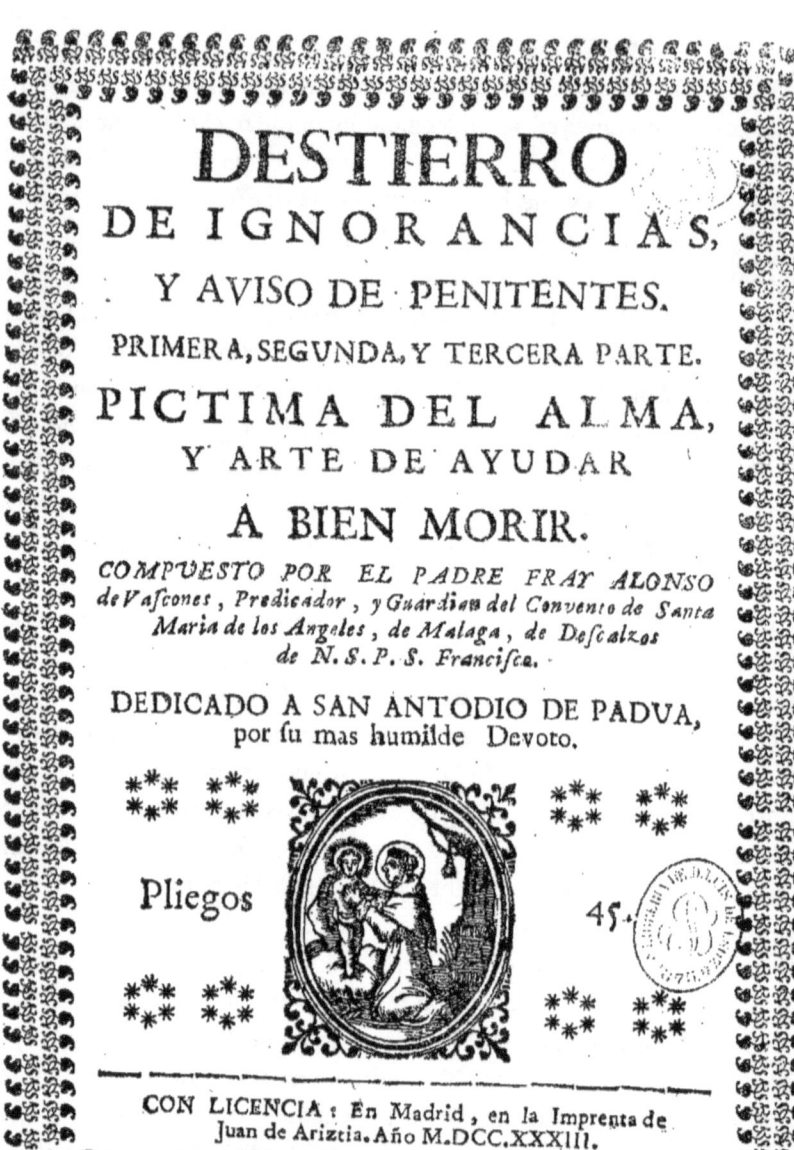

FIG. 21. Fr. Alonso de Vascones, *Destierro de Ignorancias... Arte de ayudar a bien morir* (Madrid: Imprenta de Juan de Ariztiam, 1733).

Preparation for death was an earnest task, and the treatises on the art of dying gained a lot of traction, becoming more relevant and increasingly accessible to readers from the sixteenth through the end of the eighteenth century.[9] Known as *ars moriendi*, the genre was well known in New Spain.[10] *Ars moriendi* aimed at calming fears and inspiring the living and the dying to see beyond their own mortality. Written by trained theologians, they explained the meaning of death, the process of dying, and the steps prescribed by the Church to cleanse the spirit and ensure the journey of the soul to its final destination. The advice was for not just the friars helping others die well but for friars—and secular priests—as individuals who had to reconcile with God before dying. A classic example of the *ars moriendi* was Cardinal Roberto Bellarmino's *Arte de Bien Morir*, originally written in Latin and published in 1619, which became a "classic" in its time and a universal reading among members of the Church.[11] Bellarmino's work was more than a mere manual on "how to help" a moribund person. It explained how the principles of the faith gave meaning to life and death. Those whose deaths were still distant in the future should follow the guidelines that would give them greater confidence in the salvation of their soul. The rules began with the notion that to reach a good death, one must live a righteous life, understanding and practicing the theological virtues (faith, hope, and charity) and the moral virtues (temperance, justice, and piety) and paying obedience to the Ten Commandments. For those privileged men and women who lived in a religious order, there was no greater duty than to seek a total disengagement from worldly concerns and dedicate themselves to following the precepts of a good life to attain a good death. A bad death was for those fools (*necios*) who never learned the art of dying well and reaped what they had sown, eternal condemnation. For those who chose well, the prize was eternal life.

The second part of his book offered practical emotional support to those experiencing the process of dying. It began by describing the beauty of paradise: its peace and security and abundance of an infinite number of "goods"—the type that people would pursue in the world—available in a place where there was "no time." He continued with the explanation of the rituals to be followed at death: confession, viaticum, extreme unction, and Communion. Bellarmino also explained the activities of Satan during the transit. The devil hovered over the dying, hoping to snatch their souls. The last battle the dying person had to win was the safe passage of his or her soul from the sinister menace of an aggressive demon. The presence of Satan was balanced by the potential intervention of the saints, who could appear to comfort the true believers and help them follow the right path and remain strong during the transit. Bellarmino even discussed the possibility that God could visit the dying, comfort and assist them, and free them from their fears so that they could experience the joy of a happy death. Among the practices he described as helpful against the devil were holding holy images and relics, using holy water, reading the passion of Christ, or saying a prayer used by the apostle Paul for the occasion. If the moribund person could not physically pray, those assisting him or her should do it and ask for God's help to evict Satan from the premises. For Bellarmino, the most important benefit of dying a good death was the relief from further persecutions, torments, and other incommodities of life. The hope of the end of suffering and the beauty awaiting in the afterlife, "the crown of light," was the backbone of his message and one that was repeated time and over again in funeral sermons and chronicles in Catholic countries.

Other treatises on the art of death had the more practical purposes of teaching the priests how to perform the rites of death and the moribund how to follow them, such as those written by Fr. Juan de Salazar, *Arte de Ayudar y Disponer a bien Morir a todo género de personas*, published in 1608, and Fr. Antonio Alvarado, *Arte de Bien Morir y Guía del Camino de la Muerte*, published in 1611.[12] These authors taught those at death's door how to follow the rites prepared by the Church, the prayers to obtain the favor of Mary and the saints, and what they could do if they were tempted to disbelieve the principles of the faith in those last trying moments. The dying should never doubt the possibility of their own salvation. Any lack of trust in the principles proposed by the Church was a challenge to the will of God and could hurt the outcome of the engagement in the battle with death. Salazar also had advice for the priest helping the dying person. He should modulate his voice, please the moribund, and decide what to do with those who did not want to confess or were not confident of their salvation. There were prescriptions on the procedures to follow with those dying of a mortal wound and without time for any preparation as well as for those convicted to death for their crimes. The *ars moriendi* proposed a one-on-one relationship between the priest and the moribund despite the probable presence of others. Alvarado and Salazar forbade the presence of the close members of the family in the final moments of the sick person's death so that he or she would not be distracted by their grief and could concentrate on the rites preceding death.

Death in the Chronicles and Biographies

Death was an indispensable part of chronicles and biographies, whether of seculars, saints, or illustrious members of the Church. As a literary element, it was the expected "golden brooch" closure to any life story. As an opportunity for imparting a moral and spiritual lesson, it was pure gold. Writers, naturally, selected model men who had an arsenal of good deeds and virtues accumulated throughout their lives and could pass Bellarmino's test on the expectations of a good death. Recounting the virtues and sacrifices of the outstanding men of his order, the writer could impart a precious message of calm, fortitude, and righteousness to their brothers in religion and to the secular readers who sought clues on how to imitate them. In narrating the deaths of exemplary friars, it was imperative to present them as mortals who, while subject to temptations and weaknesses throughout their lives, were capable of understanding and overcoming them and preparing themselves for their own good deaths. One chronicler arranged the biographies of his brothers not according to their birth date but by the date of their death as the event that delivered them to their expected eternal life.[13]

Chronicles "painted" the deaths of friars with details that had the visual power and effectiveness of a painting.[14] The richly detailed scenes portrayed death taking place in an unforgettable scenario and experienced by spiritually gifted men. The chronicler chose the intimacy of the last moments as a counterperspective to the otherwise very public lives of their subjects. He opened to the readers a world totally closed to all but the members of the friary to convey a lesson in spirituality and reaffirm the value of the precepts of the *ars moriendi*. Since the inclusion of all incidents preceding and surrounding the deaths of chosen friars was justified as part of a moral lesson, the descriptions are full of important details about the actual moment of death.[15] Some authors were not exempt from indulging in the inclusion of extraordinary events of divine nature, but the intimacy of the circumstances and the sense of "place" they convey were a fitting end to satisfy the readers' interest in how friars proved their spiritual mettle in their final hours. The scene was expected to stir the intellect with elevated thoughts and fill the heart and soul with emotions strong enough to orient the reader toward the heights of heaven and the ultimate reward. The few examples gathered in this chapter are also particularly appealing for their literary quality. The chroniclers were well-trained writers who knew how to lend a sense of "drama" to the narrative, rearranging the elements of reality to convey a memorable historical scene.

For early modern people, the anguish of eternal condemnation was truly heartfelt. However, the prescience of death was understood as a divine favor. It allowed those chosen to prepare themselves well for the transit and experience it "properly" and without fear. Contrariwise, the possibility—or the experience—of an accidental or sudden death without the proper preparations elicited anguish not only among the laity but among brothers in religion. The best possible death would happen in the friar's home—his convent—and among his brothers, who were his family. The intimacy of his cell was the best place for dying, since it had been the friar's site for prayer, work, and rest. However, a good number of friars who died in the convent most likely died in the infirmary. Death in either setting was a shared experience. It was a duty as well as an act of ultimate charity for any friar to be present at his brother's last moments. When the attending physician admitted to the lack of further medical hope, the rituals of death began. The community was recalled with the sound of wood tablets (*matracas*), and all the brothers gathered in or outside the cell to follow the canonical rituals administered by the ordained priest and, if possible, to offer words of consolation. A brother's death was a moment worth living and remembering. It reminded all present of the fragility of life and the levity of all of life's vanities. The brothers present at this moment were also rehearsing the rites that would someday accompany their own deaths. If the moribund was able to speak, he could engage in prayers that the others would follow. The community sang the Creed when it became obvious that the brother was expiring. This mise-en-scène was vividly depicted by many authors as a worthwhile and edifying reading.

If the dying retained their faculties, they could arrange the last material details of their lives and call for assistance to take care of the spiritual ones. The preparation for death revealed the friar's personality. It was *his* moment to call for divine attention and establish a dialogue with God concerning the fate of his soul. The desired "happy death" would end his bodily suffering and worldly cares and take him to his true celestial motherland (*patria celestial*).

Augustinian chronicler Fr. Juan de Grijalva narrates how Fr. Juan Cruzate, prior of the convent of San Agustín in Mexico City, assumed control of the preparations for his death in a style that satisfied his aesthetic and spiritual feelings. After learning of the inevitability of his death,

> he went to the Oratory where the Blessed Sacrament was kept and had it dressed up with the best ornaments and many odorous flowers. There he received the Viaticum [accompanied by] popular music, stating that he was celebrating the eucharist as Christ had celebrated his with his disciples. . . . After having received it and given thanks, he returned to his cell and lied down in his bed, dressed as he was, and had the Indians sing some villancicos and the psalm *In te Domine Speravi*. He thus finished his peregrination in full command of his senses, a serene spirit and full confidence.[16]

Grijalva admired the friar's choice to follow a different path in observing the rituals of his own death. Fr. Juan re-created Christ's last supper in his own style, inserting local music and asking the Indians to whom he had preached to sing him a psalm of his choice rather than the traditional and ritually approved Creed. This was certainly an out-of-the-ordinary "death moment," but it makes Fr. Juan a more "human" subject as he sought his final consolation among the humblest and with music sung by the less exalted. As a last wish, it was certainly unusual and worth recording.

The memory of Fr. Juan Cruzate's arrangements for his own funeral indicates that friars, unless very sick, were fully aware of their roles as protagonists of their own deaths. An unconscious moribund was not memorable for the chronicler because he had no message to convey. Those friars who addressed the community in their last moments were sufficiently aware of being suppliants expecting their ultimate reward, and if strong enough, they expressed words of personal hope, established a dialogue with God and the saints, and perhaps even "saw" the expected angels and divine beings listening to their prayers. Whether it was traditional or sui generis, and there were cases of both, the moribund's words had the weight of being his last. People hardly ever got any information about a living friar's conversations, but his last words could be quotable and were rare and desired elements of the death scene. Grijalva had this edifying objective in mind when he inserted the last words of Fr. Alonso de la Veracruz, the distinguished sixteenth-century

Latinist and theologian and one of the stars of the order. Veracruz died of "urinary disease" in July 1584. When his physician gave up any hope of recovery, he told the friar, "Master, tonight you will have supper with God in heavens." After receiving Communion, Vera Cruz addressed God before his community *in Latin*, a language that he mastered:

> You know well, my Lord, that after I entered religion, I have not offended you, in my understanding, with any mortal sin. I have governed this Province several times, and my conscience tells me I have never caused pain to anyone; I have loved all as my sons, and wished them to love and serve you. I hated no one and never intended to take vengeance on anyone. However, my Lord, if in my ignorance there is something that I have not understood and I have offended you, your blood was spilled in the cross for that purpose, and the merits of your passion [are] recreated by me in this sacred body that I now receive as viaticum and for the health of my soul.[17]

It was an elegant and obviously prepared speech that conveyed humility, but it was also transactional. It made a case for the suppliant and reminded God that he, Fr. Alonso, expected God to fulfill the promise of redemption to all repentant humans through the blood of Christ and that God would save him too, for he had loved, not hated, and if he had offended God, it was due to misunderstanding, not intention. It was a perfect last-moment oration by a man of strong faith.

While the most notable friars received the most attention and longer descriptions, in some instances the death of lesser-known figures is also treated with much care. Dominican Agustín Dávila Padilla paid careful attention to the story of Agustín Tomás San Juan, a friar from Oviedo who accompanied Fr. Domingo de Betanzos and was among the first Dominicans in New Spain. He was a humble man with a limited education but a strong and determined sense of his role as an evangelizer. Dávila Padilla understood the religious significance of Fr. Agustín's efforts to found the confraternity of the Holy Rosary in Puebla, Mexico City, and Coyocán. Those confraternities were the pillars of popular religion and the spiritual links between Spain and New Spain in those early years of the viceroyalty.[18] By introducing the worship of Mary through prayer, the confraternity began to make inroads into the Native religions. Membership in the confraternity ensured a respectful Christian burial and offered spiritual and material help to their dying members, since the care of the sick and the dead was among the most important of the services it rendered. Fr. Agustín was among those who had a premonition of his death and set a precedent for the acceptance of this experience. None other than the Virgin Mary appeared in his cell, announcing the hour of his death and the glory that awaited him in the heavens.[19] He was sick in bed, but after the vision, he asked for help to get up and began a joyful dance, and as the chronicler remarks, "And thus he, who could hardly stand up before, danced while singing praises to the Virgin." After he finished dancing, he returned to bed "full of pleasure and contentment." Dávila Padilla piously added that Fr. Agustín's soul rested in the hands of the Virgin Mary, "who carried him to the eternal happiness that he is enjoying." This dancing scene on the threshold of death evoked more comedy than tragedy and indicated to the reader that death could be joyful and that the blessed, regardless of their status in the orders or in society, would receive happiness and rewards. That was something worthy of celebration.

Another death scene worth remembering for visual effects as well as spiritual content was that of Augustinian Fr. Diego de Villarubia, an admired and beloved member of the community of his convent of Michoacán. His last moments were witnessed by two chroniclers, Fr. Juan González de la Puente and Fr. Diego de Basalenque. González de la Puente published the first chronicle of the province of San Nicolás Tolentino in 1621, and Basalenque published his in 1644.[20] González de la Puente wrote the biographies of twelve notable Augustinians, but none of their deaths received as much attention as Villarrubia's. Born in Puebla, Villarubia professed in the Augustinian convent of Colegio de San Pablo in Mexico City. He was an intellectual man, becoming a master in theology and eventually becoming the prior of the convents of Valladolid, Tacámbaro, and Michoacán. Describing his death scene, the chronicler's main intention was to pontificate on the difference between the man who prepares himself for death throughout his life and the man who, blinded by material interests, makes a shipwreck of his life and dies badly. The chroniclers' long moral disquisitions were closer to those of a preacher, not a historian—that is, the chronicler wrote a sermon under the guise of history.[21] According to González de la Puente, Villarubia was granted the favor of learning in advance of the day of his death from the

Virgin Mary. Afflicted with a cold, Villarubia made a general confession, disregarding the doctor's opinion that he was not in danger. He asked for the viaticum, which he received while kneeling on his bed and chanting litanies with tears in his eyes. On Christmas Day he stated he had a great battle with demons but had defeated them with the help of Christ and the Virgin. He could devote his attention to his death preparations. Villarrubia requested that his brothers be present in his cell and help him in that last trance. He proceeded to make a list of his few belongings and donated his only possession, five pesos, to the poor. He also requested to have his habit and cape ready for his burial and, as the rules of the Augustinian order stated, to wash his feet and tie his legs with a string he had readied for this ritual. When extreme unction was applied, he intoned the penitential psalms with those present.[22] He also addressed the community, advising them to gain as many indulgences for him as they could because he was uncertain about his own efforts in that regard. After kissing the prior's hand, he requested from him an order to die, since according to biblical sources, Moses and Aaron had died as they contemplated the promised land but had failed to obey God's commands.[23] Unlike them, Villarubia wanted to obey his prelate. He then embraced all the brothers present in his cell and requested a cross. After kissing the cross, he sat down and raised it, exclaiming in Latin that there was nothing to fear as long as he held the sign of God and life, addressing the cross with many endearing words. He also requested an icon of Saint Catherine and, embracing it, stated he would soon see the "original" in the heavens. Yet another request followed: a reading of Christ's passion according to Saint John while he repeated it himself. He also invoked Mary and several saints and vocalized the letter of the hymns written by Saint Bernard of Clairvaux honoring Christ.[24] Embracing a cross in the fashion of Saint Francis, he commended himself to God with such fervor and resounding voice that his brothers in religion assumed that at that precise moment, his spirit had flown to God, because after that, he relaxed and remained in peaceful rest through the night, dying on the following day at the hour he had predicted. The chronicler noted that his body was swollen and that his hair and beard had turned white, but to him, it was also patent that the strength of his spirit had overcome the pains of his body. The righteous dies a smooth and sweet death, not in fear or in darkness, because he dies obeying God. It was a highly "staged" death—by volition and by tradition.

A deeply religious friar like Villarubia had assimilated all the theatricality of religious ceremonies and rituals, and it was natural that he performed his own death following the script of devotional readings.

Decades later, Fr. Diego de Basalenque, who had also witnessed Villarrubia's death, wrote his own version for the chronicle of the order. The availability of two versions of the same death invites comparison. Basalenque added some significant details and avoided De la Puente's pontifications.[25] He concurred with De la Puente's testimony on Villarrubia's preparedness for death, but he added an additional layer of meaning by using martial language. Dying was a battle against death. As such, his praise of the friar's behavior during the process conveyed the vision of the Church triumphant through one of its soldiers. The friar's decision to move to the convent in Pátzcuaro to prepare himself to die was understood as a strategic maneuver, because he who arrives first chooses the best location and ensures victory. In Basalenque's narrative, Villarrubia's preparations for death were like those of a soldier planning to engage in battle.

Villarubia personally wrote two letters. One he sent to his provincial, telling him about his impending death and asking the community to pray for him and request a "happy victory" against his enemies. He asked that his robe be placed next to him on the bed and gave instructions on how to treat his body after his death. He understood his death was close, and not wanting to waste time, he asked two visiting Jesuits to administer extreme unction immediately, correcting one of them when he made a mistake in the wording. He declined to make any "final" statements because at the moment of death, he said, everything done in life felt like an indictment of one's behavior. Thus, he begged his brothers' forgiveness and the blessings of the prior. Basalenque also makes it clear that his body had suffered the ravages of poor medical practice and his own sickness. The bloodletting ordered by the doctors when he first felt ill was performed so poorly, his swollen arm hardly fit into the sleeve of his robe, and his body remained swollen after his death. The doctor was very contrite, but Villarubia consoled him by saying that because it was God's will that he died, God had obstructed any remedies to the body. It was time to administer the remedies to the soul.

Basalenque added small details such as the fact that his last confession was taken by a young priest who had been his student and not by a friend who had promised but had failed to come. He noted the "mistakes" made in the ritual by one of the two visiting Jesuits.[26] Villarubia died fully aware and in total control of his transit as an exemplar religious. Following standard writing practice, the chronicler remarked that his face "was prettier and more beautiful than in life." This after-death transformation was interpreted as a sign of eternal salvation. The body became beautiful as it reflected the good virtues of the spirit. The long passage on Villarrubia's transit fixed the reader not on the deterioration of the body but on the spiritual progress of a friar who faced death with equanimity and full of fervor and confidence.

Villarubia's death took place in a small and largely Indigenous community. The news spread by the toll of bells requesting the presence of the townsfolk in the friary's church to render the appropriate honors and bid Villarubia their farewell.[27] The most endearing note of his funeral was the presence of many children. The town's children entered the convent and crowded in his cell, crying and kissing his habit, with their elders joining them in the expression of their sadness. The Jesuit rector who had administered the last rites declared that he had never witnessed such a general display of emotions in people of all ages and stated that they were the voice of God. The picture of a cell full of children added an unusual touch of tenderness to the story. Basalenque also added the personal comment of the Franciscan who performed the rites during the burial; he believed that Villarubia had already gone to heaven. The transfer of the corpse three years later to a special burial site in the church corroborated what other hagiographic narratives took as evidence of the special fate of the deceased. His body was in very good condition with a minimal degree of corruption. His hands were as beautiful and flexible as when he performed the Mass. Traditionally, the challenge to the corruptibility of the flesh was assumed to corroborate the favor of an after-death life among those elected by God.

Two other vignettes of death in the eighteenth century illuminate the variety of circumstances and the similarities of responses. The deaths of Fr. Antonio Margil and Fr. Junípero Serra took place in their own convents and were witnessed and recorded by their biographers as fitting ends to lives well spent in the missionary field.[28] Fr. Isidro de Espinosa, a master chronicler and a missionary himself, was a companion to Fr. Antonio, and he wrote his first biography. He was following a historical tradition, cultivating a genre that was no longer a flourishing intellectual activity among the religious orders in the late eighteenth century.

After many years of outstanding missionary journeys throughout the territories of central New Spain; the provinces of Texas, Sonora, Nuevo León, Yucatán, and Guatemala; and beyond in Central America, Fr. Antonio Margil returned to his College of Santa Cruz in Querétaro in 1726. He had just finished urban missionary duties in Jalisco and Michoacán.[29] In Querétaro he collapsed and lost consciousness for one hour. It may have been a heart attack. He was nearing seventy and was in delicate health. These circumstances persuaded the Franciscan commissary general, who was in Querétaro at the time, to order him to travel to Mexico City to be nursed in the infirmary of the main Franciscan convent. Margil left Querétaro on July 2, on foot, with two conventual brothers as company. Despite being increasingly ill, he stopped in several places to preach and perform the Mass, experiencing high fever and increasing weakness. On August 1, 1726, a coach picked him up in the small town of Cuautitlán and took him to Mexico City. Before leaving he requested his two traveling companions to have a Mass said for him in the sanctuary of Nuestra Señora de Guadalupe. He arrived in the city on August 2 and died on August 6. In those four days, he confessed, received the viaticum, begged the forgiveness of his brothers, and received the extreme unction totally conscious and repeating Franciscan expressions of faith and thanks (*jaculatorias*) in Latin. At one point he asked for and received an icon of baby Jesus from the nuns of San Juan de la Penitencia, and an icon of Nuestra Señora de los Remedios from the convent of Santa Clara.

The last days of a notable figure were always public news, and people from all walks of life stopped by the convent to pray for Margil, crowding the porter's room and the nearby streets. The day before his death, four brothers visited Margil asking for his blessing. He seemed to have been delirious at times, and he was reported to have said to his companions, in a loud voice, that he had wished to die in a forest among wild animals and not in that saintly place, but he was accepting God's will that he should die where he was. Near the end he seemed to have been wording his last thoughts (*amorosos coloquios*) until, between one and two in the afternoon, the infirmary brother told him, "Time to see God," to which the moribund inclined his head in agreement. He seemed to be sleeping in his last hours. The vicar of the convent's choir sang the Creed with the community, and Margil expired while the choir sang the canticle *Nunc dimittis servum tuum*, embracing a cross and with his eyes fully open.[30] He died at almost seventy years of age, having served fifty-three years as a Franciscan. Margil's death was regarded as exemplary because he defied his own physical decline and continued performing his pastoral duties, the dominant leitmotif of his life.

Margil's final days in the Franciscan convent's hospital were far from peaceful and restful. Men of recognized spiritual gifts had little choice on the matter, especially if they died in a large city. All the local notables wanted to have the honor and opportunity of expressing their sentiments; brothers in religion also hoped to see him for the last time, receive his blessing, and perhaps hear his last words. In Margil's case someone commissioned a final "portrait," and a sketch was quickly made. Espinosa mentions that the noted eighteenth-century painter Juan Rodríguez Juárez, who was called to make the portrait sketch, declared that he had trouble drawing it. He sweated copiously and stated that the task of rendering Margil's features was almost impossible.[31] Margil's last confession was shared publicly by the confessor and repeated by the chronicler so that readers had the privilege of learning what should have been kept in secrecy. Obviously, someone was taking notes of the "event" to save it for posterity. Secrecy did not apply under those circumstances.

Following his death on August 6, 1726, the prelates attempted to prevent the pious excesses committed by the faithful during a funeral. The dead body could be desecrated by those seeking relics. Anything the dead touched or owned was believed to be infused with his spiritual power and capable of rendering protection and performing miracles. To preserve Fr. Antonio's articles of personal use, the minister provincial ordered that no one could take anything from his body or from the cell. However, his body suffered another type of inspection to determine special features of "grace." Legs and arms were handled to ascertain their flexibility, the facial features were inspected for serenity and rejuvenation, and the air in the room was sniffed to detect the lack of deterioration odor. In Margil's case his feet called for special attention. Since he had walked almost always barefoot (or with only the thinnest of sandals) for thousands of miles, his feet appeared to be soft and smooth rather than calloused and worn, a sign of being "special." A master surgeon, Joseph Benitez, signed an affidavit describing the softness and warmth of the body and the good color of the face ten hours after death.[32] This was another physical sign of the saintly nature of his spirit. Once the body was dressed in his habit, his coffin was moved from a smaller chapel close to the infirmary to the main chapel of the church. The doors of the temple were locked to prevent the populace from rushing in. However, members of the social elite and the church had privileged access. The vigil lasted three days to accommodate the many who wanted to see the body.

Those who came to render homage and pay respects to the late friar kissed his feet or his habit, pressed handkerchiefs or medals to his body, and took flowers from his coffin.[33] Espinosa and others were saddened by the assault on the body. Notwithstanding the precautions taken by the Franciscans, they were unable to stop people from taking pieces of the habit, and it was necessary to change his shroud three times.[34] In fact, Fr. Manuel de las Heras, his companion and last confessor, signed a writ stating that Carmelites and Jesuits had torn pieces of Margil's habit in the "old fashion" just before his burial.[35] By 1726, the religious orders were trying to put an end to those practices but could not prevent their own members from engaging in them. Before the funeral Mass, his coffin left the convent and made a short tour of the adjacent streets, returning to the main chapel. This ritual gave people outside the convent and the church the opportunity to share the funerary rituals. The Mass was performed by the notable savant Dr. Juan de Castorena y Ursúa. A religious witness stated that his funeral elicited such emotion that it could compare with that of Saint Anthony of Padua or Saint Francis Xavier.[36] On August 8, 1726, prelates of the mendicant orders and members of the city *cabildo* carried his coffin to the burial site in the church and deposited it at the site reserved for the Counts of the Valley of Orizaba at the nobleman's own request. Fr. Antonio may have been stunned by such a display of etiquette and popularity. He had once expressed his desire to be buried in the wild. However, he had once said that anyone honoring a man of God was really honoring God because the friars and clergy were venues to spread God's word. The theatrical nature of the vigil and the burial ceremonies was in sharp contrast with the most intimate experience of the friar's personal search for the spiritual comfort of his faith in his last moments of life. Margil had not wanted any kind of mundane attention to himself, as one of the preachers at his funeral stated in his sermon. Vicente Navarro, the preacher, affirmed that Margil had declined any honors he could receive after his death, transferring them to his chosen mission: "These honors are not for me, a miserable wicked man; they are for the dignity of the apostolic ministry and for Jesus Christ . . . whose person I represent in this highest employment as a missionary."[37]

Another missionary's death worth remembering was that of Fr. Junípero Serra (1713–84), who represented a second generation of Propaganda Fide missionaries. Born in Majorca, he arrived in New Spain in 1749 destined for the Colegio de Propaganda Fide of San Fernando in Mexico City.[38] Serra shared with Margil the experience of "live missions" among "gentiles"—the yet-to-be-evangelized Indians. He spent his first several years in New Spain among the Pames of the Sierra Gorda, part of the Sierra Madre Oriental, northeast of Mexico. From there he was sent to found missions in Upper California in 1769, a task he shared with his brother in religion Fr. Francisco Palou, a disciple and friend for over forty years. Palou witnessed Serra's death in mission San Carlos de Monterrey, California, on August 28, 1784, and administered him the last sacraments. Palou was in the San Francisco Bay mission when Serra requested his presence, feeling that his days were coming to an end. He called Serra's death "exemplary," not *dichosa*, or "happy."[39] In this, he differed from the style of previous hagiographers. Palou's strong personal bond with Serra is not betrayed in his terse and clear prose, abundant in details and intent on being objective.

In mid-1784 Serra was in his headquarters, the San Carlos de Monterrey mission. He had been in San Diego in September 1783 confirming neophytes, and despite his increasing weakness and the "heaviness" in his chest, he returned to mission San Carlos on foot, arriving in January 1784. The journey had not been free of problems. He was very sick and had to rest in Mission San Gabriel. He was still longing for the foundation of another mission in the Santa Barbara Channel—one of his most desired and frustrating projects. On July 16, 1784, he learned that the College of San Fernando could not afford to send him missionaries for the project owing to the short number of friars available for that purpose. Palou believed that the bad news was the final stroke determining his death. After receiving the letter, Serra wrote to the missionaries in the southern mission, bidding them goodbye. He also wrote the missionaries in San Antonio de Padua and San Luis Obispo—twenty-five and fifty leagues away, respectively—and to Palou, who was currently in the San Francisco mission, requesting their presence.[40] In his last days, Serra wished nothing more than to die among his brothers in religion.

Palou had a premonition of what the letter meant and traveled forty-two leagues (around 126 miles) by land, arriving in San Carlos on August 18. Serra was not well, still suffering from "a heavy chest," maybe severe asthma or a weak heart. Despite his condition Serra went to prayers with his neophytes as he did every afternoon, singing the verses that Fr. Antonio Margil had composed for the Feast of the Assumption on August 15.[41] He also sang with the neophytes for the Mass on August 19. On the Friday of that week, he carried out the exercises of the Via Crucis, a favorite devotion of the Propaganda Fide Franciscans honoring the final path followed by Jesus on his way to the cross. All the town shared in the exercise.

On July 23 a paquebot with merchandise arrived in Monterrey, and the surgeon of the ship visited Serra, proposing and carrying out a "hot cure" to relieve him from the oppression in the chest. It had no effect. Serra never complained about his health. Quite the contrary, the moment he got the fabric brought by the boat, he began cutting clothes for his neophytes. By the twenty-sixth Serra knew his end was close, and after spending his day by himself, he made a general confession with Palou. He wanted to spend the night alone. Early on the twenty-seventh Palou found him already reading the breviary early in the morning, and after Palou said his early Mass, Serra asked for the viaticum, walking to the church aided by the presidio's commandant, who had come to Mass. They were accompanied by all the Indians from the mission. Much to Palou's surprise, Serra sang the *Tantum Ergo Sacramentum* with a sonorous voice but with tears in his eyes.[42] Back in his cell, Serra called the carpenter to have him make his coffin. He spent his day sitting and deep in his thoughts. After receiving extreme unction, he knelt all night long against his bed, seeking some relief from his chest. Neophytes crowded his cell, and Serra spent some time reclined in their arms. That night he received the plenary absolution from Palou and the plenary indulgence to which Franciscans were entitled. On the twenty-eighth, Saint Augustine's Day, the captain of the frigate, José Cañizares, and the presidio's royal chaplain sat together with Serra, recalling memories of the trips they had shared. Cañizares had been the captain of the boat on Serra's first trip to California in 1769, and Serra had been the boat's chaplain on another trip in 1779. He asked Cañizares and the chaplain the favor of scattering some earth on his tomb. He asked Palou to be buried in the church next to his former companion Fr. Juan Crespí. Amid tears Palou asked Serra to ask the Holy Trinity to favor him and all those present. Serra promised, hoping the Lord would concede him that great happiness. They both expressed hopes for the conversion of the gentiles. Suddenly, Serra confessed a great fear and begged Palou to cast holy water in the cell and read the commendation for his soul.[43] His companion Fr. Matías Noriega and the shipmen joined. Serra then declared that he was relieved of his fears, left his cell, and smiled when the captain told him that he had begged Saint Anthony for his health so that they could travel together again. After having a cup of broth for lunch, he left his company for a "rest" and returned to his cell. Serra lay in his bed with his blanket and holding a cross he had owned since his novitiate. Palou knew he had not slept well the night before and was pleased he was resting. He and the rest of the visitors went out for lunch. After a while Palou went to check on him and found that Serra had expired. It was close to 2 p.m., August 28, 1784. Serra was nearly eighty years of age. He had lived nearly fifty-four years as a Franciscan and over thirty-five years as a missionary. Palou and his companions felt they had suddenly become "orphans."

It was necessary to close the door of the cell to hold back Indians and sailors expressing their sadness. Serra laid in his coffin with six candles during the day to allow people to pray and press medals against his hands and face. He received full funerary rituals in the nearby church all night long. Two soldiers guarded the body against "holy theft," but he still lost part of his habit and some hair. Around six hundred neophytes of the mission, four priests, sailors, and the soldiers from the presidio were present at his burial. Palou was happy that he was accompanied by some "Spanish" people and that his beloved teacher had received a funeral as respectful as possible under the circumstances.[44] Interestingly, he decided to tear Serra's undertunic and two of his handkerchiefs to distribute the pieces among the sailors as relics to make scapularies. He had to find other relics for the presidio soldiers and gave them some medals that Serra kept as gifts for the believers. He later wrote that "for his brothers and subjects," there was nothing but sorrow and the pain of being deprived of such an amiable father, prudent prelate, and learned and exemplary teacher.[45]

Palou wrote one of the finest descriptions of death in conventual chronicles. His terse prose is free from the verbal pyrotechnics of baroque writing and elicits emotion and intellectual engagement from the reader. Serra's biography was a straight account with precise details based on the knowledge of the missions' internal and official documentation. As an "insider" Palou was scrupulous in handling the sources. His account of Serra's death contains a great deal of repressed personal emotion that any reader can detect. He was a man of faith as much as Serra was, and both held the firm belief that there was a heaven where they would meet God and each other after death. This explains the request to petition God on their behalf and the belief, stated in his biography's introduction, that Serra had succeeded in his petition to God to favor the conversion of the gentiles because since his death, an inordinate number of them had requested instruction and baptism.

The treatment of death could be masterful in the hands of experienced writers, but it also had some odd examples and variations in the chronicles. For example, Dominican Dávila Padilla lingered on the unusual death of Fr. Antonio Garcés of the convent of Oaxaca. Fr. Antonio was burned to death trying to rescue the holy vessels from his modest church in the town of San Ildefonso when it caught fire. His body was recovered from the ashes, and lacking any other verifiable information to describe his death, Dávila Padilla picked up a local hagiographic story. Some had seen a ball of fire like a comet appearing in the eastern sky over the small town. The phenomenon was interpreted as a sign of the ascent of Fr. Antonio's soul to the heavens, especially since another friar had a vision of the deceased who, speaking to him, said he was already enjoying the other life.[46] Other dramatic deaths were those of missionaries dying of hunger or thirst. Fr. Francisco Fuentes, a Franciscan of the province of Jalisco and guardian of the convent Guaxicori, among other remote posts, was a trekker in the western mountains. He died of dehydration in one of his trips searching for the elusive Cora Indians of that area.[47]

Some friars chose to add drama to their own deaths for the purpose of evangelization. Augustinian Fr. Juan de Grijalva recorded an unusual staging of the death of Fr. Antonio de la Rea, a sixteenth-century missionary who believed in emotion and theater as didactic tools. He oversaw the Indians of the town of Molango (today's state of Hidalgo). In 1563 he became sick, and with the understanding of his approaching death, he decided to return to his mother convent in Mexico City to be buried with his brothers in his spiritual home. However, he would not leave town before reiterating his Christian message to the townspeople. He gathered them for a final sermon, summing up all the key points of the Christian doctrine he had taught them for so many years. Then he decided to stage the final judgment and the rigorous punishment awaiting the sinners by jumping into a circle of fire he had started next to the pulpit and preaching on the flames of hell that burned the souls and the impossibility of escaping them. The chronicler confessed to being impressed by the story, especially since the friar was able to jump out of the fire without any harm.[48] Fr. Antonio's final days were spent between the city of Mexico and the town of Coyocán, where he was sent to rest and prepare for death. Grijalva could not abstain from narrating some details of his last three days, when he lay in bed without speaking but with his eyes open until one hour before his death on September 14, 1726, when he said his last words, commending himself to God. Grijalva chose his life, he stated, because being such a public person and having so many witnesses of his death, Fr. Antonio—like other saintly friars—earned a place of remembrance in his order's memory.

Fr. Francisco de Burgoa, whose dense chronicles of the Dominicans in Oaxaca recorded the lives of the notable men of his province, was also careful to record the final days of some of his brothers with enough detail to induce an emotional reaction in his readers, including admiration for their pious acceptance of death. One of his choices was the death of Fr. Juan Martínez, a provincial of the order and a man of delicate health who had suffered from a long sickness. Fr. Juan fell from a horse while visiting a small town. Disregarding internal pain, he spent the day confessing, spent a sleepless night in the church, and prepared himself for Mass on the following day. While engaged in a procession within the church in honor of the Holy Rosary, he collapsed and was taken by the participating Indian dignitaries to the sacristy, where he expired shortly thereafter, holding a cross.[49] A sudden death such as this was not welcomed by the friars because they missed the opportunity to "prepare" for it. The drama of this death must have had a great impact on the small rural community.

Burgoa also recorded the disruption created by people wanting to tear relics from a dead friar's habit. Fr. Lope de Cuellar, who arrived in Mexico from Extremadura as a child, attempted a novitiate in another order in Puebla. Having failed this trial, he eventually professed with the Dominicans of Oaxaca. Blinded during an attempt to repair his cataracts by a lay brother turned physician, he became addicted to ascetic practices and also experienced many revelations and visions.[50] When he died in October 1623, the just recently arrived bishop requested special protection for his body and a quick funeral, since the celebration of his own consecration was still pending. The main chapel was closed to prevent the people clamoring outside to enter the inner temple to pay their "respects" and have the opportunity to snatch a relic from the body. Before internment his body was taken in a solemn procession in the galleries around the conventual patio. At this point the body was "attacked" by a "variety" of people who had been admitted to the cloister and who sought pieces of his habit. They closed on the corpse, tearing his cape, and the body lost a toe before it was rushed into his grave by his concerned brothers.[51]

Death Remembered: Funeral Sermons

Chronicles recorded the moment of death for potential readers. Funeral sermons delivered the meaning of death for the living—those who attended church and accompanied the dead friars before their bodies were interned. These texts were the first steps in the construction of the biography of a chosen member of the order. Above all, sermons were oral means of communication between the priest and the faithful who gathered in the church to receive messages of ethics and edification.[52] The priest's words carried the weight of traditional religion charged with the emotional appeal of a "live" spectacle. Sacred oratory was a popular genre conveying didactic, moral, and spiritual teachings and had gained traction in seventeenth-century New Spain.

Any type of oratory is ephemeral in nature unless it is printed. The regular faithful did not "read" printed sermons; they listened to them and watched the priest deliver them. The "live" delivery was what mattered to people and drew them to the church. To convey his message to his listeners, the preacher learned how to speak for an audience and how to use dramatic effects to make the strongest impression. His performance had to appeal to the ears and to the eyes. From the elevated and prominent scenario of the pulpit, he modulated his voice and learned when to pause, gesture, cry, or whisper during his speech to persuade the audience of the truth of his message.[53] These techniques were learned by reading books on the subject and by practicing in the early years of a priest's training.[54] The objective was to make the experience of the sermon unforgettably emotional and thus ensure the permanence of its key message in the audience's memory.

Hundreds of sermons were preached yearly in New Spain, but despite their ubiquity in daily life, only a fraction was printed, and most of those available for reading were devoted not to the eulogy of people but to the eulogy of the divine.⁵⁵ The texts of most sermons remained as handwritten notes for the use of the preacher or others of his order.⁵⁶ In 1994 Carlos Herrejón Peredo calculated that there were well over two thousand remaining examples of sermons preached in New Spain.⁵⁷ Of those, the majority were devoted to saints and delivered at the celebrations of the sacraments of the church or dedicated to the memory of royalty.⁵⁸ Herrejón Peredo states that only around 25 percent of the sermons he studied were delivered at funeral services. The cost of printing was most probably one of the key reasons for this relatively low number. In the case of sermons dedicated to eulogizing a dead friar, finding a patron to cover its costs was difficult unless he was someone really charismatic or had a relative or a friend willing to pay for the publication. It is not surprising that only a small number of available sermons addressed the deaths of friars. In fact, sermons dedicated to nuns are more abundant, since nuns had sermons preached at the time of their profession as well as their funeral.

It is appropriate to review how death was portrayed and understood in these sermons. Unlike chronicles and biographies, sermons did not describe the act of death itself; they addressed its meaning. Mendicant orders kept a very close relation with religious values generated in Spain. Although he did not preach in Mexico during his life, Luis Bertrand (1526–81) was a source of inspiration for many other sacred orators of the colonial period. He was a Dominican born in Valencia who preached in South America for several years. He was canonized in 1671, and among his many sermons, one especially addressed the dead (*difuntos*) in a generic fashion.⁵⁹ The key message was "Mihi vivere Christus est, et mori lucrum" (For me to live is Christ, and death is profit). Bertrand addressed the living gathered to mourn the dead by asking them what was the cause of their sadness. Certainly, he argued, it was not for the dead person, who was in a better place; their sadness was for themselves to satisfy the emotional need created by the loss of the deceased. He implied that the living were simply selfish and did not quite understand the meaning of death. If death appeared to be a disastrous event, the living might as well ask God why he created death if it really was so terrifying and destructive. Bertrand answered that hypothetical question by reminding the audience that God had no plan for death: it was created by the sin of Adam. Yet, he continued, one could and should see profit in death, not fear or horror. For all good Christians, death was profit: it was the end of their labors, the end of their personal battles, the beginning of their reward, and the gate to the glory of God. A seed cannot fructify without its own death, and the corruption of the body is necessary after death. He challenged the mourners that not all the dead were among the blessed. The blessed were those who died in God. Those who gathered in the church to honor the dead must understand that.

Franciscans customarily commissioned sermons for their dead brothers on the occasion of the celebration of their chapters. Capuchin Fr. Francisco de Guadiz, of Andalucía, delivered one in 1686 to explain the meaning of death.[60] "Divine lessons," he stated, teach people that all ends in the sepulcher. Even Christ inclined his head to death. However, members of the church—and his order—had a special privilege. The mother province assisted her sons while they lived, loving them, granting them the safest and most valuable honors in life, and assisting them after death with honors and prayers for their spiritual rest. In exchange, Guadiz requested that those who were already dead and "in the sovereign presence of [their] creator" remember those who still lived in this vale of tears so that the living would observe the precepts of religion to the letter and focus their attention on achieving the glory in which the dead already rested. Guadiz's sermon was classic in its statements of reverence for the dead, hope for the living, and the contractual relationship between both. The dead retained agency; they had the power to help the living, and the latter, in their role as suppliants, should recognize that power and expect its benefits. He also underlined another important intellectual element bonding the living and the dead. It was the notion of belonging to a spiritual family. The dead and the living were all brothers who shared a generous mother—the Church—who looked after them and prayed for them after their death. That understanding should comfort all friars.[61]

Nearly one hundred years after Guadiz delivered his sermon, Fr. Manuel Antonio de Pazos, custodian and preacher of the Franciscan province of Zacatecas, composed a sermon similar in intent and spirit during the meeting of the province's chapter in November 1782.[62] Being an eighteenth-century example of sacred oratory, it lacked the burden of the baroque verbal artifice that characterized Guadiz's sermon. However, although separated by one century, Pazos echoed some of the themes developed by Guadiz because they shared a similar intellectual understanding of the response of the living to death and the bond that death created among all members of their respective orders. After death, friars could count on the help of the living. Pazos assumed his living and dead brothers had a spiritual bond that permitted a clear line of communication, love, and responsibility between them. He acknowledged that some brothers had died with some slight imperfections and small transgressions that caused them to purify themselves in purgatory. It was their living brothers' duty to help them with their prayers until they left purgatory and reached the realm of the eternal kingdom of Jerusalem. Pazos reassured his listeners that the slight failures of some friars in no way put a stain on their religious province. Reviewing its history, he had found many exemplary men comparable in valor to biblical figures. They had imperfections, but they had all risked their lives. Their mother province had much to show for their work: twelve convents, seven vicars, four bishops, and many distinguished members.[63] This was a perfect example of how funeral sermons were bonding mechanisms among friars in any given community: they created brotherhood and togetherness in the face of death.

Other sermons disclose variations in engaging with death and the dead. The Dieguinos—discalced Franciscans—must have felt honored when Isidro Sariñana y Cuenca, bishop of Oaxaca, delivered the funeral eulogy of one of their members, Fr. Cristóbal Muñoz de la Concepción, on June 27, 1689.[64] Sariñana's sermon was a typical baroque piece, heavily doused with Latin quotes to show his biblical and theological knowledge. It dwelled on the theme of how God favors his "friends," those friars who suffer for God in the battle against the temptations of the devil. Sariñana introduced a trilogy of actions performed by those chosen friars: they "fight, they suffer, and they escape" the temptations of the world. He envisioned the deceased Fr. Cristóbal among those who had lived in a continuous inner battle ("the fight and the suffering") against all temptations, especially chastity, and succeeded in escaping (the "escape") from them. He did not use the word *conquer*. In fact, spiritual victory was represented as an "escape" from weakness and temptation, a subtle yet significant change that introduced a spirituality based on interiority, not on outward deeds. Sariñana eulogized Muñoz's careful self-examination of his own behavior, his personal confrontation with his inner doubts (*escrúpulos*), and the intensity of his penitence. He submitted willingly to the judgment of his prelate and lived in lifelong austerity. He also praised his strong belief in the protective power of prayers and his diligent practice of liturgical rituals. The bishop revealed that he had read a book of the friar's writings, a manuscript of spiritual exercises that he compared to the works of Molina, who I assume was the Carthusian Antonio de Molina, a well-known and widely read spiritual writer.⁶⁵ Thus, he revealed the existence of spiritual writings from the pen of a rather obscure friar. Nuns engaged frequently in this kind of meditation, but there is little evidence that friars also wrote this type of intimate literature. If they did, the community either destroyed or shelved the writings after their deaths.

Bishop Sariñana delineated the profile of a penitent and observant friar who followed the model of the spirituality promoted since the mid-sixteenth century: someone who was totally vested in practicing the virtues that would further interiority and remove him from the cares of the world. In fact, Muñoz was the antithesis of the evangelizing friars from Propaganda Fide, founded in 1683, just a few years before this sermon was delivered, to promote missionary involvement in the cities and the remotest boundaries of New Spain. Of course, the Dieguinos had a different spiritual agenda from that of the friars of Propaganda Fide and, for that matter, other mendicants. The eulogy of a model of the ascetic friar in the seventeenth century should not be surprising. Seventeenth-century religiosity lingered on blood, sacrifice, anguish, and redemption through penitence.⁶⁶ Sariñana also delivered a sermon in eulogy of the twenty-one Franciscans who had been martyred in New Mexico in August 1680. It has been examined in the chapter on martyrs, but it seems appropriate to state here that he praised them as fearless men who disregarded death to follow their stated mission in life. It seems that the bishop adapted his message to "fit" the two types of male spirituality that coexisted in seventeenth-century New Spain.

How much of that dual type of religiosity lingered in the eighteenth-century sermons? Reviewing the sermons preached after Fr. Antonio de Jesús Margil's death, we see some nuances of the past as well as new modes of religious praise caused by the renaissance of active evangelization led by members of Propaganda Fide. Margil did not *officially* die in the "odor of sanctity," but the emotional response to his death indicates that he was regarded as a living saint by his contemporaries. Margil (1657–1726) lived half of his life as a seventeenth-century Franciscan. His spiritual formative years were those of that century. Unlike Fr. Cristobal Muñoz, and despite being a man of intense spiritual life, he was praised for his complete engagement with the world. Immediately after his death, the man who was called *santo* by his many followers began to emerge as a potential candidate for sainthood, and that explains, in part, the literary production generated by his death. He has the lion's share in terms of eulogies: two official biographies and five known funeral sermons.⁶⁷ Here I briefly review three of them. The first one was preached by Fr. Juan López de Aguado on August 21, 1726, two weeks after his death.⁶⁸ Aguado had been a missionary with Margil in the northern frontiers of New Spain, and at the time of Margil's death, he was guardian of the Franciscan convent in Valladolid (today's Michoacán). In his sermon Aguado described Margil's uniqueness as a missionary, praising his virtues and achievements as a selfless member of the order. His sermon was based on Psalm 68, "Who rides the heights of the ancient heavens, who sends forth his voice as a mighty voice?" to represent Margil's voice as a preacher.⁶⁹ Margil's voice, he wrote, had three modes: high, soft, and clear. In his high missionary voice, Margil addressed the "wild" and "ferocious Indians" in his many geographical peregrinations and conquered them—sometimes with his mere presence. Mostly, he communicated with them effectively, occasionally inexplicably, since he did not know the language.⁷⁰ With his soft, persuasive voice, he conveyed fervor, sweetness, and wisdom. He was everywhere when he was needed because he was a man destined by heaven to remedy the needs of all. He gave himself to all—not just the neophytes but his brothers in religion as well.⁷¹ His "clear" voice was that of a teacher of the sacred who imparted with his own example all the virtues of his state: poverty, chastity, penitence, obedience, hope, and observance of the Franciscan rules. For López de Aguado, Margil was a fearless spiritual man who forgot his comforts and preached to the last day of his life. The key message was that there is no death to a voice when it is used to praise God and convey God's message to the people. This emphasis on locution reminds historians that not a single one of Margil's "sermons" has survived. A preacher's ability as a communicator was the least likely to endure, especially—as in Margil's case—if this ability was spent in rural areas.

One year later after Aguado's sermon, in 1727, the Colegio de la Santa Cruz published the sermon preached by Fr. Diego de Alcántara.⁷² Alcántara's key theme was the Old Testament story of Josiah, king of Judea, and the mourning for his death.⁷³ In the case of Fr. Antonio, his loss was worth crying for. Josiah protected the sinners from God's punishment but was also full of love for the creator. When Josiah died Jerusalem was orphaned. Margil's death had left his flock without an intercessor. To illustrate Margil's key virtues,

Alcántara peppered his sermon with anecdotes about Margil's words and deeds gathered and recorded before his death by his brothers in religion. Margil seems to have been unaware that others were collecting information about him and that his words circulated either by the grapevine or in written form. Alcántara used them as the mainstay of his sermon to display Margil's many virtues: his purity and success in taming the forces of concupiscence through his penitential practices, his poverty, his abstinence in matters of food, his obedience to the rules of the community, and his self-effacing personality. They were similar to those praised by Bishop Sariñana several decades before when speaking about Fr. Cristobal Muñoz. This is not surprising because Margil was a seventeenth-century man in his religious formation and in his spirituality, but Margil accommodated his interiority to his missionary work.

Alcántara also praised Margil as a man who could inspire bishops to imitate his behavior. This was probably an allusion to the bishops' duty of visiting their jurisdiction. Margil knew the land probably better than some bishops. Bishops were expected to visit the entire physical area of their jurisdiction at least once, but they were not expected to trek as evangelizing friars, as Margil did. Alcántara invited a comparison between the canonical power of the secular clergy and the evangelizing spirit of a missionary friar, especially one he saw as selfless and closer to the original intention of the evangelical words of Christ. Alcántara was trying to enhance the prestige of the mendicant orders and that of his own college. Margil had advanced deep into the remote southern areas of the Isthmus of Panama to carry out evangelizing activities among the hostile and largely unconverted Indigenous of that region. His success there, stated Alcántara, was in contrast with his service in Texas, where the "fruit" of his preaching had been meager. His opinion was questionable. Central America had a well-established Christianized core in Guatemala City that Margil used as a springboard for his fearless incursions into the territories of still largely independent and "gentile" tribes. There's no evidence that his presence in the isthmus made any difference in tribal beliefs. Alcántara was incorrectly implying that Margil had converted them, but in sermons the "image" was more important than the facts. Alcántara ended his sermon with a statement about the meaning of one's actions in life: "Deeds are the seeds that we plant in this world to gather the fruit in the other." That message was the guiding light of missionary work, and therefore, the audience should believe that Margil was already enjoying "celestial and everlasting happiness." Alcántara then requested the deceased Margil to intercede for those still living in this "valley of misery" and protect the colleges and their brothers, all of whom were praying for his eternal rest. As pointed out, the request for personal intercession from those believed to be in heaven was part of the culture of hope and salvation that the sermon was expected to deliver.

In Spain, cleric Vicente Navarro, a member of the University of Valencia, praised the memory of Margil in a sermon delivered in that city on October 26, 1728.[74] Margil had been baptized in Valencia, and Navarro felt obliged to render honor to such a notable "son." Navarro based the theme of his sermon on Proverbs 21:21 and said, "Whoever pursues justice and mercy, finds life, justice and honor."[75] He narrated Margil's life with some appealing anecdotes lacking much originality. He praised his humility, his penitential practices such as the Via Sacra, and his poverty, obedience, and purity, the latter resulting from the control he exercised over his body.[76] His love for God easily overcame his love for everyone else, including that for his own mother, whom he had left, never to see her again. Given the fact that Margil's first biography by Fr. Isidro de Espinosa was not published until 1737, Navarro's information must have been a novelty in Valencia. The biographical data indicate that Navarro had read Fr. Diego de Alcántara's sermon, a fact Navarro acknowledged on page twenty-one of his address. While this sermon lacks originality, it underlines the connections between members of the order in the peninsula and in the viceroyalty. The bond between the Spanish colleges and those in New Spain was strong. In its first decades, Propaganda Fide's success in New Spain depended on the Spanish volunteers who replenished the colleges across the ocean. As a clergyman Navarro shared the bond of brotherhood with all men of the cloth and the pride in a Native son.

Other mid-eighteenth-century sermons offer further nuances not only in literary style but also in the model of religious behavior they proposed. While sermons about Margil praised the sound of his voice as a venue for his message, Augustinian Fr. Felipe Mariano Pardo chose the eyes and their tears as venues for the expression of grief for a deceased brother in religion, Fr. Joseph Ochoa.[77] Pardo's theme was Ecclesiastes 38:16: "My child, shed tears over the dead, lament for the dead to show your sorrow."[78] Ochoa had been several times prior in the Augustinian convent of San Luis Potosí and a member of the chapters of the order as well as its provincial. At the time of his death, he was the Augustinian's legal representative in the vicereal court. Those many offices and titles made him worthy of a printed sermon paid for by his own carnal brother, who was also an Augustinian. Ochoa's funeral was special. He had a *túmulo* or *pira funeraria*, a temporary funeral construction built for the funeral Mass of distinguished members of the church and the laity. They were most often seen in royal funerals and those of the highest members of the church.[79] The first *túmulo* in New Spain was built in honor of the death of Charles V in 1558.[80] The bishop of Michoacán, Fr. Antonio de San Miguel, who died on June 18, 1804, had a magnificent funeral service and an impressive *túmulo* only minutely described by a contemporary source.[81]

It seems that the Augustinians spared no expense to honor Fr. Joseph. The printed sermon was preceded by an unusual description of the fifteen plates (*tarjas*) adorning the four levels of the *túmulo* and several poems of various genres explaining their symbolic meaning.[82] The protagonist of the plates was a dove that represented the soul of Fr. Joseph in various poses and in several key situations: dropping an olive branch pointing to his memorialized name; under attack by a symbol of death; sitting next to a fountain that reflected the shadow of a hawk, the symbol of expectant death; sitting in a nest on a rock as though taking refuge in his convent; using its feathers to build a nest for its chicks, his brothers and subjects; feeding its chicks as a protecting father; and shining, resplendent, in the sunlight, displaying the brightness of his kindness. The thirteenth emblem showing three doves ailing from an arrow's shot represented Fr. Joseph as son of the province and father of his community. The province was a mother left in a state of mourning widowhood.

Unlike other sermons, Pardo's information on the friar's life was circumscribed to his role as a member of the order and the convent, highlighting his generosity and his concern for the community's spiritual well-being. The preacher expressed the complexity of the friar's relation to his convent with a conceptual triple knot suggested in the *túmulo* representation of three ailing doves. The province, as mother of all her sons, cried for this particular one. At the same time, Fr. Joseph had been a protective father for the province and his conventual brothers. Thus, the community was also crying for a father. As such, he had been a father to his own mother. Pardo relaxed his convoluted metaphors in his final comments, stating that while there was cruelty in death, having died on September 12, when all honored the Virgin Mary as the Virgin of Guadalupe, they should assume that she had taken him to a better place. Then the preacher contradicted himself by stating that Fr. Joseph had not really died. Since his brother stayed in the convent as a professed friar, the community still had "another" Joseph who resembled the deceased closely in character and virtues. This was a most unusual sermon, relying on visual imagery, emblematic symbols, and a sense of theater. The word *pomp*, often associated with public events, applied to the *túmulo* and the funeral rituals of this friar. It seems that the Ochoa family and the Augustinians were invested in impressing the clerical and the secular entities of the city and rivaling the ostentatious funerals in the capital of the viceroyalty.

The sermon dedicated to Fr. Joseph de Castro, Franciscan chaplain of the convent for Indigenous nuns of Corpus Christi in Mexico City, used eulogy of a different kind. Whereas most sermons focused on the spiritual qualities of the deceased, this one was a eulogy of his agency and dedication to one material end: the building of the convent of Corpus Christi for Indian nuns. Castro died on July 3, 1753, and his funeral sermon was preached on August 8 by Fr. Manuel Ximenez de Arellano, vicar and chaplain of the convent. He had been one of Fr. Joseph's students.[83] Ximenez de Arellano, like others before him, appealed to sentiment through the tears shed by the community, which was deep in sorrow upon losing such an exemplary man. He praised the fact that where there was love, there were tears because the eyes revealed the quality of the love.[84] Beyond the expression of deep loss, the sermon extolled the material benefits that Castro brought to the convent. Ximenez gave a thorough account of Castro's total engagement in the improvement of the convent's building throughout his eight years as its vicar. He argued that Castro had left no stone unturned and no potential donor unsolicited for the improvement of the cloister and the convent's church for the "apples of his eyes," a phrase borrowed from one of his Franciscan brothers. The sermon's body is largely a description of Castro's administration and the architectural improvement of the convent. Ximenez described in detail the condition of the roof, the walls, the windows, and the floors and how they had all been restored for the safety and comfort of the nuns. Under Castro's direction practically the entire building was renovated, and its church was endowed with altars and all the necessary paraphernalia for a respectable performance of the religious services.

Ximenez had some comments on the negative influence some individuals had over the affairs of the convent throughout its formative years, although he abstained from mentioning names. He was referring to the problems created by the admission of white novices under Commissary General Fr. Pedro Navarrete in 1743. The disturbances within and outside the convent are not mentioned in the sermon, but they were serious enough to cause a civil suit with appeals to the Crown and several years of tensions. Before his death Fr. Joseph must have been strongly affected by that turn of events, as suggested by the discreet references made in his funeral eulogy by his student and brother in religion.[85]

The lengthy discussion of Castro's efforts on behalf of the material needs of the convent brings this sermon closer to those dedicated to secular patrons who endowed religious institutions. Ximenez sought to express the gratitude of the convent and the order for Fr. Joseph's dedication to Corpus Christi as well as his uprightness and personal commitment to the cause of a group of humble and devout women. The lengthy description of financial and architectural issues overshadowed the sermon's expected pious eulogies. It was closer to a bureaucrat's *relación de méritos* than a funeral sermon. However, the writer was clear in his mind: a convent and its temple were a tribute to God. The best means to express faith and religiosity was to provide shelter for those who worshipped God. Fr. Joseph's dedication and efforts were comparable to those of the missionaries who built churches for their converts in the borderlands of the viceroyalty.

An appreciation of the material legacy of some friars—in contrast to their spiritual legacy—was also present in Fr. Diego Bringas de Manzaneda's 1781 eulogy of the martyrs of Yuma. A fuller review of that sermon is available in the chapter on martyrs. Here I want to comment on Bringas de Manzaneda's understanding of how death could render service to purposes beyond the spiritual redemption of the soul. He understood and praised the Christian inspiration of these men, but he was just as interested in their contributions to the viceroyalty and increasing the number of subjects for the king.[86] The preacher brought a significant measure of history, geography, and biography into his sermon, informing the listeners about the long distances the missionaries walked and what it cost them to explain sophisticated theological concepts to those unlikely to understand them. Additionally, in their efforts to learn the Indigenous people's languages and customs, the missionaries

SERMON
QUE EN LAS SOLEMNES HONRAS
CELEBRADAS EN OBSEQUIO
DE LOS VV. PP. PREDICADORES APOSTÓLICOS

Fr. Francisco Tomas Hermenegildo Garcés:
Fr. Juan Marcelo Diaz:
Fr. José Matias Moreno:
Fr. Juan Antonio Barreneche:

MISIONEROS DEL COLEGIO

de *Propaganda fide* de la Santa Cruz de Queretaro, Fundadores de las Conversiones de la Purísima Concepcion, y de S. Pedro y S. Pablo del Rio Colorado entre los Gentiles Yumas, y muertos en ellas gloriosamente á manos de los mismos Bárbaros en los dias 17 y 19 de Julio de 1781

DIXO

EN LA IGLESIA DE DICHO COLEGIO
EL 19 DE JULIO de 1794
EN QUE SE SEPULTARON SUS CENIZAS

Fr. DIEGO MIGUEL BRINGAS DE MANZANEDA y Encinas, Misionero Apostólico, é Hijo del mismo Seminario, que reverente lo consagra á las Doctísimas, Religiosísimas y Santas Provincias de Franciscanos Observantes de la antigua y nueva España, á nombre del expresado Colegio de Misioneros de la Santa Cruz de Queretaro.

MADRID, AÑO 1819.
EN LA IMPRENTA DE D. FERMIN VILLALPANDO,
IMPRESOR DE CAMARA DE S. M.

FIG. 22. Fr. Diego Miguel Bringas de Manzaneda, *Sermón... en las Solemnes Honras de los... Misioneros del Colegio de Propaganda Fide en 1794* (Madrid, 1819).

became the disciples of those whom they intended to teach, a true act of humility in the preacher's mind. Despite his intent to underline the political benefits brought by the friars' missionary activities, Bringas de Manzaneda could not fail to interpret their deaths as "heroic," because knowing that they had little chance to survive an attack from the hostile Indigenous, they returned to the camp, obeying their superiors and fulfilling their duty. That decision cost them their lives. Bringas de Manzaneda refrained from assigning them the *intention* of martyrdom—only the church could emit such judgment—but he argued that they had all the qualifications of martyrs. His sermon addressed the heroic, not the quotidian, as well as the notions of predestination, peregrination, selflessness, courage, and manliness. They were not the usual topic of funeral sermons, but times and circumstances explained the difference.

There was a considerable disparity between the space assigned to death in the chronicles, which was considerable, and the meager number of sermons that reached the printed stage. Nonetheless, the latter let us appreciate how in the friars' spiritual world, death was the gate to another life and a necessary transit that could be faced with intelligence and fortitude. The living were separated from the dead by a transparent wall that allowed a clear view of the other side. Those who lived in God could see purgatory and redemption. Those who abandoned God saw the fires of hell. The choice of what awaited the believer was in his or her hands.

Chronicles and sermons are two different genres sharing one objective: to call attention to the closure of life as envisioned and experienced by the friars and their communities. It was a vision they shared with the faithful as a "common good." In both instances, these texts stop short of any excess of morbidity in the description of the decay of the body or the horror of death, excluding those addressing martyrdom. Chronicles and sermons aimed at showcasing the friars' faith, but they also disclosed a sense of beauty in the decorum the friars observed in their last days, when they surrendered to their own mortality and drew on the wealth of religious aid offered by the church. There was a purpose in all the official rites of death, and as the dying friar went methodically through them, he became an example to his own brothers and to the laity. The principles of the *ars moriendi*—death understood as an aesthetic experience—are some of the most intriguing intellectual products of the late Middle Ages. It reached its peak in seventeenth-century Spain, where it found fertile ground in the baroque sensibility for drama and the cultural exploration of human fate. In keeping with the intellectual transformation that encouraged thoughts on death, the passion of Christ and the image of his crucifixion had become preeminent in art and the religious imagination since the low Middle Ages. The discussion of death was of cultural import to the New World and welcomed by the theologians of the mendicant orders, rapidly assimilated to their religious discourse, and expressed either directly or indirectly in biographies and sermons. However, the sense of beauty and awe inspired by the expected rewards the soul would encounter in the other world was not as important to mendicants, who wrote on the topic as the moral and spiritual obligation of living a "good" life and helping others make a proper transit to the promise of eternal life.

Epilogue

Mendicant friars were ubiquitous figures in the streets of cities and in rural environments. Traveling on foot or riding, they became familiar in the human landscape of New Spain after the conquest of the land. Maps throughout time show small churches wherever a mission or a secular church was located. They became visual markers for travelers and testimonies of the physical and spiritual presence of the robed men almost everywhere in the land. For 350 years the friars represented faith and God to many generations of men and women of all races and social extractions. This work has not attempted to synthesize that history or explore the many highs and lows of the orders as institutions. Focusing on the friars' lived experience as men and using the arc of life, from childhood to death, as a guide, they emerge from the records as approachable figures devoid of the labels attached to them throughout years of historical interpretation. Not all of them are "likable." They were neither heroes nor devils. They were men trying to make sense of their lives, as most of us do.

It was my intention to understand them as representatives of one expression of manhood that made sense in their times and had multiple forms of expression. Some were idiosyncratic, like that of the friar explorer and the recorders of new landscapes and peoples, intrepid men who are still remembered with awe. Others expressions of masculine behavior were culturally expected and less physically daring, like that of the recorders of the history of their own orders and their outstanding members. As biographers and historians, friars became part of the intellectual elite who helped forge a unique cultural landscape in the new society of which they were a part. While that aspect of their story is not covered in this book, the records they produced are the cornerstones of personal and institutional history.

What do we gain from seeing friars over the course of a life cycle? We can see the construction of masculinity in their personal and institutional behavior. Those men recorded here were not necessarily conscious of becoming "models" of a specific form of masculinity. As children they assimilated "models" of behavior that prepared them for their chosen path in life. Since there were many routes to masculinity, the one chosen by the men studied in this book was socially distinctive, acceptable, and accepted. There was masculinity in learning how to control the flesh in the novitiate and channel one's behavior toward less physically oriented models of manhood. There was also the masculinity of renunciation, which was the guiding principle of life as a lay brother who renounced power to become a model of humble service. Renouncing the pleasures of the flesh was an essential form of denial, although its value was only appreciated because it was often breached by those who were unable to meet the challenge. There were failures of the spirit and victories of the flesh when the realities of virility overcame ethical and spiritual restraints. There were many instances of conflict, not an unlikely feature of male behavior that was often associated with dominant masculinity. Rivalry among individuals was not uncommon. Beyond that, there were other forms of conflict created either by the exercise of power or by its rejection. There was also conflict between the principles of the peace and love preached by Christianity and the social violence implied in the material and spiritual conquest of the Indigenous. That specific conflict was accepted and acceptable as part of the mores of the times. Thus, the violence of imposing their religion was not acknowledged as such; it was seen as the achievement of an exalted theological purpose carried out by a strong and dedicated form of masculine behavior.

Contesting masculinities were a reality among members of the bureaucracy and the church, landowners and mine owners throughout the colonial period. The tensions between the friars and the men engaged in the physical conquest of the land flared frequently and were prolonged into the eighteenth century in the outlying areas of a viceroyalty still expanding its frontiers, such as in the disputes between the governors of Baja California and the Franciscan order and between Fr. Junípero Serra and the military in charge of Alta California. Masculinity was not always a form of contestation, however. There was also a committed form of spirituality and manly strength in the acceptance of martyrdom as a result of a personal commitment to one's religious beliefs. A peculiar form of male resolve was behind the decision to face danger with equanimity and as a form of spiritual redemption. All these forms of behavior beg for reinterpretation as expressions of paradigms of masculinity. Beyond the historical information furnished by *Men of God*, I trust readers will see this work as an invitation to expand the frontiers of the study of manhood throughout the colonial period and, in particular, among not only the members of not only the mendicant orders but all members of the Church.

NOTES

1. Childhood

Epigraph: Ojea, *Libro Tercero*, 54.

1. Aries, *Centuries of Childhood*; Hawes and Hiner, *Children in Historical and Comparative Perspective*; Heywood, *A History of Childhood*; Rodríguez and Mannarelli, *Historia de la infancia*; Hecht, *Minor Omissions*; Lavrin, "La niñez en México e Hispanoamérica," 41–69; Lavrin, "Mexico," 221–45; González and Premo, *Raising an Empire*; Lipsett-Rivera, "The Emotional Life of Boys," 351–61; "Model Children," 52–72; and *The Origins of Macho*.
2. Karras, *From Boys to Men*; Ruiz Martínez, "La moderación como prototipo de santidad," 49–66; Lavrin, "La construcción de la niñez," 121–44.
3. Gonzalbo Aizpuru, "El Virreinato y el Nuevo Orden," 36–66. Apprentices began their technical education around the ages of eight or ten, and the training lasted for three or four years. Gonzalbo Aizpuru, "La familia educadora en Nueva España," 43–56; Loreto, "La casa y la educación familiar," 57–82.
4. Tanck de Estrada, "El Siglo de las Luces," 67–98.
5. Katzew, *Casta Painting*; Moreno Navarro, *Los Cuadros del Mestizaje Americano*. Whether or not these paintings reflect the reality of mestizaje in New Spain, they are *visually* helpful to document children in the midst of their families and in social activities.
6. See Anonymous, *Eighteenth-Century Mexican Children*, n.d., Dr. Robert H. Lamborn Collection, 1903–29, Philadelphia Museum of Art; *Retrato de la familia Fagoaga Arozqueta* (ca. 1730, Colección particular); Tanck de Estrada, "Imágenes infantiles en los años de la insurgencia," 227–79; Moriuchi, "The Art of Conversation."
7. Juan Rodríguez Juárez, *Portrait of the Child Joaquín Manuel Fernández De Santa Cruz*, Museo Nacional de Arte, Mexico City, https://memoricamexico.gob.mx/swb/memorica/Cedula?oId=3kXtG8BprXWc885Z1K8.
8. Anonymous, *Portrait of Niños Miguel José, Mariana Micaela Josefa and Manuel Miguel María Malo y Hurtado de Mendoza*, 1756, Museo Nacional de Historia,

Castillo de Chapultepec, Mexico. In another anonymous painting of a mother with her three children, the boy is dressed up in the habit of what looks like the Dominican order. See "18th Century Mexican Colonial Family Portrait," located at https://www.liveauctioneers.com/item/77879519_18th-century-mexican-colonial-family-portrait-mother/.

9. Ardanaz, "Iconografía Familiar en la Edad Moderna," 159–83.
10. I focus on the education of men who qualified to become friars. Since the majority of male Indigenous were excluded from professions in the orders, I will not address their education or socialization. See Mendieta, *Historia Eclesiástica Indiana*, vol. 2, chaps. 12–16; Escobar, *Americana Thebaida*, 86–87; Luque Alcaide, *La educación* (1970); Moon, "The Imperial College of Tlatelolco"; and Morales, "The Native Encounter," 137–59.
11. Propertied women of the nobility and upper classes, nuns, and women writers used special venues to gain authority and respect, but their socialization as women was more restricted than that of men. Those who succeeded in becoming publicly prominent were the exception, not the rule.
12. Beneyto, "Burocracia y derecho público," 15–38.
13. *Reglas de la buena crianza*; Gallego Barnés, "Refranes de mesa," 139–76; Chartier, "Los manuales de civilidad," 246–83; Revel, "The Uses of Civility," 167–205.
14. González and Premo, *Raising an Empire*, 7–9.
15. Lipsett-Rivera, *The Origins of Macho*, 15–44.
16. Twinam, *Public Lives*, 158–215.
17. Chocano Mena, *La fortaleza docta*; Weckmann, *La herencia medieval de Mexico*.
18. The development of Mexican self-awareness, or *mexicanidad*, is a complex cultural topic not dealt with here. See, among others, Grudzinska, "Del Novohispanismo a la Mexicanidad," 65–79; and Alberro, *Del gachupín al criollo*.
19. Dávila Padilla, *Historia de la Fundación*, Prólogo al Lector. He thought that being born in the Indies would corroborate the veracity of his narrative as a real witness.
20. See chapters on epic poetry, poetry, religious theater, and works in prose in New Spain in Cuarón and Baudot, *Historia de la Literatura Mexicana*, 1:286–335; Buxó, "Los artificios," 87–100.
21. González and Gutiérrez Rodríguez, "Los catedráticos novohispanos," 83–102; Barrio Moya, "La librería," 489–96.
22. According to Twinam, infancy, as defined by the legislation of the *Fuero Real* (1255), extended from birth to age three, when mothers took care of their children. After age three fathers assumed responsibility for the child. However, most children remained in the nursery until they were five or six. Twinam, *Public Lives*, 160–83.

23. Salguero, *Vida del venerable*, 6–9.
24. Dávila Padilla, *Historia de la Fundación*, 489.
25. Some Spanish men who later joined the mendicant orders had previously served in the army. Military experience could begin early in life. Ferdinand Alvarez de Toledo, the future Duke of Alba, chose to join his first military campaign when he was sixteen, not bothering to ask permission from his family. See Kamen, *The Duke of Alba*, 8.
26. By *didactic literature* I mean works addressed to character formation. The teaching of the first letters, reading, and writing are not under consideration here. Nieves Baranda states that there was little innovation in the teaching of writing for over two centuries. See Baranda, "La literatura del didactismo," 25–34.
27. Franco, *Segunda Parte de la Historia*, 313: "Que no es lo menos que deben cuidar los padres si quieren ver logrados a sus hijos, buscarles en sus tiernos años maestros que le enseñen lo bueno, de que han de usar cuando mayores."
28. Twinam, *Public Lives*, 59–125.
29. Cátedra, "Límites de control," 327–49.
30. Saavedra Fajardo, *Idea de un príncipe*, 777.
31. González, *Libro de doctrina christiana*. The author charged men of all social levels with the moral task of doing their best, not for vainglory but to live an honest life. He blamed parents for the lack of interest in the formal education of their children and expected them to use the principles he proposed in his book. See also Guillaume-Alonso, "Ecole et catheqeuse," 237–52; Cruz García de Enterría, "El adoctrinamiento 'popular,'" 275–90; Iannuzzi, "Educar a los cristianos."
32. Zumárraga, *Doctrina breve* (1543); de Gante, *Doctrina cristiana*, 1547, and *Doctrina cristiana*, 1546. *Doctrinas cristianas* in Indigenous languages and in Spanish were staple publications during the colonial period.
33. Torre Revello, "Las cartillas," 214–34; González del Campo, *Cartillas*; Framiñán de Miguel, "La Doctrina cristiana," 5–46.
34. González, *Doctrina Christiana*, 1564.
35. Anunciación, *Doctrina Christiana*, 1565; de Vargas, *Doctrina Christiana* (1576).
36. Civil, "La formation morale," 253–77; Rosales, *Catón Christiano* (1807). This book was available in Mexico in 1761, printed by Bibliotheca Mexicana. Domínguez, *Catón Cristiano* (1795); Castañeda, *La educación*.
37. Murillo, *Instrucción*, 1:6, 15–32.
38. Twinam, *Public Lives*; Johnson and Lipsett-Rivera, *Sex, Shame, and Violence*; Martínez, "A vueltas con la honra," 1–10.
39. González, *Libro de doctrina christiana*, 74–75.
40. Bolufer, "'Ciencia del mundo,'" 143–85, and "'Hombres de Bien,'" 7–31; Martínez Góngora, *El hombre atemperado*, 17–60.

41. Rodríguez Cacho, "La frustración," 61–73. Torquemada was the secretary of the Count of Benavente.
42. Hoffman, *Raised to Rule*, 2011.
43. Huarte de San Juan, *Examen* (1652). The first edition of this book (1575) was placed in the *Index* for assumptions contrary to the faith. A second expurgated edition was published in 1594. Foreign editions in several languages throughout the eighteenth century were not expurgated.
44. Giglioni, "Between Galen and St. Paul," 114–34.
45. Rincón González, "Criterios," 135–46. Huarte de San Juan did not mingle words on the lack of abilities in some men. "The beast that goes to Rome returns a beast" (*Examen*, 12). See also Gondra, "Juan Huarte de San Juan."
46. Castiglione, *Libro llamado El Cortesano* (1544). There are editions for 1561 and 1574.
47. Erasmus of Rotterdam, *Familiar Colloquies*; De Courcelles, "Autour de la formation," 13–26; Bataillon, *Erasmo y España*; Herrejón Peredo, "Marcel Bataillon," 187–200. For a compendium of Bataillon's articles on Erasmus, see Bataillon, *Erasmo y el erasmismo*.
48. Guevara, *Libro Áureo* (1650). Antonio de Guevara (ca. 1481–1545) was the bishop of Mondoñedo when he wrote two books for the education of princes, the *Libro Aúreo*, his best-known work, and the *Reloj de Príncipes*. The latter is a revised and expanded version of the former. See his *Obras Completas* (1994); and Ana Isabel Buescu, "Corte, Poder e Utopia" (2009). His *Reloj de Príncipes* was a wild publishing success, with succeeding versions in French, English, Dutch, Hungarian, Polish, and Latin. It was still read in the late eighteenth century when the Polish version was published in 1773. Guevara also published several other books, among which the *Epístolas Familiares* (1539, 1541) also contain key ideas on the upbringing of men. In *Oratorio de religiosos y ejercicio de virtuosos* (1545), he proposed strong ethical values for men of the cloth.
49. Guevara, *Libro Áureo*, lv.
50. Guevara, *Libro Áureo*, 175–98.
51. Guevara, *Epístolas Familiares*, 157.
52. *Diálogos*'s original title was *Exercitatio linguae Latina*. Few women are mentioned in Vives's text, and when they appear, it is briefly and either as fretting females or as manipulative mothers, servants, or market women. See Bravo-Villasante, "Diálogos escolares," 2006, http://www.cervantesvirtual.com/obra/los-dilogos-escolares-de-juan-luis-vives-0/.
53. Vives, *Diálogos*. This work was published in 1538. See Moreno Gallego, *La recepción* (2006); Gallego Barnés, "El impacto," 213–23. The use of dialogue in the instruction of Latin was fairly common.

54. Cervantes de Salazar, *Mexico en 1554*. Cervantes de Salazar was born in Toledo and studied at Salamanca. He met Luis Vives in the Low Countries and moved to Mexico around 1550. There he taught rhetoric and eventually became rector of the University in the late 1560s and early 1570s. He was also dean of the Cathedral Chapter and consultant for the Inquisition. He finished his life as a doctor in theology. See Sanchis Amat, "La recepción," 39–55.
55. Gnophoso [Cristóbal de Villalón], *El Crótalon*. Villalón penned several works, of which *El Crótalon* is the best known, although it has been argued that he is not its real author. He also wrote a travel account, a grammar, and an ethical appraisal of financial practices. He was ordered as a clergyman in 1543. The dates of his birth and death vary and have been cited as being either 1510–62 or 1505–81.
56. The sense of sight brought lust, love of colors, and luxury. The sense of smell degenerated into making some men love all sort of creams and perfumes, which they used before they approached their wives or paramours, seeking to incite their lust with such enervating odors. Villalón eulogized female virginity but delivered a misogynous message throughout his work, which ends with a tirade against women as temptresses of men, who were advised to keep their guard up against female plots and dishonesty.
57. Echoing standard Christian denunciation, he condemned any nonheterosexual sexual practices. He even briefly called attention to cases of incest and bestiality. His conclusion was that men could be worse than animals in failing to control their sexual appetites. Indeed, compared to human vices, a simple pig was much better. *First Canto*, 17–24.
58. Villalón shunned the Italianate dream of a perfect courtesan painted by Castiglione, who was very popular in Spain. He favored the poverty and humility of the monks of the order of Saint Bernard, who lived employing themselves in humble occupations. He praised Bernard of Clairvaux, who, having been a "dissolute young man" and an "effeminate" courtesan, found his salvation in adopting the monastic life. The popularity that some regular orders enjoyed for some time in Spain in the sixteenth century is reflected in his opinion and explains the respect that some religious reformers were seeking when they adopted more stringent observance.
59. Palmireno, *El estudioso de la aldea*, 1568, and *El estudioso cortesano* (1573). See works by Andrés Gallego Barnés and Anne Milhou-Roudie. Palmireno followed Erasmus, whose *Colloquios* were translated into Spanish between 1520 and 1533. See Bonilla y San Martin, *Erasmo en España* (1907); and Puyol, "Los 'Coloquios de Erasmo.'"
60. Fernández García, "El discurso" (2019); Truman, *Spanish Treatises* (1999); Galindo Carrillo, *Los tratados* (1948); Buescu, "The Utopia," 599–605; Bizzarri, "Sermones y espejos" (2012); Sánchez-Molero, *El aprendizaje*, and *Felipe II* (1527–1545).

61. López, "La conceptualización," 113–23.
62. Martínez Góngora, *El hombre atemperado*, 61–105.
63. Monzón and Rodrígues, *Libro Primero* (1544).
64. Ribadeneyra, *Tratado* (1595). Also in *Obras escogidas* (1868), 449–587. Ribadeneyra supported the association of religion and politics. He hoped his work would strengthen the principles of religion and virtue that had so far saved Spain from being the state imagined by Machiavelli. Hubeñak, "El antimaquiavelismo."
65. Torres, *Philosophia* (1596). Gómez de Dávila, Marquis of Velada, was chosen by Phillip II as a tutor for his son. Torres advised the tutor on how to carry out his task with discretion. Like other authors, he mixed religious indoctrination with advice on teaching liberal arts and science and considered his teachings useful for young men of all social levels.
66. Mendo, *Príncipe* (1662). The first edition was issued in 1626. Martín López, "La conceptualización," 113–23. On emblems, see Dimler, *Studies* (2007); and Praz, *Studies* (1975).
67. Mendo, *Príncipe*, 1–6.
68. Attempting a more entertaining venue for his didactic advice, Francisco de Ledesma used poetry, delivering the message of proper personal and social behavior in a short poem followed by several religious compositions, possibly added by an editor. See Ledesma, *Documentos* (1658).
69. Saavedra Fajardo, *Idea de un príncipe*.
70. Saavedra Fajardo, *Idea de un príncipe*, 4.
71. The trivium included grammar, rhetoric, and logic; the quadrivium, arithmetic, astronomy, geometry, and music.
72. Saavedra Fajardo, *Idea de un príncipe*, Dedicatoria.
73. Saavedra Fajardo, *Idea de un príncipe*, 17–18, 21–23.
74. Saavedra Fajardo, *Idea de un príncipe*, 659.
75. Saavedra Fajardo, *Idea de un príncipe*, 189. See also pp. 121–22, 180–81, 185, 189, 194–97, 598, 600. He criticized war but recommended the strengthening of the army. While supporting religion and the Church, he condemned extremes of piety and superstition.
76. *Reglas de la buena crianza* (1781). The work is a translation of a foreign author who is not mentioned. The translator was a canon of Barcelona, and an unknown clergyman made some additions.
77. Vila y Camps, *El noble* (1776).
78. Malo de Medina, *Guía* (1787).
79. Sigüenza y Góngora, *Theatro de virtudes* (1680). Also see his *Obras Históricas*, 229–361.
80. Díaz de Gamarra, *Máximas* (1983).

81. Álvarez del Palacio, "La consideración del cuerpo," 41–60. For children's games, see Vives, *Diálogos*, 33, 35–43.
82. González and Gutiérrez Rodríguez, "Los catedráticos novohispanos," 83–102.
83. Vetancurt, *Menologio* (1697).
84. Ojea, *Libro Tercero* (1897); Romero Galván, *Contexto y texto* (2007).
85. One of the problems facing chroniclers in Mexico writing the biographies of men born in Spain was the lack of access to their family histories. Thus, Fr. Antonio Garrigós, writing the biography of Fr. Joseph Marquez of the Franciscan province of Jalisco, knew his place of origin and the date of his birth but could not add any further comment on his family owing to "the long distance between the place of his death and that of his birth and childhood." Biographers often faced the same problem. See Garrigós, *Vida admirable*.
86. Molina, *Arte de la lengua mexicana*, 14–15.
87. This statement does not deny the great interest taken by some friars in Indigenous history and culture. However, indoctrination was the most important task assigned to the friars. The works of a Fr. Bernardino de Sahagún and Fr. Diego Durán demonstrate their sensitivity to other people's cultures.
88. Campos, "Los criollos novohispanos," 15–40.
89. Cárdenas, *Primera Parte* (1591). For a modern edition, see the 1988 publication by Alianza Editorial.
90. Cárdenas, *Primera Parte*, 171, 176–82.
91. Franco, *Segunda Parte*, 190–91.
92. Franco, *Segunda Parte*, 170. Fr. Antonio de los Reyes, a son of "noble parents" in the city of Toro, Castile, was sent to the house of the Marquises of Alcañices to be raised as a page and improve his chances in life.
93. Burgoa, *Palestra Historial*, 318–21, 426–27.
94. Burgoa, *Palestra Historial*, 114, 234, 264, 339, 514.
95. Burgoa, *Palestra Historial*, 114–23.
96. Salguero, *Vida del venerable*, 1–18. The intellectual star of the Augustinian order in the sixteenth century was Fr. Alonso de la Veracruz, founder of the classic studies in the province of Michoacán. His biographer, Fr. Matías de Escobar, wrote that as soon as he was old enough, his well-to-do parents sent him to study to the University of Alcalá, from where he moved to the more prestigious University of Salamanca. That was all the information that merited being recorded from his early years. Escobar, *Americana Thebaida*, 155.
97. Ponce de León, *Historia* (1686); Morales, "Los hermanos laicos."
98. Conover, "A Saint in the Empire," and *Pious Imperialism*. For a typical biography, see Ferruvino, *Vida de El Glorioso Protomártir*; and Medina, *Vida, martirio y beatificación*.

99. Ponce de León, *Historia*, 17. He also discards the possibility of Felipe being a silver craftsman apprentice. The hagiographer preferred a version presenting Felipe as possibly sticking to his studies with the Jesuits.
100. *Breve resumen de la vida y martirio*, 28, 37–38. The author reiterates that while in Japan, he had never engaged in behavior alien to any "hombría de bien." In other words, he tried to preserve his reputation by adhering to strict social behavior approved by the church.
101. Dávila Padilla, *Historia*, 599–602.
102. González de la Puente, *Primera Parte*, 202, 248, 288, 340.
103. Cervantes, *El rufián dichoso*. See also Zugasti, "Algo más sobre las fuentes," 493–513.
104. Espinosa, *El Peregrino*; Vilaplana, *Vida portentosa*, 9. Vilaplana follows Espinosa very closely in his narrative.
105. Vilaplana, *Vida portentosa*, 8.
106. Espinosa, *El Peregrino*, 6–17.
107. Espinosa, *El Peregrino*: "Sentir del R.P. Fr. Manuel Bravo de Acuña" (n.p.).
108. Franco, *Historia*, 275. He rode to the convent in his fashionable clothes and on his beautiful horse to make his choice of giving up the world more poignant and exemplar.
109. For a comparison between the childhood experience of boys entering religion and that of girls who became nuns, see Lavrin, "La construcción de la niñez," 121–44.

2. The Threshold of Religious Life

Epigraph: Arbiol, *Vocación eclesiástica*, n.p.
1. García, *Política regular*, 106, 108.
2. Malvido, "Los novicios," 719, 722; Medina, *Chronica*, 16–17.
3. See Myers and Powell, *A Wild Country*, 63–100; Lavrin, *Brides of Christ*, 74–77; and Lavrin, "María Marcela Soria," 105–8, for the recollection of María Marcela's novitiate.
4. Arbiol, *Vocación eclesiástica*; Rosell, *El Monacato*, 268–71; Vizuete Mendoza, "Novicios, maestros," 126–47.
5. Ulloa, *Los predicadores*, 224–28.
6. Burgoa, *Palestra Historial*, 466–69. Burgoa never gives dates in his narrative. We assume that Abrego was among the first-generation Dominicans in Oaxaca.
7. Pope Paul IV issued a *breve* on September 8, 1573, *Consuevit Romanus Pontifex*, confirming the prohibition of descendants of Muslims, Jews, or condemned heretics. However, Gregory XIII, on August 1, 1583, approved the admission of such men in the order of Mínimos, a much-debated and probably not obeyed

papal order. The statutes of *limpieza* remained in the Rules of the orders. See Poutrin, "Conflictos," 243–52. The topic of purity of blood in Spain has a complex bibliographical history that cannot be accommodated here. See, as examples, Hernández Franco, "Permanencia de la ideología," 73–79. For recent literature, see Ingraham, *The Conversos*, vols. 1–4; Nieva, "De la raza a la conducta," 192–201; Ruiz Ibáñez and Hernández Franco, *Conflictividad social*; Hernández Franco, *Cultura y limpieza de sangre*, 73–92; and Hering Torres, "La limpieza de sangre," 32–55.

8. Morales, *Ethnic and Social Background*, 132–41.
9. Lundberg, "The Ordination," 297–322; Woods, "Racial Exclusion," 69–92.
10. Mora Reyes, "Los Dominicos," 154. Fr. Bartolomé de Las Casas, the passionate defender of the humanity of the Indigenous peoples, was not an active evangelizer in New Spain.
11. Morales, *Ethnic and Social Background*, 7–17, 38–53. According to Morales, the prohibition of Indian ordination was official in 1569, although a statute on the subject dated back to 1539. He states that the mechanisms of exclusion were more frequently applied in the eighteenth century. Ulloa, *Los predicadores*, 228–34; *Concilios Provinciales*, 106; Poole, "Church Law," 637–50; Martínez, *Genealogical Fictions*.
12. Africans were disqualified for being descendants of slaves and the assumption of their lack of ability, not unsimilar to that established for the common Indian population, but their rejection was stronger and without any leniency in its application. *Castas* of African descent were also excluded.
13. Morales, *Ethnic and Social Background*, 52–53. See also Morales, "Orden Franciscana," 1663–1703.
14. Ulloa, *Los predicadores*, 226–34; Pita Moreda, *Los predicadores*, 44–63. Pita Moreda verified the smaller number of criollo professions, although she has advisory comments on the statistical verifiability of the sources. See also Romero Galván, "Tratado primero," 9–44.
15. Mora Reyes, "Los Dominicos," 156, 161, 170–71.
16. Basalenque, *Historia*, 2:327–31, 333.
17. Mora Reyes, "Los Dominicos," 164–66.
18. Morales, *Ethnic and Social Background*, 74. There are no similar studies for the Augustinians or the Dominicans. *Hijos de provincia* were Spaniards who took the vows in Mexico.
19. Rubial García, *El convento agustino* (1989), and *Una monarquía criolla*, 66–71, 99–100. According to Rubial, the Augustinian order relaxed its rules of admission to increase its declining membership, and by 1675 they had admitted some mestizo novices who were subsequently expelled by the visiting inspector of the order.

20. Malvido, "Los novicios," 699–738, esp. 707.
21. Rex Galindo, *To Sin No More*, 71–116.
22. *Estatutos y Ordenaciones*, 3. These ordinances were written for the college in Pachuca.
23. Chapter 3 of this work deals with lay brothers.
24. Calvo, "'Concubinato y mestizaje,'" 203–12, and "The Warmth of the Hearth," 287–312; Twinam, *Public Lives*, 1999.
25. Morales, *Ethnic and Social Background*, 142.
26. Morales, *Ethnic and Social Background*, 73. This figure includes lay brothers, since the Puebla novitiate only admitted candidates for that choice.
27. Malvido, "Los novicios." Malvido calls novices coming from outside Mexico City "hijos de provincia," which is not the meaning it had in the sixteenth and seventeenth centuries (710). Her erroneous nomenclature changes the meaning of the numbers.
28. Rex Galindo, "Propaganda Fide," 147.
29. González Marmolejo, *Los novicios*, 175, 181.
30. Medina, *Chronica* (1682).
31. Vázquez Conde, "Religiosidad," 104–6, 111–12. Dominican chronicler Franco was of the opinion that it was better to dismiss a novice than to expel a professed friar. He recalled the prescience of Prior Fr. Cristóbal de Ortega, who in 1593 detected a bad inclination in a novice and recommended his dismissal, but he was overruled by the conventual prelates and the master of novices. The lay brother proved to be "badly inclined" and totally incorrigible, and he was finally dismissed. There is no detail as to what was incorrigible behavior; orders preferred not to advertise or explain their failures. See Franco, *Historia*, 184.
32. *Cartilla y Doctrina Espiritual* (1775), 10. This guidebook was a reissue of the 1721 publication at the request of Fr. Juan Bautista Dosal, twice a definidor of the province of the Holy Gospel.
33. Miranda, *Exposición*, 157–61; Herize, *Instrucción y doctrina*, 24.
34. A friar's habit consisted of several parts. The friars wore underwear trousers, a shorter undertunic, and an outer ankle-length tunic, which was held close to the body with a rope or a belt. The scapular was a long piece of cloth with a hole for the head that hanged over the shoulders, covering chest and back. The capuce was a hood attached to a round piece of cloth that fell over the shoulders. It could be detachable or attached to the habit according to the order. An ankle-length cape covered the entire outer tunic with its own detachable hood. The Franciscans wore sandals, but the Dominicans and Augustinians wore shoes.
35. Ximénez, *Exposición de la Regla*, 16.
36. Dávila Padilla, *Historia*, 469–72.

37. Murcia, *Questiones*, 15. I follow Murcia's text as he explained the vows.
38. González de la Puente, *Primera Parte*, 441.
39. *Regla de N.P.S. Agustín*, 47.
40. Veedor, *Instrucción y Doctrina* (1685); *Cartilla y Doctrina Espiritual* (1721). The 1721 edition was licensed to be printed in Guatemala. In 1775 Fr. Juan Bautista Dosal requested a new edition that was published by Felipe de Zúñiga y Ontiveros.
41. Herize, *Instrucción y doctrina*. Herize ordered the writing and publication of this work. The text was written by an anonymous brother.
42. Grijalva, *Crónica* (1623). For the sake of comparison, see Francisco de S. Buenaventura, *Instrucción* (1734); *Instrucción para criar novicios* (1725).
43. Franco, *Segunda parte*, 43. See also pp. 11, 29, 276. Fr. Jordán de Santa Catarina in Oaxaca was master of novices between ten and twelve times over a period of forty years (52).
44. *Cartilla y Doctrina Espiritual* (1775), 2. For metaphors of the family, see Lavrin, "La familia," 125–60.
45. La Rea, *Crónica*, 316, 375.
46. Ojea, *Libro Tercero*, 26–27. Another of Fr. Alonso's students was chronicler Agustín Dávila Padilla, who, according to Franco, learned much "virtue" from his teacher, Fr. Cristóbal de la Cruz. See Franco, *Segunda parte*, 92.
47. Franco, *Segunda parte*, 47.
48. Guevara, *Oratorio*, chap. 7, 14v–15v. See also chap. 6, 13v.
49. Espinosa, *Guía de religiosos*. Espinosa belonged to the order of Saint Bernard. He followed the Carthusian tradition as well as sixteenth-century *recogimiento* notions that had influenced the reformed mendicants who first missionized New Spain.
50. Espinosa, *Guía de religiosos*, 33–34.
51. Espinosa, *Guía de religiosos*, 122, 126.
52. Veedor, *Instrucción y Doctrina*, 3v, 6–7.
53. Romero, *Avisos para el Noviciado* (1722).
54. Espinosa, *Guía de religiosos*, 23–70, 83–92.
55. Herize, *Instrucción y doctrina*, 28, 158–73.
56. Basalenque, *Historia*, 2:20, 213.
57. Acosta Africano, *Tratado*, 161–161v. See also *Cartilla y Doctrina espiritual* (1775), 7.
58. Sigüenza, *Historia de la Orden*, 253.
59. *Cartilla y Doctrina Espiritual* (1775), 69–71. This manual covers the novice's personal hygiene and behavior in the common rooms of the cloister, in his room, and in the chapel choir. It also details how to follow the liturgy properly.
60. Romero, *Avisos para el Noviciado*, 115–20.

61. Franco, *Historia*, 368. Fr. Alonso was a brother in profession of Fr. Sebastián Montaño, who died as a martyr not far from Zacatecas during a rebellion of the Tepehuán Indians. See pp. 373-775 for a description of the uprising.
62. *Cartilla y Doctrina Espiritual* (1775), 84.
63. Castro, *Directorio*, 25-27.
64. The choir (*coro*) was the area between the nave and the altar, behind the apse of the church, where the friars carried out their liturgical prayers.
65. *Cartilla y Doctrina Espiritual*, 22. See chap. 5, pp. 19-30, for the complete set of ceremonial behavior.
66. Veedor, *Instrucción y Doctrina*, 12, 19. On daily life in convents, see Vázquez Conde, "Un acercamiento a la vida," 43-61.
67. Ponce de León, *Historia*, 71-71v. A bath should not mean excessive vanity about the cleanliness of one's body (*Regla de S. Augustín*, 15-16).
68. *Cartilla y Doctrina Espiritual*, 41-41v; Veedor, *Instrucción y Doctrina*, 141v-143. *Advertencia para el gobierno del P. Maestro que no estuviere instruido en las costumbres de este colegio*, folio 3, Fondo Franciscano, Biblioteca Nacional de México, Mexico City (hereafter cited as BNFF).
69. Veedor, *Instrucción y Doctrina*, 11.
70. Franco, *Segunda Parte*, 52-53.
71. Salguero, *Vida del venerable*, 18-19. *Invitatorios*, *introitos*, and *comunicandas* are liturgical texts for the Mass using specific hymns in Gregorian chants. The first edition of his biography was published in 1664.
72. González de la Puente, *Primera Parte*, 443-61.
73. Rubial García, *El convento agustino*, 136-38.
74. Vetancurt, *Tratado de la ciudad de Mexico*. The *Tratado* is a separate part of the *Teatro*, with its own pagination. See also Gonzalbo Aizpuru, *Historia*, 289-305.
75. Herrera Feria and Torres Domínguez, "Los estudios conventuales," 112-26.
76. *Constituciones y Leyes* (1667).
77. *Constituciones y Leyes* (1667), 5-9; Medina, *Chronica*, 56, 61. In his *Tratado de la Ciudad de Mexico* and *Tratado de la Ciudad de Puebla*, as parts of *Teatro Mexicano*, Vetancurt supplies information on those convents with studies in higher education for its members (see pp. 40, 56, 61).
78. Herize, *Instrucción y doctrina*, 18.
79. Among those masters of "interiority" were Cardinal Jiménez de Cisneros, Francisco de Osuna, Fr. Juan de Ávila, Fr. Juan de la Cruz, Teresa de Ávila, and Fr. Luis de Granada.
80. Murillo, *Instrucción para enseñar la Virtud*; Peñalver, *La mística española* (1997); Pego Puigbo, *El Renacimiento espiritual* (2005); Po-Chia Hsia, *The World of Catholic Renewal*; Birley, *The Refashioning of Catholicism* (1999).

81. Romero, *Avisos para el Noviciado*, 121.
82. Franco, *Segunda Parte*, 350. As a *corista*, Francisco Villegas was guardian of the novices. He practiced rigorous disciplines in his cell.
83. Espinosa, *Guía de religiosos*, 404–5.
84. Herize, *Instrucción y doctrina*, 18. Worldly temptation and doubts about their ability to follow the rules of the order were common sources of anxiety among novices and some professed friars.
85. Prayers in honor of Mary were established at least since the eleventh century. They have variations in the hymns, lessons, and prayers. See Ibarra, *Oficio Parvo de Nuestra Señora* (1781).
86. Alvalate, *Doctrina Christiana*, 240–45; Sandoval, *Tratado del Oficio Eclesiástico*; Rex Galindo, *To Sin No More*, 122.
87. Salvador Vázquez Conde, "Religiosidad y vida," 132.
88. *Canto llano*, or "plainsong," was used in the Western Christian liturgy following the Roman rite. It is a monodic, or single-lined, chant sung *a capella*, or without musical accompaniment. All mendicants carried out their liturgy in plainsong, and novices had to learn it in their first year. The *Ceremonial Dominicano* of Fr. Joseph de San Joan had a section dedicated to teaching and learning *canto llano*. See San Joan, *Ceremonial Dominicano*.
89. San Joan, *Ceremonial Dominicano*, 21v. See also *Instrucción y Doctrina de Novicios*, 76.
90. Castro, *Ceremonial*, 1701.
91. A *loa* is a short theatrical piece introducing a longer play, although some stand on their own, such as this one. They were popular in seventeenth- and eighteenth-century literature in Spain and Spanish America. On Fr. Juan, see Ymhoff Cabrera, *Fray Juan*, 139–52; and Viveros Maldonado, "Dramaturgia," 433–56. Fr. Juan professed in the Carmelite convent of Nuestra Señora de los Remedios, Puebla, in 1708. He wrote religious poetry, theater, and secular poems. See Pérez Álvarez, "Siete loas de Fray Juan de la Anunciación" (2011); García Gómez, "Poesía dramática de Fray Juan de la Anunciación" (2010).
92. La Rea, *Crónica*, 335–37. Fr. Juan de la Cerpa, Portuguese by birth and a well-to-do farmer "experiencing many disappointments in that occupation," joined the Franciscan convent of Tzinzuntzan, endowing the convent with many fine ornaments (309).
93. Franco, *Historia*, 148–49.
94. See Franco, *Historia*, 209–12, 214, for Fr. Gaspar de Segura, another ex-soldier who served as general administrator of the conventual finances.
95. Ojea, *Libro Tercero*, 24–25.
96. Sanz López, *Compendio* (1785).

97. Sanz López, *Compendio*, 26. To contextualize this quote, it is important to remember that according to canonical sources, all Christians should aspire to a perfect life to achieve the love of God. However, within the Church, bishops and members of the orders had an advantage because of their vows and their complete dedication to those goals. Ávila, *Pureza emblemática* (1668).

98. Espinosa, *Guía de religiosos*, 109–18. Espinosa cited Abraham, who left his land and people to follow God, and the apostles, who left their own families to follow Christ. See also Pimentel Pontes Filho, "Os filhos e 'afilhados' de São Francisco de Assis."

99. Rubin, *Mother of God*; Warner, *Alone of All Her Sex*.

100. Lavrin, *Brides of Christ*, 107–15, 331–44.

101. "Toda su consideración ha de ser en su devoto y celestial esposo Jesu-Christo... que ha de ser el dueño de su alma, y el que viva en ella, y la rija, y gobierne" (Navarrete, *Directorio*, 6). See also Dávila Padilla, *Historia*, 553–55. Describing the death of Fr. Alonso Garcés in a fire in a small town (Saint Ildefonso) in Oaxaca, Dávila Padilla puts in his mouth a long speech in which the friar addressed Christ as his groom, and his death is described as the final return to the arms of his beloved husband. See also Walker Bynum, "Jesus as Mother and Abbott as Mother," 18–43, and *Jesus as Mother*.

102. Burgoa, *Palestra historial*, 18.

103. La Rea, *Crónica*, 309.

104. La Rea, *Crónica*, 81.

105. Medina, *Chronica* (1682). Quotes from his Dedicatoria, "Al humilde seráfico maestro," n.p.

106. Romero, *Avisos para el Noviciado*, 8.

107. Rubial García, *Una monarquía criolla*, 129–30. See also his "Votos pactados," 51–83, "Fray Diego Velázquez de la Cadena," 173–94, and "La mitra y la cogulla," 239–72.

3. Lay Brothers

1. Arlegui, *Crónica*, 29.

2. Sempat Assadourian, *Zacatecas* (2008).

3. Arlegui, *Crónica*, 31, 35, 217, 235, 278–87. *Donados* or *oblates* were men who lived in the convent to serve its needs and enjoy the benefices of the spiritual blessings of the community. On the origins of the lay brothers, see France, *Separate but equal* (2012); and García de Cortázar and Teja Casuso, *Monasterios* (2008). Fr. Alonso Franco mentions an Indian *donado* in the convent of Santo Domingo in Mexico. See Franco, *Segunda Parte*, 495–97.

4. Arlegui, *Crónica*, 262–72.

5. Barbado de la Torre y Angulo, *Compendio Histórico*, 38. Lay brothers were also known as *conversos* in the Dominican order. This appellative had no relation whatsoever to the *converso* understood as a Jewish or Muslim convert to the Christian faith. Another historic term applied to them was *illiterate*, meaning "unable to read or write," which separated from the educated friars.
6. *Regla de los Frayles Menores*, 9–9v, 27–27v; Anunciación, *Avisos religiosos*, 161–74; Santa María, *Chronica*, 284.
7. Dávila Padilla, *Historia*, 103–4.
8. Dávila Padilla, *Historia*, 197.
9. Dávila Padilla used the life of Fr. Bartolomé de Calzadilla, an abstinent, penitent, and hardworking lay brother, as illustrative of the virtues of lay brothers. Calzadilla died six months after the Dominicans arrived in New Spain and was the first lay brother of the order.
10. San Benito, *Vida Interior y Cartas* (1746).
11. Basalenque, *Historia*, 2:78–79.
12. Vetancurt, *Teatro Mexicano*, 121.
13. Barbado de la Torre y Angulo, *Compendio*. Barbado used a Portuguese text that he translated and expanded. He never identified the author of the original, which was probably a chronicle dating back to the sixteenth century.
14. Barbado de la Torre y Angulo, *Compendio*, 39.
15. Barbado de la Torre y Angulo, *Compendio*, 412, 419. Benito was beatified in 1712.
16. Vélez de Cosío, *Reglas Comunes*, preface, 10. This was a summary of the essential rules of observance summarized from seventeenth- and eighteenth-century Franciscan minor rules.
17. Around 1607 there were between twelve and fifteen lay brothers in the Dominican convent of Mexico City, serving the needs of forty ordained friars, between fifty and sixty novices, and several guests. See Ojea, *Libro Tercero*, 20; Pita Moreda, *Los predicadores*; Ulloa, *Los predicadores*; and Mora Reyes, "Los Dominicos."
18. Rubial García, *El convento Agustino*. In this work, see the appendix, Cuadro X and XI, "Distribución de los religiosos en los principales conventos urbanos"; Cuadro II, "Número de religiosos profesos en el convento de San Agustín de Mexico (1537–1630)"; and Gráficas 1A and 1B, "Profesiones de religiosos en el convento de la ciudad de Mexico." There's no information on novices or lay brothers for other Augustinian convents.
19. Morales, "Los hermanos laicos," 460–67. For a seventeenth-century survey of the Franciscan brothers in New Spain and the rest of the continent, see Hernández Aparicio, "Estadísticas Franciscanas," 555–92.
20. Morales, "Los hermanos laicos," 465.

21. Pita Moreda, *Los predicadores*, 28; Mora Reyes, "Los Dominicos," 155. Mora Reyes mentions lay brothers without offering much information.
22. Acuña, "Actas Capitulares de la Provincia," 151–84.
23. Mora Reyes, "Los Dominicos," 140–41, 179–80, 187n131. She also notes that only 30 percent of the friars of the province of Santiago—as opposed to that of Oaxaca—lived in rural convents by 1667.
24. Rex Galindo, *To Sin No More*, 75–77.
25. Cervantes Aguilar, *Fray Simón del Hierro*, 241.
26. BNFF, vol. 123, *Alegato presentado al Santo Concilio en Mexico*, 1771, by Fr. Rafael Verger, punto 17.
27. This document is not dated. Francisco Morales, OFM, places it as in the 1770s or early 1780s. BNFF, vol. 134. For the convent of San Francisco, see BNFF, vol. 123.
28. BNFF, vol. 123, *Memorial Tercero*, February 25, 1772. This document does not furnish information on novices.
29. Torre Curiel, *Vicarios*, 158–59. The number of novices (*assumed* to be for the ordained state) was small and declined from twelve to seven between 1740 and 1784. The *coristas* declined from forty in 1740 to nineteen in 1776. In 1784 the number remained the same. This did not bode well for the future of the order.
30. Age is not always provided in conventual records.
31. BNFF, vol. 134, *Nómina de los religiosos que tiene esta Provincia de Nuestro Padre San Francisco de Zacatecas*. Undated and ascribed to the last decades of the eighteenth century. The list divided the community between criollos and Spaniards. Even the lay brothers were classified according to their ethnic provenance. There were 130 criollos and 33 friars from Spain. Among the lay brothers, 18 were criollos and 4 came from Spain. Lay brothers were 13.4 percent of the total number of friars in the convent.
32. Age did not necessarily imply poor health and mental decline. Men well over sixty were active as writers and missionaries. Lay brother Beato Aparicio, as cited in this chapter, was active and apparently healthy into his nineties.
33. BNFF, vol. 101, *Nómina de Religiosos, Colegio de Nuestra Sra. de Guadalupe de Zacatecas*.
34. BNFF, vol. 134.
35. *Constituciones de la Provincia de San Diego*, 7.
36. Avilés, *Regla*, preface.
37. Ximenez, *Regla de N.P.S. Agustín* (1787). Sáenz was a lay brother of the convent of San Pablo in Seville. He praised the Dominicans for their benevolent treatment of lay brothers, who enjoyed privileges not available in other orders. He argued that Dominican lay brothers were better fed and dressed, had lighter

duties, received more spiritual indoctrination, and were allowed more frequent attendance to the divine offices than in other mendicant orders.

38. For Bishop Bernardo Acuña de Alburquerque, see Gay, *Historia*, 392–405; and Acuña, "Actas Capitulares de la Provincia," 151–84.
39. The title page of Barbado de la Torre y Angulo's *Compendio* announced information on "the greatness, glories, excellences and prerogatives of the humble status of lay brothers."
40. Avilés, *Regla*, 29, 30, 32, 58–59, 82.
41. Avilés, *Regla*, 85–86.
42. BNFF, vol. 134, *Nómina de Religiosos de San Francisco de Mexico*, 1781.
43. BNFF, vol. 134, *Nómina de los Religiosos, convento de las Llagas de Ntro. S P. S. Francisco de la ciudad de la Puebla*, 1778.
44. On the Christian care of the sick, see Arbiol, *Visita de enfermos*.
45. Convents were supposed to have their own pharmacies. Documentation on how lay brothers administered medical care in male convents is not readily available. Religious hospitals had pharmacies and were regulated by the Protomedicato, the institution in charge of legislating on medicine and public health. See Pardo-Tomas, *La medicina*. For further readings on pharmacopeia in convents, see Rodríguez, "Legislación"; Morales Cosme and Aceves Pastrana, "Negocio," 45–64; Rui Pita and Pereira, "A arte farmacêutica," 227–68; and Sánchez-Téllez, "La medicina," 33–40.
46. Tello, *Libro Segundo*, 879–80.
47. Franco, *Segunda Parte*, 135. Information on Fr. de Juan de Paz, lay brother.
48. BNFF, vol. 134, *Nómina de Religiosos de San Francisco de Mexico*, 1781.
49. Mendieta, *Historia Eclesiástica Indiana*, 2:210.
50. BNFF, vol. 134, *Nómina de Religiosos de San Francisco de Mexico*, 1781.
51. BNFF, vol. 134, *Nómina de Religiosos, Convento de San Francisco de Puebla*, 1778; *Lista de los religiosos residentes en este colegio de Tlatelolco*, n.d. (possibly in the 1780s, when convents were ordered to submit lists of their populations).
52. BNFF, vol. 101, untitled document, 1771, n.p.
53. The fanega is roughly the equivalent of 1.58 bushels; 1,410 to 1,430 pounds; and 648.7 kilos. These are approximate equivalents. *Alverjón* or *almorta* (Indian or grass pea) is a legume planted and eaten in Spain and, we now learn, also in Mexico. People ate it as seed or used it as flour. Eaten in large amounts, it causes lathyrism, or paralysis of the legs.
54. Cervantes Aguilar, *Fray Simón del Hierro*, 77–88.
55. Avilés, *Regla*, 90–94; Rubial, *Una monarquía criolla*, 85. They also had slaves to help in the convent and in their properties. No prelate challenged the usage.
56. Basalenque, *Historia*, 2:175–80.

57. Ojea, *Libro Tercero*, 38.
58. The Dominicans enjoyed inherited properties from many donors and used Indian labor in their properties.
59. Franco, *Segunda Parte*, 126–27; Ojea, *Libro Tercero*, 39–41.
60. The Augustinians were well-known landowners in Michoacán and New Galicia. See Moreno García, *Los Agustinos*, 35–37.
61. Prior to Mendieta, in 1585 Fr. Diego Muñoz wrote a description and brief history of the Franciscan province of San Pedro y San Pablo of Michoacán. It remained unpublished until recently. See his *Descripción de la provincia*.
62. Mendieta, *Historia Eclesiástica Indiana*, 2:154.
63. García Oro, *Cisneros* (1971); Andrés Martin, "La espiritualidad," 465–79; Nieva Ocampo, "Incorporarse," 39–67; Guadalupe, *Historia*.
64. Mendieta, *Historia Eclesiástica Indiana*, 2:166; Oré, *Account of the Martyrs* (2017).
65. Mendieta, *Historia Eclesiástica Indiana*, 2:201.
66. Mendieta, *Historia Eclesiástica Indiana*, 2:204.
67. Mendieta, *Historia Eclesiástica Indiana*, 2:223.
68. Dávila Padilla, *Historia*, 103, 185, 196, 464, 472, 575. As a chronicler, Dávila Padilla forgave some of the lay brothers for personal misbehavior in their pasts. Such was the case of Fr. Bartolomé Mateos, who escaped from a Spanish prison where he had landed after supporting Gonzalo Pizarro's insurrection against the Crown in Peru. In another instance, one friar abandoned the order and then returned after he squandered his money. Such blunders were forgiven after personal repentance and subsequent adherence to the rules of the order and conventual discipline.
69. Ojea, *Libro Tercero*, 27–28.
70. Ojea, *Libro Tercero*, 27–28.
71. Ojea, *Libro Tercero*, 49, 51, 52–53, 58–62.
72. González Polvillo, *Decálogo*, 2011.
73. Ojea, *Libro Tercero*, 63–67. Fr. Pedro Martínez, lay brother, was a man of humble origins. He is praised for the directness and simplicity of his faith and practices. He died in the Philippines, showing how a man of little means could travel by serving the church.
74. Franco, *Segunda Parte*, 156–57.
75. Ojea, *Libro Tercero*, 58; Franco, *Segunda Parte*, 200.
76. La Rea, *Crónica*.
77. Vetancurt, *Menologio Franciscano*, bound with his *Teatro Mexicano*.
78. Vetancurt, *Menologio Franciscano*, 89.
79. Vetancurt, *Menologio Franciscano*, 111.
80. Vetancurt, *Menologio Franciscano*, 100.

81. Arricivita, *Apostolic Chronicle*, 317–20.
82. Arricivita, *Apostolic Chronicle*, 312–17.
83. Dávila Padilla, *Historia*, 460.
84. Medina, *Chronica*, 95–103.
85. León, *Historia*, 23–24. Hagiographic accounts evoked miracles of prior times. Stopping the locusts elicited the memory of a story of how, in "earlier times," an Augustinian friar had stopped the annoying noise of frogs in a nearby lagoon, which distracted the community during Mass. See León, *Historia*, 23–24. These were not "heroic" deeds but understandably meaningful in the course of daily life.
86. Rubial García, "Imprenta," 43–52.
87. Morales, "Los hermanos laicos," 458.
88. Rodríguez, *Vida prodigiosa* (1769). Rodríguez was the official chronicler of the Franciscan order and custodian of the province of the Holy Gospel. For Aparicio, see also San Miguel, *Parayso* (1695); *Vida de varios santos*, 25–35; Ragon, "Sebastián de Aparicio," 17–45; Morales, "La biografía," 137–63; Durán, "La Construcción," 165–201; Shean, "'From His Roots,'" 17–50; Rubial, *La santidad*, 35–42; and "Los rituales de la esperanza" in "Culto y hagiografía de los venerables y siervos de Dios novohispanos," Undated paper, Facultad de Filosofía y Letras, UNAM.
89. My narrative is based on the information provided by Rodríguez, *Vida prodigiosa*; *Vida de varios Santos*; and the works of Pierre Ragon and Francisco Morales.
90. Torquemada, *Vida y Milagros* (1602). This book preceded Torquemada's history of the Franciscan order. According to Pierre Ragon, it is very rare.
91. Rubial, "Invención," 121–32.
92. Vetancurt, *Menologio Franciscano*, 16–24. Morales assigns his popularity to his simplicity. See Morales, "La biografía," 137–63.
93. Rodríguez, *Vida prodigiosa*. This work was dedicated by the author to D. Manuel Ventura Figueroa of the Council of Castille. It was also hoped by the new biographer that his beatification would enhance the rebirth of piety of Spain under the reign of Charles III and help ease tensions between the Spanish Crown and the Vatican.
94. See Biempica, *La sencillez* (1791). Today, the cult of *beato* Aparicio is firmly entrenched in Puebla. His preserved body lies in a glass sarcophagus and he is venerated in his own chapel in the Church of San Francisco.
95. Ponce de León, *Historia* (1686).
96. Ponce de León, *Historia*, 13v, 16.
97. León, *Historia*, 27–27v.
98. Ponce de León, *Historia*, 45–47.

99. Ponce de León, *Historia*, 34–35. Rita of Cascia (1381–1457) was an Italian Augustinian nun beatified in 1627. John of Sahagún (1419–79) was a Spanish member of the order of Hermits of Saint Augustine and was declared a "blessed" in 1601. Clare of Montefalco (1268–1308) was an Italian Augustinian abbess whose canonization process began in 1328 but was not completed until 1737. She is addressed as a saint in the narrative. Tomás de Villanueva (1488–1555) was an Augustinian professor at Alcalá de Henares and a well-known preacher who sent the first Augustinians to New Spain and was canonized in 1658. Nicholas Tolentino (1245–1306) was canonized in 1446.
100. Ponce de León, *Historia*, 12.
101. Ponce de León, *Historia*, 53, 54, 76v, 88.
102. Ponce de León, *Historia*, 106 118. The letter is barely one printed page, recto and verso, but the writer treated it as a theological work, showing extraordinary capacities of amplification.
103. Espinosa, *El Cherubin*. My narrative of his life is based on this work. It is his only biography from that century.
104. Espinosa, *Chronica Apostólica* (1746), and *El Peregrino Septentrional* (1737); McCloskey, "Fray Isidro Félix," 228–95.
105. This story resembles the conversion experience of Francisco de Borja, third general of the Society of Jesus, who was canonized in 1670. The sight of the decomposed body of Isabel of Portugal, Charles V's wife, convinced Borja of the vanity and meaningless of the world. See Nieremberg, *Vida* (1644).
106. Espinosa, *El Cherubin*, 47, 58, 60–62.
107. Espinosa, *El Cherubin*, 113, 125. His confessor of twelve years, Fr. Ángel García Duque, is said to have gathered information in preparation for writing Fr. Antonio's biography. Fr. Isidro does not explain when or why this project was dropped.
108. Espinosa, *El Cherubin*, 63, 82, 139.
109. Espinosa, *El Cherubin*, 76, 81–82. Fr. Antonio used to do this exercise by himself as well as with a companion who remained unnamed until Margil joined him. Fr. Margil was his confessor for an unspecified period of time. See p. 112.
110. Espinosa, *El Cherubin*, 74.
111. Bonding existed in some nunneries. Religious authorities condemned the practice of "private friendships," but there is evidence in some nun's writings. Espinosa provides evidence that such relationships could be formed within male convents as well.
112. Espinosa, *El Cherubin*, dedication. Saint Anthony of Padua served as a humble brother in the kitchen of the Franciscan hospice of San Paolo, near Forli in Northern Italy. Unlike him, Fr. Antonio never preached. Cherubims are celestial

beings second to seraphims in the hierarchy of angels. They are sent to earth to perform very important tasks and direct the soul to knowledge. They have the power to know and see divinity. Gregory the Great described them as full of love of God and neighbor. See Chase, *Angelic Spirituality*, 100.

113. Espinosa, *El Cherubin*, 49–50, 63, 67, 76, 104, 151–55; Arricivita, *Apostolic Chronicle*, 245–312.
114. Espinosa, *El Cherubin*, 69.
115. Espinosa, *El Cherubin*, 122. The original in Spanish reads, "Enjugad y secar las humedades de los apetitos. Deshaced las tinieblas de los pecados, convirtiéndolos en agua de lágrimas y penitencia. Enciéndase el fuego de vuestro divino amor en mi alma." Translations from the Spanish source are my own.
116. Ponce de León, *Historia*, 87. Fr. Cristóbal de Molina did not eat until the Blacks and slaves in the convent had eaten and treated them as his equals. The biographer extols this trait as exemplary and a "great deed" (*grande hazaña*).

4. Sexuality

1. Gen. 1:22; 1:28, 91; 9:7; 8:17; 35:11 (NIV). These are a few of the many instances of the command to multiply cited in Genesis.
2. Brown, *The Body and Society*. In this chapter I review only those cases involving members of the mendicant orders, excluding others such as the Mercedarians, Carmelites, Jesuits, and secular clergy.
3. On celibacy, see Heid, *Celibacy*; Parish, *Clerical Celibacy*; Stickler, *The Case for Clerical Celibacy*; Raverty, "Are We Monks?," 269–91; Hadley, *Masculinity in Medieval Europe*; Frazee, "The Origins of Celibacy," 149–67; Tentler, *Sin and Confession*; Cullum and Lewis, *Holiness and Masculinity*; Murray, *Conflicted Identities*; and Thibodeaux, *The Manly Priest*.
4. Po-Chia Hsia, *The World*; Birley, *The Refashioning of Catholicism*.
5. Traslosheros, *Historia Judicial*, 21–42; Alberro, *Inquisición y Sociedad*.
6. Heid, *Celibacy*. On analyzing celibacy, Heid assumes that single aspirants to ecclesiastical positions were "virginal." He cites three categories of aspirants: virginal, widowed, and married men. We cannot be certain that "single" male aspirants were necessarily virgins unless they were very young.
7. Murray, "'Mystical Castration,'" 73–110.
8. Noble, *A World without Women*. In parts 1 and 2 of his work, Noble discusses the rise of sexual asceticism in early Christian times and the revival of clerical celibacy in the Middle Ages.
9. The sacraments of the Catholic Church are as follows: baptism, the Eucharist, confirmation, penance, the anointment of the sick, marriage, and ordination in the holy orders.

10. Alejandre, *El veneno de Dios*; Haliczer, *Sexuality in the Confessional*; Sarrión Mora, *Sexualidad y confesión*; Martínez Ferrer, "Las Órdenes mendicantes," 47–68; González Marmolejo, *Sexo y confesión*, and "Clérigos solicitantes, perversos de la confesión"; García Mendoza, "Casos de curas solicitantes," 25–44. In their role as evangelizers, the orders gave preference to the Indians over the Spaniards on the issue of confession in the sixteenth century. However, this situation would change in the seventeenth and eighteenth centuries. As their role as evangelizers diminished, the mendicants became confessors to a more heterogeneous flock.

11. Galván Rodríguez, "La praxis," 109. Punishment also applied to fictitious confession, when penitent and confessor pretended to be confessing to carry out "dishonest" conversations.

12. Haliczer, *Sexuality in the Confessional*, 42–62.

13. San Antonio, *Resumen de la Theologia Moral*, 535–42. Solicitation could involve women, men, and children of both sexes. See also Galván Rodríguez, "La praxis inquisitorial," 118.

14. Sarrión Mora, *Sexualidad y confesión*, 70. The papal bull also condemned false accusations of confessors by anyone and prescribed excommunication to those guilty of such action. Cardinal Iudice, general inquisitor, cleared up the false notion that women involved with solicitants had no obligation to denounce the transgression to the Inquisition. This edict was circulated in Mexico in 1713. Ramo Inquisición, vol. 753, exp. 1, Archivo General de la Nación, Mexico City (hereafter cited as Ramo Inquisición).

15. On Pedro Moya de Contreras, see Poole, *Pedro Moya de Contreras*; and García-Molina Riquelme, "Instrucciones," 85–100.

16. Ramo Inquisición, vols. 261–89.

17. Ramo Inquisición, vol. 295. This list may not cite cases registered in previous years.

18. Ramo Inquisición, vol. 334, exp. 2; vol. 337, exp. 2. Not included in the figures are cases from Guatemala, Nicaragua, and Manila. Most of the Dominican cases were reported from Oaxaca, their key evangelizing area.

19. Ramo Inquisición, vol. 376, exp. 11. The town of origin was Tlalixtac. He was probably a Dominican.

20. Morales, *Ethnic and Social Background*.

21. González Marmolejo, *Sexo y confesión*, 186–88, 192. Marmolejo used the most complete records of *condemned* solicitants, not all the cases of solicitation before the Inquisition. In terms of age, Marmolejo found that the majority of his cases were men in their late thirties and forties, in the prime of their virility. In Spain, as in Mexico, the Franciscans accounted for the majority of those accused of sexual solicitation. See Rawlings, *The Spanish Inquisition*, 128; and Sarrión Mora, *Sexualidad y confesión*, 234.

22. Ramo Inquisición, vol. 435. There were six expedientes, but two of them concerned the same case.
23. Ramo Inquisición, vol. 578, exp. 2. A few cases were fifteen years old or less and were listed as "current" or active, but it is clear that they had no chance of being followed up.
24. Review of Inquisition volumes 1179 through 1205. Inquisitorial records are not neatly ordered by year. The best attempt at a global survey is by volumes, and there are glaring inconsistencies in the ordering of the expedients, or cases, in each volume. Also, the Mexican Inquisition received cases from Central America and the Philippines. A review of inquisitorial records in search of solicitations is useful in assessing the degree of attention—or lack thereof—paid to them by the institution in charge of punishing deviant clergy.
25. In New Spain, it was customary to send the accused confessor to the secret jail of the Inquisition. Sarrión Mora proves that this was not the case for the jurisdiction of Cuenca in Spain, where most accused confessors either stayed in their convents or had the freedom of the city as their "prison" in the cases of secular priests. See Sarrión Mora, *Sexualidad y Confesión*, 324.
26. González Marmolejo, *Sexo y confesión*, 66–75. Alejandre's work, *El veneno de Dios*, follows the process clearly and methodically, with an abundance of examples for Spain.
27. Ramo Inquisición, vol. 544, exp. 27 (1701). This example shows how a case could be ignored despite evidence. There was a complete statement from the victim and one witness informing the inquisitors that the confessor had taken the penitent to his cell, had given her wine, and had intended further sexual advances. She managed to leave after threatening to scream. The attorney ordered it to be shelved pending further notice. The decision may have been prompted by the lack of a second witness, the abandonment of the cause by the victim, or simply the technicality that the sexual attempt had taken place outside the confessional and that it was a case for the ecclesiastic tribunals, not the Inquisition.
28. The records held at the Archivo Histórico Nacional in Simancas, Spain, appear to be more complete. I have not consulted that source, but many cases are replicated in Mexico.
29. Homza, *Religious Authority*, 113–75. The author focuses on the secular clergy, but much of her analysis can be applied to the regular orders. See also Mayer and de la Torre Villar, *Religión, poder y autoridad*.
30. For typical manuals for confessors, see Dueñas, *Remedio de pecadores*; Villalobos, *Manual de Confesores*; Azpilcueta Navarro, *Manual de confesores*; Gavarri, *Noticias Singularissimas*; Echarri, *Directorio Moral*; and O'Banion, "'A Priest Who Appears Good,'" 333–48. O'Banion underscores the popularity of manuals for

confessors, some of which went through as many as eighty editions. That was the case of Martin de Azpilcueta's *Manual*, which was printed eighty-one times and translated into foreign languages ninety-two times. Usually cited as "el Doctor Navarro," his work was well known in Spanish America. See González Sánchez, *Los mundos del libro*, 92, 213, 218, 243.

31. Muro Abad, "La castidad del clero bajomedieval."
32. Ramo Inquisición, vol. 1150, exp. 3. Information circulating through the grapevine was called *de voz pública*. According to an Augustinian friar, his prior, Fr. Gregorio Bouza, visited a "bad" woman very frequently and stayed with her until 9 p.m. He also visited another young lady with whom he shared lunch and slept the siesta. This information was provided in an inquisitorial deposition by a nun of the convent of Nuestra Señora de la Soledad in Oaxaca. His behavior was known even inside women's convents, and it was a good example of *voz pública*.
33. Ramo Inquisición, vol. 753, exp. 2, fols. 654–58, 1713. It is always surprising to find out that men in charge of the spiritual needs of female convents faced charges as solicitants—both with nuns and with lay women in their communities.
34. Ramo Inquisición, vol. 1322, exp. 9.
35. González Marmolejo, *Sexo y confesión*, 64–65.
36. Ramo Inquisición, vol. 957, fols. 366–84, 1758. For further cases on solicitation among nuns in Mexico, see Lavrin, *Brides of Christ*, 209–43.
37. Ramo Inquisición, vol. 1178, exp. 10.
38. Ramo Inquisición, vol. 1759 bisbis, 1757–63.
39. Ramo Inquisición, vol. 1759 bisbis, 1757–63.
40. See Ramo Inquisición, vol. 1206, exp. 3.
41. He was, by no means, the worst. García-Molina Riquelme cites a Dominican who confessed to having solicited 150 Indian women and having carnal access with 80 of them. He apparently committed all these acts in Guatemala and was banished in perpetuity form the province in 1603. See García-Molina Riquelme, "Instrucciones," 94.
42. Ramo Inquisición, vol. 1168, exp. 2; vol. 1160, exp. 13. According to his account, he was originally from the Franciscan convent in Burgos and served as a missionary of the Colegio de Propaganda Fide, Querétaro, in the missions of Coahuila and Río Grande del Norte. He acted as an intermediary between the Franciscans and Teodoro de Croix, who was in charge of administrating the Provincias Internas. His name appears as *Condon* or *Cordon* in other documents but is spelled as *Conlon* in the records of the AGN. Subsequent paragraphs in this chapter refer to this source.
43. Raya Guillén, "Los clérigos solicitantes," 37–66. See p. 44 for details on a confessor giving sexual information to his confessants.

44. Ramo Inquisición, vol. 1322, exp. 9.
45. Ramo Inquisición, vol. 1179, exp 6. All details about this case follow this expediente. See also vol. 1344 for a copy of the case.
46. For information of some moral trespasses of friars in New Mexico, see Greenleaf, "Inquisition."
47. Ecclesiastical courts under the jurisdiction of the bishop reviewed sexual infractions of the clergy. Armstrong-Partida, "Priestly Marriage."
48. Ramo Inquisición, vol. 435, exp. 180 (1650). Francisca de Peralta was seen and eventually denounced after entering the confessional numerous times to "tratar de amores" (talk about love) with her confessor.
49. Ramo Inquisición, vol. 1322, exp. 9. Some of the women dealing with Fr. Francisco Castellanos voluntarily prolonged their confessional visits and the conversation with him.
50. Confessors frequently visited sick people in their homes in case they required a final confession before death. See Ramo Inquisición, vol. 520, exp. 42 (1681). Feigning sickness to have a confessor visit a woman in her room was a trick used by willing partners in seductions, as indicated elsewhere in this chapter.
51. Ramo Inquisición, vol. 1159, exp. 15, fols. 323–28.
52. Ramo Inquisición, vol. 913, exp. 3 (1749).
53. Ramo Inquisición, vol. 435, 29, 30, 168 (1650).
54. Ramo Inquisición, vol. 455, exp. 17 (1612). Fr. Lorenzo Cortés was the guardian of the convent in Calpulalpan. At this time, solicitation was reaching a surprising number of incidences, especially among Franciscan friars.
55. Ramo Inquisición, vol. 295, exp. 16 (1614).
56. Ramo Inquisición, vol. 1179. She only proceeded with the denunciation under pressure of another confessor. Popado was also accused by a married woman of making verbal propositions to her, and she seemed to have been inclined to accept, but their encounter never took place.
57. Twinam, *Public Lives*.
58. Ramo Inquisición, vol. 622, exp. 6 (1773–83).
59. Ramo Inquisición, vol. 622, exp. 13.
60. Ramo Inquisición, vol. 20, exp. 42 (1681).
61. For a case against a Franciscan who had solicited a Black woman, see Ramo Inquisición, vol. 435, exp. 150 (1690). For other ethnic and racial groups, see vol. 337, exp. 3 (1621); and vol. 435, exps. 145 and 147 (1650).
62. Ramo Inquisición, vol. 295, exp. 34 (1617). The husband of Tomasina Ribera, a married woman in Pachuca, attacked him in the street. Subsequently, the Franciscans sent Alva away and the husband left town, leaving the woman to live with her parents as a penalized victim of these two men.

63. Ramo Inquisición, vol. 1206, exp. 3.
64. Closed confessionals, where the confessor sat inside and the penitent knelt outside the confessional, were not universal in New Spain in the sixteenth or seventeenth century. They were also not available in many rural areas during the colonial period. In rural areas men and women confessed kneeling before the confessor in several places of the church and even in makeshift confessional areas outdoors. See Galván Rodríguez, "La praxis inquisitorial," 125. See Ramo Inquisición, vol. 295, exps. 57 and 59 (1620), for women who refused advances.
65. Ramo Inquisición, vol. 1344, exp. 7 (1798).
66. Ramo Inquisición, vol. 295, exp. 15 (1614); exp. 21 (1615).
67. Ramo Inquisición, vol. 335, exp. 8. This case is bound inside a process against Fr. Alonso Onrrubia. There are two other unnumbered denunciations for solicitation for that year involving other women living in Tlatelolco, one Indian and the other a free *mulata*. The accused were two different Franciscans. There is no indication these cases were acted upon.
68. Ramo Inquisición, vol. 435, exp. 145 (1650).
69. Ramo Inquisición, vol. 435, exp. 145 (1650). For Agustina de Hinojosa, see exp. 148. For María Ramos, see exp. 126.
70. See Ramo Inquisición, vol. 295, exps. 16 (1614), 29, and 31 (1617), for widows. See exps. 19 (1614), 57, and 59 (1620), for offers of a better life.
71. Domingo Báñez (1528–1604) was a distinguished Dominican theologian and counselor to Santa Teresa de Jesús. It is unlikely that Báñez would have supported any article contravening the Inquisition's directives.
72. Ramo Inquisición, vol. 335, exp. 8. In 1614 a secular priest in Tabasco was reported as saying that simple fornication was not a sin. This report was in conjunction with a denunciation that he was soliciting Indian women. See Ramo Inquisición, vol. 578, exp. 7B.
73. Chuchiak, "Procedimientos y conflictos jurídicos."
74. Ramo Inquisición, vol. 376, exp. 19 (1634).
75. See Ramo Inquisición, vol. 1435, exp. 19 (1804).
76. Ramo Inquisición, vol. 122, exps. 1–10 (1580).
77. Ramo Inquisición, vol. 295, exp. 1 (1612).
78. Chuchiak, "The Secrets behind the Screen."
79. Ramo Inquisición, vol. 485, exp. 28 (1658), fols. 285–86. Given her description I assume she had confessed outside the church. This case follows that of another solicitant, Fr. Miguel de los Ángeles, and because it is archived within it, it is not described in the index for exp. 28. For other examples of cases in the northern areas of New Spain, see Ramo Inquisición, vol. 1147, exp. 33 (1772); and vol. 1395, exp. 3 (1798). These regions were still "remote" in the mid-eighteenth century.

80. Ramo Inquisición, vol. 245, exp. 10 (1598). They were in a chapel of the convent in a presumably empty church.
81. Slaves had very little choice regarding suffering sexual violence. Although not concerning a member of the mendicant orders, it is useful to cite here the accusation of a Jesuit by a slave in the hacienda of San Francisco Javier (Matanza) near Pachuca. At age thirty-five Monica Guadalupe decided to denounce her rape and subsequent pregnancy (she was fourteen at the time of the assault) by the chaplain in charge of confessing the slaves. The chaplain used her sexually for eight months. When her pregnancy became obvious and the Jesuits learned who was responsible, they exiled him. She denounced the case after so many years to discharge her conscience, since there could be no redress for her. See Ramo Inquisición, vol. 913, exp. 5 (1740).
82. Ramo Inquisición, vol. 435, exp. 150 (1650).
83. Ramo Inquisición, vol. 376, exp. 14 (1625–31).
84. Lavrin, *Brides of Christ*, 209–43.
85. Matt. 2:27–28 (ESV).
86. Ramo Inquisición, vol. 552, 2d part, exp. 53 (1717–18); and vol. 729.
87. Borda, *Práctica de confesores*, 44–45. For nuns, even thinking of corporal "delights" was a mortal sin, since such thoughts were against the vow of chastity (Borda, *Práctica de confesores*, 47, 72).
88. Ramo Inquisición, vol. 957, exp. 2.
89. Ramo Inquisición, vol. 552, exp. 40 (1684–90).
90. Lavrin, "La religiosa y su confesor," 455–78.
91. Ramo Inquisición, vol. 985, exp. 2 (1758).
92. Ramo Inquisición, vol. 1150, exp. 3 (1777–87). All the information on this case is based on this source.
93. In September 1787 this case came out of the shelves at the request of one inquisitor. Guardia had apparently died, since the word *murió* is written on the front page.
94. Solange Alberro calls attention to the character weaknesses of the inquisitors. See chap. 1 of her work, *Inquisición y sociedad en Mexico*. See also Chuchiak, "Corruption and Careerism," 376–97.
95. See San Joseph, *Breve Exposición*, 220–50 and 225–28, for cases of a sexual nature. Sexual relations with a person consecrated to God was considered a sacrilege. See, for example, Noydens, *Promptuario moral*, 133–34.
96. Accusations of solicitation could be made years after the event took place and with such sparse information as to make them impossible to investigate. In 1798 a white woman who knew how to sign and was remarried to a man with the appellative "Don" was induced by her confessor to denounce a verbal case of solicitation that took place seven years before, when she lived in the presidio of San Carlos de Buenavista in Sonora. She could not furnish any information

on the whereabouts of the confessor and wrote the denunciation simply to be absolved by her current confessor. Such a cause went to the ignored *despreciadas* lot. Ramo Inquisición, vol. 1395, exp. 3.

97. Galván Rodríguez, "La praxis inquisitorial," 108, 115. Attorneys used metaphors of dirt, mud, ill-smelling wells, and perfidy to condemn solicitants in their writings, whether in Spain or New Spain.
98. Ramo Inquisición, vol. 527, exp. 3 (1692). Oliva was deprived of confessional rights in perpetuity and sentenced to reclusion for one year in his convent in Guadalajara. He was forbidden from performing Mass for four years.
99. Ramo Inquisición, vol. 122, exp. 4 (1581); vol. 1322, exp. 9.
100. San Christoval [Estella], *El Tratado de la vanidad del mundo*, 298. He advised readers never to come too close to the "enemy" (women) because the closer one came, the stronger the attraction.
101. Busembaum, *Médula de la teología Moral*, 236.
102. Ramo Inquisición, vol. 1322, exp. 9.
103. Ramo Inquisición, vol. 729, exp. 1.
104. A "doctrine" was an Indian jurisdiction in charge of a minister. The Dominicans were in charge of evangelizing the region of Oaxaca since the sixteenth century, and Fr. Juan held a position of great responsibility, which he obviously did not discharge well.
105. In 1716, Palacio del Hoyo was reviewed by a *visitador* and recalled to the Spanish court for some unknown cause, but after receiving a warning, he and others were allowed to return to their posts. In fact, Palacio del Hoyo was promoted to the Valladolid (Spain) Tribunal. He died on his way, in Havana, in 1730. Medina, *Historia del Tribunal del Santo Oficio*, 354; Méndez, *Secretos del Oficio*, 12, 15, 20, 143; Aguirre Beltrán, *Medicina y magia*, 95.
106. "Abusando de él como hombre vicioso y escandalizando con sus torpezas, dichos y hechos, al pueblo Cristiano, solicitando a sus hijas espirituales para actos torpes y deshonestos, tomando por capa y cubierta de sus sensualidades una cosa tan sagrada como el sacramento de la penitencia y usando lugar tan sagrado (como) cisterna inmunda de pecados, lo que es fuente de salud [y] de la gracia."
107. Noydens, *Promptuario moral de questiones*, 136: "Peca mortalmente el religioso que frecuenta locutorios y mantiene devociones en los monasterios de monjas."
108. San Joseph, *Breve exposición de los preceptos*.
109. Ramo Inquisición, vol. 914, exp. 14.
110. These punishments were very close in terms and nature to those imposed by the Inquisition in Sevilla. There, condemned priests could perform the Mass after a probation period. See Alejandre, *El veneno de Dios*, 194–210.

111. The pattern of leniency is similar to that of other inquisitorial tribunals in Spain. See Berco, "Social Control," 338.
112. Ramo Inquisición, vol. 1206, exp 3. See also vol. 1759 bisbis for another case.
113. Lavrin, "The Erotic as Lewdness," 35–57.
114. García-Molina Riquelme, "Instrucciones," 98.
115. Ramo Inquisición, vol. 340, exp. (1622); vol. 753, exp. 2 (1716). When Fr. Joseph de Rivera self-denounced for having physical contact with a young boy, he claimed not to have had a "venereal" contact. At the same time, he declared a platonic relationship with a woman. Proven sodomy cases should not be conflated with the solicitation of male confessants even though the Inquisition sometimes confused them.
116. García-Molina Riquelme, "Instrucciones," 98.
117. Ramo Inquisición, vol. 518, exp. 37. Fr. Francisco de Araúz only desisted from forcing himself on a woman he had taken to his cell when she began screaming. Fr. Pedro Alfonso de Valladolid, a Dieguino, raped a young woman between thirteen and fifteen years old and offered her 300 pesos to buy her silence (vol. 971, exp. 1 [1754]). He was a recidivist who had escaped from the convent in Puebla, where he was imprisoned for his many instances of solicitation. The Francisans requested his internment in the Inquisition's jail.
118. Giraud, "Viol et société colonial"; Castañeda, *Violación, estupro, y sexualidad*.

5. Missionaries

Epigraphs: Espinosa, *Chronica Apostólica*, 48; Fr. Fermín de Lasuén, letter to Fray Francisco Pangua, April 23, 1774, in Kenneally, *Writings*, 1:37–38.

1. McCloskey, *The Formative Years*; Rex Galindo, *To Sin No More*.
2. Ricard, *The Spiritual Conquest*; Cruz Rangel, *Chichimecas, misioneros, soldados*; Jackson, *Pames, Jonaces, and Franciscans*. The many titles of historian John L. Kessel deal with the northern frontier of New Spain, although it is presented as the history of the North American Southwest. See his *Spain in the Southwest, Friars, Soldiers, and Reformers*, and *The Missions of New Mexico*. See also Wade, *Missions, Missionaries*.
3. Melvin, *Building Colonial Cities of God*.
4. Dunne, *Pioneer Black Robes*; Hu-DeHart, *Missionaries, Miners, and Indians*.
5. Benavides, *Memorial*. See an early translation by Ayer, *The Memorial of Fray Alonso de Benavides*.
6. Nogar, *Quill and Cross*.
7. Perea, *Verdadera relación* (1632) and *Segunda Relación* (1633).
8. Zárate Salmerón, "Relaciones."

9. Zárate Salmerón, "Relaciones," fol. 18–19. He did not forget the availability of pastureland and water for cattle: "bellos campos y pastos para ganados y muchas aguas" (fol. 23v).
10. Zárate Salmerón, "Relaciones," fol. 21–22.
11. Zárate Salmerón, "Relaciones," fol. 29, 35.
12. Calvo, *Los Albores*, 285.
13. Caballero Carranco, "Viaje y entrada." Carranco explored the area for only ten days, but he was successful in reaching places unknown to other missionaries and returned safely to his convent.
14. Caballero Carranco had a very low opinion of the Natives' intelligence. He thought that their "animal" part dominated their "rational" part: "Tienen todos los gentiles y apóstatas más ejercicio de la parte animal que la racional, y así primero se ha de obrar en la parte animal agasajándolos, dándoles de comer y otras cosillas para que, como si fueran puros animales brutos, nos cobren amor, que después entra bien el predicador a enseñarles" ("Viaje y entrada," 175).
15. Nesvig, *Promiscuos Power*, 40–44.
16. Gómez Canedo, *Sierra Gorda*; Abundis, "The San Fernando College's Sierra Gorda Missions."
17. Cruz Rangel, *Chichimecas, misioneros, soldados*. My summary of the missionary activities of three mendicants in this area is based on this well-researched work. For the decline in the population, see Jackson, *Frontiers of Evangelization*, and "The Chichimeca Frontier," 45–91.
18. Gómez Canedo, *Primeras exploraciones*.
19. Rex Galindo, *To Sin No More*. The colleges were founded in Querétaro (1682), Zacatecas (1704–7), San Fernando (1733), Pachuca (1799), and Zapopan (1816). See also McCloskey, *The Formative Years*; and Escandón, "La Crónica."
20. Espinosa, *El Peregrino*.
21. Margil, *Formulario de Misiones*.
22. Margil, *Nothingness Itself*; Espinosa, *El Peregrino*; Sotomayor, *Historia*.
23. See chapter 7 of this work for an account of his death.
24. Cárdenas, "José de Escandón," 2–3.
25. Osante, *Orígenes del Nuevo Santander*, 107–35, and "Estrategia colonizadora," 17–44.
26. Villaseñor E., "El coronel Don José de Escandón," 1157–1210; Osante, *Testimonio*.
27. The Provincias Internas were created in 1776 and were a separate government unit from New Spain with a commandant captain general at the head. The *provincias* comprised the current territories of Sonora, Sinaloa, Nueva Vizcaya, Alta California and Baja California, New Mexico, Nuevo Santander, the Reino de

León, Texas, and Coahuila. See Navarro García, *José de Gálvez*; and Velázquez, *El estado de Guerra* (1973), and *Establecimiento y pérdida* (1974).

28. Barnaby, *Teodoro de Croix*; Velázquez, "La comandancia general," 163–77.
29. For a work focusing on the indoctrination of the Indians in California, see Sandos, *Converting California*. On the controversial nature of missionary activity, see Hackel, *Children of Coyote*. For the role of women, see Reyes, "Apolinaria Lorezana (1793–?)," and *Private Women*. Although Reyes's works focus largely on the nineteenth century, they raise issues on women and gender relations in the missions that remain unexplored.
30. Magaña Mancillas, "Sobre nuevo método." There were at least seven responses to how to carry out the spiritual and material governance of the missions, and they remain to be studied as a unit.
31. Gómez Canedo, *Fray Rafael Verger*, 551–75. Verger was guardian from 1770 to 1774.
32. Beebe and Senkewicz, *Junípero Serra*, 363–70.
33. Geiger, "Fray Rafael Verger," 205–31. Report addressed to the *fiscal* (prosecutor) of the *audiencia*, Manuel Lanz de Casafonda, on August 3, 1771.
34. Pimería Alta was the region north of the Altar River and beyond, up to the Gila River in today's Arizona.
35. Pimería Baja had present-day Hermosillo at its center, with the Sonora and Yaqui Rivers as its man boundaries.
36. Bolton, *Anza's California* (1930).
37. Brown, *With Anza to California* (2011); Bolton, *Anza's California Expeditions* (1933). Font's diary has been known since 1913. See Teggart, *The Anza Expedition*.
38. Montané Martí, *Fray Pedro Font*.
39. Torre Curiel, *Vicarios*, 323–25.
40. Matson, "Letters," 268.
41. In his letter from November 30, 1776, he states, "The grief and pain caused by these sad events (I speak at least for myself on account of the agitation and dread in my heart at every movement or bit of news) make us feel that instead of life, this is a prolonged death" (Matson, "Letters," 277). He cites fear and grief again in his letter dated January 20, written from the mission of Tubutama (see p. 283).
42. Matson, "Letters," 276–77.
43. Matson, "Letters," 277–78.
44. Matson, "Letters," 279.
45. Matson, "Letters," 285–88.
46. Matson, "Letters," 288. The method had been tried for eighty years, and "no material product has been gained from that land" after spending millions on those missions.

47. Matson, "Letters," 288–89.
48. Matson and Fontana, *Friar Bringas*, 103.
49. Matson, "Letters," 289: "The subordination and subjection of the Indians to the Father."
50. Radding, *Wandering Peoples*, 66–99. Only Pimería Alta missions followed that system toward the end of the century.
51. Torre Curiel, "Decline and Renaissance," 51–73.
52. Kessel, *Friars*, chap. 8.
53. Matson, "Letters," 292. The enemy were the Apaches and others engaged in continuous raids.
54. Born in Aragón, he arrived at the Colegio de la Santa Cruz in 1770 and served as a missionary until his death in Aconchí in 1800. He served as president of the missions of Pimería Alta twice, from 1777 to 1783 and from 1791 to 1795. He was fluent in Opata and Pima and wrote sermons, catechisms, prayers, and a vocabulary in that language. I base the analysis of Barbastro's ideas on his 1793 report, published by Fr. Lino Gómez Canedo. See Gómez Canedo, *Sonora*.
55. Barbastro, "Deberes y obligaciones." He submitted his recommendations to his guardian at Colegio Santa Cruz for final approval.
56. See the chapter on martyrs in this work. They were Fr. Francisco Garcés, Fr. Juan Díaz, Fr. José Moreno, and Fr. Juan Barreneche.
57. Gómez Canedo, *Sonora*, 61.
58. Gómez Canedo, *Sonora*, 75–77.
59. Gómez Canedo, *Sonora*, 72. See Torre Curiel, "Decline and Renaissance," for an explanation of the missionary economic system. Barbastro believed that merchants who were not getting orders for merchandise from the missions were giving false information negatively affecting the relationship between missions and the secular authorities. Torre Curiel offers a broader explanation.
60. For the mission of San Pedro de Aconchí under the Jesuits, see Radding, *Wandering Peoples*, 75–88.
61. Radding, *Wandering Peoples*, 155–69.
62. Gómez Canedo, *Sonora*, 77–80.
63. Gómez Canedo, *Sonora*, 86–88.
64. Gómez Canedo, *Sonora*, 88–89. Barbastro provided the supplies and paid an Indian to be his helper.
65. Gómez Canedo, *Sonora*, 87–90. "Los indios tienen más talento que las demás gentes de esta Provincia: que es más fácil enseñarles a ellos que a los españoles: que han de ser más útiles, estando enseñados, que el resto de las gentes, y que ellos son los que podrán ordenar los Señores Obispos sin escrúpulo, y de los demás hallarán pocos" (87). "Prueba que los indios tienen talento igual, a lo menos, yo

quería decir mayor, que estas gentes de razón. . . . Que tienen más disposición para ser ordenados que la mayor parte que por acá se llaman españoles . . . que ordenados habían de ser utilísimos para la administración se deja ver tan claro que no necesita de probación" (90). He soft-pedaled this recommendation by stating that at first, Indians could serve as aides to elderly priests during a test period to allow the church to assess their performance.

66. Gómez Canedo, *Sonora*, 102.
67. Jiménez, *El Gran Norte*, 432–33; Stagg, *The First Bishop*, 41.
68. Stagg, *The First Bishop*, 42. He also advocated the allocation of land to the Indians for cultivation because "the Indians of these old missions have always preferred to cultivate their own wheat, maize and other crops. They find communal farming onerous and contrary to their interests, so it should be prohibited, leaving them to their natural freedom without the obligation to serve or work on a communal basis, as has been necessary in the new conversions."
69. Péron, *Le Mexique* (2005). Péron corroborates a definite decline in the Franciscan missions in the province of Jalisco from 1780 to 1800. She calls that period "the end of the illusion" (see pp. 223–38).
70. My survey is based on his letters in Spanish, as in Vicedo and Fernández-Largo, *Escritos* (hereafter cited as Serra, *Escritos*). Tibesar, *Writings of Junípero Serra*; Beebe and Senkewicz, *Junípero Serra*; Hackel, *The Worlds of Junípero Serra*.
71. Álvarez Icaza Longoria, *La secularización*.
72. Kino and the Jesuits had visited parts of Alta California not far from the mouth of the Colorado River. See Rex Galindo, "Grey Friars," 157–70.
73. "Nuestra peregrinación por una tierra desierta y solo poblada de infidelidad con innumerables gentiles" (Serra, *Escritos*, 1:167). See also Beebe and Senkewicz, *Junípero Serra*, 169; and Geiger, "Fray Junípero," 195–330.
74. Torre Curiel, "El Confesional," 150–87.
75. Serra, *Escritos*, 1:259–66.
76. Serra, *Escritos*, 2:19–36.
77. Benoist and Flores, *Documents* (1994).
78. In 1779 he wrote, "La conquista espiritual camina prósperamente, gracias a Dios, aunque con más lento paso del quisiéramos." His concern about his flock is often mixed with other themes in his reports to Viceroy Bucareli or his guardian at San Fernando.
79. Serra, *Escritos*, 2:156–63, 213–29.
80. Serra, *Escritos*, 2:189, 228–29.
81. Serra was suggesting a system similar to that adopted by the Franciscan missions in Sonora in the late 1760s. See Torre Curiel, "Decline and Renaissance."
82. Serra, *Escritos*, 3:178–81.

83. Serra, *Escritos*, 4:7–20.
84. Focher, *Itinerario*. This was the classic instruction book for missionaries since its publication in 1574.
85. Beebe and Senkewicz, *Junípero Serra*, 398–99.
86. For Pedro Fages, see Sánchez, "Pedro Fages," 281–94, and *Spanish Bluecoats*. Fages was present in the founding of San Diego in 1769 and traveled widely in California, helping to found San Francisco. His quarrels with Fr. Junípero Serra ended his early career in California. In 1774 he was posted to Sonora, and in 1781 he was sent to quell the revolt of the Yuma Indians that left four missionary martyrs. In 1782 he was appointed governor of the Californias, replacing Felipe de Neve. His service there lasted through 1791. He did not seem to have had any personal issues with Fr. Fermín Francisco de Lasuén, second president of the California missions after Serra's death. See also Priestley, *The Colorado River Campaign* (1913).
87. This behavior was reported independently by Fr. Luis Jayme in a letter to Guardian Fr. Rafael Verger, dated October 17, 1772. He very explicitly refers to the rape of Indian women by soldiers and Fages's studied personal indifference to this issue. See Geiger, *Letter of Luis Jayme*.
88. Serra, *Escritos*, 2:62–77. San Buenaventura would create a Christian enclave among the Indigenous population of the Santa Barbara Channel, an area heavily populated and not entirely safe for the missionaries. At that point Serra had already founded three missions—San Antonio de Padua, San Gabriel, and San Luis Obispo.
89. Beebe and Senkewicz, *Junípero Serra*, 227–44; Serra, *Escritos*, 2:82.
90. Beebe and Senkewicz, *Junípero Serra*, 281–85; Serra, *Escritos*, 3:68–70.
91. Font, *Diario Íntimo*, 181.
92. Serra, *Escritos*, 3:99–105.
93. *Reglamento e Instrucción* (1784). Also available in *Instrucciones y Reglamentos de Indias*.
94. Serra, *Escritos*, 5, 59–63, Letter to Teodoro de Croix, April 26, 1782.
95. Beebe and Senkewicz, *Junípero Serra*, 339–74. Neve was appointed commandant general of Provincias Internas in 1783 but died in 1784. See Beilharz, *Felipe de Neve*.
96. Confirmation is administered only to baptized persons seven years or older. For this incident, see Evans, "The Confirmation Controversy"; and Beebe and Senkewicz, *Junípero Serra*, 372–74.
97. Serra, *Escritos*, 5:44–47. In 1790 Fermín de Lasuén, president of the missions, reaffirmed the missionaries' right to administer confirmation. See Kenneally, *Writings*, 1:214.

98. Serra, *Escritos*, 5:59–63. *Doctrina* was a juridically incorrect nomenclature, as Serra tried to explain to him.
99. Serra, *Escritos*, 5:91–96.
100. Teodoro de Croix (1730–92) was a nephew of Viceroy Carlos Francisco de Croix, Marquis of Croix (1766–71). As a career soldier he was appointed commandant general of the internal provinces in 1776 and viceroy of Peru in 1783. His successor as commandant was Felipe de Neve.
101. Serra, *Escritos*, 4:114. Serra thought that missions would provide spiritual food and material goods better than the planned towns the Crown had in mind.
102. López Arguedas, "La formación del predicador," 9–33; Moreno Basurto and González Ramírez, *El humanismo de Fray Antonio Margil de Jesús*.
103. Conover, *Pious Imperialism*, 209.
104. Garcés, *Record of Travels*, 101. Garcés believed in the friendly disposition of the Indigenous and relied on his relatively successful personal experience with several tribes in Arizona who had welcomed him. He was wrong in believing in "the open arms" reception. He met his death at the hands of the Yuma Indians on July 19, 1781, but the above statement was written in 1777. The Indigenous groups used their friendship with the Spaniards as a shield in their feuds with other tribes. Their allegiance to the Spaniards was ephemeral.
105. Garcés, *Record of Travels*, December 13 [1775]. Narrative between December 9–23, 26–28 and January 3–August 27, 1776. He spent the best part of 1776 traveling on his own with the occasional aid of some Indians.
106. Garcés, *Record of Travels*, 89–102. He suggested where the presidios would be built, stressing the need to establish a commanding presidio at the Colorado and Gila Rivers that would oversee that of San Diego. This would ensure a continuous contact by either land or sea, the routes that would provide trade between Monterrey and New Mexico.
107. Matt. 13:47: "Again, the kingdom of heaven is like a dragnet that was cast into the sea and gathered fish of every kind" (NASB).
108. Such questions, he wrote, could be applied to many other people living in the world. That is why it was so relevant to him, a man well read in Christian theology. Font, *Diario Íntimo*, 120–25.
109. Montané Martí, *Fray Pedro Font*, 380–81, 392. See the translation of Font's diary by Bolton, *Anza's California Expeditions*.
110. Geiger, *Letter of Luis Jayme*, 41–48.
111. Font was not fond of the Indians, but he was moved once in a while. Such was the occasion on meeting a group of Indians in San Francisco Bay who gave him and Anza a warm welcome. As they appeared to be sad when their guests departed, Font confessed, "A mí me enterneció el ver aquella alegría con que

nos recibieron estos pobres indios" (Font, *Diario Íntimo*, 291; I was moved to tenderness at seeing the joy with which we were welcomed by those poor Indians).

112. Solís, "Diary of a Visit." The order to write the report was handed down by Fr Tomás Cortés, guardian of the Colegio de Propaganda Fide of Zacatecas. The report runs from November 15, 1767, through October 13, 1768. The situation of the missions in the northern frontier was dismal. Pimas, Seris, Yuta, Apaches, and Comanches were in open revolt and made constant incursions through these territories. Following the acquisition of Louisiana (1769), a reorganization of the presidios followed in 1772, with the suppression of many eastern Texas missions. Rubí was in favor of the extermination of all Apaches. See Bolton, *Texas*, 317, 321–24, 381–82.

113. Solís, "Diary of a Visit," 43. This mission was founded in 1717 by Fr. Antonio Margil de Jesús. In 1768 it had three hundred inhabitants of several nations.

114. Solís, "Diary of a Visit," 50, 51.

115. Weber, *Bárbaros*.

116. Fr. Alonso de Benavides had praised the inclination of some New Mexican Natives willing to be baptized and learn trades, but he warned about treacherous Picuris, for example. However, he noted a general lack of inclination to work in European occupations or work for Spanish civilians. His opinion resulted from his desire to attract support for the Franciscans. Missionaries could not pull the rug from under their own feet, and those most politically involved sorted out contradictory issues by mixing the sweet with the sour. Benavides, *Memorial*.

117. Crespí, *Diario y Descripción*, 232. While he referred to some Natives as "humildes y mansos" (meek and docile), he also noted the tendency to theft among others (268–69, 71). The Natives took objects that attracted them because they were true novelties and would probably be used for adornment or to barter.

118. Serra, *Diario de la expedición*, 173: "Su bello talle, deporte, afabilidad y alegría nos han enamorado a todos." "En fin, todos los gentiles me han robado el corazón" (178). This was written on the twenty-third day of his journey.

119. Serra, *Escritos*, vol. 5, letter to Fermín Francisco Lasuén, April 29, 1782.

120. Serra, *Escritos*, vol. 5, letter to Fr. Francisco Pangua, December 8, 1782.

121. Crespí, *Diario y Descripción*, 196. Crespí's journal describes the trek from Misión Santa María de los Ángeles to San Diego in 1767.

122. Crespí, *Diario y Descripción*, 198.

123. Serra, *Diario de la expedición*, 121. This diary was written in 1769 on his trip to establish the mission of Monterrey.

124. Crespí, *Diario y Descripción*, 204–6, 272, "Estrecho abrazo," "cariños y atenciones."

125. Serra, *Diario de la expedición*, 134.

126. Serra, *Diario de la expedición*, 120–31.

127. Keneally, *Writings*, 1:84.
128. Guest, *Fermín Francisco de Lasuén*, 207–17.
129. Guest, *Fermín Francisco de Lasuén*, 248.
130. Kenneally, *Writings*, 2:239.
131. Kenneally, *Writings*, 1:386–87.
132. Keneally, *Writings*, 1:82–85.

6. Martyrs

1. Mendieta, *Historia Eclesiástica Indiana*, 2:227.
2. Torquemada, *Tercera Parte*, 673: "La primera es, que al tormento recibido siga la muerte natural del cuerpo. . . . La segunda . . . que sea por la defensa de la Fe de Jesu-Christo. . . . La tercera, que el martirio sea voluntario; y esto enseña Santo Tomás . . . ¿Pues que estos Benditos Religiosos hayan muerto de esta manera, quien lo dudará?" This is Torquemada's own argument, not present in Mendieta, from whose work he borrowed extensively.
3. Rubial, "El mártir en el Japón," 129–60.
4. Cañeque, *Un imperio de mártires*, 13–61, and "Letting Yourself Be Skinned," 197–223.
5. Castillo Maldonado, "Prudencio y los mártires," 65–75; González Blanco, "Los santos mártires," 77–86; González Echegaray, "El culto a los santos," 271–83.
6. Most authors base their narratives on the writings of Saint Eulogius, a ninth-century churchman who was beheaded in 859. See also Coope, *The Martyrs of Córdoba*; Haines, *Christianity and Islam*; Sánchez Domingo, "La narración de la memoria," 571–92.
7. Gregory, *Salvation at Stake*, 250–314. During the short reign of Mary Tudor (1516–58), daughter of Henry VIII and Catherine of Aragon, Catholics took a vengeful turn against Protestants, turning them into victims of religious persecution and martyrdom. During Elizabeth I's reign (1558–1603), the order reversed, and Catholics became the target. Chauncy, *The History of the Sufferings*. This work is a translation of a 1539 Latin manuscript left by Dom Maurice Chauncey.
8. For a comparative study of martyrdom in early modern Europe, see Gregory, *Salvation at Stake*; Baldwin Smith, *Fools, Martyrs, Traitors*; Rodríguez G. de Ceballos, "El mártir, héroe cristiano," 83–99; and Rubial, *La Justicia de Dios*, 169–218.
9. Van Nierop, *Treason in the Northern Quarter*; Darby, *The Origins and Development of the Dutch Revolt*; Parker, *Spain and the Netherlands* and *The Dutch Revolt*. Of particular interest to Spain was the translation into Spanish of the history of the persecutions of Catholics in England. See Personio, *Relación de algunos martyrios*; Houston, *Elizabethan England*; and Dillon, *The Construction of Martyrdom*.

10. The religious darts between England and Spain continued with the publication of Ribadeneira, *Historia eclesiástica del cisma de Inglaterra*. See the recent translation, Ribadeneyra, *Ecclesiastical History*.
11. In her *Martyrdom and Memory*, Castells argues that spectacle is a crucial dimension of martyrology (7). In the New World there was only the audience of readers and the spectacle created by the pen of the writer.
12. Torre Curiel, "Santidad y martirio"; Reff, "'The Predicament of Culture,'" 63–90.
13. Torquemada, *Tercera Parte*, 673.
14. On the meaning of blood as a symbol of life beyond death, see Bynum, *Wonderful Blood*, 147, 187, 212–13. On martyrdom and the body of the martyrs, see also Freeman, *Holy Bones, Holy Dust*; Stylianou, "Martyrs' Blood"; Christofis, "The Notion of Martyrdom"; and Rubial, "Mártires y predicadores," 50–71.
15. Sempat Assadourian, *Zacatecas*; Carrillo Cazares, *El Debate sobre la Guerra Chichimeca*; Jiménez Núñez, *El Gran Norte de Mexico*.
16. Mecham, "The Martyrdom of Father Juan de Santa Maria," 308–21.
17. López Cogolludo, *Historia de Yucathan*, 543, 547–48; Chuchiak, "By Faith, Not Arms."
18. Torquemada, *Tercera Parte*, 392–93.
19. On the Spanish arguments for punishing the Chichimec incursions, see the following testimonials in Sempat Assadourian, *Zacatecas*: "Relaciones," testimonial of Pedro de Ahumada, 1562, 336–47, and of Juan Alonso Velázquez, 1583, 449–48; "Información" of Dr. Maldonado, 1561, 324–36, and of Pedro de Ahumada, 1562, 336–47; "Exposición del Dr. Orozco," 1580, 440–49; "Carta de Fray Luis Olid de Biedma a Su Majestad," 1584, 513–16.
20. Castro, *La rebelión*.
21. Castro, *La rebelión*, 124–25. For further readings on war and resistance, see Chance, *Conquest of the Sierra*; Jones, *Maya Resistance*; Schroeder, *Native Resistance*; Yetman, *Conflict in Colonial Sonora*; MacLeod, "Instruments for the Voiceless"; and Durán, *Un dios y un reino para los indios*.
22. The Mixtón War took place in 1540–42. See Altman, *Contesting Conquest*, and *The War for Mexico's West*.
23. Deeds, *Defiance*, 23.
24. Arlegui, *Crónica de la Provincia*, 174–86. This rebellion caused a lot of destruction and decimated the Tepehuán population. The numbers of deaths in the 1616 rebellion are, at best, estimates, but the net result of this and other rebellions was a decline of the number of Indigenous living in the mountains of the western Sierras. For a recent profile of Arlegui as a historian, see Orozco Hernández, "San Francisco de Zacatecas."
25. Deeds, *Defiance*, 31–38.

26. Espinosa, *The Pueblo Indian*, 18, 24.
27. For a sampler of different opinions on the cause of this revolt, see Weber, *What Caused the Pueblo Revolt*; Kessel, *Pueblos, Spaniards*; Knaut, *The Pueblo Revolt of 1680*; and Baldwin, *Intruders Within*. Ramón Gutiérrez detected the desire of martyrdom nurtured by the New Mexico missionaries and noted the brutal and mocking treatment meted to them. See Gutiérrez, *When Jesus Came*, 127–37.
28. The lower Gulf Coast—today, Tamaulipas—was a neglected settler and missionary area. An attempt at colonization in the 1740s was followed with weak and unsuccessful attempts to build missions in that area. See Osante, *Orígenes del Nuevo Santander*, "Estrategia colonizadora," 17–44, and "Presencia misional en Nuevo Santander," 107–35.
29. Gómez Canedo, *Primeras exploraciones*. The governor of Texas, Joseph de Azlor y Vito de Vera, made incursions into the land in 1721 and suggested the separation of Texas from Coahuila. Bolton, *Texas*.
30. Cunningham, "The Domingo Ramón Diary," 38–67.
31. Presidios were populated by militia and their families. The presidio soldiers were assumed to patrol frontier areas and defend the evolving frontier against Indian attacks. See Moorhead, *The Presidio*; Naylor and Polzer, *The Presidio and Militia*, vol. 2, part 1; and Schroeder, *Native Resistance*. For a general narrative of the history of the region, see Kessell, *Spain in the Southwest*.
32. Romero de Terreros, "The Destruction"; Simpson and Weddle, *The San Sabá Papers*; Wade, McWilliams, and Boyd, *Spanish Colonial Documents*.
33. Zepeda, Molina, and Granados y Gálvez, *La tragedia de la misión de San Sabá*, 37–48.
34. Cervantes Aguilar, *Fray Simón del Hierro*, 245, 317. No further information is furnished for this martyr.
35. I engage on the Franciscan experience only.
36. Gage, *The English-American*, 23. The same night, an attack by the islanders left three Jesuits dead and two wounded. A fourth one and a Dominican later died of their wounds. Gage remarked that the zeal of the friars cooled down very fast after the encounter.
37. He reported to be elated with the college of Querétaro because it was more rigorous than those of the Carthusians. In northern Mexico the possibilities of suffering martyrdom were "greater than those imagined by so many Franciscan saints." See Arricivita, *Apostolic Chronicle*, 537–38.
38. Arricivita, *Apostolic Chronicle*, 400. For the strict daily routine of the friars, see Espinosa, *Chronica Apostólica*, 52–53; and *Estatutos y Ordenaciones*. These rules were adopted by the Colegio de Propaganda Fide in Pachuca.
39. Mendieta, *Historia Eclesiástica Indiana*, 2:231–35; Muñoz, *Descripción*, 92.

40. Arlegui, *Crónica*, 11–13, 18. After they left there was no attempt at conversion until three Franciscan friars from the province of Michoacán returned to formalize a conventual foundation in 1558.
41. Rey, "Missionary Aspects."
42. Arlegui, *Crónica*, 23.
43. Walking long distances was part of the European mendicant tradition that was carried to the New World. Fr. Martín de Valencia, one of the founders of the Franciscan province of the Holy Gospel, traveled from Spain to Rome on foot. See Mendieta, *Historia Eclesiástica Indiana*, 2:134. Fr. Antonio Margil's trips to Guatemala and the Mexican north became a matter of hagiographical wonder. See Espinosa, *El Peregrino*.
44. One *legua* was roughly between 4.2 and 5.5 kilometers. These are approximate values given the erratic standards of measurements of the time. Chardon, "The Elusive Spanish League," 294–302.
45. Arlegui, *Crónica*, 215, 217.
46. Mendieta, *Historia Eclesiástica Indiana*, 2:248.
47. Arlegui, *Crónica*, 199–200, 201–10.
48. Giudicelli and Pierre Ragon, "Les martyrs," 3.
49. Arlegui, *Crónica*, 209–15; Mendieta, *Historia Eclesiástica Indiana*, 2:237. Mendieta sustained that the first Franciscan martyr was Fr. Juan Calero, while Arlegui claimed that honor for Bernardo Cossin.
50. Murillo Gallegos, "Las voces bajo el discurso," 35–55.
51. Arlegui, *Crónica*, 224.
52. See chapter 7 in this work on the end of life for the alternative presentation of death under normal circumstances.
53. Arlegui, *Crónica*, 212–13.
54. Arlegui, *Crónica*, 239.
55. Mendieta, *Historia Eclesiástica Indiana*, 2:244. Fr. Francisco Lorenzo, preacher among the Chichimecs of Nueva Galicia, had been told he would die among them. Thus, when in his last trip he heard that the rebels had attacked the town, he prepared himself to die. He told his companion, "It is time to win heaven. He knelt before the altar, lit some candles, and died there from a *macana* blow."
56. Torquemada, *Tercera Parte*, 620; Mendieta, *Historia Eclesiástica Indiana*, 2:242. Torquemada borrows line by line from Mendieta. The over two hundred Indians surrounding them changed their minds, which the writer attributed to the miraculous intercession of God. Unfortunately, Fr Francisco Lorenzo died a martyr some years later. Neither Mendieta nor Torquemada are precise with their chronology and give no dates.

57. Lizana, *Historia de Yucatán*, 121–22. In both instances the attack was deemed treacherous by the chronicler because the Spaniards were first received amicably and with expressions of joy. Fr. Juan Enríquez had gone to the interior of the peninsula, obeying the orders of his provincial, but had taken the precaution of making a final confession before leaving because he did not expect to return. Like others, he was concerned about the salvation of his soul, not death.
58. Gregory, *Salvation at Stake*, 97–138.
59. Franco, *Segunda parte*, 367–80.
60. Arlegui, *Crónica*, 66–67.
61. Ignacio de la Barrera y Bastida (1645–1709). He was consecrated as bishop of Durango in 1707.
62. Arlegui, *Crónica*, 66–67.
63. Arlegui, *Crónica*, 95–97. That was the case of Mission Santa Ana del Torreón in Nueva Vizcaya.
64. A similar tactic of wearing robes to escape Indian attacks is reported by Juan de Torquemada. A man searching for mines in the western post of Guaynamota wore a Franciscan robe. The Natives let him know that they were not fooled, but since they respected the habit, they would not bother him. Torquemada, *Tercera Parte*, 391.
65. A league is between 2.6 and 3 miles or 4.2 and 4.83 km. However, there are variations on account of changes throughout time.
66. Arlegui, *Crónica*, 202–7, 253. Arlegui notes that the Indians of that zone were interested in clothes, animals, and merchandise. A missionary in Atotonilco, a place northwest of Zacatecas, witnessed an "attack" of over two hundred Indians who did not touch him but took everything in his cell. The same friar was also attacked walking toward San Juan del Río. His two companions were hurt by arrows, but he persuaded the attackers to spare their lives. The Indians gave him a horse to reach town and returned his clothes and his breviary. The three survivors rode the horse and reached the closest town, where the Natives recovered. No date is given, but on narrating similar displays of charity by the Indigenous, Arlegui commented that such charity required a prayer to God to "save them from falling into such bloody and harsh hands because such demonic piety is not to be desired but to run away from them" (204).
67. Arlegui, *Crónica*, 255.
68. Arlegui, *Crónica*, 118–19, 189–90.
69. Arlegui, *Crónica*, 207.
70. Arlegui, *Crónica*, 255–56.
71. Espinosa, *The Pueblo Indian Revolt*; Liebman, *An Archeological History of Pueblo Resistance*; Gutiérrez, *When Jesus Came*; Knaut, *The Pueblo Revolt of 1680*; Baldwin,

Intruders Within; Kessell, *Pueblos, Spaniards*. For a documentary history of the 1680 revolt, see Hackett, *Revolt of the Pueblo Indians*; and Kessell et al., *That Disturbances Cease*.

72. Espinosa, *The Pueblo Indian Revolt*, 194.
73. Espinosa, *The Pueblo Indian Revolt*, 195.
74. Espinosa, *The Pueblo Indian Revolt*, 234.
75. Espinosa, *The Pueblo Indian Revolt*, 224–25.
76. Espinosa, *The Pueblo Indian Revolt*, 200, 229. Casañas was the author of a report on the Indians of eastern Texas. See "Relación sobre los indios del este de Texas, por Fray Francisco Casañas (1691)," in Gómez Canedo, *Primeras exploraciones*, 77–101.
77. Espinosa, *The Pueblo Indian Revolt*, 223, 231–32.
78. Espinosa, *The Pueblo Indian Revolt*, 219–23.
79. Roldán-Figueroa, *The Martyrs of Japan*.
80. Sariñana y Cuenca, *Oración fúnebre*.
81. Sariñana, *Oración fúnebre*, 22.
82. Sariñana, *Oración fúnebre*, 23.
83. Bringas de Manzaneda y Encinas, *Sermón*. The sermon took many years to be printed. Bringas de Manzaneda was also the author of a report to the king on the status of the Gila River tribes and the missions in that area. See Matson and Fontana, *Friar Bringas Reports* (a second edition of this work was issued in 2017). Bringas was politically conservative and supported the royalist cause during the years of "rebellion" of the Mexicans against the Spanish Crown. See Cuellar, "Imposed Silence."
84. See Phil. 1:20, 21 and 1:28, 29 (NKJV).
85. He was using information culled from Fr. Antonio Barbastro, who wrote notes on the history of the Sonoran missions.
86. Arricivita, *Apostolic Chronicle*. For information on Garcés and the missions, see pp. 450–510. For information on other martyrs of the Tiburón Island, San Diego mission, and Colorado River missions, see pp. 504–47.
87. Garcés, *Diario de exploraciones*.
88. Of course, Spain had already accomplished that status, since its imperial territory was much larger than that of ancient Rome, but the "classic" orientation of clergymen's studies made the comparison imperative.
89. See Bringas de Manzaneda y Encinas, *Sermón*, 76. The call of the rivers possibly referred to Garcés's travels along the Colorado River and some of the waterways of the Southwest.
90. Sicardo, *Christiandad del Japón*; Morales, "De la utopía a la locura," 57–83.
91. González de la Puente, *Primera parte*, 276–300; Franco, *Segunda parte*, 263, 278–313, 399–415.

92. Franco, *Segunda parte*, 380.
93. Fernández, *Historia y Anales*, book 8, part 6, pp. 249–250v.
94. Medina, *Vida, Martyrio y Beatificación*; Ribadeneyra, *Historia de las Islas del Archipelago*; *San Felipe de Jesús Protomártir*; Santa María, *Chronica*; Conover, *Pious Imperialism*; Durán, "La retórica del martirio," 77–107; Kawata, "Historia del culto a San Felipe de Jesús," 1–17.
95. Sicardo, *Christiandad del Japón*, 239–46. Sicardo wrote his work following strict lines of historical corroboration, including letters of the friars and reports from the Manila province. See Rubial, "El Mártir colonial" and "El mártir en el Japón."
96. It precedes the *Libro Quinto*, the second part of his *Historia Eclesiástica*.
97. *Macanas* were long and thick wood sticks with a row of sharp stones in one edge. They were used to kill by strong blows to the head of the enemy.
98. Propaganda Fide also missionized among the Catholic flock, since its mission was inclusive and applicable to established Catholics as well as those new to the faith.
99. Espinosa, *Chronica Apostólica*, 585–86.
100. Arlegui, *Crónica*, 195–97.
101. Arricivita, *Apostolic Chronicle*, 528–29.
102. Arricivita, *Apostolic Chronicle*, 334.
103. Arricivita, *Apostolic Chronicle*, 536–39.
104. Arricivita, *Apostolic Chronicle*, 547–52.
105. Arricivita, *Apostolic Chronicle*, 545.
106. Spears, *Early Churches of Mexico*.
107. These metaphors have been culled from several biographies and chronicles.
108. The literature on the incorruptible flesh of martyrs and Christian beliefs on the relation of flesh and spirit is extensive, especially for the early and late medieval periods. There are fewer titles for the 1500–1800 period. In relation to martyrs, see Bynum, *The Resurrection of the Body*; and Freeman, *Holy Bones, Holy Dust*.
109. Arlegui, *Crónica*, 221–22, 227, 235.
110. Arlegui, *Crónica*, 251–52.
111. Arlegui, *Crónica*, 228.
112. Geiger, *Letter of Luis Jayme*, 49.
113. Arlegui, *Crónica* 229.

7. Death

Epigraph: Espinosa, *El Cherubin*, 165.
1. Erasmus, "Preparing for Death"; Sieruta, "The Art of Dying."
2. Basalenque, *Historia*, 2:285.
3. Rubial, "Imprenta, criollismo y santidad" and "Las crónicas religiosas."

4. For the sake of the continuity of the narrative in this chapter, I present the historical information on the death of friars first, followed by the sermons that remembered them, although in terms of *writing*, the sermon came first and the chronicle or biography appeared many years later.
5. Dávila Padilla, *Historia*, 483. See also 303, 327, 548, 648.
6. Pinamonti, *Breves Meditaciones* (1789). There are editions by other printers and in Puebla for the years 1777, 1792, 1793, and 1804.
7. Ledesma, *Despertador*.
8. Rylands, Bullen, and Compton Price, *Ars Moriendi*. As examples of works on the art of dying, see Bellarmino, *Arte de bien morir*; Gracián de la Madre de Dios, *Arte de Bien Morir*; Salazar, *Arte de Ayudar*; Venegas, *Agonía*; Yebra, *Libro*; Arbiol, *Visita de enfermos*; Sánchez, *Rosario*; Salzedo y Azcona, *Muerte prevenida*; and López de Mariscal and Rodríguez Domínguez, *Arte de bien morir*.
9. For the conceptualization of death, see Eire, *From Madrid to Purgatory*; Martínez Gil, *Muerte y Sociedad*; Rodríguez Álvarez, *Usos y costumbres*; Von Wobeser and Vila, *Muerte y Vida*; Harries, *The Passion in Art*; Landsberg, *L'art en croix*; and Binski, *Medieval Death*.
10. Baz Sánchez, "'Por el feliz tránsito,'" 340–407.
11. Bellarmino, *Arte de Bien Morir*. Bellarmino reviewed the situation of those who did not die in their beds, such as criminals in jail, sailors at sea, and soldiers on the battlefield. He insisted on the need to be prepared for death at all times.
12. Salazar, *Arte de Ayudar*; Alvarado, *Arte de Bien Morir*.
13. Franco, *Segunda parte*.
14. Historians of art call this technique "painting with words." See Fernández Salvador, "Palabras que pintan," 208–39.
15. The bibliography on death is extensive. Some works deal with the rituals of death; others with the legal implications, such as wills; and yet others with the spiritual and intellectual culture of death in a given period. See the works of Philippe Aries and Michel Vovelle, the founders of the studies on death. Vovelle, *Mourir autrefois* and *La mort*; Aries, *Western Attitudes*; Le Goffe, *The Birth*; Pinar, *Actitudes religiosas*; Zárate, *Los nobles*; González Lopo, "El ritual de la muerte"; Lomnitz, *Death*; Rubial, "La muerte"; Will de Chaparro and Achim, *Death and Dying*; Lavrin, "Los espacios de la muerte"; Cruz Ocaña and Magaña Ochoa, "Estudios sobre la muerte"; Terán Elizondo, Chávez Ríos, and Fernández Montemayor, *In hoc túmulo*.
16. Ps. 31, "In thee, O Lord, do I put my trust" (KJV). See also Grijalva, *Crónica*, 18–19, 202, 207–9, 213–213v.
17. Grijalva, *Crónica*, 189v–190. The chronicler translated his speech into Spanish.
18. Sotomayor Sandoval, "La cofradía," 11–25.

19. Dávila Padilla, *Historia*, 388–89.
20. González de la Puente, *Primera parte*.
21. González de la Puente, *Primera Parte*, 498–509.
22. The penitential psalms are Psalms 6, 32, 38, 51, 102, 130, and 143. They express grief and repentance.
23. Villarubia wanted to die under his prelate's order and contemplating the promised land. The biblical sources are quite clear: Moses and Aaron died without entering the promised land because they had not acknowledged God's power for bringing water to Israel. Unlike Moses and Aaron, Villarubia expected to be received in the celestial promised land. See Exod. 17; Num. 20:10 and 20:23–29; and Deut. 34:4–5 (NKJV).
24. Bernard of Clairvaux (1090–1153) is reputed to have written sacred poetry mostly dedicated to Jesus, parts of which were translated into hymns commonly performed in the services of friaries and nunneries.
25. Basalenque, *Historia*, 2:270–84.
26. The Jesuits did not expect to participate in any ritual of death during their visit. The mistake was made out of not ignorance but nervousness.
27. On the language of the bells, see Loreto, "Los barrocos sonidos."
28. Fr. Antonio Margil de Jesus (1657–1726) was born in Mallorca. He began his task as a missionary for Catholics in the cities of Querétaro and Mexico City in 1683. In April 1684 he was sent to missionize in Yucatán and Guatemala via Veracruz. After serving in Guatemala for fourteen years, Margil was recalled as guardian to the Colegio de la Santa Cruz de Propaganda Fide in Querétaro in 1696, arriving in April 1697. In 1701 he was again sent to Guatemala to found a college in that city, and in 1707 he was sent to found another one in Zacatecas that would take charge of missionary activity in Nayarit. He was later deployed to New Leon, Coahuila, and Texas in 1713, returning to Zacatecas in 1721. In 1725 Fr. Antonio was in Guadalajara and its environs and in Michoacán carrying out an urban mission.
29. A detailed account of Margil's last mission is available in Cervantes Aguilar, *Fray Simón del Hierro*, 292–301.
30. Espinosa, *El peregrino*, 301–17. *Nunc dimittis* is based on Luke 2:29–32.
31. Espinosa, *El peregrino*, 318.
32. Espinosa, *El peregrino*, 320.
33. Espinosa, *El peregrino*, 321–23.
34. Espinosa, *El peregrino*, 28. The first miracle caused by a string that had touched Margil's body one year before it was registered on May 28, 1728 (322–23).
35. Espinosa, *El peregrino*, 327–28.
36. Espinosa, *El peregrino*, 317–30.

37. "These honors are not for me, a miserable wicked man; they are for the dignity of the apostolic ministry and for Jesus Christ . . . whose person I represent in this highest employment of a missionary" (quoted in Navarro, *Oración fúnebre*, 25).
38. Beebe and Senkewicz, *Junípero Serra*. See also Vicedo and Fernández-Largo, *Escritos*; Geiger, *The Life and Times*.
39. Palou, *Relación histórica*.
40. The letters were "forgotten" in the presidio in Monterrey and were not received on time by their addressees. As soon as they learned of Serra's bad health, they began their journey, but they missed his death. Fr. Buenaventura Sitjar from San Antonio arrived on time for his burial, and Fr. Antonio Paterna, from San Luis, arrived for the September 4 funeral Mass.
41. This reference shows a spiritual link among the missionaries and the fact that Margil had composed now lost vocal music for his missionary activities. Serra suffered *dolor de pecho* (chest pain) for many years.
42. "Therefore, so great Sacrament." This is the last line of another sacred hymn, the *Pange lingua*, the hymn of the glorious body dating back to the thirteenth century and attributed to Saint Thomas Aquinas. It was sung during the veneration and benediction of the holy sacrament.
43. His fear might have been ignited by the belief in the presence of the devil's minions in his room, a widely held belief at the time. The commendation of the soul is a prayer with several variants requesting God's mercy and commending the soul to its creator. It was intoned by the priest, but the moribund (and others) could join it. See http://www.ibreviary.com/m2/preghiere.php?tipo=Rito&id=371#poc.
44. Palou indulged in a great deal of detail in his hour-by-hour account of Serra's death. The purpose was consonant with the principles of the *ars moriendi*. He felt that those non-Indians present represented the faith as established and not as recently acquired. In his eyes, this probably added weight and value to the ceremonies.
45. Palou, *Relación histórica*, 284.
46. Dávila Padilla, *Historia*, 554.
47. Tello, *Libro Segundo*, 625, 851–52.
48. Grijalva, *Crónica*, 106–106v. For his biography, see pp. 98–107v. At this time, Augustinians evangelized in the northeast of the capital city and the Huasteca coastal area facing the Gulf of Mexico.
49. Burgoa, *Palestra Historial*, 448–49.
50. Burgoa, *Palestra Historial*, 337–401.
51. Burgoa, *Palestra Historial*, 396–97.

52. Witschorik, *Preaching Power*; Núñez Beltrán, *La oratoria*; Martínez de Sánchez, *Oralidad y escritura*; Herrejón Peredo, *Del sermón*.
53. Bitulli, "Los mocos del predicador"; D. León y Moya, *Aforismos*; Barcia y Zambrano, *Despertador Christiano*.
54. On the art of writing sermons, see Granada, *Los seis libros*; and Estrada Gijón, *Arte de predicar*.
55. There is an abundance of historical and literary studies on sermons. See, as examples, Medina, *La imprenta*; Ramírez Leyva, *Cartas pastorales*; Chinchilla Pawling, "Sobre la retórica"; Godinas, "Oratoria sagrada"; López de Mariscal and Dyer, *El sermón novohispano*; Reed, *Sermons, Preaching*; and Zaragoza, "La oratoria sagrada." For an acerbic critique of sacred oratory, see Rivera, *Principios*. Rivera has partial reproductions of the texts of many sermons.
56. See, as an example, "Libro de pláticas y sermones de Fr. Juan José Sáenz Gumiel," Papeles del convento de Propaganda Fide de la Santa Cruz de Querétaro, H, cuaderno 7, Archivo Histórico de la Provincia Franciscana de San Pedro y San Pablo, Michoacán, Mexico.
57. Herrejón Peredo, *Del sermón al discurso cívico*, 17; Herrejón Pereda, "Oratoria en Nueva España." The number of sermons available has increased by now due to additional research.
58. Cortés Ortiz, "Sermones impresos." This work does not attempt to provide the total number of sermons printed in New Spain; rather, it analyzes the themes and authors. See her "Estadísticas finales" (81, 83). Franciscans led in numbers of authored sermons with 20 percent of the total, followed closely by the Dominicans with nearly 18 percent. Juan de Ávila, OFM (1499–1569), was the most cited and reprinted preacher, with twelve printed sermons. He has been declared doctor of the Catholic Church.
59. Bertrán, *Tomo Segundo*, 322–25.
60. Guadiz, *Sermón fúnebre predicado*. The body of the sermon is dedicated to an emblematic analysis of the meaning of letters in several words associated with death and is a perfect example of baroque literary excesses.
61. Lavrin, "La familia en un contexto religioso."
62. Pazos, *Sermón fúnebre*. This sermon was published by a benefactor.
63. The names of the dead brothers preceded the tables of the chapter, thus honoring their memory.
64. Sariñana y Cuenca, *Sermón*.
65. Molina, *Ejercicios espirituales*. Molina was a bestseller. He was translated into English and French and remained a beacon of spirituality throughout the seventeenth century. He followed the school of interior spirituality and meditation

dating back to Luis de Granada and advanced by the Company of Jesus. See also De la Puente, *Meditaciones espirituales*.

66. Maravall, *La cultura del barroco*.
67. Velasco y Arellano, *Tierno recuerdo*; Alcántara, *Memoria de Josías*; Navarro, *Oración fúnebre*. Joseph Luis de Velasco also published a series of funeral poems penned by other friars.
68. López Aguado, *Vozes, que hicieron eco*.
69. Psalm 68 is also known as 67. López Aguado was using 67:34 (Biblia Sacra Vulgata): "Qui ascendit super caelum caeli ad orientem ecce dabit voci suae vocem virtutis?" (Who mounts on the heavens, the immemorial heavens, and utters his word in a voice of thunder?).
70. In Guatemala, López Aguado states, his interpreters left him alone many times, and yet he communicated with some of the mountain people, although how he preached and how the Indians understood him only God knew. Margil's own brothers must have been gathering information on his life before he died, and the first venue for their diffusion were these early sermons.
71. "Esta suavidad se debe dar a conocer en el fervor, dulzura y sabiduría con que ha de persuadir a todos." "No se negaba a ninguno, como hombre a quien destino el cielo para remedio de todos." See López Aguado, *Vozes, que hicieron eco*, 24, 28.
72. Alcántara, *Memoria de Josías*. The cost of printing was covered by Captain Gaspar García del Rivero, member of the Real Tribunal del Consulado of New Spain.
73. See 2 Chron. 35:20–27 (NIV); Kings 23:25 (NIV); and Jer. 20:10 (NKJV): "Weep not for the dead, nor bemoan for him but weep sore for him that goes away, for he shall return no more, nor see his native country."
74. In his sermon he acknowledged two previous sermons in America, assumed to be New Spain, and two in Valencia.
75. *Qui sequitur justititiam et misericordiam inveniet vitam et justitiam et gloriam.*
76. The Via Sacra is a penitential exercise that imitates the steps of Christ as he walked to the cross and his crucifixion.
77. Pardo, *Doble llanto de una madre*. The sermon was preached on November 10, 1759. Pardo was the prior of the convent of Santa María de Gracia in Valladolid.
78. *Fili, in mortuum produc lacrimas, et quasi dira passus incipe plorare.* The following verse, "then bury your body with due ceremony and do not fail to honor the grave" (Biblia Católica Online), conveys the intention of the ceremonial pomp. See also García, *Sermones Panegíricos*, 430.
79. Vargas Lugo, "Dos piras funerarias barrocas"; Francisco de la Maza, *Las piras funerarias*.
80. Bazarte and Malvido, "Los túmulos funerarios."
81. *Descripción y prospecto de la pira*.

82. There were sonnets, *octavas, décimas quintillas,* and *liras.* None of the compositions is signed. One was in Latin; the rest in Spanish. Unfortunately, there is no description of the *túmulo* itself, only its decoration. Having four tiers, it must have been a large monument.
83. Ximenez de Arellano, *Tiernos Recuerdos.* The printing of the sermon was paid for by his brother, who was a member of the *audiencia* and administrator of the mercury monopoly in the viceroyalty. The theme for the sermon was taken from 2 Macc. 4:37, recording the sadness felt by King Antiochus upon the death of Onias III, an honorable and upright high priest.
84. Ximenez de Arellano, *Tiernos recuerdos,* 2. "Cuando hay amor hay sentimientos." "Sean tus ojos fuentes de lágrimas . . . que a todos sea aparente lo fino de tu amor."
85. For the problems faced by the Indigenous nuns, the Franciscan order, and viceregal authorities, see Lavrin, *Brides of Christ,* 244–74; Díaz, *Indigenous Writings.*
86. Bringas de Manzaneda y Encinas, *Sermón.*

BIBLIOGRAPHY

Archives

Biblioteca Digital Hispánica. Biblioteca Nacional de España, Madrid, Spain.
Fondo Franciscano. Biblioteca Nacional de México, Mexico City.
Genaro García Collection. Benson Library. University of Texas at Austin.
Papeles del Convento de Propaganda Fide de la Santa Cruz de Querétaro, H, cuaderno 7. Archivo Histórico de la Provincia Franciscana de San Pedro y San Pablo, Michoacán, Mexico.
Ramo Inquisición. Archivo General de la Nación, Mexico City.

Published Works

Abundis, Jaime. "The San Fernando College's Sierra Gorda Missions." *Voices of México* (2018): 78–84.
Acosta Africano, Christoval. *Tratado en Contra y Pro de la Vida solitaria.* Venetia: Giacomo Cornessi, 1592.
Actas del Simposium. *La Orden de San Jerónimo y sus monasterios.* 2 vols. San Lorenzo del Escorial, 1999.
Acuña, René. "Actas capitulares de la Provincia de Santiago de México, 1547." *Nova Tellus* 16, no. 1 (1998): 151–84; *Viator* 40, no. 2 (2009): 221–53.
Aguirre Beltrán, Gonzalo. *Medicina y magia. El proceso de aculturación en la estructura colonial.* Mexico: Instituto Nacional Indigenista, 1963.
Alberro, Solange. *Del gachupín al criollo, O de cómo los españoles de Mexico dejaron de serlo.* Mexico: Colegio de Mexico, 1992.
———. *Inquisición y sociedad en Mexico, 1571–1700.* Mexico: Fondo de Cultura Económica, 1998.
Alcántara, Diego de. *Memoria de Josías: Renovada en las honras que el Colegio de la Santa Cruz de Querétaro de misioneros apostólicos hizo a su V. Padre Fr. Antonio Margil de Jesús [. . .].* Mexico: Joseph Bernardo de Hogal, 1727.

Alejandre, Juan Antonio. *El veneno de Dios. La Inquisición de Sevilla ante el delito de solicitación en confesión*. Madrid: Siglo XXI de España, 1994.

Altman, Ida. *Contesting Conquest: Indigenous Perspectives on the Spanish Occupation of Nueva Galicia, 1524–1545*. University Park: Pennsylvania State University Press, 2017.

———. *The War for Mexico's West: Indians and Spaniards in New Galicia, 1524–1540*. Albuquerque: University of New Mexico Press, 2010.

Alvalate, Joaquín de. *Doctrina Christiana, Regular y Mística del Frayle Menor*. 3rd ed. Alcalá: Imprenta de la Real Universidad, 1794.

Alvarado, Antonio de. *Arte de Bien Morir y Guía del camino de la muerte*. Valladolid: Francisco Fernández de Córdoba, 1611.

Álvarez del Palacio, Eduardo. "La consideración del cuerpo en la educación humanista. Las actividades físico-lúdicas como medio de transmisión de valores en la literatura pedagógica del siglo XVI." *Revista Española de Educación Física y Deportes* 10 (January–March 2009): 41–60.

Álvarez Icaza Longoria, María Teresa. *La secularización de doctrinas y misiones en el arzobispado de Mexico, 1749–1789*. Mexico: UNAM, 2015.

Álvarez Santaló, León Carlos, and Carmen Griñán, eds. *Mentalidad e ideología en el Antiguo Régimen*. 2 vols. Murcia: Universidad de Murcia, 1993.

Andrés Martin, Melquiades. "La espiritualidad franciscana en España en tiempos de las observancias (1380–1517)." *Studia Histórica: Historia Moderna* 6 (1988): 465–79.

Anonymous. *Breve resumen de la vida y martirio del ínclito mexicano y proto mártir del Japón, el beato Felipe de Jesús*. Mexico: Oficina Madrileña, 1802.

———. *Doctrina cristiana . . . publicada en Mexico por mandamiento del reverendísimo señor D. Fr. Juan de Zumárraga*. México: Juan Pablos, 1546.

———. *In Memoriam. El Illmo. Y Rmo. Sr. Mtro. Don Fr Antonio de S. Miguel, 33° Obispo de Michoacán. En el 1er Centenario de su Muerte, 1804–1904*. Valladolid: J. I. Guerrero y Cía., 1804.

———. *Reglas de la buena crianza civil y christiana, utilísimas para todos y singularmente para los que cuydan de la educación de los niños*. Barcelona: Imprenta de Eulalia Piferrer, Viuda, 1781.

Anunciación, Domingo de la. *Doctrina Christiana . . . en lengua Castellana y Mexicana*. Mexico: Pedro Ocharte, 1565.

Anunciación, Juan de la. *Avisos religiosos que a los descalzos de nuestra Señora del Carmen escribe en carta pastoral su general*. Madrid, 1697.

Arbiol, Antonio. *Visita de enfermos y ejercicio santo de ayudar a bien morir*. 4th ed. Zaragoza: Pedro Carreras, 1722.

———. *Vocación eclesiástica examinada con las divinas escrituras, sagrados concilios, santos padres y bulas apostólicas*. Zaragoza: Pedro Carreras, 1716.

Ardanaz, Naiara. "Iconografía Familiar en la Edad Moderna." In *Padres e Hijos en España y el Mundo Hispánico. Siglos XVI y XVII*, edited by Jesús M. Usunáriz y Rocío García Bourrellier, 159–83. Madrid: Visor Libros, 2008.

Aries, Philippe. *Centuries of Childhood: A Social History of Family Life*. New York: Vintage Books, 1962.

———. *Western Attitudes toward Death: From the Middle Ages to the Present*. Baltimore: Johns Hopkins University Press, 1974.

Aries, Philippe, and Georges Duby, eds. *A History of Private Life*. Vol. 3. Cambridge MA: Harvard University Press, 1989.

Arlegui, Joseph de. *Crónica de la provincia de N.S.P.S Francisco de Zacatecas*. 1737. Reprint, Mexico: Cumplido, 1851.

Armstrong-Partida, Michelle. "Priestly Marriage: The Tradition of Clerical Concubinage in the Spanish Church." *Viator* 40, no. 2 (2009): 221–53.

Arricivita, Juan Domingo. *Apostolic Chronicle of Juan Domingo Arricivita: The Franciscan Mission Frontier in the Eighteenth Century in Arizona, Texas, and the Californias*. Translated and edited by George P. Hammond and Agapito Rey. Revised and indexed by Vivian C. Fisher. 2 vols. Berkeley: University of California Press, 1996. Originally published as *Chronica seráfica y apostólica del Colegio de Propaganda Fide de la Santa Cruz de Querétaro* (Mexico: Felipe de Zúñiga y Ontiveros, 1792).

Augustine of Hippo. *The Monastic Rules*. Hyde Park NY: New City Press, 2004.

Ávila, Juan de. *Pureza emblemática*. Mexico: María de Benavides, 1668.

Avilés, Francisco de. *Regla de San Agustín y Constituciones de su Religión, Compendiadas y Traducidas del Latín en Castellano*. Madrid: Juan Sanz, 1719.

Ayer, Mrs. Edward E., trans. and ed. *The Memorial of Fray Alonso de Benavides, 1630*. Chicago, 1916. Reprint, Alburquerque: Horn and Wallace, 1965.

Azpilcueta Navarro, Martin de. *Manual de confesores y penitentes*. Valladolid: Francisco Fernández de Córdova, 1560.

Baldwin, Louis. *Intruders Within: Pueblo Resistance to Spanish Rule and the Revolt of 1680*. New York: Franklyn Watts, 1995.

Baldwin Smith, Lacey. *Fools, Martyrs, Traitors*. Easton IL: Northwestern University Press, 1999.

Baranda, Nieves. "La literatura del didactismo." *Criticón* 58 (1993): 25–34.

Barbado de la Torre y Angulo, Manuel. *Compendio Histórico, Lego-Seraphico*. Madrid: Imprenta Joseph González, 1745.

Barbastro, Francisco Antonio. "Deberes y obligaciones temporales de los misioneros en el Norte de Nueva España." May 6, 1780. MS G227, Benson Library, University of Texas at Austin.

Barcia y Zambrano, Joseph de. *Despertador Christiano de sermones doctrinales sobre particulares asuntos*. Cádiz: Christoval de Requena, 1693.

Barnaby, Thomas A. *Teodoro de Croix and the Northern Frontier of New Spain, 1776–1783*. Norman: University of Oklahoma Press, 1968.

Barrio Moya, José Luis. "La librería de Don Antonio Álvarez de Castro, presidente de la Audiencia de Guadalajara (México) durante el reinado de Carlos II." *Anuario de Historia del Derecho Español* 60 (1990): 489–96.

Bartolomé Martínez, Bernabé. "Educación y formación intelectual de Palafox." In *Palafox: Iglesia, cultura y Estado en el siglo XVII*, edited and published by Congreso Internacional IV Centenario del Nacimiento de Don Juan de Palafox y Mendoza, 83–91. Navarra: University of Navarra Press, 2000.

Basalenque, Diego de. *Historia de la Provincia de San Nicolás Tolentino de Michoacán*. 1673. México: Edición de la "Voz de México," 1886.

Bataillon, Marcel. *Erasmo y el erasmismo*. Barcelona: Crítica, 2000.

———. *Erasmo y España*. Madrid: Fondo de Cultura Económica, 1983.

Bazarte, Alicia, and Elsa Malvido. "Los túmulos funerarios y su función social en Nueva España. La cera uno de sus elementos básicos." In *Espacios de mestizaje Cultural: Anuario Conmemorativo del V Centenarios de la llegada de España a America*, 3 vols., 67–88. Mexico: Universidad Autónoma Metropolitana, Unidad Azcapotzalco, 1991.

Baz Sánchez, Sara Gabriela. "'Por el feliz tránsito de aquel moribundo.' Tradición y continuidad en las preparaciones para la muerte en el ámbito de Nueva España, siglos XVI–XVIII." PhD diss., Colegio de Mexico, 2015.

Beebe, Rose Marie, and Robert M. Senkewicz. *Junípero Serra: California, Indians, and the Transformation of a Missionary*. Norman: University of Oklahoma Press, Academy of Franciscan History, 2015.

———. "Uncertainty on the Mission Frontier: Missionary Recruitment and Institutional Stability in Alta California in the 1790s." In *Francis in America: Essays on the Franciscan Family in North and South America*, edited by John Frederick Schwaller, 295–322. Washington DC: Academy of American Franciscan History, 2008.

Beilharz, Edwin A. *Felipe de Neve, First Governor of California*. Vol. 49. San Francisco: California Historical Society, 1971.

Bellarmino, Robert. *Arte de bien morir compuesto por el eminentísimo Cardenal Roberto Bellarmino*. Madrid: Pedro García Sodruz, 1650.

Benavides, Alonso de. *Memorial que Fray Juan de Santander de la Orden de san Francisco, Comisario General de Indias, presenta a la Majestad católica del rey don Felipe Cuarto, nuestro Señor, hecho por el padre Fray Alonso de Benavides, Comisario del Santo Oficio, y Custodio que ha sido de las Provincias y conversiones del Nuevo México*. Madrid: Imprenta Real, 1630.

Beneyto, Juan. "Burocracia y derecho público: la conciencia y los medios del estado en la España moderna." *Revista de Estudios Políticos* 95 (September/October 1957): 15–38.

Benoist, Howard, and Maria Eva Flores, eds. "Guidelines for a Texas Mission: Instructions for the Missionary of Mission Concepción in San Antonio." In *Documents Relating to the Old Spanish Missions of Texas*, vol. 1. San Antonio: Our Lady of the Lake University, 1994.

Berco, Cristian. "Social Control and Its Limits: Sodomy, Local Sexual Economies, and Inquisitors during Spain's Golden Age." *Sixteenth-Century Journal* 36, no. 2 (2005): 31–358.

Bergamo, Ilarione da. *Daily Life in Colonial Mexico: The Journey of Friar Ilarione da Bergamo, 1761–1768*. Translated by William J. Orr. Edited by Robert Ryal Miller and William J. Orr. Norman: University of Oklahoma Press, 2000.

Bernabéu Albert, Salvador. "Las Californias en la Historiografía española (1940–1989)." *Revista de Indias* 49, no. 187 (1989): 817–27.

———, ed. *Reglamento para el gobierno de la provincia de Californias*. Madrid and La Paz: Doce calles and Ayuntamiento de La Paz, 1994.

Bertrán, San Luis. *Tomo Segundo de las de las obras y sermones que predicó y dejó escritos el glorioso padre y apostólico varón san Luis Bertrán de la Sagrada orden del Predicadores*. Valencia: Imprenta de Jayme de Bordazar, 1690.

Biempica, Salvador. *La sencillez hermanada con la sabiduría. Oración panegírica... en la beatificación de B. Sebastián de Aparicio*. Mexico: Felipe de Zúñiga y Ontiveros, 1791.

Binski, Paul. *Medieval Death: Ritual and Representation*. Ithaca NY: Cornell University Press, 1996.

Birley, Robert. *The Refashioning of Catholicism, 1450–1700*. Washington DC: Catholic University of America Press, 1999.

Bitulli, Juan. "Los mocos del predicador: Cuerpo, gestualidad y auto-control en el púlpito barroco." *ZAMA* 6 (2014): 167–82.

Bizzarri, Hugo O. "Sermones y espejos de príncipes castellanos." *Anuario de Estudios Medievales* 42, no. 1 (January–June 2012): 163–81.

Blanco, Emilio, ed. *Antonio de Guevara. Obras Completas*. 3 vols. Madrid: Turner, 1994.

Bolton, Herbert Eugene. *Texas in the Middle Eighteenth Century: Studies in Spanish Colonial History and Administration*. Berkeley: University of California Press, 1915.

Bolufer, Mónica. "'Ciencia del mundo.' Concepto y prácticas de civilidad en la España del siglo XVIII." *Cheiron: materiali e instrumenti di aggiornamento storiografico*, no. 2 (2002): 143–85.

———. "'Hombres de Bien': Modelos de masculinidad y expectativas femeninas entre la ficción y la realidad." *Cuadernos de Ilustración y Romanticismo* 15 (2007): 7–31.

Bonilla y San Martín, Adolfo. *Erasmo en España*. New York, 1907.

Borda, Andrés de. *Práctica de confesores de monjas*. Mexico: Francisco de Ribera Calderón, 1708.

Bravo-Villasante, Carmen. "Los 'Diálogos escolares' de Juan Luis Vives." Biblioteca Virtual Cervantes, 2006. https://www.cervantesvirtual.com/portales/al_tall/obra/los-dilogos-escolares-de-juan-luis-vives-0/.

Bringas de Manzaneda y Encinas, Diego Miguel. *Sermón que en las solemnes honras celebradas en obsequio de los VPP predicadores apostólicos Fr Francisco Tomas Hermenegildo Garcés; Fr. Juan Marcelo Diaz; Fr. José Matías Moreno; Fr. Juan Antonio Barreneche, Misioneros del Colegio de Propaganda Fide de la Santa Cruz de Querétaro, fundadores de las conversiones de la Purísima Concepción, y de S. Pedro y S. Pablo del Rio Colorado entre los gentiles Yumas y muertos gloriosamente a manos de los mismos barbaros en los días 7 y 9 de julio de 1781.* Madrid: Imprenta de Fermín Villalpando, 1819.

Brown, Alan K., ed. and trans. *With Anza to California, 1775–76: The Journal of Pedro Font, O.F.M.* Norman: University of Oklahoma Press, 2011.

Brown, Peter. *The Body and Society: Men, Women, and Sexual Renunciation in Early Christianity.* New York: Columbia University Press, 1988.

Buenaventura, Francisco de San. *Instrucción para Novicios de la Religión Bethlemitica.* Mexico: Joseph Bernardo de Hogal, 1734.

Buescu, Ana Isabel. "Corte, Poder e Utopia: O Relox de Príncipes (1529) de Fr. Antonio de Guevara e sua Fortuna na Europa de sécule XVI." *Estudios Humanísticos. Historia* 8 (2009): 69–101.

———. "The Utopia." *History of European Ideas* 16, no. 4 (1993): 599–605.

Burgoa, Francisco de. *Palestra Historial . . . de la Sagrada orden de Predicadores en este Nuevo Mundo de la America en las Indias Occidentales.* 1670. 3rd ed. Mexico: Editorial Porrúa, 1989.

Busembaum, Hermann. *Médula de la teología Moral.* Madrid: Bernardo de Villadiego, 1667.

Buxó, José Pascual. "Los artificios de la inmortalidad: Impresores e impresos novohispanos del siglo XVII." *Mester* 30, no. 1 (2001): 87–100.

Bynum, Caroline Walker. *The Resurrection of the Body in Western Christianity, 200–1336.* New York: Columbia University Press, 2017.

———. *Wonderful Blood: Theology and Practice in Late Medieval Northern Germany and Beyond.* Philadelphia: University of Pennsylvania Press, 2007.

Caballero Carranco, Juan. "Viaje y entrada que hizo el padre lector Fray Juan Caballero Carranco a el Nayarit, Año 1669." In *Franciscanos eminentes en territorios de fronteras*, edited by Amaya Cabranes and Thomas Calvo, 159–78. Zamora and San Luis: Colegio de Michoacán / Colegio de San Luis, 2014.

Cabranes, Amaya, and Thomas Calvo, eds. *Franciscanos eminentes en territorios de fronteras.* Zamora and San Luis: Colegio de Michoacán / Colegio de San Luis, 2014.

Calvo, Thomas. "'Concubinato y mestizaje en el medio urbano': el caso de Guadalajara en el siglo XVII." *Revista de Indias* 44, no. 173 (1984): 203–12.

———. *Los Albores de un nuevo mundo. Siglos XVI y XVII*. Mexico: Universidad de Guadalajara / Centre d Études Mexicaines et Centroaméricaines, 1990.

———. "The Warmth of the Hearth: Seventeenth Century Guadalajara Families." In *Sexuality and Marriage in Colonial Latin America*, edited by Asunción Lavrin, 287–312. Lincoln: University of Nebraska Press, 1989.

Camacho Domínguez, Sara Angela. "Fray José de Sigüenza. Instrucción de maestros, escuela de novicios, arte de perfección religiosa y monástica." PhD diss., Universidad de Huelva, 2015.

Campos, Carlos Federico. "Los criollos novohispanos frente a la teoría de la degeneración: De la Apologética a la reivindicación." *Enclaves del Pensamiento* 11, no. 21 (January–July 2017): 15–40.

Cañeque, Alejandro. "Letting Yourself Be Skinned Alive: Jerónimo de Gracián and the Globalization of Martyrdom." *Journal of Early Modern History* 24, no. 3 (2020): 197–223.

———. *Un imperio de mártires. Religión y poder en las fronteras de la Monaquía Hispánica*. Madrid: Marcial Pons, 2020.

Cárdenas, Juan de. *Primera Parte de los Problemas y secretos maravillosos de las Indias*. Mexico: Pedro Ocharte, 1591.

Cárdenas, Mario A. "José de Escandón: The Classical Creation of a Conquistador." *World History Review* 1 (Fall 2003): 2–38.

Carranza, Miguel Alfonso de. *Primera parte del Cathecismo y doctrina de religiosos novicios, profesos y monjas*. Valencia: Juan Chrysostomo Garriz, 1605.

Carrillo Cazares, Alberto. *El Debate sobre la Guerra Chichimeca, 1531–1585*. 2 vols. Zamora: Colegio de Michoacán / Colegio de San Luis, 2000.

Cartilla y Doctrina Espiritual para la crianza y educación de los Novicios que tomaren el Hábito en la Orden de nuestro Padre San Francisco. México, Herederos de la Viuda de Miguel de Rivera Calderón, 1721. http://catarina.udlap.mx/xmLibris/projects/biblioteca_franciscana/xml/myPage.jsp?key=book_jbc014.xml&id=libro_antiguo_sace&objects=/ximg&db=/db/xmlibris/system/metadata/.

Cartilla y Doctrina Espiritual para la Crianza y Educación de los Novicios que tomaren el Hábito en la Orden de N.P.S. Francisco. 1721. Reprint, Mexico: Imprenta de D. Felipe de Zúñiga y Ontiveros, 1775.

Castañeda, Carmen. *La educación en Guadalajara durante la colonia, 1552–1821*. Mexico: Centro de Investigaciones y Estudios Superiores en Antropología Social, 2012.

———. *Violación, estupro, y sexualidad en la Nueva Galicia, 1790–1821*. Guadalajara: Editorial Hexágono, 1989.

Castañeda, Carmen, with Luz Elena Galván Lafarga and Lucía Martínez Moctezuma, coords. "Libros para la enseñanza de la lectura en la Nueva España, siglos XVII y XIX: cartillas, silabarios, catones y catecismos." In *Lecturas y lectores en la Historia de Mexico*, n.p. Mexico: Universidad Autónoma del Estado de Morelos, 2004.

Castells, Elizabeth A. *Martyrdom and Memory: Early Christian Culture Making*. New York: Columbia University Press, 2004.

Castiglione, Baldassare. *Libro llamado El Cortesano traducido agora nuevamente en nuestro vulgar castellano por Boscán*. Enveres: Casa de Martin Nucio, 1544.

Castillo Maldonado, Pedro. "Prudencio y los mártires Calagurritanos." *Kalakorikos* 5 (2000): 65–76.

Castro, Antonio de. *Ceremonial según el Romano y el uso de los religiosos de nuestro padre san Agustín. Útil y provechosos para todos los eclesiásticos asi regulares como seculares*. Madrid, 1701.

Castro, Felipe. *La rebelión de los indios y la paz de los españoles*. Mexico: CIESAS / Instituto Nacional Indigenista, 1996.

Cátedra, Pedro. "Límites de control del libro infantil (reformas religiosas y 'cartillas' escolares en el primer tercio del siglo XVI)." In *La formation de l'enfant en Espagne aux XVIe et XVIIe siècles*, coordinated by Augustine Redondo, 327–49. Paris: Presses de la Sorbonne Nouvelle, 1996.

Cervantes, Miguel de. *El rufián dichoso*. Biblioteca Virtual Miguel de Cervantes. Accessed June 21, 2024. http://www.cervantesvirtual.com/obra-visor/el-rufian-dichoso--0/html/ff31ea1a-82b1-11df-acc7-002185ce6064_2.html.

Cervantes Aguilar, Rafael. *Fray Simón del Hierro (1700–1765)*. Mexico: UNAM, 1986.

Cervantes de Salazar, Francisco. *Mexico en 1554. Tres diálogos latinos*. Edited by Miguel León Portilla. Mexico: UNAM, 2001.

Chance, John K. *Conquest of the Sierra: Spaniards and Indians in Colonial Oaxaca*. Norman: University of Oklahoma Press, 1989.

Chapa, Juan Bautista. *Texas and Northeastern Mexico, 1630–1690*. Edited and with an introduction by William C. Foster. Austin: University of Texas Press, 1997.

Chardon, Roland. "The Elusive Spanish League: A Problem of Measurement in Sixteenth-Century New Spain." *HAHR* 60, no. 2 (1980): 294–302.

Chartier, Roger. "Los manuales de civilidad. Distinción y divulgación: la civilidad y sus libros." In *Libros, lecturas y lectores en la Edad Moderna*, by Roger Chartier and Mauro Armiño, 246–83. Madrid: Alianza Editorial, 1993.

Chase, Steven. *Angelic Spirituality: Medieval Perspectives on the Ways of Angels*. New York: Paulist Press, 2002.

Chauncy, Maurice. *The History of the Sufferings of Eighteen Carthusians in England*. New York: Catholic Publication Society, 1890.

Chinchilla Pawling, Perla. "Sobre la retórica sacra en la era barroca." *Estudios de Historia Novohispana* 29 (July–December 2003): 97–122.

Chocano Mena, Magdalena. *La fortaleza docta. Elite letrada y dominación social en Mexico colonial [siglos XVI–XVII]*. Barcelona: Ediciones Bellaterra, 2000.

Christofis, George. "The Notion of Martyrdom According to St. John Chrysostom." Master's thesis, Durham University, 1984.

Chuchiak, John F., IV. "By Faith, Not Arms: Franciscan Reducciones, the Frontier Mission Experience, and the Subjugation of the Maya Hinterland, 1602–1697." In *St. Francis in America: The Franciscan Experience in the Americas*, edited by John F. Schwaller, 119–42. Washington DC: Academy of American Franciscan History, 2006.

———. "Corruption and Careerism in New Spain: Don Alonso de Peralta y Robles, Creole Inquisitor, 1594–1610." *Colonial Latin American Review* 29, no. 3 (2020): 376–97.

———. *El castigo y la represión: el Juzgado del Provisorato de Indios y la extirpación de la idolatría maya en el obispado de Yucatán 1563–1763*. Mexico: UNAM / Universidad Anáhuac Veracruz, 2022.

———, ed. and trans. *The Inquisition in New Spain, 1536–1820: A Documentary History*. Baltimore: Johns Hopkins University Press, 2012.

———. "Procedimientos y conflictos jurídicos en el uso de testimonios indígenas por la comisaria de la Inquisición en Yucatán colonial, 1570–1770." In *Los indios de Nueva España ante la justicia local: traducción, autoridad, y mediadores culturales*, edited by Yanna Yannakakis, Martina Schrader-Kniffki, and Luis Arrioja, 79–109. Zamora: Colegio de Michoacán / Emory University, 2019.

———. "The Secrets behind the Screen: Solicitantes in the Colonial Diocese of Yucatan, 1570–1770." In *Religion in New Spain*, edited by Susan Schroeder and Stafford Poole, 113–46. Albuquerque: University of New Mexico Press, 2007.

Chuchiak, John F., IV, and Luis René Guerrero Galván. *Los edictos de la fe del Santo Oficio de la Inquisición de la Nueva España: Estudio Preliminar y Corpus Facsimilar*. Mexico: UNAM / Instituto de Investigaciones Jurídicas–UNAM, 2018.

Civil, Pierre. "La formation morale de l'enfant au XVIè siècle à travers les 'Catones.'" In *La formation de l'enfant en Espagne aux XVIe et XVIIe siècles*, edited by Augustine Redondo, 253–77. Paris: Presses de la Sorbonne Nouvelle, 1996.

Comentarios del desengañado. Vida de D. Diego Duque de Estrada escrita por el mismo. In *Colección de documentos, opúsculos y antigüedades que publica la Real Academia de la Historia*, vol. 19. Madrid: Imprenta Nacional, 1860.

Concilios Provinciales Primero y Segundo celebrados en la muy noble y muy leal ciudad de Mexico . . . en los años de 1555 y 1556. México: Imprenta del Superior Gobierno, 1768.

Connell, R. W. *The Men and the Boys*. Berkeley: University of California Press, 2000.

Conover, Cornelius. "Catholic Saints in Spain's Empire." In *Empires of God: Religious Encounter in Early Modern Atlantic*, edited by Linda Gregerson and Susan Justar, 87–105. Philadelphia: University of Pennsylvania Press, 2011.

———. *Pious Imperialism: Spanish Rule and the Cult of Saints in Mexico City*. Albuquerque: University of New Mexico Press, 2019.

———. "Saintly Biography and the Cult of San Felipe de Jesús in Mexico City, 1597–1697." *The Americas* 67, no. 4 (April 2011): 441–66.

———. "A Saint in the Empire: Mexico City's San Felipe de Jesús, 1597–1820." PhD diss., University of Texas at Austin, 2008.

Constituciones de la provincia de san Diego de Mexico de los Menores Descalzos de la más estrecha observancia Regular de N.P.S. Francisco en esta Nueva España. Mexico: Viuda de Francisco Rodríguez Lupercio, 1698.

Constituciones y Leyes Municipales de esta Provincia del S. Evangelio hechas y recopiladas en el Capítulo Provincial celebrado en el convento de N. P. S. Francisco de Mexico. Mexico: Viuda de Bernardo Calderón, 1667.

Coope, Jessica A. *The Martyrs of Córdoba: Community and Family Conflict in an Age of Mass Conversion*. Lincoln: University of Nebraska Press, 1995.

Cortés Ortiz, Angélica. "Sermones impresos novohispanos del siglo XVII: la edición del sermonario *Historias varias moralizadas en sermones* de Antonio Delgado y Buenrostro." PhD diss., Universidad de Salamanca, 2015.

Courcelles, Dominique de. "Autour de la formation de l'enfant dans l'Espagne du XVIe siècle: 'La Silva de varia lección' du sevillan Pedro Mexia (1540–1550)." In *La formation de l'enfant en Espagne aux XVIe et XVIIe siècles*, edited by Augustín Redondo, 13–26. Paris: Presses de la Sorbonne Nouvelle, 1996.

Crespí, Juan. *Diario y Descripción . . . desde la misión llamada Santa María de los Ángeles hasta los puertos de San Diego, Monterey y San Francisco, en . . . 1769–1770*. In *Diario de la expedición de Fray Junípero Serra desde la misión de Loreto a San Diego en 1769*, by Junípero Serra and Juan Crespí, edited by Ángel L. Encinas Moral and Teófilo Ruiz. Madrid: Ediciones Miraguano, 2011.

Cruz García de Enterría, María. "El adoctrinamiento 'popular' del niño en el siglo XVII." In *La formation de l'enfant en Espagne aux XVIe et XVIIe siècles*, edited by Augustín Redondo, 275–90. Paris: Presses de la Sorbonne Nouvelle, 1996.

Cruz Ocaña, Luis Ernesto, and Jorge Magaña Ochoa. "Estudios sobre la muerte en Mexico: Un estado de la cuestión." *Presente y Pasado. Revista de Historia* 22, no. 44 (July–December 2017): 11–28.

Cruz Rangel, José Antonio. *Chichimecas, misioneros, soldados y terratenientes. Estrategias de colonización, control y poder en Querétaro y la Sierra Gorda Siglos XVI–XVIII*. Mexico: Archivo General de la Nación, 2003.

Cuellar, Gregory Lee. "The Imposed Silence of Idealized Memories." In *El sermón novohispano como texto de cultura. Ocho Estudios*, edited by Blanca López de Mariscal and Nancy Joe Dyer, 53–166. New York: Idea/Igas, 2012.

Cullum, Patricia, and Catherine J. Lewis, eds. *Holiness and Masculinity in the Middle Ages*. Cardiff: University of Wales Press, 2004.

Cunningham, Debbie S. "The Domingo Ramón Diary of the 1716 Expedition into the Province of the Tejas Indias: An Annotated Translation." *Southwestern Historical Quarterly* 110, no. 1 (July 2006): 38–67.

Darby, Graham. *The Origins and Development of the Dutch Revolt*. London: Routledge, 2001.

Dávila Padilla, Agustín. *Historia de la Fundación y Discurso de la Provincia de Santiago de Mexico, de la Orden de Predicadores, por las vidas de sus varones insignes y casos notables de Nueva España*. Bruselas: Casa de Juan de Meerbeque, 1625.

Descripción y prospecto de la pira y análisis de las poesías que para las solemnes exequias del Illmo. Y Rmo. Señor Mro. D. Fray Antonio de San Miguel Yglesia, celebradas en la Santa Iglesia Catedral de Valladolid de Michoacán, dirigió y compuso . . . el Br. D. Manuel de la Torre Lloreda. Valladolid, 1804.

Diaz, Mónica. *Indigenous Writings from the Convent: Negotiating Ethnic Autonomy in Colonial Mexico*. Tucson: University of Arizona Press, 2013.

Díaz de Gamarra, Juan Benito. *Máximas de Educación, Academia de Filosofía, Academia de Geometría*. Zamora: Colegio de Michoacán, 1983.

Dimler, Richard G. *Studies in the Jesuit Emblem*. New York: AMS Press, 2007.

Doctrina cristiana . . . publicada en Mexico por mandamiento del reverendísimo señor D. Fr. Juan de Zumárraga. México: Juan Pablos, 1546.

Documentos para la Historia de México. 4th series. Vol. 2. Mexico: Imprenta de Vicente García Torres, 1856.

Domínguez, D. Juan María. *Catón Cristiano de la Santa Escuela de Christo Nuestro Señor*. Mexico: Oficina del Br. D. Joseph Fernández Jauregui, 1795.

Domínguez, Francisco Atanasio, and Silvestre Vélez de Escalante. *Diario de la expedición Domínguez-Escalante por el Oeste Americano (Nuevo Mexico, Colorado, Utah y Arizona)*. Edited by Javier Torre Aguado. Madrid: Miraguano Ediciones, 2016.

Donahue, William H. "The Missionary Activities of Fray Antonio Margil de Jesus in Texas, 1716–1722." *The Americas* 14, no. 1 (July 1957): 45–55.

Douglas, John G., and William M. Graves, eds. *New Mexico and the Pimería Alta: The Colonial Period in the American Southwest*. Boulder: University Press of Colorado, 2017.

Dueñas, Juan de. *Remedio de pecadores por otro nombre llamado confesionario*. Valladolid: Juan de Villaquirán, 1545.

Dunne, Peter M. *Pioneer Black Robes on the West Coast*. Berkeley: University of California Press, 1940.

Duque de Estrada, Diego. *Comentarios del desengañado. Vida de D. Diego Duque de Estrada escrita por el mismo.* In *Colección de documentos, opúsculos y antigüedades que publica la Real Academia de la Historia*, vol. 19. Madrid: Imprenta Nacional, 1860.

Durán, Norma. "La Construcción de la subjetividad en las hagiografías. Un caso: Sebastián de Aparicio." In *Camino a la Santidad. Siglos XVI–XX*, edited by Manuel Ramos Medina, 165–20. México: Centro de Estudios de Historia de México Condumex, 2003.

———. "La retórica del martirio y la formación del sufriente en la vida de San Felipe de Jesús." *Historia y Grafía* 26 (2006): 77–107.

Echarri, Francisco. *Directorio Moral*. 2 vols. 7th ed. Madrid: Imprenta de D. Pedro Marin, 1780.

Eire, Carlos, M. N. *From Madrid to Purgatory: The Art and Craft of Dying in Sixteenth-Century Spain*. New York: Cambridge University Press, 1995.

Engelhardt, Zephyrin. *The Missions and Missionaries of California*. 4 vols. San Francisco: James H. Barry Company, 1908–15.

Erasmus of Rotterdam, Desiderius. "Preparing for Death (De preparatione ad mortem)." In *Spiritualia and Pastoralia*, translated by John N. Grant, edited by John W. O'Malley, vol. 70, *The Collected Works of Erasmus*, 389–450. Toronto: University of Toronto Press, 1998.

———. *The Whole Familiar Colloquies*. London: Hamilton, Adams, and Co., 1877.

Escobar, Matías de. *Americana Thebaida. Vitas Patrum de los religiosos hermitaños de Nuestro Padre San Augustín, de la Provincia de San Nicolás Tolentino de Michoacán*. Morelia: Imp. y Lit. en la Escuela de Artes, 1890.

Espinosa, Isidro Felis [sic] de. *El Peregrino Septentrional Atlante delineado en la ejemplarísima vida del venerable padre F. Antonio Margil de Jesús*. México: Joseph Bernardo de Hogal, 1737.

Espinosa, Isidro Félix de. *Chronica Apostólica y Seraphica de todos los colegios de Propaganda Fide de esta Nueva España de Misioneros Franciscanos Observantes*. Mexico: Viuda de D. Joseph Bernardo de Hogal, 1746.

———. *El Cherubin Custodio de el Árbol de la Vida, la Santa Cruz de Querétaro. Vida del V^e. Siervo de Dios, Fray Antonio de los Ángeles Bustamante*. Mexico: Joseph Bernardo de Hogal, 1731.

Espinosa, José Manuel. *The Pueblo Indian Revolt of 1696 and the Franciscan Missions in New Mexico: Letters of the Missionaries and Related Documents*. Norman: University of Oklahoma Press, 1988.

Espinosa, Valeriano de. *Guía de religiosos. Contiene una instrucción para principiantes que pasan del siglo a la Religión*. Valladolid: Gerónimo Murillo, 1703.

Estatutos y Ordenaciones según las bulas [que] Inocencio XI expidió para los Colegios de Misioneros. Acomodadas a la más estrecha observancia que se practica en la Seráfica Descalcez. Madrid: Don Benito Cano, 1791.

Estrada Gijón, Juan de. *Arte de predicar la palabra de Dios para su mayor honra y provecho de las almas*. Madrid: Imprenta Melchor Sánchez, 1667.

Evans, Willian E. "The Confirmation Controversy of 1779: Serra vs Neve; A Rationale." *Southern California Quarterly* 51, no. 2 (June 1969): 85–96.

Fernández, Alonso. *Historia y Anales de la Devoción y Milagros del Rosario desde su origen hasta el año de mil seiscientos y veinte y seis*. Madrid: Juan González, 1627.

Fernández García, Eduardo. "El discurso sobre la virtud política en los espejos de príncipes de los Austrias. Valentía y templanza en la teoría política entre el Renacimiento y el Barroco." PhD diss., Universidad de León, 2019.

Fernández Salvador, Carmen. "Palabras que Pintan y Pinturas que Hablan: Retórica e Imágenes en el Quito Colonial (siglos XVII y XVIII)." In *Las artes en Quito en el cambio del Siglo XVII and XVII, Memorias del Seminario Internacional, 11 de octubre de 2007*, 208–39. Quito: Fonsal, 2009.

Ferruvino, Domingo de. *Vida de El Glorioso Protomártir de El Japón San Phelipe De Jesús*. Mexico: Joseph Bernardo de Hogal, 1733.

Fiume, Giovanna. "St. Benedict the Moor: From Sicily to the New World." In *Saints and Their Cults in the Atlantic World*, edited by Margaret Joan Cormack, 16–51. Columbia: University of South Carolina Press, 2007.

Flores Melo, Raymundo. "Casos de sodomía ante la Inquisición de México en los siglos XVII y XVIII." In *Inquisición Novohispana*, vol. 2, edited by Noemí Quezada, Martha Eugenia Rodríguez, and Marcela Suárez Escobar, 45–61. Mexico: UNAM, Instituto de Investigaciones Antropológicas, 2000.

Framiñán de Miguel, Jesús. "La Doctrina Cristiana de Gregorio de Pesquera (Valladolid 1554): esbozo de análisis y contextualización histórico-literaria." *Criticón* 96 (2006): 5–46.

France, James. *Separate but Equal: Cistercian Lay Brothers, 1120–1350*. Collegeville MN: Liturgical Press, 2012.

Franch Benavent, Roberto, Fernando Andrés Robres, and Rafael Benítez Sánchez-Blanco, eds. *Cambios y resistencias sociales en la Edad moderna. Un análisis comparativo entre el centro y la periferia mediterránea de la Monarquia Hispánica*. Madrid: Silex, 2014.

Franco, Alonso. *Segunda Parte de la Historia de la Provincia de Santiago de México Orden de Predicadores en la Nueva España*. 1645. Reprint, México: Imprenta del Museo Nacional, 1900.

Frazee, Charles A. "The Origins of Celibacy in the Western World." *Church History* 41, no. 2 (June 1972): 149–67.

Freeman, Charles. *Holy Bones, Holy Dust: How Relics Shaped the History of Medieval Europe.* New Haven CT: Yale University Press, 2011.
Gage, Thomas. *The English-American: A New Survey of the West Indies*, London: G. Routledge and Sons, 1928.
Galindo Carrillo, María Ángeles. *Los tratados sobre la educación de príncipes, Siglos XVI y XVII.* Madrid: Instituto San José de Calazans de Pedagogía / Consejo Superior de Investigaciones Científicas, 1948.
Gallego Barnés, Andrés. "El impacto de las ideas pedagógicas de Luis Vives en el 'Studi general' de Valencia a través de la labor docente y de la actividad editorial de Juan Lorenzo Palmireno." In *Actas del II Seminario de Historia de la Filosofía Española*, vol. 2, 213–23. Salamanca, 1982.
——. "Refranes de mesa, salud y buena crianza." *Criticón* 105 (2009): 139–76.
Galván Rodríguez, Eduardo. "La praxis inquisitorial contra confesores solicitantes. Tribunal de la Inquisición de Canarias, años 1601–1700." *Revista de la Inquisición* (1996): 103–85.
Gante, Pedro de. *Doctrina cristiana en lengua mexicana.* México: Attributed to Juan Cromberger, 1547.
Garcés, Francisco. *Cartas del Reverendo Padre Fray Francisco Garcés.* In *Documentos para la Historia de México*, 4th series, vol. 2, 365–77. Mexico: Imprenta de Vicente García Torres, 1856.
——. *Diario de exploraciones en Arizona y California en los años de 1775 y 1776.* México: UNAM, 1968.
——. *A Record of Travels in Arizona and California, 1775–1776.* Translated and edited by J. Galvin. San Francisco: John Howell Books, 1965.
García, Gerónimo. *Política regular y religiosa república.* Tomo primero. Zaragoza: Real Hospital de Nuestra Señora, 1649.
García, Pantaleón. *Sermones Panegíricos, de varios misterios, festividades y santos.* Vol. 3. Madrid: Gómez Fuentenebro y Compañía, 1804.
García de Cortázar, José Ángel, and Ramón Teja Casuso, coords. *Monasterios cisterciences en la España medieval.* Aguilar del Campo, Palencia: Fundación Santa María la Real, 2008.
García Gómez, María Eugenia. "Poesía dramática de Fray Juan de la Anunciación. Edición y estudio de las carmelitas del siglo XVIII." PhD diss., UNAM, 2010.
García Mendoza, Jaime. "Casos de curas solicitantes ante el Santo Oficio de Tasco (1580–1630)." In *Inquisición Novohispana*, edited by Noemí Quezada, Martha Eugenia Rodríguez, and Marcela Suárez, 25–44. México: UNAM / Universidad Autónoma Metropolitana, 2000.
García-Molina Riquelme, Antonio M. "Instrucciones para procesar a solicitantes en el tribunal de la inquisición de México." *Revista de la Inquisición* 8 (1999): 85–100.

García Oro, José. *Cisneros y la reforma del clero español en tiempos de los reyes católicos.* Madrid: CSI, Instituto Jerónimo Zurita, 1971.

García Santa Olaya, Angelica Sofia. "Futuros Vasallos de la Monarquía Católica. Textos para Niños Novohispanos en la Segunda Mitad del Siglo XVIII." Master's thesis, CONACYT, 2010.

Garrigós, Antonio. *Vida admirable del V.P.F Joseph Marques, hijo de la Santa Provincia de Santiago de Xalisco.* MS 5695, fol. 11, Biblioteca Nacional, Madrid.

Garza Cuarón, Beatriz, and Georges Baudot, eds. *Historia de la Literatura Mexicana desde sus orígenes hasta nuestros días.* Vol. 1, *Las literaturas amerindias de Mexico y la literatura en español del siglo XVI.* Mexico: Siglo XXI / Facultad de Filosofia y Letras de la UNAM, 1996.

Gavarri, Fr Joseph. *Noticias Singularissimas ... de las preguntas necesarias que deben hacer los PP. Confesores [...].* Barcelona: Imprenta de Antonio Ferrer, 1677.

Gay, José Antonio. *Historia de Oaxaca.* Tomo primero. México: Imprenta del Comercio, de Dublán y Cía., 1881.

Geiger, Maynard. "Fray Junípero Serra: Organizer and Administrator of the Upper California Mission, 1769–1784." *California Historical Society Quarterly* 42, no. 3 (September 1963): 195–330.

———, ed. and trans. "Fray Rafael Verger, O.F.M., and the California Mission Enterprise." *Southern California Quarterly* 49, no. 2 (June 1967): 205–23.

———, ed. and trans. *Letter of Luis Jayme, O.F.M., San Diego, October 17, 1772.* Los Angeles: San Diego Public Library, 1970.

———. *The Life and Times of Fray Junípero Serra, O.F.M., or The Man Who Never Turned Back, 1713–1784: A Biography.* Washington DC: Academy of American Franciscan History, 1959.

Giglioni, Guido. "Between Galen and St. Paul: How Juan Huarte de San Juan responded to Inquisitorial Censorship." *Early Science and Medicine* 12, no. 1/2 (2018): 114–34.

Giraud, François. "Viol et société colonial: Le cas de la Nouvelle Espagne au XVIIIè siècle." *Annales* 41, no. 3 (May–July 1986): 625–63.

Godinas, Laurette. "Oratoria sagrada y vida cultural en el Mexico Virreinal." *Destiempos* 3, no. 14 (March–April 2008): 484–94.

Gómez Canedo, Lino. *Fray Rafael Verger en San Fernando de Mexico (1750–1782).* Monterrey, Mexico: Centro de Estudios Humanísticos de la Universidad de Nuevo León. Sobretiro del Anuario "Humanitas," 3, no. 3, (1962): 551–575.

———. *La educación de los marginados durante la época colonial: Escuelas y colegios para indios y mestizos en la Nueva España.* Mexico: Editorial Porrúa, 1982.

———. *Primeras exploraciones y poblamiento de Texas (1686–1694).* Mexico: Editorial Porrúa, 1988.

———. *Sierra Gorda. Un típico enclave misional en el centro de Mexico (Siglos XVII–XVIII)*. Pachuca: Centro Hidalguense de Investigaciones Históricas, 1976.

———. *Sonora hacia fines del siglo XVIIII: Un informe del misionero francisano Fray Francisco Antonio Barbastro, con otros documentos complementarios. Estudio preliminar, edición y notas por Lino Gómez Canedo*. Guadalajara, Mexico: Librería Font, 1971.

Gondra, José María. "Juan Huarte de San Juan y las diferencias de inteligencia." *Anuario de Psicología* 60 (1994): 13–34.

Gonzalbo Aizpuru, Pilar. "Buenos cristianos y jóvenes letrados en Santa Cruz de Tlatelolco (Mexico)." In *Historia de la infancia en América Latina*, coordinated by Pablo Rodríguez and María Emma Mannarelli, 109–20. Bogotá: Universidad Externado de Colombia, 2007.

———. "El Virreinato y el Nuevo Orden." In *Familia y educación en Iberoamérica*, coordinated by Pilar Gonzalbo Aizpuru, 43–56. México: Colegio de México, 1999.

———. *Historia de la educación en la época colonial. La educación de los criollos y la vida urbana*. Mexico: Colegio de Mexico, 1990.

———. "La familia educadora en Nueva España: Un espacio para las contradicciones." In *Familia y Educación en Iberoamérica*, coordinated by Pilar Gonzalbo Aizpuru, 43–56. México: Colegio de México, 1999.

González, Enrique, and Víctor Gutiérrez Rodríguez. "Los catedráticos novohispanos y sus libros: tres bibliotecas universitarias del siglo XVI." In *Dalla lectura allé e-learning*, edited by Andrea Romano, 83–102. Bologna: CLUEB, 2015.

González, Gutierre. *Doctrina Christiana*. Toledo: Miguel Ferrer, 1564.

———. *Libro de doctrina christiana . . . para imponer y enseñar perpetuamente los niños y otras cualesquiera personas que la quisieren aprender*. Sevilla, 1532.

González, Ondina E., and Bianca Premo, eds. *Raising an Empire: Children in Early Modern Iberia and Colonial Latin America*. Albuquerque: University of New Mexico Press, 2007.

González Blanco, Antonio. "Los santos mártires y el obispado de Calahorra." *Kalakorikos* 5 (2000): 77–86.

González de la Puente, Juan. *Primera parte de la Choronica Augustiniana de Mechoacán en que se tratan y escriben las vidas de nueve varones apostólicos augustinianos*. 1624. In *Colección de Documentos Inéditos y Raros para la Historia Eclesiástica Mexicana, publicados por el Illmo. Sr. Obispo de Cuernavaca D. Francisco Plancarte y Navarrete*, tomo 1. Cuernavaca: Tipografía "El Arte," 1907.

González del Campo. *Cartillas de la Doctrina Cristiana, impresas por la catedral de Valladolid y enviadas a America desde 1583*. Navarra: Publicaciones de la Universidad de Navarra, 1990.

González Echegaray, Jorge. "El culto a los santos: Emeterio y Celedonio en Santander." *Kalarokiros* 5 (2000): 271–84.

González Leyva, Alejandra. "Los centros de estudio y colegios dominicos de la época novohispana." *Revista Grafía* 10 (January–July 2013): 112–26.

González Lopo, Domingo Luis. "El ritual de la muerte, barroca la hagiografía como paradigma del buen morir cristiano." *Semata* 17 (2005): 299–320.

González Marmolejo, Jorge René. "Clérigos solicitantes, perversos de la confesión." In *De la santidad a la perversión. O de porqué no se cumplía la ley de Dios en la sociedad novohispana*, edited by Sergio Ortega Noriega, 229–44. Mexico: Grijalbo, 1986.

———. "El delito de solicitación en el Obispado de Puebla durante el siglo XVIII y principios del XIX." Master's thesis, ENAH, 1982.

———, ed. *Estatutos y ordenaciones según bulas que nuestro santísimo padre Inocencio XI expidió para el Colegio de Propaganda Fide*. Mexico: INAH, 2010.

———. *Los novicios del Colegio de la Santa Cruz de Querétaro (1691–1819)*. Querétaro: Fondo Editorial Universidad Autónoma de Querétaro, 2018.

———. *Misioneros del desierto. Estructura, organización y vida cotidiana de los Colegios Apostólicos de Propaganda Fide, siglo XVIII*. Mexico: Instituto Nacional de Antropología e Historia, 2009.

———. *Sexo y confesión. La iglesia y la penitencia en los siglos XVIII y XIX en la Nueva España*. México: Conaculta / Plaza y Valdés, Editores, 2002.

González Polvillo, Antonio. *Decálogo y gestualidad social en la España de la Contrarreforma*. Sevilla: Secretariado de Publicaciones de la Universidad de Sevilla, 2011.

González Sánchez, Carlos Alberto. *Los mundos del libro. Medios de difusión de la cultura occidental en las Indias de los siglos XVI y XVII*. Sevilla: Diputación de Sevilla / Universidad de Sevilla, 2001.

Gracián de la Madre de Dios, Gerónimo. *Arte de Bien Morir*. Bruselas: Roger Vellpio y Huberto Antonio, 1614.

Granada, Luis de. *Los seis libros de la Rhetorica eclesiástica o de la manera de predicar*. 5th ed. Barcelona: Juan Jolis y Bernardo Plá, 1778.

Greenleaf, Richard E. "The Inquisition in Eighteenth-Century New Mexico." *New Mexico Historical Review* 60, no. 1 (1985): 29–60.

Gregerson, Linda, and Susan Justar, eds. *Empires of God: Religious Encounter in Early Modern Atlantic*. Philadelphia: University of Pennsylvania Press, 2011.

Gregory, Brad S. *Salvation at Stake: Christian Martyrdom in Early Modern Europe*. Cambridge MA: Harvard University Press, 2001.

Grijalva, Juan de. *Crónica de la Orden de San Agustín en las provincias de la Nueva España*. Mexico: Imprenta de Juan Ruiz, 1624.

Grudzinska, Grazyna. "Del Novohispanismo a la Mexicanidad. Reflexiones sobre la Ilustración Americana." *Itinerarios* 16 (2012): 65–79.

Guadalupe, Andrés de. *Historia de la Santa Provincia de los Ángeles*. Madrid: Mateo Fernández, 1662.

Guadiz, Francisco de. *Sermón fúnebre predicado en las solemnes exequias que a sus religiosos difuntos celebra en todos los capítulos de la Seraphica y religiosísima provincia de Capuchinos de Andalucía*. Sevilla: Juan Antonio Tarazona, 1687.

Güereca Durán, Raquel E. *Un dios y un reino para los indios: la rebelión indígena de Tutotepec, 1769*. Mexico: Bonilla Artigas Editores, 2014.

Guest, Francis F. *Fermín Francisco de Lasuén (1736–1803): A Biography*. Washington DC: Academy of American Franciscan History, 1973.

Guevara, Antonio de. *Epístolas Familiares Partes Primera y Segunda*. Madrid: Juan de la Cueva, 1618.

———. *Libro Áureo del Gran Emperador Marco Aurelio con el Reloj de Príncipes*. Madrid: Carlos Sánchez, 1650.

———. *Obras Completas*. Edited by Emilio Blanco. Madrid: Turner, 2004.

———. *Oratorio de religiosos y ejercicio de virtuosos*. Valladolid: Juan de Villaquirán, 1545.

Guidicelli, C., and Pierre Ragon. "Les martyrs ou la Vierge? Frères, martyrs et images outragées dans le Mexique du Nord (XVIe–XVIIe siècles)." *Nuevo Mundo Mundos Nuevos*, 2005. Accessed July 27, 2024. https://doi.org/10.4000/nuevomundo.615.

Guillaume-Alonso, Araceli. "Ecole et cathequese en Andalusie occidental, au XVIè siècle, selon Jean d' Ávila. Quelques examples." In *La formation de l'enfant en Espagne aux XVIe et XVIIe siècles*, coordinated by Agustín Redondo, 237–52. Paris: Presses de la Sorbonne Nouvelle, 1996.

Gutiérrez, Ramón A. *When Jesus Came, the Corn Mothers Went Away: Marriage, Sexuality, and Power in New Mexico, 1500–1846*. Stanford: Stanford University Press, 1991.

Gutiérrez Román, José Francisco, Leticia Ivonne del Río Hernández, and Alberto Carrillo Cazares, coords. and eds. *Los colegios Apostólicos de Propaganda Fide, su historia y su legado*. Zacatecas: Gobierno del estado de Zacatecas / Universidad Autónoma de Zacatecas / Ayuntamiento de Guadalupe, 2001–4.

Hackel, Steven W. *Children of Coyote, Missionaries of Saint Francis: Indian-Spanish Relations in Colonial California, 1769–1850*. Raleigh: University of North Carolina Press, 2005.

———, ed. *The Worlds of Junípero Serra: Historical Contexts and Cultural Representations*. Oakland: University of California Press, 2018.

Hackett, Charles W., ed. *Revolt of the Pueblo Indians of New Mexico and Otermin's Attempted Reconquest 1680–1682*. 2 vols. Translated by Charmion Clair Shelby. Albuquerque: University of New Mexico Press, 1942.

Hadley, Dawn M. *Masculinity in Medieval Europe*. Harlow: Addison Wesley Longman, 1998.

Haines, Charles Reginald. *Christianity and Islam in Spain, AD 756–1031*. Vol. 20. London: K. Paul, Trench & Co., 1889.

Haliczer, Stephen. *Sexuality in the Confessional: A Sacrament Profaned.* New York: Oxford University Press, 1996.

Harries, Richard. *The Passion in Art.* London: Routledge, 2004.

Harrison, Jay T. "Franciscan Missionaries and Their Networks: The Diffusion of Missionary Concepts in Eighteenth-Century New Spain." *Catholic Historical Review* 105, no. 3 (Summer 2019): 457–79.

Hawes, Joseph M., and N. Ray Hiner, eds. *Children in Historical and Comparative Perspective: An International Handbook and Research Guide.* New York: Greenwood Press, 1991.

Hecht, Tobias. *Minor Omissions: Children in Latin American History and Society.* Madison: University of Wisconsin Press, 2002.

Heid, Stefan. *Celibacy in the Early Church: The Beginning of Obligatory Continence for Clerics in East and West.* San Francisco: Ignatius Press, 2000.

Hering Torres, Max S. "La limpieza de sangre. Problemas de interpretación: acercamientos históricos y metodológicos." *Historia Crítica* 45 (September–December 2011): 32–55.

Herize, Joseph de. *Instrucción y doctrina de novicios, sacada de la de san Buenaventura, con la que se crían los hijos de la Santa provincia de San Diego de México.* Mexico: Joseph Bernardo de Hogal, 1738.

Hernández Aparicio, Pilar. "Estadísticas Franciscanas del S. XVII." *Archivo Iberoamericano* 50, no. 97 (1990): 555–92.

Hernández Franco, Juan. *Cultura y limpieza de sangre en la España Moderna.* Valencia: Ediciones Universidad de Valladolid, 2003.

———. "Permanencia de la ideología nobiliaria y reserva del honor a través de los estatutos de limpieza de sangre en la España moderna." In *Mentalidad e ideología*, vol. 2, edited by León Carlos Álvarez Santaló and Cremades Griñán, 73–92. Murcia: Universidad de Murcia, 1993.

Hernández Triviño, Ascensión. "Fray Pedro de Gante (1480?–1572)." *Boletín de la Sociedad Española de Historiografía* 9 (2014): 29–46.

Herrejón Peredo, Carlos. *Del sermón al discurso cívico. Mexico, 1760–1834.* Zamora, Michoacán: Colegio de Michoacán / Colegio de Mexico, 2003.

———. "Marcel Bataillon y el humanismo mexicano en el siglo XVI." *Relaciones* 21, no. 81 (Winter 2000): 187–200.

———. "Oratoria en Nueva España." Discurso de recepción a la Academia Mexicana de la Historia, septiembre 7, 1993.

Herrera Feria, María de Lourdes, and Rosario Torres Domínguez. "Los estudios conventuales en el colegio de San Luis de Puebla de los Ángeles y sus constituciones." *Revista Electrónica de Fuentes y Archivos* 8, no. 8 (2017): 678–94.

Heywood, Colin. *A History of Childhood: Children and Childhood in the West from Medieval to Modern Time.* Cambridge: Polity Press, 2001.

Hoffman, Martha K. *Raised to Rule: Educating Royalty at the Court of the Spanish Habsburgs, 1601–1634*. Baton Rouge: Louisiana State University Press, 2011.

Homza, Lu Ann. *Religious Authority in the Spanish Renaissance*. Baltimore: Johns Hopkins University Press, 2000.

Huarte de San Juan, Juan. *Examen de Ingenios para las Sciencias*. 3rd ed. Leyden: Oficina de Juan Maire, 1652.

Hubeñak, Florencio. "El antimaquiavelismo de Ribadeneyra en la educación de príncipes." V Jornadas Internacionales "De Iustitia et Iure en el siglo de oro." Buenos Aires: Pontificia Universidad Católica Argentina, 2010.

Hu-DeHart, Evelyn. *Missionaries, Miners, and Indians: Spanish Contact with the Yaqui Nation of Northwestern New Spain, 1533–1820*. Tucson: University of Arizona Press, 1981.

Iannuzzi, Isabella. "Educar a los cristianos: Fray Hernando de Talavera y su labor catequética dentro de la estructura familiar para homogeneizar la sociedad de los reyes católicos." *Nuevo Mundo / Mundos Nuevos*, January 20, 2008. http://journals.openedition.org/nuevomundo/19122.

Ibarra, Joaquín. *Oficio Parvo de Nuestra Señora según el Breviario Romano*. Madrid: Joaquín Ibarra, 1781.

Infantes, Víctor. *De las primeras letras. Cartillas españolas para ensenar a leer de los siglos X y XVI*. Salamanca: Ediciones Universidad de Salamanca, 1998.

Ingraham, Kevin, ed. *The Conversos and Moriscos in Late Medieval Spain and beyond: Departures and Change*. 4 vols. Leiden: Brill, 2009–21.

Instrucciones y Reglamentos de Indias. 1776–1818. Library of Congress. https://www.loc.gov/resource/llnsm.201800338452846/?sp=349&r=-0.107,0.507,1.149,0.706,0.

Instrucción para criar novicios del Orden descalzo de N.S. del Carmen. Puebla: Francisco Xavier de Morales, 1725.

Instrucción y Doctrina de Novicios con la cual se han de criar los nuevos religiosos de esta Santa Provincia de San Joseph, de los Descalzos de la Regular Observancia de los Menores. Madrid: Oficina de Antonio Marín, 1733.

Instrucción y Doctrina de Novicios con la cual se han de criar los nuevos religiosos en esta Santa Provincia de San Joseph de los descalzos de la regular Observancia de los Menores. Madrid: Antonio Marin, 1734.

Jackson, Robert H. "The Bourbon-Era Mission Reform." *Estudios de Historia Novohispana*, no. 65 (July–December 2021): 13–53.

———. "The Chichimeca Frontier and the Evangelization of the Sierra Gorda, 1550–1770." *Estudios de Historia novohispana* 47 (July–December 2012): 45–91.

———. *Conflict and Conversion in Sixteenth-Century Central Mexico: The Augustinian War on and beyond the Chichimec Frontier*. Leiden: Brill, 2013.

———. *Frontiers of Evangelization: Indians in the Sierra Gorda and Chiquitos Missions.* Norman: University of Oklahoma Press, 2017.

———. *Pames, Jonaces, and Franciscans in the Sierra Gorda: Mecos and Missionaries.* Newcastle upon Tyne: Cambridge Scholars, 2017.

Jiménez Núñez, Alfredo. *El Gran Norte de Mexico: Una frontera imperial en la Nueva España (1540–1820).* Madrid: Editorial Tébar, 2006.

Johnson, Lyman, and Sonya Lipsett-Rivera, eds. *Sex, Shame, and Violence: The Faces of Honor in Colonial Latin America.* Albuquerque: University of New Mexico Press, 1998.

Jones, Grant D. *Maya Resistance to Spanish Rule: Time and History on a Colonial Frontier.* Albuquerque: University of New Mexico Press, 1989.

Kamen, Henry. *The Duke of Alba.* New Haven CT: Yale University Press, 2005.

Karras, Ruth. *From Boys to Men: Formations of Masculinity in Late Medieval Europe.* Philadelphia: University of Pennsylvania Press, 2003.

Katzew, Ilona. *Casta Painting: Images of Race in Eighteenth-Century Mexico.* New Haven CT: Yale University Press, 2004.

Kawata, Reiko. "Historia del culto a San Felipe de Jesús en Mexico. Transformación en sus imágenes (siglos XVII–XIX)." *Estudios de Arte Español y Latinoamericano* 21 (2020): 1–17.

Kenneally, Finbar, ed. and trans. *Writings of Fermín Francisco de Lasuén.* 2 vols. Washington DC: Academy of American Franciscan History, 1965.

Kessell, John L. *Friars, Soldiers, and Reformers: Hispanic Arizona and the Sonora Mission Frontier, 1767–1856.* Tucson: University of Arizona Press, 1976.

———. *Miera y Pacheco: A Renaissance Spaniard in Eighteenth-Century New Mexico.* Norman: University of Oklahoma Press, 2013.

———. *The Missions of New Mexico.* Albuquerque: University of New Mexico Press, 1980.

———. *Pueblos, Spaniards and the Kingdom of New Mexico.* Norman: University of Oklahoma Press, 2010.

———. *Spain in the Southwest: A Narrative History of Colonial New Mexico, Arizona, Texas, and California.* Norman: University of Oklahoma Press, 2002.

Kessell, John L., Rick Hendricks, Meredith D. Doge, and Larry D. Miller, eds. *That Disturbances Cease: The Journals of Don Diego De Vargas, New Mexico, 1697–1700.* Albuquerque: University of New Mexico Press, 2000.

Kirk, Stephanie, and Sarah Rivett, eds. *Religious Transformations in the Early Modern Americas.* Philadelphia: University of Pennsylvania Press, 2014.

Kittel, Robert A. *Franciscan Frontiersmen: How Three Adventurers Charted the West.* Norman: University of Oklahoma Press, 2017.

Knaut, Andrew L. *The Pueblo Revolt of 1680: Conquest and Resistance in Seventeenth Century New Mexico.* Norman: University of Oklahoma Press, 1995.

Lacson, Albert. "Making Friends and Converts: Cloth and Clothing in Early California History." *California History* 92, no. 1 (2015): 6–26.

Lamb, Ursula, ed. *The Globe Encircled and the World Revealed.* London: Routledge, 2016.

Landsberg, Jacques de. *L'art en croix. Le Theme de la crucifixion dans l'historie de l'art.* Tournai, Belgium: La Renaissance du livre, 2001.

Lara, Jaime. "Slippery Dominicans and Headless Bishops: Franciscan Visual Violence." ResearchGate, May 31, 2019, 1–22. https://www.researchgate.net/publication/333520442_Slippery_Dominicans_and_Headless_Bishops_Franciscan_Visual_Violence.

La Rea, Alonso. *Crónica de la Orden de N. Seráfico P.S. Francisco, Provincia de San Pedro y San Pablo de Mechoacan en la Nueva España.* Mexico: Viuda de Bernardo Calderón, 1643.

Lavrin, Asunción. *Brides of Christ: Conventual Life in Colonial Mexico.* Stanford: Stanford University Press, 2008.

———. "El Umbral de la Vida Religiosa: El noviciado de los frailes mendicantes." In *De la historia económica a la historia social y cultural. Homenaje a Gisela von Wobeser,* coordinated by María del Pilar Martínez López-Cano, 235–61. Mexico: UNAM, 2015.

———. "The Erotic as Lewdness in Spanish and Mexican Religious Culture during the Sixteenth and Seventeenth Centuries." In *Eroticism in the Middle Ages and the Renaissance: Magic, Marriage, and Midwifery,* edited by Ian Frederick Moulton, 35–57. Turnhout, Belgium: Brepols, 2016.

———. "Franciscan Missionaries as Witnesses of Nature in Colonial Mexico." *Archivum Franciscanum Historicum* 115 (2022): 237–85.

———. "La construcción de la niñez en la vida religiosa. El caso Novohispano." In *Historia de la infancia en América Latina,* coordinated by Pablo Rodríguez and María Emma Mannarelli, 121–44. Bogotá: Universidad Externado de Colombia, 2007.

———. "La familia en un contexto religioso: el caso de la Nueva España." In *Familias y Redes Sociales. Cotidianidad y realidad del mundo iberoamericano y mediterráneo,* coordinated by Sandra Olivero Guidobono, Juan Jesús Bravo Caro, and Rosalva Loreto López, 125–60. Madrid: Iberoamericana-Vervuert, 2021.

———. "La niñez en Mexico en Hispanoamérica: rutas de exploración." In *La familia en el mundo iberoamericano,* edited by Pilar Gonzalbo Aizpuru and Cecilia Rabel, 41–69. Mexico: Universidad Nacional Autónoma de Mexico, 1994.

———. "La religiosa y su confesor. Epistolario de una clarisa mexicana, 1801–1802." *Archivum* 105 (2012): 455–78.

———. "Los espacios de la muerte." In *Espacios en la Historia. Invención y transformation de los espacios sociales*, edited by Pilar Gonzalbo Aizpuru, 49–73. Mexico: Colegio de Mexico, 2014.

———. "Mexico." In *Children in Historical and Comparative Perspective: An International Handbook and Research Guide*, edited by Ray Hiner and Joseph M. Hawes, 221–45. Westport CT: Greenwood Press, 1991.

———. "Viceregal Culture." In *The Cambridge History of Latin American Literature*, vol. 1, edited by Roberto González Echeverría and Enrique Pupo-Walker, 286–335. Cambridge: Cambridge University Press, 1996.

Lavrin, Asunción, and Rosalva Loreto L., eds. *Diálogos Espirituales. Manuscritos Femeninos Hispanoamericanos. Siglos XVI–XIX*. Puebla: BUAP/UDLA, 2006.

Lazcano, Francisco Javier. *Índice practico moral para los sacerdotes que auxilian moribundos*. Mexico: Colegio de Ildefonso, 1750.

Leandro de Murcia. *Questiones selectas y regulares y exposición sobre la Regla de los frailes menores*. Madrid: Gregorio Rodriguez, 1645.

Ledesma, Clemente de. *Despertador de noticias teológicas morales que apuntan y despiertan las letras del ABC al cura y al Confesor*. México: María de Benavides, 1698.

Ledesma, Francisco de. *Documentos de Buena crianza, compuestos por el poeta y maestro Francisco de Ledesma y agora nuevamente enmendados y añadidos con algunas reglas de buen vivir por Juan de Lagunas*. Madrid: María de Quiñones, 1658.

Le Goffe, Jacques. *The Birth of Purgatory*. Chicago: University of Chicago Press, 1981.

León, Nicolas. *San Felipe de Jesús Protomártir*. Mexico: Talleres de la Librería Religiosa, 1898.

León y Moya, D. *Aforismos y reglas para más bien ejercer el alto oficio de la predicación*. Antequera: Manuel Botello de Payve, 1629.

Liebman, Matthew. *An Archeological History of Pueblo Resistance and Revitalization in 17th Century New Mexico*. Tucson: University of Arizona Press, 2014.

Lipsett-Rivera, Sonya. "The Emotional Life of Boys in Eighteenth-Century Mexico City." In *Routledge History Handbook of Gender and the Urban Experience*, edited by Deborah Simonton, 351–61. London: Routledge, 2017.

———. "Model Children and Models for Children in Early Mexico." In *Minor Omissions: Children in Latin American History and Society*, edited by Tobias Hecht, 52–72. Madison: University of Wisconsin Press, 2002.

———. *The Origins of Macho, Men and Masculinity in Colonial Mexico*. Albuquerque: University of New Mexico Press, 2019.

Lizana, Bernardo de. *Historia de Yucatán. Devocionario de Ntra. Sra. De Izamal y Conquista espiritual*. 1633. Reprint, Mexico: Museo Nacional de Mexico, 1893.

Lomnitz, Claudio. *Death and the Idea of Mexico*. New York: Zone Books, 2008.

López, David Martín. "La conceptualización del *Príncipe Christiano* en la tratadística jesuítica entre los siglos XVI y XVII." In *Actas de la XI Reunión Científica de la Fundación Española de Historia Moderna: Comunicaciones*, 113–23. Granada: Editorial Universidad de Granada, 2012.

López Aguado, Juan. *Vozes, que hicieron eco, en la religiosa pyra que en las honras del V.P. Fr. Antonio Margil de Jesús* [. . .]. Mexico: Joseph Bernardo de Hogal, 1726.

López Arguedas, Esteban. "La formación del predicador: de la Rhetorica Christiana de Fray Diego de Valadés a Antonio Margil de Jesús." *Kañina* 44, no. 2 (August 2020): 9–33. https://www.scielo.sa.cr/scielo.php?script=sci_arttext&pid=S2215-26362020000200009.

López Cogolludo, Diego. *Historia de Yucathan*. Madrid: Juan García Infanzón, 1688.

López de Mariscal, Blanca, and Nancy Joe Dyer, eds. *El sermón novohispano como texto de cultura. Ocho estudios*. New York: Idea/Igas, 2012.

López de Mariscal, Blanca, and Guadalupe Rodríguez Domínguez. *Arte de bien morir y la contienda del cuerpo y el alma, un incunable toledano de 1500*. Mexico: Iberoamericana, 2019.

Loreto, Rosalva. "La casa y la educación familiar en una ciudad novohispana. Los hogares poblanos del siglo XVIII." In *Familia y educación en Iberoamérica*, coordinated by Pilar Gonzalbo Aizpuru, 57–82. México: Colegio de México, 1999.

———. "Los barrocos sonidos del poder. Representaciones, orden y control urbano. Puebla de los Ángeles, siglos XVII y XVIII." In *Expresiones y estrategias. La iglesia en el orden social novohispano*, coordinated by María del Pilar Martínez López-Cano and Francisco Javier Cervantes Bello, 113–54. Mexico: UNAM, Instituto de Investigaciones Históricas / Benemérita Universidad Autónoma de Puebla, 2017.

Lundberg, Magnus. "The Ordination of Indians in Colonial Spanish America: Law, Prejudice, and Practice during Three Centuries." *Swedish Missiological Themes*, no. 91 (2003): 297–322.

Luque Alcaide, Elisa. *La educación en Nueva España en el siglo XVIII*. Sevilla: Escuela de Estudios Hispano-Americanos, 1970.

MacLeod, Murdo. "Instruments for the Voiceless: Indian Riots and Rebellions in Colonial Central America, 1530–1720." In *The Globe Encircled and the World Revealed*, edited by Ursula Lamb, 277–29. London: Routledge, 2016.

Magaña Mancillas, Mario Alberto. "Sobre nuevo método de Gobierno espiritual de misiones de California, por Fray Rafael Verger, 1772." *Relaciones* 35, no. 139 (June–August 2014): 197–229.

Malo de Medina, Francisco Gabriel. *Guía del niño instruido y padre educado. Cartilla y Catón para todas artes*. Madrid: Imprenta Real, 1787.

Malvido, Elsa. "Los novicios de San Francisco en la ciudad de Mexico. La Edad de Hierro (1649–1749)." *Historia Mexicana* 36, no. 4 (1987): 699–738.

Maravall, José Antonio. *La cultura del barroco: análisis de una estructura histórica.* Barcelona: Editorial Planeta, 2012.

Margil, Antonio de Jesús. *Formulario de Missiones que hizo, y dicto N.V.P. Fr. Antonio Margil de Jesús.* Undated manuscript. Genaro García Collection, Benson Library, University of Texas at Austin.

———. *Nothingness Itself: Selected Writings of Ven. Fr. Antonio Margil 1690–1724.* Edited by Marion A. Habig. Translated by Benedict Leutenegger. Chicago: Franciscan Herald Press, 1976.

Martínez, María Elena. *Genealogical Fictions. Limpieza de Sangre, Religion, and Gender in Colonial Mexico.* Stanford: Stanford University Press, 2008.

Martínez, María Victoria. "A vueltas con la honra y el honor. Evolución conceptiva de la honra y el honor en las sociedades castellanas desde el medioevo al siglo XVII." *Revista Borradores* 8–9 (2008): 1–10.

Martínez de Adame, Joseph. *Sermón de San Felipe de Jesús.* Mexico: Felipe de Zúñiga y Ontiveros, 1781.

Martínez de Sánchez, Ana María. *Oralidad y escritura. Práctica de las palabras: los sermones.* Córdoba: Universidad Nacional de Córdoba, Centro de Estudios Avanzados, 2008.

Martínez Ferrer, Luis. "Las Órdenes mendicantes y el sacramento de la confesión en Nueva España (siglo XVI)." *Revista Complutense de Historia de América* 24, no. 47 (1998): 47–68.

Martínez Gil, Fernando. *Muerte y Sociedad en la España de los Austria.* Cuenca: Universidad de Castilla–La Mancha, 2000.

Martínez Góngora, Mar. *El hombre atemperado. Autocontrol, disciplina y masculinidad en textos españoles de la temprana modernidad.* New York: Peter Lang, 2005.

Martínez López-Cano, María del Pilar, coord. *De la historia económica a la historia social y cultural. Homenaje a Gisela von Wobeser.* Mexico: UNAM, 2015.

Matson, Dan S. "Letters of Friar Pedro Font, 1776–1777." *Ethnohistory* 22, no. 3 (Summer 1975): 263–93.

Matson, Daniel S., and Bernard L. Fontana, eds. and trans. *Friar Bringas Reports to the King: Methods of Indoctrination on the Frontier of New Spain, 1796–97.* Tucson: University of Arizona Press, 1977.

Mayer, Alicia, and Ernesto de la Torre Villar, eds. *Religión, poder y autoridad en la Nueva España.* Mexico: UNAM, 2004.

Maza, Francisco de la. *Las piras funerarias en la historia y en el arte de Mexico.* México: Instituto de Investigaciones Estéticas, 1946.

McCloskey, Michael N. *The Formative Years of the Missionary College of Santa Cruz de Querétaro, 1683–1833.* Washington DC: Catholic University of America Press, 1955.

———. "Fray Isidro Félix de Espinosa: Companion and Biographer of Margil." *The Americas* 7, no. 13 (January 1951): 228–295.

Mecham, J. Lloyd. "The Martyrdom of Father Juan de Santa Maria." *Catholic Historical Review* 6, no. 3 (October 1920): 308–21.

Medina, Baltasar de. *Chronica de la S. Provincia de S. Diego de Mexico de Religiosos Descalzos de N.S.P.S. Francisco en la Nueva España. Vidas de Ilustres y venerables Varones, que la han edificado con excelentes virtudes*. Mexico: Juan de Ribera, 1682.

———. *Vida, Martyrio y Beatificación del Invicto Proto-Martyr de el Japón, San Felipe de Jesús*. 2nd ed. Madrid: Imprenta de los Herederos de la Viuda de Juan García Infanzón, 1751.

Medina, José Toribio. *Historia del Tribunal del Santo Oficio de la Inquisición*. Santiago de Chile: Imprenta Elzeviriana, 1903.

Medina Bustos, José Marcos. "La población en Sonora en 1785, según el informe del obispo Fray Antonio María de los Reyes." Paper presented at the 2004 XVII Simposium Sociedad Sonorense de Historia, Hermosillo, Mexico, 2004.

———. *La imprenta en Mexico, 1539–1821*. 8 vols. Santiago de Chile, 1907–12.

Melvin, Karen. *Building Colonial Cities of God: Mendicant Orders and Urban Culture in New Spain*. Stanford: Stanford University Press, 2012.

Memorial que Fray Juan de Santander de la Orden de san Francisco, Comisario General de Indias, presenta a la Majestad católica del rey don Felipe Cuarto, nuestro Señor, hecho por el padre Fray Alonso de Benavides, Comisario del Santo Oficio, y Custodio que ha sido de las Provincias y conversiones del Nuevo México. Madrid: Imprenta Real, 1630.

Méndez, Águeda. *Secretos del oficio: Avatares de la Inquisición novohispana*. Mexico: Colegio de Mexico / UNAM, 2001.

Mendieta, Jerónimo de. *Historia Eclesiástica Indiana*. Edition of Francisco Solano y Pérez-Lila. 2 vols. Biblioteca de Autores Españoles, vols. 260–61. Madrid: Atlas, 1973.

Mendo, Andrés de. *Príncipe Perfecto y Ministros Ajustados. Documentos Políticos y Morales en Emblemas* León, France: Horacio Boissat and George Remeus, 1662.

Messerschmidt, James W. *Hegemonic Masculinity: Formulation, Reformulation, and Amplification*. Lanham MD: Rowman and Littlefield, 208.

Milhou-Roudie, Anne. "Erasme et Dyonysius Caton: Deux Modèles de Savoir Vivre pour le jeune espagnol. Civilité et education en Espagne du XVIe au XVIIIè siècles." In *La Formation de l'enfant en Espagne aux XVIᵉ et XVIIᵉ siècles*, coordinated by Augustine Redondo, 121–30. Paris: Presses de la Sorbonne Nouvelle, 1996.

Miranda, Luis de. *Exposición de la regla de ls Frailes Menores de la Orden de Nuestro G. P. S. Francisco*. Salamanca: Antonio Vásquez, 1622.

Molina, Alonso. *Arte de la lengua mexicana y castellana*. Edited by Ascensión Hernández de León Portilla. Mexico: UNAM, Instituto de Investigaciones Históricas / Fideicomiso Felipe Teixido y Montserrat Alfau de Teixidor / Instituto Tecnológico y de Estudios Superiores de Monterrey, 2014.

Molina, Antonio de. *Ejercicios espirituales de las excelencias, provecho, y necesidades de la oración mental, reducidos a doctrina y meditaciones, sacadas de los santos padres y doctores de la Iglesia*. Barcelona: Rafael Figueroa, 1613.

Montané Martí, Julio César, ed. *Fray Pedro Font, Diario Íntimo y Diario de Fray Tomás Eixarch*. Mexico: Plaza y Valdés / Universidad de Sonora, 2000.

Monzón, Francisco de, and Luis Rodrígues. *Libro Primero del Espejo del Príncipe Cristiano que se trata como se ha de criar un príncipe o niños generosos desde su tierna niñez con todos los ejercicios y virtudes que le convienen hasta ser varón perfecto*. Lisboa: Casa de Luis Rodríguez, 1544.

Moon, Silver. "The Imperial College of Tlatelolco and the Emergence of a New Nahua Intellectual Elite in New Spain (1500–1760)." PhD diss., Duke University, 2007.

Moorhead, Max L. *The Presidio: Bastion of the Spanish Borderlands*. Norman: University of Oklahoma Press, 1975.

Morales, Francisco. *Ethnic and Social Background of the Franciscan Friars in Seventeenth-Century Mexico*. Washington DC: Academy of Franciscan History, 1974.

———. "De la utopía a la locura. El Asia en la mente de los franciscanos de Nueva España: del siglo XVI al XIX." In *Órdenes religiosas entre América y Asia. Ideas para una historia misionera de los espacios coloniales*, edited by Elisabetta Corsi, 57–83. Mexico: Colegio de Mexico, 2008.

———. "La biografía del beato Sebastián de Aparicio." In *Camino a la Santidad*, coordinated by Manuel Ramos Medina, 137–63. México: Centro de Estudios de Historia de México Condumex, 2003.

———. "Los hermanos laicos en las provincias de Mexico, Siglos XVI y XVII. Dos temas por estudiar: evangelización y sociedad." *Archivum Franciscanum Historicum* 112 (2019): 433–68.

———. "The Native Encounter with Christianity: Franciscans and Nahuas in Sixteenth Century Mexico." *The Americas* 65, no. 2 (2008): 137–59.

———. "Orden Franciscana y Movilidad social, Siglo XVII." *Historia Mexicana* 65, no. 4 (2016): 1663–1708.

———. "Pedro de Gante, Martin de Valencia, Toribio Motolinía." *Arqueología mexicana* 21, no. 127 (2014): 37–42.

Morales Cosme, Alba, and Patricia Aceves Pastrana. "Negocio, reglamentación y profesionalización farmacéutica: la botica del Hospital general de san Andrés (1770–1809)." *Montalbán* 36 (2003): 45–64.

Mora Reyes, María Fernanda. "Los Dominicos de la Provincia de Santiago de Mexico en las ciudades novohispanas (1570–1661)." PhD diss., Universidad Nacional Autónoma de Mexico, 2021.

Moreno Basurto, Salvador, and Manuel González Ramírez, coords. *El humanismo de Fray Antonio Margil de Jesús en el Septentrión novohispano Estudios y reflexiones desde el siglo XXI*. Zacatecas: Universidad Autónoma de Zacatecas, 2018.

Moreno Gallego, Valentín. *La recepción hispana de Juan Luis Vives*. Valencia: Biblioteca Valenciana, 2006.

Moreno García, Heriberto. *Los Agustinos. Aquellos misioneros hacendados*. Mexico: SEP, 1985.

Moreno Navarro, Isidoro. *Los Cuadros del Mestizaje Americano. Estudio Antropológico del Mestizaje*. Madrid: Ediciones José Porrúa Turanzas, 1973.

Moriuchi, Mey-Yen. "The Art of Conversation: Eighteenth-Century Mexican Casta Painting." *Shift: Graduate Journal of Visual and Material Culture* 5 (2012): 1–25.

Muñoz, Diego. *Descripción de la provincia de los apóstoles S. Pedro y S. Pablo en las Indias de la Nueva España*. Celaya, Guanajuato: Edición de la Provincia Franciscana de San Pedro y San Pablo, 2015.

Murcia, Leandro de. *Questiones selectas y regulares y exposición sobre la Regla de los frailes menores*. Madrid: Gregorio Rodriguez, 1645.

Murillo, Diego. *Instrucción para enseñar la Virtud a principiantes y escala espiritual para la perfección evangélica*. Zaragoza: Lorenzo de Robles, 1598.

Murillo Gallegos, Verónica. "Las voces bajo el discurso: los indígenas en la composición de textos lingüísticos-misionales novohispanos." *Entre caníbales. Revista de literatura* 3, no. 10 (June 2019): 35–55.

Muro Abad, Juan Roberto. "La castidad del clero bajomedieval en la diócesis de Calahorra." *Historia. Instituciones. Documentos* 20 (1993): 261–82.

Murray, Jacqueline, ed. *Conflicted Identities and Multiple Masculinities: Men in the Medieval West*. New York: Garland, 1999.

———. "'Mystical Castration': Some Reflections on Peter Abelard, Hugh of Lincoln and Sexual Control." In *Conflicted Identities and Multiple Masculinities: Men in the Medieval West*, edited by Jacqueline Murray, 73–110. London: Routledge, 2013.

Myers, Kathleen A., and Amanda Powell, eds. *A Wild Country out in the Garden: The Spiritual Journals of a Colonial Mexican Nun*. Bloomington: Indiana University Press, 1999.

Navarrete, Pedro. *Directorio para informaciones de los pretendientes del santo habito de N. Seraphico P.S. Francisco [. . .]*. Mexico: María de Ribera, 1737.

Navarro, Vicente. *Oración fúnebre en las exequias de . . . Fr. Antonio Margil de Jesús . . . celebradas el día 26 de octubre de . . . 1728 . . . Díjola . . . el Dr. Vicente Navarro*. Valencia: Antonio Bordazar, 1729.

Navarro García, Luis. *José de Gálvez y la Comandancia General de las Provincias Internas*. Sevilla: Escuela de Estudios Hispano-Americanos de Sevilla, Consejo Superior de Investigaciones Científicas, 1964.

Naylor, Thomas H., and Charles W. Polzer, comps. and eds. *The Californias and Sinaloa-Sonora, 1700–1765*. Tucson: University of Arizona Press, 1997.

———, comps. and eds. *The Presidio and Militia on the Northern Frontier of New Spain: A Documentary History, 1570–1700*. 2 vols. Tucson: University of Arizona Press, 1986 and 1997.

Nesvig, Martin. *Promiscuous Power: An Unorthodox History of New Spain*. Austin: University of Texas Press, 2018.

Nieremberg, Juan Eusebio. *Vida del Santo Padre y Gran Siervo de Dios el B. Francisco de Borja*. Madrid: María de Quiñones, 1644.

Nieser, Albert Bertrand. "The Dominican Mission Foundations in Baja California, 1769–1822." PhD diss., Loyola University, 1960.

Nieto, J. C. "Christian Doctrine ad the Christian Instruction for Children." *Bibliothèque d' Humanisme et Renaissance* 36, no. 2 (1974): 253–72.

Nieva, Guillermo René. "De la raza a la conducta: informaciones de 'limpieza de sangre' en los conventos dominicos de Castilla (ss. XVI–XVII)." *eHumanista/Conversos* 5, no. 11 (2017): 192–201.

Nieva Ocampo, Guillermo. "Incorporarse a Jesucristo: prácticas sacramentales y penitencias entre los dominicos castellanos en el siglo XVI." *Hispania Sacra*, no. 58 (January–June 2006): 39–67.

Noble, David F. *A World without Women: The Christian Clerical Culture of Western Science*. New York: Alfred A. Knopf, 1992.

Nogar, Anna. *Quill and Cross in the Borderlands: Sor Maria de Agreda and the Lady in Blue, 1628 to the Present*. Notre Dame: University of Notre Dame Press, 2018.

Noydens, Benito Remigio. *Promptuario moral de questiones prácticas y casos repentinos en la teología moral para examen de curas y confesores*. Barcelona: Antonio Lacavalleria, 1668.

Núñez Beltrán, Miguel Ángel. *La oratoria sagrada de la época del barroco. Doctrina, cultura y actitud ante la vida desde los sermones sevillanos del siglo XVII*. Sevilla: Universidad de Sevilla / Fundación Focus-Abengoa, 2000.

O'Banion, Patrick J. "'A Priest Who Appears Good': Manuals of Confession and the Construction of Clerical Identity in Early Modern Spain." In *The Formation of Clerical and Confessional Identities in Early Modern Europe*, edited by Winm Njanse and Barbara Pitkin, 333–48. Leiden: Brill, 2006.

Ojea, Hernando de. *Libro Tercero de la historia religiosa de la provincia de Mexico de la Orden de Sto. Domingo*. Mexico: Museo Nacional de Mexico, 1897.

Oré, Luis Jerónimo de. *Account of the Martyrs in the Province of La Florida*. Edited and translated by Raquel Chang-Rodriguez and Nancy Vogeley. Albuquerque: University of New Mexico Press, 2017.

Orozco Hernández, María Angélica. "San Francisco de Zacatecas: José de Arlegui." In *Historiografía mexicana*, vol. 2, *Historiografía eclesiástica*, coordinated by Rosa Camelo and Patricia Escandón, 973–85. Mexico: UNAM, 2012.

Ortega, Emmanuel. "Hagiographical Misery and the Liminal Witness: Novohispanic Franciscan Martyr Portraits and the Politics of Imperial Expansion." In *Visualizing Sensuous Suffering and Affective Pain in Early Modern Europe and the Spanish Americas*, edited by Lauran G Kilroy-Ewbank and Heather Graham, 234–65. Leiden: Brill, 2018.

———. "Testimonies of Violence: Images of Franciscans Martyrs in the Provinces of New Spain." PhD diss., University of New Mexico, 2017. https://digitalrepository.unm.edu/cgi/viewcontent.cgi?article=1061&context=arth_etds.

Ortega Noriega, Sergio, ed. *De la santidad a la perversión. O de porqué no se cumplía la ley de Dios en la sociedad novohispana*. Mexico: Grijalbo, 1986.

Osante, Patricia. "Estrategia colonizadora en el Nuevo Santander, siglo XVIII." *Estudios de Historia novohispana*, no. 30 (2004): 17–44.

———. *Orígenes del Nuevo Santander (1748–1772)*. Mexico: UNAM, 1997.

———. "Presencia misional en Nuevo Santander en la segunda mitad del Siglo XVIII. Memoria de un infortunio." *Estudios de Historia Novohispana*, no. 17 (1997): 107–35.

———. *Testimonio acerca de la causa formada en la colonial del Nuevo Santander al coronel don José de Escandón*. Mexico: UNAM / Universidad Autónoma de Tamaulipas / Instituto Tamaulipeco para la Cultura y las Artes, 2000.

Osuna, Francisco de. *Norte de los estados*. Sevilla: Bartolomé Pérez, 1531.

Palafox y Mendoza, Juan de. *Vida interior del ilustrísimo, excelentísimo y venerable D. Juan de Palafox y Mendoza*. Sevilla: Lucas Martin, 1691.

Palmireno, Juan Lorenzo. *El estudioso cortesano*. Valencia: Petri a Huete, 1573.

———. *El estudioso de la aldea*. Valencia: Casa de Joan Mey, 1568.

Palou, Francisco. *Cartas desde la península de California (1768–1773)*. Edited by José Luis Soto Pérez. Mexico: Editorial Porrúa, 1994.

———. *Recopilación de Noticias de la Antigua y Nueva California (1767–1783)*. Edited by José Luis Soto Pérez. Mexico: Editorial Porrúa, 1998.

———. *Relación histórica de la vida y apostólicas tareas del Venerable Padre Fray Junípero Serra, y de las misiones que fundo en la California Septentrional, y nuevos establecimientos del Monterey*. Mexico: Felipe Zúñiga y Ontiveros, 1787.

Pardo, Felipe Mariano. *Doble llanto de una madre conque manifestó al doble su sentimiento por la muerte de un hijo que fue su padre. Sermón Fúnebre*. Mexico: Imprenta de la Bibliotheca Mexicana, 1760.

Pardo-Tomas, José. *La medicina de la conversión: el convento como espacio de cultura medica novohispana*. Mexico: UNAM, 2014.

Parish, Helen. *Clerical Celibacy in the West: c.1100–1700*. London: Ashgate, 2010.

Parker, Geoffrey. *The Dutch Revolt*. London: Penguin Books, 1988.

———. *Spain and the Netherlands, 1559–1659: Ten Studies*. London: Fontana Press, 1990.

Pazos, Manuel Antonio de. *Sermón fúnebre que, en el aniversario de difuntos, que, en su Capítulo Provincial, hace la Provincia de N.S.P.S. Francisco de Zacateca*. Mexico: Imprenta Nueva Madrileña de los Herederos del Lic. D. Joseph de Jáuregui, 1783.

Pego Puigbo, Armando. *El Renacimiento espiritual. Introducción literaria a los tratados de oración españoles (1520–1566)*. Madrid: Ministerio de Ciencias y Tecnología / Consejo Superior de Investigaciones Científicas, 2005.

Peñalver, Patricio. *La mística española (siglos XVI y XVII)*. Madrid: Akal, 1997.

Perea, Estevan de. *Segunda relación de la grandiosa conversión que ha habido en el Nuevo Mexico*. Sevilla: Luis Estupiñán, 1633.

———. *Verdadera relación, de la grandiosa conversión que ha habido en el Nuevo Mexico: Enviada por el padre Fray Estevan de Perea, custodio de las provincias del Nuevo Mexico, al muy reverendo P. Fr. Francisco de Apodaca, Comisario general de toda la Nueva España*. N.p., 1632.

Pérez Álvarez, Lucía Elvira. "Siete loas de Fray Juan de la Anunciación." Master's thesis, UNAM, 2011.

Pérez Álvarez, María José, and Alfredo Martín García, eds. *Campo y campesinos en la España Moderna. Culturas Políticas en el Mundo Hispano*. León: Fundación Española de Historia Moderna, 2012.

Péron, Mylène. *Le Mexique, Terre de Mission Franciscaine (XVIe–XIXe siècle). La Province de Xalisco*. Paris: L'Harmattan, 2005.

Pimentel Pontes Filho, Antônio. "Os filhos e 'afilhados' de São Francisco de Assis: a construção da identidade religiosa e do parentesco da família franciscana." *Tempo da Ciência* 13, no. 26 (2006): 9–24.

Pinamonti, Giovanni Pietro. *Breves Meditaciones sobre los Novísimos repartidas por los días del mes. Con la Regla para vivir bien*. México: Herederos de Joseph de Jauregui, 1789.

Pinar, Francisco J. Lorenzo. *Actitudes religiosas ante la muerte en Zamora en el siglo XVI: Un estudio de mentalidades*. Zamora: Instituto de Estudio Zamoranos, "Florián de Ocampo," 1989.

Pinilla, Miguel Ramón. *Breve relación de la vida de la Madre Sor María Antonia de el Espíritu Santo Maldonado*. Biblioteca del Centro de Estudios Históricos Condumex (now Carso), fondo 238-1.1, siglo XVIII.

Pita Moreda, María Teresa. *Los predicadores novohispanos del siglo XVI*. Salamanca: Editorial San Esteban, 1992.

Plumbensi, Nicolao. *Opusculum Vitae, Virtutum, et Miraculorum. Ven Servi Dei Fr. Sebastian Ab Apparitio.* Romae: Ex Officina Reveredae Camerae Apostolicae, 1696.

Po-Chia Hsia, R. *The World of Catholic Renewal, 1540–1770.* Cambridge: Cambridge University Press, 1998.

Ponce de León, Nicolás. *Historia de la singular vida de el venerable hermano Fray Christoval de Molina, religioso lego de la Orden de N. P. San Agustín.* Puebla de los Ángeles: Diego Fernández de León, 1686.

Ponce Hernández, Carolina, coord. *Innovación y tradición en Fray Alonso de la Veracruz.* Mexico: UNAM / Facultad de Filosofia y Letras, 2007.

Poole, Stafford. "Church Law on the Ordination of Indians and Castas in New Spain." *Hispanic American Historical Review* 61, no. 4 (1981): 637–50.

———. *Pedro Moya de Contreras: Catholic Reform and Royal Power in New Spain, 1571–1591.* 2nd ed. Norman: University of Oklahoma Press, 2011.

Portilla, Miguel. León. *Mexico en 1554. Tres diálogos latinos de Francisco Cervantes de Salazar.* Mexico: UNAM, 2001. https://historicas.unam.mx/publicaciones/publicadigital/libros/mexico1554/383_04_03_mexico_1554.pdf.

Poutrin, Isabelle. "Conflictos sobre normas. Judíos, musulmanes y conversos en los Consilia de Martin de Azpilcueta." In *Cambios y resistencias sociales en la edad moderna. Un análisis comparativo entre el centro y la periferia mediterránea de la Monarquia Hispánica,* edited by Fernando Andrés Robres, Rafael Benítez Sánchez-Blanco, and Ricardo Franch Benavent, 243–52. Madrid: Silex, 2014.

Praz, Mario. *Studies in Seventeenth Century Imagery.* 2nd ed. Roma: Edizione di Storia e Letteratura, 1975.

Priestley, Herbert I., ed. *Diary of Pedro Fages.* Academy of Pacific Coast History, vol. 3, no. 2. Berkeley: University of California Press, 1913.

Puente, Luis de la. *Meditaciones espirituales.* Valladolid: Juan de Bostillo, 1605.

Puyol, Julio. "Los Coloquios de Erasmo." *Boletín de la Real Academia de la historia* 108, no. 2 (April–June 1936): 25–51. https://www.cervantesvirtual.com/partes/720168/boletin-de-la-real-academia-de-la-historia-1.

Radding, Cynthia. "The Function of the Market in Changing Economic Structures in the Mission Communities of Pimería Alta, 1768–1821." *The Americas* 34, no. 2 (October 1977): 155–69.

———. *Wandering Peoples: Colonialism, Ethnic Spaces, and Ecological Frontiers in Northwestern Mexico, 1700–1850.* Durham NC: Duke University Press, 1997.

Ragon, Pierre. "Sebastián de Aparicio: Un Santo Mediterráneo en el Altiplano Mexicano." *Estudios de Historia Novohispana* 123 (June 2000): 17–45.

Ramírez Leyva, Edelmira. *Cartas pastorales, elogios fúnebres, oraciones panegíricas, sermones y otros géneros de oratoria sagrada de la colección Lafragua del Fondo Reservado de la Biblioteca Nacional de Mexico.* Mexico: UNAM, 1992.

Ramos Medina, Manuel. *Camino a la santidad, siglos XVI–XX*. Mexico: Centro de Estudios Históricos Condumex, 2003.
Raverty, Aaron. "Are We Monks or Are We Men? The Monastic Masculine Gender Model According to the Rule of Benedict." *Journal of Men's Studies* 14, no. 3 (Fall 2006): 269–91.
Rawlings, Helen. *The Spanish Inquisition*. Malden MA: Blackwell Publishing, 2006.
Raya Guillén, Adriana Lucero. "Los clérigos solicitantes del obispado de Michoacán ante el Santo Oficio novohispano, 1731–1794." *Ulua* 16 (July–December 2010): 37–66.
Redondo, Augustine, coord. *La formation de l'enfant en Espagne aux XVIe et XVIIe siècles*. Paris: Presses de la Sorbonne Nouvelle, 1996.
Reed, Benjamin Daniel. *Sermons, Preaching, and Ideological Production: A Case Study of Seventeenth Century New Spain*. Bloomington: Indiana University Press, 2006.
Reff, Daniel T. "'The Predicament of Culture' and Spanish Missionary Accounts of the Tepehuan and Pueblo Revolts." *Ethnohistory* 42, no. 1 (Winter 1995): 63–90.
Regla de los Frayles Menores. Mexico: Casa de Pedro Balli, 1595.
Regla de N.P.S. Agustín, y Constituciones de la Sagrada Orden de Predicadores . . . para el uso de sus Religiosos Legos. Barcelona: Bernardo Plá, Impresor, 1787.
Regla de S. Augustín y Constituciones de su Religión. Madrid: Juan Sanz, 1719.
Reglamento e Instrucción para los Presidios de la Península de Californias, erección de nuevas Misiones y fomento del pueble y extensión de los Establecimientos de Monterey. Mexico: Felipe de Zúñiga y Ontiveros, 1784.
Restall, Matthew, Amara Solari, John F. Chuchiak IV, and Tracy Arden. *The Friar and the Maya: Diego de Landa and the Account of the Things of Yucatan*. Denver: University of Colorado Press, 2023.
Revel, Jacques. "The Uses of Civility." In *A History of Private Life*, vol. 3, edited by Phillipe Aries and Georges Duby, 167–205. Cambridge MA: Harvard University Press, 1989.
Rex Galindo, David. "Grey Friars and Indians in the Spanish Upper California, 1769–1820." *Espacio, Tiempo y Forma*, serie IV, Historia Moderna, 20 (2007): 157–70.
———. "Propaganda Fide: Training Franciscan Missionaries in New Spain." PhD diss., Southern Methodist University, 2010.
———. *To Sin No More. Franciscans and Conversion in the Hispanic World, 1683–1830*. Stanford: Stanford University Press / Academy of Franciscan History, 2017.
Rey, Agapito. "Missionary Aspects of the Founding of New Mexico." *New Mexico Historical Review* 23, no. 1 (1948): 22–31.
Reyes, Barbara O. *Private Women, Public Lives: Gender and the Missions of California*. Austin: University of Texas Press, 2009.
Ribadeneyra, Marcelo de. *Historia de las Islas del Archipelago y Reynos de la Gran China*. Barcelona: Emprenta de Gabriel Graells y Giraldo Dotil, 1601.

Ribadeneyra, Pedro de. *Ecclesiastical History of the Schism of the Kingdom of England: A Spanish Jesuit's History of the English Reformation*. Edited and translated by Spencer J. U. Weinreich. Leiden: Brill, 2017.

———. *Historia eclesiástica del cisma de Inglaterra*. 1588. Reprint, Madrid: Imprenta y Libreria de D. Manuel Martin, 1781.

———. *Obras escogidas de Pedro de Rivadeneira*. Edited by Vicente de la Fuente. Madrid: M. Rivadeneira, 1868.

———. *Tratado de la religión y virtudes que debe tener el príncipe christiano, para gobernar y conservar sus estados. Contra lo que Nicolas Machiavelo, y los políticos de este tiempo enseñan*. Madrid: Imprenta de P. Madrigal, 1595.

Ricard, Robert. *The Spiritual Conquest of Mexico: An Essay on the Apostolate and the Evangelization Methods on the Mendicant Orders in New Spain, 1523–1572*. Berkeley: University of California Press, 1966.

Rincón González, María Dolores. "Criterios de selección." *Elucidario* 1 (March 2006): 135–46.

Río, Ignacio del. "La adjudicación de las misiones de la antigua California a los padres dominicos." *Estudios de Historia Novohispana* 18 (1998): 69–82.

Rivera, Agustín. *Principios Críticos sobre el Virreinato de la Nueva España i la revolución de independencia*. Vol. 2, *La oratoria sagrada en España en los siglos XVII, XVII i XIX*. Lagos: Tipografía de Vicente Veloz, 1888.

Rivera Guerrero, Sergio. "Iconografía sobre Fray Antoni Margil de Jesús." *Mirada Docta* 1, no. 2 (February 2018): 24–37.

Rodríguez, Joseph Manuel. *Vida prodigiosa del V. Siervo de Dios Fray Sebastián de Aparicio*. Mexico: Imprenta de D. Phelipe de Zúñiga y Ontiveros, 1769.

Rodríguez, Martha Eugenia. "Legislación sanitaria y boticas novohispanas." *Estudios de Historia Novohispana* 17 (1997): 151–69.

Rodríguez, Pablo, and María Emma Mannarelli, coords. *Historia de la infancia en América Latina*. Bogotá: Universidad Externado de Colombia, 2007.

Rodríguez Álvarez, Ma. de los Ángeles. *Usos y costumbres funerarias en la Nueva España*. Zamora: Colegio de Michoacán / Colegio Mexiquense, 2001.

Rodríguez Cacho, Lina. "La frustración del humanista escribiente en el siglo XVI: el caso de Antonio de Torquemada." *Criticón* 44 (1988): 61–73.

Roldán-Figueroa, Rady. *The Martyrs of Japan: Publication History and Catholic Missions in the Spanish World (Spain, New Spain, and the Philippines, 1597–1700)*. Leiden: Brill, 2021.

Romero, Francisco. *Avisos para el Noviciado*. Madrid: Juan Sanz, 1722.

Romero de Terreros, Juan M. "The Destruction of the San Sabá Apache Mission: A Discussion of the Casualties." *The Americas* 60, no. 4 (April 2004): 617–29.

Romero Galván, José Rubén. "Tratado primero. El cronista y su mundo." In *Contextos y Texto de una Crónica. Libro Tercero de la Historia Religiosa de la Provincia de Mexico de la Orden de Santo Domingo de Fray Hernando de Ojea, O.P.*, 9–44. Mexico: UNAM, 2007.

Rosales, Gerónimo. *Catón Christiano y catecismo de la Doctrina Christiana. Para la educación y buena crianza de los niños, y muy provechoso para personas de todos los estados.* Pamplona: Viuda de Rada, 1807.

Rossell, Basilio Tomas. *El Monacato o Tardes Monásticas.* Valencia: Imprenta de Salvador Faulí, 1787.

Rubial García, Antonio. *El convento agustino y la sociedad colonial (1533–1630).* Mexico: UNAM, 1989.

———. "El Mártir colonial. Evolución de una figura heroica." In *Coloquio Internacional: El héroe, entre el mito y la historia,* 169–218. Mexico: Educación y Cultura / Trama Editorial, 2010.

———. "El mártir en el Japón." In *La santidad controvertida,* 129–60. Mexico: UNAM / Fondo de Cultura Económica, 1999.

———. "Fray Diego Velázquez de la Cadena, un eclesiástico cortesano del siglo XVII." *Anuario de Estudios Hispanoamericanos* 46 (1989): 173–94.

———. "Imprenta, criollismo y santidad. Los tratados hagiográficos sobre venerables, siervos de Dios y beatos Novohispanos." *Redial, Revista Europea de Información y Documentación sobre América Latina* 8 (1997): 43–52; 9 (1998): 117–31.

———. "Invención de prodigios. La literatura hierofánica novohispanica." *Historias* 69 (January–April 2008): 121–32.

———. *La justicia de Dios. La violencia física y simbólica de los santos en la historia del cristianismo.* México: Trama Editorial, 2011.

———. "La mitra y la cogulla: La secularización palafoxiana y su impacto en el siglo XVII." *Relaciones* 19 (Winter 1998): 239–72.

———. "La muerte como discurso retórico en algunos textos religiosos novohispanos." *Anuario de Historia* 1 (2007): 25–142.

———. *La santidad controvertida.* Mexico: UNAM / Fondo de Cultura Económica de Mexico, 1999.

———. "'Las órdenes mendicantes' evangelizadoras en Nueva España y sus cambios estructurales durante los siglos virreinales." In *La iglesia en Nueva España. Problemas y perspectivas de investigación,* coordinated by María de Pilar Martínez López-Cano, 215–36. México: Universidad Nacional Autónoma de México / Instituto de Investigaciones Históricas, 2010.

———. "Los rituales de la esperanza. Culto y hagiografía de los venerables siervos de Dios novohispanos." Paper delivered at the Vigésimo Congreso Internacional de LASA, Guadalajara, April 17–19, 1995. http://bibliotecavirtual.clacso.org.ar/ar/libros/lasa97/rubialgarcia.pdf.

———. *Una monarquía criolla. La provincia agustina de Mexico en el siglo XVII*. México: CONACULTA, 1990.

———. "Un caso raro. La vida y desgracias de sor Antonia de San Joseph, monja profesa en Jesús María." In *Memoria del II Congreso Internacional, El Monacato femenino en el Imperio Español. Monasterios, beaterios, recogimientos y colegios*, coordinated by Manuel Ramos Medina, 351–57. Mexico: CONDUMEX, 1995.

———. "Votos pactados. Las prácticas políticas entre los mendicantes novohispanos." *Estudios de Historia Novohispana* 26 (January–June 2002): 51–83.

Rubial García, Antonio, and Patricia Escandón. "La crónica de los colegios franciscanos de *propaganda fide*." In *Historiografía Mexicana*, vol. 2, *La creación de una imagen propia. La tradición española*, tomo 2, *Historiografía eclesiástica*, coordinated by Rosa Camelo and Patricia Escandón, 1017–27. Mexico: UNAM / Instituto de Investigaciones Históricas, 2012.

———. "Las crónicas religiosas del siglo XVIII." In *Historia de la literatura mexicana*, vol. 3, coordinated by Manuel Ramos and Nancy Vogeley, 269–307. México: Siglo XXI / UNAM, 2011.

Rubin, Miri. *Mother of God: A History of the Virgin Mary*. New Haven CT: Yale University Press, 2009.

Rui Pita, Joâo, and Ana Leonor Pereira. "A arte farmacêutica no século XVIII, a farmácia conventual e o inventário da Botica do Convento de Nossa Senhora do Carmo (Aveiro) Agora." *Estudos Classicos en Denate* 14, no. 1 (2012): 227–68.

Ruiz, Julio Juan. "Nicolas Maquiavelo en el Pensamiento Político del Siglo de Oro Español." *Revista de Estudios Histórico-Jurídicos* 35 (2013): 771–81.

Ruiz, Vicky L., and Virginia Sánchez-Korroll, eds. *Latinas in the United States: A Historical Encyclopedia*. 3 vols. Bloomington: University of Indiana Press, 2006.

Ruiz Ibáñez, José Javier, and Juan Hernández Franco. *Conflictividad social en torno a la limpieza de sangre en la España Moderna*. Valladolid: Ediciones Universitarias, 2003.

Ruiz Martínez, Cristina. "La moderación como prototipo de santidad: una imagen de la niñez." In *De la santidad a la perversión. O de porqué no se cumplía la ley de Dios en la sociedad novohispana*, edited by Sergio Ortega Noriega, 49–66. México: Grijalbo, 1986.

Rylands, William Harry, George Bullen, and Francis Compton Price, eds. *Ars Moriendi*. ca. 1450. Reprint, London: Holbein Society, 1881.

Saavedra Fajardo, Diego de. *Idea de un príncipe político cristiano. Representada en cien empresas*. Amberes: Casa de Ieronymo y Juan Baptista Verdussen, 1655.

Salazar, Juan de. *Arte de ayudar y disponer a bien morir a todo género de personas*. Roma: Carlo Vulliet, 1608.

Salguero, Pedro. *La vida del muy Reverendo y Venerable Maestro Fray Diego Basalenque.* 1660. MS 2561, Biblioteca Digital Hispánica, Biblioteca Nacional de España, Madrid, Spain.

———. *Vida del venerable y ejemplarísimo varón, el M.F. Diego Basalenque, provincial que fue de la Provincia de San Nicolás de Michoacán.* 2nd ed. Roma: Imprenta de los Herederos de Barbielini, 1761.

Salzedo y Azcona, Luis. *Muerte prevenida o cristiana preparación para una buena muerte.* 2 vols. Madrid: Imprenta de Miguel Escribano, 1773.

San Antonio, Miguel de. *Resumen de la Theologia Moral.* Madrid: Imprenta de Ángel Pascual Rubio, 1719.

San Benito, Joseph de. *Vida Interior y Cartas.* Madrid: Antonio Marin, 1746.

San Buenaventura, Francisco de. *Instrucción para Novicios de la Religión Bethlemitica.* Mexico: Joseph Bernardo de Hogal, 1734.

Sánchez, Joseph P. "Pedro Fages in Sonora, 1767–1768 and 1777–1782." *New Mexico Historical Review* 51, no. 4 (1976): 281–94.

———. *Spanish Bluecoats: The Catalonian Volunteers in Northwestern New Spain, 1767–1810.* Albuquerque: University of New Mexico Press, 1990.

Sánchez, Juan. *Rosario de agonizantes.* Puebla: Viuda de Miguel Ortega, 1753.

Sánchez Banon, Julio. "El Septentrión Novohispano: La Comandancia General de las Provincias Internas." PhD diss., Universidad Complutense de Madrid, 2015.

Sánchez Domingo, Rafael. "La narración de la memoria histórica y de la tradición: los mártires de Cardeña (Burgos) en la memoria colectiva de la Castilla Medieval." In *El culto a los santos, cofradías, devoción, fiestas y arte,* 571–92. San Lorenzo del Escorial: Ediciones Escurialenses, 2008.

Sánchez-Molero, José Luis Gonzalo. *El aprendizaje cortesano de Felipe II, 1527–1546: La formación de un príncipe del renacimiento.* Madrid: Sociedad Estatal para la Conmemoración de los Centenarios de Felipe II y Carlos V, 1999.

———. *Felipe II: la educación de un "felicísimo príncipe" (1527–1545).* Madrid: Consejo Superior de Investigaciones Científicas / Polifemo, 2013.

Sánchez-Téllez, María. "La medicina misionera en Hispanoamérica y Filipinas durante la época colonial." *Estudios de Historia Social y Económica de América* 6 (1990): 33–40.

Sanchis Amat, Víctor Manuel. "La recepción de los Diálogos de México en 1554 de Francisco Cervantes de Salazar: Apuntes bibliográficos." *Tiempo y Escritura* 28 (January–July 2015): 39–55.

San Christoval [Estella], Diego de. *El Tratado de la vanidad del mundo, dividido en tres libros y tratado de meditaciones devotísimas del amor de Dios.* Madrid: Imprenta de Joseph Otero, 1787.

Sandos, James A. *Converting California: Indians and Franciscans in the Mission.* New Haven CT: Yale University Press, 2004.

Sandoval, Bernardo de. *Tratado del Oficio Eclesiástico Canónico.* Toledo: Francisco de Guzmán, 1563.

San Felipe de Jesús Protomártir Mexicano. Extracto de las informaciones auténticas para la beatificación de los veintiséis Mártires del Japón. Mexico: Talleres de la Librería Religiosa, 1898.

San Joan, Joseph de. *Ceremonial Dominicano en el cual se trata de las cosas que conducen al modo uniforme y orden de celebrar los oficios divinos, con las ceremonias del Orden de Predicadores.* Madrid: Viuda de D. Francisco Nieto, 1694.

San Joseph, Martin de. *Breve Exposición de los Preceptos que en la regla de los Frayles Menores obligan a pecado mortal.* Zaragoza: Hospital Real y General de N. Señora de Gracia, 1638.

San Miguel, Isidro de. *Parayso cultivado de la sencilla prudencia. Virtudes practicadas en la Inocentísima vida del V. siervo de Dios, y portentoso varón Fr. Sebastián de Aparicio.* Nápoles: Stamperia de Juan Vernuccio y Nicolas Layno, 1695.

Santa María, Juan de. *Chronica de la Provincia de San Joseph de los Descalzos de la Órden de los Menores de Nuestro Seraphico Padre S. Francisco. Parte Primera.* Madrid: Imprenta Real, 1615.

———. *Chronica de la Provincia de San Joseph de los Descalzos de la Orden de los Menores de Nuestro Seráfico Padre San Francisco. Parte Segunda.* Madrid: Imprenta Real, 1618.

Santander, Juan *Memorial que Fray Juan de Santander de la Orden de san Francisco, Comisario General de Indias, presenta a la Majestad católica del rey don Felipe Cuarto, nuestro Señor, hecho por el padre Fray Alonso de Benavides, Comisario del Santo Oficio, y Custodio que ha sido de las Provincias y conversiones del Nuevo México.* Madrid: Imprenta real, 1630.

Santiago, Mark. *Massacre at the Yuma Crossing: Spanish Relations with the Quechans, 1779–1782.* Tucson: University of Arizona Press, 2010.

Sanz López, Juan. *Compendio de la doctrina regular y mística más necesaria y útil a los frayles menores. Para instrucción de los novicios y dirección de los profesos en su estado religioso.* Madrid: Imprenta de Don Andrés de Soto, 1785.

Sariñana y Cuenca, Isidro. *The Franciscan Martyrs of 1680.* Santa Fe: Historical Society of New Mexico, no. 7, New Mexican Printing Company, 1906.

———. *Oración fúnebre que dijo el doctor D. Ysidro Sariñana y Cuenca . . . el día 20 de marzo de 1681 . . . en las exequias de veinte y un religiosos de la Regular Observancia del Seraphico P.S. Francisco, que murieron a manos de los Indios Apóstatas de la Nueva Mexico, en diez de agosto del año de 1680.* Mexico: Viuda de Bernardo Calderón, 1681.

———. *Sermón que en las honras de. V.P. Fr. Christoval Muñoz de la Concepción, hijo, y definidor habitual de la Santa Provincia de S. Diego de Religiosos Descalzos de N.P.S. Francisco de esta Nueva España*. México: María de Benavides, 1689.

Sarrión Mora, Adelina. *Sexualidad y confesión: la solicitación ante el Tribunal del Santo Oficio*. Cuenca: Ediciones de la Universidad de Castilla–La Mancha, 2010.

Schroeder, Susan, ed. *Native Resistance and the Pax Colonial in New Spain*. Lincoln: University of Nebraska Press, 1998.

Schroeder, Susan, and Stafford Poole, eds. *Religion in New Spain*. Albuquerque: University of New Mexico Press, 2007.

Schwaller, John F. *The Stations of the Cross in Colonial Mexico: The Via Crucis en Mexicano by Augustin de Vetancurt, and the Spread of a Devotion*. Norman: University of Oklahoma Press, 2022.

Sempat Assadourian, Carlos. *Zacatecas. Conquista y transformaciones de la frontera en el Siglo XVI. Minas de plata, guerra y evangelización*. Mexico: Colegio de Mexico, 2008.

Serra, Junípero. *Escritos de Fray Junípero Serra*. Edited by Salustiano Vicedo. Introduction by Jacinto Fernández-Largo. 5 vols. Petra, Mallorca: Imprime Apóstol y Civilizador, Petra, 1984.

Serra, Junípero, and Juan Crespí. *Diario de la expedición de Fray Junípero Serra desde la misión de Loreto a San Diego en 1769*. Edited by Ángel L. Encinas Moral and Teófilo Ruiz. Madrid: Ediciones Miraguano, 2011.

Shean, Julie A. "'From His Roots a Branch Will Bear Fruit': The Development of Missionary Iconography in Late Eighteenth-Century Cult Images of Sebastián de Aparicio (1502–1600)." *Colonial Latin American Review* 18, no. 1 (2009): 17–50.

Sicardo, Joseph. *Christiandad del Japón, y dilatada persecución que padeció. Memorias sacras de los mártires de las ilustres religiones de Santo Domingo, San francisco, Compañía de Jessy y crecido número de seglares, y con especialidad, de los religiosos del Orden de N.P. S. Augustin*. Madrid: Francisco Sanz, 1698.

Sieruta, Dominka. "The Art of Dying Well According to Erasmus of Rotterdam and Teresa De Avila." *Lumen et Vita* 9, no. 2 (2019): 67–76.

Sigüenza, José de. *Historia de la Orden de San Jerónimo*. 1600. Reprint, Madrid: Baylly, Balliere e Hijo Editores, 1907.

———. *Instrucción de maestros y escuela de novicios. Arte de perfección religiosa y monástica*. Madrid: Joseph Rodríguez, 1793.

Sigüenza y Góngora, Carlos. *Obras Históricas*. 2nd ed. Mexico: Editorial Porrúa, 1950.

———. *Theatro de virtudes políticas que constituyen un príncipe*. Mexico: Viuda de Bernardo Calderón, 1680.

Simpson, Lesley Byrd, and Robert S. Weddle. *The San Sabá Papers: A Documentary Account of the Founding and Destruction of San Sabá Mission*. Dallas: Southern Methodist University Press, 2000.

Solís, Gaspar de. "Diary of a Visit of Inspection of the Texas Missions Made by Fray Gaspar José De Solís in the Year 1767–68." *Southwestern Historical Quarterly* 35, no. 1 (July 1931): 28–76.

Sotomayor, José Francisco. *Historia del Apostólico Colegio de Nuestra Señora de Guadalupe de Zacatecas*. Vol. 1. Zacatecas: Imp. y Encuadernación de "La Rosa," 1889.

Sotomayor Sandoval, Susana Alejandra. "La cofradía de Nuestra Señora del Santísimo Rosario de indios mixtecos y zapotecos extravagantes del señor santo Domingo de la ciudad de México 1594–1753." *Itinerantes*, no. 3 (2013): 11–25.

Spears, Beverly. *Early Churches of Mexico: An Architect's View*. Albuquerque: University of New Mexico Press, 2017.

Stagg, Albert. *The First Bishop of Sonora: Antonio de los Reyes, O.F.M.* Tucson: University of Arizona Press, 1976.

Stickler, Alfons Maria. *The Case for Clerical Celibacy: Its Historical Development and Theological Foundations*. San Francisco: Ignatius Press, 1995.

Stylianou, Anastasia. "Martyrs' Blood in Reformation England." PhD diss., University of Warwick, 2018.

Tanck de Estrada, Dorothy. "El Siglo de las Luces." In *Historia Mínima de la educación en Mexico*, 67–98. Mexico: Colegio de Mexico, 2010.

———, coord. *Historia Mínima de la educación en Mexico*. Mexico: Colegio de Mexico, 2010.

———. "Imágenes infantiles en los años de la insurgencia, El grabado popular, la educación y la cultura política de los niños." *Historia Mexicana* 59, no. 1 (2009): 227–79.

———. *Pueblos de indios y educación en el México colonial, 1750–1821*. México: Colegio de México, 1999.

Teggart, Frederick J., ed. and trans. *The Anza Expedition of 1775–1776: Diary of Pedro Font*. Berkeley: University of California Press, 1913.

Tello, Antonio. *Libro Segundo de la Crónica Miscelánea en que se trata de la conquista espiritual y temporal de la Santa Provincia de Jalisco en el Nuevo Reino de la Galicia y Nueva Vizcaya*. Guadalajara: Imprenta La República Literaria, 1891.

Tentler, Thomas N. *Sin and Confession on the Eve of Reformation*. Princeton NJ: Princeton University Press, 1977.

Terán Elizondo, Isabel, Víctor Manuel Chávez Ríos, and María del Carmen Fernández Montemayor, coords. *In hoc túmulo. Escritura e imagen de la muerte en Mexico*. Zacatecas: Universidad Autónoma de Zacatecas, 2017.

Terrones Aguilar de Caño, Francisco. *Arte o instrucción, y breve tratado que dice las partes que ha de tener el predicador evangélico, como ha de componer el sermón, que cosas ha de tratar, y en qué manera las ha de decir. Granada: Bartolomé de Lorenzana, 1617.

Thibodeaux, Jennifer D. *The Manly Priest: Clerical Celibacy, Masculinity and Reform in England and Normandy, 1066–1300*. Philadelphia: University of Pennsylvania Press, 2015.

Tibesar, Antonine. *Writings of Junípero Serra*. 4 vols. Washington: Academy of Franciscan History, 1955–56.

Torquemada, Juan de. *Tercera Parte de los Veinte y Un Libros Rituales. Monarchia Indiana*. Madrid: Nicolás Rodríguez, 1723.

———. *Vida y Milagros del sancto confessor de Cristo, F. Sebastián de Aparicio*. Mexico: Santiago Tlatelolco, 1602.

Torre Curiel, José Refugio de la. "Santidad y martirio en testimonios jesuitas y franciscanos sobre la cristianización del noroeste novohispano. Siglos XVII y XVIII." *Relaciones* 37, no. 145 (March 2016): 63–107.

———. *Vicarios en Entredicho. Crisis y desestructuración de la Provincia Franciscana de Santiago De Xalisco, 1749–1860*. Zamora: Colegio de Michoacán, 2001.

Torre Revello, José. "Las cartillas para enseñar a leer a los niños en la América Española." *Thesaurus* 15, nos. 1-2-3 (1960): 214–34.

Torres, Juan de. *Philosophia moral de príncipes para su buena crianza y gobierno, y para personas de todos estados*. Burgos: Philippe de Iunta y Juan Baptista Varesio, 1596.

Torre Villar, Ernesto de la. "Fray Pedro de Gante, maestro y civilizador de America." *Estudios de Historia Novohispana* 5, no. 5 (October 1974): 1–81.

Traslosheros, Jorge. *Historia Judicial Eclesiástica de la Nueva España. Materia, Métodos y Razones*. Mexico: Editorial Porrúa / UNAM / Instituto de Investigaciones Históricas, 2014.

Truman, Ronald W. *Spanish Treatises on Government, Society and Religion in the Time of Phillip II: The "De Regimin Principium" and Associated Traditions*. Leiden: Brill, 1999.

Twinam, Ann. *Public Lives Private Secrets: Gender, Honor, Sexuality, and Illegitimacy in Colonial Spanish America*. Stanford: Stanford University Press, 1999.

Ulloa, Daniel. *Los predicadores divididos. Los dominicos en Nueva España, siglo XVI*. Mexico: Colegio de Mexico, 1977.

Van Nierop, Henk. *Treason in the Northern Quarter: War, Terror and the Rule of Law in the Dutch Revolt*. Princeton NJ: Princeton University Press, 1999.

Vargas, M. de. *Doctrina Christiana . . . en castellano, mexicano y Otomí*. Mexico: Pedro Balli, 1576.

Vargas Lugo, Elisa. "Dos piras funerarias barrocas." *Mexico: Anales del Instituto de Investigaciones Estéticas* 14, no. 53 (1983): 49–63. https://doi.org/10.22201/iie.18703062e.1983.53.1210.

Vázquez Conde, Daniel Salvador. "Religiosidad y vida cotidiana en la provincia de franciscanos descalzos de San Diego de Mexico, 1599–1821." Tesis de Licenciatura en Etnohistoria, Mexico: Escuela Nacional de Antropología e Historia, 2007.

———. "Un acercamiento a la vida cotidiana de los 'Dieguinos' o franciscanos descalzos novohispanos." *Legajos. Boletín del Archivo general de la Nación* 4 (April–June 2010): 43–61.

Veedor, Joseph. *Instrucción y Doctrina de Novicios sacada de la de San Buenaventura y de la de las Provincias de descalzos de N.P. San Francisco, de San Joseph, y de San Pablo, nuevamente enmendada añadida, y ajustada al uso y estilo de ésta de San Diego en México.* Puebla: Diego Fernández de León, 1685.

Velasco y Arellano, José Luis. *Tierno recuerdo de la incansable solicitud e infatigable anhelo del V.P. Fr. Antonio Margil de Jesús.* Mexico: Francisco Rivera y Calderón, 1726.

Velázquez, María del Carmen. *El estado de Guerra en Nueva España, 1760–1808.* Mexico: Colegio de Mexico, 1950.

———. *Establecimiento y pérdida del Septentrión de Nueva España.* Mexico: Colegio de Mexico, 1974.

———. "La comandancia general de las Provincias internas." *Historia Mexicana* 27, no. 2 (October–December 1977): 163–77.

Vélez de Cosío, Mauricio. *Reglas Comunes de los clérigos regulares menores.* Madrid: Viuda de Barco López, 1818.

Venegas, Alejo. *Agonía del Tránsito de la muerte con los avisos y consuelos acerca de ella.* Alcalá: con licencia, 1565.

Vetancurt, Agustín de. *Menologio Franciscano, in Teatro Mexicano.* Mexico: María de Benavides, viuda de Juan de Ribera, 1697.

———. *Teatro Mexicano. Crónica de la Provincia del Santo Evangelio de Mexico.* 1696. Reprint, México: Editorial Porrúa, 1971.

———. *Teatro Mexicano. Descripción Breve de los Sucesos Ejemplares, Históricos, Políticos, Militares, y Religiosos del nuevo mundo Occidental de las Indias.* Mexico: María de Benavides, viuda de Juan de Ribera, 1697.

———. *Tratado de la ciudad de Mexico y las grandezas que la ilustran después que la fundaron españoles.* Mexico: María de Benavides, viuda de Juan de Ribera, 1697.

Vicedo, Salustiano, and Jacinto Fernández-Largo. *Escritos de Fray Junípero Serra.* 5 vols. Petra, Mallorca: Publicaciones Apóstol y Civilizador, 1984.

Vida de varios santos y beatos canonizados y beatificados en el presente siglo. Vol. 1. Barcelona: Sierra, Oliver y Marte, 1795.

Vilaplana, Hermenegildo de. *Vida portentosa del Americano Septentrional Apóstol, el V. P. Fr. Antonio Margil de Jesús.* México: Imprenta de la Bibliotheca Americana, 1763.

Vila y Camps, Antonio. *El noble bien educado. Instrucción político-moral de un maestro a su discípulo.* Madrid: Oficina de Don Miguel Escribano, 1776.

Villalobos, Enrique de. *Manual de Confesores*. Alcalá: Antonio Vázquez, 1640.

Villalón, Cristóbal [Christophoro Gnophoso]. *El Crótalon*. Madrid: Sociedad de Bibliófilos Españoles, 1871.

Villaseñor E., Roberto. "El coronel Don José de Escandón y la conquista del Nuevo Santander." *Boletín del Archivo General de la Nación*, 2nd ser., 8, nos. 3–4 (1967): 1157–1210.

Viveros Maldonado, Germán. "Dramaturgia de Fray Juan de la Anunciación." *Literatura Mexicana* 4, no. 2 (1993): 433–56.

Vives, Juan Luis. *Diálogos*. 9th ed. Madrid: Plácido Barco López, 1792.

Vizuete Mendoza, J. Carlos. "Novicios, maestros y la obra de Fray José de Sigüenza." In *Actas del Simposium (I), La Orden de San Jerónimo y sus monasterios*, 125–47. San Lorenzo del Escorial: Publicaciones del R. C. U. Escorial–María Cristina, Ediciones Escurialenses, 1999.

Von Wobeser, Gisela, and Enriqueta Vila, coords. *Muerte y vida en el más allá: España y América, siglos XVI–XVIII*. Mexico: UNAM, 2009.

Vovelle, Michel. *La mort et l'Occident: De 1300 a Nos Jours*. Paris: Gallimard, 1983.

———. *Mourir autrefois: Attitudes collectives devant la mort aux XVII et XVII siècles*. Paris: Gallimard, 1974.

Wade, Maria F. *Missions, Missionaries, and Native Americans: Long-Term Processes and Daily Practices*. Gainesville: University Press of Florida, 2008.

Wade, Maria F., Jennifer K. McWilliams, and Douglas K. Boyd. *Spanish Colonial Documents Pertaining to Mission Santa Cruz de San Sabá (41MN23), Menard County, Texas*. Austin: Texas Department of Transportation, 2007.

Walker Bynum, Carolyn. "Jesus as Mother and Abbott as Mother: Some Themes in Twelfth-Century Cistercian Writing." In *Medieval Religion: New Approaches*, edited by Constance Hoffman Berman, 18–43. New York: Routledge, 2005.

———. *Jesus as Mother: Studies in the Spirituality of the High Middle Ages* Berkeley: University of California Press, 1987.

Warner, Marina. *Alone of All Her Sex: The Myth and the Cult of the Virgin Mary*. Oxford: Oxford University Press, 2013.

Weber, David J. *Bárbaros: Spaniards and Their Savages in the Age of Enlightenment*. New Haven CT: Yale University Press, 2005.

———. *What Caused the Pueblo Revolt of 1680*. Boston: Bedford / St. Martin's, 1999.

Weckmann, Luis. *La herencia medieval de Mexico*. 2 vols. Mexico: Colegio de México, 1984.

Will de Chaparro, Martina, and Miruna Achim. *Death and Dying in Colonial Spanish America*. Tucson: University of Arizona Press, 2011.

Witschorik, Charles A. *Preaching Power: Gender, Politics, and Official Catholic Church Discourse in Mexico City, 1720–1875*. Eugene OR: Pickwick Publications, 2013.

Woods, Damon. "Racial Exclusion in the Mendicant Orders from Spain to the Philippines." UCLA *Historical Journal* 11 (1991): 69–92.

Ximénez, Juan. *Exposición de la Regla de los frayles menores*. Valencia: Pedro Patricio Mey, 1622.

Ximenez, Matteo. *Compendio della vita del beato Sebastiano d'Apparizio* [. . .]. Roma: Stamperia Salomoni, 1789.

Ximenez de Arellano, Manuel. *Tiernos recuerdos que excitan el llanto de las religiosas descalzas Indias Caciques del convento de Corpus Christi de México, por la muerte del Rev. Padre Fr. Joseph de Castro, hijo de la Provincia del santo Evangelio* [. . .]. Mexico: Imprenta de la Bibliotheca Mexicana, 1753.

Yannakakis, Yanna, Martina Schrader-Kniffki, and Luis Arrioja, eds. *Los indios de Nueva España ante la justicia local: traducción, autoridad, y mediadores culturales*. Zamora: Colegio de Michoacán, Atlanta: Emory University Press, 2019.

Yebra, Melchor de. *Libro llamado Refugium Infirmorum . . . para ayudar a bien morir a los que están en lo último de su vida*. Madrid: Luys Sánchez, 1593.

Yetman, David. *Conflict in Colonial Sonora: Indians, Priests, and Settlers*. Albuquerque: University of New Mexico Press, 2012.

Ymhoff Cabrera, Jesús. *Fray Juan de la Anunciación, Poemas religiosos y profanos*. Toluca: Editorial del Gobierno del Estado de Mexico, 1985.

Yunes Vincke, Estefanía. "The Doctrina Christiana En Lengua Mexicana of Fray Pedro De Gante: A Pedagogical Tool for the New World." *Estudios de Historia Novohispana*, no. 59 (July–December 2018): 111–37.

Zaragoza, Verónica. "La oratoria sagrada novohispano: una revisión bibliográfica." San Miguel de Tucumán, XI Jornadas Interescuelas / Departamentos de Historia. Facultad de Filosofía y Letras. Universidad de Tucumán, 2007.

Zárate, Verónica. *Los nobles ante la muerte en Mexico: Actitudes, ceremonias y memoria, 1750–1850*. Mexico: Colegio de Mexico, 2000.

Zárate Salmerón, Gerónimo de. "Relaciones de todas las cosas que en el Nuevo México se han visto y sabido, así por mar como por tierra desde el año de 1538 hasta el de 1676." Ca. 1676. MS 6882, Biblioteca Nacional de España, Madrid, Spain.

Zepeda, Nicolás de, Miguel de Molina, and Joseph Joaquín Granados y Gálvez. *La tragedia de la misión de San Sabá y otras Relaciones de la insumisión indigena*. Mexico: Planeta/Conaculta, 2002.

Zugasti, Miguel. "Algo más sobre las fuentes de 'El Rufián dichoso' de Cervantes." Actas del XII Congreso Internacional AITENSO, 2005. http://www.cervantesvirtual.com/obra/algo-mas-sobre-las-fuentes-de-el-rufian-dichoso-de-cervantes.

Zumárraga, Juan de. *Doctrina breve muy provechosa de las cosas que pertenecen a la fe católica*. México: Juan Cromberger, 1543.

INDEX

Page numbers in *italics* refer to figures.

Aaron (biblical character), 264, 337n23
Abraham (biblical character), 306n98
Abrego, Jerónimo de, 42
absolution, 122, 319n96
Acevedo, Pablo de, 249
Aconchí Indians, 188
Acosta, Francisco de, 34
Acuña de Alburquerque, Bernardo, 87–88
adultery, 152
Africans, 42–43, 91, 301n12. *See also* Blacks
Ágreda, María de, 115
Agüero, Christobal de, 73
Alburquerque, Duke, 173
Alcántara, Diego de, 280–82
Alcántara, Juan de, 159–60, 320n104
Alcántara, Pedro de, 57
Alcázar, Diego de, 37, 300n108
Alderete, Agustín de, 44
Alfonso de Valladolid, Pedro, 321n117
Almodóvar, Lucas de, 97
alms. See *limosneros*
Alva, Antonio de, 134, 162
Alvarado, Antonio, 258–59; *Arte de Bien Morir y Guía del Camino de la Muerte*, 258

Álvarez, Antonio, 154
Álvarez de Toledo, Ferdinand, 295n25
Ángeles Bustamante, Antonio de los, 104, 112–17, *114*, 253, 312n112
Anthony of Padua, 116, 312n112
Anunciación, Domingo de la, 34
Anunciación, Juan de la, 67–68, 305n91
Apache Indians, 170, 177, 183, 188, 206–7, 221–22, 231, 328n112
Aparicio, Sebastián, 68, 80, 104–9, *105*, 308n32, 311n94
Apodaca, Francisco de, 170
Araúz, Francisco de, 321n117
Arbiol, Antonio, 40
Arbizu, José, 234
Arias y Saavedra, Antonio, 171
Arlegui, Joseph, 76, 225, 227, 231, 232–33, 245, 246, 249, 250, 333n66
Armenta, Joseph de, 153
Arozqueta, Josefa, 5–6
Arricivita, Juan Domingo, 102, 224, 245, 246–48
ars moriendi, 257, 258–59, 287–88, 338n44
Arte de Ayudar y Disponer a bien Morir a todo género de personas (Salazar), 258

Arte de Bien Morir (Bellarmino), 257, 336n11

Arte de Bien Morir y Guía del Camino de la Muerte (Alvarado), 258

Arte de la lengua mexicana y castellana (Molina), 29

aspirants, 39, 40, 42–44, 46–47, 48–49, 52, 75, 81, 313n6

attorneys, convent, 94

attorneys, Inquisition, 126–27, 132, 148–49, 157–62, 315n57, 320n97

audiencia, ecclesiastical, 121

Augustine of Hippo, 121–22

Augustinians: areas active in, 167, 172; and death, 264, 282–83, 284; lay brothers in, 80–81, 88, 90–91, 93, 111; martyrdom in, 240; membership in, 80–81; novitiate training in, 52; property ownership by, 93, 310n60; racial issues in, 44–45, 301n19; violence against, 172; on war, 219

Ávila, Juan de, 304n79, 339n58

Ávila, Teresa de, 304n79

Avilés, Francisco de, 87, 88

Avisos para el Noviciado (Romero), 74

Azlor y Vito de Vera, Joseph de, 331n29

Baltasar Carlos (Prince), 21

Báñez, Domingo, 147, 318n71

baptism, 167, 200

Barbado de la Torre y Angulo, Manuel, 79–80, 102

Barbastro, Antonio Francisco, 181, 188–91, 324n54, 324n59, 324nn64–65; *Deberes y obligaciones*, 187

Barboza, Antonio de, 69

Barreneche, Juan Antonio, 223, 247

Barrera, Ignacio de la, 231, 333n61

Barri, Felipe, 198

Basalenque, Diego de, 32–33, 58, 62, 63, 93–94, 254, 263, 265–66

Basterra, Dionisio de, 210

Bautista de Orozco, Juan, 147

beatification, 33, 104, 108–9, 242–43

beheading, 245–46

Bellarmino, Roberto: *Arte de Bien Morir*, 257–58, 336n11

Benavides, Alonso de, 169–70, 328n116

Benedict XIV (Pope), 124

Benítez, Esteban, 249

Benítez, Joseph, 268

Bernard of Clairvaux (Saint), 65, 264, 297n68, 337n24

Bertrand, Luis, 276

Betanzos, Domingo, 43, 87

biographies and biographers: childhood overlooked by, 1, 28, 30–31, 33, 35–36; on death, 253, 254, 259, 266, 272–73, 275, 288; influence of, 108; information lacking for, 299n85; on lay brothers, 101, 104, 108–13, 115–18; on martyrs, 235–36, 240; on masculinity, 56–57; on missionaries, 202; on novitiates, 62

birth, as religious metaphor, 73–74, 253–54

bishops, 199, 281, 306n97

Blacks, 81, 102, 110, 150–51, 313n116. *See also* Africans

Bonaventure (Saint), 67

Book of Professions from the Convent of Saint Augustine, Mexico City, 41

books, 12–13, 24–25, 27, 52–53, 54–56, 57–58, 116

Borda, Andrés de, 152

Borja, Francisco de, 312n105

Bourbon dynasty, 176–77, 179

Bouza, Gregorio, 154–56, 316n32

boys, 32–33, 37, 39. *See also* childhood
Bravo, Manuel, 36
Bringas de Manzaneda, Diego Miguel, 238–40, 285, 287, 334n83; *Sermón*, 286
Bucareli, Antonio María, 179, 180, 190–91, 193, 197–98
Buenaventura Pérez, Fr., 131–32
Burgoa, Francisco de, 32, 42, 274–75
Bustamante, Antonio de. *See* Ángeles Bustamante, Antonio de los

Caballero Carranco, José, 171–72, 322nn13–14
Cadaval, Manuel, 139–40
Cadena, Diego de la, 76
Calero, Juan, 172, 225, 244
California, 178, 182, 191–92, 195–96, 197–200, 209–11, 221, 251, 326n86
Calvillo, María Manuela, 145–46
Calzadilla, Bartolomé de, 307n9
Cañeque, Alejandro, 214
Cañizares, José, 271
canto llano, 67, 69, 305n88
Carbonel, Antonio, 234–35
Cárdenas, Juan de, 29–30
Carranco, Anna Josefa, 136
Carranco, Juana Josefa, 136
cartillas, 12, 27, 52–53, 54, 56
Castellanos, Francisco, 138, 158–59, 317n49
Castells, Elizabeth A.: *Martyrdom and Memory*, 330n11
Castiglione, Baldassare, 297n58; *The Courtier*, 15
Castorena y Ursúa, Juan de, 269
Castro, Joseph de, 284–85
catechism and catechization, 25, 83, 102–3, 145, 192, 201

Catholic Church: conversion goals of, 242–43; and death, 253–54; and education for boys, 6; influence of, 12; and martyrdom, 214–15; and minority groups, 42–43; and missionary work, 166–67, 212; and Protestants, 329n7; rejection of, 220; sacraments of, 313n9; and sexuality, 18, 120–23, 134; and suicide, 70; and visions, 70
catones, 12–13, 27
Celedonio (Roman soldier), 214
celibacy, 120–23, 313n6
cells, as spiritual refuges, 65–66
Cerda, Ginés de la, 143–44
Ceremonial Dominicano (San Joan), 305n88
Cervantes de Salazar, Francisco, 18, 297n54
charity, 71, 90, 97–98, 102, 238, 255, 333n66
chastity, vow of, 48–49, 120, 152, 319n87
Chavarría, Diego de, 233
cherubims, 116, 312n112
Chichimecs (ethnic groups), 106, 172, 217–19, 228, 243, 332n55
childhood: behavioral education during, 14–19, 21–22, 24–27; character reform in, 34–35; intellectual education during, 6–10; legitimacy of, 9, 45; moral education during, 11–14, 295n26; as overlooked stage, 1–2, 28–29, 31–32, 299n96; social education during, 1–6; stages of, 10–11, 294n22
childhood, in writings: birthplace considered in, 29–31; as overlooked stage, 28–29, 31–32; and redemption, 34–35; stereotyped, 32–34, 35–37

Christ, 73, 237, 238, 252, 253, 306n101
Christian Doctrine (Gante), 96
Christians and Christianity, 6–7, 66, 95–96, 226, 227–28, 237, 273, 276, 306n97
chronicles and chroniclers: about, 28, 95; challenges for, 299n85; on death, 253–54, 259–60, 263, 275, 287; on lay brothers, 95, 98, 99–100, 118; on martyrs, 214, 216, 224, 228–30, 235–36, 240, 245–46, 248; methods of, 103; subjects emphasized by, 69, 76; subjects neglected by, 31, 61; on virginity, 121
Chuchiak, John, 149
Clairvaux, Bernard de, 65–66, 264, 297n58, 337n24
Clare of Montefalco, 312n99
Clemente XIII (Pope), 109
Clement VIII (Pope), 40, 42
Cobián, María Antonia, 136
Colegio de la Santa Cruz, 113, 179, 183
Colegio de San Francisco de Sales, 25–26
Colegios. *See* Propaganda Fide
Comanche Indians, 206–7, 221–22
commendation of the soul, 272, 338n43
communication, 89, 186, 227, 236, 275, 280, 340n70
Communion, 12, 122, 255
concubinage, 121, 141
confession, act of: about, 122, 163; and death, 317n50; feigning, 133, 314n11; and legal issues, 122–24, 131, 141–42, 145–46, 163; racial issues in, 314n10
confessionals: banishment from, 133, 156; and legal issues, 153; misuse of, 152–53, 159–60; physical forms of, 318n64; significance of, 130, 158, 163

confessors: authority of, 8; consequences for misbehavior of, 156–57, 162–64, 315n25, 315n27; falsely accused, 314n14; manuals for, 315n30; and novices, 57; role of, 122, 128, 314n10, 317n50; sexual solicitation by, 122–25, 128, 130–34, 135; writings asking advice from, 116
confessors, women's relationships with: and Blacks, 150–51; and Indians, 141–43, 146–50; and *mulatas*, 146–47; and nuns, 152–56; and Spanish, 141–46, 159–60, 319n96
confirmations, 200
Congo, Catalina, 150
Conlon, Francisco, 134–38, 316n42
Consuevit Romanus Pontifex, 300n7
convents: in dangerous situations, 226, 248; as family, 73, 208, 283–84; lay brothers in, 77–78, 80–82, 83–85, 88–94; nuns in, 151, 153; pharmacies in, 309n45; physical presence of, 284–85; training in, 64–65
conversions: and behavior changes, 100; challenges to, 171–72, 216–17, 218, 225–26; death encouraging, 113, 312n105; governance of, 176–77, 200–201; and martyrdom, 242–43; as military operations, 248; optimism about, 169
Córdoba, Andrés de, 97
coristas, 40, 64, 67, 77, 82, 83, 84, 305n82, 308n29
coro (choir area), 60–61, 66–67
Cortés, Alonso, 142
Cortés, Lorenzo, 317n54
Cossin, Bernardo, 172, 227–28
Council of Trent (1540–63), 39, 40, 42, 65, 66, 121, 122

The Courtier (Castiglione), 15
Crespí, Juan, 192, 207–8, 209–10, 271, 328n117
criollos, 9–10, 29–30, 43–45, 46, 308n31
Croix, Carlos Francisco de, 200–201, 327n100
Croix, Teodoro de, 178, 185, 198, 199, 200–201, 316n42, 327n100
Crown, Spanish: in California, 191, 199; and conversion, 217; and exploration of new land, 170; and France, 220–21; and Indians, 180, 192, 201; and legal issues, 285; and martyrdom, 220, 251; and Mary, mother of Jesus, 71; missions controlled by, 181, 202; rebellion against, 334n83
Cruz, Ana de la, 151
Cruz, Cristóbal de la, 34–35, 303n46
Cruz, Juana de la, 146
Cruz, Juan de la, 304n79
Cruzate, Juan, 261
Cuber y Linián, Tomas, 160–61
Cuellar, Antonio de, 225
Cuellar, Lope de, 274
Cueva, Pedro de la, 32
Cum sicut nuper, 123

Dantí, Antonio, 210–11
Dávila, Gómez de, 298n65
Dávila Padilla, Agustín, 10, 30–31, 34–35, 77–78, 98–99, 255, 262–63, 273, 306n101, 310n68
death: approaches to differing, 273–75; as birth, 253–54; chronicles on, 259–60; conversions prompted by, 113, 312n105; figurative, in life changes, 56; and lay brothers, 89; lifelong preparation for, 255–57, 336n11; prescience of, 260–64; rituals for, 257–59; social

leveling from, 102. *See also* martyrdom; martyrs; sermons, funeral
Deberes y obligaciones (Barbastro), *187*
Delgado, Diego, 229
denunciations: ambivalence of, 141, 142, 318n72; discouragement of, 123–24; disregarded, 124–25, 140; encouragement of, 132, 314n14, 317n56; false, 314n14; motivations for, 319n96; and nuns, 159; procedures dealing with, 125–27, 145; of secular women, 317n48; by slaves, 150–51, 319n81; standards for, 297n57; statistics on, 125–26; by women of color, 146–51, 318n67. *See also* self-denunciations
depression, mental, 210, 232–33
Destierro de Ignorancias (Vascones), *256*
the devil, 69, 100, 252, 257–58, 278, 338n43. *See also* Satan
Diálogos (Vives), 17–18, 296n52
diaries, 205–6, 207–8
Diario Íntimo (Font), *183*
Díaz, Juan, 223, 247
Díaz de Gamarra, Juan Benito: *Máximas de educación en la piedad Cristiana*, 25–26
Dieguinos, 278, 279
Doctrinas Cristianas, 12, 14
Dominicans: areas active in, 167, 172–73, 221, 320n104; and death, 262, 273, 274; lay brothers in, 78, 81–82, 87, 88, 93–94, 307n5, 307n17, 308n37; martyrdom in, 240, 242; membership in, 81–82; novitiate training in, 52, 60, 64; professions in, 34; property ownership by, 93–94, 310n58; racial issues in, 29, 43, 44–45; sermons of, 339n58; suicide attempts in, 69–70; traditions in, 48, 66; on war, 219

Index 391

donados, 32, 76–77, 81, 83, 92, 98, 101, 107, 306n3
doncellas, 135, 136, 143–44, 147
Durán, Diego, 108, 299n87

Education of a Christian Prince (Erasmus of Rotterdam), 15
Eighteenth-Century Mexican Children, 5
Eighteenth-Century Mexican Elite Family, 4
El Crótalon (Villalón), 18–19, 297n55
El discreto estudiante, 23
El estudioso cortesano (Palmireno), 19
El estudioso de la aldea (Palmireno), 19
Emeterio (Roman soldier), 214
Enríquez, Juan, 229, 333n57
Enríquez, Nicolas: *Fr. Antonio Margil de Jesús*, 175
Erasmus of Rotterdam, 254; *Education of a Christian Prince*, 15; *Familiar Colloquies*, 15
Escalona, Juan de, 171
Escandón, José de, 176–77
Espejo del Príncipe Cristiano (Monzón), 19
Espinareda, Pedro de, 76, 226–27
Espinosa, Juan de, 53
Espinosa, Valeriano de, 56–57, 65–66, 245–46, 303n49; *Guía de religiosos*, 56, 71, 72, 306n98
evangelization: dangers in process of, 173; and death, 273, 279, 281; in decline, 191; and lay brothers, 76, 96; and martyrdom, 216, 217, 226; and military, 180; and racial beliefs, 43, 314n10

Fages, Pedro, 197, 198, 250, 326nn86–87
Fagoaga, Francisco, 5–6
Fagoaga-Arozqueta family, 5–6
Familiar Colloquies (Erasmus of Rotterdam), 15
fanegas, 309n53
fathers, biological, 4, 6, 9, 11, 16, 294n22
fathers, metaphorical, 25, 53, 54, 71, 283
fear, among missionaries, 206, 207, 232–33, 235, 246, 271–72
Felipe de Jesús (friar), 33–34, *241*, 242–43, 300nn99–100
Félix de Espinosa, Isidro, 36, 112–13, 115, 116, 166, 245–46, 253, 266, 268, 269.
Font, Pedro, 181–83, 184–86, 189, 190–91, 199, 204–6, 327n111; *Diario Íntimo*, 183; map of California trip, *182*
Francis (Saint), 237, 264
Franciscans: areas active in, 76, 167, 168–69; and death, 267–68, 271, 277; lay brothers in, 79–80, 81–82, 84–87, 86, 91–92, 97, 100–101, 107–9; martyrdom in, 34, 219–21, 226–27, 231–32, 237–38, 240, 244, 245–46, 248; membership in, 308n29; missionary activity by, 168–74, 176–77, 217, 225; missions declining in, 325n69; novitiate training in, 52–53, 56–58, 60–61, 64–65, 66, 71; racial issues in, 43–44, 45–47, 81; sermons of, 277, 339n58; and sexual matters, 125, 133–35, 140, 143, 148–49, 161, 314n21, 317n54; traditions in, 47–48; on war, 219
Franco, Alonso: as biographer, 31; on lay brothers, 90, 94, 98, 99–100, 306n3; on martyrs, 230, 240, 242; on novitiates, 53–54, 61–62, 302n31, 303n46
Fr. Antonio Margil de Jesús (Enríquez), *175*
French settlers, 173, 220–21

friars: and aspirant selection, 38–40, 42; birthplaces of important, 45; childhood of, 2; and death, 254, 259–62, 273–74, 277–79; humility in, 90; and Indian culture, 299n87; Indians' view of, 225–27; languages necessary for, 96; lay brothers as, 79, 80–85, 87, 93–94, 111; as martyrs, 227–33, 236–40; numbers of, 81–83, 84, 209; and sexual matters, 120, 133–36, 139–43, 147–51, 154–56, 163–65
Fr. Junípero Serra Preaching to All People, 194
Fuente, María Antonia de, 135–36
Fuentes, Francisco, 273
Fuero Real (1255), 294n22
Fuster, Vicente, 196

Gage, Thomas, 223–24, 331n36
Galarza, Joseph, 147
Galindo, Felipe, 173
Gallina, Juan, 53
Gálvez, José de, 178, 179–80, 181, 193
Ganacia, Joseph, 141
Gante, Pedro de, 79, 95–96; *Christian Doctrine*, 96
Garcés, Antonio, 247–48, 273, 306n101
Garcés, Francisco Tomás Hermenegildo, 186, 203–5, 223, 239–40, 327n104
García, Estevan, 109–10
García del Santísimo Rosario, José Joaquín, 177
García Duque, Ángel, 116, 312n107
García Marín, José, 234
García-Molina Riquelme, Antonio M., 316n41
Garnica, Alberto de, 94
Gasol, José, 211
Gastore, Juan Ignacio, 210

Giraldo de Terreros, Alonso, 221–22
girls, expectations for, 2, 3, 5–6
Giudicelli, C., 227
Gnophoso, Christophoro. *See* Villalón, Cristóbal de
God: in childhood education, 24, 28; and death, 262, 264, 273, 276–77; and lay brothers, 78, 119; and life choices, 38; and martyrdom, 216, 237, 246, 248; missionary view of, 203, 204–5, 206; and novitiates, 59, 60–61, 70–71; and sexuality, 122, 158; and vow of obedience, 48
González, Ondina E., 9
González de la Puente, Juan, 31, 49, 240, 263–64, 265
González Marmolejo, René, 46, 125, 314n21
Granada, Luis de, 57, 99, 304n79
Gregory, Brad, 215, 230
Gregory XIII (Pope), 300n7
Gregory XV (Pope), 123
Grijalva, Juan de, 52, 261–62, 273–74
Grimarest, Enrique de, 190
Guadalcanal, Diego de, 98
Guadalupe, Mónica, 319n81
Guardia, Francisco, 154–56
Guerrero, Pedro, 31
Guevara, Antonio de: *Libro Áureo*, 16; *Oratorio de religiosos*, 54, 55; *Reloj de Príncipes*, 16
Guía de religiosos (Espinosa), 56, 71, 72, 306n98
Guillén, Felipe, 188, 189, 246–47
Gutiérrez, Bartolomé, 243
Gutiérrez, Juan, 142–43
Gutiérrez, María Ignacia, 137
Gutiérrez, Pedro, 250
Guzmán, Luis, 173

habits (clothing), 47–48, 110–11, 231, 269, 274–75, 302n34, 333n64
hagiography, 35–36, 101, 104, 111, 229, 249, 270, 273, 311n25
Heras, Manuel de las, 269
Herize, Joseph de, 57–58, 65, 66
Hermosillo, Gonzalo de, 242
Hernández, Salvador, 68–69
Herrejón Peredo, Carlos, 276
Hierro, Simón del, 93, 177
hijos de provincia, 45, 301n18, 302n27
Hinojosa, Agustina de, 147
Historia Eclesiástica Indiana (Mendieta), 244
Holy Gospel province, 43, 45–46, 74
Holy Office. *See* Inquisition, in sexual matters
Hopi Indians, 170, 204
Huarte de San Juan, Juan, 14–15

Idea de un príncipe político cristiano (Saavedra Fajardo), 20, 21–22
Index, 14, 15, 296n43
Indians: aggression by, 183–84, 188, 217–20, 224, 231–32, 326n86, 327n104, 328n112, 330n24, 331n36; agricultural work of, 184–85, 325n68; attitudes toward, 179, 180–81, 203–8, 236–37, 239, 322n14, 328nn116–17; and confessions, 314n10; educational plans for, 190–91, 324n64; expectations for, 188–89; governmental approach to, 199–200, 201; as laborers, 310n58; and martyrdom, 215–16, 223–28; and military, 217–18, 220–23; missionaries spared by, 231, 332n56, 333n66; missionary work accepted by, 220; missionary work resisted by, 169–71, 172–73, 217–18, 220–23; ordination suggested for, 190, 324n65; preinvasion culture of, 218; and racial issues, 42–44, 301n11; rebellions by, 220–23; and settlers, 217–18, 220–23; and sexual solicitation, 147–50, 318n72; suppression of, 176–78; writings on, 244–45
Indigenous peoples. *See* Indians
Ines (Apache woman), 149–50
Inquisition, in sexual matters: common knowledge about, 161–62; confessions to, 135; consequences meted out by, 315n25, 320n110; follow-through lacking, 124–26, 315n27; gender issues in, 163–64; inquisitors' role in, 156–61, 162; and nuns, 152–56; procedures of, 126–27; and racial issues, 147–51; records of, 134, 315n24; role of, 121, 123–24; and seduction by women, 142–43; specific cases in, 130–34, 139–42; statistics about, 125; trust as issue for, 162–63; and victims' responses, 147–51
The Inquisition vs. Fr. Joseph María López Aguado, for Solicitation 1788, 129
Instrucción y Doctrina de Novicios (1685, Veedor), 50
Instrucción y Doctrina de Novicios (1733), 51
interiority, 65, 278–79, 281, 304n79
Iriarte, Gregorio de, 160–61
Isabel de Santiago, 159
Islam, 214
Iudice (Cardinal), 314n14

Japan and Japanese, 243
Javier de Silva, Francisco, 177, 222

Jayme, Luis, 196, 206, 222–23, 250, 326n87
Jesuits, 33, 168, 221, 223, 230, 265–66, 319n81, 337n26
Jesús María Casañas, Francisco de, 234
Jesús y Torres, Bartolomé de, 102
Jiménez de Cisneros, Alonso, 233–34
Jiménez de Cisneros, Francisco, 304n79
John of Sahagún, 312n99
Josiah (biblical character), 280
Juárez, Juan, 101

La Purísima Concepción, 65
La Rea, Alonso de, 53, 68–69, 73–74, 100
La Rea, Antonio, 273–74
Lasuén, Fermín Francisco de, 167, 180, 191–92, 196, 201, 210–11
La Suprema, 121, 127, 164
lay brothers: about, 76–80, 117–19; actions of, 95–97, 101–3, 107, 110–13, 115; age of, 86, 308n32; appreciation of, 308n37; backgrounds of, 97, 98–101, 104, 106–7, 109, 113; changes requested by, 87–88; character of, 98, 99, 102; deaths of, 97, 103; duties of, 88–94; ethnicity of, 308n31; forgiveness for, 310n68; friendships among, 115–16; in memory, 108–9; numbers of, 82–87, 307n17; reasons for becoming, 33, 69; reasons for leaving, 47; recruitment of, 82–83; terms for, 307n5; unusual individuals as, 107–8; virtues of, 307n9; and vows, 110–11, 116; writings by, 116–17
legumes, 309n53
Leite, Juana Gertrudis, 143, 317n56
Leiva, Fernando de, 97–98

Lent, 146, 148
León, Luis de, 99
letters: and death, 265, 270, 338n40; guidance in, 112, 116–17, 312n102; help sought in, 210; informative, 183–84, 193; and martyrdom, 224, 230, 233–35; and sexual matters, 123, 147–48, 153–54
Libro Áureo (Guevara), 16
life, stages of, 10–11, 29, 294n22
limosneros, 84, 91–93, 101, 102, 107
limpieza de sangre, 42, 43–44, 45, 81, 300n7
Lipsett-Rivera, Sonya, 9
liturgy, 58, 60–61, 67, 88, 305n88
Lizana, Bernardo de, 229
Llinás, Antonio, 166–67
loas, 67–68, 305n91
López, Francisco, 79
López, Lucía, 150
López, Melchor, 102
López de Aguado, Juan, 280, 340n70
Lorenzo, Francisco, 229, 245, 332nn55–56
Lucas (*donado*), 76
Lugo, Cristóbal de. *See* Cruz, Cristóbal de la
Luna, Antonio de, 130

macanas, 222, 244, 245, 335n97
Machiavelli, Niccoló: *The Prince*, 15, 21
Macías, Josefa, 138
Magdalena, Jerónimo de la, 93–94
Malaviar, María Josefa, 144
Malo de Medina, Francisco Gabriel, 24–25
Malvido, Elsa, 39, 302n27
manhood. *See* masculinity
Map of California, 1777 (Font), 182

Margil de Jesús, Antonio, *175*; about, 35–36; as composer, 271, 338n41; death of, 266–69; funeral sermons for, 279–82; and lay brothers, 102; miracles associated with, 337n34; as missionary, 173–74, 176, 202, 328n113, 332n43, 337n28, 340n70; relationships with colleagues of, 115–16, 312n109

María Catarina de Jesús Nazareno, 154–56

María de San Nicolás Obispo Herrera, 154

María Ignacia del Niño Jesús, 153–54

María Manuela de la Luz, 154

María Mónica de Santa Catalina, 154–56

Marini, Diego, 87

Mariscal, Manuel, 137

marriages, 106–7, 137

marriages, metaphorical, 68, 73

Martínez, Juan, 32, 274

Martínez, Pedro, 99, 310n73

martyrdom: about, 213–16; acceptance of, 223–25, 229–32; circumstances surrounding, 227–28; high point of, 220, 331n37; military metaphors for, 248–49, 252; and mission expansion, 218, 219, 221; negative views of, 234–35; and politics, 251; positive views of, 228–29, 235–40; premonitions of, 229–30, 332n55; significance of, 248–52; study of, 330n11; theological bases for, 238–39. *See also* death

Martyrdom and Memory (Castells), 330n11

martyrs: acceptance of death by, 252, 279; behavior patterns in, 227–28; eulogized, 240, 242–48; fear among, 232–33; lay brothers as, 80; legacies of, 285; Protestants as, 329n7; remains of, 242, 249; sorrow expressed for, 235–36; suffering of, 237; writings on death of, 240, 242. *See also* death

Mary, mother of Jesus, 71, 262–64, 305n85

masculinity: alternate form of, 37, 38, 56–57, 74, 118–19, 120, 201, 289–91; and celibacy, 122; factors influencing, 3, 6; general, 24; in martyrdom, 238, 252; in military, 197, 201; outward signs of, 7–8; proper, 14, 18–19; proscribed for missionaries, 27; secular, 107; and solicitants, 164–65; youthful, 35

Mass, 64, 88, 161, 162

masters, of novices, 49, 52, 53–54, 58, 65, 303n43. *See also* teachers

Mateos, Bartolomé, 310n68

Máximas de educación en la piedad Cristiana (Díaz de Gamarra), 25–26

Medellín, Diego de, 99–100

Medina, Baltasar de, 74, 103; *Vida, martirio y beatificación del invicto protomártir de el Japón San Felipe de Jesús, patrón de Mexico*, 241

men: boys becoming, 37; childhood of ignored, 1–2; as fathers, 11; friendships among, 115–16, 312n111; guidance for, 15–18; indecision of, 34; masculinity as entitlement for, 3, 6–8; misbehavior of allowed, 33, 38; perfection as goal of, 74; religious life suiting, 56; and sexual matters, 18–19, 107, 120–21, 128, 164–65, 297nn56–57; as writers, 13; writings for, 19, 21–22, 24–27; writings on, 117–19

mendicant orders: behavioral expectations in, 13–14; bonding activities in, 66–67; and death, 288; and martyrdom, 249; member selection by, 2; novitiate in, 38, 39–40; racial issues in, 43–45; in secular world, 65; service in, 77; sexual matters in, 123, 125, 127; Spanish influence on, 7, 276; vows in, 48–49; writings on training in, 54, 56
Mendieta, Jerónimo de, 90, 95–98, 213, 218–19, 227, 244–45, 332n49, 332n56; *Historia Eclesiástica Indiana*, 244
Mendo, Andrés: *Príncipe Perfecto y Ministros Ajustados*, 21
Mendoza, Gerónimo de, 225, 226
Menologio (Vetancurt), 31, 101, 108
Mercado, Diego de, 171
mestizos, 43, 301n19
Mexican Inquisition, 124, 164, 315n25
Mexico. *See* New Spain
Mezquia, Marcos de, 232
Michoacán province, 73–74
military, 56, 172–73, 176–78, 180, 184, 191–92, 196–201, 220–21, 295n25
miracles, 100–101, 103, 110, 111, 170, 249, 311n85, 337n34
missionaries: administration by, 179–81, 191–93, 195–96; Antonio de Jesús Margil representing, 173–76; challenges to, 166–68; changing situation for, 202, 212; continuing need for, 43; criollos as, 46; declining numbers of, 325n69; disagreements on role of, 181, 183–86, 187–91; expansion as goal of, 168–70; expectations of unrealistic, 170–71; Indians resisting, 168, 171–73, 328n12; isolation affecting, 208–12; as martyrs, 331n36; military

oversight of, 196–201; reactions to mixed, 333n57; royal oversight of, 176–78, 191–92; and secular authorities, 324n59; self-image of, 203–8. *See also* martyrdom; martyrs
Mixtón War (1541–42), 218
mocedad, 11, 28, 35, 38
Moctezuma, Count of, 173
Molina, Alonso de: *Arte de la lengua mexicana y castellana*, 29
Molina, Antonio de, 278–79, 339n65
Molina, Cristóbal de, 33, 103, 104, 109–12, 312n102, 313n116
Molina, Miguel de, 222
Monarquía Indiana (Torquemada), 216
Montalvo, Juan, 31
Montano, Jacinto, 140
Montaño, Sebastián, 230, 240, 242, 304n61
Monzón, Francisco de: *Espejo del Príncipe Cristiano*, 19
Morales, Francisco, 43–44, 45–46, 81, 104, 301n11
Mora Reyes, María Fernanda, 44, 81–82
Moreno, Joseph Matías, 223, 224, 247, 331n37
Moses (biblical character), 264, 337n23
Mota, María Dolores, 143–44
mothers, biological, 4, 6, 9, 12, 26–27, 294n22
mothers, metaphorical, 53, 54, 71, 73–74, 277, 283
Motolinía, Toribio, 108
Moya de Contreras, Pedro, 124
mulatas, 130, 146–47, 151
Muñoz, Francisco, 147
Muñoz de la Concepción, Cristóbal, 278–79
Muñoz-Rivera, Alonso, 149

Murcia, Leandro de, 48–49
Murillo, Diego, 13

Nahuatl language, 29, 96
Navarrete, Pedro, 73, 285
Navarro, Vicente, 269, 282
Nesvig, Martin, 172
Neve, Felipe de, 197, 198, 199, 200, 326n95, 327n100
New Mexico, 169–71, 220, 235, 237
New Spain: administration of, 178; attitudes toward, 10; childhood in, 30; death in, 262, 279; education in, 25, 32–33; lay brothers in, 76, 95, 117–18; literature in, 104, 108–9; martyrdom in, 214, 215, 223, 239, 240–42, 243; racial issues in, 9, 27, 42–43, 45; sermons in, 275–76; sexual matters in, 315n25
Nicholas III (Pope), 77
novices: about, 39–40; age of, 68–69; cells of, 65–66; clothing of, 47–48; dismissal of, 302n27; duties of, 90; leaving the order, 34; numbers of, 308n29; personal lives of, 69–70; profession by, 67–68; and racial issues, 301n19; regimen of, 58–62; selection of, 42–47; and sexual solicitation, 131; spiritual family of, 70–71, 73–75; training of, 48–49, 52–54, 62, 64–65, 66–67; writings on training of, 54–58
Núñez de San Pablo, Juan, 94
nuns, 40, 112, 151–56, 159, 276, 284, 312n111, 316nn32–33, 319n87

obedience, vow of, 48–49, 53, 56, 99
Ochoa, Joseph, 282–84
Ojea, Hernando de, 53–54, 98–100

Ojea, Juan de, 69–70
Ojeda y Parra, Margarita, 136
Ojeda y Parra, Rosalía, 136
Oliva, Joseph de, 158, 320n98
Olmedo, Ana María, 141
Onrrubia, Alonso, 147, 318n67
Opata Indians, 188, 189
Oratorio de religiosos (Guevara), 54, 55
ordination, 40, 67–68, 190, 301n11
Ortega, Antonio Francisco, 199
Ortiz, Alonso, 100–101
Ortiz, Miguel, 98
Osuna, Francisco de, 304n79

Palacio del Hoyo, Francisco Antonio de, 159–60, 320n105
Palmireno, Juan Lorenzo: *El estudioso cortesano*, 19; *El estudioso de la aldea*, 19
Palos, Juan de, 97
Palou, Francisco, 202, 270–73, 338n44
Pame Indians, 172
Pangua, Francisco, 195–96, 210
papal bulls, 123–24, 314n14
papal orders, 300n7
Pardo, Felipe Mariano, 282, 283–84, 340n77
parents, 11–12, 71, 295n31
Pascuala (Black woman), 151
Paul (Saint), 238, 246
Paul IV (Pope), 300n7
Paz, Juan de, 69, 99
Pazos, Manuel Antonio de, 277–78
penance, 122, 156, 160
penitents, 122–24, 158, 162–63, 279
Peralta, Francisca de, 317n48
Peralta, Manuela, 137
Perdomo, Joaquín, 133
Perea, Estevan, 169–70

Pereyra, Juan de, 102
Pérez, Alonso, 52, 53–54, 303n46, 304n61
Pérez, Josefa, 137
Pérez, Ramón, 154, 156
perfection, 29, 48, 71, 74–75, 306n97
Péron, Mylène, 325n69
Petra, María Jacinta, 136
pharmacies, 309n45
physical exercise, 22, 24, 26
Pico, Juan Antonio, 144
Pima Indians, 189
Pimería Alta missions, 181, 183–84, 186, 188, 246, 247, 324n50, 324n54
Pimería Baja missions, 183
Pita Moreda, María Teresa, 81
Pius IV (Pope), 123
poetry, 67–68, 298n68, 337n24
Ponce de León, Nicolás, 109–12
Popado, Manuel, 143, 317n56
Porras, Mateo de, 124–25
Portilla, Alonso de la, 150–51
Portrait-Drawing of Fr. Diego de Basalenque (Salguero), 63
portraits, 3–6, 37, 116, 268
postulants, 11, 37, 43–44, 47, 67
poverty, vow of, 48–49, 110–11
prayer, 60–61, 66–67, 88–89, 305n85
prelates, 59–60, 67, 77
Premo, Bianca, 9
presidios, 139–40, 186, 327n106, 331n31
priests: and death, 258, 275; Indians as, 324n65; lay brothers compared with, 77–79, 82, 86, 92; and marriage, 68; respect for, 8; and sexual matters, 121, 141, 318n72; skills needed, 40; training of secular, 190
The Prince (Machiavelli), 15, 21
princes, education for, 14, 16, 19, 21–22, 296n48

Príncipe Perfecto y Ministros Ajustados (Mendo), 21
professions, religious, 34, 38, 40, 41, 67, 73, 82, 146, 301n14
Propaganda Fide: chronicles on, 246; founders of, 35–36; membership statistics in, 85–86; and military, 177, 180; and missionary work, 166, 179, 270; racial policy of, 45, 46; recruitment by, 82–83, 84; role of, 173–74, 202, 212, 335n98; sexual matters in, 134–35, 139, 140, 162; Spaniards in, 282; variation in, 279
Protestants, 214–15, 239n7
Protomedicato, 309n45
Provincias Internas, 178, 189, 322n27
provisorato, 121
Pueblo Revolt (1680), 168–69, 171, 220, 233–34, 235, 251
purity of blood. See *limpieza de sangre*

Quiteria, Catalina, 150

Radding, Cynthia, 185–86
Ragon, Pierre, 108–9, 227
Ramos, Juana, 142–43
Ramos, María, 147
rape, 137, 138, 139, 148, 149–51, 152, 164, 319n81, 321n117, 326n87
Rebullida, Pedro, 245
refectories, 59–60
Reglas de la buena crianza civil y christiana, 22–24, 23
Reloj de Príncipes (Guevara), 16
Rentería, Joseph de, 232
renunciations, 34, 48, 70, 95, 120, 290
Revillagigedo, Count de, 177
revolt (New Mexico, 1696), 220, 233, 251
Rex Galindo, David, 45, 46, 82

...tonio de los, 31–32, 190–91, 299n92, 325n68
Ribadeneira, Pedro de, 298n64; *Tratado del Príncipe Cristiano*, 21
Ribera, Tomasina, 317n62
Río, Juan del, 249
Rita of Cascia, 312n99
Rivera, Jacinta, 136
Rivera, Joseph de, 321n115
Rivera y Moncada, Fernando de, 196, 197, 198–99
Rocha, Ignacio de la, 109
Rodríguez Juárez, Juan, 268
Romero, Francisco, 57, 60, 65; *Avisos para el Noviciado*, 74
Romero de Terreros, Pedro, 221
Rubial García, Antonio, 80, 104, 214, 301n19

Saavedra Fajardo, Diego de, 298n75; *Idea de un príncipe político cristiano*, 20, 21–22
sacraments, 70, 122, 123–24, 136–37, 142, 152, 161, 313n9
Sacramentum poenitentiae, 124, 314n14
Sáenz, Francisco, 87–88, 108
Sahagún, Bernardino de, 108, 299n87
saints, 214, 258. *See also* names of individual saints
Salazar, Juan de, 258–59; *Arte de Ayudar y Disponer a bien Morir a todo género de personas*, 258
Salguero, Pedro, 10, 32–33; *Portrait-Drawing of Fr. Diego de Basalenque*, 63
San Benito, José de, 78
San Buenaventura College, 64, 65, 326n88
Sánchez, Agustín, 144
Sánchez Calderón, Marcos, 103

Sánchez Cosío, Ignacia, 136
Sancho de Valls, Manuel, 153–54
San Cosme friary, 39, 46
San Cristoval, Diego de, 158, 320n100
San Diego (Franciscan order), 87
San Diego (Franciscan province), 46–47, 52, 66, 74
San Diego mission, 195, 196
San Francisco, Jacinto de, 76, 225
San Joan, Joseph de, 67; *Ceremonial Dominicano*, 305n88
San José de San Miguel de Aguayo mission, 207, 328n113
San Joseph, Martin de, 160
San Juan, Agustín Tomás de, 262–63
San Miguel, Antonio de, 283
San Pablo, Hernando de, 41
San Pedro y San Pablo mission, 188, 247
San Sabá Mission, 221, 250
Santa Catarina, Jordán de, 61–62, 303n43
Santa María, Diego de, 101
Santa María, Gregorio de, 49
Santa María, Juan de, 151, 217
Santa María, Vicente de, 196
Santiesteban, Joseph, 222
Santiesteban, Juan de, 140
San Xavier del Bac church, 188–89
Sanz López, Juan, 70–71
Sariñana y Cuenca, Isidro, 236–38, 278–79
Sarrión Mora, Adelina, 315n25
Satan, 216, 252, 257–58. *See also* the devil
Sebastiana de San Agustín, 159
secularization, 177, 190, 192, 200
seduction: and confessions, 317nn48–50; by men, 134–40, 144–45; by women, 140–44

self-denunciations, 128, 130, 321n115
Sena, Juan de, 99
senses, physical, 18, 22, 297n56
Seris Indians, 183, 188
Sermón (Bringas de Manzaneda), *286*
sermons, funeral: chronicles compared to, 275–76, 287; on death and the dead, 278–82, 340n70; on death and the living, 276–78; on death's meaning, 275–77, 287–88, 339n60; on martyrdom, 236–38, *286*; as spoken message, 236, 275–76; themes in, 282–87, 341nn82–83
Serra, Junípero, *194*; about, 35–37; as administrator, 191–93, 195–96, 327n101; death of, 201, 202, 266, 270–74, 338n40, 338nn43–44; health of, 338n41; on Indians, 208; military interacting with, 196–201; and missionary expansion, 180–81, 326n88; missionary vision of, 201; relationships with colleagues of, 209–10, 338n40; training of, 173
Sicardo, José, 240
sickness, feigned, 137, 141–42, 317n50
Sigüenza y Góngora, Carlos: *Theatro de virtudes políticas que constituyen un príncipe*, 25
slaves, 110, 150–51, 219, 309n55, 313n116, 319n81
socialization, of females, 294n11
socialization, of males, 1–3, 8, 9, 19, 26, 31, 32, 294n11
sodomy, 139, 164, 321n115
solicitants, sexual: about, 128, 130; accusations fought by, 131–34; actions against, 123, 315n25; mitigation denied for, 124–25; self-denunciation of, 128, 130, 321n115

solicitation, sexual: about, 122–24; accusations of, 319n96; ignored, 315n27; individual cases of, 158–62; investigations of, 124–26; and nuns, 151–56; procedures dealing with, 126–27, 156–58; as public knowledge, 316n32; racial issues in, 144, 318n67; ramifications of, 162–65; reactions to, by targeted, 144–51; records on, 315n24; seduction in, by men, 134–40, 144–45; seduction in, by women, 140–44; statistics on, *125*, 314n21; targets of, 147, 314n13
Solís, Gaspar José de, 206–7
Solórzano, Pedro de, 99
Spain, 9–10, 16, 214–15, 239, 329n9, 334n88
Spaniards: birthplace important to, 29–31, 308n31; blood purity important to, 42–43, 97; and confession, 314n10; inexperience in missionizing of, 232; influence of, 6–7; as invaders, 218–21; in mendicant orders, 44–45; military experience of, 295n25; relationships with Indians of, 205–6, 226, 327n104; resistance to missions of, 171–73; as settlers, 170–71, 189, 204. *See also* criollos
spectacle, 103, 232, 275, 330n11
strings, in miracles, 337n34
submission, in behavior, 57, 60–61, 252
suicide, 69–70, 214
Supreme Council of the Holy Office, 133
Supreme Council of the Inquisition, 121, 127, 164

Tabares, Francisco, 89–90
Takanawa (Japanese lord), 243

Tapia, Juan de, 76, 249
teachers: character of important, 16; in convents, 94; as disciplinarians, 27; funerals for, 272; and novitiates, 40, 49, 52–54, 57–58, 60–61, 66; obedience to important, 25–26; responsibilities of, 8, 21
Tello de Sandoval, Francisco, 35
Ten Commandments, 99
Tepehuán Indians, 219–20, 230, 250–51, 304n61, 330n24
Testal, Francisco, 132–34
Texas, 173, 221, 331n29
texts. *See* books
Theatro de virtudes políticas que constituyen un príncipe (Sigüenza y Góngora), 25
Tolentino, Nicholas, 312n99
Topia Indians, 228
Torquemada, Juan de, 108, 213–14, 332n56; *Monarquía Indiana*, 216
Torre Curiel, José Refugio de la, 84, 186
Torres, Juan de, 21, 298n65
torture, 159, 214
Tratado del Príncipe Cristiano (Ribadeneira), 21
Trujillo, Joseph, 149–50
túmulos, 283, 341n82
Twinam, Ann, 9, 12, 294n22

Universi Dominici gregis, 123–24
urbanity, 8, 13–14

Valdés, Ignacia, 137
Valle, Juan del, 230
Vallejo, Raymundo, 146
Valverde de Padilla, Margarita, 159–60
Vargas, Diego de (fray), 150
Vargas, Diego de (governor), 233

Vargas, Francisco de (fray), 233
Vascones, Alonso de: *Destierro de Ignorancias*, 256
Vázquez Conde, Daniel Salvador, 46
Vázquez de Vega, Pedro, 101
Veedor, Joseph, 57; *Instrucción y Doctrina de Novicios*, 50
Veracruz, Alonso de, 64, 261–62, 299n96
Verger, Rafael, 179–81, 195, 326n87
Vertavillo, Diego de, 52
Vetancurt, Agustín de, 31, 79, 101; *Menologio*, 31, 101, 108
Via Crucis, 115
Via Sacra, 102, 116, 340n76
victims: and martyrdom, 228, 248, 329n7; of military, 206; of solicitants, 126, 132, 144, 147, 150, 156–57, 163, 164, 315n27
Vida, martirio y beatificación del invicto protomártir de el Japón San Felipe de Jesús (Medina), 241
Vilaplana, Hermenegildo de, 36
Vila y Camps, Antonio, 24
Villalba, Francisco, 148–49
Villalón, Cristóbal de, 297nn55–58; *El Crótalon*, 18–19, 297n55
Villanueva, Tomás de, 312n99
Villarubia, Diego de, 49, 64, 254, 263–66, 337n23
virginity, 106, 121–22, 135–36, 297n56, 313n6
visions, 69–70, 169, 263, 273, 274
Vives, Luis: *Diálogos*, 17–18, 296n52
vows: and economic matters, 188; and lay brothers, 110; and novitiates, 40, 48–49, 67, 70–71, 306n97; ranking of, 53; and sexual matters, 120, 122–23, 142, 152, 319n87
voz pública, 128, 316n32

walking, 59, 226, 332n43
widows, 121, 137, 142–43
women: attitudes toward, 3; distrust of, 22, 297n56, 320n100; Eve representing, 27; family role of, 7–8, 11–12, 26–27; Mary, mother of Jesus, representing, 71; societal roles of, 294n11; stereotypes about, 296n52. *See also* nuns
women, sexually solicited: about, 135, 144, 145–46; approaches to, 131–33; consequences for, 317n62; cooperation by, 136–38, 140–44; denunciations by, 15, 132, 146, 314n14; expectations for, 145; manipulation of, 160; neglect of, 156–57; rape of, 138; resistance by, 146–47; as victims, 163–64

Ximenez, Diego, 183
Ximenez de Arellano, Manuel, 284–85

Yaqui Indians, 189
Ymhoff Cabrera, Jesús, 305n91
Yucatán (province), 147, 149
Yuma Indians, 188, 205, 238, 247
Yuma massacre (1781), 224, 251, 326n86, 327n104

Zacatecas (city), 76, 106
Zacatecas (province), 225, 246
Zamora, Juan Antonio, 243, 245
Zamora, Miguel de, 103
Zárate, Jerónimo de, 169, 170–71
Zárate, Martín de, 32

In the Confluencias series:

The Sonoran Dynasty in Mexico: Revolution, Reform, and Repression
By Jürgen Buchenau

The Enlightened Patrolman: Early Law Enforcement in Mexico City
By Nicole von Germeten

Men of God: Mendicant Orders in Colonial Mexico
By Asunción Lavrin

Strength from the Waters: A History of Indigenous Mobilization in Northwest Mexico
By James V. Mestaz

Informal Metropolis: Life on the Edge of Mexico City, 1940–1976
By David Yee

To order or obtain more information on these or other University of Nebraska Press titles, visit nebraskapress.unl.edu.

www.ingramcontent.com/pod-product-compliance
Lightning Source LLC
Chambersburg PA
CBHW051241300426
44114CB00011B/844